Modern Real Estate Practice in New York

Edith Lank
Second Edition

For Salespersons & Brokers

REAL ESTATE EDUCATION COMPANY/CHICAGO

Copyright © 1986, 1983 by Longman Group USA Inc.

Published by Real Estate Education Company/Chicago, a division of Longman Financial Services Publishing, Inc.

86 87 88 10 9 8 7 6 5 4 3 2

Library of Congress Cataloging-in-Publication Data

Lank, Edith.
   Modern real estate practice in New York for salespersons & brokers.

   Includes index.
   1. Vendors and purchasers—New York (State)
2. Real estate business—Law and legislation—New York (State) I. Title.
KFN5166.L36   1986   346.74704'37   86-10171
ISBN 0-88462-679-2   347.4706437

Sponsoring Editor: Jeny Sejdinaj
Copy Editor: Carole Bilina
Production Editor: Gloria Ball

Real Estate Education Company Series

Bellairs, Helsel & Caldwell	Modern Real Estate Practice in Pennsylvania, 4th Edition
Coit	Introduction to Real Estate Law, 2nd Edition
Cyr & Sobeck	Real Estate Brokerage: A Success Guide
Danks	Real Estate Advertising
Floyd	Real Estate Principles, 2nd Edition
Friedman & Henszey	Protecting Your Sales Commission: Professional Liability in Real Estate
Gaddy & Hart	Real Estate Fundamentals, 2nd Edition
Gaines & Coleman	Basic Real Estate Math, 3rd Edition
Galaty, Allaway & Kyle	Modern Real Estate Practice, 10th Edition
Gibson, Karp & Klayman	Real Estate Law
Greynolds & Aronofsky	Practical Real Estate Financial Analysis: Using The HP-12C Calculator
Hinds & Ordway	International Real Estate Investment
Kyle	Property Management, 2nd Edition
Lank	Modern Real Estate Practice in New York, 2nd Edition
Martin & Jackson	New Jersey Supplement for Modern Real Estate Practice, 4th Edition
Mettling	Modern Residential Financing Methods: Tools of the Trade
Pivar	Classified Secrets
Pivar	Power Real Estate Listing
Pivar	Power Real Estate Selling
Developed by Real Estate Education Company	Professional Real Estate Selling Skills
Developed by Real Estate Education Company	Straight Talk Newsletter
Developed by Real Estate Education Company in conjunction with Grubb & Ellis Company	Successful Industrial Real Estate Brokerage, 3rd Edition Successful Leasing & Selling of Office Property, 2nd Edition Successful Leasing & Selling of Retail Property, 2nd Edition

Contents

Law of Contracts 74

Land-Use Regulations 94

Real Estate Financing 106

8   License Law and Ethics 130

9   Valuation and Listing Procedures 164

23   **Voluntary and Involuntary Alienation 408**

24   **Liens and Easements 416**

Preface

This second edition of *Modern Real Estate Practice in New York* is dedicated to the thousands of real estate students and instructors whose enthusiastic acceptance has made it the best-selling real estate textbook in the state. Many valuable suggestions for this new edition have come from those who have used the book.

The organization of the text remains the same. It provides standard basic material for real estate education adapted for New York in *a single textbook fitting both 45-hour license courses.* Part One covers material for the salesperson's course and Part Two includes all the state-mandated topics for the broker's course. The text has been updated throughout, with particular attention to changes in financing, investment, construction, and license law. End-of-chapter questions have been reworked in a uniform multiple-choice format. The revision reflects much-appreciated advice, corrections, and suggestions from more than 35 instructors and various real estate specialists.

This textbook was originally adapted from the classic text, *Modern Real Estate Practice,* by Fillmore W. Galaty, Wellington J. Allaway, and Robert C. Kyle, which has sold more than a million copies since it was first published in 1959.

Approximately one-half of New York's licenses are issued for New York City and its environs, the other half for Upstate. Local customs (and, occasionally, law) vary considerably in some matters between these areas. Because the licensee is authorized to practice real estate anywhere in the state, care has been taken to point out regional differences in such topics as preparation of a purchase contract, settlement procedures, and rent regulations.

Excerpts from the Department of State's study booklets have been placed at the ends of relevant chapters; instructors may wish to assign this material. The glossary includes all terms mentioned in the glossary of the state study booklet.

Special thanks are due to the following reviewers for their valuable assistance in the development of *Modern Real Estate Practice in New York*, second edition:

Thomas E. DeCelle, Executive Director, Southern Tier Institute of Real Estate Studies
Judith J. Deickler, Real Estate Education Consultant
Peter A. Karl, III, State University of New York-Utica Rome College of Technology
Leon Katzen, Esq., St. John Fisher College
John Mataraza, President, Real Estate Training Center
James R. Myers, Esq., Ulster County Community College

Special contributions to the first edition came from Charles E. Davies, William A. Lange, Jr., Esq., George E. Lasch, and Dorothy Tymon.

Thanks are also due to Attorneys Abraham Berkowitz, Ronald Friedman, David Henehan, Benjamin Henszey, Ezra Katzen, James Loeb, Louis Ryen, Karen Schaefer, Sally Smith, and Christine F. Van Benschoten; and to REALTORS® Ronald Baroody, Thomas Carozza, John Cyr, Barry Deickler, Thomas Galvin, Harold Kahn, Norman Lank, William Lester, Robert Michaels, Joan Sobeck, Thomas

Wills III, and Rex Vail. Special assistance came from the many instructors who responded to a call for their suggestions and from Larry Rockefeller, Esther Vail, Professor Kenneth Beckerink, Cindy Faire, Jim Foley, John Keaton, Willard Roth, and Longman Financial Services Publishing's Anita Constant, senior vice president, Rich Hagle, senior editor, Jeny Sejdinaj, sponsoring editor, and Carole Bilina, senior copy editor.

For permission to use forms and figures, thanks go to Julius Blumberg, Inc.; National Association of REALTORS®, Economics and Research Division; New York Department of State; Real Estate Board of Rochester, NY, Inc.; and Stephen Roulac and Company.

Edith Lank
Rochester, New York

About the Author

Edith Lank has been a licensed broker in New York since 1969 and has taught license-qualifying courses at St. John Fisher College since 1976. Her award-winning weekly column on real estate has appeared in newspapers in Buffalo, Rochester, Syracuse, Schenectady, Amsterdam, Elmira, Brooklyn, Binghamton, Kingston, Ithaca, Middletown, Westchester, and Rockland counties and Long Island, as well as in newspapers across the country.

She appears weekly on public radio and has hosted her own television show. She is the author of *Home Buying* and *Selling Your Home With an Agent*. Her work has been honored by the Monroe County Bar Association, Women in Communications, Real Estate Board of Rochester, National Assocation of REALTORS®, National Association of Real Estate Editors, Real Estate Educators Association, and Governor Mario Cuomo. A graduate of Syracuse University, she is a member of Phi Beta Kappa.

Part One

Real Estate Salesperson

1

What is Real Estate?

Overview   Tens of thousands of men and women in New York State work in some aspect of the real estate industry as brokers, salespersons, appraisers, or property managers. They aid buyers, sellers, and investors in making decisions that involve billions of dollars in property each year. But what exactly is real estate? This chapter will discuss the nature of land, real estate, and real and personal property and will introduce you to the many facets of the real estate industry.

Real Estate Transactions

The purchase of *real estate* involves an entirely different type of transaction from the purchase of *personal property*, like groceries, clothing, fuel, automobiles, or television sets. *Even the simplest of real estate transactions brings into play a body of complex laws.*

Real estate has often been described as a **bundle of legal rights.** When a person purchases a parcel of real estate, he or she is actually buying the rights previously held by the seller. These *rights of ownership (see* Figure 1.1) include the right to *possession,* the right to *control the property* within the framework of the law, the right of *enjoyment* (to use the property in any legal manner), the right of *exclusion* (to keep others from entering or occupying the property), and the right of *disposition* (to be able to sell or otherwise convey the property). Within these ownership rights are included further rights to will, devise, mortgage, encumber, cultivate, explore, lease, license, dedicate, give away, share, trade, or exchange the property.

**Figure 1.1
Bundle of Legal Rights**

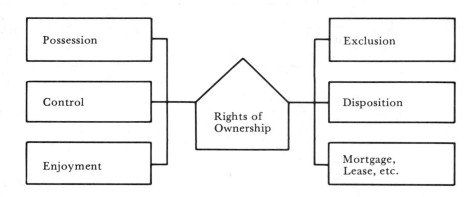

Land, Real Estate, and Real Property

The words *land, real estate,* and *real property* often are used to describe the same commodity. There are, however, important differences in their technical meanings.

Land

The term *land* refers to more than just the surface of the earth; it includes the underlying soil and things that are permanently attached to the land by nature, such as trees and water. From a legal standpoint, land ownership also includes possession and control of the minerals and substances below the earth's surface together with the airspace above the land up to infinity.

Thus, **land** is defined as *the earth's surface extending downward to the center of the earth and upward to infinity, including things permanently attached by nature, such as trees and water (see* Figure 1.2).

A specific tract of land is most commonly referred to as a **parcel.**

Real Estate

The term *real estate* is somewhat broader than the term *land* and includes not only the physical components of the land as provided by nature but also all man-made permanent improvements on and to the land. The word **improvement** applies to the buildings erected on the land as well as to streets, utilities, sewers, and other man-made additions to the property.

Real estate, therefore, is defined as *the earth's surface extending downward to the center of the earth and upward into space, including all things permanently attached to it by nature or by people (see* Figure 1.2).

Figure 1.2
Land/Real Estate

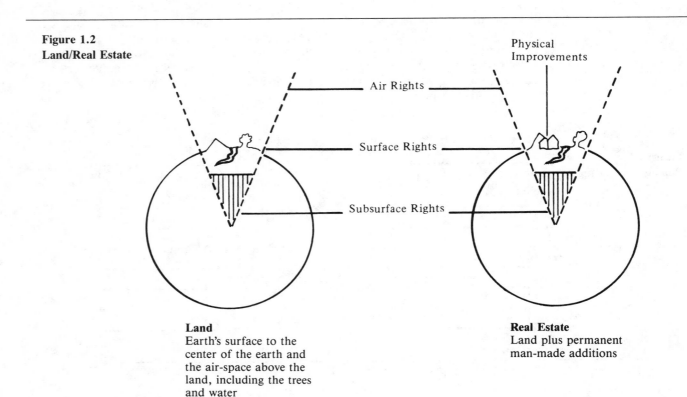

Physical Improvements

Air Rights

Surface Rights

Subsurface Rights

Land
Earth's surface to the center of the earth and the air-space above the land, including the trees and water

Real Estate
Land plus permanent man-made additions

In practice, the term *real estate* is most often used to describe that commodity with which the real estate broker and salesperson are concerned. It is sometimes referred to as *realty*.

Real Property

The term *real property* is broader still. It refers to the physical surface of the land, what lies below it, what lies above it, and what is permanently attached to it, as well as to the *legal rights of real estate ownership.*

Thus, **real property** is defined as *the earth's surface extending downward to the center of the earth and upward into space, including all things permanently* *attached to it by nature or by man, as well as the interests, benefits, and rights inherent in the ownership of real estate (see Figure 1.3).*

Figure 1.3
Real Property

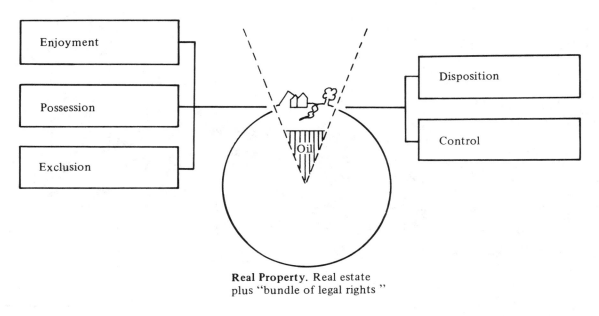

Real Property. Real estate
plus "bundle of legal rights"

Subsurface rights. Ownership of real estate includes ownership of all minerals and other substances in the ground. **Subsurface rights,** the rights to the natural resources lying below the earth's surface, may be sold separately.

For example, a landowner may sell to an oil company his or her rights to any oil and gas found in the land. Later the same landowner can sell the land to a purchaser and in the sale reserve the rights to all coal that may be found in the land. After these sales, three parties have ownership interests in this real estate: (1) the oil company owns all oil and gas, (2) the seller owns all coal, and (3) the purchaser owns the rights to all the rest of the real estate.

Mineral rights also may be leased, and much of the farmland in southwestern New York State is subject to oil and gas leases.

Air rights. As with the rights to minerals that lie below the surface of the land, the rights to use the air above the land may be sold or leased independently of the land itself. Such **air rights** are an increasingly important part of real estate, particularly in large cities, where air rights over railroads have been purchased to construct huge office buildings like the Pan-Am Building in New York City. For the construction of such a building, the developer must purchase not only the air rights above the land but also numerous small portions of the actual land in order to construct the building's foundation supports, called *caissons* (see Figure 1.4).

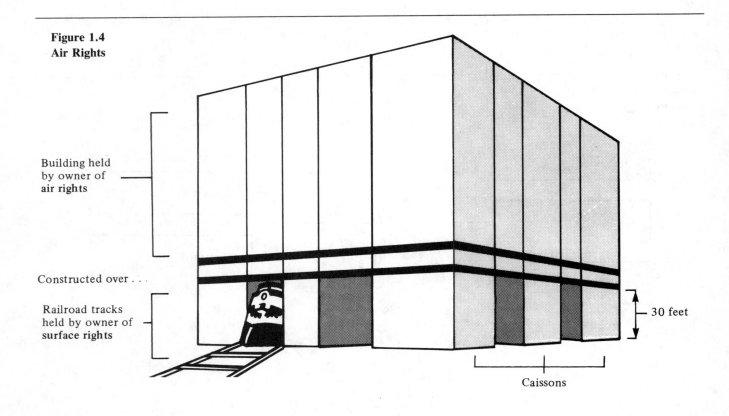

**Figure 1.4
Air Rights**

Building held
by owner of
air rights

Constructed over . . .

Railroad tracks
held by owner of
surface rights

30 feet

Caissons

Until the development of airplanes, a property's air rights were considered to be unlimited. Today, however, the courts permit reasonable interference with these rights, such as is necessary for aircraft, as long as the owner's right to use and occupy the land is not unduly lessened. Governments and airport authorities often purchase air rights adjacent to an airport to provide glide patterns for air traffic.

With the continuing development of solar power, air rights—more specifically, *sun rights*—may be redefined by the courts. They may consider tall buildings that block sunlight from smaller buildings to be interfering with the smaller buildings' rights to solar energy.

In summary, one parcel of real property may be owned by many people. There may be: (1) an owner of the surface rights, (2) an owner of the subsurface mineral rights, (3) an owner of the subsurface gas and oil rights, and (4) an owner of the air rights.

Riparian rights are the owner's rights in land bordering a river. In New York, persons owning land bordering navigable streams own the property to the high-water mark; the riverbed belongs to the state. Persons owning land bordering non-navigable streams own the land to the midpoint of the stream (*see* Figure 1.5).

Closely related to riparian rights are the **littoral rights** of owners whose land borders on large, navigable lakes and oceans. Owners with littoral rights may enjoy unrestricted use of available waters but own the land adjacent to the water only up to the mean high-water mark. All land below this point is owned by the government. Riparian and littoral rights are appurtenant (attached) to the land and are not usually retained when the property is sold.

Figure 1.5
Riparian Rights

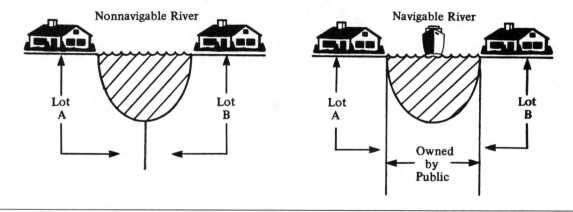

Where land adjoins streams or rivers, an owner is entitled to all *accretions,* or increases in the land resulting from the deposit of soil by the natural action of the water. An owner may also lose land through *avulsion* due to a sudden change in the channel of a stream.

Real Estate versus Personal Property

Property may be classified as either real estate or personal property. Real estate has already been defined as a part of the earth including the permanent additions or growing things attached to it, the air space above it, and the minerals below it.

Personal property, on the other hand, is *all property that does not fit the definition of real estate.* Thus, personal property has the unique characteristic of being *movable.* Items of personal property, also referred to as **chattels,** *movables,* or **personalty,** include such tangibles as refrigerators, drapes, clothing, money, bonds, and bank accounts (*see* Figure 1.6).

The distinction between personal and real property is of great importance to the real estate practitioner. Buyers and sellers must be guided to clear written agreements about what "goes with" property being sold. The distinction also is significant with regard to taxation when property is sold: Personal property may be subject to sales tax, real property to transfer tax.

It is possible to change an item of real estate to personal property. A growing tree is real estate, but if the owner cuts down the tree and thereby severs it from being permanently attached to the earth, it becomes personal property.

The reverse situation is also true. Personal property can be changed to real estate. If an owner buys cement, stones, and sand and constructs a concrete walk on a parcel of real estate, the component parts of the concrete, which were originally personal property, are converted into real estate because they have become a permanent improvement on the land.

Figure 1.6
Real versus Personal Property

Real Estate
Land and anything permanently attached to it

Personal Property
Movable items not attached to real estate; items severed from real estate

Fixture
Item of personal property converted to real estate by attaching it to the real estate with the intention that it become permanently a part thereof

Trade Fixture
Item of personal property attached to real estate that is owned by a tenant and is used in a business; legally removable by tenant

Trees and crops are generally considered in two classes: (1) trees, perennial bushes, and grasses that do not require annual cultivation are considered real estate, and (2) annual crops of wheat, corn, vegetables, and fruit, known as *emblements,* generally are considered personal property.

Classification of Fixtures

Fixtures. *An article that was once personal property but has been so affixed to land or to a building that the law construes it to be a part of the real estate is a* **fixture.** Examples of fixtures are heating plants, elevator equipment in high-rise buildings, radiators, kitchen cabinets, light fixtures, and plumbing fixtures. Almost any item that has been added as *a permanent part* of a building is considered a fixture.

Trade fixtures. An article owned by a tenant and attached to a rented space or building for use in conducting a business is a **trade fixture.** Examples of trade fixtures are bowling alleys, store shelves, bars, and restaurant equipment. Agricultural fixtures such as chicken coops and toolsheds also are included in this definition (*see* Figure 1.6). Trade fixtures must be removed on or before the last day the property is rented. Trade fixtures that are not removed become the real property of the landlord.

Trade fixtures differ from other fixtures in the following ways:

1. Fixtures belong to the owner of the real estate but trade fixtures are usually owned and installed by a tenant for his or her business use.

2. Fixtures are considered a permanent part of a building but trade fixtures are removable. (The tenant must, however, restore the property to its original condition, repairing holes left by bolts, for example.)
3. Fixtures are legally construed to be real estate but trade fixtures are legally construed to be personal property.

Legal tests of a fixture. Courts apply four basic tests to determine whether an article is a fixture (and therefore a part of the real estate) or removable personal property. These tests are based on: (1) the adaptation of the article to the real estate, (2) the method of annexation of the item, (3) the intention and relationship of the parties, and (4) the existence of an agreement.

The adaptation of an article to use in a particular building is a test of the nature of the article. Air conditioners installed by a landlord into wall slots specifically constructed for that purpose would be considered fixtures even though they readily could be removed.

The permanence of the manner of annexation, or attachment, often provides a basis for court decisions relating to fixtures. For instance, a furnace, although it is removable, is usually attached in such a way that it cannot be taken out without causing extensive damage to the property. Moreover, the furnace is considered an essential part of the complete property and as such is a fixture.

The intent of the parties at the time an article was attached generally is considered the most important factor in deciding whether or not an article is a fixture. A tenant who opens a jewelry store may bolt her sale and display cases to the floor. If she wishes to remove them later, she can do so. Because these items are an integral part of her business property and it was never her intent to make them a permanent part of the structure, they would be considered removable trade fixtures. The best evidence of intent may be a written agreement.

Although these three tests seem simple, there is no uniformity in court decisions regarding what constitutes a fixture. Articles that appear to be permanently affixed sometimes have been held by the courts to be personal property, while items that do not appear to be permanently attached have been held to be fixtures. The front door key, although not attached, is clearly a fixture that belongs with a house.

Real Estate Law

Buying real estate is usually the biggest financial transaction of a person's life. At the center of this important and sensitive transaction there is generally a middleman—the real estate **broker.** A real estate **salesperson** works on behalf of the broker. The broker and the salesperson generally represent the seller and seek a buyer for his or her property. After they have found a prospective buyer, they bring the parties together. Then both seller and buyer look to the broker and their respective lawyers to guide and facilitate the transfer of the real estate from one party to the other.

Certain specific areas of law are important to the real estate practitioner. These include the *law of contracts,* the *real property law,* the *law of agency* (which covers the obligations of a broker to the person who engages his or her services), and the *real estate license law,* all of which will be discussed in this text.

A person engaged in the real estate business need not be an expert on real estate law but should have a knowledge and understanding of the basic principles of the law under which he or she operates. A real estate practitioner must be able to recognize the technical legal problems involved in transactions that he or she will negotiate and should appreciate the necessity of referring such problems to a competent attorney. *An* **attorney** *is a person trained and licensed to represent another person in court, to prepare documents defining or transferring rights in property, or to give advice or counsel on matters of law.* Brokers and salespeople must be aware of their limitations in such areas.

Extreme care should be taken in handling all phases of a real estate transaction. Carelessness in handling the documents connected with a real estate sale can result in expensive legal contests. In many such cases costly court actions could have been avoided if the parties handling negotiations had exercised greater care and employed competent legal counsel.

Real estate license laws. Because real estate brokers and salespeople are engaged in the business of handling other people's real estate and money, the need for regulation of their activities has long been recognized. In an effort to protect the public from fraud, dishonesty, or incompetence in the buying and selling of real estate, all 50 states, the District of Columbia, Puerto Rico, and all Canadian provinces have passed laws that require real estate brokers and salespeople to be licensed. New York first required licensing in 1922. The license laws of the various states are similar in many respects but differ in details.

Under these laws a person must obtain a license in order to engage in the real estate business. The applicant must possess certain stated personal and educational qualifications and must pass an examination to prove an adequate knowledge of the business. In addition, in order to qualify for license renewal and continue in business, the licensee must meet continuing education requirements and follow certain prescribed standards of conduct in the operation of business. Chapter 8 describes in detail New York's license laws and the required standards.

Real Estate—A Business of Many Specializations	Some people think of the real estate business as being made up only of brokers and salespeople. Today's real estate industry, however, employs scores of well-trained, knowledgeable individuals in areas other than real estate brokerage. Modern real estate practice provides many specializations for people who want to serve the community and earn a better-than-average income.
Real Estate Specialists	The specializations that make up the real estate business include brokerage, appraisal, property management, real estate financing, property development, counseling, education, syndication, and insurance. To be truly competent a real estate licensee must possess at least a basic knowledge of all phases of the business.

Brokerage. The bringing together of people interested in making a real estate transaction is *brokerage.* Typically, the broker acts as an *agent;* that is, he or she negotiates the sale, purchase, or rental of property on behalf of others for a fee or commission. The agent's commission is generally a percentage of the amount involved in the transaction. It usually is paid by the seller. Brokerage is discussed further in Chapter 2.

Appraisal. The process of estimating the value of a parcel of real estate is *appraisal*. Although brokers must have some understanding of valuation as part of their training, an appraisal specialist generally is employed when property is financed or sold by court order and large sums of money are involved. The appraiser must have sound judgment, experience, and a detailed knowledge of the methods of valuation. Appraisal is covered in Chapter 16.

Property management. A real estate agent who operates a property for its owner is involved in *property management*. The property manager may be responsible for soliciting tenants, collecting rents, altering or constructing new space for tenants, ordering repairs, and generally maintaining the property. The manager's basic responsibility is to protect the owner's investment and maximize the owner's return on the investment. Property management is discussed in Chapter 19.

Financing. The business of providing the funds necessary to complete real estate transactions is *financing*. Most transactions are financed by means of a mortgage loan in which the property is pledged as security for the eventual payment of the loan. However, there are other forms and methods of financing real estate in addition to mortgages. Real estate financing is examined in Chapter 7.

Property development. *Property development* includes the work of subdividers who purchase raw land, divide it into lots, build roads, and install sewers; the skills of land developers who improve the building lots with houses and other buildings and who sell the improved real estate, either themselves or through brokerage firms; and the work of builders and architects who plan and construct the houses and other buildings. Property development is discussed in Chapter 20.

Counseling. Providing competent, independent advice, guidance, and sound judgment on a variety of real estate problems, including the purchase, use, and investment of property, is *counseling*. A counselor attempts to furnish his or her client with direction in choosing among alternative courses of action.

Education. Both the real estate licensee and the consumer can learn more about the complexities of the real estate business through *education*. Colleges, schools, real estate organizations, and continuing education programs conduct courses and seminars in all areas of the business. New York State requires that courses for licensure or continuing education credit be taught by instructors with five years' experience in the subjects being taught.

Syndication. Syndication is the bringing together of groups of investors for large ventures. In New York State sale of syndications requires a special securities license.

Insurance. *Insurance* is sometimes included among the major services of the real estate business. In many real estate offices, the real estate broker is also an insurance broker; however, *insurance brokerage is a separate business that requires a separate state license.*

Uses of Real Property

Just as there are many areas of specialization within the real estate industry, so too are there many different types of property in which to specialize (*see* Figure 1.7). Real estate can generally be classified into one of the following categories according to its use.

Figure 1.7
Uses of Real Property

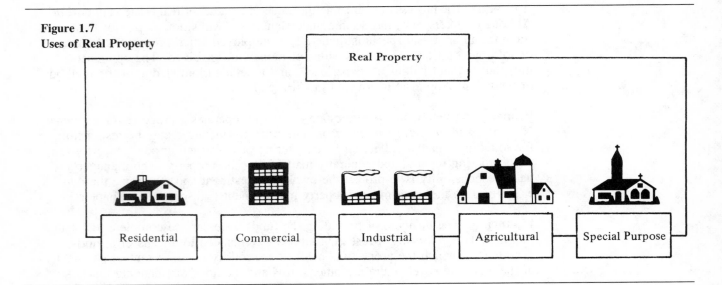

1. **Residental**—all property used for housing, from acreage to small city lots, both single-family and multifamily, in urban, suburban, and rural areas.
2. **Commercial**—business property, including offices, shopping centers, stores, executive offices, theaters, hotels, and parking facilities.
3. **Industrial**—warehouses, factories, land in industrial districts, and research facilities.
4. **Agricultural**—farms, timberland, pasture land, ranches, and orchards.
5. **Special purpose**—churches, schools, cemeteries, and government-held lands.

The market for each of these types of properties can be further subdivided into: (1) the sale market, which involves the transfer of title, and (2) the rental market, which involves the transfer of space on a rental basis.

In theory, a real estate person or firm can perform all the aforementioned services and handle all five classes of property. This is rarely done, however, except in small towns. Most real estate firms tend to specialize to some degree, especially in urban areas. The vast majority of real estate firms performs two or more services for two or more types of property. One firm may provide brokerage and management services for residential property only; another firm may perform all services but specialize in industrial or commercial property.

Because the greatest number of individuals in the real estate field are involved in residential brokerage, most people tend to think of the marketing of real estate as the primary activity in the field. But many other people are also a part of the real estate business; for example, people associated with mortgage banking firms and those who negotiate mortgages for banks and savings and loan associations, people in property management firms and real estate departments of corporations, and officials and employees of such government agencies as zoning boards and assessing offices.

Summary

Even the simplest real estate transactions involve a complex body of laws. When a person purchases real estate, he or she is, in effect, purchasing not only the land itself but also the *legal rights* to use the land in certain ways that formerly were held by the seller.

Although most people think of *land* as the surface of the earth, the definition of this word really applies not only to the *earth's surface* but also to the *mineral deposits under the earth* and the *air above it*. The term *real estate* further expands this definition to include *all natural and man-made improvements attached to the land*. *Real property* is the term used to describe real estate plus the "bundle of legal rights" associated with its ownership.

The same parcel of real estate may be owned and controlled by different parties, one owning the *surface rights*, one owning the *air rights*, and another owning the *subsurface rights*.

Ownership of land encompasses not only the land itself but also the right to use the water on or adjacent to it. The common-law doctrine of *riparian rights* gives the owner of land adjacent to nonnavigable water ownership of the stream to its midpoint. *Littoral rights* are held by owners of land bordering large lakes and oceans and include rights to the water and ownership of the land up to the high-water mark.

All property that does not fit the definition of real estate is classified as *personal property*, or *chattels*. When articles of personal property are permanently affixed to land, they may become *fixtures* and as such are considered a part of the real estate. However, personal property attached to real estate by a tenant for a business purpose is classified as a *trade fixture* and remains personal property.

The real estate business is a dynamic industry employing hundreds of thousands of men and women. Every state and Canadian province has some type of *licensing requirement* for real estate brokers and salespeople.

Although selling is the most widely recognized activity of the real estate business, the industry also involves many other services such as *appraisal, property management, property development, counseling, property financing, education, syndication,* and *insurance*.

Real property can be classified according to its general use as either *residential, commercial, industrial, agricultural,* or *special purpose*. Although many brokers deal with more than one type of real property, they usually specialize to some degree.

Questions

1. Real estate is often referred to as a *bundle of legal rights*. Which of the following is *not* among these rights?

   a. Right of exclusion
   b. Right to use the property for private purposes, legal or otherwise
   c. Right of enjoyment
   d. Right to sell or otherwise convey the property

2. The definition of *land* does *not* include:

   a. minerals in the earth.
   b. the air above the ground up to infinity.
   c. trees.
   d. buildings.

3. A specific tract of land is known as a:

   a. bundle.   c. chattel.
   b. parcel.   d. littoral.

4. An important characteristic of land is that it may be modified. Such modifications become a part of and tend to increase the value of real estate. Which of the following is *not* a modification?

   a. New access roads   c. New houses
   b. Utilities   d. Crops

5. Man-made, permanent additions to land are called:

   a. chattels.   c. improvements.
   b. parcels.   d. trade fixtures.

6. Which of the following best defines real estate?

   a. Land and the air above it
   b. Land and all that there is above or below the surface and all the improvements thereon
   c. Land, the buildings thereon, and anything permanently affixed to the land and/or buildings
   d. Land and the mineral rights in the land

7. Dell Hicks, owner of a large farm in Livingston County, may lease to a gas-drilling company his:

   a. riparian rights.   c. air rights.
   b. subsurface rights.   d. littoral rights.

8. When a building is to be constructed over land owned by another, the builder purchases the landowner's:

   a. riparian rights.   c. air rights.
   b. subsurface rights.   d. littoral rights.

9. Molly Malone owns land along the Mohawk River and as such has certain:

   a. riparian rights.   c. air rights
   b. subsurface rights.   d. littoral rights.

10. The definition of real estate includes many elements and parts. Which of the following items would *not* be a part of real estate?

    a. Fences
    b. Permanent buildings
    c. Farm equipment
    d. Growing trees

11. Steve Jackson rents a detached, single-family home under a one-year lease. Two months into the rental period, Jackson installs awnings over the building's front windows to keep the sun away from some delicate hanging plants. Which of the following is true?

    a. Jackson must remove the awnings before the rental period is over.
    b. Because of their permanent nature, the awnings are considered to be personal property.
    c. Jackson may not remove the awnings.
    d. The awnings are removable trade fixtures.

12. When the Hair Zoo moved in, the hairdresser installed three shampoo basins, four large plate-glass mirrors, and custom work-station counters. Just before the expiration of the lease, the hairdresser has the right to remove:

    a. everything but the shampoo basins because they are attached to the plumbing.
    b. only the mirrors, and then only if holes in the walls are repaired.
    c. all of the items mentioned above.
    d. nothing because all the items became fixtures when they were attached.

13. Legal tests for a fixture do *not* include:

    a. annexation.   c. accretion
    b. adaptation.   d. intention.

14. The purchase of real estate:
    a. is generally the largest financial investment in a person's lifetime.
    b. involves a complex body of laws.
    c. is usually facilitated by a real estate broker.
    d. All of the above

15. Areas of law that are of particular importance to the real estate broker include:
    a. the law of contracts.
    b. the law of agency.
    c. the real property law.
    d. All of the above

16. The bringing together of people interested in making a real estate transaction is known as:
    a. appraisal.   c. cooperation.
    b. brokerage.   d. development.

17. Harry Wales buys farmland outside New York City, splits it into lots, and installs roads and utilities. He is acting as a:
    a. broker.   c. manager.
    b. developer.   d. subdivider.

18. Special-purpose real estate includes:
    a. apartment houses.
    b. churches.
    c. factories.
    d. shopping plazas.

19. Property that is part of the commercial market includes:
    a. office buildings for lease.
    b. apartments for rent.
    c. churches.
    d. factories.

20. Peter Dickinson is a real estate broker in a large Upstate city. Chances are his real estate firm:
    a. performs most or all of the various real estate specializations.
    b. deals only in farm property.
    c. deals only in insurance.
    d. performs two or more of the various real estate specializations for at least two types of property.

2

Law of Agency

Key Terms

Agency coupled with an interest
Agent
Antitrust laws
Broker
Buyer's broker
Client
Commission
Customer
Dual agency
Employee
Fiduciary relationship
Fraud
General agency
Independent contractor

Kickbacks
Latent defects
Law of agency
Listing agreement
Meeting of the minds
Power of attorney
Principal
Procuring cause of sale
Puffing
Ready, willing, and able buyer
Salesperson
Special agency
Subagency
Universal agency

Overview

Real estate brokers (and the salespersons assisting them) bring together buyers and sellers. Real estate brokerage today is a complex operation involving strictly defined legal relationships. The broker generally acts as the authorized agent of the seller. This chapter will discuss the laws governing agency and also will examine the nature of the real estate brokerage business itself.

Brokerage Defined	The business of bringing buyers and sellers together in the marketplace is *brokerage.* In the real estate business a **broker** is defined as a person who is licensed to buy, sell, exchange, or lease real property for others and to charge a fee for services. Working on behalf of and licensed to represent the broker is the real estate **salesperson.**

The **principal** who employs the broker may be a seller, a prospective buyer, an owner who wishes to lease his or her property, or a person seeking property to rent. The real estate broker acts as the **agent** of the principal, who usually compensates the broker with a **commission.** This commission is contingent upon the broker's successfully performing the service for which he or she was employed, which is generally procuring a prospective purchaser, seller, lessor, or lessee who is ready, willing, and able to complete the contract. The principal is also known as the **client.** In the usual real estate transaction the seller is the client, to whom specific duties are owed; the buyer is merely the agent's **customer,** to whom the agent owes only fair and trustworthy treatment.

Agency	The role of a broker as the agent of his or her principal is a **fiduciary relationship** that falls within the requirements of the body of law that governs the rights and duties of the principal, agent, and third parties known as the **law of agency.** The fiduciary relationship is one of trust and confidence in which an agent (such as a broker or an attorney) is responsible for the money and/or property of others. It requires putting the principal's interest above all others', including the broker's own interest. The agent is also known as a fiduciary.

Types of Agencies	An agent is someone who is authorized by another to negotiate contracts for that person. An agent may be classified as a universal agent, general agent, or special agent based upon his or her authority.

A **universal agent** is someone who is empowered to represent the principal in *all matters* that can be delegated. The universal agent has the power to enter into *any* contract (such as the selling and buying of property) on behalf of the principal without prior permission. This type of agency is created by a written document known as a **power of attorney,** which grants the agent unlimited authority in the principal's financial and other matters.

A **general agent** is someone empowered to represent the principal in a *specific range of matters.* The general agent may bind the principal to any contracts within the scope of his or her authority. This type of agency is also created by a power of attorney that stipulates the specific areas of authority in which the agent may act.

A **special agent** is authorized to represent his or her principal in *one specific transaction or business activity only.* A real estate broker is generally a special agent hired by a seller to find a ready, willing, and able buyer for the seller's property. As a special agent, the broker is *not authorized* to sell the property or to bind the principal to any contract.

An **agency coupled with an interest** is an agency relationship in which the agent is given an interest in the subject of the agency (the property being sold). Such an agency *cannot be revoked by the principal nor can it be terminated upon the principal's death.* For example, a broker might supply the financing for a condominium development provided the developer agrees to give the broker the exclusive right to sell the completed condo units. Because this is an agency coupled with an interest, the developer would not be able to revoke the listing agreement after the broker provided the financing.

Creation of Agency
An agency relationship is created by an agreement of the parties; the broker-seller relationship is generally created by an employment contract, commonly referred to as a **listing agreement.**

In New York State a listing agreement may be implied or expressed. A written listing agreement is required only if it is for a period of one year or more. Oral agreements of agency for a shorter period of time are binding. Most brokers, however, require that all agreements be in writing and signed by the principal. The possibilities of misunderstanding and the difficulty of proving an oral agreement dictate written listings as good business practice.

Termination of Agency
An agency between a principal and an agent may be terminated at any time, except in the case of an agency coupled with an interest. An agency may be terminated for any of the following reasons:

1. Death or incompetency of either party.
2. Destruction or condemnation of the property.
3. Expiration of the terms of the agency.
4. Mutual agreement to terminate the agency.
5. Renunciation by the agent or revocation by the principal.
6. Bankruptcy of either party.
7. Completion or fulfillment of the purpose for which the agency was created.

Since an amendment to New York State law in 1975, agency does not automatically terminate upon the incompetency of the principal; the power-of-attorney document contains wording that determines the matter.

In New York the principal acting in good faith always has the power to cancel the agency but may be answerable to the broker for damages if he or she cancels before the agency's expiration.

Buyer as Principal
Usually, a real estate broker is hired by a seller to locate a buyer for the seller's real property. In some cases, however, a broker may be hired by a potential buyer to find a parcel of real estate for purchase.

A prospective purchaser seeking commercial or industrial property is particularly likely to hire a broker for this reason. In this situation the broker and the buyer usually will draw up an agreement commonly referred to as a finder's agreement. This document sets forth in detail the nature of the property desired and the amount of the broker's compensation.

In recent years more sophisticated buyers, who realize that the usual agent is supposed to put the seller's interests first, have started employing their own

buyer's brokers. The broker who is working for the buyer must, of course, make the exact situation known to all parties.

Agent's Responsibilities to Principal

The broker, as an agent, owes his or her principal certain duties. An agent has a *fiduciary relationship* with his or her principal, that is, a relationship of trust and confidence between employer and employee. This confidential relationship carries with it certain duties that the broker must perform—the duties of **care, obedience, accounting,** and **loyalty,** easily remembered as the word COAL (see Figure 2.1) A final duty is *notice.*

Figure 2.1
Agent's Responsibilities

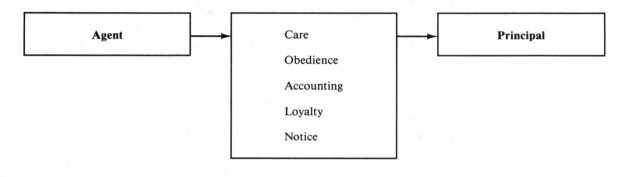

Care. The broker, as an agent, must exercise a reasonable degree of care while transacting business entrusted to him or her by the principal. The broker is liable to the principal for any loss resulting from negligence or carelessness.

Obedience. The broker is obligated to act in good faith and in conformity with his or her principal's instructions and authority. Again, a broker is liable for any losses incurred by the principal due to any acts the broker performs that are not within the scope of authority granted. The broker is not, however, required to obey unlawful or unethical instructions.

Accounting. The broker must be able to report the status of all funds entrusted to him or her. Real estate license laws require brokers to give duplicate originals of all documents to all parties affected by them and to keep copies of such documents on file for three years. In addition, the license laws require the broker to immediately deposit all funds entrusted to him or her in a special trust, or escrow, account. The laws make it illegal for the broker to commingle such monies with personal funds or to retain any interest they earn.

Loyalty. An agent must always place a principal's interests above those of other persons. Thus, an agent cannot disclose such information as the principal's financial condition, the fact that the principal (if the seller) will accept a price lower than the listing price, or any similar confidential facts that might harm the principal's bargaining position.

New York forbids brokers or salespersons from buying property listed with them for their own accounts or for accounts in which they have a personal interest without first notifying the principal of such interest and receiving his or her consent. By law neither brokers nor salespersons may sell property in which they have a personal interest without informing the purchaser of that interest. It is prudent to make such a disclosure in writing.

Notice. Along with these four responsibilities goes the duty of notice. It is the broker's duty to keep the principal fully informed at all times of all facts or information the broker obtains that could affect the principal's business or decisions. In certain instances the broker may be held liable for damages for failure to disclose such information. The broker must volunteer pertinent information whether or not the seller knows enough to ask.

Agent's Responsibilities to Third Parties

In dealing with a buyer, a broker, as an agent of the seller, must exercise extreme caution and be aware of the laws and ethical considerations that affect this relationship. For example, brokers must be careful about the statements they or their staff members make about a parcel of real estate. Statements of opinion are permissible as long as they are offered as opinions and without any intention to deceive. Making such statements when selling real estate is called **puffing.**

Statements of fact, however, must be accurate and questions must be answered honestly. The broker must be alert to ensure that none of his or her statements can in any way be interpreted as involving **fraud.** Fraud encompasses all deceitful or dishonest practices intended to harm or take advantage of another person. If a contract to purchase real estate is obtained as a result of misstatements made by a broker or his or her salespersons, the contract may be disaffirmed or renounced by the purchaser. In such a case the broker will lose a commission. If either party suffers loss because of a broker's misrepresentations, the broker can be held liable for damages. Fraud is discussed in detail in Chapter 14.

Brokers and salespersons should be aware that the courts have ruled that a seller is responsible for revealing to a buyer any hidden or **latent defects** in a building. *A latent defect is one that is not discoverable by ordinary inspection.* As an agent of the seller, a broker is likewise responsible for disclosing such *hidden defects.* Buyers have been able to either rescind the sales contract or receive damages in such instances. Examples of such circumstances are cases in which a house was built over a ditch that was covered with decaying timber, a buried drain tile caused water to accumulate, or a driveway was built partly on adjoining property. New York courts have not completely ruled in this area.

Dual agency. In dealing with buyers, the broker must be careful of any situation that might be considered a **dual,** or **double, agency.** Sometimes a broker may have the opportunity to receive compensation from both the buyer and seller in a transaction. Theoretically, however, an agent cannot be loyal to two or more distinct principals in the same transaction. Thus real estate license laws prohibit a broker from representing and collecting compensation from both parties to a transaction without their prior mutual knowledge and consent.

Before entering into a listing agreement a licensee should fully explain to a seller/principal the nature of the agency relationship and the provisions of the document that creates it. Also, to avoid potential problems arising from misunderstanding under the usual agency arrangement in which the seller is principal, a licensee should inform each buyer/customer that he or she represents the seller and owes the seller 100-percent loyalty. However, giving this information does not relieve the licensee from dealing fairly and honestly with the buyer/customer.

Nature of the Brokerage Business	A broker has the right to reject agency contracts that in his or her judgment violate the ethics or high standards of the office. However, after a brokerage relationship has been established, the broker represents the person who has engaged him or her. The broker owes that person, the principal, the duty to exercise care, skill, and integrity in carrying out instructions.
Broker-Salesperson Relationship	A person licensed to perform any real estate activities on behalf of a licensed real estate broker is known as a real estate salesperson. *The salesperson is responsible to the broker under whom he or she is licensed.* A salesperson can carry out only those responsibilities assigned by that broker.

A broker is licensed to act as the principal's agent and thus can collect a commission for performing his or her assigned duties. A salesperson, on the other hand, has no authority to make contracts or receive compensation directly from a principal. The broker is fully responsible for the actions of all salespeople licensed under him or her. *All of a salesperson's activities must be performed in the name of his or her supervising broker.*

The salesperson functions as a **subagent** of the broker; so do cooperating brokers who choose to work on the broker's listings. In a multiple listing cooperative sale, both listing broker and selling broker have a fiduciary relationship with the seller unless the buyers have specifically retained their own agent.

Independent contractor vs. employee. Salespersons are engaged by brokers as either employees or independent contractors. The agreement between a broker and a salesperson should be set down in a written contract that defines the obligations and responsibilities of the relationship. The independent contractor relationship is discussed in detail in Chapter 13.

The nature of the employer-employee relationship allows a broker to exercise certain *controls* over salespeople who are employees. The broker may require an **employee** to adhere to regulations concerning such matters as working hours, office routine, and dress standards. As an employer a broker is required by the federal government to withhold social security tax and income tax from wages paid to employees. He or she also is required to pay unemployment compensation tax on wages as defined by state and federal laws. A broker may provide employees with such benefits as health insurance.

A broker's relationship with an independent contractor is different. The **independent contractor**-salesperson operates more independently than an employee and the broker may not control his or her activities in the same way. Basically the broker may control *what* the independent contractor will do but not *how* it will be done. An independent contractor assumes responsibility for paying his or her own income and social security taxes and must provide his or her own health insurance if such coverage is desired. An independent contractor receives nothing from his or her broker that could be construed as an employee benefit.

In June 1982, the Court of Appeals, New York State's highest court, overturned an attempt to collect unemployment insurance premiums from a New York broker. The court found the brokerage "exercises no control over the results produced by its salespersons or the means used . . . the salespersons are therefore appropriately to be considered independent contractors." Among evidence cited were the facts that the salespersons were paid a commission upon gross sales and were not entitled to draw against commissions; that they were permitted to work whatever hours they chose and were free to engage in outside employment; that neither attendance at sales meetings nor initial training was mandatory; that the salespersons paid their own premiums in a group insurance plan; and that most leads were generated by the salespersons themselves.

The federal Internal Revenue Service has provided "safe harbor" guidelines under which independent contractor status will not be challenged where the associate is licensed, has fluctuating income based on commissions, and works under a written contract specifying independent contractor status.

Figure 2.2
Employee versus
Independent Contractor

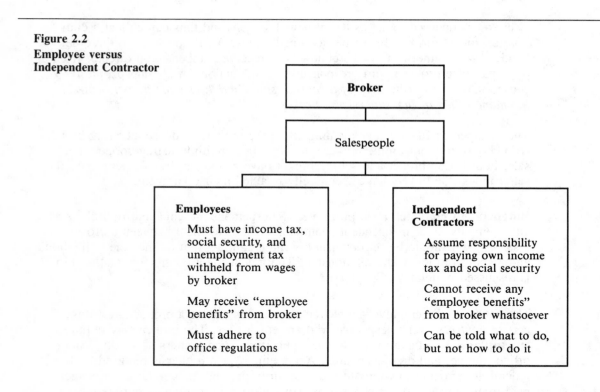

Broker's Compensation

The broker's compensation is specified in the listing agreement, management agreement, or other contract with the principal and is subject to negotiation between the parties. Compensation usually is computed as a *percentage of the total amount of money involved.* Such commission is usually considered to be earned when the broker has accomplished the work for which he or she was hired. After a seller accepts an offer from a ready, willing, and able buyer, the seller technically is liable for the broker's commission regardless of whether or not the buyer completes the purchase. **A ready, willing, and able buyer** is one who is *prepared to buy on the seller's terms, is financially capable, and is ready to take positive steps toward consummation of the transaction.*

Figure 2.3
Broker's Compensation

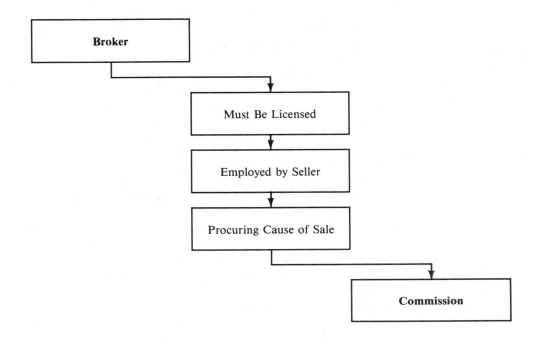

A broker who has produced a buyer who is ready, willing, and able to meet the listing terms is usually still entitled to a commission if the transaction is *not* consummated for any of the following reasons:

1. The owner changes his or her mind and refuses to sell.
2. There are defects in the owner's title that are not corrected.
3. The owner commits fraud with respect to the transaction.
4. The owner is unable to deliver possession within a reasonable time.
5. The owner insists on terms not in the listing (for example, the right to restrict the use of the property).
6. The owner and the buyer agree to cancel the transaction.

In other words, *a broker generally is due a commission if a sale is not consummated because of the principal's default.*

The broker is entitled to a fee if he or she is the **procuring cause of a sale** or lease, produces a ready, willing, and able buyer, or brings about a **meeting of the minds.** It is customary in New York that the broker collect the commission at the closing of title even though the fee actually is earned when all conditions of the sale are met. Generally, the broker is considered to have earned a fee if buyer and seller have established the price, the amount of cash to be paid, the duration of the mortgage, the interest rate, and amortization. A carefully drafted agency agreement that sets forth such specifics as the property's address, the price, terms, expiration date of agency, and percentage rate of commission can help the broker prevent enforcement problems.

New York allows a broker who fears avoidance of commission to file an affidavit of entitlement or, in some cases, a lien (financial claim) against property. The process is detailed in Chapter 24.

The rate of a broker's commission is *negotiable in every case.* Any attempt, no matter how subtle, to impose uniform commission rates would be a clear violation of state and federal antitrust laws (which will be discussed later in this chapter).

New York's license laws make it illegal for a broker to share a commission with someone who is not licensed as a salesperson or broker. This has been construed to include the giving of certain items of personal property (for instance, a new TV to "a friend" for providing a valuable lead) and other premiums (vacations and the like) as well as finder's fees and portions of the commission. **Kickbacks,** the return of part of the commission as gifts or money to buyers or sellers, are also prohibited.

Salesperson's compensation. The compensation of a salesperson is set by a mutual agreement between the broker and salesperson. A broker may agree to pay a salary or a share of the commissions from transactions originated by a salesperson. Some brokers require salespeople to pay all or part of the expenses of advertising listed properties. The salesperson may never accept compensation from any buyer, seller, or broker except the one broker with whom he or she is associated.

Duncan and Hill Decision

An important court decision in 1978, *Duncan and Hill v. the Department of State,* involved a Rochester real estate firm. The court considered the question: To what extent can a real estate agent participate in the preparation of a real estate offer and counteroffer? In a complaint precipitated by the broker's refusal to return a $200 deposit to the prospective purchaser, the charge was made that the broker, not being an attorney, illegally prepared legal documents: an offer, counteroffer, and acceptance. The court ruled that by inserting detailed terms of the mortgage into the offer, the broker was indeed illegally practicing law. Among the terms cited were "callable in 10 years," "prepayment privileges," and "standard default in 10 days." The court cautioned brokers to refrain from inserting any provision that requires exercise of legal expertise and to confine themselves to a general description of the property, price to be paid, and mortgaging to be secured. The court also said that brokers may readily protect themselves from the charge of the unlawful practice of law by inserting in the document that it is subject to the approval of the respective attorneys for the parties.

Antitrust Laws

The real estate industry is subject to federal and state **antitrust laws.** Generally, these laws prohibit monopolies and contracts, combinations, and conspiracies that unreasonably restrain trade. The most common antitrust violations that can occur in the real estate business are price-fixing and allocation of customers or markets.

Illegal *price-fixing* occurs when brokers conspire to set prices for the services they perform (sales commissions, management rates) rather than let those prices be established through competition in the open market.

Real estate licensees must be scrupulously careful to dissociate themselves from the slightest discussion of commission rates with any member of a competing firm. In the past a number of New York brokers and real estate boards have suffered from charges under antitrust laws.

Allocation of customers or markets involves an agreement between brokers to divide their markets and refrain from competing with each other's business. Allocations may take place on a geographic basis with brokers agreeing to specific territories within which they will operate exclusively. The division may also take place along other lines; for example, two brokers may agree that one will handle only residential properties less than $100,000 in value, while another will handle residential properties more than $100,000 in value.

The penalties for such acts are severe. For example, under the Sherman Antitrust Act people who fix prices or allocate markets may be found guilty of a misdemeanor, punishable by a maximum $100,000 fine and three years in prison. In a civil suit a person who has suffered a loss because of the antitrust activities of a guilty party may recover triple the value of the actual damages plus attorney's fees and costs.

Summary

Real estate brokerage is the bringing together, for a fee or commission, of people who wish to buy, sell, exchange, or lease real estate.

An important part of real estate brokerage is the *law of agency*. A real estate broker is the *agent,* hired by either a buyer or a seller of real estate to sell or find a particular parcel of real estate. The person who hires the broker is the *principal.* The principal and the agent have a *fiduciary relationship* under which the agent owes the principal the duties of care, obedience, accounting, loyalty, and notice.

The broker's compensation in a real estate sale generally takes the form of a *commission,* which is often a percentage of the real estate's selling price. The broker is considered to have earned a commission when he or she procures a *ready, willing, and able buyer* for a seller or brings about a *meeting of the minds*.

A broker may hire salespeople to assist him or her in this work. The salesperson works as a subagent on the broker's behalf as either an *employee* or an *independent* contractor.

Many of the general operations of a real estate brokerage are regulated by the real estate license laws. In addition, state and federal *antitrust laws* prohibit brokers from conspiring to fix prices or allocate customers or markets.

Questions

1. The term *fiduciary* refers to:
   a. the sale of another's property by an authorized agent.
   b. principles by which a real estate broker must conduct his or her business.
   c. one who acts as a trustee for another and has legal authority to act on behalf of that person.
   d. the principal in a principal-agent relationship.

2. A person who has the authority to enter into contracts concerning all business and legal affairs of another is called a(n):
   a. general agent.   c. special agent.
   b. universal agent.   d. attorney.

3. The legal relationship between broker and seller is generally a(n):
   a. special agency.   c. ostensible agency.
   b. general agency.   d. universal agency.

4. The real estate broker usually is hired as an agent through the document known as a:
   a. listing agreement.
   b. finder's agreement.
   c. meeting of the minds.
   d. procuring contract.

5. The statement "a broker must be employed to recover a commission for his or her services" means:
   a. the broker must work in a real estate office.
   b. the seller must have made an agreement to pay a commission to the broker for selling the property.
   c. the broker must have asked the seller the price of the property and then found a ready, willing, and able buyer.
   d. the broker must have a salesperson employed in the office.

6. Any listing agreement in New York State must be in writing if:
   a. the broker intends to collect a commission.
   b. it is for a period of more than one year.
   c. the broker produced a buyer ready, willing, and able.
   d. the property previously was listed with another broker.

7. A listing may be terminated when either broker or principal:
   a. gets married.
   b. goes bankrupt.
   c. overfinances other property.
   d. becomes 21 years of age.

8. The salesperson who sincerely tries to represent both buyer and seller is in danger of falling into:
   a. fraud.   c. dual agency.
   b. puffing.   d. general agency.

9. A seller who wishes to cancel a listing agreement in New York:
   a. must cite a legally acceptable reason.
   b. may not cancel without the agent's consent.
   c. may be held liable for money and time expended by the broker.
   d. may not sell the property for six months after.

10. A broker is entitled to collect a commission from both the seller and the buyer:
    a. when the broker holds a state license.
    b. when the buyer and the seller are related.
    c. when both parties agree to such a transaction.
    d. when both parties have attorneys.

11. Miss Mollie's father bought the house in 1940 for $4,500. She asks Bob Broker to list it and instructs him to see if he can get as much as $35,000 "because she's heard houses have gone up in value." Bob knows the property might bring $55,000. In such a case:
    a. Bob should take the listing as instructed, knowing he can produce a prompt, trouble-free sale for Miss Mollie.
    b. Bob should buy the house himself for the full $35,000, making sure his purchase contract reveals that he is a licensed broker.
    c. Bob should buy the house only through his cousin, who has a different last name, in order to avoid a breach of fiduciary duty.
    d. Bob has an obligation to tell Miss Mollie that he believes the house is worth much more.

12. An example of a latent defect would be a:
    a. large crack in the dining-room ceiling.
    b. roof with warped shingles.
    c. used-car lot next door.
    d. malfunctioning septic tank.

13. An independent contractor may be paid:
    a. regular draw against earnings.
    b. reimbursed car expenses.
    c. commissions on sales.
    d. two-week vacations each year.

14. Commissions usually are earned:
    a. when the buyer makes a purchase offer.
    b. when the seller accepts the buyer's offer without conditions.
    c. when a new mortgage has been promised by the lender.
    d. when title to the property transfers.

15. Even if a proposed transaction does not go through, the broker sometimes may collect a commission where:
    a. the buyer turned out to be financially unable.
    b. the seller refused to do repairs required by the lender.
    c. the seller simply backed out.
    d. the lender did not appraise the house for the sale price.

16. A meeting of the minds occurs when the:
    a. seller signs a listing agreement.
    b. buyer is introduced to seller.
    c. buyer and seller agree on price and terms of sale.
    d. final closing (settlement) of the transaction takes place.

17. Commission rates are set by:
    a. state law.
    b. local custom.
    c. the broker.
    d. agreement between seller and broker.

18. Henry Householder lists his house with Larry Lister. Henry offers a bonus commission of $500 to the salesperson who brings a good buyer before Thanksgiving. Sam Salesman, who is associated with the cooperating firm of Olive Otherbroker, effects the sale on November 1. Sam may collect that bonus from:
    a. Henry.   c. Olive.
    b. Larry.   d. no one.

19. The Duncan and Hill decision warned real estate licensees against:
    a. drawing up legal documents.
    b. entering into dual agency.
    c. committing fraud.
    d. puffing.

20. At a booth in the neighborhood coffee shop, Bob Broker is seated with his friendly rival, Olive Otherbroker. Olive says, "Did you hear about that firm that's charging a flat fee for selling property? Do you think they'll make it?" Bob's proper response is to:
    a. explain to Olive that flat fees are allowed by law, just as commissions are.
    b. assure Olive that his commission rates are not going to change.
    c. caution Olive about the dangers of discussing commission rates with competing firms.
    d. say "goodbye" immediately and walk out.

Appendix: Excerpts from New York State's Study Booklet for Brokers

SUMMARY OF THE LAW OF AGENCY RELATING TO REAL ESTATE BROKERAGE

The law of agency (or principal and agent) governs the relationship between real estate brokers and salespersons and their clients—the owners and buyers.

Authorization—employment. The foundation of an agency is an authorization or contract of employment, the terms of which may be either expressed or implied. An expressed agreement is one in which the terms have been discussed and agreed to by the parties, either verbally or in writing. An implied contract is one which arises from the act of the parties, as where an owner lists property as being for sale or rent with a real estate broker, or sells or leases property to a person introduced as a buyer or lessee by a broker, or by the appropriation of the labors of the broker. The law of New York State does not require that an authorization must be in writing unless, by its terms, it is not to be performed within one year, in which event a written contract is required to be signed by the party to be bound. . . .

A broker can bind the owner only insofar as the broker has been authorized. The broker's powers or authority are limited to those actually conferred by the owner. Hence, employment to sell or lease is mere authority to find a buyer or lessee and to act as an intermediary between them. There must be express authority to accept deposits or sign a contract.

Duration and termination of broker's employment. The employment of a real estate broker may or may not be for a definite time. . . .

It should be noted that a principal has the unquestionable power to cancel the authority or agency given by the principal to a broker. That power stems from the inalienable right of an owner to dispose of or refuse to dispose of his/her property. . . . Where the authority is for a fixed time, the principal is answerable for damages for the cancellation of the broker's authority prior to the expiration date whereas where the authority

is for an unspecified time, the principal acting in good faith, may cancel the broker's authority at will. . . . Authority . . . is terminable upon the occurrence of any of the following events: (a) when the object has not been performed during the specified period or, where the period of authority is unspecified, the object has not been performed or accomplished within a reasonable time, (b) death or insanity of a broker or principal, (c) bankruptcy of either, (d) destruction of the subject matter, (e) broker's fraudulent conduct for own benefit, or (f) sale by another broker if the authority is for an unspecified time.

Dual employment. A broker may be employed by both the seller and buyer of real estate, neither of whom can avoid payment of compensation if either knew and consented that the broker also represent the other party.

Interpretation of authorization. The law of the place of the contract governs its enforcement. An authorization made in New York is enforceable in accordance with the provisions of the laws of New York, irrespective of the location of the land the broker is employed to sell or lease.

When commissions are earned. To entitle a broker to compensation, the broker's services must have been the procuring cause of the sale or lease. A broker is not entitled to a commission until the buyer and seller agree, not only as to the respective price, but as to the terms of the transaction and all other points material thereto. A broker may not be entitled to commission where, although the broker introduced the purchaser to the seller, the broker did not bring them to an agreement and the transaction was subsequently negotiated by another broker.

In the absence of a special agreement, the services rendered by a broker to an owner of real property generally fall into one of two categories: (1) where an owner has given the broker full and complete terms upon which the owner is willing to sell the property and not merely the asking price thereof; (2) where the owner has the property for sale and may or may not have set an asking price thereof, and has not fixed the terms of the transaction, leaving them to be determined thereafter. In the first case the broker's duty is fulfilled when the broker produces a customer ready, able and willing to comply with all the terms fixed by the owner. In the second case, the broker's commissions may not be earned until the customer produced by the broker reaches an agreement with owner upon the price and terms upon which a sale can be made. This of course, does not mean that a contract in writing must be signed by the parties, but that they are in agreement not only upon price but upon all the essential terms which they reasonably consider to be essential. The terms essential to effect a meeting of minds are: (1) Price; (2) Amount of Cash; (3) Duration of Mortgages; (4) Rate of Interest; and (5) Amortization. Having rendered the services described in these two transactions, the broker's right to the commissions is undisturbed even though the transaction was not consummated by the principals.

Commission rates. The commission or compensation of a real estate broker is not regulated by statute; nor is it legally fixed by the regulations of the real estate board in a particular community, as many suppose. The broker and the employer may agree upon any reasonable rate of compensation, or the method or time of payment thereof, that is mutually acceptable. But, in the absence of such an agreement, the broker is entitled to commissions, or compensation for services, only at the rate customarily paid for similar services in the community in which the broker's services were rendered.

Conflicting commission claims: "procuring cause". Where an owner employs a number of brokers to negotiate a transaction, the broker whose services are the procuring cause of the sale or lease is entitled to compensation, usually this means the broker who first induces the customer to agree to the owner's terms. The broker who actually negotiates a sale or lease may be entitled to compensation, notwithstanding the fact that the owner has erroneously paid a full commission on the same transaction to another broker.

"Ready, willing and able." The words "ready" and "willing" are synonymously used to mean that the broker's customer is prepared to enter into a contract with the broker's principal on his/her terms. The word "able" refers to the customer's ability to enter into a contract with the broker's principal on his/her terms. It refers to financial ability to buy the property offered to the customer and in the event of an exchange it refers to the ownership or right to the property owned by the customer and offered in exchange. If the prospective purchaser is able to tender the sums or deeds required at the time of the execution of a contract such customer is considered "able" to perform the contract. However, the above discussed elements of the broker's customer's ability to buy or exchange must be proved in a case where no binding contract has been signed by the principals. Where the principals entered into a written contract they are both treated as being mutually satisfied of each other's ability to perform.

Disclosure of customer. Where the disclosure of the name of the customer is not requested by the broker's employer, a broker is not bound to disclose to the client the identity of the customer. However, a broker may not be entitled to commissions where the broker did not inform the client of the name of the prospective customer and, after negotiations failed, the purchaser sought out the owner and affected a sale directly. A broker may lose commissions where the broker failed to disclose name of buyer for fear the price would be increased by the seller and later the property is sold to the same buyer. It is obvious that without disclosure of the name of the customer, the employer is unable to investigate the customer.

Commissions payable. Unless otherwise provided in the authorization, a broker's commission is due and payable when it has been earned. A broker employed to negotiate a sale of real property, for instance, earns a commission when the broker produces a purchaser who is ready, able and willing to buy on the seller's terms. It is not imperative, however, that a broker shall produce a customer who will buy or lease upon the terms specified in the listing. The broker is entitled to a commission if the broker brings the client and the customer together and, after mutual bargaining, they come to an agreement; even at a price and on terms materially different from those specified in the authorization.

Deferment of payment of commissions. The original commission agreement between a broker and employer may contemplate that the commission will be earned by the broker only if and when title passes to the buyer. Even if such a provision was not in the original commission agreement, the broker may still agree, subsequently, to waive payment of commission unless and until title passes. . . . However, the courts have refused to enforce such waiver of commission agreements, where the broker's employer was found to be at fault for the nonconsummation of the transaction. It is not uncommon for a broker to agree to waive the payment of commissions where the failure to effect transfer of title is due for any cause whatsoever, including the fault of the client. Brokers are therefore cautioned to seek advice of counsel before entering into such waiver of commission agreements.

Default by owner. In order to deprive a broker of a commission, an owner cannot, in bad faith, terminate a broker's employment and make a sale or lease directly. A broker is entitled to compensation where the owner refuses to sign a contract of sale on the terms the owner originally proposed or where, because of some defect, the title to the property is unmarketable, or where the owner is guilty of misrepresentation or mistake as to size of property or is guilty of a misstatement of the amount of rentals. . . .

Default by buyer. A broker is not entitled to a commission unless the buyer is ready and able to comply with the terms of the agreement to buy or lease. If a contract is entered into between a buyer and seller, the broker's right to commission is not affected by the buyer's . . . refusal or failure to perform. When a binder, signed by a prospective customer, provides that the customer will pay the broker's commission the customer is liable for the commission if he or she fails or refuses to consummate the negotiation or fails or refuses to complete the transaction.

Duty to owners. An agent is bound, not only to good faith, but to reasonable diligence and such skill as is generally possessed by persons of ordinary capacity in the same business. A broker may not profit by deceiving the owner. An owner may hold the broker to strict loyalty and require the broker to account fully for the profits of a transaction wherein the owner was defrauded.

If a broker submits any offer of purchase to the owner, the broker is duty bound to reveal any other better offers that have been made. If a broker fails to do so, the broker cannot recover commissions. A broker must disclose higher offers even if the higher offer has less cash. A broker is not entitled to any commission where the broker induced the owner to accept less than the asking price after the buyer has indicated a willingness to pay the asking price. A broker cannot claim commissions where the broker has induced the owner to accept less than the asking price knowing the property is of special value to the buyer. A broker is duty bound to reveal any facts in the broker's possession concerning the buyer's intention to resell at an increased price.

A broker cannot take a position which is not in the best interest of an owner. Hence, a broker employed to sell cannot purchase for himself or herself without a full disclosure of the broker's interest. A broker cannot sell the owner's property to a corporation or partnership in which the broker is interested without similar disclosure.

Duty to buyers. Brokers should guard against inaccuracies in their representations to buyers. If a misstatement is made as to a matter of fact by a broker, it may have the most serious consequences, both to the broker and to the owner. Such a misrepresentation, if it is material and intentional, may be fraudulent and may justify a refusal by a buyer to take title and afford the owner a defense to the broker's claim for a commission. It is not the duty of the broker to verify all representations made by the owner. Nonetheless, if the broker knows or has reason to know that the owner has made misrepresentations, or has failed to disclose material defects, then the broker is under a duty not to perpetuate such misrepresentations.

Deposit money. A real estate broker, by reason of the nature of the broker's work, is in a position to come into possession of funds belonging to others. The question often arises as to whom such money belongs and what disposition should be made of the funds by the broker. A real estate broker who is duly authorized to manage real property is authorized to collect rents. With relation to such moneys, there is never any question but that the money belongs to the owner and must be kept in a separate bank account and must be duly accounted for to the broker's client.

However, where a real estate broker has been employed by an owner to find a buyer, it is customary for the broker to take a deposit from the prospective buyer, issue a receipt and have the prospective purchaser execute an offer to buy subject to acceptance by the owner. . . . Experience has demonstrated that brokers may become involved in difficulties and may place their licenses in jeopardy when they do not take time to learn their responsibilities with relation to other people's money. Brokers should be thoroughly familiar with the law of agency and the rules applicable to deposits to avoid the pitfalls encountered in the handling of funds belonging to third persons.

3

Real Estate Instruments: Estates and Interests

Key Terms

Beneficiary
Common elements
Condominium
Cooperative
Co-ownership
Corporation
Curtesy
Dower
Easement
Easement appurtenant
Easement by necessity
Easement in gross
Easement by prescription
Encroachment
Encumbrance
Estate in land
Fee simple
Fee on condition
Freehold estate
General partnership
Homestead

Joint tenancy
Leasehold estate
License
Lien
Life estate
Limited partnership
Partition
Partnership
Qualified fee
Remainder interest
Restriction
Reversionary interest
Right of survivorship
Severalty
Syndicate
Tenancy by the entirety
Tenancy in common
Trust
Trustee
Trustor
Undivided interest

Overview

Ownership of a parcel of real estate is not necessarily absolute. An owner may or may not be able to pass property on to heirs. Sometimes ownership may exist only as long as property is used for one specific purpose. In addition other persons may possess certain interests in one's real estate. Purchasers must consider many different forms of ownership before they take title to a parcel of real estate. The choice of ownership form will affect such matters as the owner's legal right to sell without the consent of others, right to choose heirs, and the future rights of creditors. Estate and gift tax consequences also may need to be considered. This chapter will discuss various interests in real estate and the basic forms of real estate ownership.

Estates in Land

The degree, quantity, nature, and extent of interest that a person has in real property is an **estate in land.** Estates in land are divided into two major classifications: (1) freehold estates and (2) leasehold estates (those involving tenants).

Freehold estates *are estates of indeterminable length,* such as those existing for a lifetime or forever. The freehold estates recognized in New York are: (1) fee simple, (2) qualified (determinable) fee, (3) fee on condition, and (4) life estates.

The first three of these estates continue for an indefinite period and are inheritable by the heirs of the owner; the fourth terminates upon the death of the person on whose life it is based.

Leasehold estates are *estates for a fixed term of years.* They are classified as:

Estate for years: Commonly established by a lease, written or (if for a period of less than one year) oral, an estate for years gives the tenant possession of the property for a specific period of time. No notice is necessary from either party to end the tenancy at the expiration of the term

Periodic estate, estate at will, estate at sufferance: These leasehold estates are covered at length in Chapter 22. Each lasts for an indefinite length of time. If the premises are let on a month-to-month tenancy, New York State law requires 30 days' notice to terminate, from the day the rent is due, typically the first day of the month.

The various estates and interests are illustrated in Figure 3.1.

Fee Simple Estate

An estate in **fee simple** is the *highest type of interest in real estate recognized by law.* A fee simple estate is one in which the holder is entitled to all rights incident to the property. There is no time limit on its existence—it is said to run forever. It is complete ownership. Upon the death of its owner the estate passes to heirs. The terms *fee, fee simple,* and *fee simple absolute* are basically the same. New York law provides that a grant of real property conveys an estate in fee simple unless the terms of the grant show a clear intention to convey a lesser estate.

Qualified Fee Estate

In New York a **qualified fee,** also known as a determinable fee or estate on limitation, is an estate in land that terminates *automatically* on the occurrence or nonocurrence of a specified event. The words "while," "until," and "so long as" generally signify the conveyance of a qualified fee estate. For example, Smith conveys 1,000 acres to the Jones Foundation "so long as it is maintained as a wildlife preserve and used for no other purpose." Five years later the Jones Foundation decides to build its corporate headquarters on this land. Title to the land automatically reverts to Smith or his heirs. This future interest is called a *possibility of reverter.*

Figure 3.1
Estates and Interests in
Real Estate

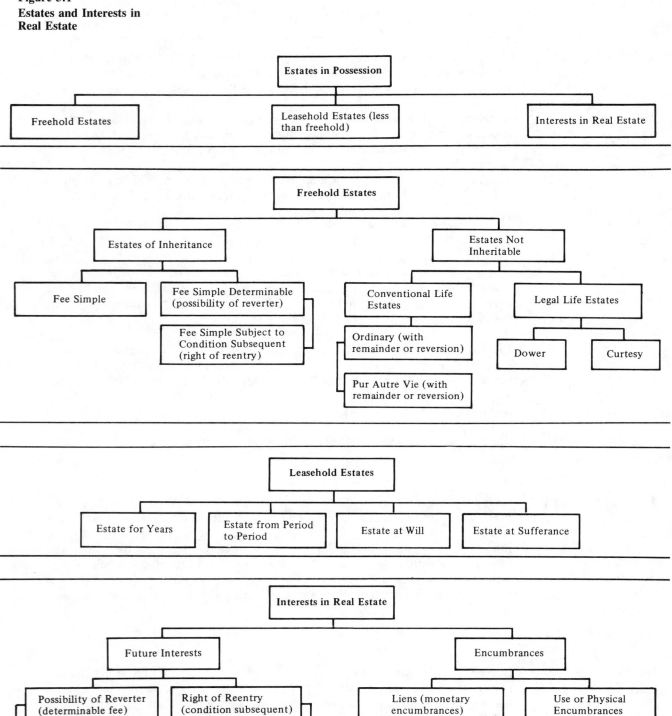

Fee on Condition

A fee on condition differs from a qualified fee in that the occurrence or nonoccurrence of a specified condition *may* terminate the estate created by the grant. The occurrence of such a condition creates a *right of reentry* for the grantor but *does not automatically terminate* the estate in that person's favor. Thus, if Smith conveyed his land to the Jones Foundation, "provided it be used solely as a wild-life preserve," Jones's subsequent use of the land as its corporate headquarters would create a right for Smith or his heirs to recover title to the land. Title would remain with Jones, however, until Smith filed suit in court to recover it. New York court opinions harbor many subtle distinctions between qualified estates and estates on condition.

Conventional Life Estates

A conventional **life estate** is *limited in duration to the life of some designated person.* The owner does not have the right to pass ownership to heirs because the estate terminates at the death of the owner. Life estates may be *ordinary* or *pur autre vie.*

An *ordinary* life estate lasts as long as the life tenant is alive. It ends with the death of the person to whom it was granted. A may leave property to B, who will be complete owner in fee simple for the rest of his or her life. B does not, however, have the right to leave the property to anyone at death.

A life estate *pur autre vie* (for another life) lasts as long as some third person is alive. Mrs. A might, for example, leave her home to neighbor B, to be owned by B "as long as my cat, Felix, is alive and living in the home." B (or even B's heirs) would be complete owner of the property but only until the cat's death.

Remainder and reversion: The owner creating a life interest provides for the eventual disposal of the property. After the death of the life tenant, the property may pass to some third party or return to the original owner.

1. **Remainder interest:** Mr. A may leave the family homestead to the second Mrs. A for her lifetime with the provision that it pass, at her death, to the son of his first marriage, A, Jr. During Mrs. A's lifetime, A, Jr. owns a *remainder interest* and is known as a *remainderman.*

2. **Reversionary interest:** Mr. A may give his home to poor relative B for B's lifetime with the provision that at B's death, ownership reverts to A (or, if A has died, to A's heirs). During B's lifetime, Mr. A owns a *reversionary interest.*

A life tenant's interest in real property is a true ownership interest. In general, the life tenant is not answerable to the *remainderman.* The life tenant cannot, however, perform any acts that would permanently injure the land or property. Such injury to real estate is known in legal terms as *waste.*

A life tenant is entitled to all income and profits arising from the property during his or her term of ownership. A life interest may be sold, leased, or mortgaged but it always will terminate upon the death of the person against whose life the estate is measured.

Legal Life Estates

Curtesy and dower. A husband's life estate in the real estate of his deceased wife is called **curtesy.** **Dower** is the life estate that a wife has in the real estate of her deceased husband. New York law no longer recognizes dower and curtesy as legal life estates. Brokers should be alert, however, to possible rights of dower and curtesy in property owned by couples married before September 1, 1930.

Homestead

In New York homestead is not an estate but rather the right to protection of a principal residence against certain creditors' claims, particularly in bankruptcy. The homestead exemption protects up to $10,000 of a homeowner's equity from the court-ordered sale of his or her home to satisfy *unsecured* debts. An unsecured debt is one in which there is no collateral—the person's home has not been given as security for payment of the loan. A charge account or personal loan would be an example of an unsecured debt.

Encumbrances

A claim, charge, or liability that attaches to and is binding on real estate is an **encumbrance.** It is a right or interest held by a party who is not the owner of the property. An encumbrance may lessen the value or obstruct the use of the property but it does not necessarily prevent a transfer of title.

Encumbrances may be divided into two general classifications: (1) liens (usually monetary), which affect the title, and (2) encumbrances that affect the physical condition of the property, such as restrictions, easements, licenses, and encroachments.

Liens

A charge against property that provides security for a debt or obligation of the property owner is a **lien.** If the obligation is not repaid, the lienholder, or creditor, has the right to have it paid out of the debtor's property, usually from the proceeds of a court sale.

Real estate taxes (discussed at more length in Chapter 25) have first claim against the proceeds of such a sale. *Judgments* are court orders to pay a debt, for example, an outstanding hospital bill. They may be filed against any real estate owned by the debtor in the county where the judgment was obtained or in any county in the state.

Mechanics' liens are placed against a specific property by workmen who have not been paid for labor or materials used in construction or repairs. A claim for a mechanic's lien must be placed within four months of the completion of the work on a single dwelling and eight months on other buildings.

Liens will be discussed in detail in Chapter 24.

Restrictions

Private agreements placed in the public record that affect the use of land are **deed restrictions** *and covenants.* They usually are imposed by an owner of real estate when he or she sells the property and they are included in the seller's deed to the buyer. Deed restrictions typically would be imposed by a developer or subdivider to maintain specific standards in a subdivision. Deed restrictions are discussed further in Chapter 6.

Easements

A right acquired by one party to use the land of another party for a special purpose is an **easement.** Easements are discussed in detail in Chapter 24.

Easement appurtenant. The permanent right to use another's land is an **easement appurtenant.** In Figure 3.2, for example, B has the right to cross A's land to reach the lake. The easement was granted (given) by A and is owned by B. B's property, which benefits from the arrangement, is known as the *dominant tenement,* A's is the *servient tenement.* An easement appurtenant *runs with the land,* so that if B sells the property to C, C acquires the same right-of-way over A's land.

Figure 3.2.
Easements

The owner of Lot A has an **easement by necessity** across Lot B to gain access to his property from the paved road. The owner of Lot B has an **easement appurtenant** across Lot A so that B may reach the lake. The utility company has an **easement in gross** across both parcels of land for its electric power lines.

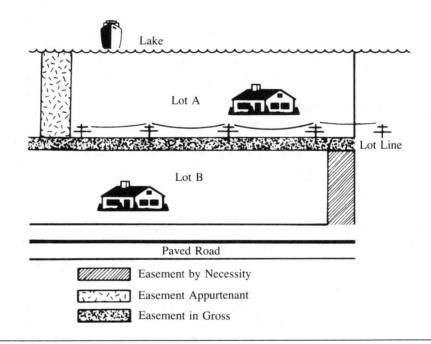

Easement in gross. A simple right to use the land of another is an **easement in gross.** In Figure 3.2, the power company owns an easement in gross on the boundary line of both lots.

Easement by necessity. If the only access to a parcel is through another's property, the owner may acquire an **easement by necessity** in order to reach his or her land. In Figure 3.2, A owns an easement by necessity, from the road, across B's land.

Easement by prescription. Under specific circumstances, one may acquire the right to use another's property by doing so for a period of ten years, creating an **easement by prescription. Tacking** allows consecutive owners to accumulate the ten years' usage.

Party walls. A wall shared by two buildings and constructed on the boundary line between two owners' lots is shared by the owners. Each owns his or her side of the wall and an easement right in the other half.

Creating an easement. Today easements commonly are created by written agreement between the parties establishing the easement right. The methods of creating easements by prescription and terminating easements are discussed in Chapter 24.

Licenses

A privilege to enter the land of another for a specific purpose is a **license.** It is not a permanent right and may be withdrawn. Examples of license include permission to park in a neighbor's driveway and permission to erect a billboard.

Encroachments

When a building (or some portion of it), fence, driveway, or any other installation illegally *extends beyond the land of its owner* and covers some land of an adjoining owner or a street or alley, an **encroachment** arises. Encroachments usually are disclosed by either a physical inspection of the property or a survey. A survey shows the location of all improvements on a property and whether any improvements extend over the lot lines. If the building on a lot encroaches on neighboring land, the neighbor may be able to recover damages or secure removal of the portion of the building that encroaches. Encroachments of long standing (for the prescriptive ten-year period) may give rise to easements by prescription. For encroachments of six inches or less, the prescriptive period may be as little as one or two years.

Forms of Ownership

A fee simple estate in land may be held (1) in **severalty,** where title is held by one owner, (2) in **co-ownership,** where title is held by two or more persons, or (3) in **trust,** where title is held by a third person for the benefit of another, called the beneficiary.

The form by which property is owned is important to the real estate broker's work for two reasons: (1) *the form of ownership existing when a property is sold determines who must sign the various documents involved* (listing contract, acceptance of offer to purchase, sales contract, and deed), and (2) *the purchaser must determine in what form he or she wishes to take title.* When questions about these forms are raised by the parties to a transaction, the real estate broker should recommend that the parties seek legal advice.

Ownership in Severalty

When title to real estate is *vested in* (presently owned by) one person or one organization, that person or organization is said to own the property *in severalty.* This person also is referred to as the *sole owner.*

Co-Ownership

When title to one parcel of real estate is vested in (owned by) two or more persons or organizations, those parties are said to be **co-owners** or *concurrent owners* of the property. New York recognizes (1) tenancy in common, (2) joint tenancy, (3) tenancy by the entirety, and (4) partnership property.

Tenancy in Common

The ownership of a **tenant in common** is an **undivided interest.** Although a tenant in common may hold, say, a one-half or one-third interest in a property, it is impossible to distinguish physically which specific half or third of the property is owned. The deed creating a tenancy in common may or may not state the fractional interest held by each co-owner; if no fractions are stated and two people hold title to the property as co-owners, each has an undivided one-half interest.

The second important characteristic of a tenancy in common is that *each owner* can sell, convey, mortgage, or transfer that interest *without the consent* of the other co-owners. Upon the death of a co-owner, his or her undivided interest passes to his or her heirs or devisees according to his or her will (*see* Figure 3.3).

Figure 3.3
Tenancy in Common

A and B are tenants in common.

A	B
1/2	1/2

B dies and wills his interest to C and D equally.

A	C	D
1/2	1/4	1/4

In New York a conveyance to two or more persons not married to each other creates a tenancy in common unless otherwise stated in the deed. Property passing to two or more persons by intestacy (when a person dies without a will) is also taken by them as tenants in common.

Joint Tenancy

The basis of **joint tenancy** is *unity of ownership*. Only one title exists and it is vested in a unit made up of two or more people. The death of one of the joint tenants does not destroy the unit; it only reduces by one the number of people who make up the owning unit. The remaining joint tenants receive the interest of the deceased tenant by **right of survivorship** (see Figure 3.4).

Figure 3.4
Joint Tenancy with Right of Survivorship

A, B, and C are joint tenants.

A, B, C

B dies, then

A

C dies, then

A + B

A dies and wills his interest to **D** and **E**.

D	E
½	½

D and E are tenants in common.

This right of survivorship is the distinguishing characteristic of joint tenancy. As each successive joint tenant dies, the surviving joint tenants acquire the interest of the deceased joint tenant. Only the last survivor may dispose of the property by will.

Creating joint tenancies. To create a right of survivorship in New York, language in the deed must expressly state that title is to be taken in joint tenancy. Acquisition of property by two more executors, trustees, or guardians creates in them a joint tenancy.

Four unities are required to create a joint tenancy:

1. unity of *time*—all joint tenants acquire their interest at the same time.
2. unity of *title*—all joint tenants acquire their interest by the same deed.
3. unity of *interest*—all joint tenants hold equal ownership interests.
4. unity of *possession*—all joint tenants hold an undivided interest in the property.

These four unities are present when title is acquired by *one deed, executed and delivered at one time and conveying equal interests to all the grantees who hold undivided possession of the property as joint tenants.*

In New York two individuals may become joint tenants of property owned by one of the parties if he or she directly conveys the property to himself or herself and the other as joint tenants with the right of survivorship.

Terminating joint tenancies. A joint tenancy is destroyed when any one of the essential unities of joint tenancy is terminated. Thus, while a joint tenant is free to convey his or her interest in the jointly held property, doing so will destroy the unity of interest and, in turn, the joint tenancy. For example, if, A, B, and C hold title as joint tenants and A conveys her interest to D, then D will own an undivided one-third interest as a tenant in common with B and C, who will continue to own their undivided two-thirds interest as joint tenants (*see* Figure 3.5).

**Figure 3.5
Combination of
Tenancies**

A, B, and C are joint tenants.

A sells her interest to D.

A, B, C

| D 1/3 | B + C 2/3 |

D becomes a tenant in common with B and C as joint tenants.

Joint tenancies also may be terminated by operation of law, as in bankruptcy or foreclosure sale proceedings.

**Termination of
Co-Ownership by
Partition Suit**

Tenants in common or joint tenants who wish to terminate their co-ownership of real estate may file in court a suit to **partition** the land. The right of partition is a legal way to dissolve a co-ownership when the parties do not voluntarily agree to its termination. If the court determines that the land cannot actually be divided into parts, it will order the real estate sold and divide the proceeds of the sale among the co-owners according to their fractional interests.

Tenancy by the Entirety

A **tenancy by the entirety** is a *special joint tenancy between husband and wife*. The distinguishing characteristics of this tenancy are: (1) the owners must be husband and wife at the time of the grant; (2) the owners have rights of survivorship; (3) during the owners' lives, title can be conveyed *only by a deed signed by both parties* (one party cannot convey a one-half interest); and (4) there generally is no right to partition.

In New York a conveyance to a man and a woman who are legally married to each other creates in them a tenancy by the entirety unless the deed expressly states otherwise.

When a couple becomes divorced, the tenancy by the entirety is broken and they immediately become tenants in common. (Tenancy by the entirety is not used in all states.)

Community Property Rights

The concept of community property originated in Spanish law rather than English common law and was adopted by eight of the western and southwestern states. New York does not recognize this concept.

Types of Co-Ownership

To clarify the concepts of co-ownership further:

1. A deed conveys title to A and B. The intention of the parties is not stated so ownership as tenants in common is created. If A dies, her one-half interest will pass to her heirs or according to her will.
2. A deed conveying title one-third to C and two-thirds to D creates a tenancy in common, with each owner having the fractional interest specified.
3. A deed to H and W as husband and wife creates a tenancy by the entirety.
4. A conveyance of real estate to two people (not husband and wife) by such wording as "to Y and Z, as joint tenants and not as tenants in common" creates a joint tenancy ownership. Upon the death of Y, the title to the property passes to Z by right of survivorship.

Trusts

Property owners may provide for their own financial care and/or that of their families by establishing a trust. Such trusts may be created by agreement during a property owner's lifetime (living trust), or established by will after his or her death (testamentary trust).

The individual creating a trust *(trustor)* makes an agreement with a *trustee* (usually a corporate trustee) by which the individual conveys his or her assets (real and/or personal) or a certain portion of them to the trustee with the understanding that the trustee will assume certain duties. These duties include the care and investment of the trust assets to produce an income. After payment of operating expenses and trustee's fees, this income is paid or used for the benefit of the *beneficiaries*. These trusts may continue for the lifetimes of the beneficiaries or the assets can be distributed when the beneficiaries reach certain predetermined ages.

Ownership of Real Estate by Business Organizations

Ownership by a business organization makes it possible for many people to hold an interest in the same parcel of real estate. There are various ways in which investors may be organized to finance a real estate project. Some provide for the real estate to be owned by the entity itself; others provide for direct ownership of the real estate by the investors. Business organizations may be categorized as: (1) partnerships, (2) corporations, or (3) syndicates. The purchase or sale of real estate by any business organization involves complex legal questions and legal counsel usually is required.

Partnerships

An association of two or more people to carry on a business as co-owners and share in the business's profits and losses is a **partnership.** Partnerships are classified as general and limited. In a **general partnership** all partners participate to some extent in the operation and management of the business and may be held personally liable for business losses and obligations. A **limited partnership** includes general partners as well as limited, or silent, partners. The business is run by the general partner or partners. The limited partners do not participate and each can be held liable for the business's losses *only* to the extent of his or her investment. The limited partnership is a popular method of organizing investors in a real estate project.

General partnerships are dissolved and must be reorganized if one partner dies, withdraws, or goes bankrupt. In a limited partnership, the agreement creating the partnership may provide for the continuation of the organization upon the death or withdrawal of one of the partners.

Corporations

A **corporation** is an artificial person or legal entity created under the authority of the laws of the state from which it receives its charter. Because the corporation is a legal entity, real estate ownership by a corporation is an *ownership in severalty.* A corporation is managed and operated by its *board of directors.* A corporation's charter sets forth the powers of the corporation, including its right to buy and sell real estate after passage of a resolution to that effect by its board of directors. Some charters permit a corporation to purchase real estate for any purpose; others limit such purchases to land that is needed to fulfill the entity's corporate purpose.

As a legal entity, a corporation exists in perpetuity until it is formally dissolved. The death of one of the officers or directors does not affect title to property that is owned by the corporation.

Individuals participate, or invest, in a corporation by purchasing stock. Because stock is *personal property,* stockholders do not have a direct ownership interest in real estate owned by a corporation. Each stockholder's liability for the corporation's losses usually is limited to the amount of his or her investment.

Syndicates

Generally, a **syndicate** is a *joining together of two or more people or firms in order to make and operate a real estate investment.* A syndicate is not in itself a legal entity; however, it may be organized into a number of ownership forms, including co-ownership (tenancy in common, joint tenancy), partnership, trust, or corporation. A *joint venture* is an organization of two or more people or firms to carry out a *single business project.* Joint ventures are characterized by a time limitation resulting from the fact that the joint venturers do not intend to establish a permanent relationship. More will be said about these organizations in Chapter 17.

Cooperative and Condominium Ownership

Apartment dwellers have turned in the past few decades to arrangements under which they own their living space. **Cooperative** ownership was the first to develop; **condominium** ownership appeared more recently.

Cooperative Ownership

Under the usual **cooperative** arrangement, title to land and building is held by a **corporation.** Tenants buy stock in the corporation and receive in return proprietary leases to their apartments. As stockholders they exercise control over the administration of the building. Barring any violation of antidiscrimination laws, tenants often can approve or disapprove of prospective purchasers of the apartment leases.

However, the corporation is vulnerable to financial problems. If other tenants cannot pay their monthly charges, the owner-occupant may lose out in the event of a forced sale of the property. Cooperative ownership typically is found in and around New York City.

Condominium Ownership

The **condominium** form of occupant ownership has gained increasing popularity in recent years. The occupant-owner of each apartment holds a *fee simple title* to his or her apartment and a percentage of the indivisible parts of the building and land, known as the **common elements.** The individual unit owners in a condominium own these common elements together as *tenants in common,* but with *no right to partition.*

The condominium form of ownership usually is used for apartment buildings. These may range from freestanding high-rise buildings to townhouse arrangements. The common elements include such items as the land, walls, hallways, elevators, stairways, and roof. Lawns and recreational facilities such as swimming pools, clubhouses, tennis courts, and golf courses also may be considered common elements. In addition the condominium form of ownership is used for such other types of properties as commercial property, office buildings, or multiuse buildings that contain offices and shops as well as residential units.

Ownership. A condominium unit is *owned in fee simple.* The owner receives a separate tax bill and may mortgage the individual living unit.

Default in the payment of taxes or a mortgage loan by one unit owner may result in a foreclosure sale of that owner's unit but does not affect the ownership of the other unit owners. A condominium unit may be owned in severalty or in any form of co-ownership.

Operation and administration. The condominium property is administered by an association of unit owners according to the bylaws set forth in the declaration. The association may be governed by a board of directors or other official entity. It may manage the property on its own or it may engage a professional property manager to perform this function.

Townhouse ownership is a hybrid form. The townhouse occupant owns the land directly beneath his or her unit, and the living unit including roof and basement, in fee simple. A town house owner also becomes a member of a homeowners' association, which owns the common elements.

Timesharing is a variation of condominium ownership in which the buyer receives the right to use a living unit, usually in a resort area, for a specific portion of a year. The buyer might own an undivided one-twelfth interest together with a right to use the facility for one month of the year.

New York State regulations on the formation and administration of condominiums and cooperatives will be discussed at length in Chapter 21.

Summary

An *estate* is the degree, quantity, nature, and extent of interest a person holds in land. *Freehold estates* are estates of indeterminate length. Less-than-freehold estates are those for which the length can be accurately determined. These are called *leasehold estates* and they concern landlords and tenants.

Freehold estates are further divided into fee estates and life estates. Estates of inheritance include *fee simple* and *qualified fee* estates. There are two types of life estates: (1) conventional life estates, which are created by acts of the parties, and (2) legal life estates, which are created by law. Legal life estates include *curtesy* and *dower*. Curtesy and dower have been abolished in New York. Homestead in New York is not an estate but a right to partial exemption of the equity in a residence from seizure for unsecured debts, as in bankruptcy.

Encumbrances against real estate may be in the form of liens, deed restrictions, easements, licenses, and encroachments.

An *easement* is the right acquired by one person to use another's real estate. *Easements appurtenant* involve two separately owned tracts. The tract benefited is known as the *dominant tenement;* the tract that is subject to the easement is called the *servient tenement.* An *easement in gross* is a personal right such as that granted to utility companies to maintain poles, wires, and pipelines.

A *license* is permission to enter another's property for a specific purpose. A license usually is created orally, is of a temporary nature, and can be revoked.

An *encroachment* is physical intrusion of some improvement upon another's land.

Sole ownership or *ownership in severalty* indicates that title is held by one person or entity.

There are several ways in which title to real estate can be held concurrently by more than one person, called *co-ownership.* Under *tenancy in common* each party holds an undivided interest. An individual owner may sell his or her interest. Upon the death of an owner his or her interest passes to heirs. When two or more parties hold title to real estate, they will hold title as tenants in common unless there is an expressed intention otherwise. *Joint tenancy* indicates two or more owners with the right of survivorship. The intention of the parties to establish a joint tenancy with right of survivorship must be clearly stated and four *unities* must exist.

Tenancy by the entirety is a joint tenancy between husband and wife. It gives the husband and wife the right of survivorship in all lands acquired by them *jointly* during marriage. During their lives both must sign the deed for any title to pass to a purchaser.

Real estate ownership also may be held in *trust*. In creating a trust, title to the property involved is conveyed to a *trustee,* who administers it for the benefit of a *beneficiary*.

Various types of business organizations may own real estate. A *corporation* is a legal entity and holds title to real estate in severalty. A *partnership* may own real estate in its own name. A *syndicate* is an association of two more people or firms to make an investment in real estate. Many syndicates are *joint ventures* and are organized for only a single project. A syndicate may be organized as a co-ownership, trust, corporation, or partnership.

Cooperative ownership of apartment buildings indicates title in one entity (corporation or trust) that must pay taxes, mortgage interest and principal, and all operating expenses. Reimbursement comes from shareholders or beneficiaries through monthly assessments. Shareholders have proprietary, long-term leases entitling them to occupy their apartments. Under *condominium ownership* each occupant-owner holds fee simple title to his or her apartment unit plus a share of the common elements. Each owner receives an individual tax bill and may mortgage his or her unit as desired. Expenses for operating the building are collected by an owners' association through monthly assessments. In *townhouse ownership* each occupant also owns the land directly below the unit.

Questions

1. The most complete ownership recognized by law is a(n):

   a. life estate.
   b. fee simple estate.
   c. leasehold estate.
   d. estate at will.

2. Herbert Kramer devises a parcel of land to New York University "so long as it is used for an experimental farm." Two years after Kramer's death the university begins to build a cafeteria on the land. In this case:

   a. Kramer's heirs automatically become owners.
   b. Kramer's heirs may take legal action to regain the property.
   c. Kramer's heirs own the land but the university owns the cafeteria.
   d. Kramer's heirs have no claim on the land.

3. Which one of the following best describes a life estate?

   a. An estate conveyed to A for the life of Z, and upon Z's death to B
   b. An estate held by A and B in joint tenancy with right of survivorship
   c. An estate upon condition
   d. An estate given by law to a husband

4. New York State no longer recognizes the rights of:

   a. curtsey and dower.
   b. homestead.
   c. tenancy by the entirety.
   d. testamentary trust.

5. When a homeowner who is entitled by state law to a homestead exemption is sued by his or her creditors, then the creditors:

   a. can have the court sell the home and apply the full proceeds of the sale to the debts.
   b. have no right to have the debtor's home sold.
   c. can force the debtor to sell the home to pay them.
   d. can have a court sale and apply the sale proceeds, in excess of $10,000, to the debts.

6. Encumbrances include:

   a. encroachments.
   b. liens.
   c. easements.
   d. All of the above

7. Deed restrictions are created by a:

   a. seller.
   b. buyer.
   c. neighborhood association.
   d. governmental agency.

8. After Peter Desmond purchased his house and moved in, he discovered that his neighbor regularly used Desmond's driveway to reach a garage located on the neighbor's property. Desmond's attorney explained that ownership of the neighbor's real estate includes an easement appurtenant that gives him the driveway right. Desmond's property is properly called:

   a. the dominant tenement.
   b. a tenement.
   c. a leasehold.
   d. the servient tenement.

9. Mary buys a house and automatically receives the same right the seller had: to use a neighbor's party wall. Mary owns an

   a. estate at sufferance.
   b. emblement.
   c. encroachment.
   d. easement.

10. A town's right to run a drainage ditch across the back of someone's property is an example of an easement:

    a. in gross.
    b. by prescription.
    c. by necessity.
    d. in common.

11. John owns a small country house and gives a neighboring farmer permission to plant crops on the two acres around his house. John changes his mind and decides to put in a lawn. He may withdraw the permission because the farmer had only a(n):

    a. estate at sufferance.
    b. easement by necessity.
    c. license.
    d. life estate.

12. A license is an example of a(n):
    a. easement.   c. encumbrance.
    b. encroachment.   d. restriction.

13. Ownership of real property by one person without the ownership participation of others is called ownership in:
    a. trust.   c. solety.
    b. severalty.   d. condominium.

14. A parcel of real estate was purchased by Howard Evers and Tinker Chance. Evers paid one-third of the cost and Chance paid the balance. The seller's deed received at the closing conveyed the property "to Howard Evers and Tinker Chance," without further explanation. Thus:
    a. Evers and Chance are joint tenants.
    b. Evers and Chance are tenants in common, each owning a one-half undivided interest.
    c. Evers and Chance are tenants in common, with Evers owning an undivided one-third interest.
    d. Evers and Chance are general partners in a joint venture.

15. If property is held by two or more owners as tenants in common, upon the death of one owner the ownership of his or her interest will pass:
    a. to the remaining owner or owners.
    b. to the heirs or whoever is designated under the deceased owner's will.
    c. to the surviving owner and/or his or her heirs.
    d. to the deceased owner's surviving spouse.

16. The right of survivorship is closely associated with a:
    a. corporation.   c. trust.
    b. cooperative.   d. joint tenancy.

17. In New York a deed conveying property to a married couple, such as: to "Frank Peters and Marcia Peters, husband and wife," creates a:
    a. joint tenancy.
    b. tenancy by the entirety.
    c. tenancy in common.
    d. periodic tenancy.

18. Which of the following statements applies equally to joint tenants and tenants by the entireties?
    a. There is no right to file a partition suit.
    b. The survivor becomes owner.
    c. A deed signed by one will convey a fractional interest.
    d. A deed will not convey any interest unless signed by both spouses.

19. Henry's will provides that the local bank will receive his real estate and administer it for the benefit of his children until they reach the age of 18. Henry has established a:
    a. life estate.   c. testamentary trust.
    b. joint venture.   d. tenancy in common.

20. An artificial person created by legal means is known as a:
    a. trust.   c. limited partnership.
    b. corporation.   d. joint tenancy.

21. A syndicate formed to carry out a single business project is commonly known as a:
    a. joint venture.   c. limited partnership.
    b. corporation.   d. joint tenancy.

22. Dorothy bought an apartment in Manhattan and received shares in a corporation and a proprietary lease to her unit. Her building is organized as a:
    a. cooperative.   c. joint venture.
    b. condominium.   d. syndicate.

23. Other residents of the building reserve the right to approve or disapprove of potential buyers in which form of joint ownership?
    a. Cooperative   c. Joint venture
    b. Condominium   d. Tenancy in common

24. A condominium is a form of:
    a. apartment building.   c. living unit.
    b. co-ownership.   d. townhouse.

25. Townhouse ownership differs from condominium arrangements because the occupant also owns in fee simple:
    a. shares in a corporation.
    b. a proprietary lease.
    c. the land directly under the living unit.
    d. part of the golf course.

4

Real Estate Instruments: Deeds and Mortgages

Key Terms

Acceleration clause
Acknowledgment
Alienation clause
Arrears
Attorney-in-fact
Bargain and sale deed
Bargain and sale deed with covenant
Benchmark
Bond
Datum
Deed
Default
Deficiency judgment
Delivery and acceptance
Due-on-sale clause
Estoppel certificate
Foreclosure
Grantee/Grantor
Granting clause
Habendum clause

Legal description
Lessee/Lessor
Lien theory
Metes and bounds
Monument
Mortgage
Mortgagee/Mortgagor
Note
Plat of subdivision
Point of beginning
Quitclaim deed
Rectangular (government) survey system
Satisfaction of mortgage
Section
"Subject to" clause
Title
Title theory
Transfer tax
Warranty deed

Overview

This chapter will discuss deeds—the documents used to transfer ownership of real property—and mortgages—the documents used to pledge real property as security for debts. Because "the big house at the corner of Oak and Main" is insufficient identification for these important instruments, the standard system of legal descriptions also will be discussed.

Legal Descriptions

A deed is the instrument that conveys title to real property—in laymen's terms, the written document that transfers ownership. One of the essential elements of a valid deed is an adequate description of the land being conveyed (the deed does not usually mention improvements on the land). A **legal description** is an *exact way of describing real estate in a contract, deed, mortgage, or other document that will be accepted by a court of law.*

Land can be described by three methods: by metes and bounds, by government survey, or by reference to a plat (map) filed in the county clerk's office in the county where the land is located. A legal description in New York may combine different descriptive methods.

Legal descriptions should not be changed, altered, or combined without adequate information from a competent authority such as a surveyor or title attorney. Legal descriptions always should include the name of the county and state in which the land is located.

Metes and Bounds

A **metes-and-bounds description** makes use of the boundaries and measurements of the land in question. Such a description starts at a definitely designated point called the **point** or **place of beginning** (abbreviated POB) and proceeds clockwise around the boundaries of the tract by reference to linear measurements and directions. A metes-and-bounds description always ends at the point where it began (the POB).

In a metes-and-bounds description **monuments** are fixed objects used to establish real estate boundaries. In the past, natural objects such as stones, large trees, lakes, streams, and intersections of major streets or highways, as well as man-made markers placed by surveyors, were commonly used as monuments. Today man-made markers are the more common monuments because it is recognized that natural objects may change or be removed. Measurements often include the words ''more or less''; the location of the monuments is more important than the distance stated in the wording.

It is absolutely essential in a metes-and-bounds description that the boundary ultimately return to the point of beginning so that the tract being described is fully enclosed. Metes-and-bounds descriptions are complicated and should be handled with extreme care. When they include compass directions of the various lines and concave or convex curved lines, they can be difficult to understand. In such cases the advice and counsel of a surveyor should be sought.

An example of a metes-and-bounds description of a parcel of land (pictured in Figure 4.1) follows:

A tract of land located in the City of Elmira, County of Chemung, State of New York, described as follows: Beginning at the intersection of the east line of Jones Road and the south line of Skull Drive; thence east along the south line of Skull Drive 200 feet; thence south 15° east 216.5 feet, more or less, to the center thread of Red Skull Creek; thence northwesterly along the center line of said creek to its intersection with the east line of Jones Road; thence north 105 feet, more or less, along the east line of Jones Road to the place of beginning.

Figure 4.1
Metes-and-Bounds
Tract

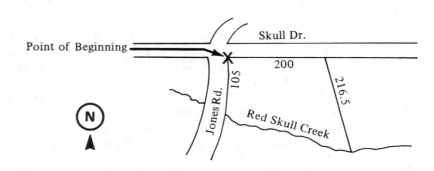

Rectangular (Government) Survey System

The **rectangular survey system,** sometimes called the *government survey method,* was established by Congress in 1785, soon after the federal government was organized. The system was developed as a standard method of describing all lands conveyed to or acquired by the federal government, including the extensive area of the Northwest Territory. It is seldom used in New York State.

The rectangular survey system is based on sets of two intersecting lines: principal meridians and base lines. The *principal meridians* are north and south lines and the *base lines* are east and west lines. Both are exactly located by reference to degrees of longitude and latitude.

Townships. Using these meridians and base lines, land is surveyed into six-mile square *townships*, each with identifying reference numbers. Each township contains 36 square miles.

Sections. A township is further divided into 36 numbered **sections.** Sections are numbered 1 through 36, as shown in Figure 4.2. Section 1 is always in the northeast, or upper righthand, corner. By law each section number 16 has been set aside for school purposes and is referred to as a *school section.* The sale or rental proceeds from this land originally were available for township school use.

As illustrated in Figure 4.3, each section contains one square mile, or *640 acres,* and is divided into *quarters* for reference purposes. One could refer to the southeast quarter, which is a 160-acre tract; this would be abbreviated as SE¼. Quarter sections can be divided into quarters or halves, and such parts can be further divided by quarters. The SE¼ of SE¼ of SE¼ of Section 1 would be a ten-acre square in the lower right-hand corner of Section 1.

Figure 4.2
Sections in a
Township

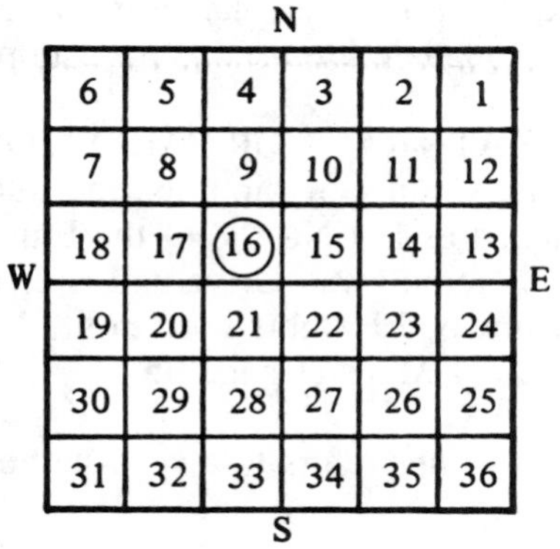

Recorded Plat of Subdivision

The third method of land description is by *lot and block number* referring to a **plat of subdivision** filed with the clerk of the county where the land is located.

The first step in subdividing land is the preparation of a *plat of survey* by a licensed surveyor or engineer, as illustrated in Figure 4.4. On this plat the land is divided into blocks and lots, and streets or access roads for public use are indicated. The blocks and lots are assigned numbers or letters. Lot sizes and street details must be indicated completely and must comply with all local ordinances and requirements. When properly signed and approved, the subdivision plat may

Figure 4.3
A Section

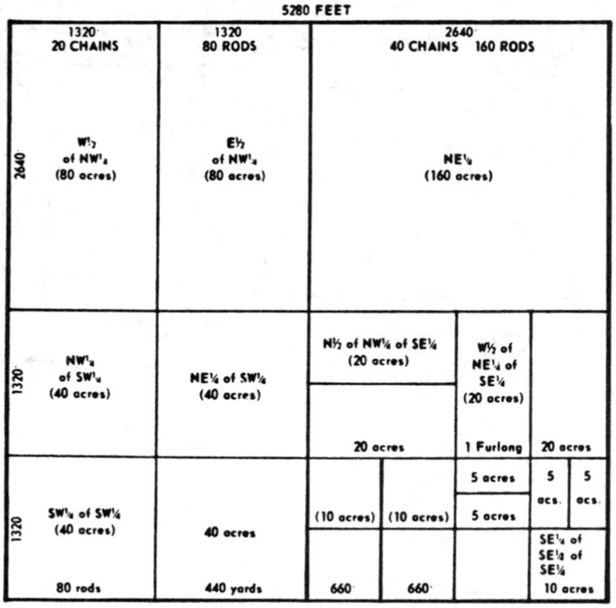

be recorded in the county in which the land is located; it thereby becomes part of the legal description. In describing a lot from a recorded subdivision plat, the lot and block number, name or number of the subdivision plat, and name of the county and state are used. For example:

> THAT TRACT OR PARCEL OF LAND, situate in the Town of Brighton, County of Monroe, and State of New York, known and designated as Lot No. 58 of the Elmwood Heights Tract. Said Lot is situate on Hemingway Drive and is of the dimensions shown on a map of Elmwood Heights filed in the Monroe County Clerk's Office in Liber 125 of Maps at page 95.

The word *liber* refers to a specific book of maps in the county clerk's office.

Figure 4.4
Subdivision Plat Map

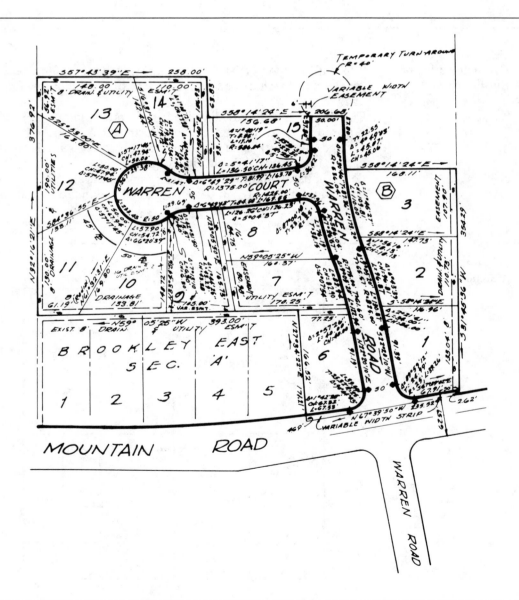

Preparation and Use of a Survey

A licensed surveyor is trained and authorized to locate a given parcel of land and to determine its legal description. The surveyor does this by preparing a *survey*, which sets forth the legal description of the property. A survey map shows the location and dimensions of the parcel and the location, size, and shape of buildings located on the lot. Surveys may be required for (1) conveying a portion of a given tract of land, (2) placing a mortgage loan, (3) showing the location of new construction, (4) locating roads and highways, and (5) determining the legal description of the land on which a particular building is located.

Measuring Elevations

Air Lots

The owner of a parcel of land may subdivide the air above his or her land into *air lots*. This type of description is found in titles to tall buildings located on air rights, generally over railroad tracks. (*See* the discussion of air rights in Chapter 1.) Similarly a surveyor in preparing a subdivision plat for condominium use describes each condominium unit by reference to the elevation of the floors and ceilings on a vertical plane above the city datum.

Datum

A point, line, or surface from which elevations are measured or indicated is a **datum.** The United States Geological Survey defines *datum* as the mean sea level at New York harbor. It is of special significance to surveyors in determining the height of structures, establishing the grade of streets, and similar situations. Many large cities have established a local official datum.

Benchmarks. To aid surveyors, permanent reference points called **benchmarks** have been established through the United States (*see* Figure 4.5). Local benchmarks simplify surveyors' work because measurements may be based on them rather than on the basic benchmark, which may be miles away.

**Figure 4.5
Benchmark**

Condominium Descriptions

A sufficient description of condominium property to be conveyed must include: (1) a description of the land on which the building and improvements are located; (2) a designation of the unit conveyed as listed in the declaration, filed in accordance with the *New York Condominium Act;* and (3) a description of the common interest conveyed with the unit.

undivided % ownership (interest)

Deeds

A **deed** is a *written instrument by which an owner of real estate intentionally conveys to a purchaser his or her right, title, or interest in a parcel of real estate. All deeds must be in writing in accordance* with the requirements of the statute of frauds. The owner (who sells or gives the land) is referred to as the **grantor** and the purchaser (who acquires the title) is called the **grantee**. A deed is *executed* (or signed) by the grantor.

Requirements for a Valid Conveyance

Although the formal requirements for a valid deed are not uniform in all states, certain requirements are basic. These are:

1. a *grantor* having the legal capacity to execute (sign) the deed;
2. a *grantee* named with reasonable certainty, so that he or she can be identified;
3. a recital of *consideration*;
4. a *granting clause* (words of conveyance);
5. a *habendum clause* (to define ownership in deed);
6. designation of any *limitations* on the conveyance of a full fee simple estate;
7. an *adequate description* of the property conveyed;
8. *exceptions and reservations* affecting the title (**"subject to" clause**);
9. the *signature of the grantor, acknowledgment;* and
10. *delivery* of the deed and *acceptance* by the grantee to pass title.

Grantor. In New York both grantee and grantor must be identified by residence if the deed is to be recorded.

In New York a person must be of sound mind and have reached the age of 18 in order to effect a valid conveyance. A contract executed by an incompetent or a minor is *voidable* by the courts; that is, it may be set aside in a lawsuit conducted by a representative of the incompetent or minor. A minor may disaffirm a contract upon reaching the age of 18. A minor who is married may convey property used as a home as if he or she had reached the age of 18. A grantor generally is held to have sufficient mental capacity to execute a deed if he or she is capable of understanding the action.

Grantee. To be valid a deed must name a grantee and do so in such a way that he or she is readily identifiable.

Consideration. In order to be valid all deeds must contain a clause acknowledging the grantor's receipt of a consideration. *Consideration* is defined as something of value given in an exchange. The amount of consideration must be stated in dollars. When a deed conveys real estate as a gift to a relative, "love and affection" may be sufficient consideration. It is customary to recite a *nominal* consideration such as "$10.00 and other good and valuable consideration." The full dollar amount of consideration seldom is set forth in the deed, except when the instrument is executed by an administrator, an executor, corporation or trustee, or pursuant to court order.

Granting clause (words of conveyance). A deed of conveyance transfers a present interest in real estate. It must contain words in the **granting clause** that state the grantor's intention to convey the property. Depending on the type of deed and the obligations agreed to by the grantor, the wording generally is either "convey and warrant," "grant," "grant, bargain, and sell," or "remise, release, and quitclaim."

If more than one grantee is involved, the granting clause should cover the creation of their specific rights in the property. The clause might state, for example, that the grantees will take title as joint tenants or tenants in common. This is especially important because specific wording is necessary to create a joint tenancy.

The granting clause also should indicate what interest in the property is being conveyed by the grantor. Deeds that convey the entire fee simple interest of the grantor usually contain wording such as "to Jacqueline Smith and to her heirs and assigns forever." If the grantor is conveying less than his or her complete interest, such as a life estate to property, the wording must indicate this limitation. For example, a deed creating a life estate would convey property "to Jacqueline Smith for the duration of her natural life."

Habendum clause. When it is necessary to define or explain the ownership to be enjoyed by the grantee, a **habendum clause** follows the granting clause. The habendum clause begins with the words "to have and to hold." Its provisions must agree with those set down in the granting clause.

Description of real estate. For a deed to be valid, it must contain an adequate description of the real estate conveyed. Land is considered adequately described if a competent surveyor can locate the property from the description used.

Exceptions and reservations. A grantor may reserve some right in the land for his or her own use (an easement, for instance). A grantor also may place certain restrictions on a grantee's use of the property. A developer, for example, may restrict the number of houses that may be built on a one-acre lot in a subdivision. Such restrictions may be stated in the deed or contained in a previously recorded document (such as the subdivider's master deed) that is expressly cited in the deed.

Signature of grantor. To be valid a deed must be signed by *all grantors* named in the deed. New York permits a grantor's signature to be signed by an attorney-in-fact acting under a power of attorney. An **attorney-in-fact** is any person who has been given power of attorney (specific written authority) to execute and sign legal instruments for a grantor. In such cases it usually is necessary for an authorizing document known as a *power of attorney* to be recorded in the county where the property is located. Because the power of attorney terminates upon the death of the person granting such authority, adequate evidence must be submitted that the grantor is alive at the time the attorney-in-fact signs the deed.

A grantor who is unable to write is permitted to sign his or her name by *mark*. With this type of signature two persons other than the notary public taking the acknowledgment must witness the grantor's execution of the deed and sign as witnesses. A corporation must use its seal beside the signature of a corporate officer if the seal is mentioned in the acknowledgment.

Acknowledgment. An **acknowledgment** is a form of declaration made voluntarily by a person who is signing a formal, written document before a notary public or authorized public officer. This acknowledgment usually states that the person signing the deed or other document is known to the officer or has produced sufficient identification. The acknowledgment provides evidence that the signature is genuine.

Usually an acknowledgment is made before a *notary public;* however, it also can be taken by a judge, justice of the peace, or other qualified person (*see* Chapter 4 Appendix). The form of a *certificate of acknowledgment* varies from state to state. The certificate form authorized by the state where the property is located should be used even if the party signing is a resident of another ("foreign") state. In other words, the laws of the state where the land is located govern the procedure.

Although an acknowledgment is not required to make a deed valid, in New York all deeds, mortgages, and similar documents affecting an interest in real estate must be acknowledged before they can be recorded. Each document must be signed before a notary public or other authorized public official or before a witness, who must attest to the validity of the grantor's signature. The signature of the witness must then be acknowledged before an authorized public official.

From a purely practical point of view a deed that is not acknowledged is not a satisfactory instrument.

Although an unrecorded deed is valid between the grantor and the grantee, it is often not a valid conveyance against subsequent innocent purchasers. For this reason a grantee would not in effect secure good title to the property. To help assure good title a grantee should always require acknowledgment of the grantor's signature on a deed, so that it may be recorded. Further requirements before a deed may be recorded are detailed in Chapter 11.

Delivery and acceptance. Before a transfer of title by conveyance can take effect, there must be an actual **delivery** of the deed by the grantor and either actual or implied **acceptance** by the grantee. *Title is said to pass when a deed is delivered.* The effective date of the transfer of title from the grantor to the grantee is the date of delivery of the deed itself.

Execution of Corporate Deeds

Under the law a corporation is considered to be a legal entity. Some basic rules must be followed when corporations are to convey real estate:

1. A corporation can convey real estate only upon a proper resolution passed by its *board of directors.* If all or a substantial portion of a corporation's real estate is being conveyed, it is also usually required that a resolution authorizing the sale be secured from the *stockholders.*
2. *Deeds to real estate can be signed only by an authorized officer* and in most states the officer's signature is required. The authority of the officer must be granted by a resolution properly passed by the board of directors.
3. The corporate *seal* need not be affixed to the conveyance unless the acknowledgment mentions the seal.

Rules pertaining to religious corporations and not-for-profit corporations vary widely. Because the legal requirements must be followed explicitly it is advisable to consult an attorney for all corporate conveyances.

Types of Deeds

The most common forms of deed in New York are:

1. full covenant and warranty deed;
2. bargain and sale deed with covenant against grantor's acts;

3. bargain and sale deed without covenant against grantor's acts;
4. quitclaim deed;
5. executor's deed; and
6. referee's deed.

Warranty deeds. For a purchaser of real estate, a **full covenant and warranty deed** (shown in Figure 4.6) provides the *greatest protection* of any deed. It is referred to as a warranty deed because the grantor is legally bound by certain covenants or warranties. The warranties usually are implied by the use of certain words, which include: "convey and warrant," "warrant generally," and, commonly in New York, "grant and release." In some localities the grantor's warranties are expressly written into the deed itself. The basic warranties are:

1. *Covenant of seisin:* The grantor warrants that he or she is the owner of the property and has the right to convey title to it. The grantee may recover damages up to the full purchase price if this covenant is broken.
2. *Covenant against encumbrances:* The grantor warrants that the property is free from any liens or encumbrances except those specifically stated in the deed. Encumbrances generally would include such items as mortgages, mechanics' liens, and easements. If this covenant is breached, the grantee may sue for expenses to remove the encumbrance.
3. *Covenant of quiet enjoyment:* The grantor guarantees that the grantee's title is good against third parties who might bring court actions to establish superior title to the property. If the grantee's title is found to be inferior, the grantor is liable for damages.
4. *Covenant of further assurance:* The grantor promises to obtain and deliver any instrument needed in order to make the title good.
5. *Covenant of warranty forever:* The grantor guarantees that if at any time in the future the title fails, he or she will compensate the grantee for the loss sustained.

These covenants in a warranty deed are not limited to matters that occurred during the time the grantor owned the property; they extend back to its origins. (The differences among a warranty deed, a bargain and sale deed, and a quitclaim deed are illustrated in Figure 4.7.)

In addition, a warranty deed in New York contains a *lien covenant,* stating that in accordance with Section 13 of the Lien Law, the seller holds the proceeds of the sale in trust against unpaid improvements to the property.

In New York State the seller need not deliver a full covenant and warranty deed unless the purchase agreement stipulates it. In many Upstate areas the warranty deed is the one most commonly used.

Bargain and sale deed without covenant. A **bargain and sale deed without covenant** contains no warranties against encumbrances. It does, however, *imply* that the grantor holds title to the property. Because the warranty is not specifically stated the grantee has little legal recourse if defects later appear in the title. The bargain and sale deed without covenant is used in foreclosure and tax sales.

Bargain and sale deed with covenant against grantor's acts. A covenant may be added under which grantors covenant that they have done nothing to encumber the property while it was in their possession. This deed often is used by

Figure 4.6
Full Covenant and
Warranty Deed

P 1688—Warranty Deed : Full Covenants, Corp. or Ind.   JULIUS BLUMBERG, INC., LAW BLANK PUBLISHERS
Stat. Form AA with Lien Covenant. I Side Recording.
THIS IS A LEGAL INSTRUMENT AND SHOULD BE EXECUTED UNDER SUPERVISION OF AN ATTORNEY.

THIS INDENTURE, made the   day of   19
BETWEEN

                                                                                        grantor

                                                                                        grantee

WITNESSETH, that the grantor, in consideration of
                                                                         Dollars, paid by the grantee
hereby grants and releases unto the grantee, the heirs or successor and assigns of the grantee forever,
     ALL

TOGETHER with the appurtenances and all the estate and rights of the grantor in and to said premises.
TO HAVE AND TO HOLD the premises here granted unto the grantee, the heirs or successors and assigns forever,
                                        AND the said grantor covenants as follows:
FIRST.—That the grantor is seized of the said premises in fee simple, and has good right to convey the same;
SECOND.—That the grantee shall quietly enjoy the said premises;
THIRD.—That the said premises are free from incumbrances;
FOURTH.—That the grantor will execute or procure any further necessary assurance of the title to said premises;
FIFTH.—That the grantor will forever warrant the title to said premises;
This deed is subject to the trust provisions of Section 13 of the Lien Law.
     The words "grantor" and "grantee" shall be construed to read in the plural whenever the sense of this deed so requires.
IN WITNESS WHEREOF, the grantor has executed this deed the day and year first above written.

In presence of:
                                                                              .... L. S.

                                                                              .... L. S.

STATE OF NEW YORK, COUNTY OF   ss.:
     On the   day of   19   , before
me personally came   to me known,
who, being by me duly sworn, did depose and say that deponent resides
at No.
deponent is   of
                          the corporation described in and which
executed, the foregoing instrument; deponent knows the seal of said
corporation; that the seal affixed to said instrument is such corporate
seal; that it was so affixed by order of the Board of Directors of said
corporation; deponent signed deponent's name thereto by like order.

STATE OF NEW YORK, COUNTY OF   ss.:
     On the   day of   19   , before
me personally came

to me known to be the individual   described in, and who executed
the foregoing instrument, and acknowledged that   he   executed
the same.

𝔇𝔢𝔢𝔡

WARRANTY — FULL COVENANTS

TO

Dated,   19

STATE OF NEW YORK

County of_____ **ss.**

RECORDED ON THE

..........day of.................................., 19......

     at............o'clock.........M.

in Liber.................of Deeds

at Page.................and examined

....
                                        CLERK

PLEASE RECORD AND RETURN TO:

Forms may be purchased from Julius Blumberg, Inc., New York, NY 10013, or any of its dealers.
Reproduction prohibited.

Figure 4.7
Types of Deeds

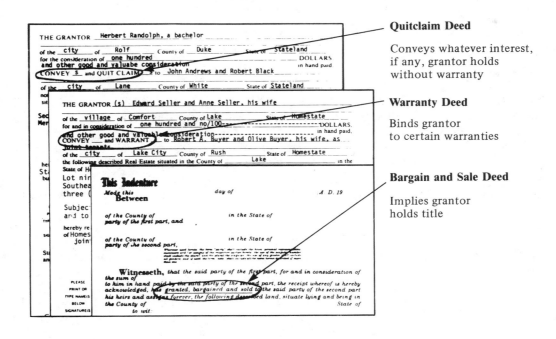

Quitclaim Deed

Conveys whatever interest, if any, grantor holds without warranty

Warranty Deed

Binds grantor to certain warranties

Bargain and Sale Deed

Implies grantor holds title

fiduciaries: executors, trustees, and corporations. The grantors are willing to warrant about the time they owned the property but not about previous owners.

The **bargain and sale deed with covenant (against grantor's acts)** often is used in real estate transactions in the New York City area.

Quitclaim deeds. A **quitclaim deed** provides the grantee with the least protection of any deed. It carries no covenant or warranties and conveys only such interest, if any, as the grantor may have when the deed is delivered. By a quitclaim deed the grantor only "remises, releases, and quitclaims" his or her interest in the property to the grantee.

If the grantor has no interest in the property the grantee will acquire nothing, nor will he or she acquire any right of warranty claim against the grantor. A quitclaim deed can convey title as effectively as a warranty deed if the grantor has good title when he or she delivers the deed, but it provides no guarantees.

A quitclaim deed commonly is used for simple transfers within a family and for property transferred during divorce settlements. It also can be used to clear a cloud on a title when persons who may or may not have some claim to property are asked to "sign off."

Executor's and referee's deeds. An *executor's deed* is a bargain and sale deed with covenant; a *referee's deed* contains no covenants or warranties although it does *imply* seisin (ownership). One characteristic of such instruments is that the *full consideration* (sale price) usually is stated in the deed. This is done because the deed is executed pursuant to a court order; and because the court has authorized the sale of the property for a given amount of consideration, this amount should be *exactly* stated in the document.

Mortgages

United States Mortgage Law

Some states recognize a lender as the owner of mortgaged land. These states are called **title theory** states. Connecticut, for example, is a title theory state.

New York, however, interprets a mortgage purely as a lien on real property and is called a **lien theory** state. If a mortgagor defaults, the lender is required to foreclose the lien (generally through a court action), offer the property for sale, and apply the funds received from the sale to reduce or pay off the debt.

Security and Debt

Generally, any interest in real estate that may be sold may be pledged as security for a debt. The basic principle of property law, that a person cannot convey greater rights in property than he or she actually has, applies equally to the right to mortgage. So the owner of a fee simple estate can mortgage the fee and the owner of a leasehold or subleasehold can mortgage that leasehold interest. A large retail corporation renting space in a shopping center, for example, may mortgage its leasehold interest in order to finance some remodeling work.

As discussed in Chapter 3, the owner of a cooperative interest holds a personal property interest, not an interest in real estate. A cooperative owner has a leasehold interest generally acceptable to lenders as collateral. The owner of a condominium unit, however, can mortgage his or her fee interest in the condominium apartment.

Mortgage Loan Instruments

By itself a mortgage document is basically a pledge of property given by a borrower to a lender to secure a loan. Because a pledge of security is not legally effective unless there is a debt to secure, a note is also required. *Both documents must be executed in order to create an enforceable mortgage loan.*

Therefore, when a property is to be mortgaged, the owner must execute, or sign, two separate instruments:

1. The **note,** or the **bond,** which is similar to a note, is the promise, or agreement, to repay the debt in definite installments with interest. The mortgagor executes one or more promissory notes to total the amount of the debt.
2. The **mortgage** is the document that creates the lien as *security* for the debt.

Trust deeds. In some areas of the country, and in certain situations, lenders prefer to use a three-party instrument known as a *trust deed,* or *deed of trust,* rather than a mortgage document. A trust deed conveys the real estate as security for the loan to a third party, called the *trustee.*

Provisions of the Note	In general, the promissory note (or bond) executed by a borrower (known as the *maker* or *payor*) states the amount of the debt, the time and method of payment, and the rate of interest. If the note is used with a mortgage, it names the mortgagee as the payee. It also may refer to or repeat several of the clauses that appear in the mortgage document. The bond, like the mortgage, should be signed by all parties who have an interest in the property. Figure 4.8 is an example of a note and mortgage commonly used in some areas of New York State.

Provisions of the Mortgage Document

The mortgage document refers to the terms of the note and clearly establishes that the conveyance of land is security for the debt. It identifies the lender as well as the borrower and it includes an accurate legal description of the property. It should be signed by all parties who have an interest in the real estate. The instrument also sets forth the obligations of the borrower and the rights of the lender.

The essentials of a valid mortgage are listed in the excerpts from the New York State study booklet in the Appendix to this chapter.

Duties of the Mortgagor

The borrower is required to fulfill many obligations. These usually include the following:

1. payment of the debt in accordance with the terms of the note;
2. payment of all real estate taxes on the property given as security;
3. maintenance of adequate insurance to protect the lender if the property is destroyed or damaged by fire, windstorm, or other hazard;
4. obtainment of the lender's authorization before making any major alterations on the property;
5. maintenance of the property in good repair at all times; and
6. obtainment of the lender's authorization before placing a second mortgage (junior lien) against the property.

Failure to meet any of these obligations can result in a borrower's **default** on the note. When this happens the mortgage usually provides for a grace period (30 days, for example) during which the borrower can meet the obligation and cure the default. If he or she does not do so, the lender has the right to foreclose the mortgage and collect on the note. The most frequent cause of default is the borrower's failure to meet monthly installments.

Most mortgages contain a late-payment clause. New York allows a late-payment penalty 15 days after payment is due. An individual may charge a two percent penalty: a lending institution, four percent.

Provisions for Default

The provisions of a mortgage include an **acceleration clause** to assist the lender in a foreclosure. If a borrower defaults the lender has the right to accelerate the maturity of the debt—to declare the *entire* debt due and owing *immediately*.

Other clauses in a mortgage enable the lender to take care of the property in the event of the borrower's negligence or default. If the borrower does not pay taxes or insurance premiums or make necessary repairs on the property, the lender may step in and do so to protect his or her security (the real estate). Any money

Figure 4.8
Sample Note and
Mortgage

P 666—Note and Mortgage, short form,   © 1978 BY JULIUS BLUMBERG, INC.,
plain English format, 11-78   PUBLISHER, NYC 10013

CONSULT YOUR LAWYER BEFORE SIGNING THIS FORM—THIS FORM SHOULD BE USED BY LAWYERS ONLY.

NOTE AND MORTGAGE

$...   Date...

Parties   Mortgagor

                   Mortgagee
                   Address

Promise   Mortgagor promises to pay to Mortgagee or order the sum of
to pay
principal   dollars ($
amount (debt)
interest   with interest at the rate of   % per year from the date above until the debt is paid in full.
payments   Mortgagor will pay the debt as follows:

Application   The Mortgagee will apply each payment first to interest charges and then to repayment of the debt.
of payments

Address   Payment shall be made at Mortgagee's address above or at any other address Mortgagee directs.
for payment

Transfer of   **Additional promises and agreements of the Mortgagor:**
rights in
the Property   1. The Mortgagor hereby mortgages to the Mortgagee the Property described in this Note and Mortgage. Mort-
                   gagor can lose the Property for failure to keep the promises in this Note and Mortgage.

Property   2. The Property mortgaged (the "Property") is All
Mortgaged

Future   3. The Mortgagee may make advances in the future to the Mortgagor or future owners of the Property. In ad-
advances   dition to the above Debt this Note and Mortgage is intended to secure any more debts now or in the future owed
                   by the Mortgagor to the Mortgagee. The principal amount of the above Debt shall be the maximum amount of debt
                   secured by this Note and Mortgage. Mortgagee is not obligated to make future advances.

Insurance	4. Mortgagor will keep the buildings on the Property insured against loss by fire and other risks included in the standard form of extended coverage insurance. The amount shall be approved by Mortgagee, but shall not exceed full replacement value of the buildings. Mortgagor will assign and deliver the policies to Mortgagee. The policies shall contain the standard New York Mortgage clause in the name of Mortgagee. If Mortgagor fails to keep the buildings insured Mortgagee may obtain the insurance. Within 30 days after notice and demand, Mortgagor must insure the Property against war risk and any other risk reasonably required by Mortgagee.
Maintenance	5. Mortgagor will keep the Property in reasonably good repair.
No sale or alteration	6. The Mortgagor may not, without the consent of Mortgagee, (a) alter, demolish or remove the buildings and improvements on the Property, or (b) sell the Property or any part of it.
Taxes, etc.	7. Mortgagor will pay all taxes, assessments, sewer rents or water rates within 30 days after they are due. Mortgagor must show receipts for these payments within 10 days of Mortgagee's demand for them.
Mortgagee's right to cure	8. Mortgagor authorizes Mortgagee to make payments necessary to correct a default of Mortgagor under Paragraphs 4 and 7 of this Mortgage. Payments made by Mortgagee together with interest at the rate provided in this Note and Mortgage from the date paid until the date of repayment shall be added to the Debt and secured by this Mortgage. Mortgagor shall repay Mortgagee with interest within 10 days after demand.
Statement of the amount due	9. Within five days after request in person or within ten days after request by mail, Mortgagor shall give to Mortgagee a signed statement of the amount due on this Note and Mortgage and whether there are any offsets or defenses against the Debt.
Title	10. Mortgagor warrants the title to the Property. Mortgagor is responsible for any costs or losses of the Mortgagee if an interest in the Property is claimed by others.
Lien law section 13	11. Mortgagor will receive the advances secured by this Note and Mortgage and will hold the right to receive the advances as a trust fund. The advances will be applied first for the purpose of paying the cost of improvement. Mortgagor will apply the advances first to the payment to the cost of improvement before using any part of the total of the advances for any other purpose.
Default, when full amount of debt due immediately	12. Mortgagee may declare the full amount of the Debt to be due and payable immediately for any default. The following are defaults: (a) Mortgagor fails to make any payment required by this Note and Mortgage within 15 days of its due date; (b) Mortgagor fails to keep any other promise or agreement in this Note and Mortgage within the time set forth, or if no time is set forth, within a reasonable time after notice is given that Mortgagor is in Default.
Sale	13. If Mortgagor defaults under this Note and Mortgage and the Property is to be sold at a foreclosure sale, the Property may be sold in one parcel.
Receiver	14. If Mortgagee sues to foreclose the Note and Mortgage, Mortgagee shall have the right to have a receiver appointed to take control of the Property.
Payment of rent and eviction after Default	15. If there is a Default under this Note and Mortgage, Mortgagor must pay monthly in advance to Mortgagee, or to a receiver who may be appointed to take control of the Property, the fair rental for the use and occupancy of the part of the Property that is in the possession of the Mortgagor. If Mortgagor does not pay the rent when due, Mortgagor will vacate and surrender the Property to Mortgagee or to the receiver. Mortgagor may be evicted by summary proceedings or other court proceedings.
Applicable law	16. Mortgagee shall have all the rights set forth in Section 254 of the New York Real Property Law in addition to Mortgagee's rights set forth in this Note and Mortgage, even if the rights are different from each other.
No oral changes	17. This Note and Mortgage may not be changed or ended orally.
Notices	18. Notices, demands or requests may be in writing and may be delivered in person or sent by mail.
Who is bound	19. If there are more than one Mortgagor each shall be separately liable. The words "Mortgagor" and "Mortgagee" shall include their heirs, executors, administrators, successors and assigns. If there are more than one Mortgagor or Mortgagee the words "Mortgagor" and "Mortgagee" used in this Mortgage includes them.
Signatures	Mortgagor has signed this Note and Mortgage as of the date at the top of the first page.

WITNESS   MORTGAGOR..

....

Note and Mortgage

▬▬▬▬▬▬▬▬▬▬▬▬

TO

▬▬▬▬▬▬▬▬▬▬▬▬

Dated,   19

▬▬▬▬▬▬▬▬▬▬▬▬

STATE OF NEW YORK

County of_____

RECORDED ON THE

........day of...,19......

     at...........o'clock..........M.

in Liber....................of Mortgages

at Page.....................and examined

....

CLERK

STATE OF NEW YORK, COUNTY OF   ss.:

    On   19   , before me personally came   to me known, who, being by me duly sworn, did depose and say that deponent resides at No.

deponent is   of

       the corporation described in and which executed the foregoing instrument; deponent knows the seal of said corporation; that the seal affixed to said instrument is such corporate seal; that it was so affixed by order of the Board of Directors of said corporation; deponent signed deponent's name thereto by like order.

STATE OF NEW YORK, COUNTY OF   ss.:

    On   19   , before me personally came

to me known to be the individual   described in, and who executed the foregoing instrument, and acknowledged that   he executed the same.

advanced by the lender to cure such defaults is either added to the unpaid debt or declared immediately due and owing from the borrower.

Assignment of the Mortgage

A note or bond is a *negotiable instrument;* as such it may be sold to a third party, or assignee. An *estoppel certificate* executed by the borrower will verify the amount owed and interest rate. Upon payment in full, or satisfaction of the debt, the assignee is required to execute the satisfaction, or release, of mortgage. In the event of a foreclosure the assignee (not the original mortgagee) files the suit.

Recording Mortgages

The mortgage document must be recorded in the recorder's office of the county in which the real estate is located. The recordation gives constructive notice to the world of the borrower's obligations and establishes the lien's priority.

First and Second Mortgages

Mortgages and other liens normally have priority in the order in which they have been recorded. A mortgage on land that has no prior mortgage lien on it is a *first mortgage*. When the owner of this land later executes another mortgage for additional funds, the new mortgage becomes a *second mortgage,* or *junior lien,* when recorded. The second mortgage is subject to the first mortgage; the first has prior claim to the value of the land pledged as security.

The priority of mortgage liens may be changed by the execution of a *subordination agreement* in which the first lender subordinates his or her lien to that of the second lender. To be valid such an agreement must be signed by both lenders.

Satisfaction of the Mortgage Lien

When all mortgage loan payments have been made and the note paid in full the mortgagor wants the public record to show that the debt has been paid and the mortgage lien satisfied. In the usual mortgage, when the note has been fully paid the mortgagee is required to execute a *release of mortgage,* or **satisfaction of mortgage.** This document reconveys to the mortgagor all interest in the real estate that was conveyed to the mortgagee by the original recorded mortgage document. By having this release entered in the public record the owner shows that the mortgage lien has been removed from his or her property.

Buying Subject to or Assuming a Seller's Mortgage

A person who purchases real estate that has an assumable mortgage on it may take the property *subject to* the mortgage or may *assume* it and *agree to pay* the debt. This technical distinction becomes important if the buyer defaults and the mortgage is foreclosed.

When the property is sold *subject to* the mortgage the purchaser is not personally obligated to pay the debt in full. The new owner has bought the real estate knowing that he or she must make the loan payments and that, upon default, the lender will foreclose and the property will be sold by court order to pay the debt. But if the sale does not pay off the entire debt, the new owner is not liable for the difference.

In contrast, when the new owner not only purchases the property subject to the mortgage but *assumes and agrees to pay* the debt, then he or she becomes personally obligated for the payment of the *debt.* If the mortgage is foreclosed in such a case and the court sale does not bring enough money to pay the debt in full, a deficiency judgment against both the assumer and the original borrower can be obtained for the unpaid balance.

Alienation clause. Frequently, when a real estate loan is made, the lender wishes to prevent some future purchaser of the property from being able to assume that loan, particularly at its old rate of interest. For this reason some lenders include an **alienation clause** (also known as a *resale clause* or *due-on-sale clause*) in the note. An alienation clause provides that upon the sale of the property by the borrower to a buyer who wants to assume the loan, the lender has the choice of either declaring the entire debt to be immediately due and owing or permitting the buyer to assume the loan at such conditions as the mortgagee may require.

In New York a mortgage is assumable unless the document contains a specific alienation clause.

Foreclosure

When a borrower defaults in making payments or fulfilling any of the obligations set forth in the mortgage the lender can enforce his or her rights through a foreclosure. A **foreclosure** is a legal procedure whereby the property that is pledged as security is sold to satisfy the debt. The foreclosure procedure passes title to a third party who purchases the realty at a *foreclosure sale*. Property thus sold is *free of the mortgage and all junior liens* but subject to any prior liens.

Methods of Foreclosure

There are two general types of foreclosure proceedings—judicial and strict foreclosure. Strict foreclosure rarely is used; judicial foreclosure is the procedure followed in the majority of cases. The borrower has the right to redeem the property until the moment of sale by producing full payment including back interest and costs incurred in the foreclosure proceedings.

In New York, however, the defaulting borrower does not have the right to redeem the property after the foreclosure sale.

The purchaser at a foreclosure sale receives a referee's deed. The referee is appointed by the court and executes the deed by virtue of the authorization given to him or her by the court.

Judicial foreclosure. Upon a borrower's default the lender may *accelerate* the due date of all remaining monthly payments. The lender's attorney can then file a suit to foreclose the lien. The property is ordered sold. A public sale is advertised and held and the real estate is sold to the highest bidder.

Deed in Lieu of Foreclosure

An alternative to foreclosure would be for the lender to accept, or "buy," a *deed in lieu of foreclosure* from the borrower. This is sometimes known as a *friendly foreclosure* because it is by agreement rather than by civil action. The major disadvantage to this manner of default settlement is that the mortgagee takes the real estate subject to all junior liens, while foreclosure eliminates all such liens.

Deficiency Judgment

If the foreclosure sale does not produce sufficient cash to pay the loan balance in full after deducting expenses and accrued unpaid interest, the mortgagee may be entitled to seek a *personal judgment* against the signer of the note for the unpaid balance. Such a judgment is called a **deficiency judgment.** It may be obtained against any endorsers or guarantors of the note and any owners of the mortgaged property who may have assumed the debt by written agreement. If, on the other hand, there are any surplus proceeds from the foreclosure sale after the debt is paid off and expenses are deducted, they are paid to the borrower.

Other Real Estate Instruments

Among other important instruments used in the practice of real estate are listing agreements, which will be discussed in detail in Chapter 9; leases, the subject of Chapter 22; purchase and sale contracts, option agreements, and land contracts, which will be treated in Chapter 5.

Leases. Through a lease the owner of property, the **lessor,** allows some other person to use it in exchange for periodic payments. The tenant, or **lessee,** has a leasehold estate. Four different types of tenancy are discussed in Chapter 22.

In New York, leases for a period of one year or less need not be written. Leases for a period of three years or more may, if properly acknowledged, be entered into the public records. Leases may be assigned or sublet unless the lease expressly prohibits the tenant from doing so. If the building contains four or more units, subletting may not be prohibited in this state.

A lease *survives a sale;* it is still valid after any transfer of title.

Summary

Documents affecting or conveying interests in real estate must contain a *legal description* that accurately identifies the property involved. There are three methods of describing land in the United States: (1) metes and bounds, (2) rectangular (government) survey, and (3) recorded plat of subdivision. A legal description is a precise method of identifying a parcel of land.

In a *metes-and-bounds description,* the actual location of monuments is the most important consideration. When property is being described by metes and bounds the description always must enclose a tract of land; the boundary line must end at the point at which it started.

The *rectangular survey system* is not used in New York. It involves surveys based on principal meridians. Land is surveyed into squares 36 miles in area, called *townships.* Townships are divided into 36 *sections* of one square mile each.

Land can be subdivided into lots and blocks by means of a *recorded plat of subdivision.* An approved plat of survey showing the division into blocks, giving the size, location, and designation of lots, and specifying the location and size of streets to be dedicated for public use is filed for record in the recorder's office of the county in which the land is located.

A survey prepared by a surveyor is the usual method of certifying the legal description of a certain parcel of land. When a survey also shows the location, size, and shape of the buildings located on the lot, it is referred to as a *survey map*. Surveys customarily are required when a mortgage or new construction is involved.

Air lots, condominium descriptions, and other measurements of vertical elevations may be computed from the United States Geological Survey *datum*, which is the mean sea level in New York harbor. Most large cities have established local survey datums for surveying within the area. The elevations from these datums are further supplemented by reference points, called *benchmarks*, placed at fixed intervals from the datums.

The voluntary transfer of an owner's title is made by a *deed*, executed (signed) by the owner as *grantor* to the purchaser or donee as *grantee*.

Among the most common requirements for a valid deed are: a grantor with legal capacity to contract, a readily identifiable grantee, a granting clause, a legal description of the property, a recital of consideration, exceptions and reservations on the title (''subject to'' clause), and the signature of the grantor. In addition the deed should be acknowledged before a notary public or other officer in order to provide evidence that the signature is genuine and to allow recording. Deeds are subject to state transfer taxes when they are recorded. Title to the property passes when the grantor delivers a deed to the grantee and it is accepted.

The obligation of a grantor is determined by the form of the deed. A *general warranty deed* provides the greatest protection of any deed by binding the grantor to certain covenants or warranties. A *bargain and sale deed with covenant* warrants only that the real estate has not been encumbered by the grantor. A *bargain and sale deed* carries with it no warranties but implies that the grantor holds title to the property. A *quitclaim deed* carries with it no warranties whatsoever and conveys only the interest, *if any*, the grantor possesses in the property.

Mortgage loans provide the principal sources of financing for real estate operations. Mortgage loans involve a borrower, called the *mortgagor*, and a lender, the *mortgagee*.

Some states recognize the lender as the owner of mortgaged property; these are known as *title theory states*. Others recognize the borrower as the owner of mortgaged property and are known as *lien theory states*. New York is a lien theory state.

The borrower is required to execute a *note* agreeing to repay the debt and a *mortgage* placing a lien on the real estate to secure his or her note. This is recorded in the public record in order to give notice to the world of the lender's interest. Payment in full of the note by its terms entitles the borrower to a *satisfaction*, or *release*, which is recorded to clear the lien from the public records. Default by the borrower may result in *acceleration* of payments and a *foreclosure* sale. If the sale proceeds fail to clear the debt the mortgagee may seek a deficiency judgment against the borrower. A subsequent owner who *assumed* the loan is also personally responsible and liable to a deficiency judgment; one who *took* the property *subject to* the mortgage is not.

Questions

1. Monuments, angles, and distances are used in which type of legal description?
   a. Plat
   b. Government survey
   c. Metes and bounds
   d. Tape location map

2. According to the plat map, which of the following lots has the most frontage on Manassas Lane?
   a. Lot 10, Block B
   b. Lot 11, Block B
   c. Lot 8, Block A
   d. Lot 1, Block A

3. On the plat, how many lots have easements?
   a. One
   b. Two
   c. Three
   d. Four

4. A person legally authorized to locate land and give a legal description of it is a(n):
   a. assessor.
   b. surveyor.
   c. abstractor.
   d. recorder.

5. It is essential that every deed be signed by the:
   a. grantor.
   b. grantee.
   c. grantor and grantee.
   d. devisee.

6. Title to property transfers at the moment a deed is:
   a. signed.
   b. acknowledged.
   c. delivered and accepted.
   d. recorded.

7. Consideration in a deed refers to:
   a. gentle handling of the document.
   b. something of value given by each party.
   c. the habendum clause.
   d. the payment of transfer tax stamps.

8. A declaration before a notary or other official providing evidence that a signature is genuine is an:
   a. affidavit.
   b. acknowledgment.
   c. affirmation.
   d. estoppel.

9. In order to be recorded a document must be:
   a. witnessed.
   b. sealed.
   c. acknowledged.
   d. considered.

10. Alvin Rosewell executes a deed to Sylvia Plat as grantee, has it acknowledged, and receives payment from the buyer. Rosewell holds the deed, however, and arranges to meet Plat the next morning at the courthouse to deliver the deed to her. In this situation at this time:
    a. Plat owns the property because she has paid for it.
    b. title to the property will not officially pass until Plat has been given the deed the next morning.
    c. title to the property will not pass until Plat has received the deed and recorded it the next morning.
    d. Plat will own the property when she has signed the deed the next morning.

11. The grantee receives greatest protection with what type of deed?
    a. Quitclaim
    b. Warranty
    c. Bargain and sale with covenant
    d. Executor's

12. A bargain and sale deed with covenant against grantor's acts is commonly used:
    a. in Manhattan.
    b. Upstate.
    c. in divorce settlements.
    d. to clear cloud from a title.

13. Which of the following types of deeds most usually recites the full, actual consideration paid for the property?
    a. Full covenant and warranty deed
    b. Quitclaim deed
    c. Bargain and sale deed
    d. Referee's deed

14. The bond accompanying a mortgage is signed by the:
    a. mortgagor.
    b. mortgagee.
    c. grantor.
    d. lessee.

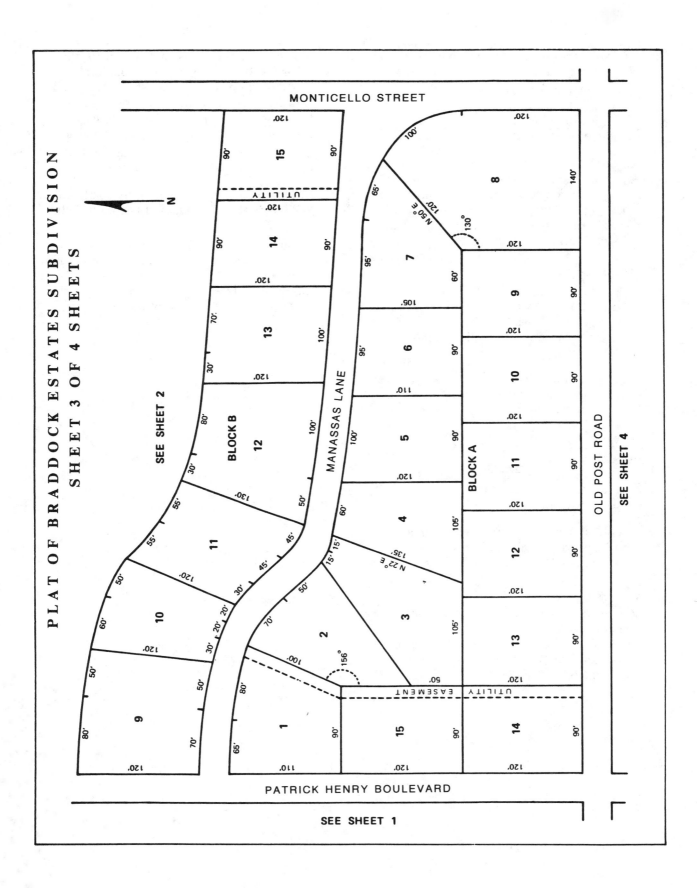

PLAT OF BRADDOCK ESTATES SUBDIVISION
SHEET 3 OF 4 SHEETS

15. The borrower proves a mortgage has been paid off by recording a:

    a. reduction certificate.
    b. certificate of estoppel.
    c. certificate of satisfaction.
    d. notice of default.

16. All on the same parcel: Charlie Feckless gives A a mortgage in return for a loan of $15,000. A fails to record the mortgage. Charlie then borrows an additional $40,000 from B, who records the mortgage. Charlie then persuades C to lend him $50,000 and C records his mortgage. Which is now the first mortgage against the property?

    a. A's because it was the loan first made
    b. B's because it was the one first recorded
    c. C's because it was for the largest amount
    d. None because Charlie failed to pay his income tax

17. Gloria Glamour allows Ron Rocker to take over the mortgage on her property when he buys the house. She will receive the most protection if Ron:

    a. takes the property subject to the existing loan.
    b. assumes the existing loan.
    c. alienates the present loan.
    d. accelerates the loan.

18. A mortgage document requires the mortgagor to perform certain duties; which of the following is *not* one of these?

    a. Maintain the property in good condition at all times
    b. Obtain the mortgagee's permission before renting a room to a boarder
    c. Maintain adequate insurance on the property
    d. Obtain the lender's permission before making major alterations to the property

19. A savings and loan association lent Bob Bluecollar $60,000 to buy a house. The local factory closed down and real estate values fell. At a foreclosure auction the property sold for only $50,000. To make up its loss the lender may seek a deficiency judgment against:

    a. Bob.   c. the appraiser.
    b. the new owner.   d. no one.

20. Jim has a lease until June on his apartment at $400 a month. The building is sold in February. Jim:

    a. must vacate by March 30.
    b. should negotiate a new lease with the new owner.
    c. can stay if he pays an extra month's rent.
    d. can abide by the terms of the original lease.

Appendix: Excerpts from New York State's Study Booklet for Brokers

DEEDS

Ordinarily, a "deed" is understood to be an instrument in writing duly executed and delivered, that conveys title to real property. A deed is "duly executed" when it is signed and acknowledged by the maker thereof, who is usually termed the "grantor."

Essentials of a valid deed. They are as follows:
1. It must be in writing;
2. The grantor thereto must be competent (sane adult);
3. It must contain an adequate expression of intent to convey real property;
4. There must be a definite description of the real property conveyed;
5. It must include an "habendum" clause ("to have and to hold the above granted premises unto the party of the second part, ..., his heirs and assigns forever");
6. It must be signed by the grantor;
7. There must be an acknowledgment of its execution by grantor (see Acknowledgments);
8. It must be delivered to the grantee (purchaser).

Kinds of deeds. The forms of deeds in general use in the State of New York are: (a) deed with full covenants; (b) bargain and sale deed, without covenant against grantor; (c) bargain and sale deed with covenant against grantor; (d) quitclaim deed; (e) executor's deed; and (f) referee's deed. Short forms of all the foregoing conveyances are prescribed by the Real Property Law.

Deed with full covenants. This form of conveyance is usually styled a "full covenant and warranty deed" and is most advantageous to the purchaser of real property, because it must contain, at least, the five covenants prescribed in the statutory short form of such a deed. A purchaser of real property is not entitled to a deed with full covenants unless a provision to that effect is included in the contract for the sale of the property described in the deed. In case a sale contract does not set forth the form of deed to be delivered to the buyer, the buyer may be required to accept a bargain and sale deed, without even a covenant therein that the grantor "has not done or suffered anything whereby the said premises have been incumbered in any way."

The following are the five covenants found in the full covenant and warranty deed:

First. That said..............is seized of said premises in fee simple, and has good right to convey the same;

Second. That the party of the second part shall quietly enjoy the said premises;

Third. That the said premises are free from incumbrances;

Fourth. That the party of the first part will execute or procure any further necessary assurance of the title to said premises;

Fifth. That said..............will forever warrant the title to said premises.

Bargain and sale deed without covenant against grantor. This is the simplest form of a deed. It is generally used when the purpose is to convey all the right, title and interest of the owner of record in the real property described in the document, and the grantor is not under contract to deliver a deed containing specified covenants.

Bargain and sale deed with covenant against the grantor. This form of deed contains the following covenant by the grantor: "And the party of the first part covenants that he has not done or suffered anything, whereby the said premises have been incumbered in any way whatever." In all other respects the statutory short form thereof is identical with the short form of a bargain and sale deed, without covenant against the grantor, as prescribed by the statute and quoted above.

Quitclaim deed. The usual purpose of this form of deed is to remove a cloud from the title to real property. Its statutory short form is practically identical with the short form of a bargain and sale deed, without covenant against the grantor as prescribed by the statute and hereinbefore quoted, the only difference being the use of the word "quitclaim" in the conveying clause of the deed so named.

Executor's deed. This form of deed is used to convey title to a decedent's real property. It will be noted that the statutory short form of such a deed, contains only the covenant against incumbrances that is included in the form of bargain and sale deed with covenant against grantor, prescribed by the statute.

Referee's deed. This form of deed is used for the conveyance of real property sold pursuant to a judicial order, in an action for the foreclosure of a mortgage or for partition. This deed does not contain any covenants.

MORTGAGES

The term "mortgage" means an instrument in writing, duly executed and delivered, that creates a lien, upon the real property described therein, as security for the payment of a specified debt, which may be in the form of a bond or note. Essentials of a valid mortgage:

1. It must be in writing;

2. The parties thereto must be competent (sane adults);

3. Its purpose must be stated (to secure payment of a specified bond or obligation);

4. There must be an appropriate mortgaging clause (the mortgagor hereby mortgages to the mortgagee'');

5. The description of the property mortgaged must be stated definitely;

6. It must be signed by the mortgagor;

7. It must be acknowledged by the mortgagor;

8. It must be delivered to the mortgagee.

The statutory short form of mortgage contains the following covenants:

1. That the mortgagor will pay the indebtedness as hereinbefore provided.

2. That the mortgagor will keep buildings on the premises insured against loss by fire for the benefit of the mortgagee.

3. That no building on the premises shall be removed or demolished without the consent of the mortgagee.

4. That the whole of said principal sum shall become due after default in the payment of any installment of principal or of interest for..........

days, or after default in the payment of any tax, water rate or assessment for...........days after notice and demand.

5. That the holder of this mortgage in any action to foreclose it, shall be entitled to the appointment of a receiver.

6. That the mortgagor will pay all taxes, assessments or water rates, and in default thereof, the mortgagee may pay the same.

7. That the mortgagor within...........days upon request in person or within..............days upon request by mail will furnish a statement of the amount due on this mortgage.

8. That notice and demand or request may be in writing and may be served in person or by mail.

9. That the mortgagor warrants the title to the premises.

Bond. A bond is evidence of the debt which creates the obligation for repayment of a loan, while a mortgage is the security for the debt with specific property as a pledge.

In addition to a statutory short form of mortgage, there is also a statutory short form of bond and mortgage. This includes all of the provisions enumerated in the short form of mortgage, as well as an acknowledgement of indebtedness by the mortgagor.

Priority of lien. Mortgages are frequently referred to as first, second and third mortgages, as the case may be. This reference indicates their relative priority in lien upon the mortgaged premises. The lien of the first mortgage has priority over the liens of subsequently recorded mortgages, which means that in case of the sale of the mortgaged premises by court order (in an action to foreclose a mortgage, for instance), the indebtedness secured by the first mortgage must be paid, whether or not there is any money left to apply on the second or third mortgage debt.

Assignment of mortgage. A mortgage may be sold by the holder thereof, in which case it is customary for the holder to execute and deliver to the purchaser a document known as an assignment of mortgage, in which it is advisable for the assignee (purchaser) to require that there shall be included a covenant, setting forth the amount due of principal and interest on account of the mortgage debt.

Estoppel certificate. Usually the purchaser of a mortgage upon real property requires that the mortgagee shall furnish a certificate, duly executed by the mortgagor, substantially providing that the mortgage is a valid lien, that a certain amount of principal and interest is due and that there are no defenses or offsets to the mortgage. This acknowledgment by the mortgagor of the validity of the mortgage lien and of the amount of the debt precludes the mortgagor from asserting contrary claims thereafter.

Satisfaction or assignment of mortgage. When the owner of property incumbered by a mortgage pays the mortgage debt, the owner should not only require the holder of the mortgage to return the mortgage and the bond or other obligation secured by it, but should insist that the mortgagee deliver to the owner a duly executed and acknowledged "satisfaction piece," which will authorize the mortgage to be discharged of record.

Alternatively, the owner usually may require the mortgage holder to execute an assignment of the mortgage to a third party, without recourse against the mortgage holder.

Mortgage foreclosure. One of the mortgagee's remedies for the failure of the mortgagor to pay interest upon or installments of the principal of the mortgage debt, as agreed, or for the violation of any other of the mortgagor's covenants, is by way of an action for the foreclosure of the lien of the mortgage. Such an action usually culminates in a judgment directing the sale of the property covered by the mortgage, and the application of the proceeds of the sale toward the payment of the mortgage debt.

ACKNOWLEDGMENTS

Technically, the term "acknowledgment" means both the act and the evidence thereof made by the officer taking the acknowledgment. Practically, an acknowledgment is the certificate of an officer, duly empowered to take an acknowledgment or proof of the conveyance of real property, that on a specified date "before me came ...., to me known to be the individual described in, and who executed the foregoing instrument and acknowledged that he executed the same."

The Real Property Law provides:

Acknowledgments and proofs within the state. The acknowledgment or proof, within this state, of a conveyance of real property situate in this state may be made:

1. At any place within the state, before (a) a justice of the supreme court; (b) an official examiner of title; (c) an official referee; or (d) a notary public.

2. Within the district wherein such officer is authorized to perform official duties, before (a) a judge or clerk of any court or record; (b) a commissioner of deeds outside of the city of New York, or a commissioner of deeds of the city of New York within the five counties comprising the city of New York; (c) the mayor or recorder of a city; (d) a surrogate, special surrogate, or special county judge; or (e) the county clerk or other recording officer of a county.

3. Before a justice of the peace, town councilman, village police justice or a judge of any court of inferior local jurisdiction, anywhere within the county containing the town, village or city in which he is authorized to perform official duties.

A certificate of authentication of an acknowledgment made anywhere in the State as to the execution of a conveyance, is required to entitle a conveyance to be recorded when acknowledged or proved before a commissioner of deeds, justice of the peace, town councilman or village police justice.

The usual form of acknowledgment by an individual is as follows:

STATE OF NEW YORK,

ss.:

County of ....

On this .... day of ....:..............., before me came ...., to me known to be the individual described in, and who executed the foregoing instrument, and acknowledged that he executed the same.

....

Notary Public,

..........................County, No......

The form of acknowledgment by a corporation is set forth in section 309 of the Real Property Law.

When a certificate of acknowledgment on a conveyance is made by a notary public in another state, it is acceptable for recording without further authentication. A certificate of acknowledgment or proof of conveyance made by a notary public in a foreign country other than Canada requires a certificate of authentication.

In addition to providing a conveyance by acknowledgment pursuant to the above section, a conveyance may also be proved by a subscribing witness. However, this is not the usual and ordinary method of proof.

5

Law of Contracts

Overview

"Get it in writing" is a phrase commonly used to warn one party to an agreement to protect his or her interests by entering into a written *contract* with the other party, outlining the rights and obligations of both. The real estate business makes use of many different types of contracts, including listing agreements, leases, and sales contracts. Brokers and salespeople must understand the content and uses of such agreements and must be able to explain them to buyers and sellers.

This chapter first will deal with the legal principles governing contracts in general and then will examine the types of contracts used in the real estate business in particular.

Contracts

Brokers and salespeople use many types of contracts and agreements in the course of their business in order to carry out their responsibilities to sellers, buyers, and the general public. Among these are listing agreements, sales contracts, option agreements, installment contracts, and leases.

Before studying these specific types of contracts the student must first understand the general body of law that governs the operations of such agreements, known as *contract law*.

Contract Law

A **contract** may be defined as a *voluntary agreement between legally competent parties to perform or refrain from performing some legal act, supported by legal consideration.*

Depending on the situation and the nature or language of the agreement, a contract may be: (1) expressed or implied; (2) unilateral or bilateral; (3) executory or executed; and (4) valid, unenforceable, voidable, or void.

Express and Implied Contracts

Depending on how a contract is created, it may be express or implied. In an **express contract** the parties state the terms and show their intentions in words. An express contract may be either oral or written. In an **implied contract** the agreement of the parties is demonstrated by their acts and conduct.

In the usual agency relationship a listing agreement is an *express* contract between the seller and the broker that names the broker as the fiduciary representative of the seller. However, the courts have held that a broker may, under certain situations, also have an *implied* contract to represent a buyer.

Bilateral and Unilateral Contracts

According to the nature of the agreement made, contracts also may be classified as either bilateral or unilateral. In a **bilateral contract** both parties promise to do something; one promise is given in exchange for another. A real estate sales contract is a bilateral contract because the seller promises to sell a parcel of real estate and deliver title to the property to the buyer who promises to pay a certain sum of money for the property. "I will do this *and* you will do that." "Okay."

A **unilateral contract**, on the other hand, is a one-sided agreement whereby one party makes a promise in order to induce a second party to do something. The second party is not legally obligated to act; however, if the second party does comply the first party is obligated to keep the promise. An offer of a reward would be an example of a unilateral contract; under this agreement a law enforcement agency offers a monetary payment (reward) to anyone who can aid in the capture of a criminal. "I will do this *if* you will do that." "Okay."

Executed and Executory Contracts

A contract may be classified as either executed or executory, depending on whether or not the agreement is completely performed. A fully **executed contract** is one in which both parties have fulfilled their promises and thus performed the contract. An **executory contract** exists when something remains to be done by one or both parties.

Validity of Contracts

A contract can be described as either valid, void, voidable, or unenforceable (*see* Table 5.1), depending on the circumstances.

Table 5.1
Legal Effects of Contracts

Type of Contract	Legal Effect	Example
Valid	Binding and Enforceable on Both Parties	Agreement Complying with Essentials of a Valid Contract
Void	No Legal Effect	Contract for an Illegal Purpose
Voidable	Valid, but May Be Disaffirmed by One Party	Contract with a Minor
Unenforceable	Valid Between the Parties, But Neither May Sue to Force Performance	Certain Oral Agreements

A **valid contract** complies with all the essential elements (which will be discussed later in this chapter) and is binding and enforceable on both parties.

A **void contract** is one that has no legal force or effect because it does not meet the essential elements of a contract. For example, one of the essential conditions in order for a contract to be valid is that it be for a legal purpose; thus a contract to commit a crime is void.

A **voidable contract** is one that seems on the surface to be valid but may be rescinded, or disaffirmed, by one of the parties. For example, a contract entered into with a minor usually is voidable; a minor generally is permitted to disaffirm a real estate contract within a reasonable time after reaching legal age. A voidable contract is considered by the courts to be a valid contract if the party who has the option to disaffirm the agreement does not do so within a prescribed period of time.

An **unenforceable contract** also seems on the surface to be valid; however, neither party can sue the other to force performance. Unenforceable contracts are said to be "valid as between the parties" because after the agreement is fully executed and both parties are satisfied, neither has reason to initiate a lawsuit to force performance.

Elements Essential to a Valid Contract

The essentials of a valid contract vary somewhat from state to state. Those elements that are uniformly required are:

1. **Competent parties:** To enter into a binding contract in New York a person must be at least 18 years old and of sound mind. A married person under 18 may be considered adult. Persons under 18 may enter into a valid contract but the contract is voidable by the minor at any time before he or she reaches majority. A contract performed by a person judicially declared insane may be held void. Contracts for the sale of real property entered into on Sunday are enforceable in New York.

2. **Offer and acceptance:** This requirement, also called *mutual assent,* means that there must be a "meeting of the minds." The wording of the contract must express all the agreed-upon terms and must be clearly understood by the parties.

3. **Consideration:** The agreement must be based upon good or valuable consideration. Consideration is what the parties promise in the agreement to give to or receive from each other. Consideration may consist of legal tender, exchange of value, or love and affection. The price or amount must be definitely stated and payable in exchange for the deed or right received.

4. **Legality of object:** To be valid and enforceable a contract must not contemplate a purpose that is illegal or against public policy.

5. **Agreement in writing and signed:** New York's **statute of frauds** requires certain types of contracts to be in writing. These include all contracts for the sale of real estate and for leasing beyond the period of one year.

In addition to these elements, a real estate sales contract must contain an adequate description of the property being conveyed. The **parol evidence** rule states that the written contract takes precedence over oral agreements or promise.

Undue influence and duress. Contracts signed by a person under duress or undue influence are voidable (may be canceled) by such person or by a court. Extreme care should be taken when one or more of the parties to a contract is elderly, sick, in great distress, or under the influence of drugs or alcohol. To be valid every contract must be signed as the "free and voluntary act" of each party.

Performance of Contract

[handwritten marginalia: Statute of frauds vitiated by performance but contract needed because]

Occasionally a contract may call for a specific time at or by which the agreed-upon acts must be completely performed. In addition many contracts provide that **"time is of the essence."** This means that the contract must be performed within the time limit specified and any party who has not performed on time is guilty of a breach of contract. This powerful phrase is a two-edged sword and brokers should leave its use to attorneys.

When a contract does not specify a date for performance, the acts it requires should be performed within a reasonable time. The interpretation of what constitutes a reasonable time will depend upon the situation.

Assignment and Novation

Often, after a contract has been signed one party may want to withdraw without actually terminating the agreement. This may be accomplished through either assignment or novation.

Assignment refers to a transfer of rights and/or duties under a contract. Generally, rights may be assigned to a third party unless the agreement forbids such an assignment. Obligations also may be assigned but the original obligor remains secondarily liable for them (after the new obligor) unless he or she is specifically released from this responsibility. A contract that requires some personal quality or unique ability of one of the parties may not be assigned. Most contracts include a clause that either permits or forbids assignment.

A contract also may be performed by **novation,** or the substitution of a new contract for an existing agreement. The new agreement may be between the same parties or a new party may be substituted for either (this is *novation of the parties*). The parties' intent must be to discharge the old obligation. For example, when a real estate purchaser assumes the seller's existing mortgage loan (*see* Chapter 7), the lender may choose to release the seller and substitute the buyer as the party primarily liable for the mortgage debt.

Discharge of Contract

A contract may be completely performed, with all terms carried out, or it may be breached (broken) if one of the parties defaults. In addition there are various other methods by which a contract may be discharged (canceled). These include:

1. *Partial performance* of the terms along with a written acceptance by the person for whom acts have not been done or to whom money has not been paid.
2. *Substantial performance,* in which one party has substantially performed the contract but does not complete all the details exactly as the contract requires. Such performance may be sufficient to force payment with certain adjustments for any damages suffered by the other party.
3. *Impossibility of performance,* in which an act required by the contract cannot be legally accomplished.
4. *Mutual agreement* of the parties to cancel.
5. *Operation of law,* as in the voiding of a contract by a minor, or as a result of fraud or the expiration of the statute of limitations, or as a result of a contract being altered without the written consent of all parties involved.

Default—Breach of Contract

A **breach** of contract is a violation of any of the terms or conditions of a contract without legal excuse, as when a seller breaches a sales contract by not delivering title to the buyer under the conditions stated in the agreement.

If the seller defaults, the buyer has three alternatives:

1. The buyer may *rescind, or cancel, the contract* and recover the earnest money.
2. The buyer may file a court suit, known as an **action for specific performance,** to force the seller to perform the contract (i.e., convey the property).
3. The buyer may *sue the seller for compensatory damages.*

A suit for damages seldom is used in this instance, however, because in most cases the buyer would have difficulty proving the extent of damages.

If the *buyer defaults,* the seller may pursue one of the following courses:

1. The seller may *declare the contract forfeited.* The right to forfeit usually is provided in the terms of the contract and the seller usually is entitled to retain the earnest money and all payments received from the buyer.
2. The seller may *rescind the contract;* that is, he or she may cancel, or terminate, the contract as if it had never been made. This requires the seller to return all payments the buyer has made.
3. The seller may *sue for specific performance.* This may require the seller to

offer, or tender, a valid deed to the buyer to show the seller's compliance with the contract terms.

4. The seller may *sue for compensatory damages.*

Statute of Limitations. New York allows a specific time limit of *six years* during which parties to a contract may bring legal suit to enforce their rights. Any party who does not take steps to enforce his or her rights within this **statute of limitations** may lose those rights.

Contracts Used in the Real Estate Business

As mentioned earlier the types of written agreements most commonly used by brokers and salespeople are listing agreements, real estate sales contracts, option agreements, contracts for deed, and leases.

Broker's Authority to Prepare Documents

The manual for real estate brokers issued by the New York Department of State expressly states that the real estate broker's license does not confer the right to draw legal documents or give legal advice. A recent decision by the New York Appellate Court stated that a broker has a right to draw a simple contract. No court decisions have yet been made as to what constitutes a ''simple'' contract. The preparation of legal documents by a broker may result in the loss of commissions, revocation of the license, or other penalties or damages. In Upstate areas, many brokers fill in the blanks on forms or simple sales contracts; in the New York City area, the seller's attorney often prepares the contract.

Contract forms. *Printed forms* are used for all kinds of contracts because most transactions basically are similar in nature. The use of printed forms raises three problems: (1) what to *fill in the blanks,* (2) what printed matter is not applicable to a particular sale and can be *ruled out* by drawing lines through the unwanted words, and (3) what additional clauses or agreements (called *riders*) are to be *added.* All changes and additions usually are initialed by both parties.

Listing Agreements

Listing agreements are *instruments used by the real estate broker in order to legally represent a principal.* They are contracts that establish the rights of the broker as agent and of the buyer or seller as principal. Explanations of the types of listing agreements will be presented in Chapter 9.

Sales Contracts

A **real estate sales contract** sets forth all details of the agreement between a buyer and a seller for the purchase and sale of a parcel of real estate. Depending on the locality this agreement may be known as an *offer to purchase, contract of purchase and sale, earnest money agreement, binder and deposit receipt,* or other variations of these titles. New York does not mandate any specific form of listing or sales contract. An example of a real estate contract form used by some members of the Real Estate Board of Rochester appears as Figure 5.1.

In a few localities, notably in and around New York City, some brokers prepare a **memorandum of sale.** This sheet of information states the essential terms of the agreement and negotiations of terms. The parties agree to have a formal and complete contract of sale drawn up by an attorney. Throughout the state a memorandum might be used in any situation where the details of the transaction are too complex for the standard sales contract form.

Figure 5.1
Real Estate Sales
Contract

PURCHASE AND SALE CONTRACT
FOR RESIDENTIAL PROPERTY

Plain English Form Published by the Real Estate Board of Rochester, N.Y., Inc. and the Monroe County Bar Association.

COMMISSIONS OR FEES FOR REAL ESTATE SERVICES TO BE PROVIDED ARE NEGOTIABLE BETWEEN REALTOR AND SELLER.
When Signed, This Document Becomes A Binding Contract. Buyer And Seller May Wish To Consult Their Own Attorney.

TO: _____Mary and John Public_____ (Seller) FROM: _____Debra and Arthur Byer_____ (Buyer)

OFFER TO PURCHASE

Buyer offers to purchase the property described below from Seller on the following terms:

1. PROPERTY DESCRIPTION.
Property known as No. _____240 Hemingway Drive_____ in the (Town) (City) (Village) of _____Brighton (Rochester 14620)_____ State of New York, also
known as Tax No. _____080-557_____, including all buildings and any other improvements and all rights which the Seller has in or with the property.
Approximate Lot Size: _____85' x 185'_____
Check if Applicable: [ ] As described in more detail in the attached description.

Description of Buildings on Property:

_____8-room frame one-story house and attached one-car garage_____

2. OTHER ITEMS INCLUDED IN PURCHASE. The following items, if any, now in or on the property are included in this purchase and sale: All heating, plumbing, lighting fixtures, flowers, shrubs, trees, windows shades, venetian blinds, curtain and traverse rods, storm windows, storm doors, screens, awnings, TV antennae, water softeners, sump pumps, window boxes, mail box, tool shed, fences, wall-to-wall carpeting and runners, exhaust fans, hoods, garbage disposal, electric garage door opener and remote control devices, intercom equipment, humidifier, security systems, smoke detectors, all fireplace screens and enclosures, swimming pool and all related equipment and accessories, and all built-in cabinets, mirrors, stoves, ovens, dishwashers, trash compactors, shelving, and air conditioning (except window) units. Buyer agrees to accept these items in their present condition. Other items to be included in the purchase and sale are:

_____all drapes, washer, and dryer._____

Seller represents _____all of the above except built-in dishwasher_____ to be in good working order.
Items not included are: _____dining-room chandelier._____

Seller represents that he has good title to all of the above items to be transferred to Buyer, and will deliver a Bill of Sale for the same at closing.

3. PRICE: AMOUNT AND HOW IT WILL BE PAID. The purchase price is _____Ninety-eight Thousand_____ Dollars
$ _____$98,000.00_____. Buyer shall receive credit at closing for any deposit made hereunder. The balance of the purchase price shall be paid as follows: (Check and complete applicable provisions.)

[ ] (a) Seller agrees to pay a loan fee of up to _____% of the mortgage amount as stated in paragraph 4 (a).

xxx(b) All in cash, or certified check at closing.

[ ] (c) By Buyer assuming and agreeing to pay according to its terms, the principal balance of the mortgage in the approximate amount of $ _____
held by _____, provided that the mortgage is assumable without the holder's approval. Buyer
understands that the mortgage bears interest at the rate of _____% per year and the monthly payments are $_____ which includes principal,
interest, taxes and insurance (strike out any item not included in payment), with the last payment due on approximately _____, 19_____. Buyer agrees to pay the
balance of the purchase price over the amount of the assumed mortgage in cash or certified check at closing. Buyer understands that principal balance may be lower at time of closing because
of monthly payments made after this contract is signed. If the mortgage to be assumed provides for graduated or balloon payments, then a copy of the original bond and mortgage shall be
furnished to Buyer's attorney for approval within ten days after acceptance of this offer.

[ ] (d) By Buyer delivering a purchase money bond and mortgage to Seller at closing. This purchase money bond and mortgage shall be in the amount of $_____
shall be for a term of _____ years, shall bear interest at the rate of _____% per year, and shall be paid in monthly installments of
$_____, including principal and interest. The entire principal balance shall be all due and payable _____ years from date of closing.

The mortgage shall contain the statutory clauses as to payment, insurance, acceleration on default of thirty days, taxes, assessments, and water rates and also shall provide for late charges of
2% of any monthly payment which is not paid within 15 days after it is due and for recovery of reasonable attorney's fees if the mortgage is foreclosed.

The mortgage shall allow Buyer to prepay all or part of the mortgage without penalty at any time but shall also provide that the mortgage be paid in full if Buyer sells the property, unless Seller
consents in writing to assumption of the mortgage debt. The balance of the purchase price will be paid at closing in cash, or certified check.

4. CONTINGENCIES. Buyer makes this offer subject to the following contingencies. If any of these contingencies is not satisfied by the dates specified, then either Buyer or Seller may cancel
this contract by written notice to the other.

[ ] (a) **Mortgage Contingency.** This offer is subject to Buyer obtaining a _____ mortgage loan in the amount of $_____ for a term of
_____ years. Buyer shall immediately apply for this loan and shall have until _____, to obtain a written mortgage commitment. The conditions of any such
mortgage commitment shall not be deemed contingencies of this contract but shall be the sole responsibility of Buyer. If the loan commitment requires repairs, replacements, or improvements
to be made, or painting to be done, before closing, then Seller shall do the work and install the materials and improvements needed or have the same done, at his expense, not to exceed,
however, $_____. If the cost of doing so is more than that amount, Buyer will be allowed either to receive credit at closing for such amount and incur the
necessary expenses to comply with the loan commitment requirements, or to cancel this contract by written notice to Seller and receive back his deposit.

[ ] (b) **Mortgage Assumption Contingency.** This offer is subject to Buyer obtaining permission to assume the existing mortgage loan balance referred to above (3c) by _____ 19____.
If the mortgage holder requires that the interest rate be increased for such approval to be given, Buyer agrees to assume the mortgage at such rate as long as it does not exceed _____%
at the time of commitment.

xxx(c) **Sale Contingency.** This offer is contingent upon Buyer securing a firm contract for the sale of his property located at ___91 Salem Drive, Islip, NY___
no later than __May 1,19--__. If Buyer is unable to obtain a firm contract for the sale of his property by such date, then either he or Seller may cancel this contract by written notice to the
other. If Seller receives another acceptable purchase offer, Seller may notify Buyer in writing that Seller wants to accept the other offer and Buyer will then have 5 banking days to
remove this sale contingency by written notice to the Seller. If Buyer does not remove this contingency after receiving notice from Seller, Buyer's rights under this contract shall end, and Seller
shall be free to accept the other purchase offer and Buyer's deposit shall be returned. Buyer may not remove this contingency by such notice to Seller if Buyer's mortgage loan commitment
requires the sale and transfer of his property as a condition of the mortgage lender disbursing the mortgage loan proceeds, unless Buyer has a contract for the sale of his property which is not
then subject to any unsatisfied contingencies.

xxx(d) **Attorney Approval.** This offer is subject to approval by Buyer's and Seller's Attorney within ___3___ banking days after acceptance.

[ ] (e) **Waiver of Attorney Approval.** This offer is not subject to the Buyer's Attorney approval.

[ ] (f) **Other Contingencies.** _____
_____

5. Closing Date and Place. The transfer of title shall take place at the __Monroe__ County Clerk's Office on or before the ___1___ day of __July__ , 19--.

6. Buyer's Possession of Property. Buyer shall have possession of the property on the day of closing.

7. Title Documents. Seller shall provide the following documents in connection with the sale:

A. Deed. Seller will deliver to Buyer at closing a properly signed and notarized Warranty Deed with lien covenant (or Executor's Deed, Administrator's Deed or Trustee's Deed, if Seller holds title as such).

B. Abstract, Bankruptcy and Tax Searches, and Instrument Survey Map. Seller will furnish and pay for and deliver to Buyer or Buyer's attorney at least 10 days prior to the date of closing, fully guaranteed tax, title and
United States Court Searches dated or redated after the date of this contract with a local tax certificate for Village, or City taxes, if any, and an instrument survey map dated or redated after the date of this contract. Seller
will pay for the map or redated map and for continuing such searches to and including the day of closing. Any survey map shall be prepared or redated and certified to meet the standards and requirements of Buyer's
mortgage lender and of the Monroe County Bar Association.

8. Marketability of Title. The deed and other documents delivered by Seller shall be sufficient to convey good marketable title in fee simple, to the property free and clear of all liens and encumbrances.
However, Buyer agrees to accept title to the property subject to restrictive covenants of record common to the tract or subdivision of which the property is a part, provided these restrictions have not been violated, or if
they have been violated, that the time for anyone to complain of the violations has expired. Buyer also agrees to accept title to the property subject to public utility easements along lot lines as long as those easements do
not interfere with any buildings now on the property or with any improvements Buyer may construct in compliance with all present restrictive covenants of record and zoning and building codes applicable to the
property.

9. Objections to Title. If Buyer raises a valid writen objection to Seller's title which means that the title to the property is unmarketable, Seller may cancel this contract by giving prompt written notice of
cancellation to Buyer. Buyer's deposit shall be returned immediately, and if Buyer makes a written request for it, Selleh shall reimburse Buyer for the reasonable cost of having the title examined. However, if Seller gives
written notice within five (5) days that Seller will cure the problem prior to the closing date, then this contract shall continue in force until the closing date subject to Seller performing as promised. If Seller fails to cure the
problem within such time, Buyer will not be obligated to purchase the property and his deposit shall be returned together with reimbursement for the reasonable cost of having the title examined.

10. Recording Costs, Mortgage Tax, Transfer Tax and Closing Adjustments. Seller will pay the real property transfer tax and special additional mortgage recording tax, if applicable. Buyer will pay mortgage assumption charges, if any, and will pay for recording the deed and the mortgage, and for mortgage tax. Rent payments, if any, fuel oil on the premises, if any, water charges, pure water charges, sewer charges, mortgage interest, prepaid or deferred F.H.A. insurance premium, current common charges or assessments, if any, and current taxes computed on a fiscal year basis, excluding any delinquent items, interest and penalties, will be prorated and adjusted between Seller and Buyer as of the date of closing.

11. Zoning. Seller certifies that the property is in full compliance with all zoning or building ordinances for use as a __single-family dwelling.__

If applicable laws require it, Seller will furnish at or before closing, a Certificate of Occupancy for the property dated within ninety (90) days of the closing, provided Seller need not spend more than $ __N/A__ to make the property comply. If the cost of doing so is more than that amount, Buyer will be allowed either to receive credit at closing for such amount and incur the expense himself, instead of receiving a Certificate of Occupancy, or to cancel this contract by written notice to Seller. If Buyer cancels, his deposit shall be returned.

12. Risk of Loss. Risk of loss or damage to the property by fire or other casualty until transfer of title shall be assumed by the Seller. If damage to the property by fire or such other casualty occurs prior to transfer, Buyer may cancel this contract without any further liability to Seller and Buyer's deposit is to be returned. If Buyer does not cancel but elects to close, then Seller shall transfer to Buyer any insurance proceeds, or Seller's claim to insurance proceeds payable for such damage.

13. Condition of Property. Buyer(s) agree to purchase the property "as is" except as provided in paragraph 2, subject to reasonable use, wear, tear, and natural deterioration between now and the time of closing. However, this paragraph shall not relieve Seller from furnishing a Certificate of Occupancy as called for in paragraph 11, if applicable. Buyer shall have the right, after reasonable notice to seller, to inspect the property within 48 hours before the time of closing.

14. Deposit. Buyer (has deposited) ~~(will deposit upon acceptance)~~ $ __1,000.00__ in the form of a __good check__ with __Sun City Realty__ which deposit is to become part of the purchase price or returned if not accepted or if this contract thereafter fails to close for any reason not the fault of Buyer. If buyer fails to complete his part of this contract, seller is allowed to keep the deposit and may also pursue other legal rights he has against the buyer, including a law suit for any real estate brokerage commission paid by the seller.

15. Real Estate Broker.

XXX The parties agree that __Sun City Realty__ brought about this purchase and sale.

[ ] It is understood and agreed by both Buyer and Seller that no broker secured this contract.

16. Life of Offer. Buyer agrees not to withdraw this offer before __February 29__, 19__--, at __10 p.__m.

17. Responsibility of Persons Under This Contract; Assignability. If more than one person signs this contract as Buyer, each person and any party who takes over that person's legal position will be responsible for keeping the promises made by Buyer in this contract. If more than one person signs this contract as Seller, each person or any party who takes over that person's legal position, will be fully responsible for keeping the promises made by Seller. However, this contract is personal to the parties and may not be assigned by either without the other's consent.

18. Entire Contract. This contract when signed by both Buyer and Seller will be the record of the complete agreement between the Buyer and Seller concerning the purchase and sale of the property. No verbal agreements or promises will be binding.

OK for buyers
2/29/-
L.H.

Dated: __February 26, 19--__   BUYER __Debra Byer__

Witness: __Susy Salesperson__   BUYER __Arthur Byer__

ACCEPTANCE OF OFFER BY SELLER

Sellers certify that they own the property and have the power to sell the property. Sellers accept the offer and agree to sell on the terms and conditions set forth above and agree that the deposit may be held by __Sun City Realty.__

[ ] Waiver of Seller's Attorney Approval. This offer is not subject to Seller's Attorney approval.

Dated: __February 27, 19-__   SELLER __Mary Public__

Witness: __Susy Salesperson__   SELLER __John Q. Public__

Approved for sellers as to form.
J.M. 3/1/19-

OPTION CLAUSE: VETERANS ADMINISTRATION AND FEDERAL HOUSING ADMINISTRATION LOANS ONLY

It is expressly agreed that, notwithstanding any other provisions of this contract, the purchaser shall not be obligated to complete the purchase of the property described herein or to incur any penalty by forfeiture of earnest money deposits or otherwise, in those cases involving a GI loan, if the contract purchase price or cost exceeds the reasonable value of the property established by the Veterans Administration or in those cases to be insured by the Federal Housing Administration unless the seller has delivered to the purchaser a written statement issued by the Federal Housing Commissioner setting forth the appraised value of the property (excluding closing costs) of not less than $_____ which statement the seller hereby agrees to deliver to the purchaser promptly after such appraised value statement is made available to the seller. The purchaser shall, however, have the privilege and option of proceeding with the consummation of this contract without regard to the amount of the appraised valuation if made by the Federal Housing Commissioner or reasonable value established by the Veterans Administration. In those cases involving FHA, the appraised valuation is arrived at to determine the maximum mortgage the Department of Housing and Urban Development will insure. HUD does not warrant the value or the condition of the property. The purchaser should satisfy himself/herself that the price and the condition of the property are acceptable.

BUYERS: _____ and _____

SELLERS: _____ and _____

CONTRACT OF SALE

Property Address: 240 Hemingway Drive, Rochester 14620 Date 2/26/ 19 -- To Be Closed July 1, 19 --

Buyer: Debra and Arthur Byer	Seller: John Q. and Mary Public
Address: 93 Salem Drive, Islip NY 11751	Address: 240 Hemingway Drive Rochester, NY 14620
Zip: _____ Phone: (H) (516) 123-4567 (B) 123-4000	Zip: _____ Phone: (H) (716) 473-4973 (B) 271-6230
Attorney: Learned Hand, Esq.	Attorney John Marshall, Esq.
Address: 480 Powers Building, Rochester 14614	Address: Suite 1900, Executive Office Bld 14614
Zip: _____ Phone: (B) 987-6543 (H) ---	Zip: _____ Phone: (B) 555-1212 (H) 911-8000
Selling Broker Sun City	Listing Broker Sun City Realty
Address:	Address: 400 Rainbow Plaza 14601
Zip: _____ Phone: _____ Broker Code: SUNC	Zip: _____ Phone: 716-586-5028 Broker Code: SUNC
Selling Agent: Susan Salesperson Phone: (H) 473-1755	Listing Agent: J. R. Ewing Phone: (H) 271-6265

The contract of sale is the most important document in the sale of real estate because it sets out in detail the agreement between the buyer and the seller and establishes their legal rights and obligations. *The contract, in effect, dictates the contents of the deed.*

Contracts in writing. New York has adopted the common-law doctrine known as the **statute of frauds,** which provides that certain oral agreements are not enforceable in a court of law. Thus, generally, no lawsuit will be successful for the sale of real estate unless the contract is in writing and signed by the parties to the agreement. A written agreement establishes the interest of the purchaser and his or her rights to enforce that interest by court action. It prevents the seller from selling the property to another person who might offer a higher price. The contract agreement also obligates the buyer to complete the transaction according to the terms agreed upon.

Offer and acceptance. One of the essential elements of a valid contract of sale is a meeting of the minds whereby the buyer and seller agree on the terms of the sale. This usually is accomplished through the process of **offer and acceptance.**

A broker lists an owner's real estate for sale at the price and conditions set by the owner. A prospective buyer who wants to purchase the property at those terms or some other terms is found. Upstate, an offer to purchase is drawn up, signed by the prospective buyer, and presented by the broker to the seller. This is an *offer.* If the seller agrees to the offer *exactly as it was made* and signs the contract, the offer has been *accepted* and the contract is *valid.* The broker then must advise the buyer of the seller's acceptance, obtain lawyers' approval if the contract calls for it, and deliver a duplicate original of the contract to the buyer.

In some Downstate areas the broker prepares a precontract agreement known as a binder, which may or may not be legally enforceable, but which usually contains many of the essential terms that will later be included in a contract. In the New York City area purchase offers often are handled by attorneys.

Any attempt by the seller to change the terms proposed by the buyer creates a **counteroffer.** The buyer is relieved of his or her original offer because the seller has, in effect, rejected it. The buyer can accept the seller's counteroffer or can reject it and, if he or she wishes, make another counteroffer. Any change in the last offer made results in a counteroffer until one party finally agrees to the other party's last offer and both parties sign the final contract (See Figure 5.2).

An offer is not considered to be accepted until the person making the offer has been *notified of the other party's acceptance.* When the parties are communicating through an agent or at a distance, questions may arise regarding whether an acceptance, rejection, or counteroffer has effectively taken place. The real estate broker or salesperson must transmit all offers, acceptances, or other responses as soon as possible in order to avoid such problems.

Equitable title. When a buyer signs a contract to purchase real estate he or she does not receive title to the land; only a deed can actually convey title. However, after both buyer and seller have executed a sales contract the buyer acquires an interest in the land known as **equitable title.** In New York a buyer under a land contract also acquires equitable title. Acquisition of equitable title may give the buyer an insurable interest in the property. If the parties decide not to go

Figure 5.2
Offer and Acceptance

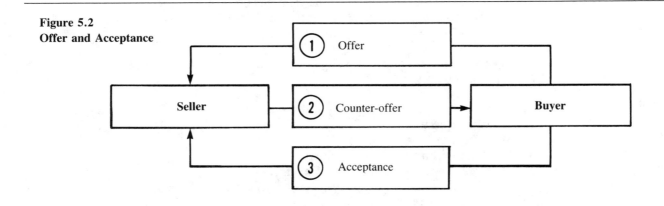

through with the purchase and sale, they usually enter into a written **release,** freeing each other from any obligation under the contract.

Destruction of premises. New York State has adopted the *Uniform Vendor and Purchaser Risk Act,* which specifically provides that the seller (vendor) bears any loss that occurs before the title passes or the buyer (vendee) takes possession.

Earnest money deposits. It is customary but not essential for a puchaser to put down a cash deposit when making an offer to purchase real estate. This cash deposit, commonly referred to as **earnest money,** *gives evidence of the buyer's intention to carry out terms of the contract.* This deposit is paid to the broker and the sales contract typically provides that the broker will hold the deposit for the parties. In some areas of New York it is common practice for deposits to be held in escrow by the seller's attorney.

The amount of the deposit is a matter to be agreed upon by the parties. Under the terms of most listing agreements a real estate broker is required to accept a reasonable amount as earnest money. Generally the deposit should be sufficient to discourage the buyer from defaulting, compensate the seller for taking the property off the market, and cover any expenses the seller might incur if the buyer defaults. A purchase offer with no earnest money is, however, valid. Most contracts provide that the deposit becomes the seller's property if the buyer defaults.

Earnest money must be held by a broker in a special *trust,* or *escrow, bank account.* This money cannot be *commingled,* or mixed, with a broker's personal funds. A broker may not use such funds for his or her own personal use; this illegal act is known as *conversion.* A broker need not open a special escrow account for each earnest money deposit received. One such account into which all such funds are deposited is sufficient. A broker should maintain full, complete, and accurate records of all earnest money deposits.

There is some uncertainty as to exactly who owns the earnest money after it is put on deposit. Until the offer is officially accepted, the money is the buyer's. After the seller accepts the offer, however, the buyer may not get the money back, even though the seller is not entitled to it until the transaction has been completed. Under no circumstances does the money belong to the broker, who must maintain it in his or her trust account. This uncertain nature of earnest money deposits makes it absolutely necessary that such funds be properly protected pending a final decision on their disbursement.

Parts of a sales contract. In New York the essentials of a valid contract for the sale of real property are:

1. Contract in writing
2. Competent parties
3. Agreement to buy and sell
4. Adequate description of the property
5. Consideration (price and terms of payment)
6. Grantor's agreement to convey (should specify type of deed)
7. Place and time of closing
8. Signatures of the parties

Usually included, but not essential for a valid contract, are provisions covering the following:

9. Encumbrances to which the deed will be made subject
10. Earnest money deposit
11. Mortgage financing the buyer plans to obtain
12. Possession by the buyer
13. Title evidence
14. Prorations and adjustments
15. Destruction of the premises before closing
16. Default by either party
17. Miscellaneous provisions

Miscellaneous Provisions

When the purchaser intends to secure an FHA or VA loan, special clauses must be included in the sales contract providing that the contract may be voided if the property appraises below the sale price. Provisions may be added stipulating that the seller will furnish satisfactory reports on such matters as termite or insect infestation, quality of a private water supply, or condition of plumbing or heating equipment. In some transfers a certificate of occupancy must be obtained from a municipality; the contract should make it clear whose responsibility this will be. The purchaser may add a stipulation that allows inspection of the property within 24 hours before settlement.

Among common provisions in the "subject to" section of the contract are: the purchaser's need to secure a specific loan, the purchaser's right to a satisfactory engineer's report on the property within a specified few days, approval of the contract by a family member or the purchaser's attorney, again within a short period of time, or the purchaser's need to sell a present home before buying the next residence. The last provision is known in some areas as a **contingency.** Where the purchaser has another home that must be sold first, the seller may insist on an **escape clause,** or kick-out. Such a provision allows the seller to accept a more favorable offer, with the original purchaser retaining the right to firm up the first sales contract (dropping the contingency) or to void the contract.

Plain Language Requirement (Sullivan Law)

New York law requires that certain written agreements for the sale or lease of residential property be written in a clear and coherent manner with words that are common in everyday usage. The copy also must be appropriately divided and captioned in its various sections. A grantor who fails to comply with this requirement is liable for actual damages plus $50. The plain language requirement does not apply to agreements involving amounts over $50,000.

Figure 5.1 is an example of a plain English contract.

Option Agreements

An **option** is a *contract by which an* optioner *(generally an owner) gives an* optionee *(a prospective purchaser or lessee) the right to buy or lease the owner's property at a fixed price within a stated period of time.* The optionee pays a fee (the agreed-upon consideration) for this option right and assumes no other obligation until deciding, within the specified time, either to: (1) exercise his or her option right (to buy or lease the property), or (2) allow the option right to expire. The owner may be bound to sell; the optionee is not bound to buy.

A common application of an option is a lease that includes an option for the tenant to purchase the property. Options must contain all the terms and provisions required for a valid contract of sale.

Installment Contracts (Land Contracts)

A real estate sale can be made under an **installment contract,** sometimes called a *contract for deed* or *land contract of sale*.

Under a typical land contract, the seller, also known as the *vendor,* retains fee ownership while the buyer, known as the *vendee,* secures possession and an equitable interest in the property. The buyer agrees to give the seller a down payment and pay regular monthly installments of principal and interest over a number of years. The buyer also agrees to pay real estate taxes, insurance premiums, repairs, and upkeep on the property. While the buyer obtains possession when the contract is signed by both parties, *the seller is not obligated to execute and deliver a deed to the buyer until the terms of the contract have been satisfied.* This frequently occurs when the buyer has made a sufficient number of payments to obtain a mortgage loan and pay off the balance due on the contract.

Real estate is occasionally sold with the new buyer assuming an existing land contract from the original buyer/vendee. Generally, the seller/vendor must approve the new purchaser.

As the mortgage market became increasingly difficult in the early 1980s, land contracts were used with greater frequency in the state outside the New York City area in an attempt to retain nonassumable mortgages or to afford greater protection for seller financing. The land contract was frequently combined with a wrap-around mortgage, described in Chapter 7. Such contracts require extensive legal input from lawyers experienced in real estate matters. The broker who negotiates a land contract should consult attorneys for both parties at every step of the way and refrain from specifying any detailed terms in the purchase agreement.

Leases

A lease is a contract in which the owner agrees to give possession of all or a part of the real estate to another person in exchange for a rental fee. Leases are discussed in detail in Chapter 22.

Local Forms

To gain familiarity with the forms used in a local area the student should go to brokers or real estate companies and ask for copies of the sales contract, listing agreement, and other forms they use. Usually such forms also can be obtained at a title or abstract company and some banks and savings and loan associations, or they may be purchased at local office supply and stationery stores.

Right of rescission. With contracts for the purchase of some types of personal property, the buyer has three days in which to reconsider and *rescind* (cancel) the contract. No such right applies to contracts for the purchase of real estate.

Borrowers who change their minds about a mortgage loan have three days in which to cancel the transaction if the mortgage was for *refinance* of presently owned property. No right of rescission, however, applies to mortgage loans used for the *purchase* of real estate.

Summary

A *contract* is defined as an agreement made by competent parties, with adequate consideration, to take or not to take some proper, or legal, action.

Contracts may be classified according to whether the parties' intentions are *expressed* or are *implied* by their actions. They also may be classified as *bilateral,* when both parties have obligated themselves to act, or *unilateral,* when one party is obligated to perform only if the other party acts. In addition, contracts may be classified according to their legal enforceability as either *valid, void, voidable,* or *unenforceable.*

Many contracts specify a time for performance. In any case all contracts must be performed within a reasonable time. An *executed* contract is one that has been fully performed. An *executory* contract is one in which some act remains to be performed.

The *essentials of a valid contract* are: (1) competent parties, (2) offer and acceptance, (3) consideration, (4) legality of object, and (5) agreement in writing and signed by the parties. A valid *real estate contract* also must include a description of the property.

In a number of circumstances a contract may be canceled before it is fully performed. Furthermore, in many types of contracts either of the parties may transfer his or her rights and obligations under the agreement by *assignment* of the contract or *novation* (substitution of a new contract).

If either party to a real estate sales contract defaults, several alternative methods of action are available. Contracts usually provide that the seller has the right to declare a sale canceled through forfeiture if the buyer defaults. In general if either party has suffered a loss because of the other's default, he or she may sue for damages to cover the loss. If one party insists on completing the transaction, he or she may sue the defaulter for *specific performance* of the terms of the contract; in this way a court can order the other parties to comply with the agreement.

Contracts frequently used in the real estate business include listing agreements, sales contracts, options, installment contracts (land contracts), and leases.

A *real estate sales contract* binds a buyer and a seller to a definite transaction as described in detail in the contract. The buyer is bound to purchase the property for the amount stated in the agreement. The seller is bound to deliver a good and marketable title, free from liens and encumbrances (except those allowed by the ''subject to'' clause of the contract).

Under an *option* agreement, the optionee purchases from the optionor, for a limited time period, the exclusive right to purchase or lease the optionor's property. For a potential purchaser or lessee an option is a means of buying time to consider or complete arrangements for a transaction. An *installment contract,* or *land contract,* is a sales/financing agreement under which a buyer purchases a seller's real estate on time. The buyer takes possession of and responsibility for the property but does not receive the deed immediately.

Questions

1. A legally enforceable agreement under which two parties agree to do something for each other is known as a(n):
   a. escrow agreement.
   b. legal promise.
   c. contract.
   d. option agreement.

2. Donna Bates drives into a filling station and tops off her gas tank. She is obligated to pay for the fuel through what kind of contract?
   a. Express   c. Oral
   b. Implied   d. Voidable

3. A contract is said to be *bilateral* if:
   a. one of the parties is a minor.
   b. the contract has yet to be fully performed.
   c. only one party to the agreement is bound to act.
   d. all parties to the contract are bound to act.

4. A seller gave an open listing to several brokers specifically promising that if one of the brokers found a buyer for the seller's real estate, the seller then would be obligated to pay a commission to that broker. This offer by the seller is a(n):
   a. executed agreement.
   b. discharged agreement.
   c. implied agreement.
   d. unilateral agreement.

5. During the period of time after a real estate sales contract is signed but before title actually passes the status of the contract is:
   a. voidable.   c. executed.
   b. executory.   d. implied.

6. Tom Jones, who is 17 years old and married, signs a contract to buy a house. The contract is:
   a. voidable.
   b. valid.
   c. executed.
   d. unilateral.

7. Broker Sam Manella has found a buyer for Joe Taylor's home. The buyer has entered into a real estate sales contract for the property for $1,000 less than the asking price and has deposited $5,000 earnest money with broker Manella. Taylor is out of town for the weekend and Manella has been unable to inform him of the signed agreement. At this point the real estate sales contract is a(n):
   a. voidable contract. c. executory agreement.
   b. offer.   d. implied contract.

8. Consideration offered in exchange for a deed might take the form of:
   a. love and affection.
   b. a purchase-money mortgage.
   c. cash.
   d. Any of the above

9. The statute of frauds requires that a contract must be in writing for:
   a. all real estate sales.
   b. all real estate contracts of any sort.
   c. all contracts.
   d. bilateral contracts only.

10. In New York State who prepares purchase contracts?
    a. Seller's attorney
    b. Buyer's attorney
    c. Real estate broker
    d. A, b, or c, according to local custom

11. If a real estate sales contract does not state that time is of the essence and the stipulated date of transfer comes and goes without a closing, the contract is then:
    a. binding for only 30 more days.
    b. novated.
    c. still valid.
    d. automatically void.

12. A suit for specific performance asks for:
    a. money damages.
    b. a new contract.
    c. a deficiency judgment.
    d. a forced sale or purchase.

13. In filling out a sales contract, someone crossed out several words and inserted others. In order to eliminate future controversy as to whether the changes were made before or after the contract was signed, the broker should:
    a. write a letter to each party listing the changes.
    b. have each party write a letter to the other approving the changes.
    c. redraw the entire contract.
    d. have both parties initial or sign on the margin near each change.

14. In New York State the statute of limitations for enforcement of a contract is:
    a. three years.   c. ten years.
    b. six years.   d. 20 years.

15. The Foxes offer in writing to purchase a house for $120,000, including the drapes. The Wolfs reply in writing accepting $120,000 but excluding the drapes. During the time limit specified in this counteroffer, who is bound?
    a. The Foxes   c. Both parties
    b. The Wolfs   d. Neither party

16. In New York State a valid contract for the sale of real estate must include:
    a. an earnest money deposit.
    b. the time and place of closing.
    c. the signatures of witnesses.
    d. All of the above

17. A happening without which a contract will become void is known as a:
    a. contingency.   c. warranty.
    b. reservation.   d. consideration.

18. An option to purchase binds:
    a. the buyer only.
    b. the seller only.
    c. neither buyer nor seller.
    d. both buyer and seller.

19. Which of the following best describes a land installment contract, or contract for deed?
    a. A contract to buy land only
    b. A mortgage on land
    c. A means of conveying title immediately while the purchaser pays for the property in installments
    d. A method of selling real estate whereby the purchaser pays for the property in regular installments while the seller retains title to the property

20. The purchaser of real estate under an installment contract:
    a. generally pays no interest charge.
    b. is called a vendor.
    c. is not required to pay property taxes for the duration of the contract.
    d. is called a vendee.

Appendix: Excerpts from New York State's Study Booklet for Brokers

CONTRACTS FOR THE SALE OR LEASE OF REAL PROPERTY

Essentials. 1. A contract for the leasing for a longer period than one year, or for the sale, of any real property, or an interest therein, is void, unless the contract, or some note or memorandum thereof, expressing the considerations, is in writing, subscribed by the party to be charged, or by the party's lawful agent thereunto authorized by writing. The other essentials of a valid contract for the sale of real property are:

2. Competent parties (sane adults):

3. An expression of their agreement to sell and buy;

4. An understandable and adequate description of the premises that are the subject of the transaction;

5. The consideration for the contemplated conveyance (price and terms of payment);

6. Agreement of grantor to convey title (although it is not essential, the contract should usually specify the form of the deed to be delivered to grantee).

7. Place and date of closing. (Again, this item may not be required to make the contract enforceable, but it is usually prudent to include this item.)

The contract speaks for itself. Care should be taken that the written contract includes all special terms and convenants that were verbally agreed upon by the parties.

For instance, if such a contract does not specifically provide that the grantor shall deliver a full covenant and warranty deed, the grantor may require the grantee to accept a bargain and sale deed. Under a contract providing that the seller shall deliver "a good and sufficient deed," the seller cannot be required to turn over a deed containing full covenants, for even a bargain and sale deed, without covenant against the grantor, is "a good and sufficient deed." A marketable title is one that a court will compel a buyer to accept in any action for specific performance of a contract.

Encumbrances. Where there are incumbrances, or other flaws in the title to the property that is the subject of the contract, it is imperative that the contract shall express the agreement of the parties respecting them. Encumbrance is a right or interest in property held by a third party, which often limits the use and diminishes the value of the property, but usually does not prevent the transferring of title. The more common forms of encumbrances are:

1. Taxes, water rents and assessments for local improvements that have become liens upon the property to which a contract or conveyance relates;

2. Mortgages, upon such property.

3. Lease of property or any part thereof;

4. Judgments against the grantor, duly recorded in the county in which the property is located;

5. Mechanics' liens for work or labor done or material furnished for use upon such property;

6. *Lis pendens* (a legal document, filed in the office of the county clerk giving notice that an action or proceeding is pending in the courts affecting the title to the property);

7. Encroachments of a building, or other structure on the property, upon a street or other public place, or upon land of an adjoining owner*;

8. Easements (rights that may be exercised by the public or individuals on, over or through the lands of others; such as rights-of-way, rights to erect poles and string wires or cables overhead, or rights to construct and maintain conduits, pipes or mains underground);

9. Restrictive covenants (limitations upon the use of property, contained in these or other written instruments in the chain of title thereto, providing that the property shall not be used for specified purposes, or that buildings thereon must be set back from the property line for a given distance, or shall not be constructed of certain materials, etc.; zoning regulations, however, are not restrictions that, in a legal sense, are encumbrances);

10. Strictly speaking, violations are not considered encumbrances, although they may diminish the value of property. Violations (written notices

* In this sense, a party wall is an encumbrance, because it is a wall built along the line separating two properties, partly on each.

from state or municipal officers, addressed to the owners, lessees or occupants of specified real property, requiring compliance with definitely stated provisions of laws or ordinances relating to such property, which it is the duty of such officers to enforce).

"Time is of the essence of this contract." This clause is frequently found in real property contracts. It is useful where a quick "turn-over" is contemplated by the purchaser, or the seller has a special reason for closing title upon the date specified in the contract. Its legal effect is to require the seller to be able to deliver the required deed and the purchaser to be prepared to make payment of the agreed purchase price, upon the exact closing date fixed in the contract. If, then, either party is unprepared, the contract is breached and the delinquent is at a serious disadvantage and may suffer substantial financial loss. Obviously, neither party to a real property contract should bind himself/herself by such a provision, unless reasonably certain that the party can make good his/her part of the agreement precisely on the closing date specified therein.

Mortgage clauses. Contracts for the sale of real property frequently contain provisions relating to existing or contemplated mortgages upon the properties to which such contracts relate. It is particularly important for the purchaser to know whether he/she is to take the property "subject to" an existing mortgage, or is assuming payment of the mortgage indebtedness; for, in the latter case, in the event of the foreclosure of the mortgage, the purchaser will be liable for the deficiency, if the property sells for less than the mortgage debt.

Again, in the purchase of land intended for subdivision into building lots, it is usually to the interest of the purchaser to have the sale contract provide that a "release clause" shall be included in the mortgage to be given by the purchaser as security for the payment of a part of the purchase price. The purpose of such a provision is to enable the purchaser to give clear title to lots in the subdivision, which is possible only upon their release from the lien of the "blanket" mortgage.

Sometimes, what is known as a "mortgage subordination clause" is included in a contract for the sale of realty. The ordinary purpose of such a provision is to subordinate the mortgage to be taken by the seller, as a part of the purchase price, to a contemplated mortgage to secure a loan required to defray the cost of erecting a new building or altering an existing building upon the property. A sale contract should be carefully scru-

tinized and, if a mortgage subordination clause is included therein, the property owner should defer signing the contract until the property owner has had the advice thereon of a competent lawyer of his/her own selection.

Action for specific performance. This is a court action to compel defaulting principal to comply with provisions of contract.

Recording land contracts. Contracts for the sale or purchase of real property are usually not recorded, for, as a rule, they are not acknowledged by the parties thereto. They are recordable, if duly acknowledged.

Recording executory contracts and powers of attorney. 1. An executory contract for the sale, purchase or exchange of real property or an instrument canceling such a contract, or an instrument containing a power to convey real property, as the agent or attorney for the owner of the property, acknowledged or proved, and certified, in the manner to entitle a conveyance to be recorded, may be recorded.

General Obligations Law

Requirements for use of plain language in consumer transactions. a. Every written agreement, for the lease of space to be occupied for residential purposes, or to which a consumer is a party and the money, property or service which is the subject of the transaction is primarily for personal, family or household purposes must be:

1. Written in a clear and coherent manner using words with common and every day meanings;

2. Appropriately divided and captioned by its various sections . . . This subdivision shall not apply to agreements involving amounts in excess of fifty thousand dollars nor prohibit the use of words or phrases or forms of agreement required by state or federal law, rule or regulation or by a governmental instrumentality.

b. A violation of the provisions of subdivision a of this section shall not render any such agreement void or voidable nor shall it constitute:

1. A defense to any action or proceeding to enforce such agreement; or

2. A defense to any action or proceeding for breach of such agreement.

c. In addition to the above, whenever the attorney general finds that there has been a violation of this section, he may proceed as provided in the executive law.

6

Land-Use Regulations

Key Terms

Allodial system
Building code
Building permit
Certificate of occupancy (C of O)
Covenant
Deed restriction
Direct public ownership
Eminent domain
Enabling acts
Escheat
Feudal system

Laches
Master plan
Nonconforming use
Police power
Special-use permit
Spot zoning
Subdivision regulations
Taxation
Variance
Zoning appeal board
Zoning ordinances

Overview

The various ownership rights a person possesses in a parcel of real estate are subject to certain public and private land-use controls such as zoning ordinances, building codes, and deed restrictions. The purpose of these controls is to ensure that our limited supply of land is being put to its highest and best use for the benefit of the general public as well as private owners. This chapter will discuss government powers, three types of land-use controls, and how they help shape and preserve the physical surface of our nation.

Government Powers

Although an individual in the United States has maximum rights in the land he or she owns, these ownership rights are subject to certain powers, or rights, held by federal, state, and local governments. Because they are for the general welfare of the community, these limitations on the ownership of real estate supersede the rights of the individual. Government rights include the following:

1. **Taxation:** Taxation is a charge on real estate to raise funds to meet the public needs of a government (*see* Chapter 25).
2. **Police power:** This is the power vested in a state to establish legislation to preserve order, protect the public health and safety, and promote the general welfare. There is no federal police power as such—it exists in this manner on a state level only. A state's police power is passed on to municipalities and counties through legislation called *enabling acts*. The use and enjoyment of property is subject to restrictions authorized by such legislation, including both environmental protection laws and zoning and building ordinances regulating the use, occupancy, size, location, construction, and rental of real estate.
3. **Eminent domain:** Through a condemnation suit, a government may exercise this right to acquire privately owned real estate for public use. Three conditions must be met: (a) the proposed use must be declared by the court to be a public use; (b) just compensation must be paid to the owner; and (c) the rights of the property owner must be protected by due process of law.

    The exercise of decision-making under the right of eminent domain is granted by state laws to quasipublic bodies such as land-clearance commissions and public housing or redevelopment authorities, as well as to railroads and public utility companies.

    Condemnation proceedings are instituted only when the owner's consent cannot be obtained. Otherwise, public agencies acquire real property through direct negotiation and purchase from the owner.
4. **Escheat:** While escheat is not actually a limitation on ownership, state laws provide for ownership of real estate to revert, or escheat, to the state when an owner dies and leaves no heirs and no will disposing of his or her real estate.

Land-Use Controls

The control and regulation of land use is accomplished in both the public and private sectors through: (1) public land-use controls, (2) private land-use controls through deed restrictions, and (3) public ownership of land—including parks, schools, and expressways—by the federal and local governments.

Public Controls

Under **police power** each state, and in turn its municipalities, has the inherent authority to adopt regulations necessary to protect the public health, safety, and general welfare. This includes limitations or controls on the use of privately owned real estate. Although the courts have traditionally been conservative in extending the scope of police power, changing social and economic conditions, along with greater concern for the general welfare of the people, have influenced the courts toward making broader interpretations of this power in recent years and the trend is likely to continue.

Our growing urban populations, the many new types of industry, and the increasing complexity of our civilization make it necessary for cities, towns, and villages to increase their controls over the private use of real estate. Police power in many areas has been increased to include controls over noise, air, and water pollution as well as population density. New problems arise every day.

The police powers of government authority that regulate privately owned real estate have been extended to include the following:

1. city plan specifications;
2. zoning;
3. subdivision regulations;
4. codes that regulate building construction, safety, and public health; and
5. environmental protection legislation.

**City Plan
Specifications**

Some concerned individuals were dissatisfied with the manner in which metropolitan areas were haphazardly developing in the late nineteenth and early twentieth centuries. During this period unofficial citizens' groups in cities like New York, Boston, and Chicago adopted city plans. One of the first plans was the McMillan Improvement Plan for Washington, D.C. Adopted in 1901, it set forth the overall strategy for the development of the famous park system of our nation's capital.

A few years later the Burnham Plan for the city of Chicago was published. The Burnham Plan was probably the most influential force in urban planning throughout the country. The subject matter of this plan encompassed rapid transit and surburban growth, a comprehensive park system, forest preserves, transportation and terminals, streets and subdivision control, and problems of the central city.

Today the country is witnessing a much broader approach to urban planning and development than that submitted under early city plans. The decentralization of the American city in the post-World War II years, coupled with the increasing popularity of the suburban shopping center, has created many satellite communities, often referred to as *bedroom communities* or *dormitory suburbs*. These references were based on the fact that most of the populace of these communities originally worked in the central city but slept in the suburbs. Today whole communities, known as *New Towns*, are being created and developed in accordance with well-developed, overall city plans. Revitalization of old, inner-city or downtown areas is also of increasing concern in city planning.

Some predict that by the end of this century a number of large urban areas will consolidate into a large configuration, known as a *megalopolis*. These large, continuous metropolitan areas may exist in many places around the country where major cities are being interconnected with other communities developed under well-defined city plans. The urban growth along the eastern seaboard from New York to Boston is an example.

Implementing urban planning. City planning includes devising a **master plan,** giving advice on planning and scheduling public works programs (especially those concerning traffic facilities and public buildings), controlling subdivision developments, and preparing, modifying, and administering zoning ordinances and regulations. In most cases a city, county, or regional *planning commission* is created for these purposes. A combination of residential, commercial, and industrial property usually is included in master plans in order to spread the tax load and provide employment for local residents.

City planning and zoning serve as means to meet the social and economic needs of our ever-changing communities. Both economic and physical surveys are essential in preparing a master plan. The plans must also include the coordination of numerous civic plans and developments to ensure orderly city growth with stabilized property values.

Zoning

Zoning ordinances are laws of local government authorities (such as municipalities and counties) that regulate and control the use of land and structures within designated districts or zones. Zoning regulates and affects such things as use of the land, lot sizes, types of structures permitted, building heights, setbacks (the minimum distance away from streets or sidewalks that structures may be built), and density (the ratio of land area to structure area or population). Often the purpose of zoning is to implement a local master plan.

Zoning powers are conferred on municipal governments by New York State **enabling acts;** there are no statewide zoning ordinances. State and federal governments may, however, regulate land use through special legislation such as scenic easement and coastal management laws.

Zoning ordinances generally divide land use into three use classifications: (1) residential, (2) commercial, and (3) industrial. A fourth use now included by many communities, is *cluster zoning,* or *multiple-use zoning,* which permits planned unit developments.

Zoning classifications found in a typical New York State community might include:

1. R-1, one-family residential;
2. R-2, multifamily residential;
3. C-1, commercial-retail;
4. C-2, heavy commercial; and
5. I-1, industrial.

Variations exist between municipalities and some may have as many as 15 classifications.

To ensure adequate control, land-use areas are further divided into subclasses. For example, residential areas may be subdivided to provide for detached single-family dwellings, semidetached structures containing not more than four dwelling units, walk-up apartments, high-rise apartments, and so forth. Some special types of zoning are listed in Table 6.1.

Adoption of zoning ordinances. Today approximately 98 percent of all cities with populations in excess of 10,000 have enacted comprehensive zoning ordinances governing the utilization of land located *within corporate limits.* New York City adopted one of the first in the country, shortly after World War I. In some cases the use of land located *within one to three miles* of an incorporated area must

Table 6.1 **Special Types of Zoning**	Type of Zoning	Primary Purpose
	Bulk Zoning	To control density and avoid overcrowding through restrictions on setback, building height, and percentages of open areas.
	Aesthetic Zoning	To require that new buildings conform to specific types of architecture
	Incentive Zoning	To require that street floors of office buildings be used for retail establishments.
	Directive Zoning	To use zoning as a planning tool to encourage use of land for its highest and best use

receive the approval and consent of the incorporated area even if the property is not contiguous to the village, town, or city.

Zoning ordinances must not violate the rights of individuals and property holders (as provided under the due process provisions of the Fourteenth Amendment of the U.S. Constitution) or the various provisions of the state constitution of the state in which the real estate is located. If the means used to regulate the use of property are destructive, unreasonable, arbitrary, or confiscatory, the legislation is usually considered void. *Tests* applied in determining the validity of ordinances often require that:

1. The power must be exercised in a reasonable manner.
2. The provisions must be clear and specific.
3. The ordinance must be free from discrimination.
4. The ordinance must promote public health, safety, and general welfare under the police power concept.
5. The ordinance must apply to all property in a similar manner.

When *downzoning* occurs in an area—for instance, when land zoned for single-family residences is rezoned to apartment use—the state usually is not responsible for compensating property owners for any resulting loss of value.

Zoning laws are enforced through local requirements that building permits be obtained before property owners build on their land. A permit will not be issued unless a proposed structure conforms to the permitted zoning, among other requirements.

Nonconforming use. In the enforcement of a zoning ordinance a frequent problem is the situation in which a building does not conform to the zoning use because it was erected prior to the enactment of the zoning law. Such a building is not a violation because when it was built there was no zoning ordinance; it is referred to as a **nonconforming use** and such use is allowed to continue. If the building is destroyed or torn down, any new structure must comply with the terms of the zoning ordinance. Local laws may say that the right to a nonconforming use is lost if it is discontinued for a certain period, usually one year.

Zoning boards of appeal. Frequently the comprehensive plan that establishes zoning ordinances has the detrimental effect of *overzoning*. **Zoning appeal boards** have been established in most communities for the specific purpose of hearing complaints about the effects of zoning ordinances on specific parcels of property. Petitions may be presented to the appeal board for exceptions to the zoning law. The board of appeals has great power and it is important to the community that the members of the board be free of personal or political influence.

Zoning variations. Each time a plan is created or a zoning ordinance enacted, some owners are inconvenienced and want to change the use of a property. Generally such owners may appeal for either a conditional-use permit or a variance to allow a use that does not meet zoning requirements. The person appealing for a variance or a change in zoning may be asked to provide an *environmental impact study* of the sort required from developers (*see* Chapter 18). This is often a simple check-off form.

A **special-use permit** is granted to allow a property owner a special use of property that is in the public interest. For example, a restaurant may be built in an industrially zoned area if it is deemed necessary to provide meal services for area workers.

A **variance** may be sought by a property owner who has suffered hardship as a result of a zoning ordinance. For example, if an owner's lot is level next to a road but slopes steeply 30 feet away from the road, the zoning board may be willing to allow a variance so the owner can build closer to the road than normally would be allowed. However, the board might refuse to allow a change if there were another possible building site on the same parcel and the only hardship that would result from using the alternate site was a longer driveway that would cost more money.

The granting of such variances is sometimes inaccurately referred to as **spot zoning.** If the proposed variance affects only a small area and is not in harmony with the general plan for that area—a chemical factory in a residential neighborhood, for instance—spot zoning is unconstitutional in New York.

Subdivision Regulations

Most communities have adopted **subdivision regulations,** often as a part of a master plan. These will be covered in detail in Chapter 18. Subdivision regulations usually provide for the following:

1. location, grading, alignment, surfacing, and widths of streets, highways, and other rights-of-way;
2. installation of sewers and water mains;
3. minimum dimensions of lots and length of blocks;
4. building and setback lines;
5. areas to be reserved or dedicated for public use, such as parks or schools; and
6. easements for public utilities.

Subdivision regulations, like all other forms of zoning or building regulations, cannot be static. They must remain flexible to meet the ever-changing needs of society.

Building Codes

Most cities and towns have enacted ordinances to *specify construction standards* that must be met when repairing or erecting buildings. These are called **building codes** and they set the requirements for kinds of materials, sanitary equipment, electrical wiring, fire prevention standards, and the like. New York has a statewide building code that is in force where no local code exists or where local codes are less restrictive.

Most communities require the issuance of a **building permit** by the city clerk or other official before a person can build a structure or alter or repair an existing building on property within the corporate limits of the municipality. Through the permit requirement officials are made aware of new construction or alterations and can verify compliance with building codes and zoning ordinances by examining the plans and inspecting the work. After the completed structure has been inspected and found satisfactory, the inspector issues a **certificate of occupancy.** The certificate *(C of O)* is also required for some transfers of existing buildings.

If the construction of a building or an alteration violates a deed restriction (discussed later in this chapter), the issuance of a building permit will *not* cure this violation. A building permit is merely evidence of the applicant's compliance with municipal regulations. Rights of adjoining owners in a subdivision to enforce subdivision restrictions usually prevail over the police power legislation of the community when there is a conflict, if the restrictions are more limiting.

The subject of city planning, zoning, and restricting the use of real estate is extremely technical and the interpretation of the law is not altogether clear. Questions concerning any of these subjects should be referred to legal counsel.

Environmental Protection Legislation

Federal and state legislators have passed a number of environmental protection laws in an attempt to respond to the growing public concern over the improvement and preservation of America's natural resources. Table 6.2 contains a brief summary of significant federal environmental legislation.

The various states have responded to the environmental issue by passing a variety of localized environmental protection laws regarding all types of pollution—air, water, noise, and solid waste disposal. For example, many states have enacted laws that prevent builders or private individuals from constructing septic tanks or other effluent-disposal systems in certain areas, particularly where public bodies of water—streams, lakes, and rivers—are concerned.

New York State's controls include the Adirondack Park Agency's rules and regulations, the *Environmental Quality Review Act (SEQRA),* the *Wetlands Act,* and the *Subdivided Lands Law.*

In addition to the states and the federal government, cities and counties also frequently pass environmental legislation of their own.

Landmark Preservation

In New York State local governments may enact regulations intended to preserve individual buildings and areas of historical or architectural significance. Regulations setting up local historic areas or landmark preservation districts may restrict an owner's right to alter certain old buildings on the exterior. Interior remodeling is typically free from regulation. Individual buildings located outside a historic area also may be designated as landmarks. The federal government, through its National Register of Historic Places, also places some restrictions on the alteration of landmark buildings.

Table 6.2	Legislation	Major purpose
Typical Federal Environmental Legislation	National Environmental Policy Act—1970	To establish a Council for Environmental Quality for land-use planning; in addition, created the Environmental Protection Agency (EPA) to enforce federal environmental legislation
	Clean Air Amendment—1970	To create more stringent standards for automotive, aircraft, and factory emission
	Water Quality Improvement Act—1970	To strengthen water pollution standards
	Resource Recovery Act—1970	To expand the solid waste disposal program
	Water Pollution Control Act Amendment—1972	To create standards for cleaning navigable streams and lakes by the mid-80s
	Clean Water Act—1974	To establish standards for water supplies
	Resource Conservation & Recovery Act—1976	To regulate potentially dangerous solid waste disposal
	Clean Water Act Amendment—1977	To update the list of potentially dangerous water pollutants under the 1974 act

Private Land-Use Controls

A real estate owner can create a **deed restriction** by including a provision for it in the deed when the property is conveyed.

There is a distinction between restrictions on the owner's rights to *sell* and restrictions on his or her right to *use*. In general, provisions in a deed conveying a fee simple estate with restrictions that the grantee will not sell, mortgage, or convey it are considered void. Such restrictions attempt to limit the basic principle of the *free alienation (transfer) of property;* the courts usually consider them against public policy and therefore unenforceable.

A subdivider may establish restrictions on the right to *use* land through a **covenant** in a deed or by a separate recorded declaration. These use restrictions are usually considered valid if they are reasonable restraints and are for the benefit of all property owners in the subdivision.

Plats of new subdivisions will frequently set forth on the face of the plat, or on a declaration attached thereto, restrictive covenants concerning the use of the land. When a lot in that subdivision is conveyed by an owner's deed, the deed refers to the plat or declaration of restrictions and incorporates these restrictions as limitations on the title conveyed by the deed. In this manner the restrictive covenants are included in the deed by reference and become binding on all grantees. Such covenants or restrictions usually relate to: (1) type of building; (2) use to which the land may be put; (3) type of construction, height, setbacks, and square footage; and (4) cost.

Most restrictions have a *time limitation*, for example, "effective for a period of 25 years from this date." Frequently the effective term of the restrictions may be extended with the consent of a majority (or sometimes two-thirds) of the owners in a subdivision. In New York, deed restrictions expire after 30 years unless documents extending them are filed. Where a deed restriction and a zoning provision cover the same subject the more limiting restriction will prevail. If deed restrictions say lots in a subidivision must measure at least two acres but the town allows half-acre lots, the two-acre restriction is enforceable.

Enforcement of deed restrictions. Subdividers place restrictions on the use of all lots of a subdivision as a *general plan* for the benefit of all lot owners. Such restrictions give each lot owner the right to apply to the court for an *injunction* to prevent a neighboring lot owner from violating the recorded restrictions. If granted, the court injunction will direct the violator to stop the violation upon penalty of being in contempt of court. The court retains the power to punish the violator for failure to obey the court order.

If adjoining lot owners stand idly by while a violation is being committed, they can *lose the right* to the court's injunction by their inaction; the court might claim their right was lost through **laches,** that is, loss of a right through undue delay or failure to assert it. In New York neighboring owners have a two-year statute of limitations on objections to violations of the general plan (type of building, height, setbacks) and ten years in which to object to violations of conditions mentioned in the deed.

Conditions in a deed are different from restrictions or covenants. A grantor's deed of conveyance of land can be subject to certain stated conditions whereby the buyer's title *may* revert (go back) to the seller. (This was discussed in Chapter 3 as a determinable fee estate.) For example, Bill Potter conveys a lot to Jane Knish by a deed that includes a condition forbidding the sale, manufacture, or giving away of intoxicating liquor on the lot and provides that in case of violation the title (ownership) reverts to Potter. If Knish operates a tavern on the lot, Potter can file suit and obtain title to the property. Such a condition in the title is enforced by a *reverter,* or *reversion,* clause.

Direct Public Ownership

Over the years the government's general policy has been to encourage private ownership of land. It is necessary, however, for a certain amount of land to be owned by the government for such use as municipal buildings, state legislature houses, schools, and military stations. **Direct public ownership** is a means of land control.

There are other examples of necessary public ownership. Urban renewal efforts, especially government-owned housing, are one way that public ownership serves the public interest. Publicly owned streets and highways serve a necessary function for the entire population. In addition, public land is often used for such recreational purposes as parks. National and state parks and forest preserves create areas for public use and recreation and at the same time help to conserve our natural resources.

At present the federal government owns approximately 775 million acres of land. Much of that is in Alaska. At times the federal government has held title to as much as 80 percent of the nation's total land area.

Summary

Government powers limiting private rights in land include *taxation, eminent domain, police power,* and *escheat.*

The control of land use is exercised in two ways: through public controls and private (or nongovernment) controls.

Public controls are ordinances based upon the states' *police power* to protect the public health, safety, and welfare. Through power conferred by state enabling acts, cities and municipalities enact city plans and zoning ordinances.

Any effective control of land requires an overall *city plan* to be developed based upon a local economic survey of the community. *Zoning ordinances* segregate residential areas from business and industrial zones and control not only land use, but height and bulk of buildings and density of populations. Zoning enforcement problems involve boards of appeal, special use permits, variances, and exceptions, as well as nonconforming uses. *Subdivision regulations* are required to maintain control of the development of expanding community areas so that growth will be harmonious with community standards.

Building codes are different from zoning ordinances. Zoning ordinances control use; building codes control construction of buildings by specifying standards for construction, plumbing, sewers, electrical wiring, and equipment.

In addition to land-use control on the local level, the state and federal governments occasionally have intervened when necessary to preserve natural resources through *environmental legislation*.

Private controls are exercised by owners, generally subdividers, who control use of subdivision lots by carefully planned *deed restrictions* that are made to apply to all lot owners. The usual recorded restrictions may be enforced by adjoining lot owners obtaining a court *injunction* to stop a violator. Reverter-type restrictions are called *conditions* and the grantors or their heirs exercise the *right of reverter* (when such right was reserved as a part of the original conveyance) to enforce the conditions.

Public ownership is a means of land-use control that provides land for such public benefits as parks, highways, schools, and municipal buildings.

Questions

1. The government's police power allows it to regulate:
   - a. law enforcement.
   - b. fire codes.
   - c. zoning.
   - d. All of the above

2. The state needs to run a new expressway through Martin's farm. Martin does not agree to sell the necessary land. The state then may try to exert its right of eminent domain through a court proceeding known as:
   - a. escheat.
   - b. variance.
   - c. condemnation.
   - d. downzoning.

3. The right of escheat allows New York State to acquire land:
   - a. through an act of condemnation.
   - b. when someone dies without leaving a will or heirs.
   - c. through a gift from a donor.
   - d. when property taxes are not paid as due.

4. Zoning ordinances control the use of privately owned land by establishing land-use districts. Which one of the following is not a usual zoning district?
   - a. Residential
   - b. Commercial
   - c. Industrial
   - d. Rental

5. A nonconforming use is allowed:
   - a. only after a condemnation suit.
   - b. if it is for a public purpose.
   - c. with the approval of two-thirds of the neighbors.
   - d. if it existed before the area was zoned.

6. Doctor Livingston goes before his local zoning board asking for permission to open an office in his residential neighborhood because the area has no medical facilities. He is asking for a:
   - a. variance.
   - b. nonconforming use.
   - c. special-use permit.
   - d. restriction.

7. Dan Hill asks the zoning board to allow him to build a fence to keep his children out of traffic on a busy corner, though he does not have room for the required ten-foot setback. He is asking for a:
   - a. variance.
   - b. nonconforming use.
   - c. special-use permit.
   - d. restriction.

8. The purpose of a building permit is:
   - a. to override a deed restriction.
   - b. to maintain municipal control over the volume of building.
   - c. to provide evidence of compliance with municipal regulations.
   - d. to regulate area and bulk of buildings.

9. Miss Muffet's Greek Revival home is located in a historic preservation district. She probably may not change:
   - a. the number of living units in the building.
   - b. the exterior of the building.
   - c. the interior of the building.
   - d. either exterior or interior.

10. Every parcel in the subdivision has a deed restriction forbidding basketball backboards on front-facing garages. Wilt puts one up anyhow. Wilt's neighbors may force him to remove it by:
    - a. calling the police.
    - b. notifying the original developer of the subdivision.
    - c. sending a petition to the town or city hall.
    - d. going to court.

7

Real Estate Financing

Key Terms

Adjustable rate mortgage (ARM)
Amortized loan
Annual percentage rate (APR)
Balloon payment
Buydown
Cap
Ceiling
Conventional loan
Fannie Mae (FNMA)
FHA loan
Freddie Mac (FHLMC)
Ginnie Mae (GNMA)
Graduated payments
Growing equity mortgage (GEM)
Imputed Interest
Index
Interest

Loan-to-value ratio (l-v-r)
Margin
Mortgage insurance premium (MIP)
PITI
Pledged account mortgage
Points
Prepayment penalty
Private mortgage insurance (PMI)
Regulation Z
Secondary market
Shared equity mortgage
Sonny Mae (SONYMA)
Straight (term) loan
Underwriting
Usury
VA loan

Overview

Rarely is a parcel of real estate purchased for cash; almost every transaction involves some type of financing. An understanding of real estate financing is of prime importance to the real estate licensee. In a recent survey a majority of buyers reported that they obtained their mortgage information from a broker or salesperson. This chapter will discuss the basic mortgage loan as well as alternative types of financing and payment plans. In addition the chapter will examine various sources of mortgage money and the role of the federal government in real estate financing.

Mortgage Financing

Liberalization of mortgage terms and payment plans over the last six decades has made the dream of home ownership a reality for over 70 percent of the population. For example, the amount of a mortgage loan in relation to the value of a home, the **loan-to-value ratio**, has increased from 40 percent in 1920 to as much as 95 or 100 percent today. Payment periods were also extended, from five years in the 1920s to 30 years or more in the 1980s.

Interest rates charged by lending institutions on home mortgage loans vary as changes occur in the money market. As interest rates move up, an established fixed-rate mortgage with a lower interest rate may be a plus in selling a home if the new owner is able to assume the existing mortgage. On the other hand, if mortgage interest rates fall, the homeowner may seek to pay off the loan and refinance at a lower rate.

To buffer the effects of an unstable money market, lenders have been offering many alternative forms of mortgages in recent years, such as adjustable interest rate and graduated payment mortgages. Seller financing also gains popularity in times of tight mortgage money.

For years potential homeowners have been able to receive assistance in obtaining low down-payment mortgage loans through the federal programs of the Federal Housing Administration (FHA) and the Veterans Administration (VA). In addition, private mortgage insurance companies offer programs to assist loan applicants in receiving higher loan-to-value ratios from private lenders than they could otherwise obtain.

Payment Plans

Many mortgage loans are **amortized loans**. Regular payments are applied first to the interest owed and the balance to the principal amount, over a term of perhaps 15 to 30 years. At the end of the term the full amount of the principal and all interest due will be reduced to zero. Such loans are also called *self-liquidating loans.*

Most amortized mortgage loans are paid in monthly installments. These payments may be computed based on a number of payment plans, which tend to alternately gain and lose favor as the cost and availability of mortgage money fluctuates. These payment plans include the following (illustrated in Figure 7.1); all are fixed-rate loans:

1. The most frequently used plan requires the mortgagor to pay a *constant amount*, usually each month. The mortgagee credits each payment first to the interest due and then applies the balance to reduce the principal of the loan. While each payment is the same, the portion applied toward repayment of the principal grows and the interest due declines as the unpaid balance of the loan is reduced. This is known as a *fully amortized loan.*
2. *A mortgagor may choose a straight payment plan* that calls for periodic payments of interest, with the principal to be *paid in full at the end of the loan term*. This is known as a **straight,** or **term, loan.** Such plans are generally used for home-improvement loans and second mortgages rather than for residential first mortgage loans.

Figure 7.1
Payment Plans

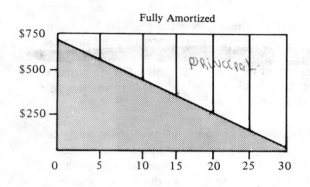

Fully Amortized

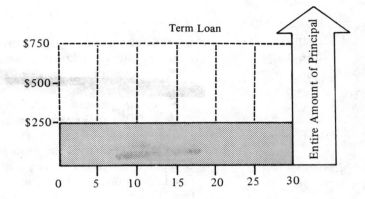

Term Loan

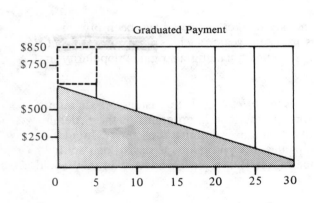

Graduated Payment

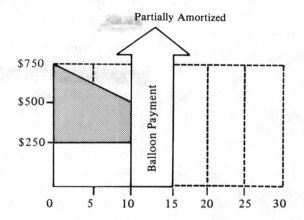

Partially Amortized

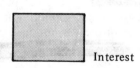 Interest

 Principal

3. The mortgagor may elect to take advantage of a *graduated payment plan,* used to enable younger buyers and buyers in times of high interest rates to purchase real estate. Under this plan a mortgagor makes lower monthly payments for the first few years of the loan (typically the first five years) and larger payments for the remainder of the term, when the mortgagor's income is expected to have increased.

4. When a mortgage loan requires periodic payments that will not fully amortize the amount of the loan by the time the final payment is due, the final payment is a larger amount than the others. This is called a **balloon payment** and this type of loan is a *partially amortized loan.*

Other payment plans include the **growing equity mortgage (GEM)**, under which the borrower pledges to increase monthly payments, often by between four percent and 7.5 percent each year, with the extra portion of each month's payment going to reduce the principal. This shortens the remaining time on the loan; a 30-year mortgage can be cut down to approximately 17 years.

Adjustable rate mortgages (ARMs) are increasingly popular when mortgage rates rise. The interest rate on an ARM can rise or fall with the money market; details will be discussed later in this chapter.

Graduated payment loans are well-suited to young professionals and other borrowers who can demonstrate to the satisfaction of lenders that they have reasonable expectations of rising income in the years ahead. With payments kept artificially low during the first few years of the loan, the borrowers can purchase property they might otherwise not qualify for. The shortfall in monthly payments may result in *negative amortization* (an increase in the principal owed) or be accounted for in some other way.

Interest

A charge for the use of money is called **interest**. A lender charges a borrower a certain percentage of the principal as interest for each year the debt is outstanding. The amount of interest due on any one installment payment date is calculated by computing the total yearly interest, based on the unpaid balance, and dividing that figure by the number of payments made each year. If the current outstanding loan balance is $50,000 with interest at the rate of 12 percent per annum and constant monthly payments of $617.40, the interest and principal due on the next payment would be computed as follows:

$$\begin{array}{ll} \$50,000 & \underline{\$500.00}\text{ month's interest} \\ \underline{\times \quad .12} & 12)\$6,000.00 \\ \$\ 6,000\text{ annual interest} & \end{array}$$

$$\begin{array}{l} \$617.40\text{ monthly payment} \\ \underline{-500.00}\text{ interest due} \\ \$117.40\text{ month's principal reduction} \end{array}$$

Interest is usually due at the end of each payment period (payment *in arrears*).

Tax-Deductible Interest Payments

Taxpayers may take that portion of each monthly payment that is applied toward interest on the loan as a deduction on their yearly income-tax returns. (Homeowners may also deduct all property taxes, prepaid interest points, and any mortgage prepayment penalties.)

Usury. The maximum rate of interest that may be charged on mortgage loans is usually set by state law. Charging interest in excess of this rate is called **usury** and lenders are penalized for making usurious loans. In New York a usurious lender may lose the entire amount of the loan in addition to the interest. Loans made to corporations are generally exempt from usury laws except for New York's criminal usury limit of 25 percent on loans up to $2,500,000.

Usury laws were enacted to protect borrowers from unscrupulous lenders who would charge unreasonably high interest rates. New York has a *floating interest rate*. The maximum rate that may be charged is adjusted up or down at specific intervals based on a certain economic standard, such as the prime lending rate or the rate of return on government bonds.

Money available for borrowing is a commodity subject to the economic laws of supply and demand, and lenders are in business to make money by lending money and charging interest. When there is plenty of money available, interest rates become fairly low. When money is scarce, interest rates go up. President Carter issued an executive order in 1980 that called for a temporary override of all state usury laws. Mortgage money had all but dried up in New York before the executive order.

Sellers taking back purchase-money mortgages always have been exempt from usury limits. While lending institutions are now also exempt, *individuals making third-party mortgage loans are still bound by New York's usury limit.*

Points. When a new mortgage is placed, the lending institution may compensate for an interest rate that is below the current true cost of money by asking for extra prepaid interest in the form of up-front **points**. Each point is one percent of the new loan. On an $80,000 loan each point would be $800; a charge of two points would total $1,600. Payment of points is a one-time affair usually at time of closing but occasionally at mortgage application or issuance of a mortgage commitment by the lender.

Except with VA loans, points may be paid by either buyer or seller, depending on the terms of the sales contract. The buyer's points are interest payments, income-tax-deductible in the year they are paid. The seller's points, because they are not paid on his or her own loan, are not deductible but merely one of the costs of selling. Points paid by investors or by refinancing homeowners must be *amortized* (deducted gradually over the period of the loan).

Annual percentage rate. If a mortgage loan is made at 12 percent but also requires three points in prepaid interest or other service fees, the loan really costs the borrower more than 12 percent. The exact rate depends on the length of the proposed mortgage and requires some complicated calculations. The rate, which would total slightly over 12 percent, is known as the **annual percentage rate (APR)**. Federal regulations require that the borrower be advised of the APR in advertisements and when a loan is placed.

 Buydowns. With some mortgage plans, lending institutions are willing to lower the interest rate in return for extra payment of points. The arrangement is known as a **buydown.** Permanent buydowns keep the interest rate low for the entire life of the loan. Others may only lower the rate for a period of time, for example, by three percent the first year of the loan, two percent the second year, and one percent the third year ("3-2-1-buydown").

Prepayment

Some mortgage notes require the borrower to pay a **prepayment premium**, or **penalty,** if the loan is paid off before its full term. For a one- to six-family dwelling, the maximum prepayment premium a lender can charge in New York is 90 days' interest on the unpaid balance of the mortgage when it is paid in full within one year of the date the mortgage is granted. Thereafter the borrower can prepay in whole or in part at any time without a premium.

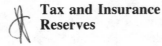 **Tax and Insurance Reserves**

Many lenders require borrowers to provide a reserve, or escrow, fund to meet future real estate taxes and insurance premiums. When the mortgage loan is made, the borrower starts the reserve by depositing funds to cover partial payment of the following year's tax bill. If a new insurance policy has been purchased, the insurance premium reserve will be started with the deposit of one-twelfth of the annual tax and insurance premium liability. Thereafter the monthly loan payments required of the borrower will include principal, interest, and tax and insurance reserves (**PITI**).

RESPA, the federal Real Estate Settlement and Procedures Act (discussed in Chapter 11), limits the amount of tax and insurance reserves that a lender may require.

Conventional, Insured, and Guaranteed Loans

Mortgage loans fall into several classifications:

1. *Conventional loans* are those arranged entirely between borrower and lending institution.
2. *Government-backed loans* include those insured by the Federal Housing Administration (FHA) or guaranteed by the Veterans Administration (VA). With both types the actual loan comes from a local lending institution.
3. *Loans directly from the government* include State of New York Mortgage Agency (SONYMA) mortgages and Farmer's Home Administration (FmHA) loans.

Coventional Loans

In making conventional loans, lending institutions set their own standards within the scope of banking regulations. As a result a variety of mortgage plans is often offered and some flexibility is occasionally available. Conventional mortgages may be fixed-rate, adjustable-rate, graduated-payment, growing-equity, or a combination of plans.

Paperwork and the time between loan application and loan commitment can sometimes be expedited with conventional loans. Most conventional mortgages are not assumable by a subsequent buyer of the property or are assumable only with the lender's approval.

Private mortgage insurance. In general, conventional loans call for higher down payments (lower loan-to-value ratio) than do government-backed mortgages. Banking theory holds that it risks depositors' money to lend more than 80 percent of the value of real estate. With any down payment below 20 percent, therefore, a conventional loan in New York State must be accompanied by **private mortgage insurance (PMI).** The borrower pays a yearly premium for insurance that protects the lender in case of loss at a foreclosure.

Adjustable rate mortgages. Until the early 1980s almost all mortgages were fixed-rate. As interest rates began to skyrocket, lenders found themselves locked in to unprofitable long-term commitments with money lent out at rates like five, six, and seven percent—far below the then current cost of money. This led to serious problems for lending institutions and many were reluctant to make any further fixed-interest loans, even at high rates.

Out of a chaotic variety of new mortgage instruments, the **adjustable rate mortgage (ARM)** emerged and became a national standard. As interest rates rose, borrowers across the country increasingly chose ARMs. The ARM shifts the risk of changing interest rates to the borrower, who also stands to benefit if rates drop during the period of the loan.

The vocabulary of ARMs includes the following:

Adjustment period: The anniversary on which interest rate adjustments may be made. Most borrowers elect one-year adjustments although they might be made more frequently or after three or five years.

Index: The interest rate on the loan may go up or down, following the trend for interest rates across the country. The lender must key changes to some national indicator of current rates. The most commonly chosen **index** is the rate at the last auction of one-year United States Treasury bills. Next most popular is the average mortgage interest rate across the country for the preceding six months.

Margin: If treasury bills are the chosen index and they are selling at ten percent interest at the time the loan is adjusted, the borrower pays a specific percentage above that index. That percentage is known as the **margin.** With a two percent margin over Treasury bills the borrower would be charged 12 percent.

Cap: The loan agreement may set a **cap** of, for example, two percent on any upward adjustment. If interest rates (as reflected by the index) went up three percent by the time of adjustment, the interest rate could be raised only two percent. Depending on the particular mortgage, the extra one percent might be treated one of three ways:

1. It could be saved by the lender to be used at the next adjustment period, even though rates had fallen in the meantime.
2. It could be absorbed by the lender with no future consequences to the borrower.
3. The shortfall (the unpaid one percent) could be added to the amount borrowed so that the principal would increase instead of decreasing (negative amortization). Another use of the word *cap* is synonymous with the word *ceiling*.

Ceiling: A **ceiling** (sometimes called a *lifetime cap*) is a maximum allowable interest rate. Typically, a mortgage may offer a five-point ceiling. If the interest rate started at 11 percent, it could never go beyond 16 percent no matter what happened to national rates. A ceiling allows the borrower to calculate the *worst case*.

Worst case: If a 30-year adjustable loan for $85,000 costs $809 a month for principal and interest at 11 percent, and if the ceiling is five percent, the worst that could happen is that the rate would go to 16 percent. The borrower can calculate in advance what that could cost—$1,143 a month.

Negative amortization: Negative amortization could result from an artificially low initial interest rate. It also could follow a hike in rates larger than a cap allows the lender to impose. Not all mortgage plans include the possibility of negative amortization. Sometimes the lender agrees to absorb any shortfalls. The possibility must always be explored, however, when an ARM is being evaluated.

Convertability: This feature offers the best of both worlds. The borrower may choose to change the mortgage to a fixed-rate at then current interest levels. With some plans any favorable moment may be chosen. More commonly the option is the available on the third, fourth, or fifth anniversary of the loan. Cash outlay for the conversion is low compared with the costs of placing a completely new mortgage; one point, or one percent of the loan, is typical.

Initial interest rate: With many loan plans the rate during the first year, or the first adjustment period, is set artificially low to induce the borrower to enter into the agreement. This enables some buyers, whose income might not otherwise qualify, to place new mortgage loans. Buyers who plan to be in a house for only a few years may be delighted with such arrangements, especially if no interest adjustment is planned for three years. Other borrowers, however, may end up with negative amortization and payment shock.

Assumability: Many ARMs are assumable by the next owner of the property with the lender's approval and the payment of one point or more in service fees.

FHA-Insured Loans

The Federal Housing Administration (FHA) was created in 1934 under the National Housing Act to encourage improvement in housing standards and conditions, provide an adequate home-financing system through insurance of housing credit, and exert a stabilizing influence on the mortgage market. The FHA was the government's response to the lack of housing, excessive foreclosures, and collapsed building industry that occurred during the Depression.

The FHA, which operates under the Department of Housing and Urban Development (HUD), neither builds homes nor lends money itself. Rather, *it insures loans on real property made by approved lending institutions.* It does not insure the property but it does insure the lender against loss. The common term **FHA loan**, then, refers to a loan that is *not made* by the agency, but insured by it.

Most FHA loans are processed through *direct endorsement* with lenders handling the paperwork within their own organizations. Other applications are forwarded to the FHA for final decision; this can add several weeks to the loan process.

FHA 203(b). The most widely used FHA mortgage is known as 203(b) and may be placed on one- to four-family residences. Among the requirements set up by the FHA before it will insure a loan:

1. In addition to paying interest, the borrower is charged a lump sum of between 2.9 and 3.8 percent of the loan as a **mortgage insurance premium (MIP).** This amount is payable at the closing or (more commonly) it may be financed for the term of the loan. If the loan is subsequently paid off within the first ten years, some refund of unused premium is due the borrower from HUD. (With FHA loans made before September 1, 1983, the borrower pays ½ percent annually as an insurance premium.)

2. The real estate must be evaluated by an FHA-approved appraiser. The required down payment will be based on the appraised value; if the purchase price is higher, the buyer must pay the difference in a higher cash down payment. On Section 203(b) loans minimum down payment requirements are:

    a. for property appraised under $50,000, three percent. A house appraised at $40,000 would require a $1,200 down with a $38,000 mortgage possible. (A more complex calculation, based on what is known as *acquisition cost,* can reduce this down payment further.)

    b. for property over $50,000, the requirement is three percent down on the first $25,000 and five percent down on the rest. A house appraised at $75,000 would require a down payment of three percent on the first $25,000 ($750) plus five percent of the remaining $50,000 ($2,500) for a total down payment of $3,250.

c. for property to be purchased by an investor rather than an owner-occupant, the down payment requirement is a minimum of 15 percent. Some lenders charge additional points for such loans.

3. The FHA sets top limits on its loans, depending on price levels in different areas. Its loan maximums vary from one county to another within the state. In the least expensive areas the limits are:

single-family dwellings	$67,500
two-family dwellings	76,000
three-family dwellings	92,000
four-family dwellings	107,000

In more expensive counties, the maximum may be as high as:

single-family dwellings	$90,000
two-family dwellings	101,300
three-family dwellings	122,500
four-family dwellings	142,650

In some areas the limits fall between these figures.

4. The FHA may stipulate repair requirements to be completed before it will issue mortgage insurance on a specific property.

Certain energy-saving improvements may be financed along with an FHA mortgage. No prepayment penalties are charged if an FHA loan is paid off before the end of the term. When the final payment is made on a long-standing FHA loan, some refund of unused premiums left in the mortgage insurance pool may be due the borrower. *An outstanding feature of all FHA loans is that like VA mortgages they are completely assumable by the next owner of the property, with no change in interest rate, no credit check on the buyer, and only a small charge for paperwork.*

Other FHA programs. Among other FHA programs, which may or may not be handled by local lenders at any given time, are:

Section 203(b) Veterans: A slightly lower down payment is required; the loan is only for owner-occupied single-family dwellings. It is available to a veteran who already may have used VA eligibility on other property.

Section 203(I): for single-family housing in rural areas located on 2.5 or more acres.

Section 203(k): for purchase and/or rehabilitation of existing one-to four-unit dwellings. The loan may include purchase price and cost of proposed rehabilitation.

Section 221(d)-2: for single-family houses purchased with no down payment, and closing costs added to the mortgage. Maximum loans vary from $31,000 in some areas to $36,000 in others on three-bedroom homes. A family of five or more may apply for loans up to $36,000, or $42,000 in a higher-cost area, on a four-bedroom home.

Section 245(a): graduated payment mortgages. The borrower has to prove enough income to qualify for initial lowered payments and reasonable expectations of rising income. No subsidy is involved; because early payments do not cover interest due, the shortfall is added to the principal owed (negative amortization).

Section 251: adjustable rate mortgages, for one- to four-family dwellings, owner-occupied.

Other FHA programs are sometimes available to finance mobile homes, manufactured housing, condominiums, and rehabilitation construction of housing.

VA-Guaranteed (GI) Loans

Under the *Servicemen's Readjustment Act of 1944* and subsequent federal legislation, the Veterans Administration is authorized to guarantee loans to purchase or construct homes for eligible veterans—those who have served a minimum of 180 days' active service since September 16, 1940 (90 days for veterans of any war). For those enlisting after September 7, 1980, active service of two full years is required. The VA also guarantees loans to purchase mobile homes and plots on which to place them. VA loans assist veterans in financing the purchase of homes with little or no down payments at comparatively low interest rates. Rules and regulations are issued from time to time by the VA setting forth the qualifications, limitations, and conditions under which a loan may be guaranteed. Table 7.1 is a comparison of VA and FHA loan programs.

There is no VA limit on the amount of the loan a veteran can obtain; this is determined by the lender. The VA does, however, set a limit on the amount of the loan that it will guarantee, currently 60 percent of the loan amount or $27,500, whichever is less, in the purchase, construction, repair, or alteration of a house, condominium, or farm residence.

Table 7.1 Comparison of FHA and VA Loan Programs	Federal Housing Administration	Veterans Administration
	1. Financing is available to veterans and non-veterans alike. 2. Financing programs for owner-occupied, rental, and other types of construction; owner-occupied has greater loan-to-value ratio. 3. Requires a larger down payment than VA. 4. FHA valuation sets the maximum loan FHA will insure but does not limit the sales price. 5. No prepayment penalty 6. Insures the loan by way of mutual mortgage insurance; premiums paid by borrower. 7. No secondary financing permitted till after closing. 8. Borrower may pay any number of points required. 9. FHA loan can be assumed without FHA approval. 10. Interest rate is negotiable between borrower and lender.	1. Financing is available only to veterans and certain unremarried widows and widowers. 2. VA financing is limited to owner-occupied residential (one- to four-family) dwellings—must sign occupancy certificate on two separate occasions. 3. Does not normally require down payment, though lender may require small down payment. 4. With regard to home loans, the VA loan may not exceed the appraised value of the home. 5. No prepayment penalty 6. Guarantees up to 60 percent of the loan or $27,500, whichever is less. 7. Secondary financing permitted in exceptional cases. 8. Borrower prohibited from paying discount points (except in refinancing and certain defined circumstances); he or she can pay a one-percent loan origination fee and must pay a one-percent funding fee to VA. 9. VA loan can be assumed by nonveteran or veteran without VA approval. 10. VA sets interest rate.

Like the term *FHA loan,* **VA loan** is something of a misnomer. The VA does not normally lend money itself; it *guarantees* loans made by lending institutions approved by the agency. The term *VA loan* refers to a loan that is not made by the agency but guaranteed by it.

To determine what portion of a mortgage loan the VA will guarantee, the veteran must apply for a *certificate of eligibility.* This certificate does not mean that the veteran automatically will receive a mortgage. It merely sets forth the amount of benefits (guarantee) the veteran is entitled to.

The veteran who has met the service requirements and whose discharge is other than dishonorable may obtain the certificate by writing to:

VA Regional Office   VA Regional Office
Federal Building   *or*   252 7th Avenue
111 West Huron Street   New York, New York
Buffalo, New York 14202   10001

The VA also will issue a *certificate of reasonable value* (CRV) for the property being purchased, stating its current market value based on a VA-approved appraisal. The CRV places a ceiling on the amount of a VA loan allowed for the property; if the purchase price is greater than the amount cited in the CRV, the veteran must pay the difference in cash.

Only in certain situations where financing is not reasonably available (such as in isolated rural areas) does the VA lend money itself; otherwise, a veteran obtains a loan from a VA-approved lending institution. The VA does not require a down payment. Although the VA guarantee is never more than $27,500, in practice the veteran may be able to obtain a 100-percent loan if the appraised valuation of the property is $110,000 or less and the veteran is entitled to a full $27,500 (the usual 25 percent down payment) guarantee.

Maximum loan terms are 30 years for one- to four-family dwellings and 40 years for farm loans. The interest rate cannot exceed the rate set periodically by the VA Administrator. Property purchased with a VA loan must be owner-occupied.

VA loans can be assumed by purchasers who do not qualify as veterans. The original veteran-borrower remains liable for the loan unless he or she obtains a release of the liability, which must be approved by the VA.

Prepayment. As with an FHA loan, the borrower under a VA loan can prepay the debt at any time without penalty. The veteran may not be required to pay more than a one-percent loan fee and one-percent vendee fee to the VA.

Creative Financing

A borrower and a lender can tailor financing instruments to suit the type of transaction and the financial needs of both parties by altering the terms of the basic mortgage and note. Especially in times of tight or expensive mortgage money, such *creative financing* gains prominence. In addition real estate may be financed using instruments other than mortgages.

Purchase-Money Mortgages

Strictly speaking, a purchase-money mortgage is any mortgage placed when property is bought. In many areas, however, a purchase-money mortgage is a note and mortgage *given by the purchaser to the seller* to finance the property ("Seller take-back financing''). A purchase-money mortgage is usually given to cover a portion of the purchase price; it may be given to finance the entire purchase price (especially in times of tight money). This may be a first or second mortgage and it becomes a lien on the property when the title passes. In the event of the foreclosure of a purchase-money mortgage, the lien takes priority over judgment liens against the borrower and homestead exemptions of the borrower and spouse. A purchase-money mortgage held by the seller is generally considered exempt from usury limitations on interest. If seller-financing is at an artificially low interest rate, the Internal Revenue Service will ''impute'' a higher rate and tax the recipient accordingly.

Imputed Interest. If the amount of seller-financing in a transaction is $2.8 million or less, the seller must charge no less than nine percent interest or a rate equal to the applicable federal rate (AFR), whichever is lower. The AFR is the rate on federal securities with terms similar to the maturity of the seller-financing note. If the seller charged a rate lower than required, he or she would be taxed as if he had received income at the required rate.

Reverse Annuity Mortgages

A *reverse annuity loan* is one in which regular monthly payments are made *to the borrower* based on the equity the homeowner has invested in the property given as security for the loan. A reverse mortgage allows senior citizens on fixed incomes to realize the equity buildup in their homes without having to sell. The borrower is charged a fixed rate of interest and the loan is eventually paid from the sale of the property or from the mortgagor's estate upon his or her death. New York allows such mortgages where the homeowner is at least 60 years old.

Pledged Account Mortgages

With a **pledged account mortgage** the borrower places the down payment in a savings account. This money is drawn upon to subsidize the borrower's own payments during the early years of the loan. The seller, meanwhile, receives full proceeds because the mortgage loan covers the full purchase price.

Shared Equity Mortgages

Under a **shared equity mortgage** the purchaser receives some financial help in the form of a contribution toward the down payment, a concessionary interest rate, or assistance with monthly payments. The ''partner'' may be a lending institution, the seller, the government, or a relative. Typically the partner receives a share of profit when the property is sold.

Package Mortgages

A package loan not only includes the real estate but also *all fixtures and appliances on the premises*. In recent years this kind of loan has been used extensively in financing furnished condominium units. Such loans usually include the kitchen range, refrigerator, dishwasher, and other appliances, as well as furniture, drapes, and carpets, as part of the real estate in the sales price of the home.

Blanket Mortgages

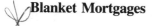

A blanket mortgage covers *more than one parcel or lot* and is used to finance subdivision developments. These mortgages often include a provision, known as a *partial release clause,* that the borrower may obtain the release of any one lot or parcel from the lien by repaying a definite amount of the loan.

Wraparound Mortgages

A wraparound mortgage is frequently used as a method of refinancing real property or financing the purchase of real property when an existing mortgage is to be retained. It is also used to finance the sale of real estate when the buyer wishes to put up a minimum of initial cash for the sale. The buyer gives a wraparound mortgage to the seller, who will collect payments on the new loan usually at a higher interest rate and continue to make payments on the old loan. The buyer should require a protective clause in the document granting him or her the right to make payments directly to the original lender in the event of a default on the old loan. Wraparound mortgages, like all creative financing, require careful study by the buyer's and seller's attorneys. The broker who negotiates one should exercise special care not to give legal advice.

Open-End Mortgages

An open-end mortgage is frequently used by borrowers to obtain additional funds to improve their property. The borrower "opens" the mortgage to increase the debt after the debt has been reduced by payments over a period of time. The lender is not obligated to advance the additional funds.

Construction Loans

A construction loan, or building loan agreement, is made to *finance the construction of improvements* on real estate (homes, apartments, office buildings, and so forth). Under a construction loan the lender disburses the loan proceeds while the building is being constructed. A building loan can be difficult to secure if an individual is not working through a recognized builder or contractor.

Payments are made from time to time to the *general contractor* or owner for that part of the construction work that has been completed since the previous payment. Prior to each payment the lender inspects the work; the general contractor must provide the lender with adequate waivers of lien releasing all mechanics' lien rights (*see* Chapter 24) for the work covered by the payment. This kind of mortgage loan generally bears a higher interest rate because of the risks assumed by the lender. This type of financing is short-term, or *interim*, financing. The borrower is expected to arrange for a permanent loan (also known as an *end*, or *take-out loan*) that will repay the construction lender when the work is completed.

Sale and Leaseback

Sale-and-leaseback arrangements are sometimes used as a means of financing large commercial or industrial plants. The land and building used by the seller for business purposes are sold to an investor such as an insurance company. The real estate is then leased back by the buyer (the investor) to the seller, who continues to conduct business on the property as a tenant. The buyer becomes the lessor and the original owner becomes the lessee. This enables a business firm that has money invested in a plant to free that money for working capital. The buyer benefits from an assured long-term tenant.

Sale-and-leaseback arrangements are complex. They involve complicated legal procedures and their success is usually related to the effects the transaction has on the firm's income-tax liability. A real estate broker should consult with legal and tax experts when involved in this type of transaction.

Installment Contracts (Land Contracts)

As discussed in Chapter 4, real estate can be purchased under an *installment contract*, also known as a contract for deed, land contract, agreement of sale, or articles of agreement for warranty deed. Real estate is often sold on contract in one of two situations: (1) when mortgage financing is not available or is too expensive or (2) when the purchaser does not have a sufficient down payment to cover the difference between a mortgage loan and the selling price of the real estate.

Investment Group Financing

Large real estate projects like high-rise apartment buildings, office complexes, and shopping centers are often financed as joint ventures through group financing arrangements such as syndicates, limited partnerships, and real estate investment trusts. These complex investment agreements are discussed in Chapter 17,"Real Estate Investment."

Sources of Real Estate Financing

Most loans to finance real estate purchases are obtained from financial institutions designed to hold individuals' savings. These institutions lend out and invest these deposits to earn interest, some of which is directed back to the savers, some of which is retained as income. Mortgage loans are generally made by institutional lenders such as savings and loan associations, commercial banks, mutual savings banks, life insurance companies, mortgage banking companies, mortgage brokers, credit unions, pension and trust funds, and finance companies. Individuals (sellers, investors, employers, brokers, and relatives) occasionally are sources for financing.

Savings and Loan Associations

Savings and loan associations are traditionally the most active participants in the home-loan mortgage market, specializing in long-term residential loans. All savings and loan associations must be chartered either by the federal government or by the state in which they are located. Savings and loans are regulated on a national level by the Federal Home Loan Bank system (FHLB). The FHLB sets up mandatory guidelines for member associations and provides depositors with savings insurance through the Federal Savings and Loan Insurance Corporation (FSLIC).

Commercial Banks

Traditionally, commercial banks have not been considered a prime source of real estate financing because they are not specifically set up to finance long-term loans. In some areas, however, commercial banks are originating an increasing number of home mortgages. Like the savings and loan associations, banks must be chartered by the state or federal government; bank deposits are insured by the Federal Deposit Insurance Corporation (FDIC).

Mutual Savings Banks

These institutions, which operate like savings and loan associations, are located mainly in New York and New England. They issue no stock and are mutually owned by their investors. They are primarily savings institutions and are highly active in the mortgage market.

Life Insurance Companies

Insurance companies amass large sums of money from the premiums paid by their policyholders. While a certain portion of this money is held in reserve to satisfy claims and cover operating expenses, much of it is invested in profit-earning enterprises such as long-term real estate loans.

Most insurance companies like to invest their money in large, long-term loans that finance commercial and industrial properties. They also invest in residential mortgage and trust deed loans by purchasing large blocks of government-backed loans (FHA-insured and VA-guaranteed loans) from the Federal National Mortgage Association and other agencies that warehouse such loans for resale in the secondary mortgage market (as discussed later in this chapter).

Mortgage Banking Companies

Mortgage banking companies operate primarily as loan correspondents. They originate mortgage loans with money belonging to other institutions such as insurance companies and pension funds or to individuals and they act as the liaison between borrower and lender. In addition many mortgage banking companies have sufficient funds of their own to make real estate loans that later may be sold to investors (with the mortgage company receiving a fee for servicing the loans). Mortgage banking companies are often involved in all types of real estate loan activities, with particular emphasis on FHA and VA loans.

The majority of mortgage banking companies are organized as stock companies. They are subject to considerably fewer lending restrictions and limitations than commercial banks or savings and loans.

Mortgage Brokers

Mortgage brokers are individuals who are licensed to act as intermediaries in bringing borrowers and lenders together. Mortgage brokers charge a fee, often of the borrower, for their services. They usually handle large commercial transactions.

Credit Unions

Credit unions are cooperative organizations in which members place money in savings accounts usually at higher interest rates than other savings institutions offer. In the past most credit unions made only short-term consumer and home-improvement loans but in recent years they have been branching out into originating longer-term first and second mortgage loans.

SONYMA

The State of New York Mortgage Agency (**SONYMA** or **Sonny Mae**) raises funds through the sale of bonds. The money is channeled into mortgages targeted for specific purposes in specific locations. Loans are made through local lending institutions, typically at below-market interest rates.

Farmer's Home Administration

The Farmer's Home Administration (FmHA) is a federal agency of the Department of Agriculture that channels credit to rural residents as well as to certain small communities. FmHA loan programs fall into two categories: (1) guaranteed loans made and serviced by a private lender and guaranteed for a specific percentage by the FmHA, and (2) insured loans that are originated, made, and serviced by the agency. For low-income first-time home buyers, mortgage interest may be subsidized as low as one percent. Only modest residences are eligible.

Application for Credit

All mortgage lenders require prospective borrowers to file an application for credit that provides the lender with the basic information needed to evaluate the acceptability of the proposed loan. The application includes information regarding the purpose of the loan, the amount, rate of interest, and the proposed terms of repayment.

A prospective borrower must submit personal information to the lender including age, family status, employment, earnings, assets, and financial obligations. Details of the real estate that will be the security for the loan must be provided including legal description, improvements, title, survey, and taxes. For loans on income property or those made to corporations, additional information is required such as financial and operating statements, schedules of leases and tenants, and balance sheets.

Through the process known as **underwriting** the lender carefully investigates the application information, studying credit reports and an appraisal of the property before deciding whether or not to grant the loan. The lender's acceptance of the application is written in the form of a *loan commitment,* which creates a contract to make a loan and sets forth the details. With borderline cases, a commitment may be made based on the lender's current financial position.

Qualifying ratios. With each mortgage plan offered a lender will specify certain *qualifying ratios* that will be applied to each borrower. A typical ratio might be 25/33; the borrower will be allowed to spend up to 25 percent of gross monthly income for housing expense or up to 33 percent of income after other payments on long-term debts have been subtracted. The lender calculates the maximum monthly payment each way and allows only the lower figure.

Government Influence in Mortgage Lending	Aside from FHA-insured and VA-guaranteed loan programs the federal government influences mortgage lending through the Federal Reserve System as well as through various federal agencies such as the Farmer's Home Administration. It also deals in the secondary mortgage market through the Government National Mortgage Association, the Federal Home Loan Mortgage Corporation, and the Federal National Mortgage Association.
Federal Reserve System	Established in 1913 under President Woodrow Wilson, the Federal Reserve System ("The Fed") operates to maintain sound credit conditions, help counteract inflationary and deflationary trends, and create a favorable economic climate. The Federal Reserve System divides the country into 12 federal reserve districts each served by a federal reserve bank. All nationally chartered banks must join the Federal Reserve and purchase stock in its district reserve banks.

The Federal Reserve regulates the flow of money and interest rates in the marketplace indirectly through its member banks by controlling their *reserve requirements* and *discount rates*.

Reserve controls. The Federal Reserve requires each member bank to keep a certain amount of its assets on hand as reserve funds unavailable for loans or any other use. This requirement was designed primarily to protect customer deposits but more importantly it provides a means of manipulating the flow of cash in the money market. By increasing its reserve requirements the Federal Reserve in effect limits the amount of money that member banks can use to make loans, causing interest rates to increase.

In this manner the government can slow down an overactive economy by limiting the number of loans that would have been directed toward major purchases of goods and services. The opposite is also true: By decreasing the reserve requirements the Federal Reserve can allow more loans to be made, thus increasing the amount of money circulated in the marketplace and causing interest rates to decline.

Discount rates. Federal Reserve member banks are permitted to borrow money from the district reserve banks. The interest rate that the district banks charge for the use of this money is called the *discount rate*. This rate is the basis on which the banks determine the percentage rate of interest that they in turn charge their loan customers. Theoretically when the Federal Reserve discount rate is high, bank interest rates are high; therefore fewer loans will be made and less money will circulate in the marketplace. Conversely a lower discount rate results in lower interest rates, more bank loans, and more money in circulation.

Government Influence in the Secondary Market

Mortgage lending takes place in both the primary and secondary mortgage markets. The *primary market,* which this chapter has dealt with thus far, includes: (1) lenders who supply funds to borrowers as an investment and keep the loans in their own *portfolio* and (2) lenders who also originate loans for the purpose of selling them to investors. Loans are bought and sold in the **secondary market** after they have been originated. A lender may wish to sell a number of loans in order to raise immediate funds when it needs more money to meet the mortgage demands in its area. Secondary market activity is especially desirable when money is in short supply because it provides a great stimulant to the housing construction market as well as to the mortgage market.

Generally when a loan has been sold the original lender continues to collect the payments from the borrower. The lender then passes the payments along to the investor who has purchased the loan and charges the investor a fee for servicing the loan. Many borrowers are never aware that their mortgage loan has been sold.

A major source of secondary mortgage market activity is a *warehousing agency,* which purchases a number of mortgage loans and assembles them into one or more packages of loans for resale to investors. The major warehousing agencies are the Federal National Mortgage Association (FNMA), the Government National Mortgage Association (GNMA), and the Federal Home Loan Mortgage Corporation (FHLMC).

Federal National Mortgage Association. The Federal National Mortgage Association (FNMA), often referred to as **Fannie Mae,** is a quasigovernmental agency organized as a privately owned corporation that provides a secondary market for mortgage loans. The corporation raises funds to purchase loans by selling government-guaranteed FNMA bonds at market interest rates. These bonds are secured by blocks, or pools, of mortgages acquired through FNMA's loan commitment program.

Mortgage banking firms are actively involved with FNMA, originating loans and selling them to FNMA while retaining the servicing functions. FNMA is the nation's largest purchaser of mortgages.

When Fannie Mae talks, lenders listen. Because FNMA eventually purchases one mortgage out of every ten, it has great influence on lending policies. When Fannie Mae announces that it will buy a certain type of loan, local lending institutions often change their own regulations to meet the stated criteria. When lenders are experimenting with new types of loans, a Fannie Mae announcement can result in standardization of the innovative mortgage plans and bring order out of chaos.

Government National Mortgage Association. The common name for the Government National Mortgage Association (GNMA) is **Ginnie Mae.** It exists as a corporation without capital stock and is a division of the Department of Housing and Urban Development (HUD). GNMA is designed to administer special assistance programs and work with FNMA in secondary market activities.

Ginnie Mae also guarantees investment securities issued by private offerors such as banks, mortgage companies, and savings and loan associations, that are backed by pools of FHA and VA mortgage loans. The *Ginnie Mae pass-through certificate* is a security interest in a pool of mortgages that provides for a monthly "pass-through" of principal and interest payments directly to the certificate holder. Such certificates are guaranteed by Ginnie Mae.

Federal Home Loan Mortgage Corporation. The Federal Home Loan Mortgage Corporation (FHLMC), or **Freddie Mac,** provides a secondary market for mortgage loans, primarily conventional loans. Freddie Mac has the authority to purchase mortgages, pool them, and sell bonds in the open market with the mortgages as security. FHLMC does not, however, guarantee payment of Freddie Mac mortgages.

Many lenders use the standardized forms and follow the guidelines issued by Freddie Mac because use of FHLMC forms is mandatory for lenders who wish to sell mortgages in the agency's secondary mortgage market. The standardized documents include loan applications, credit reports, and appraisal forms.

Financing Legislation

The federal government regulates the lending practices of mortgage lenders through the Truth-in-Lending Act, Equal Credit Opportunity Act, and the Real Estate Settlement Procedures Act.

Regulation Z

Commonly referred to as the *Truth-in-Lending Act,* **Regulation Z** requires credit institutions to inform borrowers of the true cost of obtaining credit so that the borrower can compare the costs of various lenders and avoid the uninformed use of credit. *All real estate transactions made for personal or agricultural purposes are covered.* The regulation does not apply to business or commercial loans.

The regulation requires that the customer be fully informed of all finance charges as well as the true annual interest rate, before a transaction is consummated. In the case of a mortgage loan made to finance the purchase of a dwelling the lender must compute and disclose the annual percentage rate (APR).

Advertising. Regulation Z provides strict regulation of real estate advertisements that include mortgage financing terms. Chapter 15 contains detailed information.

Penalties. Regulation Z provides penalties for noncompliance. The penalty for violation of Regulation Z is twice the amount of the finance charge with a minimum of $100 and a maximum of $1,000, plus court costs, attorney's fees, and any actual damages. Willful violation is a misdemeanor punishable by a fine of up to $5,000 or one year's imprisonment or both.

Federal Equal Credit Opportunity Act

The Federal Equal Credit Opportunity Act (ECOA) prohibits lenders and others who grant or arrange credit to consumers from discriminating against credit applicants on the basis of race, color, religion, national origin, sex, marital status, age (provided the applicant is of legal age), or dependency upon public assistance. In addition, lenders and other creditors must inform all rejected credit applicants in writing of the principal reasons why credit was denied or terminated.

Real Estate Settlement Procedures Act

The federal Real Estate Settlement Procedures Act (RESPA) was created to ensure that the buyer and seller in a residential real estate transaction involving a new first mortgage loan have knowledge of all settlement costs. This important federal law will be discussed in detail in Chapter 11.

Summary

The note for the amount of the mortgage loan usually provides for *amortization.* The note also sets the rate of *interest* at which the loan is made that the mortgagor or trustor must pay as a charge for borrowing the money. Charging more than the maximum interest rate allowed by state statute is called *usury* and is illegal.

Newly popular in recent years are *adjustable rate mortgages,* under which the interest rate is changed each *adjustment period* to a stipulated *margin* above a national *index* of current mortgage rates. A *cap* may limit the size of possible adjustments and a *ceiling* may limit the maximum adjustment over the life of the loan. In instances where monthly payments do not cover the interest due *negative amortization* is possible, with the total debt increasing, instead of decreasing as it does with normal *amortization.*

Mortgage loans include conventional loans, those *insured by the FHA or an independent mortgage insurance company,* and those *guaranteed by the VA.* FHA and VA loans must meet certain requirements in order for the borrower to obtain the benefits of the government guarantee that induces the lender to lend its funds. The fixed interest rates that must be charged for VA loans may be less than those charged for conventional loans. Lenders may charge *discount points;* each point is one percent of the new mortgage. All FHA and VA mortgages are freely assumable.

Other types of real estate financing include purchase-money mortgages, buydowns, pledged account mortgages, graduated payment loans, shared equity loans, reverse mortgages, blanket mortgages, package mortgages, open-end mortgages, wraparound mortgages, construction loans, sale-and-leaseback agreements, land contracts, and investment group financing.

The federal government affects real estate financing money and interest rates through the Federal Reserve Board's *discount rate* and *reserve requirements;* it also participates in the *secondary mortgage market*. The secondary market is composed of investors who ultimately purchase and hold the loans as investments. These include insurance companies, investment funds, and pension plans. *Fannie Mae* (Federal National Mortgage Association), *Ginnie Mae* (Government National Mortgage Association), and *Freddie Mac* (Federal Home Loan Mortgage Corporation) take an active role in creating a secondary market by regularly purchasing mortgage loans from originators and retaining, or *warehousing,* them until investment purchasers are available.

Regulation Z, the federal Truth-in-Lending Act, requires lenders to inform prospective borrowers who use their homes as security for credit of *all finance charges* involved in the loan. Severe penalties are provided for noncompliance. The *Federal Equal Credit Opportunity Act* prohibits creditors from discriminating against credit applicants on the basis of race, color, religion, national origin, sex, marital status, age, or dependency upon public assistance. The *Real Estate Settlement Procedures Act* requires lenders to inform both buyers and sellers in advance of all fees and charges for the settlement or closing of a residential real estate transaction.

Questions

1. A savings and loan institution offers a mortgage plan with an 80 percent loan-to-value ratio. On the purchase of a $120,000 property, how much down payment will be required?
   a. $20,000   c. $40,000
   b. $24,000   d. $80,000

2. A borrower obtains a $76,000 mortgage loan at 11½ percent interest. If the monthly payments of $785 are credited first on interest and then on principal, what will the balance of the principal be after the borrower makes the first payment?
   a. $75,215.00   c. $75,543.66
   b. $75,943.33   d. $75,305.28

3. When Tiny Tim buys his house, Old Scrooge allows monthly mortgage payments to be figured on a 30-year basis so that Tim can handle them. At the end of the fifth year, however, Scrooge wants the whole remaining debt paid off in a:
   a. graduated payment.
   b. shared-equity payment.
   c. balloon payment.
   d. blanket payment.

4. A homeowner may take as an income-tax deduction:
   a. mortgage insurance premium.
   b. mortgage interest paid.
   c. property insurance premium.
   d. All of the above

5. New York's usury limits still apply to interest on mortgage loans by:
   a. sellers.
   b. individuals other than sellers.
   c. regular lending institutions.
   d. the FHA.

6. Norman Emanuel sells his home for $50,000 and agrees to pay three points to his buyer's lending institution. The buyer is putting 20 percent down on the property. How much will the points cost Norman?
   a. $300   c. $1,500
   b. $1,200   d. $20,000

7. A lending institution may require the buyer to send in an extra monthly payment to cover future bills for:
   a. property taxes and insurance premiums.
   b. major repairs.
   c. possible default in monthly payments.
   d. All of the above

8. Which of the following is an example of a conventional loan?
   a. A mortgage loan insured by the Federal Housing Administration
   b. A second loan for home improvements secured through a credit union
   c. A mortgage obtained through a private lender with a VA guarantee
   d. All of the above

9. Private mortgage insurance (PMI) is required whenever:
   a. the loan is to be placed with the FHA.
   b. the property covers more than 2.5 acres.
   c. the loan exceeds $67,500.
   d. the buyer is putting less than 20 percent down on a conventional loan.

10. The Department of Housing and Urban Development insures mortgage loans made through:
    a. the FHA.   c. Fannie Mae.
    b. the VA.   d. Freddie Mac.

11. No down payment is required for loans made through:
    a. the FHA.   c. Fannie Mae.
    b. the VA.   d. Freddie Mac.

12. Money for FHA and VA mortgages comes from:
    a. different departments of the federal government.
    b. qualified local lending institutions.
    c. the Federal Reserve Bank.
    d. the secondary mortgage market.

13. The government lends money directly in which kind of loan?
    a. FHA   c. Farmer's Home
    b. VA   d. All of the above

14. The terms *index, margin,* and *cap* are used in evaluating what type of mortgage?
    a. Package   c. Conventional
    b. Blanket   d. Adjustable rate

15. The Carters purchased a residence for $75,000. They made a down payment of $15,000 and agreed to assume the seller's existing mortgage, which had a current balance of $23,000. The Carters financed the remaining $37,000 of the purchase price by executing a mortgage and note to the seller. This type of loan, by which the seller becomes the mortgagee, is called:
    a. a wraparound mortgage.
    b. a package mortgage.
    c. a balloon note.
    d. a purchase-money mortgage.

16. The bank that will make a lower-rate loan in return for the payment of extra points is offering a:
    a. reduced loan-to-value ratio.
    b. graduated payment loan.
    c. buydown.
    d. second mortgage.

17. Negative amortization refers to a situation in which:
    a. debt is gradually reduced through monthly payments.
    b. debt grows larger instead of smaller each month.
    c. regular adjustments reduce the interest rate.
    d. the interest rate may rise or fall according to an index.

18. The McBains are purchasing a lakefront summer home in a new resort development. The house is completely equipped and furnished and the McBains have obtained a loan that covers the purchase price of the residence including the furnishings and equipment. This kind of financing is called:
    a. a wraparound mortgage.
    b. a package mortgage.
    c. a blanket mortgage.
    d. an unconventional loan.

19. A developer obtains one mortgage for a whole subdivision. As he sells each lot, he obtains a release of one parcel from the:
    a. package mortgage.
    b. reverse mortgage.
    c. balloon mortgage.
    d. blanket mortgage.

20. Tom Terrific buys a local factory from a company that intends to remain and rent it from him. Tom has put together a(an):
    a. equity-sharing transaction.
    b. sale and leaseback.
    c. secondary market.
    d. reserve for escrow.

21. Which of the following best defines the *secondary market?*
    a. Lenders who exclusively deal in second mortgages
    b. Where loans are bought and sold after they have been originated
    c. The major lender of residential mortgages
    d. The major lender of FHA and VA loans

22. Fannie Mae is:
    a. the leading purchaser of mortgages on the secondary market.
    b. a lender for homes in rural areas.
    c. a government agency that regulates interest rates.
    d. an old crone who lives in a cave.

23. The public can invest in mortgage pools by buying certificates issued by:
    a. the Federal Reserve Bank.
    b. the Farmer's Home Administration.
    c. the Government National Mortgage Agency.
    d. the Guaranteed Mortgage Fund.

24. Freddie Mac:
    a. mortgages are guaranteed by the full faith and credit of the federal government.
    b. buys and pools blocks of conventional mortgages, selling bonds with such mortgages as security.
    c. affects the mortgage market through adjustment of the discount rate.
    d. forbids the charging of more than one point to the buyer.

25. Regulation Z protects the consumer from:
    a. misleading advertising.
    b. fraudulent mortgage plans.
    c. discrimination in lending.
    d. substandard housing.

Appendix: Amortization Tables

Amortization Table for the first few months of a 30-year loan of $50,000 at 13 percent with monthly payment of $553.10

Payment	Principal	Interest	Balance
1	11.43	541.67	49,988.57
2	11.56	541.54	49,977.01
3	11.68	541.42	49,965.33
4	11.81	541.29	49,953.52
5	11.94	541.16	49,941.58
6	12.07	541.03	49,929.51
7	12.20	540.90	49,917.31
8	12.33	540.77	49,904.98

Amortization Table for the monthly payment needed to amortize a loan of $1,000

	Numbers of years					
Annual interest rate	1	5	25	30	35	40
9%	87.45	20.76	8.40	8.05	7.84	7.72
10	87.92	21.25	9.09	8.78	8.60	8.50
10¼	88.04	21.38	9.27	8.97	8.79	8.69
10½	88.15	21.50	9.45	9.15	8.99	8.89
10¾	88.27	21.62	9.63	9.34	9.18	9.09
11	88.39	21.75	9.81	9.53	9.37	9.29
11¼	88.50	21.87	9.99	9.72	9.57	9.49
11½	88.62	22.00	10.17	9.91	9.77	9.69
11¾	88.73	22.12	10.35	10.10	9.96	9.89
12	88.85	22.25	10.54	10.29	10.16	10.09
12¼	88.97	22.38	10.72	10.48	10.36	10.29
12½	89.09	22.50	10.91	10.68	10.56	10.49
12¾	89.20	22.63	11.10	10.87	10.76	10.70
13	89.32	22.76	11.28	11.07	10.96	10.90
13¼	89.43	22.88	11.47	11.26	11.15	11.10
13½	89.56	23.01	11.66	11.45	11.35	11.30
13¾	89.68	23.14	11.85	11.65	11.55	11.51
14	89.79	23.27	12.04	11.85	11.76	11.72
14¼	89.91	23.40	12.23	12.05	11.96	11.92
14½	90.02	23.53	12.42	12.25	12.16	12.12
14¾	90.15	23.66	12.61	12.44	12.36	12.33
15	90.26	23.79	12.81	12.65	12.57	12.54
16	90.73	24.32	13.59	13.45	13.38	13.36
17	91.21	24.85	14.38	14.26	14.21	14.18

FHA Offices in New York State

Buffalo Area Office
Statler Building
107 Delaware Ave.
Buffalo, NY 14202
716-846-5755

Albany Service Office
Leo O'Brien Federal Building
North Pearl and Clinton Aves.
Albany, NY 12207
518-472-3567

Rochester Service Office
316 Kenneth J. Keating Federal Building
Rochester, NY 14614
716-263-5871

New York Area Office
26 Federal Plaza
New York, NY 10007
212-264-8053

New York Regional Office
26 Federal Plaza
New York, NY 10007
212-264-8053

8

License Law and Ethics

Key Terms

Apartment information vendor
Article 12A
Associate broker
Blockbusting
Branch office
Broker
Code of Ethics
Commingle
Continuing education
Denial, suspension or revocation of license
Department of State (DOS)

Designation
DOS
GRI
Irrevocable consent
Net listing
Qualifying course
Real estate license law
REALTOR®
Rules and regulations
Salesperson
Supervising (principal) broker

Overview

Broker and salesperson license applicants are required to pass state examinations designed to test their knowledge of real estate principles and laws. Foremost among these is New York's real estate license law, which sets forth strict operating standards for licensees and penalties for noncompliance. This chapter will introduce the most basic provisions of New York's law as well as the rules and regulations of the Department of State, which administers real estate licensing services. An appendix reprints portions of the law as set forth in the state's study booklet for prospective licensees.

Real Estate License Laws in All States	All states, the District of Columbia, Puerto Rico, and Canadian provinces have enacted **real estate license laws** that provide the state with the authority to license and regulate the activities of real estate brokers and salespeople. Certain details of the law vary from state to state but the main provisions of many state laws are similar.
Purposes of License Laws	Although a fee is charged for real estate licenses, raising revenues is not the primary purpose of license laws. The purposes of the laws are: (1) to protect the public from dishonest or incompetent brokers or salespeople, (2) to prescribe certain standards and qualifications for licensing brokers and salespeople, and (3) to maintain high standards in the real estate business.

Basic Provisions of License Law	The authority that controls the licenses of real estate brokers and salespeople is the New York Department of State, Division of Licensing Services. It has the power to issue licenses and enforce the real estate license law. The law is enforced through the **denial, suspension, or revocation of licenses.**

The **Department of State (DOS)** has adopted a series of **rules and regulations** that further define the basic law, provide for its administration, and set forth additional operating guidelines for brokers and salespeople. These administrative rules and regulations have the *same force and effect as the law* itself. Throughout this chapter all discussions of the license law also include the rules and regulations.

Violation of the license law is a misdemeanor punishable by up to a year in jail and a fine of up to $1,000.

The New York Real Property Law, **Article 12A,** which went into effect in 1922, is the main source of law for real estate licenses in New York. Copies of the law and regulations or a license application may be obtained by writing to the:

New York Department of State
Division of Licensing Services
162 Washington Avenue
Albany, New York 12231

or to a local office listed in Table 8.1.

Who Must Be Licensed	Any person who for another and for a fee or the expectation thereof performs any of the activities described in the license law must hold a valid real estate license unless specifically exempted. In 1985 New York State had more than 40,000 licensed brokers and 100,000 salespersons.

Broker. A real estate broker is defined in the license law as any person, firm, partnership, or corporation who for another and for a fee or the expectation of a fee perform(s) any of the following services:

Table 8.1
Offices of the
Department of State

Albany . . . . 162 Washington Ave., Albany, NY 12231
Binghamton . . . . State Office Bldg., Binghamton, NY 13901
Buffalo. . . . . 65 Court St., Buffalo, NY 14202
Hauppauge . . . . NYS Office Bldg., Veterans Hwy., Hauppauge, NY 11787
Mineola . . . . 114 Old Country Rd., Mineola, NY 11501
New York City . . . . 270 Broadway, New York, NY 10007
Rochester . . . . 189 N. Water St., Rochester, NY 14604
Syracuse . . . . Hughes State Office Bldg., Syracuse, NY 13202
Utica . . . . State Office Bldg., Utica, NY 13501

1. negotiates any form of real estate transaction;
2. lists or attempts to list real property for sale;
3. negotiates a loan secured by a mortgage;
4. negotiates or makes a lease;
5. collects rents;
6. sells a lot or parcel of land by auction;
7. exchanges real property;
8. relocates tenants; or
9. engages in resale of condominiums.

Table 8.2 shows the number of licenses by county in November 1985.

Salesperson. A real estate salesperson is one who assists in any of the services a broker performs and is associated with a broker.

To summarize, a broker is authorized to operate his or her own real estate business; a salesperson can operate only in the name of and under the supervision of a licensed broker. The salesperson may never accept any payment of commission from anyone except his or her supervising broker.

Exceptions. The provisions of the license law do not apply to:

1. public officers while they are performing their official duties.

2. persons acting in any capacity under the judgment or order of a court.

3. attorneys at law duly admitted to practice in the courts of New York. If an attorney employs real estate salespeople, however, he or she must obtain a real estate broker's license; attorneys are not required to take the licensing examination.

4. a resident manager employed by an owner to manage rental property when the leasing of units or the collection of rents is part of the resident manager's regular duties.

Licensing Procedure All applicants for a real estate license must submit a written application to the New York Department of State on forms provided by the department, accompanied by the appropriate fees. To receive a license, applicants must pass an examination administered by the Department of State. Persons who have been convicted of a felony may not obtain a New York real estate license unless they have received executive pardon subsequent to the conviction or a certificate of good conduct from a parole board. The Department of State will also consider at its

Table 8.2	COUNTY	REAL ESTATE BROKERS	REAL ESTATE SALES PERSONS	COUNTY	REAL ESTATE BROKERS	REAL ESTATE SALES PERSONS
Real Estate licensees by county in November 1985	ALBANY	736	1721	ONONDAGA	861	2159
	ALLEGANY	48	99	ONTARIO	178	587
	BRONX	789	1320	ORANGE	672	1714
	BROOME	387	1171	ORLEANS	37	140
	CATTARAUGUS	91	243	OSWEGO	99	331
	CAYUGA	89	261	OTSEGO	104	202
	CHAUTAUQUA	217	757	PUTNAM	269	719
	CHEMUNG	102	233	QUEENS	3235	10988
	CHENANGO	83	208	RENSSELAER	214	521
	CLINTON	67	159	RICHMOND	674	2868
	COLUMBIA	165	372	ROCKLAND	757	2113
	CORTLAND	55	128	ST LAWRENCE	100	285
	DELAWARE	144	287	SARATOGA	335	1612
	DUTCHESS	671	1891	SCHENECTADY	272	776
	ERIE	1304	4603	SCHOHARIE	48	206
	ESSEX	88	204	SCHUYLER	11	29
	FRANKLIN	47	108	SENECA	40	79
	FULTON	80	139	STEUBEN	100	289
	GENESEE	76	232	SUFFOLK	3899	12033
	GREENE	135	273	SULLIVAN	204	402
	HAMILTON	21	46	TIOGA	52	142
	HERKIMER	70	259	TOMPKINS	166	291
	JEFFERSON	112	305	ULSTER	390	889
	KINGS	2487	6491	WARREN	189	599
	LEWIS	16	33	WASHINGTON	63	168
	LIVINGSTON	77	225	WAYNE	105	328
	MADISON	78	233	WESTCHESTER	3159	6254
	MONROE	1510	4885	WYOMING	41	166
	MONTGOMERY	84	163	YATES	53	108
	NASSAU	4466	13290	OUTSIDE NYS	1743	570
	NEW YORK	7660	12328			
	NIAGARA	243	696			
	ONEIDA	302	738	STATE TOTAL	40570	101669

SOURCE: New York State, Department of State, Division of Licensing, "Report for the Month of November 1985."

discretion a certificate of relief from disabilities issued by a probation officer or a judge. A real estate licensee must be either a citizen of the United States or a permanent resident.

Broker's License. An applicant for the broker's license must be 19 years of age or older. The license application, shown in Figure 8.1, must include:

1. the name and address of the applicant and the name under which he or she intends to conduct business. If the applicant is a partnership or corporation, the application must state the names and addresses of each partner or officer.
2. the place or places where business will be conducted.
3. the business or occupation held by the applicant for the two years preceding the date of application.
4. proof that the applicant successfully has completed 90 hours of real estate education from an institution approved by the Department of State.

Figure 8.1
Application for Broker's
License

State of New York
DEPARTMENT OF STATE
Division of Licensing Services
162 Washington Avenue
Albany, NY 12231

FOR OFFICE USE ONLY	CLASS	KEY	REG. NO.

CASH NO.	FEE	EC
	1 0 0 00	

APPLICATION FOR LICENSE AS REAL ESTATE BROKER

INSTRUCTIONS/ELIGIBILITY—PLEASE READ CAREFULLY

Print or type all information. Send the completed application, together with any additional papers, and the $100 *NONREFUNDABLE* fee to the above address. *DO NOT SEND CASH*; make your check or money order payable to the Department of State. Effective January 1, 1986, all licenses will be issued for full two year terms, automatically expiring two years after effective date.

FOR OFFICE USE ONLY

1. APPLICANT'S NAME

LAST NAME — FIRST NAME — MIDDLE INITIAL — CONTINUE ON NEXT LINE IF NECESSARY

2. HOME ADDRESS

NUMBER AND STREET — CONTINUE ON NEXT LINE IF NECESSARY

CITY

STATE   ZIP CODE   COUNTY

3. INDIVIDUAL OR TRADE NAME

CONTINUE ON NEXT LINE IF NECESSARY

4. CORPORATION OR PARTNERSHIP NAME

CONTINUE ON NEXT LINE IF NECESSARY

5. BUSINESS ADDRESS AT WHICH YOU WILL OPERATE

NUMBER AND STREET

CITY

S____
__ __/__ __

STATE   ZIP CODE   COUNTY

B____
__ __/__ __

6. DATE OF BIRTH OF APPLICANT

MONTH   DAY   YEAR

7. I am an attorney licensed to practice in the State of New York...................... ☐ Yes ☐ No

8. A Real Estate Broker's license was last issued to me by the State of New York.   FROM 19 ___ TO 19 ___

9. A Real Estate Salesperson's license was last issued to me by the State of New York... FROM 19 ___ TO 19 ___

10. ALL NEW APPLICANTS (Except attorneys licensed to practice in New York State) MUST PASS a written examination and provide proof of work experience by submitting one of the following supplemental forms:
— Broker A/Statement of Experience as a Licensed Real Estate Salesperson, or
— Broker B/Statement of Experience Equivalent to that of a Licensed Real Estate Salesperson.

Examinations are held monthly. Please circle the city in which you wish to take your examination. You will be notified by mail of the date, time and location of the examination.

ALBANY   BINGHAMTON   BUFFALO   HAUPPAUGE   MINEOLA   NEWBURGH   NEW YORK CITY

PLATTSBURGH   ROCHESTER   SYRACUSE   UTICA   WATERTOWN

411201-570 (11/85)

Figure 8.1
(continued)

Complete applicable sections below.

TRADE NAME BROKERS ONLY:

11. The trade name has been cleared with the Division of Licensing Services.................................. ☐ Yes ☐ No

12 The trade name has been registered with the County Clerk and a copy of the certificate, certified by him/her, is enclosed.. ☐ Yes ☐ No

PARTNERSHIP BROKERS ONLY:

13. The partnership name has been cleared with the Division of Licensing Services.......................... ☐ Yes ☐ No

14. The partnership name has been registered with the County Clerk and a copy of the certificate, certified by him/her, is enclosed.. ☐ Yes ☐ No

CORPORATE BROKERS ONLY:

15. The corporate name or corporation's assumed name has been cleared with the Division of Licensing Services... ☐ Yes ☐ No

16. The corporation's assumed name has been registered.. ☐ Yes ☐ No

17. The Charter of Incorporation provides the power to engage in the business of real estate brokerage, and a copy of the receipt of incorporation in New York State is enclosed.................................... ☐ Yes ☐ No

18. A statement listing the names, titles and home addresses of all officers is enclosed...................... ☐ Yes ☐ No

19. A list of stockholders owning at least 10% of stock is enclosed...................................... ☐ Yes ☐ No

20. If the representative broker, or a stockholder, holds stock in any other licensed real estate corporation, a statement is attached with shareholders name, name of real estate corporation and amount of stock held... ☐ Yes ☐ No

ALL APPLICANTS:

21. Has any license, permit, commission or registration ever been denied, suspended, or revoked in any state, territory or foreign country?... ☐ Yes ☐ No
   • If Yes, attach a statement of details.

22. Have you ever been convicted of any crime or offense, other than minor traffic violations?.................. ☐ Yes ☐ No
   • If Yes, submit a certified copy of each conviction.

23. Have you at any time while holding a real estate broker's or salesperson's license acted as a real estate dealer buying and/or selling real estate on your own account as an individual?........................... ☐ Yes ☐ No

APPLICANT AFFIRMATION

I subscribe and affirm, under the penalties of perjury, that the statements made in this application, including statements made in any accompanying papers, have been examined by me and to the best of my knowledge are true.

X _____ _____

Signature of Applicant *Date*

NOTICE TO APPLICANT:
The information given on your application is subject to verification and investigation. In order to prevent any unnecessary return of your application, and to help us to avoid unwarranted field travel for investigation, we request your cooperation by providing us with information that will help us to contact you by telephone, if needed.

Business | Residence | Alternate

Area Code Number | Area Code Number | Area Code Number

Figure 8.1
(continued)

Broker A/ Statement of Experience as a
Licensed Real Estate Salesperson

Supplement to
Application for License as a Real Estate Broker

INSTRUCTIONS / ELIGIBILITY—

Please type or print all information. This supplemental form must be submitted with your completed "Application for License as Real Estate Broker" if you qualify for a broker's license because you:
— have been licensed as a Real Estate Salesperson for *at least one full year,* and
— have completed *at least 1,750 working hours** under the supervision of a licensed broker, and
— have successfully completed the 90-hour broker qualifying course as approved by the Secretary of State.

The sponsoring broker must complete the "Record of Real Estate Transactions" section on the reverse (both applicant and sponsor must sign the accompanying Certification). Applicants must also enclose a recent photograph and *original* school certificates.

* Equivalent to 35 hours per week for 50 weeks.

> Attach
> small
> black and
> white
> photo
> here.

SALESPERSON EXPERIENCE—I was actively engaged as a licensed real estate salesperson as indicated below:

Broker's Name and Address	Number of Hours/Week	From Mo/Day/Yr	To Mo/Day/Yr

During the above period of time, I successfully negotiated the following TOTAL NUMBER of transactions (details on back):

_____ Sales _____ Rentals or Leases _____ Listings
_____ Purchases* _____ Mortgages _____ Other _____

*A purchase is defined as that circumstance where the agent represents a real estate buyer in a transaction and commissions are paid by the buyer.

EDUCATION — I have completed the 90-hour broker qualifying course at:

_____
(Name of School)   *(Completion Date)*

_____
(Name of School)   *(Completion Date)*

CERTIFICATES OF COMPLETION ☐ Already submitted ☐ Attached

During the above periods of time, I have engaged in no other business, vocation or regular activity other than:

I, _____ , subscribe and affirm, under the penalties of perjury, that the above
(Name of Applicant— PLEASE PRINT)
statements, which are made in connection with and as a part of my application for a real estate broker's license, are true and correct.

X _____   _____
Signature of Applicant   *Date*

NOTICE TO APPLICANT:
The information given on your application is subject to verification. In order to prevent any unnecessary return of your application, we request your cooperation by providing us with information that will help us to contact you by telephone, if needed.

Business	Residence	Alternate
Area Code Number	Area Code Number	Area Code Number

411201-570 A (11/85)

Figure 8.1
(continued)

RECORD OF REAL ESTATE TRANSACTIONS — TO BE COMPLETED BY BROKER
(Attach additional sheets if necessary)

APPLICANT	SPONSORING BROKER / AGENCY
Name	Name
Home Address Number and Street	Address Number and Street
City State ZIP	City State ZIP
Date of Birth	Business Phone Area Code ( )

Date	Name of Buyer/Tenant	Name of Seller/Landlord	Address of Property	Sale Price	Net Commission

CERTIFICATION:

We, the undersigned, jointly certify that the information given above and on all attached sheets represents a true record of transactions negotiated by the named applicant during association with the named broker. We understand that any material misstatement made may result in the revocation or suspension of the license, if issued, as well as any existing license of the applicant and/or the broker.

X _____

Applicant Signature

X _____

Broker Signature

_____

Date

_____

Date

Figure 8.1
(continued)

Broker B / Statement of Experience Equivalent to that of a
                 Licensed Real Estate Salesperson

Supplement to
Application for License as a Real Estate Broker

INSTRUCTIONS / ELIGIBILITY—

Please type or print all information. This supplemental from must be submitted with your completed "Application for License as Real Estate Broker" if you qualify for a broker's license because you:
— have been engaged in the general real estate business for at least two years, and
— during that two-year period, have had experience in the real estate business equivalent to that of an active real estate salesperson, and
— have successfully completed the 90-hour broker qualifying course as approved by the Secretary of State.

Applicants are required to submit a sworn statement describing their experience in the real estate business — this form is to be used for that purpose. Describe your experience in the space provided on both sides of this form; attach additional sheets, if necessary. The description of your experience in the real estate business should be as detailed and specific as possible. You are encouraged to attach supporting documents such as copies of tax or payroll records, leases, deeds, contracts, etc., which will aid the Department of State in verifying your experience. Applicants must also enclose a recent photograph and *original* school certificates.

> Attach
> small
> black and
> white
> photo
> here.

I, _____ , depose and say:
(PRINT Name of Applicant)

THAT the statements herein made are given as proof of my experience in the general real estate business.

THAT I understand that if I make a material misstatement in this application and a license is issued, the Department of State may suspend or revoke my license.

THAT my activities in the general real estate business consisted of the transactions set forth on this form.

THAT the information contained in any separate sheets attached to this application is made a part of this statement, and the attached sheets are incorporated herein by reference.

I subscribe and affirm, under penalties of perjury, that the above statements are true and correct.

X _____
Applicant's Signature

EDUCATION — I have completed the 90-hour broker qualifying course at:

_____   _____
(Name of School)   (Completion Date)

_____   _____
(Name of School)   (Completion Date)

CERTIFICATES OF COMPLETION   ☐ Already submitted   ☐ Attached

STATEMENT OF EXPERIENCE (add additional sheets if necessary):
PURCHASES — *(DATE, GRANTEE, GRANTOR, LOCATION AND DESCRIPTION, VALUE, BOOK, PAGE)*

NOTICE TO APPLICANT:
The information given on your application is subject to verification. In order to prevent any unnecessary return of your application, we request your cooperation by providing us with information that will help us to contact you by telephone, if needed.

Business   Residence   Alternate

Area Code   Number   Area Code   Number   Area Code   Number

411201-570 B (11/85)

Figure 8.1
(continued)

STATEMENT OF EXPERIENCE, continued

SALES — *(DATE, GRANTEE, GRANTOR, LOCATION AND DESCRIPTION, VALUE, BOOK, PAGE)*

MORTGAGES — *(DATE, MORTGAGEE, MORTGAGOR, LOCATION, DESCRIPTION, AMOUNT OF MORTGAGE, BOOK, PAGE)*

LEASES — *(DATE, LEASEE, LESSOR, LOCATION, DESCRIPTION, AMOUNT OF RENT, BOOK, PAGE)*

5. an affidavit stating that the applicant has actively participated in the real estate business as a licensed real estate salesperson under a broker's supervision for at least one year or that he or she has at least two years' equivalent experience in the real estate business. The statement of experience, if used, must describe:

- any transactions entered into during the two years (or more, if applicable).
- the date and nature of each transaction, the names of the principals to each, the addresses of the subject properties, and the nature and extent of the applicant's participation in each.

6. a passport-sized photograph. The applicant must retain another such photograph and attach it to the examination admission card.

The broker who intends to do business under an assumed, partnership, or corporate name must clear the name with the Division of Licensing Services, Department of State, before filing the application for a broker's license. A corporate name also must be cleared before filing with the Division of Corporations and State Records, and a trade name must be cleared with the county clerk.

Associate Broker. A license as **Associate Broker** is available for the broker who wishes to work as a salesperson under the name and supervision of another broker. The associate broker must meet all the qualifications for a broker's license and pass the same examination but transacts business in the name of the sponsoring broker, exactly as a salesperson would. A separate application form is used and is signed not only by the applicant but also by the sponsoring broker with whose firm the new broker will be associated.

Salesperson's License. An applicant for a salesperson's license must be 18 years of age or older. The application, shown in Figure 8.2, must state:

1. the applicant's name and address;
2. the name and business address of the broker with whom the salesperson will be associated (the *supervising* or *principal broker*);
3. proof that the applicant successfully has completed 45 hours of real estate education from an institution approved by the Department of State;
4. the business or occupation held by the applicant for the two years preceding the date of application; and
5. the length of time the applicant has engaged in the real estate business, if any.

The Department of State will send the applicant an admission slip with an appointment for the license examination, and a state study booklet containing portions of the license law and other relevant laws and regulations. (Excerpts from the study booklet are reprinted at the end of this chapter and elsewhere in this textbook.)

Temporary Rent Collector's Permit. The temporary rent collector's permit is available to those applying for a real estate salesperson's license upon receipt by the Department of State of the individual's license application. Upon issuance of the permit an applicant may act as a rent collector for a period not exceeding 90 days before the written license examination. This permit is issued only once during a particular license term.

Apartment Information Vendors. An apartment information vendor's license is available to anyone over the age of 18 who is trustworthy and able to maintain

Figure 8.2
Application for
Salesperson's License

State of New York
DEPARTMENT OF STATE
Division of Licensing Services
162 Washington Avenue
Albany, NY 12231

FOR OFFICE USE ONLY	CLASS	KEY	REG. NO.
CASH NO.			FEE 2 0 0 0 EC

APPLICATION FOR LICENSE AS REAL ESTATE SALESPERSON

INSTRUCTIONS/ELIGIBILITY—PLEASE READ CAREFULLY

Print or type all information. Your sponsoring broker must complete the Statement of Association on the reverse. Send the completed application, together with any additional papers, and the $20 *NONREFUNDABLE* fee to the above address. *DO NOT SEND CASH*; make your check or money order payable to the Department of State. Effective January 1986, all license terms are for full two year terms, automatically expiring two years after date of issuance.

ATTACH ORIGINAL SALESPERSON QUALIFYING COURSE COMPLETION CERTIFICATE.

NOTE: You are *NOT* eligible to file this application for salesperson if you are either a member of the partnership, or are an officer or own voting stock in the corporation that is the sponsoring brokerage.

1. APPLICANT'S NAME
   LAST NAME — FIRST NAME — MIDDLE INITIAL — CONTINUE ON NEXT LINE IF NECESSARY

2. HOME ADDRESS
   NUMBER AND STREET — CONTINUE ON NEXT LINE IF NECESSARY

   CITY

   STATE   ZIP CODE   COUNTY

3. SPONSORING BROKER OR FIRM NAME
   (exactly as it appears on Broker license)
   CONTINUE ON NEXT LINE IF NECESSARY

4. OFFICE ADDRESS AT WHICH APPLICANT WILL BE PERMANENTLY STATIONED
   NUMBER AND STREET — CONTINUE ON NEXT LINE IF NECESSARY

   CITY

   STATE   ZIP CODE   COUNTY

FOR OFFICE USE ONLY

S _ _ _
_ _ / _ _
B _ _ _
_ _ / _ _

5. DATE OF BIRTH OF APPLICANT
   MONTH   DAY   YEAR

6. I have enclosed a separate, written request for a temporary rent collector's permit with this application........................ ☐ Yes ☐ No

7. ALL NEW APPLICANTS MUST PASS A WRITTEN EXAMINATION.
   Examinations are held weekly, except in Plattsburgh and Watertown, where they are held every other month. Please circle the city in which you wish to take your examination. You will be notified by mail of the date, time and location of the examination.

   ALBANY   BINGHAMTON   BUFFALO   HAUPPAUGE   MINEOLA   NEWBURGH   NEW YORK CITY

   PLATTSBURGH   ROCHESTER   SYRACUSE   UTICA   WATERTOWN   YONKERS

Figure 8.2
(continued)

Complete applicable sections below.

TRADE NAME BROKERS ONLY:

11. The trade name has been cleared with the Division of Licensing Services.................... ☐ Yes ☐ No

12 The trade name has been registered with the County Clerk and a copy of the certificate, certified by him/her, is enclosed.......... ☐ Yes ☐ No

PARTNERSHIP BROKERS ONLY:

13. The partnership name has been cleared with the Division of Licensing Services.................... ☐ Yes ☐ No

14. The partnership name has been registered with the County Clerk and a copy of the certificate, certified by him/her, is enclosed.......... ☐ Yes ☐ No

CORPORATE BROKERS ONLY:

15. The corporate name or corporation's assumed name has been cleared with the Division of Licensing Services.......... ☐ Yes ☐ No

16. The corporation's assumed name has been registered.......... ☐ Yes ☐ No

17. The Charter of Incorporation provides the power to engage in the business of real estate brokerage, and a copy of the receipt of incorporation in New York State is enclosed.......... ☐ Yes ☐ No

18. A statement listing the names, titles and home addresses of all officers is enclosed.......... ☐ Yes ☐ No

19. A list of stockholders owning at least 10% of stock is enclosed.......... ☐ Yes ☐ No

20. If the representative broker, or a stockholder, holds stock in any other licensed real estate corporation, a statement is attached with shareholders name, name of real estate corporation and amount of stock held... ☐ Yes ☐ No

ALL APPLICANTS:

21. Has any license, permit, commission or registration ever been denied, suspended, or revoked in any state, territory or foreign country?..........
   • If Yes, attach a statement of details. ☐ Yes ☐ No

22. Have you ever been convicted of any crime or offense, other than minor traffic violations?..........
   • If Yes, submit a certified copy of each conviction. ☐ Yes ☐ No

23. Have you at any time while holding a real estate broker's or salesperson's license acted as a real estate dealer buying and/or selling real estate on your own account as an individual?.......... ☐ Yes ☐ No

APPLICANT AFFIRMATION

I subscribe and affirm, under the penalties of perjury, that the statements made in this application, including statements made in any accompanying papers, have been examined by me and to the best of my knowledge are true.

X _____   _____
Signature of Applicant   *Date*

NOTICE TO APPLICANT:
The information given on your application is subject to verification and investigation. In order to prevent any unnecessary return of your application, and to help us to avoid unwarranted field travel for investigation, we request your cooperation by providing us with information that will help us to contact you by telephone, if needed.

Business | Residence | Alternate
Area Code Number | Area Code Number | Area Code Number

a $5,000 interest-bearing escrow account. The license is renewable annually for a $250 fee. Apartment information vendors must provide prospective tenants with a contract or receipt with specific information regarding the services they offer. They also must display a sign in all offices bearing the same information, post their license in all offices, and notify the Department of State of any changes in name or address.

Fees. The Department of State charges the following application fees:

Broker, original license and renewal:	$100
Associate broker, original license and renewal:	100
Salesperson, original license and renewal:	20
Branch office, original and renewal:	100
Temporary rent collector's permit:	20
Apartment information vendor's license:	250

License Examinations

In approximately one-half the states, but not in New York, a uniform test is used. Furnished by Educational Testing Service (ETS) of Princeton, NJ, it contains nationwide material and a special state section for matters that differ from one area to another. Another uniform test, ACT, is used in some states. New York, however, has its own examinations.

The *salesperson's examination* is given weekly in Albany, Buffalo, Happauge, Mineola, New York City, Rochester, and Syracuse; every other week in Binghamton, Newburgh, Utica, and Yonkers; monthly in Plattsburg and Watertown. The broker's examination is given monthly.

Admission slips must be accompanied by a photograph. Scrap paper is furnished and must be turned in before leaving the room. Calculators are allowed but must be noiseless and hand-held with no tape printout. All questions on each test are multiple choice and the passing grade is 70.

The salesperson's examination covers material from both the state study booklet and the 45-hour license qualifying course. One hour is allowed for the test.

The *brokers' examination* contains 100 questions and runs for 2¾ hours. In recent years it has contained considerable material based on human rights and fair housing in addition to the subjects listed in the broker's study manual: English language, deeds, mortgages, land contracts, leases, principal and agent, and real property law. Arithmetic comprises ten percent of the questions.

During 1984, before prelicensing education was mandatory, the New York Department of State administered license examinations to 25,034 prospective salespersons of whom 70 percent, or 17,547, passed. The pass rate was higher for broker applicants, with 1,636 taking the examination and 82 percent, or 1,338, passing it.

Those failing the examination are notified by mail. If the applicant has a passing grade, a license is prepared, which may take weeks. The salesperson's license will be mailed to the supervising broker. The new broker, however, may operate on his or her own and receives the license directly.

Each retake of the salesperson's examination requires an additional $20 fee; three retakes of the broker's examination within a year are allowed for the original $100 fee.

Issuing the License   Each license is issued for a two-year term. An applicant who has successfully completed the real estate license examination receives a license and pocket card from the Department of State. A salesperson's employing broker must retain the salesperson's license. The pocket card must be carried by the salesperson. If a licensee does not renew the license within two years of its expiration, he or she must retake the licensing examination.

Summary of Requirements. Table 8.3 shows the basic requirements for licensure as a real estate broker or salesperson in New York State.

**Table 8.3
Requirements for
Licensing in New
York**

Salesperson:	Broker:
At least 18	At least 19
No felony*	No felony*
Permanent resident U.S.	Permanent resident U.S.
Sponsoring broker	Full year's experience*
45-hour course	90 hours' study
Pass state exam	Pass state exam
$20 (two years)	$100 (two years)
*some exceptions possible	

The Department of State certifies certain educational institutions to offer two types of required courses, *qualifying* and *continuing education* courses.

One **qualifying course** covers the necessary 45 hours' instruction preliminary to a salesperson's license; the second 45-hour qualifying course completes the 90-hour prelicensing requirement for licensure as a broker. The courses must be taken in order. Topics to be covered and the time devoted to each are set by law.

Continuing education courses fulfill requirements for renewal of licenses. In order to renew a broker's or salesperson's license, a licensee must fulfill a continuing education requirement consisting of study at an institution approved by the Department of State, every four years. The requirement may be satisfied by successful completion during the four-year period of one of the following:

1. a 45-hour course that is *not* the original license-qualifying course, or
2. a 30-hour course with perfect attendance and a final examination, or
3. three 15-hour modules, each with perfect attendance.

Unlike qualifying courses, then, continuing education courses may take several forms and may cover any material deemed acceptable by the Department of State.

Those exempted from the continuing education requirement include:

1. anyone who is a licensed broker at the time of license renewal and who has been continuously licensed as a full-time salesperson and/or broker for the preceding 15 years.
2. any licensee who took, during the preceding four-year period, a 45-hour license *qualifying course* for either a salesperson's or a broker's license.
3. New York State attorneys.

Licensing Corporations, Partnerships, and Other Legal Entities

New York corporations, partnerships, and other legal entities may obtain a real estate license from the Department of State. A license issued to a corporation entitles the president or other designated officers to act as a broker. A license must be secured by each officer who wishes to act as a broker; the appropriate fee must be paid for each license. An officer of a corporation or a member of a partnership may not be licensed as a salesperson in the firm's name. Each partner in a partnership or each member of any other legal entity who desires to act as a broker in the firm's name also must pay a fee and obtain a license. More than one license may be issued to an individual who represents more than one legal entity.

No licensed real estate salesperson may own either singly, jointly, or indirectly any voting shares of stock in any licensed real estate brokerage corporation with which he or she is associated.

Licensing Nonresidents

Nonresidents of New York may be licensed as New York real estate brokers or salespersons by conforming to all the provisions of the license law except that they are not required to maintain a place of business within the state. The department will recognize the license issued to a real estate broker or salesperson by another state as satisfactory qualification for a New York broker's or salesperson's license if the laws of his or her home state: (1) require that real estate license applicants establish competence by written examinations; (2) permit licenses to be issued to New York licensees without requiring them to take that state's licensing examination.

A list of the states that have such reciprocity agreements with New York is found in Table 8.4. If a particular state's laws do not include these provisions, the Department of State will require that the nonresident applicant meet the examination requirement and will issue a license upon payment of a license fee and receipt of a certified copy of the license issued to the applicant by the other state.

Every nonresident applicant must file an irrevocable consent on the form prescribed by the Department of State. The **irrevocable consent** submits the applicant to the jurisdiction of the New York courts.

Table 8.4
States Offering
Reciprocity with
New York Licenses

State	Broker	Salesperson	Requirements: 2 years' licensure	Current license
Arkansas	x		x	x
Delaware	x	x	x	x
Massachusetts	x		x	x
Nebraska	x	x	x	x
New Jersey	x	x	x	x
Oklahoma	x		x	x
Ohio	x	x	x	

General Operation of a Real Estate Business

Place of Business. Every New York real estate broker must have and maintain a principal place of business within the state.

Business Name and Sign. Any business name used by a New York real estate broker must be approved by the Department of State. A sign of sufficient size to be readable from the sidewalk indicating the name and business of the applicant as a licensed real estate broker must be posted conspicuously on the outside of the building. If the office is located in an apartment building, office building, or hotel, the broker's name and the words "Licensed Real Estate Broker" must be posted in the space that lists the names of the building's occupants.

Branch Offices. A broker may maintain a branch office or offices; a supplemental license must be maintained for each branch.

Change of Business Address. Licensees must notify the department in writing of any change in their business address. A filing fee of $1 must accompany all such notifications. Failure to notify the department of a change is grounds for suspension of a license.

Display of Licenses. The broker's license must be prominently displayed at his or her place of business. Salesperson's licenses need not be displayed.

Salesperson's Transfer of Employment. When a salesperson's employment is changed or terminated the supervising broker must notify the Department of State. The new supervising broker must notify the department that he or she will be holding the salesperson's license and must submit a $1 fee.

Blockbusting Prohibited. Regulations prohibit licensees from inducing or attempting to induce an owner to sell, lease, or list any property by making representations regarding the entry or prospective entry into the neighborhood of a person or persons of a particular race, color, religion, or national origin. Property owners may petition the department to order brokers and salespeople to cease and desist from such solicitation. Failure to comply subjects the license of the brokers and salespeople to suspension or revocation after hearing.

Net Listings Prohibited. Also prohibited is the use of net listing agreements wherein the broker is promised as commission all of the sale price that exceeds an amount specified by the seller.

Offer to Purchase. All offers to purchase property must be promptly presented to the owner of the property. *they must be in writing*

Maintaining Documents. Every real estate broker must maintain a file of all listings, offers, closing statements, and other documents completed by the firm that relate to real estate transactions for a period of three years. All of these records must contain the names and addresses of the sellers, buyers, and mortgagees, the sale prices, the amount of deposit paid on contract, the commissions charged, and the expenses of procuring a mortgage loan or, if the broker has purchased for resale, the net profit and expenses that relate to the transaction. The broker must also keep copies of a statement showing all payments made by the broker. All of these records must be made available to the Department of State upon request.

ART. #20

#20 **Delivery of Documents.** A real estate broker must immediately deliver duplicate originals of any document relating to a real estate transaction prepared by the broker or one of his or her salespeople to all parties signing the document.

#18 **Care and Handling of Funds.** A real estate broker must not **commingle** money or other properties belonging to a principal with his or her own. At all times the broker must maintain a separate *bank* account to be used exclusively for the deposit of these monies and must deposit them as promptly as possible. Within a reasonable time period the broker must render an account of the funds to the client and remit any funds collected. Interest earned, if any, does not belong to the broker.

Commissions. No individual in New York may legally accept a commission or other compensation for performing any of the activities regulated by the license law, or recover such fees, unless he or she held a valid New York real estate license at the time the activity was performed. A salesperson may not accept a commission from anyone other than his or her supervising broker. Brokers and salespeople may not obtain compensation from more than one party to a transaction without the knowledge and consent of all parties involved.

Advertising. All real estate advertisements must contain the name of the broker's firm and must clearly indicate that the party who placed the ad is a real estate broker. Blind ads that contain only a telephone number are prohibited.

For Sale Signs. A broker must obtain an owner's consent to place a For Sale sign on the owner's property.

Publishers. Article 12B of the Real Property Law requires real estate and business opportunity publishers or those who print, write, or otherwise issue for the purpose of promoting for others the sale, lease, or exchange of real estate or businesses to file a statement with the Department of State for its approval.

Disclosure of Interest. Brokers may not buy or acquire an interest in property listed with them for their own account without first making their true position known to the owners involved. Similarly a broker may not sell property in which he or she has an interest nor buy such property for a client without revealing the interest to all parties to the transaction.

Substitution. The license law expressly prohibits the broker from inducing any party to a contract of sale or lease to break the contract for the purpose of substituting a new contract with another principal.

Obligations to Other Brokers. Brokers are prohibited from negotiating the sale, lease, or exchange of any property belonging to an owner who has an existing written contract that grants exclusive authority to another broker. No broker may compensate or accept the services of any other broker's associates without that broker's knowledge.

Suspension and Revocation of Licenses

The New York Department of State, Division of Licensing Services, may hear complaints and/or initiate investigations into any alleged violations of the license law or its rules and regulations. Anyone found guilty of any of the following violations may have his or her license suspended or revoked or may be fined or reprimanded:

1. making any substantial misrepresentation;
2. making any false promise likely to influence, persuade, or induce;
3. making a false statement or misrepresentation through agents, salespersons, advertising, or otherwise;
4. accepting a commission or valuable consideration (salesperson) for the performance of any service from any person except the licensed broker with whom the salesperson is associated;
5. acting for more than one party in a transaction without the knowledge of all parties involved;
6. failing within a reasonable amount of time to account for or remit any monies belonging to others that come into his or her possession;
7. being unworthy or incompetent to act as a real estate licensee;
8. paying a commission or valuable consideration (broker) to any person for services performed in violation of the law;
9. obtaining a license falsely or fraudulently or making a material misstatement in the license application;
10. engaging in any other conduct, whether of the same or of a different character from that just specified, that constitutes improper, fraudulent, or dishonest dealing; and
11. any violation of license law.

Investigation of Complaint and Hearing. If the department feels that a complaint against a licensee warrants further investigation, it will send an investigator to interview the alleged violator about the charge. In some cases the investigation is preceded by a formal letter of complaint from the department. If the investigation results in sufficient evidence, the department will conduct an administrative hearing and make a decision after the transcript of the hearing becomes available. Individuals accused of violation of the law may defend themselves at a hearing or be represented by an attorney.

Penalties. If an offender has received any sum of money as commission, compensation, or profit in connection with a license law violation, he or she may be held liable for up to four times that amount in damages in addition to having the license suspended or revoked. The Department of State may also impose a fine of up to $1,000 on an offender. If an offense constitutes a misdemeanor, a licensee may be tried in a court of special sessions in addition to the hearing. Criminal actions will be prosecuted by the Attorney General of the state of New York.

Appeal. The action of the Department of State is subject to review through a proceeding brought under Article 78 of the Civil Practice Law and its accompanying rules. Any determination in granting or renewing a license, revoking or suspending a license, imposing a fine, a reprimand, or the refusal to institute any of these penalties may be appealed.

Revocation of Employer's License. Revocation of a broker's license automatically suspends the licenses of all salespeople in the broker's employ, pending a change of employer and the reissuing of their licenses accordingly.

When a salesperson is accused of violating license law the supervising broker is also held accountable if the broker knew or should have known of the violation or if, having found out about the problem, the broker retained any fees or commission arising from the transaction.

Professional Organizations

Years ago, real estate brokers realized the need for an organization to assist them in improving their business abilities and to educate the public to the value of qualified real estate brokers. The National Association of REALTORS® (NAR) was organized in 1908 (as the National Association of Real Estate Boards) to meet this need. This association has grown with the business and today is one of the leading trade organizations in the country. It is the parent organization of most local real estate boards that operate throughout the United States and the professional activities of all REALTORS®—active members of local boards that are affiliated with the national association—are governed by the association's Code of Ethics. The term REALTOR® is a registered trademark. In 1986, NAR had 711,226 members as REALTOR® and REALTOR®-ASSOCIATES.

There are also many independent real estate boards and other professional associations that were organized to set high standards for their members, promote their members' best interests, and educate the public about the real estate profession. The National Association of Real Estate Brokers (Realtists) was founded in 1947. Its membership includes individual members, as well as brokers who belong to state and local real estate boards affiliated with the organization. The members also subscribe to a code of ethics that sets professional standards for all Realtists.

These are trade associations. Licensed brokers and salespersons are not required to join. In New York one licensee in five belongs to NAR.

The importance of adhering to a set of ethical business standards, however, cannot be overemphasized.

The NAR adopted its **Code of Ethics** in 1913. The REALTORS® Code of ethics is reproduced in Figure 8.3.

Figure 8.3
REALTORS®
Code of Ethics

Code of Ethics[1] of the National Association of REALTORS®

Revised and Approved by the Delegate Body of the Association at its 75th Annual Convention November 15, 1982

Preamble . . .

Under all is the land. Upon its wise utilization and widely allocated ownership depend the survival and growth of free institutions and of our civilization. The REALTOR® should recognize that the interests of the nation and its citizens require the highest and best use of the land and the widest distribution of land ownership. They require the creation of adequate housing, the building of functioning cities, the development of productive industries and farms, and the preservation of a healthful environment.

Such interests impose obligations beyond those of ordinary commerce. They impose grave social responsibility and a patriotic duty to which the REALTOR® should dedicate himself, and for which he should be diligent in preparing himself. The REALTOR®, therefore, is zealous to maintain and improve the standards of his calling and shares with his fellow REALTORS® a common responsibility for its integrity and honor. The term REALTOR® has come to connote competency, fairness, and high integrity resulting from adherence to a lofty ideal of moral conduct in business relations. No inducement of profit and no instruction from clients ever can justify departure from this ideal.

In the interpretation of this obligation, a REALTOR® can take no safer guide than that has been handed down through the centuries, embodied in the Golden Rule, "Whatsoever ye would that men should do to you, do ye even so to them."

Accepting this standard as his own, every REALTOR® pledges himself to observe its spirit in all of his activities and to conduct his business in accordance with the tenets set forth below.

Article 1

The REALTOR® should keep himself informed on matters affecting real estate in his community, the state, and nation so that he may be able to contribute responsibly to public thinking on such matters.

Article 2

In justice to those who place their interests in his care, the REALTOR® should endeavor always to be informed regarding laws, proposed legislation, governmental regulations, public policies, and current market conditions in order to be in a position to advise his clients properly.

Article 3

It is the duty of the REALTOR® to protect the public against fraud, misrepresentation, and unethical practices in real estate transactions. He should endeavor to eliminate in his community any practices that could be damaging to the public or bring discredit to the real estate profession. The REALTOR® should assist the governmental agency charged with regulating the practices of brokers and salesmen in his state.

1. Published with the consent of the NATIONAL ASSOCIATION OF REALTORS®, author of and owner of all rights in the Code of Ethics of the NATIONAL ASSOCIATION OF REALTORS®, © NATIONAL ASSOCIATION OF REALTORS® 1982— All Rights Reserved. The NATIONAL ASSOCIATION OF REALTORS® reserves exclusively unto itself the right to comment on and interpret the CODE and particular provisions thereof. For the NATIONAL ASSOCIATION's official interpretations of the CODE, *see* INTERPRETATIONS OF THE CODE OF ETHICS; NATIONAL ASSOCIATION OF REALTORS®.

**Figure 8.3
(continued)**

Article 4

The REALTOR® should seek no unfair advantage over other REALTORS® and should conduct his business so as to avoid controversies with other REALTORS®.

Article 5

In the best interests of society, of his associates, and his own business, the REALTOR® should willingly share with other REALTORS® the lessons of his experience and study for the benefit of the public and should be loyal to the Board of REALTORS® of his community and active in its work.

Article 6

To prevent dissension and misunderstanding and to assure better service to the owner, the REALTOR® should urge the exclusive listing of property unless contrary to the best interest of the owner.

Article 7

In accepting employment as an agent, the REALTOR® pledges himself to protect and promote the interests of the client. This obligation of absolute fidelity to the client's interests is primary but it does not relieve the REALTOR® of the obligation to treat fairly all parties to the transaction.

Article 8

The REALTOR® shall not accept compensation from more than one party, even if permitted by law, without the full knowledge of all parties to the transaction.

Article 9

The REALTOR® shall avoid exaggeration, misrepresentation, or concealment of pertinent facts. He has an affirmative obligation to discover adverse factors that a reasonably competent and diligent investigation would disclose.

Article 10

The REALTOR® shall not deny equal professional services to any person for reasons of race, creed, sex, or country of national origin. The REALTOR® shall not be party to any plan or agreement to discriminate against a person or persons on the basis of race, creed, sex, or country of national origin.

Article 11

A REALTOR® is expected to provide a level of competent service in keeping with the standards of practice in those fields in which the REALTOR® customarily engages.

The REALTOR® shall not undertake to provide specialized professional services concerning a type of property or service that is outside his field of competence unless he engages the assistance of one who is competent on such types of property or service or unless the facts are fully disclosed to the client. Any person engaged to provide such assistance shall be so identified to the client and his contribution to the assignment should be set forth.

The REALTOR® shall refer to the Standards of Practice of the National Association as to the degree of competence that a client has a right to expect the REALTOR® to possess, taking into consideration the complexity of the problem, the availability of expert assistance, and the opportunities for experience available to the REALTOR®.

Article 12

The REALTOR® shall not undertake to provide professional services concerning a property or its value where he has a present or contemplated interest unless such interest is specifically disclosed to all affected parties.

Article 13

The REALTOR® shall not acquire an interest in or buy for himself, any member of his immediate family, his firm or any member thereof, or any entity in which he has a substantial ownership interest, property listed with him without making the true position known to the listing owner. In selling property owned by himself or in which he has any interest, the REALTOR® shall reveal the facts of his ownership or interest to the purchaser.

Article 14

In the event of a controversy between REALTORS® associated with different firms, arising out of their relationship as REALTORS®, the REALTORS® shall submit the dispute to arbitration in accordance with the regulations of their board or boards rather than litigate the matter.

Article 15

If a REALTOR® is charged with unethical practice or is asked to present evidence in any disciplinary proceeding or investigation, he shall place all pertinent facts before the proper tribunal of the member board or affiliated institute, society, or council of which he is a member.

Article 16

When acting as agent, the REALTOR® shall not accept any commission, rebate, or profit on expenditures made for his principal-owner, without the principal's knowledge and consent.

Figure 8.3 (continued)

Article 17

The REALTOR® shall not engage in activities that constitute the unauthorized practice of law and shall recommend that legal counsel be obtained when the interest of any party to the transaction requires it.

Article 18

The REALTOR® shall keep in a special account in an appropriate financial institution, separated from his own funds, monies coming into his possession in trust for other persons, such as escrows, trust funds, clients' monies, and other like items.

Article 19

The REALTOR® shall be careful at all times to present a true picture in his advertising and representations to the public. He shall neither advertise without disclosing his name nor permit any person associated with him to use individual names or telephone numbers unless such person's connection with the REALTOR® is obvious in the advertisement.

Article 20

The REALTOR®, for the protection of all parties, shall see that financial obligations and commitments regarding real estate transactions are in writing expressing the exact agreement of the parties. A copy of each agreement shall be furnished to each party upon his signing such agreement.

Article 21

The REALTOR® shall not engage in any practice or take any action inconsistent with the agency of another REALTOR®.

Article 22

In the sale of property that is exclusively listed with a REALTOR®, the REALTOR® shall utilize the services of other brokers upon mutually agreed upon terms when it is in the best interests of the client.

Negotiations concerning property that is listed exclusively shall be carried on with the listing broker, not with the owner, except with the consent of the listing broker.

Article 23

The REALTOR® shall not publicly disparage the business practice of a competitor nor volunteer an opinion of a competitor's transaction. If his opinion is sought and if the REALTOR® deems it appropriate to respond, such opinion shall be rendered with strict professional integrity and courtesy.

Note: Where the word REALTOR® is used in this Code and Preamble, it shall be deemed to include REALTOR-ASSOCIATE®. Pronouns shall be considered to include REALTORS® and REALTOR-ASSOCIATES® of both genders.

The Code of Ethics was adopted in 1913. Amended at the Annual Convention in 1924, 1928, 1950, 1951, 1952, 1955, 1956, 1961, 1962, 1974, and 1982.

New York State Association of REALTORS®

The New York State Association of REALTORS® is a member board of the National Association of REALTORS® that represents more than 30,000 REALTORS® and REALTOR-ASSOCIATES® in New York State. The objectives of the state association are carried out by volunteer officers, directors, and committee members. The staff consists of an executive director, administrator, director of educational activities, and groups responsible for legislative activities, communications, and other membership services. The Commercial-Investment Division, the New York State Appraisal Society, and the Realtors Land Institute are divisions of the state association that serve specialized needs of the membership.

Educational Services. In 1969 the New York REALTORS® Institute established a structured educational program with the approval of the National Association of REALTORS®. The prescribed course of study leads to the use of the designation Graduate, REALTORS® Institute (GRI). To earn the GRI designation the candidate must successfully complete three courses. They are approved by the state for continuing education credit. GRI courses are offered during the year at various locations around the state and in summer at a week-long session at Ithaca College.

GRI course I covers residential property: valuation, listing, marketing and closings, business planning, and construction. Topics in GRI II include appraisal, financing, taxation, ethics and legal topics, and an overview of real estate management. GRI III covers commercial property: estimating cash flow, pricing, financing and appraising commercial property, federal taxation, exchanges, and syndication.

Designations

Designations analogous to college degrees are awarded after study, examinations, and experience. Various real estate bodies award these designations. Some are associated with the National Association of REALTORS and some are independent organizations. Among the more well-known designations are:

American Institute of Real Estate Appraisers: MAI, Member Appraisal Institute; and RM, Residential Member;

Realtors National Marketing Institute: CCIM, Certified Commercial-Investment Member; CRB, Certified Real Estate Brokerage Manager; and CRS, Certified Residential Specialist;

Realtors Land Institute: AFLM, Accredited Farm and Land Member; ALC, Accredited Land Consultant

Real Estate Securities and Syndication Institute: SRS, Specialist in Real Estate Securities;

Institute of Real Estate Management: CPM, Certified Property Manager;

American Society of Real Estate Appraisers: CRE, Counselor of Real Estate;

Society of Industrial and Office Realtors: SIR;

Society of Real Estate Appraisers: SRA, Senior Residential Appraiser; SREA, Senior Real Estate Appraiser; SRPA, Senior Real Property Analyst; and

American Society of Appraisers: ASA.

Summary

The real estate license law was enacted by New York State to protect the public from dishonest brokers and salespeople, prescribe certain licensing standards, maintain high standards in the real estate profession, and protect licensed brokers from unfair or improper competition.

In New York, licensees must be permanent residents of the United States, never convicted of a felony, and must pass state examinations before licensure. A salesperson must have completed a prescribed 45-hour qualifying course, be at least 18 years old, and sponsored by a licensed broker. A broker must be at least 19 years old, with an additional 45 hours of approved study and one full year's experience as a licensed salesperson. Some exceptions to these requirements are available.

The real estate license, which covers a two-year period, costs $20 for a salesperson and $100 for a broker. An associate broker license designates a fully qualified broker who chooses to remain in a salesperson's capacity under a supervising broker. Those exempt from licensing requirements include New York State attorneys, public officials while performing their public duties, persons acting under court order, and resident managers employed by one owner to collect rents and manage property.

Every broker must have a principal place of business within the state, post a sign readable from the sidewalk or in the lobby of an office building, obtain a separate license for each branch office, and display the broker's license prominently. Brokers are required to maintain a separate escrow account for deposit of other people's money and are prohibited from *commingling* their own funds with such funds. The broker must immediately deliver duplicate originals of all documents to the persons signing them and must keep a file of all documents relating to real estate transactions for at least three years.

Commissions may be collected only by the supervising broker and may be shared only with other brokers and the broker's own salespersons. Advertisements must contain the name of the broker's firm.

Laws, rules, and regulations governing licensees are administered by the New York Department of State, which may, after hearings, suspend or revoke licenses.

Many licensees subscribe to a code of ethics as members of professional real estate organizations. The *Code of Ethics* of the National Association of REALTORS® is reprinted in this chapter.

Designations are awarded after study, examinations, and experience by various organizations. The New York State Association of REALTORS® awards the GRI designation to graduates of the REALTORS® Institute.

Questions

1. Real estate license laws were instituted to:
   a. raise revenue through license fees.
   b. limit the number of brokers and salespersons.
   c. match the federal government's requirements.
   d. protect the public and maintain high standards.

2. In New York, real estate licenses are under the supervision of the:
   a. Real Estate Commission.
   b. Board of REALTORS®.
   c. Department of State.
   d. Department of Education.

3. New York's real estate license law is known as:
   a. the Statute of Frauds.
   b. Article 12A.
   c. the Law of Agency.
   d. Newton's Law.

4. A New York resident does *not* need a real estate license to perform which of the following actions?
   a. Selling a neighbor's house for a fee
   b. Offering tenants in a building that is to be rehabilitated a list of new rental spaces for a fee
   c. Entering into a lease with a prospective tenant for rental property he or she owns
   d. Buying lots in a particular area on behalf of a developer for a fee

5. Which of the following does *not* require a license in New York?
   a. Selling condominiums
   b. Selling mobile homes
   c. Selling land at auction
   d. Selling shopping plazas

6. A duly licensed salesperson may accept a bonus from:
   a. a grateful seller.
   b. a grateful buyer.
   c. another salesperson.
   d. None of the above

7. A fully qualified broker who chooses to remain as a salesperson under another broker's sponsorship is known as a(n):
   a. adjunct salesperson.   c. associate broker.
   b. sales associate.   d. principal broker.

8. To obtain a broker's license one must reach the age of:
   a. 18.   c. 20.
   b. 19.   d. 21.

9. A broker must have completed how many hours of prescribed study?
   a. 15   c. 45
   b. 30   d. 90

10. A salesperson's license application must be accompanied by a fee of:
    a. $20.   c. $100.
    b. $50.   d. $250.

11. Subjects covered by the broker's license examination include:
    a. human rights and fair housing.
    b. deeds and mortgages.
    c. the English language.
    d. All of the above

12. Every real estate license is good for a period of:
    a. one year.   c. three years.
    b. two years.   d. four years.

13. A continuing education course may consist of:
    a. a 45-hour course.
    b. a 30-hour course with examination.
    c. three 15-hour modules.
    d. Any of the above

14. A nonresident broker requesting a New York license must:
    a. post a bond of $5,000.
    b. be fingerprinted.
    c. find a New York sponsor.
    d. allow himself or herself to be sued in New York State.

15. A broker must post a sign at the place of business:

    a. inside the broker's office.
    b. on the outside door of the office.
    c. above each salesperson's desk.
    d. visible from the sidewalk or in a lobby.

16. A broker must display in the office:

    a. the broker's license.
    b. all salespersons' licenses.
    c. associate brokers' licenses.
    d. All of the above

17. A real estate broker must keep all documents pertaining to a real estate transaction on file for a period of:

    a. two years.   c. seven years.
    b. three years.   d. Indefinitely

18. The term "commingling" pertains to:

    a. mixing the broker's funds with escrow deposits.
    b. soliciting the services of another broker's salespersons.
    c. failure to deliver duplicate originals of contracts.
    d. promoting business at social gatherings.

19. Every advertisement must contain the:

    a. sales associate's full name.
    b. address of the brokerage firm.
    c. name of the brokerage firm.
    d. full listing price of the property.

20. Violation of the license law is legally classified as a(n):

    a. violation.   c. misdemeanor.
    b. offense.   d. felony.

21. The Department of State may impose a fine on an offending licensee of up to:

    a. $250.   c. $1,000.
    b. $500.   d. None of the above

22. If a principal broker loses her license, her associated salespersons must immediately:

    a. appoint one of their number to serve as supervisor.
    b. stop listing and selling.
    c. obtain brokers' licenses.
    d. move the office to another location.

23. A broker need *not* be:

    a. licensed by the state.
    b. over 19 years of age.
    c. a REALTOR®.
    d. a permanent resident of the United States.

24. The Code of Ethics is promulgated by the:

    a. National Association of REALTORS®.
    b. Department of State.
    c. Article 12A, Real Property Law.
    d. None of the above

25. The designation "GRI" stands for:

    a. general realty insurance.
    b. government regulatory institution.
    c. Graduate, REALTORS® Institute.
    d. guaranteed regular interest.

Appendix: Excerpts from New York State's Study Booklet for Brokers

SUMMARY OF ARTICLE 12-A OF THE REAL PROPERTY LAW

Purpose and effect. This statute was enacted, primarily, for the protection of the public against the dishonest practices of unscrupulous, and the costly blunderings of incompetent, real estate agents.

Real estate agents must be licensed. This statute forbids anyone who is not a duly licensed real estate broker or salesperson to negotiate any form of real estate transaction, for another and for compensation of any kind, in the State of New York. The provision covers the negotiation of mortgages and the collection of rents, as well as the making of leases of and sale by auction or otherwise of real property. In addition arranging the relocation of commercial or residential tenants for a fee is an activity restricted to real estate brokers. The negotiation of, or attempt to negotiate the sale of a lot or parcel for another, requires a real estate broker's license. A licensed broker may not employ an unlicensed person to assist in the negotiation of a real estate transaction. If the broker does, the broker forfeits rights to a commission on the transaction, is guilty of a misdemeanor and may have his/her license revoked.

Nonresident brokers. A nonresident of the State of New York may be licensed as a real estate broker in this State, upon the same terms as resident brokers, except that a nonresident broker must file a duly executed "irrevocable consent" that service of summons, complaints and other legal documents in actions and other proceedings instituted against the broker, in any court in the State of New York, may be served upon the Secretary of State, with the same force and effect as if served upon the broker personally. A nonresident who is licensed in another state must demonstrate competency in the prescribed written examination, and must maintain an office in this State, unless in his/her state a New York broker may be licensed without passing the qualifying examination that is there required of resident applicants for real estate brokers' licenses, and is not required to maintain an office in that state.

Persons exempt from application of law. The provisions of the statute do not apply to public officers while performing their official duties, to persons acting in any capacity under the judgment or order of a court, or to attorneys-at-law duly admitted to practice in the courts of New York. Where an attorney employs a salesperson or salespersons, the attorney must obtain a license as real estate broker.

Eligibility for license. Applicants for salespersons' licenses are examined only to establish their character and general intelligence. Anyone age 18 or over may be licensed as a real estate salesperson. First time real estate salesperson applicants are required to take and pass an approved 45-hour qualifying course of study as a prerequisite to licensing.

Licenses to act as real estate brokers are granted to citizens of the United States or to persons who are legal resident aliens; persons under the age of 19 years are ineligible. No one may be licensed as a real estate broker without having actively participated in the general real estate brokerage business as a licensed real estate salesperson under the supervision of a licensed real estate broker for a period of at least one year, or has had the equivalent experience in general real estate business for a period of at least two years, and has attended for at least 90 hours and has successfully completed a real estate course or courses approved by the Secretary of State . . . and has demonstrated competency to act as a broker by passing the required written examination.

Each officer of a corporation or member of a copartnership who engages in any form of real estate brokerage, in behalf of a corporation or firm, must be licensed, as its representative, as a real estate broker. Salespersons' licenses are not issued to officers of corporations nor to members of copartnerships.

No person shall be entitled to a license as a real estate broker or real estate salesperson under this article who has been convicted in this State or elsewhere of a felony, and who has not subsequent to such conviction received executive pardon therefor or a certificate of good conduct from the parole board.

Application for licenses. Persons wishing to be licensed, either as real estate brokers or salespersons, will be furnished with appropriate forms of applications, instructions, etc., by the Division of Licensing Services, Department of State, Albany, NY.

The mere filing of an application for a license does not authorize the applicant to engage in the real estate brokerage business.

Nonresident applications. The Department of State shall recognize the license issued to a real estate salesperson by another state as satisfactory qualification for license as a salesperson provided that the laws of the state of which he or she is a resident require that applicants for licenses as salespersons establish their competency by written examinations and permit licenses to be issued to residents of the State of New York duly licensed under this article, without examination.

Temporary permits. Upon receipt of an application for a real estate salesperson's license, and on express request, a permit will be issued authorizing the applicant to act as a rent collector for a period not exceeding 90 days, pending the written examination. Not more than one such permit shall be issued the same applicant during the same license term.

License fees. The nonrefundable fee for the issuance or renewal of a license authorizing a person, copartnership or corporation to act as a real estate broker is $100 and the fee for issuance or renewal of a salesperson's license is $20.

License terms. The license term for real estate brokers and salespersons is 2 years.

Renewal of license. A person who does not apply for renewal of either a broker's or salesperson's license within two years from expiration of a previously issued license must qualify by passing a written examination. No renewal license will be issued unless the licensee meets the continuing education requirement. Licensees must submit proof satisfactory to the Department of State that they have attended at least 45 hours of classroom instruction, and successfully completed a real estate course or courses approved by the Secretary of State, within the preceding 4 years. Licensed brokers with more than 15 years full-time experi-

ence and attorneys admitted to the bar in New York State are exempted from this requirement.

Pocket card. The Department of State issues a pocket card to each licensed salesperson, which must be exhibited on demand. Anyone doing business of any kind with a real estate agent should insist that credentials be shown to determine whether or not the agent is duly licensed and, if licensed, in what capacity.

Compensation of salespersons. Real estate salespersons may not demand or receive compensation from any person other than a duly licensed real estate broker with whom the salesperson is associated. Payment of a commission to a licensed salesperson by the client does not cancel the claim of the broker for the services rendered by the salesperson.

Splitting commissions. No real estate broker may pay any part of a fee, commission or other compensation received, to any person for any service, help or aid rendered to such broker in the negotiation of any real estate transaction, unless such person is a duly licensed real estate salesperson associated with the broker, or is a licensed real estate broker of this State, or is engaged in the real estate brokerage business in another state or is exempt from the application of the license law. Further, a real estate broker may not pay or agree to pay any part of a fee, commission, or other compensation received or due, or to become due to the broker to any person who is or is to be a party to the transaction. (*"Kickback"—colloquial*)

Violations and penalties. A violation by any unlicensed person of any provision of Article 12-A of the Real Property Law is a class A misdemeanor, which is punishable by a fine of not more than $1,000 or by imprisonment for not exceeding one year, or by both such fine and imprisonment. The commission of a single act prohibited by this article constitutes a violation thereof. In case the offender shall have received any sum of money, as compensation or profit by, or in consequence of offending, the offender is also liable to a civil penalty up to the sum of four times the amount of money so received by the offender, which may be sued for and recovered by the person aggrieved by the offender's misconduct. An unlicensed real estate agent cannot collect compensations for services by resort to the courts, for the agent must allege and prove that the agent is a duly licensed real estate broker or salesperson in order to be entitled to a judgment.

Disciplinary provisions. The license of any real estate broker or salesperson may be suspended pending hearing or may be suspended or revoked by the licensing authorities, after hearing and upon conviction of a violation of any provision of the license law, or for a material misstatement in the application for the broker's license, or for fraud, fraudulent practice, the use of dishonest or misleading advertising, or demonstrated untrustworthiness to act as a real estate broker or salesperson, as the case may be. The revocation of a broker's license operates to suspend the licenses of all real estate salespersons associated with the broker, pending a change of association and the reissuing of their licenses accordingly. All brokers' and salespersons' licenses and pocket cards shall be returned to the Department of State within five days after the receipt of notice of such revocation or suspension. Whenever the license of a broker or salesperson is revoked by the Department of State, such real estate broker or salesperson shall be ineligible to be relicensed either as a real estate broker or salesperson until after the expiration of a period of one year from the date of such revocation.

Drawing of legal documents. While the license as real estate broker gives the right to negotiate real estate transactions, it does not give the right to draw legal documents or give legal advice. The preparation of a legal document may result in the loss of commissions and the revocation of the license. It is essential that real estate brokers and their salespersons refrain from drawing legal instruments of any character.

Enforcement of law. The Department of State is charged with the enforcement of this statute, the routine of which is administered by the Division of Licensing Services of the Department, with the aid of an advisory committee of real estate brokers appointed by the Secretary of State.

Upon complaint of any person or on his own initiative, the Secretary of State is empowered to investigate any violation of this article or to investigate the business, business practices and business methods of any person, firm or corporation applying for or holding a license as a real estate broker or salesperson and for the purpose of exercising this power he may subpoena and bring before him any person in this State and require the production of any books or any papers which he deems relevant to the inquiry.

All communications relating to administration of the law, or to real estate agents licensed or unlicensed, should be addressed to the Division of Licensing Services, Department of State, 162 Washington Avenue, Albany, NY 12231.

Department of State
RULES AND REGULATIONS

Regulations Affecting Brokers and Salespersons

Commingling money of principal. A real estate broker shall not commingle the money or other property of his principal with his own and shall at all times maintain a separate, special bank account to be used exclusively for the deposit of said monies and which deposit shall be made as promptly as practicable. Said monies shall not be placed in any depository, fund or investment other than a federally insured bank account. Accrued interest, if any, shall not be retained by, or for the benefit of, the broker except to the extent that it is applied to, and deducted from, earned commission, with the consent of all parties.

Rendering account for client. A real estate broker shall, within a reasonable time, render an account to his client and remit to him, any monies collected for his client, and unexpecded for his account.

Managing property for client. (a) When acting as an agent in the management of property, a real estate broker shall not accept any commission, rebate or profit on expenditures made for his client without his full knowledge and consent.

(b) A person, firm or corporation licensed or acting as a real estate broker, and having on deposit or otherwise in custody or control any money furnished as security by a tenant of real property, shall treat, handle and dispose of such money (including any required interest thereon) in compliance with the requirements of the General Obligations Law. Failure to so comply, including failure to pay, apply or credit any required interest, shall constitute grounds for disciplinary or other appropriate action by the Secretary of State.

Broker's purchase of property listed with him. A real estate broker shall not directly or indirectly buy for himself property listed with him, nor shall he acquire any interest therein without first making his true position clearly known to the listing owner.

Disclosure of interest to client. Before a real estate broker buys property for a client in the ownership of which the broker has an interest, he shall disclose his interest to all parties to the transaction.

Broker's sale of property in which he owns an interest. Before a real estate broker sells property in which he owns an interest, he shall make such interest known to the purchaser.

Compensation. A real estate broker shall make it clear for which party he is acting and he shall not receive compensation from more than one party except with the full knowledge and consent of all parties.

Negotiating with party to exclusive listing contract. No real estate broker shall negotiate the sale, exchange or lease of any property directly with an owner or lessor if he knows that such owner, or lessor, has an existing written contract granting exclusive authority in connection with such property with another broker.

Inducing breach of contract of sale or lease. No real estate broker shall induce any party to a contract of sale or lease to break such contract for the purpose of substituting in lieu thereof a new contract with another principal.

Broker's offering property for sale must be authorized. A real estate broker shall never offer a property for sale or lease without the authorization of the owner.

Sign on property. No sign shall ever be placed on any property by a real estate broker without the consent of the owner.

Delivering duplicate original of instrument. A real estate broker shall immediately deliver a duplicate original of any instrument to any party or parties executing the same, where such instrument has been prepared by such broker or under his supervision and where such instrument relates to the employment of the broker or to any matters pertaining to the consummation of a lease, or the purchase, sale or exchange of real property or any other type of real estate transaction in which he may participate as a broker.

Accepting services of another broker's salesman or employee. A real estate broker shall not accept the services of any salesman or employee in the organization of another real estate broker without the knowledge of the broker and no real estate broker should give or permit to be given or directly offer to give anything of value for the purpose of influencing or rewarding the actions of any salesman or employee of another real estate broker in relation to the business of such broker or the client of such broker without the knowledge of such broker.

Termination of salesman's association with broker. A real estate salesman shall, upon termination of his association with a real estate broker, forthwith turn over to such broker any and all listing information obtained during his association whether such information was originally given to him by the broker or copied from the records of such broker or acquired by the salesman during his association.

Automatic continuation of exclusive listing contract. No real estate broker shall be a party to an exclusive listing contract which shall contain an automatic continuation of the period of such listing beyond the fixed termination date set forth therein.

Prohibitions in relation to solicitation. (a) No broker or salesperson shall induce or attempt to induce an owner to sell or lease any residential property or to list same for sale or lease by making any representations regarding the entry or prospective entry into the neighborhood of a person or persons of a particular race, color, religion or national origin.

(b) No broker or salesperson shall solicit the sale, lease or the listing for sale or lease of residential property after such licensee has received notice from the owner thereof, or from the department, that such owner does not desire to sell or lease such residential property or does not desire to be solicited to sell, lease, or list for sale or lease, such property. A notice from the department under this section shall be in writing and shall be issued when the department has received written notification from the owner of the residential property that he or she does not desire to sell or lease such property, or does not desire to be solicited to list to sell or lease the same, and requests the department to so notify a particular broker or brokers, or brokers in general.

Use of trade or corporate name. No licensed

real estate broker or applicant applying for a real estate broker's license, may use a trade or corporate name which, in the opinion of the Department of State, is so similar to the trade name or corporate name of any licensed real estate broker that confusion to the public will result therefrom.

Net listing agreements. (a) The term *net listing* as used herein shall mean an agency or other agreement whereby a prospective seller of real property or an interest therein, lists such property or interest for sale with a licensed real estate broker authorizing the sale thereof at a specified net amount to be paid to the seller and authorizing the broker to retain as commission, compensation, or otherwise, the difference between the price at which the property or interest is sold and the specified net amount to be received by the seller.

(b) No real estate broker shall make or enter into a "net listing" contract for the sale of real property or any interest therein.

Branch offices. (a) Every branch office shall be owned, maintained and operated only by the licensed broker to whom the license for such office is issued. A branch office shall not be conducted, maintained and operated under an arrangement whereby a licensed salesman or employee of the broker shall pay, or be responsible for, any expense or obligation created or incurred in its conduct, maintenance or operation, or under any other arrangement, the purpose, intent or effect of which shall permit a licensed salesman or employee to carry on the business of real estate broker for his own benefit, directly, or indirectly, in whole or in part.

(b) Every branch office shall be under the direct supervision of the broker to whom the license is issued, or a representative broker of a corporation or partnership holding such license. A salesman licensed as such for a period of not less than two years and who has successfully completed a course of study in real estate approved by the Secretary of State, may be permitted to operate such a branch office only under the direct supervision of the broker provided the names of such salesman and supervising broker shall have been filed and recorded in the division of licenses of the Department of State.

(c) Supervision of such a licensed salesman shall include guidance, oversight, management, orientation, instruction and supervision in the management and operation of the branch office and

the business of real estate broker conducted therein.

(d) No broker shall relocate his principal office or any branch office without prior approval of the department.

Supervision of salesman by broker. (a) The supervision of a real estate salesman by a licensed real estate broker shall consist of regular, frequent and consistent personal guidance, instruction, oversight and superintendence by the real estate broker with respect to the general real estate brokerage business conducted by the broker, and all matters relating thereto.

(b) The broker and salesman shall keep written records of all real estate listings obtained by the salesman, and of all sales and other transactions effected by, and with the aid and assistance of, the salesman, during the period of his association, which records shall be sufficient to clearly identify the transactions and shall indicate the dates thereof. Such records must be submitted by the salesman to the Department of State with his application for a broker's license.

(c) Participation in the general real estate brokerage business as a licensed real estate salesman shall consist of active service under the supervision of a licensed real estate broker for at least 35 hours per week for 50 weeks in each year required for qualification under the law.

Ownership of voting stock by salesmen prohibited. No licensed real estate salesman may own, either singly or jointly, directly or indirectly, any voting shares of stock in any licensed real estate brokerage corporation with which he is associated.

Records of transactions to be maintained. (a) Each licensed broker shall keep and maintain for a period of three years records of each transaction effected through his office concerning the sale or mortgage of one to four family dwellings. Such records shall contain the names and addresses of the seller, the buyer, mortgagee, if any, the purchase price and resale price, if any, amount of deposit paid on contract, amount of commission paid to broker, or gross profit realized by the broker if purchased by him for resale, expenses of procuring the mortgage loan, if any, the net commission or net profit realized by the broker showing the disposition of all payments made by the broker. In lieu thereof each broker shall keep and maintain, in connection with each such transaction a copy of (1) contract of sale, (2) commission agreement, (3) closing statement, (4) statement showing disposition of proceeds of mortgage loan.

(b) Each licensed broker engaged in the business of soliciting and granting mortgage loans to purchasers of one to four family dwellings shall keep and maintain for a period of three years, a record of the name of the applicant, the amount of the mortgage proceeds, a copy of the verification of employment and financial status of the applicant, a copy of the inspection and compliance report with the Baker Law requirements of FHA with the name of the inspector. Such records shall be available to the Department of State at all times upon request.

Advertising. (a) All advertisements placed by a broker must indicate that the advertiser is a broker or give the name of the broker and his telephone number.

(b) All advertisements placed by a broker which state that property is in the vicinity of a geographical area or territorial subdivision must include as part of such advertisement the name of the geographical area or territorial subdivision in which such property is actually located.

Disclaimer. Nothing in this Part is intended to be, or should be construed as, an indication that a salesperson is either an independent contractor or employee of a broker.

Subjects for study—real estate salesperson. The following are the required subjects to be included in the course of study in real estate for licensure as a real estate salesperson, and the required minimum number of hours to be devoted to each such subject:

Subject	Hours
Real estate instruments	6
Law of agency	5
Real estate financing	5
Valuation and listing procedures	5
Law of contracts	5
License law and ethics	5
Human rights—fair housing	4

Closing and closing costs	4
Land use regulations	3
Real estate mathematics	3

Subjects for study—real estate broker. The following are the required subjects to be included in a course of study in real estate for licensure as a real estate broker and the required minimum number of hours to be devoted to each such subject:

Subject	Hours
Operation of a real estate broker's office	10
General business law	5
Construction	3
Subdivision and development	3
Leases and agreements	3
Liens and easements	3
Taxes and assessments	3
Investment property	3
Voluntary and involuntary alienation	3
Property management	2
Condominiums and cooperatives	2
Appraisal	2
Advertising	2
Rent regulations	1

College degree major in real estate. Evidence satisfactory to the department of the successful completion of a course of study at any accredited college or university in the United States of America, approved by the Commissioner of Education of the State of New York or by a regional accrediting agency, accepted by said Commissioner of Education, which has a program leading to a recognized collegiate degree, which includes therein a major in real estate, may be deemed acceptable for educational credit provided attendance at such real estate course is not less than 90 hours in the case of an applicant for licensure as a real estate broker, and 45 hours in the case of an applicant for licensure as a real estate salesperson, and the applicant presents evidence of the issuance of a bachelor's degree and that he has passed the required course in real estate.

9

Valuation and Listing Procedures

Key Terms

Arm's-length transaction
Comparative market analysis (CMA)
Cost approach
Demand
Depreciation
Economic obsolesence
Exclusive-agency listing
Exclusive-right-to-sell listing
Functional obsolesence
Income approach
Listing agreement
Locational obsolesence

Market
Market comparison approach
Market value
Multiple-listing service (MLS)
Net listing
Nonhomogeneity
Open listing
Physical deterioration
Situs
Subject property
Supply
Value

Overview

This chapter will discuss the nature and characteristics of land and the concept of value particularly as it is tested by the influences of supply and demand in the real estate market. The listing agreement, which comprises the broker's stock in trade, can take many forms, each with its own rights and responsibilities for principal and agent. This chapter will examine these forms of listing agreements. The real estate broker needs at least a rudimentary knowledge of basic appraisal. A fuller treatment is found in Chapter 16, which some students may wish to read also at this point.

Characteristics of Real Estate

Unlike many commodities sold on the open market, real estate possesses unique characteristics that affect its use both directly and indirectly. These fall into two broad categories: economic characteristics and physical characteristics (*see* Figure 9.1).

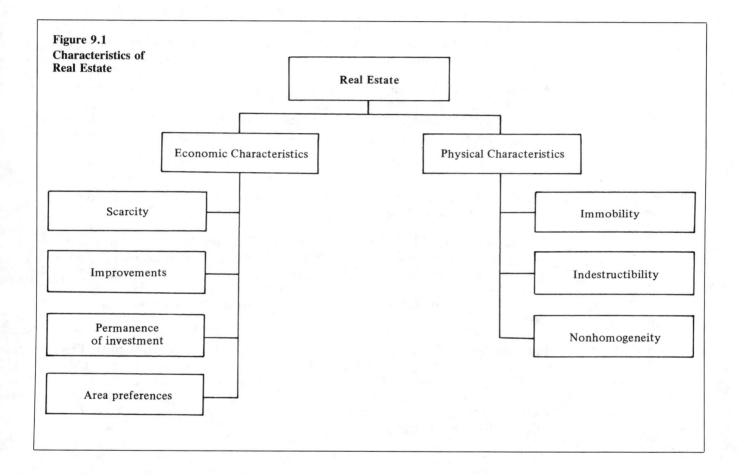

**Figure 9.1
Characteristics of
Real Estate**

Economic Characteristics

The basic economic characteristics of land are: (1) relative scarcity, (2) improvements, (3) permanence of investment, and (4) area preferences.

Relative scarcity. The total supply of land is fixed. While there is still a considerable amount of land not in use, land in a given location or of a particular quality is scarce in some areas.

Improvements. The building of an improvement on one parcel of land has an effect on the value and utilization of neighboring tracts. Not only does an improvement affect adjoining tracts, it often has a direct bearing on whole communities. For example, the improvement of a parcel of real estate by the construction of a steel plant or the selection of a site for the building of an atomic reactor can directly influence a large area favorably or unfavorably.

Permanence of investment. After land has been improved, the capital and labor needed to build the improvement represent a fixed investment. Although older buildings can be razed, improvements such as drainage, electricity, water, and sewerage remain. The income return on such investments is long-term and relatively stable and usually extends over what is referred to as the economic life of the improvement.

Area preference. This economic characteristic, often called **situs,** refers to people's choices and preferences for a given area. It is the unique quality of people's preferences that makes a house in a given location sell for twice as much as a similar one on the other side of town.

Examples of likes and dislikes are numerous. Social influences caused the rapid movement of people to suburban areas. Some are now returning to the urban areas, however, preferring the environments and amenities offered by city living to those offered by suburbia. *Area preference is the most important economic characteristic of land.*

Physical Characteristics

The basic physical characteristics of land are: (1) immobility, (2) indestructibility, and (3) nonhomogeneity.

Immobility. Land, which is the earth's surface, is immobile. It is true that some of the substances of land are removable and that topography can be changed but still that part of the earth's surface always remains. *The geographic location of any given parcel of land can never be changed.* It is rigid; it is fixed. Because land is immobile, real estate laws and markets tend to be local in character.

Indestructibility. Just as land is immobile, it is *durable* and *indestructible.* This permanence, not only of land but also of the improvements (including the buildings) that are placed on it, has tended to stabilize investments in land. The fact that land is indestructible does not, of course, change the fact that the improvements on land do depreciate and can become obsolete, thereby reducing—or possibly destroying—values.

Nonhomogeneity. The characteristic of **nonhomogeneity** stems from the fact that no two parcels of land are ever exactly the same. Although there may be substantial similarity, *all parcels differ geographically* as each parcel has its own location.

Characteristics Define Land Use

The various characteristics of a parcel of real estate affect its desirability for a specific use. Physical and economic factors that would affect land use include: (1) contour and elevation of the parcel, (2) prevailing winds, (3) transportation, (4) public improvements, and (5) availability of natural resources, such as water. Hilly, heavily wooded land would need considerable work before it could be used for industrial purposes but would be ideally suited for residential use. Flat land located along a major highway network would be undesirable for residential use but well-located for industry.

Real Estate—The Business of Value

The real estate industry deals with real estate and its value. Value is not the same as price nor is it the same as cost. Specifically **value** can be defined as *the amount of goods or services that will be offered in the marketplace in exchange for any given product.* It also has been described as the *present worth of future benefits.*

The value of real property does not remain the same. Changes in the cost of construction material can increase the objective value of property and differing standards and needs can alter a personal estimate of value. A housing shortage may increase the market value of even older, less desirable houses, while building a better road may cause the value of property along an older road to decrease. Availability of financing also may affect the property's value.

In real estate the concept of *cost* generally relates to the past, *price* to the present, and *value* to the future. Value does not rise in exact proportion to inflation or to the cost of living, as is illustrated in Table 9.1.

Table 9.1 Changing Values in Selected Cities

Median Sales Price of Existing Single-Family Homes for Metropolitan Areas			
	1983	**1984**	**1985**
Albany/Schenectady/Troy	$49,400	$52,900	$60,300
Buffalo/Niagara Falls	*	44,800	46,600
New York/Northern New Jersey/Long Island	88,900	105,300	133,600
Rochester	54,800	59,600	64,200
Syracuse	*	50,700	58,800
Boston	82,600	100,000	134,200
Chicago	76,500	79,500	81,100
Cleveland	*	62,700	63,300
Los Angeles Area	112,700	115,300	116,900
Philadelphia	59,600	60,300	68,300
Washington, D.C.	89,400	93,000	97,100
United States	70,300	72,400	75,200

SOURCE: National Association of REALTORS®.
*Not available.

The Real Estate Market

In literal terms a **market** is a place where goods can be bought and sold, where a price can be established, and where it becomes advantageous for buyers and sellers to trade. The function of the market is to facilitate this exchange by providing a setting in which the *supply and demand forces* of the economy can establish price levels.

Supply and Demand

The economic forces of supply and demand continually interact in the market to establish and maintain price levels. Essentially *when supply goes up, prices will drop; when demand increases, prices will rise* (*see* Figure 9.2).

Supply can be defined as *the amount of goods offered for sale within the market at a given price during a given time period.*

Figure 9.2
Supply and Demand

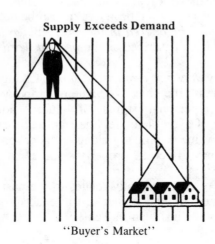

Supply Exceeds Demand

"Buyer's Market"

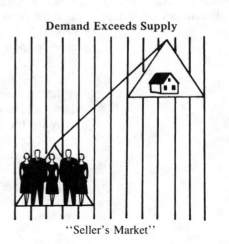

Demand Exceeds Supply

"Seller's Market"

Demand can be defined as *the number of people willing and able to accept the available goods at any given price during a given time period.*

Supply and demand in the real estate market. Because real estate is fixed in nature (immobile), it cannot be moved from area to area to satisfy the pressures of supply and demand. For this reason the real estate business has local markets where offices can maintain detailed familiarity with the market conditions and available units.

Because of its characteristics of nonstandardization and immobility, the real estate market is relatively slow to adjust to changes in supply and demand. The product cannot be removed from the market or transferred to another market, so an oversupply usually results in a lowering of price levels. But because development and construction of real estate take a considerable period of time from conception to completion, increases in demand may not be met immediately. Building and housing construction may occur in uneven spurts of activity.

Factors Affecting Supply

Factors that tend to affect supply in the real estate market include the labor supply, construction costs, and government controls and financial policies (*see* Figure 9.3).

Labor supply and construction costs. A shortage of labor in the skilled building trades, an increase in the cost of building materials, or a scarcity of materials will tend to lower the amount of housing that will be built. High interest rates also severely curtail construction. The impact depends on the extent to which higher costs can be passed on to the buyer or renter in the form of higher purchase prices or rentals.

Government controls and financial policies. The government can influence the amount of money available for real estate investment through its fiscal and/or

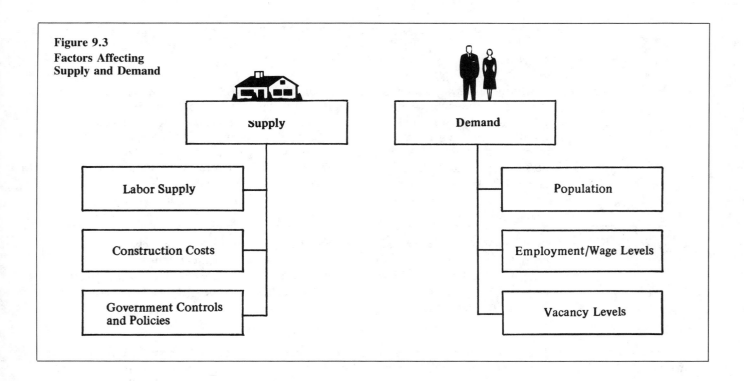

Figure 9.3
Factors Affecting
Supply and Demand

Supply

Demand

Labor Supply

Construction Costs

Government Controls
and Policies

Population

Employment/Wage Levels

Vacancy Levels

monetary policies. At the local level, policies on taxation of real estate can have either positive or negative effects. Tax incentives have been one way for communities to attract new businesses and industries to their areas. Along with these enterprises come increased employment and expanded residential real estate markets. Where land is not being used to its maximum potential, some urban areas adjust the assessment and, by taxing the land and improvements at higher levels, force a more productive use of the real estate.

Local governments also can affect market operations and the development and construction of real estate by applying land-use controls. Health, fire, zoning, and building ordinances are used by communities to control and stimulate the highest potential use of land. Community amenities such as churches, schools, and parks and efficient governmental policies are influential factors affecting the real estate market.

Factors Affecting Demand

Factors that tend to affect demand in the real estate market include population, employment and wage levels, and vacancy levels (*see* Figure 9.3).

Population. Population trends have a basic influence on the sale of real estate. Because shelter (whether in the form of owned or rented property) is a basic human and family need, the general need for housing will grow as the population grows. Although the total population of the country is increasing, this trend is not uniform in all localities.

In a consideration of the impact of population on the real estate market, the makeup of the population, or *demographics,* also must be taken into account. In recent years an increasing number of residential units are being purchased by singles or one-parent families.

Employment and wage levels. Employment opportunities and wage levels in a small community can be drastically affected in a short period of time by decisions made by major employers in the area.

Vacancy levels. Vacancy levels in a community provide a good indication of the demand for housing. A growing shortage of housing (a lower number of vacancies) will result in increasing rents. Conversely because real estate is a fixed commodity and cannot be removed from the market, an increase in vacancies will force rents down. As a rule of thumb, when the vacancy level goes below five percent, sale and rental prices tend to increase and when the vacancy level rises above five percent, prices tend to weaken.

Appraisal

Real estate usually is appraised using one of three different approaches: *cost approach, income approach,* or *market comparison approach*. Each is appropriate for a different type of real estate. Some elaborate appraisals study the **subject property** (the parcel being evaluated) through all three methods, reconciling the results for a final estimate of value.

Approaches to Appraisal

The **cost approach** estimates the amount needed to reproduce or replace the property being studied. This approach is most appropriate for non-income-producing buildings that cannot easily be compared with others: hospitals, schools, churches, fire stations. It also is used for insurance purposes. The cost approach considers not only the cost of reconstructing buildings but also the amount of **depreciation** that has already subtracted value from the property. Depreciation falls into three categories: **physical deterioration, functional obsolesence** (undesirable or outmoded features), and **economic (locational) obsolesence** (undesirable factors located beyond the property lines).

The **income approach** to appraisal estimates value by analyzing the income generated by the property being considered. It is appropriate for valuation of commercial, industrial, and rental property.

The **market comparison approach** evaluates property by careful study of similar parcels recently sold. The process is based upon research and study of data. It is most appropriate for single residences.

Market Value

Market value is an important concept defined as the *probable price a property will bring in a competitive and open market, offered by an informed seller and allowing a reasonable time to find a purchaser who buys the property with knowledge of all the uses to which it is adapted, neither buyer nor seller being under duress.*

Market value, in other words, is the best price obtainable in a free, open, and informed market. The concept of market value also supposes an **arm's-length transaction,** defined as one between relative strangers, each trying to do the best for himself or herself. A sale between mother and son, for example, is not likely to be an arm's-length transaction and may not yield full market value for the property.

Market value is not to be confused with cost or even with selling price. In an ideal market each parcel would sell for its exact value but outside factors may cause a sale to be made below market value and sometimes above market value.

Listing Property

Every real estate sale involves two parties. The first is the seller. The second is the buyer. It is the seller who furnishes the real estate broker and salesperson with the necessary inventory: that is, the *listing*. How complete and accurately priced this inventory is will determine the broker's ultimate success.

To acquire their inventories brokers and salespeople must obtain listings. As discussed in Chapter 2, a listing agreement creates a special agency relationship between a broker (agent) and a seller (principal) whereby the agent is authorized to represent his or her principal's property for sale, solicit offers, and submit the offers to the principal. Listing agreements generally are written contracts of employment although in New York oral agreements may be used if the term of the listing is for less than one year.

Only a broker can act as agent to list, sell, or rent another person's real estate. While both broker and salesperson have the authority to list, lease, and sell property and provide other services to a principal, state license laws stipulate that these acts must be done in the name and under the supervision of the broker, never in the name of the salesperson.

Listing Agreements

The forms of listing agreements, or employment contracts, used in New York are: (1) open listing, (2) exclusive-agency listing, and (3) exclusive-right-to-sell listing. Their similarities and differences are examined in Table 9.2.

Table 9.2
Listing Agreements

Type of Listing	Who Can Sell		
	Seller	Agent	Other Brokers
Open Listing	x	x	x
Exclusive-Agency Listing	x	x	
Exclusive-Right-to-Sell Listing	x		

Open listing. In an **open listing** the seller retains the right to employ any number of brokers to act as agents. The seller is obligated to pay a commission only to that broker who successfully produces a ready, willing, and able buyer. If the seller personally sells the property *without the aid of any of the brokers,* he or she is not obligated to pay any of them a commission. A listing contract generally creates an open listing unless wording that specifically provides otherwise is included.

Exclusive-agency listing. In an **exclusive-agency listing** *only one broker* is specifically authorized to act as the exclusive agent of the principal. The *seller* under this form of agreement *retains the right to sell the property himself or herself* without obligation to the broker.

Exclusive-right-to-sell listing. In an **exclusive-right-to-sell listing** one broker is appointed as sole agent of the seller and is given the exclusive right or *authorization* to represent the property in question. Under this form of contract the seller must pay the broker a commission *regardless of who sells the property* if it is sold while the listing is in effect. If the seller gives a broker an exclusive-right-to-sell listing but finds a buyer without the broker's assistance, the seller must still pay the broker a commission. (An example of this form of agreement is reproduced in Figure 9.6.)

Net listing. Not legal in this state, a net listing is based on the amount of money the seller will receive if the property is sold. The seller's property is listed for this net amount and the broker is free to offer the property for sale at any price higher than the listing price. If the property is sold, the broker pays the seller only the net amount for which the property was listed and keeps the rest. *This type of listing is illegal in New York.*

Multiple Listing

A **multiple-listing service (MLS)** is usually organized within a geographic area by a group of brokers who agree to pool their listings.

The multiple-listing agreement, while not actually a separate form of listing, is in effect an *exclusive-right-to-sell* or *exclusive agency* with an additional authority to *distribute the listing to other brokers who belong to the multiple-listing service.* The contractual obligations among the member brokers of a multiple-listing organization vary widely. Most provide that upon sale of the property *the commission is divided between the listing broker and the selling broker.* Terms for division of the commission vary by individual arrangement between brokers.

Under most multiple-listing contracts the broker who secures the listing is not only authorized but *obligated* to turn the listing over to his or her multiple-listing within a definite period of time so that it can be distributed to other member brokers.

A multiple-listing offers advantages to both the broker and the seller. Brokers develop a sizable inventory of properties to be sold and are assured of a portion of the commission if they list the property or participate in its sale. Sellers also gain under this form of listing agreement because all members of the multiple-listing organization work to sell their property.

Termination of Listings

As discussed in Chapter 2, a listing agreement—or any agency relationship—may be terminated for any of the following reasons: (1) performance by the broker, (2) expiration of the time period stated in the agreement, (3) abandonment by the broker if he or she spends no time on the listing, (4) revocation by the owner (although the owner may be liable for the broker's expenses), (5) cancellation by the broker or by mutual consent, (6) bankruptcy, death, or insanity of either party, (7) destruction of the property, or (8) a change in property use by outside forces (such as a change in zoning).

Expiration of listing period. All listings should specify a definite period of time during which the broker is to be employed. The use of automatic extensions of time in exclusive listings has been outlawed in New York.

Obtaining Listings

All legal owners of the listing property or their authorized agents as well as the listing salesperson and/or broker should sign the listing agreement. The listing salesperson can sign the contract in the broker's name if authorized by the broker.

Information needed for listing agreements. It is important to obtain as much information as possible concerning a parcel of real estate when taking a listing. This ensures that all possible contingencies can be anticipated, particularly when the listing will be shared with other brokers and salespeople in a multiple listing arrangement. This information includes the following (where appropriate):

1. names and addresses of owners;
2. legal description of the property;
3. size of lot (frontage and depth);
4. number and sizes of rooms and total square footage;
5. construction and age of the building;
6. information relative to the neighborhood (schools, churches, transportation);
7. current taxes;
8. amount of existing financing (including interest, payments, and other costs);
9. utilities and average payments;
10. appliances to be included in the transaction;
11. date of occupancy or possession;
12. possibility of seller financing;
13. zoning classification (especially important for vacant land); and
14. a detailed list of exactly what will and what will not be included in the sales price.

A real estate broker, as an agent of the seller, is responsible for the disclosure of any material information regarding the property. Getting as much initial information from the seller as possible—even if it becomes necessary to ask penetrating and possibly embarrassing questions—will pay off in the long run by saving both principal and agent from potential legal difficulties. The agent also should assume the responsibility of searching the public records for such pertinent information as legal description, lot size, and yearly taxes.

The *true tax* figure should be used, disregarding any present veteran's, aged, or religious exemption, or any addition for unpaid water bills.

In the sale of multiple dwellings the seller should be ready to present a statement of rents and expenses, preferably prepared by an accountant. Prospective buyers will want statements on leases and security deposits. The listing agent should verify zoning and the legality of existing use. The seller should be informed of any necessity for a certificate of occupancy at transfer. Arranging with tenants to show the property at reasonable times is also of vital importance.

Truth-in-Heating Law. New York's Truth-in-Heating law requires the seller to furnish upon written request two past years' heating and cooling bills to any prospective buyer of a one- or two-family home. Sellers also must furnish a statement on the extent and type of insulation they have installed together with any information the seller may have on insulation installed by previous owners.

Pricing the Property

After a listing is secured and all necessary information obtained, the pricing of the real estate is of primary importance. While it is the responsibility of the broker or salesperson to advise, counsel, and assist, it is ultimately the *seller* who must determine a listing price for his or her property. However, because the average seller usually does not have the background to make an informed decision about a fair market price, the real estate agent must be prepared to offer his or her knowledge, information, and expertise in this area. A broker should reject any listing in which the price has been substantially exaggerated.

A broker or salesperson can help the seller determine a listing price for the property through a **comparative market analysis.** This is a comparison of the prices of recently sold homes that are similar in location, style, and amenities to that of the listing seller. If no such comparison can be made or if the seller feels that his or her property is unique in some way, a full-scale real estate appraisal—a professional, detailed estimate of a property's value—may be warranted.

Although it has some resemblance to a market approach appraisal, a comparative market analysis (CMA) differs from an appraisal in several important ways. It is usually offered as a free service by a salesperson or broker, contrasting with the paid appraisal rendered by a fee appraiser. Both studies analyze recent sales of similar properties, but the CMA does so in a more superficial manner. The CMA includes material not usually considered in regular appraisals: information on nearby properties that *failed* to sell, for example, and a list of competing property currently on the market. Brokers' ethics dictate that a CMA must never be called a "free appraisal." A comparative market analysis form is illustrated in Figure 9.4.

The broker should convey to the seller the fact that the eventual selling price is set by the buying public through the operation of supply and demand in the open market. Among factors that should not determine listing price are the original cost, assessed value, replacement cost, and the amount the seller needs to realize from the property.

Sample Listing Agreement

Figure 9.5 is a typical listing agreement. The individual specifics of a listing may vary from area to area and state law may require that additional provisions be added to such contracts. Following is a section-by-section analysis of the sample agreement; numerical references are to the specific provisions of the contract.

1. *Exclusive right to sell.* The title specifies that this document is an "exclusive right to sell" real property.
2. *Date.* The date of the listing contract is the date it is executed; this may not necessarily be the date that the contract becomes effective.
3. *Names.* The names of all persons having an interest in the property should be specified and should enter into the agreement. If the property is owned under one of the forms of co-ownership discussed in Chapter 3, that fact should be clearly established.
4. *Broker or firm.* The name of the broker or firm entering into the listing must be clearly stated in the agreement.
5. *Contract.* This section establishes the document as a *bilateral contract* and states the promises by both parties that create and bind the agreement.
6, 7. *Commission rate.* This paragraph establishes the broker's rate of commission. Price fixing is illegal so a broker's commission is open to negotiation between owner and broker.

Figure 9.4
Comparative Market Analysis

Date: _____

Comparative Market Analysis for _____

Sugg. list price $ _____

Address	Style	Const	Age	No. of Rms	No. of Bdrms	No. of Baths	Gar	Fplc	Pool	C/A	Size Prop	Assess Value	Taxes	Comments & Extras	Fair Market Value

1. SIMILAR HOMES RECENTLY SOLD: These tell us what people are willing to pay . . . for this kind of home . . . in this area . . . at this time

Closed Price | Date | Adjustd Price

2. SIMILAR HOMES FOR SALE NOW: These tell us what we are competing against. Buyers will compare your home against these homes.

Askg Price | Days On Mkt.

3. EXPIRED LISTINGS — SIMILAR HOMES UNSOLD FOR 90 DAYS OR MORE: These illustrate the problems of over pricing.

PROBLEMS OF OVERPRICING:

A. HARD to get salespeople excited.
B. HARD to get people to make an offer.
C. HARD to get good buyers to look.
D. HARD to get financing.

SOURCE: John E. Cyr and Joan M. Sobeck, *Real Estate Brokerage: A Success Guide* (Chicago: Real Estate Education Company, 1982), p. 161.

Figure 9.5
Sample Listing
Agreement

SAMPLE FORM

EXCLUSIVE RIGHT TO SELL LISTING CONTRACT (1)

This agreement is made and entered into this _____ day of _____, 19_(2)_, by and between _____(3)_____ as owner or owners (referred to herein as "owner"), of the real estate described herein and _____ of _____(4)_____, Indiana, as licensed real estate broker (referred to herein as "broker"). The parties, by signing this contract, agree as follows:

1. The broker hereby agrees to list for sale the property described herein and to use his best efforts to find a purchaser for the property upon the terms and conditions set out in this agreement or upon such other terms as are acceptable to the owner. Owner agrees that broker shall have the exclusive right to sell said property for the period of this listing contract upon the terms specified herein or any other terms accepted by owner. (5)

2. In return for the broker's acceptance of this exclusive right to sell listing contract the owner hereby agrees:

    (a) that, in the event the broker, owner or other person finds a purchaser who is ready, willing and able to purchase the property described herein upon the terms specified herein or any other terms accepted by the owner, the broker shall have completed his performance under this contract and the owner shall pay the broker a commission for his services in an amount equal to _____(6)_____ (_____%) percent of the gross sales price, but not less than $ _____(7)_____;

    (b) that, in the event negotiations with a potential purchaser are begun by the broker, owner or any other person during the period of this listing contract or if negotiations are begun after its expiration date with a purchaser who was first contacted during the period of this listing contract and the property is sold to such purchaser within _____ months after the expiration date of this contract on the terms hereof or on any other terms accepted by the owner, owner shall pay the broker a commission on the same basis as set out herein unless the property at the time of sale is listed with another licensed broker. Owner hereby represents that there is not now any other listing contract in force with another licensed broker. (8)

In order to promote the purposes for which this contract is entered into and to further define the rights and duties of the owner and the broker, it is further agreed:

1. The broker is authorized to retain on behalf of the owner any earnest money deposit which may be made by the potential purchaser and to retain it until the sale is completed. In the event that a contract of sale is entered into and the purchaser defaults, the earnest money deposit shall be applied first to the broker's advertising expenses and other expenses incurred by the broker under this listing contract and the balance shall be divided between the owner and the broker. Both parties agree, however, to do whatever is necessary to enforce the contract made with such purchaser to collect any sums which may be due under such contract. (9)

2. The broker or his representatives (including other brokers or salesmen under any multiple listing arrangement to which the broker may be a party) shall have access to the property described below at all reasonable times for the purposes of showing to prospective purchasers. The broker is authorized to place a "For Sale" sign on this property, to reveal any and all information which appears in this listing contract and to advertise the property for the purpose of promoting its sale. (10)

3. The listing price includes the balances due on all mortgages, liens, assessments for municipal improvements, current real estate taxes and balances due on personal property or fixtures

**Figure 9.5
(continued)**

which are a part of the property described herein and that such balances shall be paid by the owner prior to or at the time of sale of the property unless the contract of sale provides otherwise. Seller recognizes his responsibility for and agrees to advise the broker of any municipal improvements contracted for. (11)

4. The owner represents and warrants that the property is free and clear of all encumbrances except those noted above and except easements and restrictions of record and current taxes and that the present use of the property does not violate any restriction or zoning ordinance; (12) that the owner is the sole owner of the property and that he will execute a general warranty deed or land contract (if applicable) in the event of sale and will furnish an abstract of title showing a merchantable title or a title insurance policy showing an insurable title for the amount of the sales price; (13) that all information appearing anywhere in this contract including that on the reverse side is true and correct to the best of owner's knowledge; (14) and that all operating equipment which is included in the sale of the property will be in good operating order at the time of closing of the sale except _____ (15) _____ .

5. The property is offered for sale without regard to race, creed, color or national origin in accordance with applicable State and Federal laws. (16)

The period of this listing is from _____ A.M./P.M. of _____, 19 _____, up to and including 11:00 P.M. of _____ (17) _____, 19 _____. The agreed upon listing price is $ _____, in cash or upon any other price, term, or exchange to which owner agrees. Both parties agree that this contract: is freely entered into; this writing constitutes the entire agreement; is binding upon their heirs, administrators, executors and assigns; is without relief from valuation and appraisement laws; includes the obligation to pay necessary attorney's fees of the other for its enforcement. Owner by signing below, hereby acknowledges receipt of a copy of this contract. The address and location of the listed property are: _____

_____

the legal description of which is: _____

_____

Other Conditions: _____

_____

_____   _____
       (Owner)   (Owner)

                       _____
                      (Real Estate Broker or Firm)

by_____

Title:_____

8. *Extension clause*. This section, permitted in New York, will protect the broker if the owner or another person sells the property after the listing expires to a person with whom the original broker negotiated. In other words the broker is guaranteed a commission for a set period of time after the agreement expires (generally three to six months) if he or she was the procuring cause of the sale even if the broker did not actually consummate the transaction. This extension clause does not apply, however, if the owner signs a new listing agreement with another broker after the original agreement expires.

9. *Broker's responsibilities*. This paragraph defines the rights and duties of the broker.

10. *Broker's authority*. Here the broker is given the authority to place a sign on the property and show it to buyers as well as the permission to supply the buyers with any and all information that may appear on the listing form. Without such permission this information would be confidential and could not be revealed to anyone without breaching the agency doctrine of confidence.

11. *Listing price*. The listing price is a gross sales price and the owner should understand that any obligations such as taxes, mortgages, and assessments remain his or her responsibility and must be paid out of the proceeds of the sale.

12. *Encumbrances*. This paragraph points out responsibilities of encumbrances, which are especially important to the broker because they determine whether or not the property is salable.

13. *Evidence of ownership and deed*. The type of deed to be executed and proof of ownership in the form of a title are stated here.

14. *Liabilities*. The owner protects both buyer and broker with this statement.

15. *Warranty of fitness*. Although the buyer has the duty to inspect the property, exhaustive tests of all equipment are not necessary. This generally implied warranty of fitness protects the buyer against misrepresentation.

16. *Civil rights legislation*. This clause serves to alert the owner that both federal and state legislation exist to protect against discrimination.

17. *Termination of agreement*. Both the exact time and the date serve to remove any ambiguity in regard to termination of the contract. A particular termination date does not necessarily include that day itself unless the phrase "up to and including" is used.

New York State Requirements

Regulations issued pursuant to Article 12A of the New York Real Property Law provide that the broker must have attached to or printed on the reverse side of an exclusive agreement a statement to the following effect:

An exclusive-right-to-sell listing means that if you, the property owner, find a buyer for your house or if another broker finds a buyer, you must pay the agreed-upon commission to the present broker.

An exclusive-agency listing means that if you, the property owner, find a buyer, you will not have to pay a commission to the broker. However, if another broker finds a buyer you will owe a commission to both the selling broker and your present broker.

The owner must sign the statement.

If an exclusive listing of residential property is obtained by a broker who is a member of a multiple listing service: (1) the broker must give the homeowner a list of the names and addresses of all member brokers; and (2) the listing agreement must allow the seller to choose whether all negotiated offers to purchase will be submitted through the listing broker or through the selling broker.

The statement describing various types of listings available is found at the end of the listing agreement of the Real Estate Board of Rochester, NY, Inc., as shown in Figure 9.6.

Income Tax Benefits for Home Sellers

Although sellers should be referred to their accountants or attorneys for specific information, many ask the real estate broker about the regulations on profit from the sale of real estate. Where one's own primary residence is being sold, two special tax treatments apply.

In New York State, federal tax benefits for homeowners will also apply to state income tax. Special tax breaks are available if the homeowner is over 55 at the time of sale or if the residence is replaced with another. Failing that, special tax techniques like income-averaging or installment sale may fit particular situations.

Deferment of tax. If a main residence is replaced with another within 24 months before or after the sale of the first home, profit on the first property is not immediately taxable but is "buried" in the cost basis of the new residence. It will not be taxed until some time in the future when the next home is sold. If the replacement residence costs less than the first one sold for, a portion of the profit may be immediately taxable; the rest qualifies for postponement.

In the following example a first home is sold for $107,700, of which $32,700 represents profit. A replacement residence is purchased for $100,000. Only $7,700 of the profit is taxable in the same year as the sale. The remaining $25,000 of untaxed profit is rolled over into the cost basis of the new home. Some day, when profit on the new home is figured, its cost basis will be $75,000 rather than $100,000.

Old residence adjusted sales price:		$107,700
Less cost of new home:		− 100,000
Taxable gain:		$ 7,700
Cost of new home:		$100,000
Less:		
gain from old home:	$32,700	
minus taxable gain:	− 7,700	
Deferred gain:	$25,000	− 25,000
Tax basis of new home:		$ 75,000

Over 55 exclusion. A homeowner who sells or exchanges his or her principal residence and (1) was 55 or older by the date of sale or exchange, and (2) owned and used the property sold or exchanged as a principal residence for a period totaling at least three years within the five-year period ending on the date of the sale, may exclude from his or her gross income part or all of the capital gain on that sale or exchange. Taxpayers who meet these requirements can exclude the

**Figure 9.6
Sample MLS
Listing Contract**

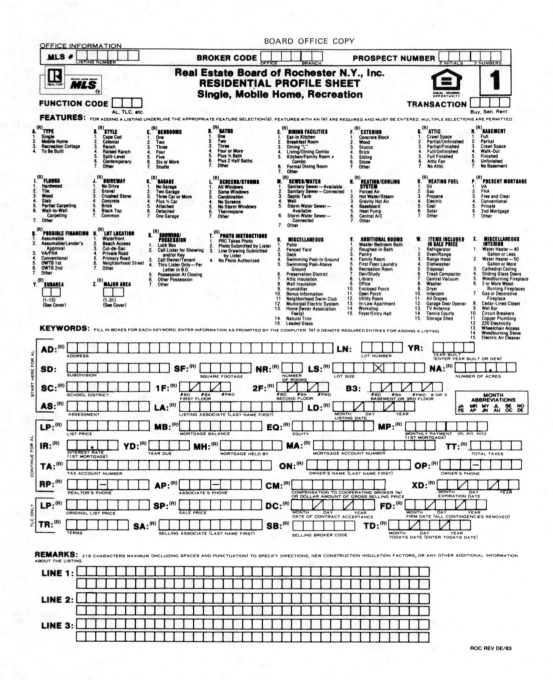

Figure 9.6
(continued)

REALTOR EXCLUSIVE RIGHT TO SELL, EXCHANGE OR LEASE CONTRACT. COMMISSIONS OR FEES FOR REAL ESTATE SERVICES TO BE PROVIDED HEREUNDER ARE NEGOTIABLE BETWEEN REALTOR® AND OWNER. IT IS UNDERSTOOD THAT THE REAL ESTATE BOARD OF ROCHESTER, N.Y., INC. (Including its MLS) IS NOT A PARTY TO THIS LISTING AGREEMENT.

A. OWNERSHIP OF PROPERTY AND POWER TO SIGN CONTRACT. I am the Owner(s) of the property located at __240 Hemingway Drive, Rochester NY 14620__ (the Property). I have complete legal authority to sell, exchange or lease the Property. I have not entered into any other contract which would affect the sale, exchange or lease of the Property; except as follows:

_____ (name or specify contract).

B. EXCLUSIVE RIGHT TO SELL, EXCHANGE OR LEASE.
__X__ I hereby hire __Sun City Realty__ _____ (Realtor) to sell or exchange the Property and I hereby grant to Realtor, the Exclusive Right To Sell the Property for the price of $ __97,000.00__ or any other price that I later agree to, and upon such terms and conditions as I may agree to or to exchange the Property upon such terms and conditions as I may agree to.

_____ I hereby hire Realtor to lease the Property and I hereby grant to Realtor the Exclusive Right To Lease the Property for a rent of _____ per _____ or any other rent that I may later agree to, and upon such terms and conditions as I may agree to.

C. PAYMENT TO REALTOR.
__X__ I will pay Realtor a commission of __6__ % of the sale price of the Property as set forth in the purchase and sale contract that I sign, or a commission of _____ if the Property is exchanged.

_____ I will pay Realtor a commission of _____ % of the gross rent for the Property as set forth in the lease contract that I sign, or such other compensation arrangement as is agreed upon in writing, a copy of which is attached.

D. SUBMISSION OF OFFERS TO PURCHASE. I agree that any offers to purchase, exchange or lease the Property shall be submitted through the (listing) (selling) broker.

E. FOR SALE, FOR RENT SIGN. I (do) (do not) want a "for sale" or "for rent" sign placed on the Property.

F. ADDITIONAL TERMS AND CONDITIONS. I agree that the "Additional Terms and Conditions" on the back of this page are part of this Contract.

G. LIFE OF CONTRACT. This Contract will last until midnight on __January 1__, 19__--__. For the purpose of Paragraph 4 of the Additional Terms and Conditions, the effective period shall be __60 days__ days after this Contract ends.

H. EXPLANATION: The owner does hereby certify that the following is understood:
An "exclusive right to sell" listing means that if you, the owner of the property, find a buyer for your house, or if another broker finds a buyer, you must pay the agreed commission to the present broker.
An "exclusive agency" listing means that if you, the owner of the property, find a buyer, you will not have to pay a commission to the broker. However, if another broker finds a buyer, you will owe a commission to both the selling broker and your present broker.

Date: __July 1, 19--__   Owner __John Q. Public__
                          Owner __Mary Public__

                          Realtor __Sun City Realty__
                          By: __Susy Salesperson__

REAL ESTATE BOARD OF ROCHESTER, N.Y., INC.

ADDITIONAL TERMS AND CONDITIONS

1. MULTIPLE LISTING SERVICE. Realtor will submit this Contract to the multiple listing service of the Real Estate Board of Rochester ("MLS") within 48 hours of my signing this Contract, excluding Saturdays, Sundays and holidays.

2. DUTIES OF REALTOR AND OWNER. Realtor will bring all offers to purchase, exchange or lease the Property to me. I agree to refer all inquiries about the Property to Realtor. I agree to cooperate with Realtor in showing the Property to possible buyers or renters at any reasonable hour. I agree that Realtor may photograph the Property listed for sale or exchange.

3. PAYMENT OF COMMISSION. I agree to pay to Realtor the commission(s) set forth in Paragraph C of this Contract on the "closing date" specified in the purchase and sale contract or when I sign a written agreement to exchange the Property or when I sign a lease for the Property. I will pay this commission to Realtor whether I, Realtor, or anyone else sells, exchanges or leases the Property during the life of this Contract. Realtor has earned the commission when I am provided with a written purchase offer which meets the price and other conditions I have set or when the purchase and sale contract becomes a binding legal commitment on the buyer, or when I sign a written agreement to exchange the Property, or when I sign a lease for the Property.

4. SALE EXCHANGE OR LEASE OF PROPERTY AFTER CONTRACT ENDS TO A PERSON WHO WAS SHOWN THE PROPERTY DURING LIFE OF CONTRACT. If I sell, exchange or lease the Property within the effective period set forth in Paragraph G of this Contract to a person who was shown the Property by Owner(s), Realtor, or anyone else during the life of this Contract, I will pay Realtor the same commission agreed to in Paragraph C of this Contract. I will not owe any commission to Realtor if such sale, exchange or lease occurs during the life of a Rochester Real Estate Board MLS contract I enter into after this Contract ends.

5. INFORMATION ABOUT PROPERTY. I have given Realtor correct information about the Property. Realtor will not be responsible to me or anyone else for the accuracy of such information. New York State Law states that Seller is legally obligated to give written information about insulation within fifteen (15) days of written request by a prospective purchaser made prior to signing of purchase agreement. I authorize Realtor to get other information about the Property if Realtor wants to do so. Realtor will use reliable sources of information, but Realtor is not responsible to me for the accuracy of the information.

6. RESPONSIBILITY OF OWNER(S) UNDER THIS CONTRACT. All Owners must sign this Contract. If more than one person signs this Contract as Owner, each person is fully responsible for keeping the promising made by Owner. My estate and/or legal heirs, and all other persons who take over my legal position, will be responsible for keeping the promises made by me in this Contract.

7. RENEWAL AND MODIFICATION OF CONTRACT. I may extend the life of this Contract by signing a renewal agreement. If I renew this Contract, Realtor will notify MLS of the renewal. All changes or modifications of the provisions of this Contract must be made in writing, signed by Owner(s) and Realtor.

8. LIST OF BROKERS. I hereby certify that Realtor has provided me with a list of names and addresses of all brokers participating in the MLS listing service.

first *$125,000* of gain. A homeowner may exclude gains under the "over 55" provision *only once in a lifetime* even if the total gain excluded is less than the $125,000 limit.

Thus if the homeowner in our example were over 55 and chose to take advantage of the once-in-a-lifetime exemption, the taxable gain would be zero. If the homeowner did not use the exemption now, it could be saved for use in future years to cover up to $125,000 piled-up profits on both homes or a string of homes.

Because one's spouse must join in the election to use the over-55 exclusion it may not be taken by anyone whose spouse has ever used the exclusion, even in a previous marriage, and even on a home owned solely by a former spouse.

Where the property sold is not one's own home several tax treatments are available. Installment treatment allows for taxation of profit year by year as it is earned. (Some adjustments are made, however, for depreciation previously claimed.)

Capital gains. The long-term gain on any property held over six months usually qualifies for a reduced tax rate with only 40 percent of the profit subject to income tax. Holding periods for capital gains treatment and the percentage excluded from taxation are frequently changed by the government.

New York State also imposes a ten percent capital gains tax on real estate transfers for property not the seller's main residence where the sale price is more than $1,000,000.

When an individual buys and sells real property as a major source of income, the Internal Revenue Service may classify the taxpayer as a *dealer* and deny capital gains treatment, taxing profits as ordinary income.

Summary

The unique nature of land is apparent in both its economic and physical characteristics. The economic characteristics consist of *scarcity, improvements, permanence of investment,* and *area preferences.* The physical characteristics are *immobility, nonhomogeneity,* and *indestructibility.*

Real estate is the business of *value.* A property's value is the present worth of its future benefits. Value is not the same as *price; price* is determined in the marketplace.

A *market* is a place where goods and services can be bought and sold and relatively stable price levels established. Because of its unique characteristics, real estate is relatively slow to adjust to the forces of supply and demand.

Supply can be defined as the amount of goods available in the market for a given price. *Demand* is defined as the number of people willing to accept those available goods at a given price.

The supply of and demand for real estate are affected by many factors including *population changes, wage and employment levels, percentage of unoccupied space, construction costs and availability of labor,* and *governmental monetary policy and controls.*

Real estate is appraised through the use of three different methods. The *cost approach* estimates the money needed to reconstruct the building and subtracts any loss in value due to *depreciation.* Depreciation may be *physical* (wear and tear), *functional* (outmoded features), or *economic* (*locational*—due to features beyond the property boundaries).

Market value is defined as the *probable price a property will bring in a competitive and open market, offered by an informed seller, and allowing a reasonable time to find a purchaser who buys the property with knowledge of all the uses to which it is adapted, neither buyer nor seller being under duress.*

To acquire an inventory of property to sell, brokers and salespeople must obtain listings. The various kinds of listing agreements include open listings, exclusive-agency listings, and exclusive-right-to-sell listings.

An *open listing* is one in which the broker's commission depends upon his or her finding a buyer before the property is sold by the seller or another broker. Under an *exclusive-agency listing* the broker is given the exclusive right to represent the seller but the seller can avoid paying the broker a commission if he or she sells the property without the broker's help. With an *exclusive-right-to-sell listing* the seller appoints one broker to represent him or her and must pay that broker a commission regardless of whether it is the broker or the seller who finds a buyer for it, if the buyer is found within the listing period. *Net listings* are illegal in New York.

A *multiple listing* is an exclusive listing with the additional authority and obligation on the part of the listing broker to distribute the listing to other brokers in his or her multiple-listing organization.

A listing agreement may be terminated for the same reasons as any other agency relationship.

The *comparative market analysis* is a rudimentary form of *market data appraisal.*

When a homeowner sells a principal residence, income tax on any gain is deferred if the homeowner purchases another residence within 24 months. Homeowners over the age of 55 are given additional benefits.

Questions

1. Any two parcels of real estate:
   a. can never be the same.
   b. can be the same only with identical tract houses.
   c. are considered the same if they have identical sale prices.
   d. are identical because of situs.

2. The benefits anticipated from property in the future are a measure of its:
   a. value.   c. obsolesence.
   b. depreciation.   d. nonhomogeneity.

3. In real estate the concept of cost is related to the:
   a. past.   c. future.
   b. present.   d. sale price.

4. If six houses are offered for sale on the same street, sale prices will probably:
   a. be identical.
   b. fall below market value.
   c. set new highs for that neighborhood.
   d. None of the above

5. Real estate markets tend to be:
   a. similar across the country.
   b. statewide in their characteristics.
   c. stable despite economic changes.
   d. local in character.

6. The three approaches to appraisal do *not* include the:
   a. cost method.
   b. income approach.
   c. comparative market analysis.
   d. market comparison method.

7. Tom Wills is asked to estimate the market value of a church. He will give most emphasis to which appraisal approach?
   a. Cost
   b. Income
   c. Competitive analysis
   d. Market comparison

8. The income approach to appraisal is most appropriate for a:
   a. tract ranch house.
   b. library.
   c. apartment house.
   d. vacant lot.

9. The market data approach to appraisal utilizes:
   a. asking prices for property on the market.
   b. building costs in the area.
   c. analysis of functional obsolesence.
   d. recent sale prices of similar parcels.

10. If the roof of a building is near the end of its useful life, an appraiser will subtract value because of:
    a. physical deterioration.
    b. functional obsolesence.
    c. economic obsolesence.
    d. situs.

11. An office building that cannot be centrally air-conditioned suffers from:
    a. physical deterioration.
    b. functional obsolesence.
    c. economic obsolesence.
    d. situs.

12. An example of economic or locational obsolesence might be a:
    a. faulty heating system.
    b. poor floor plan.
    c. tenant who will not pay rent.
    d. used car lot next door.

13. The highest price that would be paid by an informed buyer when property is widely exposed on the market is known as:
    a. cost.   c. sale price.
    b. listing price.   d. market value.

14. In the final analysis selling price for real estate is set by:
    a. the seller.
    b. the broker.
    c. comparative market analysis.
    d. the buying public.

15. Ned Neighbor tells Betty Broker over the phone that if she sells his house before Christmas, he will pay her a five percent commission. Betty produces a buyer and negotiates a sales agreement. Betty:

    a. cannot claim a commission because the listing was oral.
    b. cannot claim it because it is not an arm's-length transaction.
    c. can claim a commission only if Ned is still willing to pay.
    d. has a legal claim for commission as agreed over the phone.

16. Susy promised a commission to Broker A if he sold the property, then turned around and made the same arrangement with Broker B. Susy must be entering into a (n):

    a. open listing.
    b. exclusive-agency listing.
    c. exclusive-right-to-sell listing.
    d. net listing.

17. Leon Ericsson arranged to let Don Hotshot be his only broker, but when Leon sold the property himself, he owed Don nothing. Their agreement must have been a(n):

    a. multiple listing.
    b. exclusive-agency listing.
    c. exclusive-right-to-sell listing.
    d. net listing.

18. In the question above, Don could have claimed a commission if their agreement had been a(n):

    a. open listing.
    b. exclusive-agency listing.
    c. exclusive-right-to-sell listing.
    d. net listing.

19. In New York State every listing contract must include:

    a. an automatic extension clause.
    b. a net listing provision.
    c. the broker's license number.
    d. an explanation of types of listings.

20. Under a multiple-listing system if Broker A lists the property and Broker B with another firm sells it:

    a. no commission need be paid.
    b. Broker A is entitled to the full commission.
    c. Broker B receives the full commission.
    d. the commission is shared between the two offices.

21. The Truth-in-Heating law requires a seller to disclose to prospective buyers:

    a. any flaws in the heating system.
    b. a detailed list of which tenants pay their own utilities.
    c. two years' past heating bills.
    d. receipts for installation of furnace and air conditioner.

22. A property was listed with a broker who belonged to a multiple-listing service. It was sold for $93,500 by another broker member. The total commission was six percent of the sales price; of this commission the selling broker received 60 percent and the listing broker received the balance. How much was the listing broker's commission?

    a. $3,366   c. $5,610
    b. $2,019.60   d. $2,244

23. The Internal Revenue Service offers special income tax treatment for profit from the sale of one's primary residence. New York State:

    a. taxes such profit as ordinary income.
    b. goes along with the federal tax treatment.
    c. imposes its own capital gains tax.
    d. allows the first $10,000 of profit tax-free.

24. Tax on profit from the sale of one's home is postponed if another home of equal or greater value is bought within:

    a. six months.
    b. one year.
    c. two years.
    d. three out of five years.

25. Mr. Spock is 56 when he sells his long-time home for a profit of $110,000. If he chooses to, Mr. Spock may have income tax on his profit:

    a. postponed.   c. amortized.
    b. rolled over.   d. forgiven forever.

Appendix: Excerpt from New York State's Study Booklet for Brokers

Rule 175.24 which refers to exclusive listings of one-, two- or three-family dwellings states as follows:

(b) In all commission agreements obtained by a broker which provide for an exclusive listing of residential property, the broker shall have attached to the listing or printed on the reverse side of the listing and signed by the homeowner or the homeowner's agent the following explanations in type size of not less than six point:

"EXPLANATION:
An 'exclusive right to sell' listing means that if you, the owner of the property, find a buyer for your house, or if another broker finds a buyer, you must pay the agreed commission to the present broker.
An 'exclusive agency' listing means that if you, the owner of the property, find a buyer, you will not have to pay a commission to the broker. However, if another broker finds a buyer, you will owe a commission to both the selling broker and your present broker."

(c) If an exclusive listing of residential property is obtained by a broker who is a member of a multiple listing service,

(1) he shall give to the homeowner a list of the names and addresses of all member brokers; and

(2) the listing agreement shall provide that the homeowner shall have the option of having all negotiated offers to purchase the listed residential property submitted either through the listing broker or submitted through the selling broker.

A broker can bind his/her principal only insofar as the broker has been authorized. The broker's powers or authority are limited to those actually conferred by the principal. Hence employment to sell or lease is mere authority to find a buyer or lessee and to act as an intermediary between them. There must be express authority to accept deposits or sign a contract.

Human Rights and Fair Housing

Key Terms

Affirmative action
Affirmative marketing agreement (NAR)
Blockbusting
Cease and desist order
Civil Rights Act of 1866
Code for Equal Opportunity
Code of Ethics
Department of Housing and Urban Development
Executive Law
Federal Fair Housing Act of 1968

New York Human Rights Law
Nonsolicitation order
Office of Equal Opportunity
Real Property Law
Redlining
Reverse discrimination
State Division of Human Rights
Steering
Testers

Overview

To ensure equal opportunity in housing for everyone, federal and state governments have enacted laws that require ethical practices from real estate licensees dealing with the public. In addition brokers and salespeople have an obligation to educate their clients about fair housing laws affecting sellers and landlords. This chapter will deal with such fair housing laws and will examine the codes of ethical practices in this matter followed by most licensees.

Equal Opportunity in Housing

Brokers and salespeople who offer residential property for sale anywhere in the United States must be aware of the federal, state, and local laws pertaining to human rights and nondiscrimination. These laws, under such titles as open housing, fair housing, or equal opportunity housing, generally prohibit undesirable and discriminatory activities. Their provisions affect every phase of the real estate sales process from listing to closing and *all brokers and salespersons must comply with them.*

The goal of legislators who have enacted fair housing laws and regulations is to create a single, unbiased housing market—one in which every homeseeker has the opportunity to buy any home in the area he or she chooses provided that the home is within the homebuyer's financial means. As a potential licensee the student of real estate must be aware of undesirable and illegal housing practices in order to avoid them. Failure to comply with fair housing practices is not only a criminal act but also grounds for license revocation.

Federal Fair Housing Laws

The efforts of the federal government to guarantee equal housing opportunities to all U.S. citizens began more than 100 years ago with the passage of the **Civil Rights Act of 1866.** This law, an outgrowth of the Fourteenth Amendment, prohibits any type of discrimination based on race. "All citizens of the United States shall have the same right in every state and territory as is enjoyed by white citizens thereof to inherit, purchase, lease, sell, hold, and convey real and personal property." A summary of federal fair housing laws appears in Table 10.1.

Table 10.1
Summary of Federal Fair Housing Laws

Law	Purpose
Civil Rights Act of 1866	Prohibits discrimination in housing based on race without exception
Executive Order No. 11063	Prohibits discrimination in housing funded by FHA or VA loans
Civil Rights Act of 1964	Prohibits discrimination in federally funded housing programs
Fair Housing Act of 1968	Prohibits discrimination in housing based on race, color, religion, sex, or national origin with certain exceptions

Aside from a few isolated court decisions there was little effort to enforce the principles of fair housing until 1962, when President John Kennedy issued *Executive Order No. 11063.* This order guaranteed nondiscrimination in all housing financed by FHA and VA loans. Because of the relatively small percentage of housing affected by Executive Order No. 11063, however, it had limited impact.

The scope of the federal government's fair housing regulation was expanded by the *Civil Rights Act of 1964,* which prohibited discrimination in any housing program that receives whole or partial federal funding. However, because only a very small percentage of housing in the United States is government-funded, this law also had little impact on the housing industry.

Fair Housing Act of 1968. In 1968 two major events greatly encouraged the progress of fair housing. The first was the passage of the **Federal Fair Housing Act,** which is contained in *Title VIII of the Civil Rights Act of 1968.* This law provides that it is unlawful to discriminate on the basis of race, color, religion, sex, or national origin when selling or leasing residential property. It covers dwellings and apartments as well as vacant land acquired for the construction of residential buildings and prohibits the following discriminatory acts:

1. refusing to sell, rent, or negotiate with any person, or otherwise making a dwelling unavailable to any person;
2. changing terms, conditions, or services for different individuals as a means of discrimination;
3. practicing discrimination through any statement or advertisement that restricts the sale or rental of residential property;
4. representing to any person, as a means of discrimination, that a dwelling is not available for sale or rental;
5. making a profit by inducing owners of housing to sell or rent because of the prospective entry into the neighborhood of persons of a particular race, color, religion, or national origin;
6. altering the terms or conditions for a home loan to any person who wishes to purchase or repair a dwelling, or otherwise denying such a loan as a means of discrimination; and
7. denying people membership or limiting their participation in any multiple-listing service, real estate brokers' organization, or other facility related to the sale or rental of dwellings, as a means of discrimination.

The following exemptions to the Federal Fair Housing Act also are provided:

1. The sale or rental of a single-family home is exempted when the home is owned by an individual who does not own more than three such homes at one time and when the following conditions exist: (a) a broker, salesperson, or agent is not used, and (b) discriminatory advertising is not used. If the owner is not living in the dwelling at the time of the transaction or was not the most recent occupant, only one such sale by an individual is exempt from the law within any 24-month period.
2. The rental of rooms or units is exempted in an owner-occupied one- to four-family dwelling.
3. Dwelling units owned by religious organizations may be restricted to people of the same religion if membership in the organization is not restricted on the basis of race, color, or national origin.
4. A private club that is not in fact open to the public may restrict the rental or occupancy of lodgings that it owns to its members as long as the lodgings are not operated commercially.

In addition to the general provisions of the Federal Fair Housing Law, the Department of Housing and Urban Development has issued numerous rules and regulations that establish guidelines for the real estate industry in such specific areas as advertising and marketing procedures.

Jones vs. Mayer. The second significant fair housing development of 1968 was the Supreme Court decision in the case of *Jones vs. Alfred H. Mayer Company,* 392, U. S. 409(1968). In its ruling the Court upheld the previously discussed Civil Rights Act of 1866, which "prohibits all racial discrimination, private or public, in the sale and rental of property."

The importance of this decision rests in the fact that while the 1968 federal law exempts individual homeowners and certain groups, the 1866 law *prohibits all racial discrimination without exception.* So despite any exemptions in the 1968 law, an aggrieved person may seek a remedy for racial discrimination under the 1866 law against *any* homeowner regardless of whether or not the owner employed a real estate broker and/or advertised the property. *Where race is involved, no exceptions apply.*

Amendment to Fair Housing Law. A 1972 amendment to the Federal Fair Housing Act of 1968 instituted the use of an equal housing opportunity poster. This poster, which can be obtained from HUD (illustrated in Figure 10.1), features the equal housing opportunity slogan, an equal housing statement pledging adherence to the Fair Housing Act and support of affirmative marketing and advertising programs, and the equal housing opportunity logo shown in Figure 10.2.

When HUD investigates a broker for discriminatory practices it considers failure to display the poster evidence of discrimination.

Blockbusting and Steering

Blockbusting and steering are undesirable housing practices frequently discussed in connection with fair housing. While they are not mentioned by name in the Federal Fair Housing Act of 1968, both are prohibited by that law and by New York State law.

Blockbusting means *inducing homeowners to sell by making representations regarding the entry or prospective entry of minority persons into the neighborhood.* The blockbuster frightens homeowners into selling and makes a profit by buying the homes cheaply and selling them at considerably higher prices to minority persons. The Federal Fair Housing Act prohibits this practice.

Steering is the channeling of homeseekers to particular areas either to maintain the homogeneity of an area or to change the character of an area in order to create a speculative situation. This practice makes certain homes unavailable to homeseekers on the basis of race or national origin; on these grounds it is prohibited by the provisions of the Federal Fair Housing Act. Steering is often difficult to detect, however, because the steering tactics can be so subtle that the homeseeker is unaware that his or her choice has been limited. Steering may be done unintentionally by agents who are not aware of their own unconscious assumptions.

Redlining

The practice of refusing to make mortgage loans or issue insurance policies in specific areas without regard to the economic qualifications of the applicant is known as **redlining.** This practice, which often contributes to the deterioration of older, transitional neighborhoods, is frequently based on racial grounds rather than on any real objections to the applicant.

Figure 10.1
Equal Housing
Opportunity Poster

**EQUAL HOUSING
OPPORTUNITY**

We Do Business in Accordance With the Federal Fair Housing Law

(Title VIII of the Civil Rights Act of 1968, as Amended by
the Housing and Community Development Act of 1974)

IT IS ILLEGAL TO DISCRIMINATE AGAINST ANY PERSON BECAUSE OF RACE, COLOR, RELIGION, SEX, OR NATIONAL ORIGIN

- In the sale or rental of housing or residential lots
- In advertising the sale or rental of housing
- In the financing of housing
- In the provision of real estate brokerage services

Blockbusting is also illegal

An aggrieved person may file a complaint of a housing discrimination act with the:

U.S. DEPARTMENT OF HOUSING AND URBAN DEVELOPMENT
Assistant Secretary for Fair Housing and Equal Opportunity
Washington, D.C. 20410

HUD–928.1 (7-75) Previous editions are obsolete

Figure 10.2
Opportunity Symbol

EQUAL HOUSING
OPPORTUNITY

In an effort to counteract redlining the federal government passed the *Home Mortgage Disclosure Act* in 1975. This act requires all institutional mortgage lenders with assets in excess of $10 million and one or more offices in a given geographic area to make annual reports by census tracts of all mortgage loans the institution makes or purchases. This law enables the government to detect lending or insuring patterns that might constitute redlining. A lending institution that refuses a loan solely on sound economic grounds cannot be accused of redlining.

Enforcement

The Federal Fair Housing Act is administered by the **Office of Equal Opportunity** (OEO) under the direction of the secretary of the **Department of Housing and Urban Development** (HUD). Any aggrieved person may file a complaint with the secretary or his or her delegate within 180 days after a discriminatory action occurs. Complaints may be reported to: Fair Housing, Dept. of Housing and Urban Development, Washington, DC 20410, or to Fair Housing c/o the nearest HUD regional office. The secretary's efforts to resolve the dispute are limited to conference, conciliation, and persuasion.

After investigating a complaint HUD will decide whether or not to attempt to resolve the dispute and will notify the complainant of the decision within 30 days after the complaint is filed. If HUD decides to attempt conciliation, the complainant should wait to see if the matter can be settled out of court before filing suit; HUD will terminate all efforts at conciliation when the case actually comes to trial in court. An aggrieved person always has the option to take the alleged violator to court whether or not a complaint has been filed with HUD. If the agency is investigating the incident, however, the courts generally wait until it has completed its efforts before going ahead with the case.

If HUD is unable to obtain voluntary compliance from the accused violator within 30 days after the complaint is filed, the complainant then has another 30 days in which to file suit in the appropriate court if he or she chooses to do so. In states with fair housing laws that are substantially equivalent to federal statutes (this includes New York) such suits must be brought in state court within the time period specified by state law. If no such law exists the complaint may be taken to a U.S. district court if a suit is filed within 180 days after the discriminatory action occurs.

In addition, court actions may be brought by the attorney general in cases where accused violators of the Federal Fair Housing Act of 1968 are engaged in practices that show a pattern of discrimination.

Complaints brought under the Civil Rights Act of 1866 must be taken directly to a federal court. The only time limit for action would be three years, New York's statute of limitation for *torts,* injuries done by one individual to another.

Substantially Equivalent State Laws

Whenever a state or municipality has a fair housing law that has been ruled *substantially equivalent* to the federal law, all complaints in that state or locality, including those filed with HUD, are referred to and handled by the state enforcement agencies. In New York, HUD refers complaints to the State Division of Human Rights.

Threats or Acts of Violence

The Federal Fair Housing Act of 1968 contains criminal provisions protecting the rights of those who seek the benefits of the open housing law as well as owners, brokers, or salespeople who aid or encourage the enjoyment of open housing rights. Unlawful actions involving threats, coercion, and intimidation are punishable by appropriate civil action. In such cases the victim should report the incident immediately to the local police and to the nearest office of the Federal Bureau of Investigation.

New York Human Rights Law

Blockbusting, forbidden under federal statutes, is specifically mentioned in the **New York Human Rights Law** (Article 15, Executive Law) and is also prohibited by a Department of State regulation. A person discriminated against is able to initiate a private lawsuit (with no dollar limit mentioned under state law) and also to lodge a complaint with the Department of State if the offender is a licensed broker or salesperson. A complaint may be filed with the New York State Division of Human Rights also within a one-year period.

In certain neighborhoods in New York State, homeowners have joined together to stop all solicitation of listings, no matter what the motivation. Where they have petitioned the secretary of state, a **nonsolicitation order** to cover a certain area may have been issued. Agents who violate the order and canvass the area for listings may run into irate homeowners and face stiff penalties that have included loss of license. New salespersons and brokers are advised to make sure they are aware of any such nonsolicitation orders effective in their areas.

Individual homeowners may petition for a similar **cease and desist order.**

Under sections of the Executive Law, New York statutes broaden the nondiscrimination rules to cover commercial real estate. In addition several other categories are added in which discrimination is prohibited. These include *age, disability,* and *marital status.*

Further provisions forbidding discrimination on the basis of age apply to transactions involving commercial space and public housing but not to housing in general. The age provisions apply only to those 18 and over.

Local governments may add other groups to the list of protected categories. In 1986 New York City prohibited housing discrimination based on sexual orientation.

The **Real Property Law** forbids a landlord to deny rental housing because of children and also prohibits an eviction because of a tenant's pregnancy or new child. The rules extend to mobile homes.

Various exceptions are made to the New York State rules but these exceptions will not apply where the discrimination is racially based because the Federal Civil Rights Law of 1866, which covers *race, permits no exceptions*. With that in mind, the New York State exceptions are:

1. public housing that may be aimed at one specific age group;
2. rental of a duplex in which the owner or his or her family occupy the other unit;
3. restriction of all rooms rented to members of the same sex;
4. rental of a room in one's own home; and
5. restriction of rentals to persons 55 years of age or older.

While an owner sometimes may discriminate under these exemptions, a licensee may not participate in the transaction.

In general the New York statutes, which are reprinted at the end of this chapter, cover all fields: renting, selling, leasing, and advertising. Public accommodations are also included. The law further forbids any real estate board to discriminate in its membership because of any of the listed categories, which in this case include age. New York regulations are generally more restrictive than federal laws.

Table 10.2 summarizes the categories covered by the various federal and New York State laws.

Table 10.2 **Categories Under** **Which Discrimination** **Is Forbidden**	Civil Rights Act of 1866	Fair Housing Act of 1968	New York Executive Law
Race	Yes	Yes	Yes
Color		Yes	Yes
Religion		Yes	Yes ("creed")
National origin		Yes	Yes
Sex		Yes (1974)	Yes
Age			Yes (over 18)
Disability			Yes
Marital Status			Yes
Exceptions	No	Yes	Yes

Code for Equal Opportunity

In order to better support fair housing opportunities in its members' communities the National Association of REALTORS® has adopted a **Code for Equal Opportunity.** The Code sets forth suggested standards of conduct for REALTORS® so that they may comply with both the letter as well as the spirit of the fair housing laws. The Code provides that:

1. In the sale, purchase, exchange, rental, or lease of real property, REALTORS® and their REALTOR®-ASSOCIATES have the responsibility to offer equal service to all clients and prospects without regard to race, color, religion, sex, or national origin. This encompasses:
   a. standing ready to enter broker-client relationships or to show property equally to members of all races, creeds, or ethnic groups;
   b. receiving all formal written offers and communicating them to the owner;
   c. exerting their best efforts to conclude all transactions; and
   d. maintaining equal opportunity employment practices.

2. Members, individually and collectively, in performing their agency functions, have no right or responsibility to volunteer information regarding the racial, creedal, or ethnic composition of any neighborhood or any part thereof.

3. Members shall not engage in any activity that has the purpose of inducing panic selling.

4. Members shall not print, display, or circulate any statement or advertisement with respect to the sale or rental of a dwelling that indicates any preference, limitations, or discrimination based on race, color, religion, sex, or ethnic background.

5. Members who violate the spirit or any provision of this Code of Equal Opportunity shall be subject to disciplinary action.

The Code of Ethics and the Code for Equal Opportunity are two segments of the NAR's overall equal opportunity program, which is designed to ensure that no person is denied equal professional real estate services.

Affirmative Marketing Agreement

The National Association of REALTORS® also has entered into an agreement with HUD for a program of voluntary affirmative action to eliminate fair housing violations. After a local board of REALTORS® has voluntarily accepted the **affirmative marketing agreement,** individual member brokers are asked to join in compliance with the agreement. The broker's salespersons are referred to as associate members of the agreement.

The REALTOR® who signs the agreement takes on a five-year period of implementing fair housing. His or her board promises to advertise quarterly its commitment to affirmative action. The member's ads must carry the fair housing logo "unless overly expensive" and the logo must appear on the broker's brochures.

Within 60 days of signing the agreement, members must hold an information program for all their associates, detailing their obligations under the agreement. Associates will be monitored by their brokers to ensure that fair housing practices are being carried out. All associates must keep a careful record of each home shown every prospect. Members also are committed to actively hiring minority members for salaried positions. Requirements also provide for the dissemination of equal housing opportunity guides to all sellers. The seller *is* bound by fair housing law and it is essential that licensees explain to sellers that licensees cannot cooperate in any discriminatory actions.

Information about the affirmative marketing agreement is available from the National Association of REALTORS® and also from the following HUD offices:

Albany: Equal Opportunity Officer, HUD
                 O'Brien Federal Bldg.
                 N. Pearl & Clinton
                 Albany, New York 12207

Buffalo: Equal Opportunity Officer, HUD
                 107 Delaware Ave.
                 Buffalo, New York 14203

New York: Equal Opportunity Officer, HUD
                 26 Federal Plaza
                 New York, New York 10278

In order to be eligible for certain FHA, HUD, and VA transactions, brokers who do not belong to an affirmative marketing agreement will be asked to take equivalent steps individually.

Implications for Brokers and Salespersons

To a large extent the laws place the burden of responsibility for effecting and maintaining fair housing on real estate licensees—brokers and salespeople. The laws are explicit and widely known. Anyone who violates them, whether intentionally or unintentionally, should be aware of the legal ramifications. In such cases the complainant does not have to prove guilty knowledge or specific intent—only the fact that discrimination occurred.

How does a broker go about complying with the laws and making that policy known? HUD regulations suggest that a public statement in the form of an approved fair housing poster be displayed by a broker in any place of business where housing is offered for sale or rent (including model homes). HUD also offers guidelines for nondiscriminatory language and illustrations for use in real estate advertising.

In addition the National Association of REALTORS® suggests that a broker's position can be emphasized and problems can be avoided by the prominent display of a sign stating that it is against company policy as well as state and federal laws to offer any information on the racial, ethnic, or religious composition of a neighborhood or to place restrictions on listing, showing, or providing information on the availability of homes for any of these reasons.

If a prospect still expresses a locational preference for housing based upon race the association's guidelines suggest the following response: "I cannot give you that kind of advice. I will show you several homes that meet your specifications. You will have to decide which one you want."

Compliance with the fair housing laws involves knowing the regulations and doing as the law demands. It is, however, often hard to distinguish practices that are discriminatory in intent from those that are discriminatory in effect. A good test of whether or not an action is discriminatory is the answer to the question: Are we doing this for everyone? If the act is not done for everyone, it could be construed as discriminatory.

Discrimination involves a sensitive area, human emotions—specifically, fear and self-preservation based on considerable prejudice and misconception. The broker or salesperson who keeps his or her own actions in check by complying with the law still has to deal in many cases with a general public whose attitudes cannot be altered by legislation alone. Therefore a licensee who wishes to comply with the fair housing laws and also succeed in the real estate business must work to educate the public.

In recent years brokers sometimes have been caught in the middle when local governments enacted well-meaning *reverse discrimination* regulations. Intended to preserve racial balance in given areas, local laws sometimes run counter to federal and state rules, posing a real problem for the conscientious licensee.

From time to time real estate offices may be visited by **testers** or *checkers,* undercover volunteers who want to see whether all customers and clients are being treated with the same cordiality and are being offered the same free choice within a given price range. The courts have held that such practice is permissible as the only way to test compliance with the fair housing laws that are of such importance to American society.

When a real estate broker is charged with discrimination, it is no defense that the offense was unintentional. Citing past service to members of the same minority group is of little value as a defense.

The agent's best course is to study fair housing law, develop sensitivity on the subject, and follow routine practices designed to reduce the danger of unintentionally hurting any member of the public. These practices include careful record-keeping for each customer: financial analysis, properties suggested, houses shown, check-back phone calls. Using a standard form for all qualifying interviews is helpful. Special care should be taken to be on time for appointments and to follow through on returning all phone calls.

Besides helping to avoid human rights violations, these practices are simply good business and should result in increased business for the licensee.

For every broker and salesperson, a sincere, positive attitude toward fair housing laws is a good start in dealing with this sensitive issue. It provides effective models for all who come in contact with the licensee. Active cooperation with local real estate board programs and community committees is also an excellent idea. This evidences the licensee's willingness to serve the community and observe the laws and it helps to change public attitudes.

Summary

The federal regulations regarding equal opportunity in housing are principally contained in two laws. The *Civil Rights Act of 1866* prohibits all racial discrimination and the *Federal Fair Housing Act* (Title VIII of the Civil Rights Act of 1968) prohibits discrimination on the basis of race, color, religion, sex, or national origin in the sale or rental of residential property. Discriminatory actions include refusing to deal with an individual or a specific group, changing any terms of a real estate or loan transaction, changing the services offered for any individual or group, making statements or advertisements that indicate discriminatory restrictions, or otherwise attempting to make a dwelling unavailable to any person or group because of race, color, religion, sex, or national origin. Some exceptions apply to owners but *none to brokers,* and *none when the discriminatory act is based upon race.*

Complaints under the Federal Fair Housing Act may be reported to and investigated by the *Department of Housing and Urban Development*. Such complaints also may be taken directly to a U.S. district court. In New York, complaints are handled by state and local agencies and state courts. Complaints under the Civil Rights Act of 1866 must be taken to a federal court.

New York's *Executive Law (Human Rights Law)* adds to the grounds on which discrimination is forbidden those of age, disability, and marital status.

The National Association of REALTORS® Code for Equal Opportunity suggests an excellent set of standards for all licensees to follow.

Questions

1. After John Wilson lists a summer home with salesperson Sharon Sikes, he informs her of his general dislike of members of a particular ethnic minority group. Sikes later shows the home to two prospective buyers, one of whom is a member of this group, and both make an offer. When Wilson contacts her again she does not present him with the lower offer, which was made by the member of the minority. Sikes has violated:
   a. regulations of the New York Real Estate License Law.
   b. the law of agency.
   c. the executive law.
   d. All of the above

2. Which of the following acts is permitted under the Federal Fair Housing Act?
   a. Advertising property for sale only to a special group
   b. Altering the terms of a loan for a member of a minority group
   c. Refusing to sell a home to an individual because he or she has a poor credit history
   d. Telling an individual that an apartment has been rented when in fact it has not

3. The Civil Rights Act of 1866 is unique because it:
   a. covers only the area of race.
   b. provides no exceptions.
   c. requires a federal court suit by the complainant.
   d. All of the above

4. "I hear they're moving in; there goes the neighborhood. Better sell to me today!" is an example of:
   a. steering.   c. redlining.
   b. blockbusting.   d. testing.

5. The act of channeling homeseekers to a particular area either to maintain or to change the character of a neighborhood is:
   a. blockbusting.
   b. redlining.
   c. steering.
   d. permitted under the Fair Housing Act of 1968.

6. Which would *not* be permitted under the Federal Fair Housing Act?
   a. The Harvard Club in New York will rent rooms only to graduates of Harvard who belong to the club.
   b. The owner of a 20-unit apartment building rents to women only.
   c. A convent refuses to furnish housing for a Jewish man.
   d. All of the above

7. Jan Heath, an Ithaca homeowner selling her own home, receives a response to her ad from an Italian man who identified himself as such. She told him the house was sold, which was untrue. The next week he notices the ad in the paper again and feels he has been discriminated against. He may seek a remedy under:
   a. the Civil Rights Act of 1866.
   b. the Federal Fair Housing Act of 1968.
   c. the New York Executive Law.
   d. All of the above

8. Guiding prospective buyers to a particular area because the agent feels they belong there may lead to:
   a. blockbusting.   c. steering.
   b. redlining.   d. bird-dogging.

9. A refusal to rent to someone because they receive public assistance violates:
   a. no law.
   b. the New York Executive Law.
   c. the Fair Housing Act of 1968.
   d. the Civil Rights Act of 1866.

10. A policy of never renting to college students violates:
    a. no law.
    b. the New York Executive Law.
    c. the Fair Housing Act of 1968.
    d. the Civil Rights Act of 1866.

11. Refusing an apartment to a couple because they are unmarried violates:
    a. no law.
    b. the New York Executive Law.
    c. the Fair Housing Act of 1968.
    d. the Civil Rights Act of 1866.

12. The advertisement: "For rent: my front bed-room, shared bath, females only" violates:
    a. no law.
    b. the New York Executive Law.
    c. the Fair Housing Act of 1968.
    d. the Civil Rights Act of 1866.

13. If the seller says "I don't want to sell to any South American refugees," you are being asked to violate:
    a. no law.
    b. the Civil Rights Act of 1866.
    c. the Fair Housing Act of 1968.
    d. Executive Order No. 11063.

14. The seller who requests prohibited discrimination in the showing of a home should be told:
    a. "As your agent I have a duty to warn you that such discrimination could land you in real trouble."
    b. "I am not allowed to obey such instructions."
    c. "If you persist, I'll have to refuse to list your property."
    d. All of the above

15. A good precaution against even unconscious discrimination is:
    a. detailed record-keeping on each customer.
    b. use of a standard financial interview form.
    c. routine follow-up phone calls.
    d. All of the above

Appendix: Excerpts from New York State's Study Booklet for Brokers

DISCRIMINATORY PRACTICES

The Executive Law prohibits discrimination because of race, creed, color, national origin or sex by brokers, salespersons, employees or agents thereof in selling or renting housing or commercial space covered by the law, and in advertising the sale or rental of any housing or commercial space.

Moreover, under a rule promulgated by the Secretary of State, licensed real estate brokers and salespersons are prohibited from engaging in the practice of "blockbusting"—the solicitation of the sale or lease of property due to a change in the ethnic structure of a neighborhood.

Upon written petition of property owners revoking the implied invitation to solicitation, the Secretary may issue an order to real estate brokers and salespersons requiring them to cease and desist from such solicitation. Also the Secretary may issue a general "non-solicitation order" which prohibits all real estate brokers and salespersons from soliciting the listing of property for sale or purchase in a prohibited area. Failure to comply imperils the license of the broker or salesperson, which is then subject to suspension or revocation after hearing.

In addition, no broker or salesperson may, either directly or by implication, encourage or discourage the purchase of property by referring to the race, color, religion or national origin of persons living in or near or moving into or near to any particular neighborhood.

Except with regards to senior citizens housing subsidized, insured, or guaranteed by the federal government, it is illegal to discriminate in the rental of housing on the basis that the prospective tenant has or may have a child or children, and no broker or salesperson may participate in such discrimination.

The Department has embodied in its rules and regulations the principle that discrimination is against public policy and that licensees, in their activities, must abide by the law of the State.

Extracts from the Executive Law

It shall be an unlawful discriminatory practice for the owner, lessee, sublessee, assignee, or managing agent of publicly-assisted housing accommodations or other person having the right of ownership or possession of or the right to rent or lease such accommodations:

(a) To refuse to rent or lease or otherwise to deny to or withhold from any person or group of persons such housing accommodations because of the race, creed, color, disability, national origin, age, sex or marital status of such person or persons.

(b) To discriminate against any person because of his race, creed, color, disability, national origin, age, sex or marital status in the terms, conditions or privileges of any publicly-assisted housing accommodations or in the furnishing of facilities or services in connection therewith.

(c) To cause to be made any written or oral inquiry or record concerning the race, creed, color, disability, national origin, age, sex or marital status of a person seeking to rent or lease any publicly-assisted housing accommodations.

(d) Nothing in this subdivision shall restrict the consideration of age in the rental of publicly-assisted housing accommodations if the division grants an exemption based on bona fide considerations of public policy for the purpose of providing for the special needs of a particular age group without the intent of prejudicing other age groups.

It shall be an unlawful discriminatory practice for any real estate broker, real estate salesman or employee or agent thereof or any other individual, corporation, partnership or organization for the purpose of inducing a real estate transaction from which any such person or any of its stockholders or members may benefit financially, to represent that a change has occurred or will or may occur in the composition with respect to race, creed, color, national origin or marital status of the owners or occupants in the block, neighborhood or area in which their real property is located, and to represent, directly or indirectly, that this change will or may result in undesirable consequences in the block, neighborhood or area in which the real property is located, including but not limited to the lowering of property values, an increase in criminal or anti-social behavior, or a decline in the quality of school or other facilities.

It shall be an unlawful discriminatory practice for any real estate broker, real estate salesman or employee or agent thereof:

To refuse to sell, rent or lease any housing accommodation, land or commercial space to any person or group of persons or to refuse to negotiate because of the race, creed, color, national origin, sex, or disability or marital status of such person or persons, or in relation to commercial space because of the age of such person or persons, or to represent that any housing accommodation, land or commercial space is not available for inspection, sale, rental or lease when in fact it is so available, or otherwise to deny or withhold any housing accommodation, land or commercial space or any facilities of any housing accommodation, land or commercial space from any person or group of persons because of the race, creed, color, national origin, sex, or disability or marital status of such person or persons or in relation to commercial space because of the age of such person or persons.

The provisions of this paragraph shall not apply (1) to the rental of a housing accommodation in a building which contains housing accommodations for not more than two families living independently of each other, if the owner or members of his family reside in one of such housing accommodations, (2) to the restriction of the rental of all rooms in a housing accommodation to individuals of the same sex or (3) to the rental of a room or rooms in a housing accommodation, if such rental is by the occupant of the housing accommodation or by the owner of the housing accommodation and he or members of his family reside in such housing accommodation.

It shall be an unlawful discriminatory practice for the owner, lessee, sublessee, or managing agent of, or other person, to print or circulate or cause to be printed or circulated any statement, advertisement or publication, or to use any form of application for the purchase, rental or lease of any housing accommodation, land or commercial space or to make any record or inquiry which expresses, directly or indirectly, any limitation, specification, or discrimination as to race, creed, color, national origin, sex, or disability or marital status, or in relation to commercial space as to age; or any intent to make any such limitation, specification or discrimination.

It shall be an unlawful discriminatory practice for any real estate board, because of the race, creed, color, national origin, age, sex, or disability or marital status of any individual who is otherwise qualified for membership, to exclude or expel such individual from membership, or to discriminate against such individual in the terms, conditions and privileges of membership in such board.

The provisions of this subdivision, as they relate to age, shall not apply to persons under the age of eighteen years.

11

Closing and Closing Costs

Key Terms

Abstract of title	Liability coverage
Accrued item	Marketable title
Actual notice	Mortgage reduction certificate
Adjustments	Prepaid item
Attorney's opinion of title	Priority
Chain of title	Proration
Closing statement	Real Estate Settlement Procedures Act (RESPA)
Coinsurance clause	Real property transfer report
Constructive notice	Recording
Credit	Replacement cost
Debit	Suit to quiet title
Escrow	Title insurance
Evidence of title	Torrens system
Financing statement	Uniform Settlement Statement
Homeowner's insurance policy	

Overview

The final step in the real estate transaction is the closing, a procedure that includes both title and financial considerations. For the protection of real estate owners, taxing bodies, creditors, and the general public, public records are maintained in every county and borough. Such records help to establish ownership, give notice of encumbrances, and establish priority of liens. The placing of documents in the public records is known as *recording*. This chapter will discuss title records and then go on to the real estate closing, focusing on the licensee's role in this concluding phase of a real estate transaction. Emphasis will be placed on the computations necessary to settle all necessary expenses between buyer and seller and between seller and broker.

Public Records and Recording

Before an individual purchases a fee simple estate to a parcel of real estate, he or she wants to be sure that the seller will be able to convey a good title to the property. The present owner of the real estate undoubtedly purchased his or her interest from a previous owner so the same question of *kind and condition* of title has been inquired into many times in the past. As long as taxes are paid and liens do not become delinquent it is expected that a fee simple title will remain a marketable title.

Recording Acts

The state legislature has passed laws that allow owners or parties interested in real estate to record, or file, in the public records all documents affecting their interest in real estate in order to give *legal, public, and constructive notice* to the world of their interest. These statutory enactments are referred to as *recording acts.*

Public records are maintained by the recorder of deeds, county clerk, county treasurer, city clerk and collector, and clerks of various courts of record. Records involving taxes, special assessments, ordinances, and zoning and building records also fall into this category. All these records are open for public inspection.

Necessity for Recording

New York's laws provide that a *deed or mortgage may not be effective as far as later purchasers* are concerned unless such documents have been *recorded.* Thus the public records should reveal the condition of the title and a purchaser should be able to rely on a search of such public records. From a practical point of view the recording acts give **priority** to those interests that are recorded first.

In New York in order to give subsequent purchasers constructive notice of a person's interest, all deeds, mortgages, or other written instruments affecting an interest in real estate must be recorded in the county clerk's office of the county where the real estate is located. All documents must be properly acknowledged and show proof of payment of the real estate transfer tax on deeds or the mortgage tax on mortgages before the documents will be accepted for recording.

A deed will not be accepted for recording unless it is accompanied by a **real property transfer report,** which will be used by the New York State Board of Equalization and Assessment. A *real estate transfer gains affidavit* also must be filed.

The recording office in the county clerk's office maintains general indexes of instruments recorded in that office. Two alphabetical lists are generally maintained—one listing the names of the grantors, mortgagors, or assignors, followed by the names of the grantees, mortgagees, or assignees, and the other listing the names of the grantees, mortgagees, or assignees, followed by the names of the grantors, mortgagors, or assignors. In some counties around New York City the Lot and Block system is used for indexing. Documents are also recorded in the Office of the New York City Register in borough offices in Manhattan (New York County), Brooklyn (Kings County), Bronx, and Jamaica (Queens).

Notice

Through the legal maxim of *caveat emptor* the courts charge a prospective real estate buyer or mortgagee (lender) with the responsibility of inspecting the property and searching the public records to ascertain the interests of other parties. **Constructive notice** is a presumption of law that charges a buyer with the responsibility of learning this information. The information is available; therefore the buyer or lender is responsible for learning it.

Constructive notice, or what a buyer is charged with knowing, is distinguished from **actual notice,** or what the person actually knows (*see* Figure 11.1). After an individual has searched the public records and inspected the property, he or she has actual notice, or knowledge, of the information learned. An individual is said to have actual notice of any information of which he or she has *direct knowledge*. If it can be proved that an individual has actual knowledge of information concerning a parcel of real estate, he or she cannot rely on a lack of constructive notice such as an unrecorded deed or an owner who is not in possession.

In New York it is the *duty of the purchaser* to investigate the title of property to be conveyed. The purchaser will be held to constructive notice of any outstanding rights on the title that could be discovered by a diligent search.

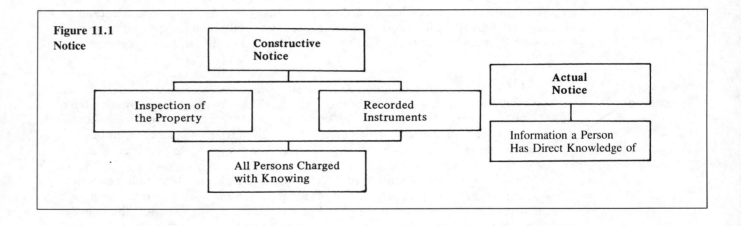

**Figure 11.1
Notice**

Real estate taxes and special assessments are automatically direct liens on specific parcels of real estate and need not be recorded. Other liens such as inheritance taxes and franchise taxes are placed by statutory authority against all real estate owned either by a decedent at the time of death or by a corporation at the time the franchise tax became a lien; these liens also are not recorded.

Recording Claims for Commission. A New York real estate broker is allowed to file an affidavit of entitlement to commissions in the office of the county clerk. While not a lien against the property, the affidavit will be indexed in the public records and places anyone reviewing title to the property on notice of the broker's claim. In addition a mechanic's lien may be filed for unpaid commissions due on the leasing of commercial property for a period of three years or more.

Recording Sales Contracts. In the case of an impending dispute it can on rare occasions be desirable to enter a contract for the sale of real property in the public records. Any document to be filed must be acknowledged. If neither the buyer nor seller can be reached for an acknowledgment, it will be sufficient if a witness to their signatures appears before a notary. The notary's statement in such a situation would read that "before me came . . . the subscribing witness to the foregoing instrument who, being by me duly sworn, did depose and say . . . that he knows the individual . . . who executed the foregoing instrument . . . was present and saw . . . execute the same, and that he, said witness, at the same time subscribed as witness thereto. . . ."

Chain of Title

The **chain of title** shows the record of ownership of the property over a period of time. An **abstract of title** is a condensed history of all the instruments affecting a particular parcel of land. In the United States chains of title in colonial states frequently date back to a grant from the king of England.

Through the chain of title, the ownership of the property can be traced from its origin to its present owner. If this cannot be done it is said that there is a *gap* in the chain. In such cases it is usually necessary to establish ownership by a court action called a **suit to quiet title,** or an Article 15 proceeding.

Evidence of Title

When dealing with an owner of real estate, a purchaser or lender requires satisfactory proof that the seller is the owner and has good title to the property. The owner is generally required to produce documentary proof called **evidence of title.**

There are four forms of title evidence: (1) abstract of title and lawyer's opinion, (2) title insurance policy, (3) Torrens certificate, and (4) certificate of title.

A deed is not evidence of title; while it conveys the interest of the grantor, even a warranty deed contains no proof of the kind or condition of the *grantor*'s title. The only effective proof must be one of the evidences of title, based upon an adequate search of the public records to *ascertain the ownership interests and condition of the title.*

Abstract of Title and Lawyer's Opinion

An abstract of title is a brief history (in abstract, or brief, form) of the instruments appearing in the county record that affect title to the parcel in question. The legal description of the property is in the abstract's caption. Abstracts usually consist of several sections, or continuations. It is necessary for each section of the abstract to begin with a search of the public record from a date immediately following the date of the previous section. If this were not done, there would be a gap in the abstract.

When an abstract is first prepared or is continued, the abstractor lists and summarizes each instrument in chronological order along with information relative to taxes, judgments, special assessments, and the like. The abstractor concludes with a certificate indicating which records were examined and when, and he or she signs the abstract. Abstractors must exercise due care because they can be liable for negligence for any failure to include or accurately record all pertinent data. An *abstractor does not, however, pass judgment on or guarantee the condition of the title.*

The abstract illustrated in Figure 11.2 shows that in 1945 Ida Hughey mortgaged her property at 47 Rowley Street to Rochester Savings Bank for $5,000. The rubber stamp on the record shows that the mortgage was paid off in 1958. The mortgage document evidently carried two legal descriptions: one by plat of sub-division, the other by metes and bounds.

In 1952 Hughey granted a five-year lease on the property to Michael and Mildred Franco, who recorded the document. The next year the Francos bought the prop-erty. This particular abstract later reports a driveway easement the Francos nego-tiated with their neighbors to the north and then traces the property through several different owners with mortgages placed and paid off along the way.

In a sale of land the seller's attorney usually orders the abstract continued to cover the current date. It is then submitted to the buyer's attorney, who must *examine the entire abstract*. Following his or her detailed examination the attorney must evaluate all the facts and material in order to prepare a written report for the purchaser on the condition of the ownership; this report is called an **attorney's opinion of title.**

As transfers of title have accumulated through the years, each abstract of title to individual property has become more and more voluminous and the time needed by an attorney to examine an abstract has therefore increased. In many ways the title evidence system of abstract examination and opinion and the certification of title by attorneys (discussed later in this chapter) are imperfect and open to objection. It is difficult to detect forged deeds or false statements including in-correct marital information and transfers involving incompetent parties or minors. An honest mistake could be made against which the owner of real estate had no recourse. To provide purchasers with protection against this type of error and to give insurance along with defense of the title, title insurance is used increas-ingly in New York. It is usually required by the lending institution when a new mortgage is to be placed.

Title Insurance

A **title insurance** policy is a contract by which a title insurance company agrees, subject to the terms of its policy, to indemnify (that is, to compensate or re-imburse) the insured (the owner, mortgagee, or other interest holder) against any losses sustained as a result of defects in the title other than those exceptions listed in the policy. The title company agrees to defend at its own expense any lawsuit attacking the title if the lawsuit is based on a defect in title against which the policy insures.

A buyer or seller seeking to obtain a title insurance policy as evidence of owner-ship makes an application to the title insurance company. The title company examines the title records and agrees to insure against certain undiscovered de-fects. Exactly which defects the company will insure against depends on the type of policy it issues; the New York State Insurance Department sets standards. A policy will usually insure against defects that may be found in the public rec-ords and such items as forged documents, documents of incompetent grantors, incorrect marital statements, and improperly delivered deeds. The company does not agree to insure against any defects in or liens against the title that are found by the title examination and specifically listed in the policy as exceptions.

Upon completion of the examination the title company usually issues a report of title, or a commitment to issue a title policy. This describes the policy that will

Figure 11.2
Portion of an Abstract

A B S T R A C T O F T I T L E

\- T O -

#47 W e s t s i d e R o w l e y S t r e e t, b e i n g
P a r t o f L o t s #27 a n d 28 o f t h e
B r o o k s T r a c t (N. P a r t) i n t h e
C i t y o f R o c h e s t e r

Maps: Liber 2 of Maps, page 120 and 138
Liber 3 of Maps, page 45
1935 Hopkins Atlas, Vol. 1, Plate 4

1 Ida May Hughey — Mortgage to secure $5000.00
-To- Dated June 3, 1947
Ack. same day
Rochester Savings Bank — Recd. same day at 12:30 P. M.
47 Main Street West
Rochester, New York — Liber 1800 of Mortgages, page 344

CORRECTLY DISCHARGED OF RECORD
BY MORTGAGEE 12/19/58
BY ASSIGNEE
NO ASSIGNMENT OF RECORD
ABSTRACT & TITLE INSURANCE CORPORATION
PER

(+) Conveys land in the City of Rochester, being on the west side of Rowley Street in said City and being part of lots Nos. 27 and 28 in the Brooks Tract as shown on a map of said Tract made by M. D. Rowley, surveyor, May 15, 1869, and filed in Monroe County Clerk's Office and counded and described as follows:

Beginning at a point in the west line of Rowely Street 15 feet northerly from the southeast corner of said lot #27; thence northerly on the west line of Rowley Street, forth (40) feet; thence westerly on a line parallel with the south line of said lot #27, 121 feet; thence southerly on a line parallel with the west line of Rowley Street, 40 feet; thence easterly 121 feet to the place of beginning.

Figure 11.2
(continued)

　　　　　　Being the same premises conveyed to the **mortgagor**
by Liber 2258 of Deeds, page 178.

　　　　　　Subject to any restrictions and public utility
easements of record.

- -

2　　Ida May Hughey, Landlord　　　Lease

　　　　　　　　-To-　　　　　　　Dated　May 23, 1952
　　　　　　　　　　　　　　　　　Ack.　　same day
　　Michael Franco　　　　　　　Rec.　　August 4, 1952
　　Mildred Franco,his wife,
　　Tenants, 17 Glendale Park,　Liber 2769 of Deeds, page 290
　　Rochester, N.Y.,(Second
　　parties not certified)

　　　　　　First party leases to second parties premises described as #47 Rowley Street, Rochester, New York, being a
12 room house for a term of 5 years commencing July 16, 1952
and ending July 15, 1957 on certain terms and conditions set
forth herein.

　　　　　　Second parties shall have the right of renewal on
the same terms and conditions as herein for an additional
period of 5 years provided that written notice of intention to
renew is served upon Landlord or her assigns at least 30 days
prior to end of initial term hereof.

- -

3　　Ida May Hughey,　　　　　　Warranty Deed

　　　　　　-To-　　　　　　　　Dated Oct. 30, 1953
　　　　　　　　　　　　　　　　Ack. Same day
　　Michele Franco, Mildred　　Rec. Same day at 10:50 A.M.
　　Franco, his wife, as
　　tenants by the entirety,　　Liber 2861　of Deeds, page 411
　　#47 Rowley St., Rochester,
　　N.Y. (Second parties not
　　certified).

　　　　　　Conveys same as #1.

　　　　　　Subject to all covenants, easements and restrictions

be issued and includes the following: (1) the name of the insured party, (2) the legal description of the real estate, (3) the estate or interest covered, (4) a schedule of all exceptions, consisting of encumbrances and defects found in the public records, and (5) conditions and stipulations under which the policy is issued. An *owner's policy will usually exclude coverage* against the following exceptions: unrecorded documents, unrecorded defects of which the policyholder has knowledge, rights of parties in possession, and facts discoverable by survey. Under the contract the title insurance company agrees to defend the title at its own expense and to reimburse the policyholder for damages sustained by reason of any defect not excepted. Title companies in New York must offer a homeowner the right to purchase insurance covering future market value.

Title companies issue various forms of title insurance policies, the most common of which are the *owner's* title insurance policy (a *fee policy*), the *mortgage* title insurance policy, and the *leasehold* title insurance policy. As the names indicate, each of these policies is issued to insure specific interests. For example, a mortgage title insurance policy ensures a mortgage company or lender that it has a valid first lien against the property. The owner's policy (usually available at a small additional charge when a mortgage policy is purchased) insures the property owner's interests.

The Torrens System

In New York the **Torrens system** of land registration is a valid method of recording title. The method, however, is used only occasionally in this state.

Under the Torrens system a written application to register a title to real estate is made with the clerk of the court of the county in which the real estate is located. If the applicant proves that he or she is the owner, the court enters an order to register the real estate and the *registrar of titles* is further directed to issue a certificate of title. At any time, the Torrens original certificate of title in the registrar's office reveals the owner of the land and all mortgages, judgments, and similar liens. It does not reveal federal or New York State taxes and some other items.

Certificate of Title

In some rural localities a *certificate of title prepared by a attorney* is used and no abstract is prepared. The attorney examines the public records and issues a certificate of title that expresses his or her opinion of the title's status. The certificate is an opinion of the validity of the grantor's or mortgagor's title and the existence of liens and encumbrances. It is not, however, a title insurance policy and does not carry the full protection of such a policy.

A lawyer's opinion of title is often oral, or implied, representation; the person who sustains damages by relying upon it may look to the lawyer for satisfaction.

Marketable Title

Under the terms of the usual real estate sales contract the seller is required to deliver marketable title to the buyer at the closing. Generally, a **marketable title** is one that is so free from significant defects (other than those specified in the sales contract) that the purchaser can be assured against having to defend the title. Proper evidence of title is proof that the title is in fact marketable. In order for title to be marketable it must: (1) be free from liens and encumbrances; (2) disclose no serious defects and not be dependent on doubtful questions of law or fact to prove its validity; (3) not expose a purchaser to the hazard of litigation or threaten the quiet enjoyment of the property; and (4) convince a reasonably well-informed and prudent person, acting upon business principles and willful knowledge of the facts and their legal significance, that he or she could in turn sell or mortgage the property at a fair market value.

A buyer cannot be forced to accept a conveyance that is materially different from the one bargained for in the sales contract; he or she cannot be forced to buy a lawsuit. Questions of marketable title must be raised by a purchaser (or his or her broker or attorney) prior to acceptance of the deed. If a buyer accepts a deed with unmarketable title, the only available legal recourse is to sue the seller under the covenants of warranty (if any) contained in the deed.

Closing the Transaction

Although salespeople usually are not burdened with the technicalities of closing, they must clearly understand what takes place. A real estate specialist should be able to assist in preclosing arrangements and advise the parties in estimating their expenses and the approximate amounts the buyer will need and the seller will receive at the closing. The closing represents the culmination of the service the broker's firm provides. The sale that the broker has negotiated is completed and the broker's commission (and thus the salesperson's commission) is generally paid out of the proceeds at the closing.

In some states a closing statement problem is part of the broker's licensing examination. This is not the case in New York State.

Generally the closing of a real estate transaction involves a gathering of interested parties at which the promises made in the *real estate sales contract* are kept, or *executed;* that is, the seller's deed is delivered in exchange for the purchase price. In many sales transactions two closings actually take place at this time: (1) the closing of the buyer's loan—the disbursal of mortgage funds by the lender—and (2) the closing of the sale.

As discussed in Chapter 5, a sales contract is the blueprint for the completion of a real estate transaction. A contract should be complete and should provide for all possibilities in order to avoid misunderstandings that could delay or even prevent the closing of the sale. Before going ahead with this exchange the parties should assure themselves that the various conditions and stipulations of their sales contract have been met.

The buyer will want to be sure that the seller is delivering good title and that the property is in the promised condition. This involves inspecting the title evidence, the deed the seller will give, any documents representing the removal of undesired liens and encumbrances, any survey, termite report, or leases, if there are tenants on the premises. The seller will want to be sure that the buyer has obtained the stipulated financing and has sufficient funds to complete the sale. Both parties will wish to inspect the closing statement to make sure that all monies involved in the transaction have been properly accounted for. In doing this the parties most likely will be represented by attorneys.

When the parties are satisfied that everything is in order, the exchange is made and all pertinent documents are then recorded. The documents must be recorded in the correct order to avoid creating a defect in the title. For example, if the seller is paying off an existing loan and the buyer is obtaining a new loan, the seller's satisfaction of mortgage must be recorded before the seller's deed to the buyer. The buyer's new mortgage must be recorded after the deed because the lender cannot have a security interest in the buyer's property until it belongs to the buyer.

Where Closings Are Held and Who Attends

Closings may be held at a number of locations including the offices of the title company, the lending institution, the office of one of the parties' attorneys, the broker's office, the office of the county clerk (or other local recording official), or an escrow company. Those attending a closing may include any of the following interested parties:

1. buyer;
2. seller;
3. real estate agent (broker and/or salesperson);
4. attorney(s) for the seller and/or buyer;
5. representatives and/or attorneys for lending institutions involved with the buyer's new mortgage loan, the buyer's assumption of the seller's existing loan, or the seller's payoff of an existing loan; and
6. representative of the title insurance company.

Broker's Role at Closing

Depending on the locality the broker's role at a closing can vary from simply collecting his or her commission to conducting the proceedings. Because a real estate broker is not authorized to give legal advice or otherwise engage in the practice of law, a broker's job is essentially over when the sales contract is signed; at that point, the attorneys take over. Even so a broker's service generally continues after the contract is signed in that he or she advises the parties in practical matters, aids the buyer with a mortgage application, and makes sure all the details are taken care of so that the closing can proceed smoothly. In this capacity the broker might make arrangements for such items as title evidence, surveys, appraisals, termite inspections, and repairs, or might suggest sources of these services to the parties.

Lender's Interest in Closing

Whether a buyer is obtaining new financing or assuming the seller's existing loan, the lender wants to protect its security interest in the property—to make sure that the buyer is getting good, marketable title and that tax and insurance payments are maintained so that there will be no liens with greater priority than the mortgage lien, and the insurance will be paid up if the property is damaged or destroyed. For this reason the lender frequently will require the following items: (1) a title insurance policy or abstract of title; (2) a fire and hazard insurance policy with receipt for the premium; (3) additional information, such as a survey, a termite or other inspection report, or a certificate of occupancy (for newly constructed buildings, multiple dwellings, and in a few areas like lower Manhattan, all buildings); (4) establishment of a reserve, or escrow, account for tax and insurance payments; and (5) representation by its own attorney at the closing.

Homeowner's Insurance

Where mortgaging is involved the buyer must bring to the closing proof of insurance on the property, and occasionally of flood insurance. The insurance policy or binder usually names the lender as lienholder and co-payee in case of loss under the policy.

Although it is possible for a homeowner to obtain individual policies for each type of risk (*see* Chapter 21 for a discussion of various kinds of available coverage), most residential property owners take out insurance in the form of a packaged **homeowner's policy.** These standardized policies insure holders against the destruction of their property by fire or windstorm, injury to others that occurs on the property, and theft of any personal property on the premises that is owned by the insured or members of his or her family.

The package homeowner's policy also includes **liability coverage** for: (1) personal injuries to others resulting from the insured's acts or negligence, (2) voluntary medical payments and funeral expenses for accidents sustained by guests or resident employees on the property of the owner, and (3) physical damage to the property of others caused by the insured. Voluntary medical payments will cover injuries to a resident employee but will not cover benefits due under any workmen's compensation or occupational disease law.

Characteristics of Homeowners' Packages

Although coverage provided may vary among policies, all homeowners' policies have three common characteristics: fixed ratios of coverage, indivisible premium, and first- and third-party insurance. *Fixed ratios of coverage* require that each type of coverage in a homeowner's policy be maintained at a certain level. The amount of coverage on household contents and other items must be a fixed percentage of the amount of insurance on the building itself. While the amount of contents coverage may be increased, it cannot be reduced below the standard percentage. In addition theft coverage may be contingent on the full amount of the contents coverage.

An *indivisible premium* combines the rates for covering each peril into a single amount. For the single rate the insured receives coverage for all the perils included in the policy (*see* the lists that follow). The insured may not pick and choose the perils to be included.

As previously discussed, *first- and third-party insurance* not only provides coverage for damage or loss to the insured's property or its contents but also covers the insured's legal liability for losses or damages to another's property or injuries suffered by another party while on the owner's property.

There are four major forms of homeowners' policies. The *basic* form, known as *HO-1*, provides property coverage against the following perils:

1. fire or lightning,
2. glass breakage,
3. windstorm or hail,
4. explosion,
5. riot or civil commotion,
6. damage by aircraft,
7. damage from vehicles,
8. damage from smoke,
9. vandalism and malicious mischief,
10. theft, and
11. loss of property removed from the premises when endangered by fire or other perils.

Increased coverage is provided under a *broad* form, known as *HO-2*, that covers the following additional perils:

12. falling objects;
13. weight of ice, snow, or sleet;
14. collapse of the building or any part of it;
15. bursting, cracking, burning, or bulging of a steam or hot water heating system, or of appliances used to heat water;
16. accidental discharge, leakage, or overflow of water or steam from within a plumbing, heating, or air-conditioning system;
17. freezing of plumbing, heating, and air-conditioning systems and domestic appliances; and
18. injury to electrical appliances, devices, fixtures, and wiring from short circuits or other accidentally generated currents.

Further coverage is provided by *comprehensive* forms *HO-3*, the most popular form, and *HO-5;* these policies cover all possible perils except flood, earthquake, war, and nuclear attack. Other policies include *HO-4*, a form designed specifically for apartment renters, and *HO-6*, a broad-form policy for condominium owners. Apartment and condominium policies generally provide fire and windstorm, theft, and public liability coverage for injuries or losses sustained within the unit but do not usually extend to cover losses or damages to the structure. The structure is insured by either the landlord or the condominium owners' association (except, in condominium ownership, for additions or alterations made by the unit owner that are not covered by the association's master policy).

Claims. Most homeowners' insurance policies contain a **coinsurance clause.** This provision requires the insured to maintain fire insurance on his or her property in an amount equal to at least 80 percent of the **replacement cost** of the dwelling (not including the price of the land). If the owner carries such a policy a claim may be made for the cost of the repair or replacement of the damaged property without deduction.

In any event *the total settlement cannot exceed the face value of the policy.* Because of coinsurance clauses it is important for homeowners to periodically review all policies to be certain that the coverage is equal to at least 80 percent of the current replacement cost of their homes. Some policies carry automatic increases in coverage to adjust for inflation.

Federal Flood Insurance Program

A subsidized program authorized by Congress requires property owners in certain areas to obtain flood damage insurance on properties financed by mortgages or other loans, grants, or guarantees obtained from federal agencies and federally insured or regulated lending institutions. The program seeks to improve future management for floodplain areas through land-use and control measures. The Department of Housing and Urban Development (HUD), which administers the flood program, has prepared maps and identified specific flood-prone areas throughout the country.

RESPA Requirements

The federal **Real Estate Settlement Procedures Act (RESPA),** enacted in 1974 and revised in 1975, was created to ensure that the buyer and seller in a residential real estate transaction have knowledge of all settlement costs. *RESPA* *requirements apply when the purchase is financed by a federally related mortgage loan.* Federally related loans include those (1) made by banks, savings and loan associations, or other lenders whose deposits are insured by federal agencies (FDIC or FSLIC); (2) insured by the FHA or guaranteed by the VA; (3) administered by the U.S. Department of Housing and Urban Development; or (4) intended to be sold by the lender to Fannie Mae, Ginnie Mae, or Freddie Mac.

RESPA regulations apply only to transactions involving new first mortgage loans. A transaction financed solely by a purchase-money mortgage taken back by the seller, an installment contract (land contract of sale, contract for deed), or the buyer's assumption of the seller's existing loan would not be covered by RESPA unless the terms of the assumed loan are modified or the lender charges more than $50 for the assumption. When a transaction is covered by RESPA, the following requirements must be met:

1. *Special information booklet:* Lenders must give a copy of the HUD booklet *Settlement Costs and You* to every person from whom they receive or for whom they prepare a loan application. This booklet provides the borrower with general information about settlement (closing) costs and explains the various RESPA provisions including a line-by-line discussion of the Uniform Settlement Statement (*see* item 3).
2. *Good faith estimate of settlement costs:* At the time of the loan application or within three business days the lender must provide the borrower with a good faith estimate of the settlement costs the borrower is likely to incur. This estimate may be a specific figure or a range of costs based upon comparable past transactions in the area. In addition if the lender requires use of a particular attorney or title company to conduct the closing, the lender must state whether it has any business relationship with that firm and must estimate the charges for this service.
3. *Uniform Settlement Statement (HUD Form 1):* RESPA provides that loan closing information must be prepared on a special HUD form, the **Uniform Settlement Statement,** designed to detail all financial particulars of a transaction. The completed statement must itemize all charges imposed by the lender. Charges incurred by the buyer and seller, contracted for separately and outside the closing, do not have to be disclosed. Items paid for prior to the closing must be clearly marked as such on the statement and are omitted from the totals. Upon the borrower's request, *the closing agent must permit the borrower to inspect the settlement statement, to the extent that the figures are available, one business day before the closing.* Lenders must retain these statements for two years after the date of closing unless the loan (and its servicing) is sold or otherwise disposed of. The Uniform Settlement Statement may be altered to allow for local custom and certain lines may be deleted if they do not apply in the area.
4. *Prohibition against kickbacks:* RESPA explicitly prohibits the payment of kickbacks, or unearned fees, such as when an insurance agency pays a kickback to a lender for referring one of the lender's recent customers to the agency. This prohibition does *not* include fee splitting between cooperating brokers or members of multiple-listing services, brokerage referral arrangements, or the division of a commission between a broker and his or her salespeople.

RESPA is administered by HUD.

The Title Procedure

On the date when the sale is actually completed, that is, the date of delivery of the deed, the buyer has a title commitment or an abstract that was issued several days or weeks before the closing. For this reason the title or abstract company is usually required to make a second search of the public records. A supplemental telephone search by the abstracting company is often made at the moment of closing.

The seller is usually required to execute an *affidavit of title*. This is a sworn statement in which the seller assures the title company (and the buyer) that since the date of the title examination there have been no judgments, bankruptcies, or divorces involving the seller, no unrecorded deeds or contracts made, no repairs or improvements that have not been paid for, no defects in the title that the seller knows of, and that he or she is in possession of the premises. This form is always required by the title insurance company before it will issue an owner's policy, particularly an extended-coverage policy, to the buyer. Through this affidavit the title company obtains the right to sue the seller if his or her statements in the affidavit prove incorrect.

Checking the Premises

In general it is important for the buyer to inspect the property to determine the interests of any parties in possession or other interests that cannot be determined from inspecting the public record. A *survey* is frequently required so that the purchaser will know the location, size, and legal description of the property. The contract will specify whether the seller is to pay for this. It is usual for the survey to ''spot'' the location of all buildings, driveways, fences, and other improvements located primarily on the premises being purchased as well as any such improvements located on adjoining property that may encroach upon the premises being bought. The survey also sets out in full any existing easements and encroachments. So that the survey will clearly identify the location of the property, the house number, if any, should be stated.

The state requires that the seller of a one- or two-family building furnish the buyer, at closing, with an affidavit stating that the residence complies with the New York fire code requirement for a working smoke alarm on the premises.

Releasing Existing Liens

When the purchaser is paying cash or is obtaining a new mortgage in order to purchase the property, the seller's existing mortgage usually is paid in full and released of record. In order to know the exact amount required to pay the existing mortgage the seller secures a current *payoff statement* from the mortgagee. This payoff statement sets forth the unpaid amount of principal, interest due through the date of payment, the fee for issuing the release, credits, if any, for tax and insurance reserves, and any penalties that may be due because the loan is being prepaid before its maturity. The same procedure would be followed for any other liens that must be released before the buyer takes title.

For transactions in which the buyer is assuming the seller's existing mortgage loan, the buyer will want to know the exact balance of the loan as of the closing date. In some areas it is customary for the buyer to obtain a **mortgage reduction certificate** from the lender, stating the exact balance due and the last interest payment made.

Closing in Escrow
In the western section of the country the majority of transactions are closed in escrow but the system is almost never used in New York State.

In an **escrow** closing a disinterested third party is authorized to act as escrow agent and coordinates the closing activities. The escrow agent may be an attorney, a title company, a trust company, an escrow company, or the escrow department of a lending institution. Buyer and seller choose an escrow agent and execute an escrow agreement after the sales contract is signed. This agreement sets forth the details of the transaction and the instructions to the escrow agent. Buyer and seller deposit all pertinent documents and other items with the escrow agent before the specified date of closing.

The escrow agent examines the title evidence. When clear title is shown and all other conditions of the escrow agreement have been met, the agent is authorized to disburse the purchase price to the seller and to record the deed and mortgage (if a new mortgage has been executed by the purchaser).

Preparation of Closing Statements
A typical real estate sales transaction involves numerous expenses for both parties in addition to the purchase price. There are a number of property expenses that the seller will have paid in advance for a set period of time or that the buyer will pay in the future. The financial responsibility for these items must be *prorated,* or divided, between the buyer and the seller. In closing a transaction it is customary to account for all these items by preparing a written statement to determine how much money the buyer needs and how much the seller will net after the broker's commission and expenses. While there are many different formats of closing statements, or settlement statements, all are designed to achieve the same results.

Closing statements in New York are prepared by the buyer's and seller's attorneys. The broker should, however, possess the necessary knowledge to prepare statements so that he or she can calculate the expenses involved in a particular sale and give the seller an accurate estimate of the property's sale costs. In addition the buyer must be prepared with the proper amount of money to complete the purchase and, again, the broker should be able to assist by making a reasonably accurate estimate.

How the Closing Statement Works
The completion of a **closing statement** involves an accounting of the parties' debits and credits. A **debit** is a charge, an amount that the party being debited owes and must pay at the closing. A **credit** is an amount entered in a person's favor—either an amount that the party being credited already has paid, an amount that he or she must be reimbursed for, or an amount the buyer promises to pay in the form of a loan.

To determine the amount the buyer needs at the closing, the buyer's debits are totaled. Any expenses and prorated amounts for items prepaid by the seller are added to the purchase price. Then the buyer's credits are totaled. These would include the earnest money (already paid), the balance of the loan the buyer is obtaining or assuming, and the seller's share of any prorated items that the buyer will pay in the future. Finally the total of the buyer's credits is subtracted from the total amount the buyer owes (debits) to arrive at the actual amount of cash the buyer must bring to the closing. Usually the buyer brings a bank cashier's check or a certified personal check.

A similar procedure is followed to determine how much money the seller actually will receive. The seller's debits and credits are each totaled. The credits would include the purchase price plus the buyer's share of any prorated items that the seller has prepaid.

The seller's debits would include expenses, the seller's share of prorated items to be paid later by the buyer, and the balance of any mortgage loan or other lien that the seller is paying off. Finally the total of the seller's charges is subtracted from the total credits to arrive at the amount the seller will receive.

Expenses

In addition to the payment of the sales price and the proration of taxes, interest, and the like, a number of other expenses and charges may be involved in a real estate transaction. These may include the following items.

Broker's commission. The broker's commission is usually paid by the seller because the broker is usually the seller's agent. When the buyer has employed the broker, the buyer pays the commission.

Attorney's fees. If either of the parties' attorneys will be paid from the closing proceeds, that party will be charged with the expense in the closing statement.

Recording expenses. The charges for recording documents may vary from one area to another. Upstate, a county may typically charge $5 for recording a document plus $3 per page. Thus a single-page deed would cost $8 to record while the charge for a four-page mortgage would be $17. These charges are established by law and are based upon the size of the document. The licensee should verify local recording charges.

The *seller* usually pays for recording charges (filing fees) that are necessary in order to clear all defects and furnish the purchaser with a clear title in accordance with the terms of the contract. Items usually charged to the seller would include the recording of satisfaction of mortgages, quitclaim deeds, affidavits, and satisfaction of mechanic's lien claims. The *purchaser* pays for recording charges incident to the actual transfer of title. Items usually charged to the purchaser include recording the deed that conveys title to the purchaser and a mortgage executed by the purchaser.

Transfer tax stamps. Any New York State conveyance is taxed at a rate of $2 per $500 or fraction thereof of the property's value minus any mortgage being assumed. Before 1983 the rate was $0.55. The transfer tax must be paid, usually by the seller, when the deed is recorded through the purchase of *stamps* from the county recorder of the county in which the deed is recorded. Local taxes also may be due.

New York City levies a transfer tax of one percent on sales of less than $500,000 and on one- to three-family dwellings. Other transfers require payment of a two percent city tax. The tax is paid by the grantor.

Personal property transferred with the real estate (drapes, for example) is covered by a bill of sale and is subject not to transfer tax but to state sales tax.

In 1985 the U.S. Supreme Court let stand a New York State capital gains tax of ten percent, due on any transfer where consideration totals more than $1,000,000. Any sale between $500,000 and $1,000,000 does not require this capital gains tax but must be accompanied by an affidavit detailing the transaction. The affidavit must be filed or the tax paid before the deed may be recorded.

State mortgage tax. New York State imposes a tax of $0.75 for each $100 or fraction thereof for every mortgage recorded within the state and in many counties there is an additional $0.25 for each $100 or fraction thereof. The first $10,000 of a mortgage for any one- or two-family residence is taxed at a rate of $0.50 for each $100. If the mortgage covers property improved by a structure with six or fewer cooking units, the mortgagee must pay a portion of the mortgage tax—$0.25 for each $100 or fraction thereof. When a land contract is recorded, mortgage tax is due on the amount "borrowed." The city of New York imposes an additional tax of $0.50 for each $100 or fraction thereof for every mortgage recorded on property located in the city. In counties that levy additional tax, none is due on the first $10,000 of the loan.

Title expenses. The responsibility for title expenses will vary according to local custom. If the buyer's attorney will inspect the evidence or if the buyer purchases title insurance policies, the buyer will be charged for these expenses. In some situations the title or abstract company is required to make two searches of the public records: the first showing the status of the seller's title on the date of the sales contract and the second continuing after the closing and through the date the purchaser's deed is recorded. In such cases the seller pays for the initial search and the purchaser pays for the "re-date" charge. The buyer often pays for title insurance in the area around New York City; Upstate custom varies in this matter.

Loan fees. When the purchaser is securing a mortgage to finance the purchase, the lender (mortgage company) will usually charge a service charge or origination fee. The fee is a flat charge and is usually paid by the purchaser at the time the transaction is closed. In addition the buyer may be charged an assumption fee if he or she assumes the seller's existing financing and in some cases may pay discount points.

The seller also may be charged discount points as discussed in Chapter 7. Also, the seller may be required to pay a prepayment charge or penalty for paying off his or her mortgage loan in advance of its due date.

Tax reserves and insurance reserves (escrows). A *reserve* is a sum of money set aside to be used later for a particular purpose. The mortgage lender usually requires the borrower to establish and maintain a reserve so that the borrower will have sufficient funds to pay general taxes and renew insurance when these items become due.

To set up the reserve the borrower is required to make a lump-sum payment to the lender when the mortgage money is paid out (usually at the time of closing). Thereafter the borrower is required to pay into the reserve an amount equal to one month's portion of the *estimated* general tax and insurance premium as part of the monthly payment made to the mortgage company.

Additional fees. An FHA borrower owes a lump sum for prepayment of the mortgage insurance premium (MIP) if it is not being financed as part of the loan. A

VA mortgagor pays a one percent fee directly to the VA at closing. If a conventional loan carries private mortgage insurance the buyer prepays one year's insurance premium at closing.

Appraisal fees. Either the seller or the purchaser pays the appraisal fees, depending on who orders the appraisal. When the buyer obtains a mortgage, it is customary for the lender to require an appraisal, which the buyer pays for.

Survey fees. If the purchaser obtains new mortgage financing, he or she customarily pays the survey fees. In some cases the sales contract may require the seller to furnish a survey.

Prorations

Most closings involve the dividing of financial responsibility between the buyer and seller for such items as loan interest, taxes, rents, fuel, and utility bills. These allowances are called **prorations** or **adjustments.** Prorations are necessary to ensure that expenses are fairly divided between the seller and the buyer. For example, where taxes must be paid in advance, the seller would be entitled to a rebate at the closing. If the buyer assumes the seller's existing mortgage, the seller usually owes the buyer an allowance for accrued interest through the date of closing.

As interest is usually paid in arrears, each payment covers interest for the preceding month. At a mid-month closing, the seller who has not made the current month's payment might owe six weeks' back interest on a mortgage.

Accrued items are items to be prorated (such as water bills and interest on an assumed mortgage) that are owed by the seller but eventually will be paid by the buyer. The seller therefore gives the buyer credit for these items at closing.

Prepaid items are items to be prorated (such as taxes or fuel oil left in the tank) that have been prepaid by the seller but not fully earned (not fully used up). They are therefore credits to the seller.

General rules for prorating. The rules or customs governing the computation of prorations for the closing of a real estate sale vary:

1. In New York it is specifically provided that the buyer owns the property on the closing date. In practice, however, either buyer or seller may be charged with that day's expenses.
2. Mortgage interest, general real estate taxes, water taxes, and similar expenses are usually computed by using *360 days in a year and 30 days in a month.* However, the rules in some areas provide for computing prorations on the basis of the actual number of days in the calendar month of closing. The sales contract may specify which method is to be used. Pocket calculators aid a trend toward using a 365-day year.
3. *Special assessments* for such municipal improvements as sewers, water mains, or streets are usually paid in annual installments over several years. In a sales transaction, the seller pays the current installment and the buyer assumes all future installments. *The special assessment installment generally is not prorated at the closing.*
4. *Rents* are usually adjusted on the basis of the *actual* number of days in the month of closing. It is customary for the seller to receive the rents for the day of closing and to pay all expenses for that day. If any rents for the

current month are uncollected when the sale is closed, the buyer often will agree by a separate letter to collect the rents if possible and remit the pro rata share to the seller.

5. *Security deposits* are generally transferred by the seller to the buyer; some leases may require the tenant's consent to such a transfer of the deposit.

6. Unpaid *wages of building employees* are prorated if the sale is closed between wage payment dates.

Accounting for Credits and Charges

The items that must be accounted for in the closing statement fall into two general categories: (1) prorations or other amounts due to either the buyer or seller (credit to) and paid for by the other party (debit to) and (2) expenses or items paid by the seller or buyer (debit only).

Items Credited to Buyer (debited to seller)

1. buyer's earnest money*
2. unpaid principal balance of outstanding mortgage being assumed by buyer*
3. earned interest on existing assumed mortgage not yet payable (accrued)
4. earned portion of general real estate tax not yet due (accrued)
5. unearned portion of current rent collected in advance
6. earned janitor's salary (and sometimes vacation allowance)
7. tenants' security deposits*
8. purchase-money mortgage (*see* Chapter 7)
9. unpaid water bills

Items Credited to Seller (debited to buyer)

1. sales price*
2. fuel oil on hand, usually figured at current market price (prepaid)
3. insurance and tax reserve (if any) when outstanding mortgage is being assumed by buyer (prepaid)
4. refund to seller of prepaid water charge and similar expenses
5. unearned portion of general real estate tax paid in advance

Other items may be included in such a list depending upon the customs of the area. The items marked by an asterisk are not prorated; they are entered in full as listed.

The *buyer's earnest money,* while credited to the buyer, *is not debited to the seller.* The buyer receives a credit because he or she has already paid that amount toward the purchase price; however, under the usual sales contract the money is held by the broker or escrow agent until the settlement, when it will be included as part of the total amount due the seller. If the seller is paying off an existing loan and the buyer is obtaining a new one, these two items are accounted for with a debit only to the seller for the amount of the payoff and a credit only to the buyer for the amount of the new loan.

Accounting for expenses. Expenses paid out of the closing proceeds are debited only to the party making the payment.

The Arithmetic of Prorating

The computation of a proration involves identifying a yearly charge for the item to be prorated, then dividing by 12 to determine a monthly charge for the item. It is usually also necessary to identify a daily charge for the item by dividing the monthly charge by the number of days in the month. These smaller portions are then multiplied by the number of months and/or days in the prorated time period to determine the accrued or unearned amount that will be figured in the settlement.

Using this general principle there are three basic methods of calculating prorations:

1. The yearly charge is divided by a *360-day year,* or 12 months of 30 days each.
2. The monthly charge is divided by the *actual number of days in the month of closing* to determine the amount.
3. The *yearly charge is divided by 365* to determine the daily charge. Then the actual number of days in the proration period is determined and this number is multiplied by the daily charge.

In some cases when a sale is closed on the fifteenth of the month the one-half month's charge is computed by simply dividing the monthly charge in two.

The final proration figure will vary slightly depending on which computation method is used.

Sample Closing Statements

Figure 11.3 details a buyer's closing statement and Figure 11.4 a seller's closing statement for the same transaction. The property is being purchased for $89,500, with $49,500 down and the seller taking back a mortgage for $40,000. Closing takes place on August 12.

Prorations. The buyer is taking over a house on which taxes have been paid, in one case until the end of the year. The buyer will therefore reimburse the seller for the time in which the buyer will be living in a tax-paid house. Specifically, the seller paid city and school taxes of $1,176.35 for the tax year that started July 1 and will receive a large portion of that back as a credit from the buyer. County taxes of $309.06 were paid January 1 for the year ahead so the buyer will also credit the seller for the four months and 18 days remaining in the year, an adjustment of $118.52.

The buyer owes the seller ("total seller's credits") the purchase price plus unearned taxes, for a total of $90,657.68. Toward this sum the buyer receives credit for an earnest money deposit of $500 in a broker's escrow account. (The seller's attorney and the broker will later take this sum into consideration when commission is paid.) The buyer also receives credit for the $40,000 bond and mortgage given to the seller at closing. The buyer therefore gives the seller cash (or a certified check) for the remaining sum, $50,157.68.

The upper half of the closing statement accounts for the transaction between buyer and seller; the lower part details each one's individual expenses. The buyer pays to record the deed and mortgage and pays the mortgage tax. The buyer also pays his or her attorney.

The seller's expenses involve last-minute payment of the school tax (plus a small late-payment penalty) for which the seller is largely reimbursed, the required

Figure 11.3
Buyer's
Closing
Statement

SELLER'S CREDITS

Sale Price _____ $ 89,500.00

ADJUSTMENT OF TAXES

School Tax 7/1/85 to 6/30/86   Amount $ 1176.35   Adj. 10 mos. 18 days $ 1,039.16

City/School Tax 7/1/ to 6/30/   Amount $_____ Adj. _____ mos._____ days $_____

County Tax 19 85   Amount $ 309.06   Adj. 4 mos. 18 days $ 118.52

Village Tax 6/1/ to 5/31/   Amount $_____ Adj. _____ mos._____ days $_____

City Tax Embellishments   Amount S_____ Adj. _____ mos. _____ days S_____

_____

_____

_____

Total Seller's Credits $ 90,657.68

PURCHASER'S CREDITS

Deposit with __Nothnagle_____ $ 500.00

(Assumed) (New) Mortgage with __Seller $480.07 p/m__ $ 40,000.00

beg. 9-12-85, 12% int., 15 yrs. _____ $_____

_____ $_____

_____ $_____

_____ $_____

_____ $_____

_____ $_____

Total Purchaser's Credits $ 40,500.00

Cash (Rec'd) (Paid) at Closing $ 50,157.68

EXPENSES OF PURCHASER		EXPENSES OF SELLER	
Mortgage Tax	$ 275.00	Title Search Fee	$_____
Recording Mortgage	$ 11.00	Transfer Tax on Deed	$_____
Recording Deed	$ 12.00	Filing of Gains Tax Affidavit	$_____
		Discharge Recording Fee	$_____
ESCROWS:		Mortgage Tax	$_____
____ mos. insurance $ _____		Surveyor's Fees	$_____
____ mos. school tax $ _____		Points	$_____
____ mos. county tax $ _____		Mortgage Payoff	$_____
____ mos. village tax $ _____		Real Estate Commission	$_____
PMI FHA Insurance $ _____		Water Escrow	$_____
Total: $_____			$_____
Bank Attorney Fee	$_____		$_____
Points	$_____		$_____
Title Insurance	$_____		$_____
Interest	$_____	Legal Fee	$_____
	$_____	Total	$_____
	$_____		
	$_____	Cash Received:	$
Legal Fee	$ 500.00	Less Seller's Expenses:	$
Total	$ 798.00	Net Proceeds:	$

Cash paid to Seller: $ 50,157.68

Plus Purchaser's Expenses: $ 798.00

Total Disbursed: $ 50,955.68

Figure 11.4
Seller's Closing Statement

SELLER'S CREDITS

Sale Price _____ $ 89,500.00

ADJUSTMENT OF TAXES

School Tax 7/1/85 to 6/30/86   Amount $ 1176.35   Adj. 10 mos. 18 days $ 1,039.16

City/School Tax 7/1/ to 6/30/   Amount $_____ Adj. _____ mos. _____ days $_____

County Tax 19 85   Amount $ 309.06   Adj. 4 mos. 18 days $ 118.52

Village Tax 6/1/ to 5/31/   Amount $_____ Adj. _____ mos. _____ days $_____

City Tax Embellishments   Amount $_____ Adj. _____ mos. _____ days $_____

Total Seller's Credits $ 90,657.68

PURCHASER'S CREDITS

Deposit with Nothnagle _____ $ 500.00

(Assumed) (New) Mortgage with seller _____ $ 40,000.00

12% interest, 15 years, payments _____ $_____

$ 480.07, beginning 9/12/85 _____ $_____

_____ $_____

_____ $_____

_____ $_____

_____ $_____

Total Purchaser's Credits $ 40,500.00

Cash (Rec'd) (Paid) at Closing $ 50,157.68

EXPENSES OF PURCHASER

Mortgage Tax .... $_____

Recording Mortgage............... $_____

Recording Deed................... $_____

ESCROWS:

_____ mos. insurance   S _____

_____ mos. school tax   S _____

_____ mos. county tax   S _____

_____ mos. village tax   S _____

PMI FHA Insurance S _____

Total: $_____

Bank Attorney Fee................. $_____

Points........................... $_____

Title Insurance.................... $_____

Interest.......................... $_____

.... $_____

.... $_____

.... $_____

Legal Fee........................ $_____

Total............................ $_____

Cash paid to Seller: $

Plus Purchaser's Expenses: $

Total Disbursed: S

EXPENSES OF SELLER

Title Search Fee .... $ 220.00

Transfer Tax on Deed .... $ 358.00

Filing of Gains Tax Affidavit .. $ 1.00

Discharge Recording Fee ...... $_____

Mortgage Tax .... $ 100.00

Surveyor's Fees .... $_____

Points .... $_____

Mortgage Payoff .... $_____

Real Estate Commission ...... $ 487.00

Water Escrow .... $_____

1985-86 school tax ...... $ 1,182.14

Federal express .... $ 14.00

.... $_____

.... $_____

Legal Fee................... $ 550.00

Total....................... $ 7,295.14

Cash Received: $ 50,157.68

Less Seller's Expenses: $ 7,295.14

Net Proceeds: $ 42,862.54

Figure 11.5
Buyer's
Closing
Statement
(New Mortgage)

STATEMENT OF CLOSING

In the matter of the _____ of premises situate _____

_____

Seller: _____ Purchaser: _____

Closed __September 12_____ 19__85__

Adjustments as of __October 28_____ 1985

SELLER'S CREDITS

Sale Price _____ $__62,000.00__

ADJUSTMENT OF TAXES

School Tax 7/1/ to 6/30/	Amount $_____	Adj. ____mos.____days	$_____
City; School Tax 7/1/ to 6/30/	Amount $_____	Adj. ____mos.____days	$_____
County Tax 19_85_	Amount $_631.16_	Adj. _4_mos. _2_days	$__213.90__
Village Tax 6/1/85 to 5/31/86	Amount $_382.80_	Adj. _9_mos. _2_days	$__289.22__
City Tax Embellishments	Amount $_____	Adj. ____mos. ____days	$_____

Rent 8/28 – 9/12 – 15 days @ $ 14.12/day   211.80

Total Seller's Credits $__62,714.92__

PURCHASER'S CREDITS

Deposit with _Nothnagle Gallery of Homes_	$__1000.00__
(Assumed) (New) Mortgage with _Nothnagle Home Securities_	$_58,900.00_
(assigned to Citibank)	$_____
Adjustable Rate Mortgage (see reverse for term)	$_____
1st due 11/1/85	$_____
Monthly payments (see below)	$_____
1985-86 school tax $738.24, adj. 1 mo. 28 days	$__118.92__
_____	$_____

Total Purchaser's Credits $__60,018.92__

Cash (Rec'd) (Paid) at Closing $__2,696.00__

EXPENSES OF PURCHASER		EXPENSES OF SELLER	
Mortgage Tax	$__416.75__	Title Search Fee	$_____
Recording Mortgage	$__35.00__	Transfer Tax on Deed	$_____
Recording Deed	$__12.00__	Filing of Gains Tax Affidavit	$_____
		Discharge Recording Fee	$_____
ESCROWS:		Mortgage Tax	$_____
_2_ mos. insurance $_43.50_		Surveyor's Fees	$_____
_2_ mos. school tax $_123.04_		Points	$_____
_9_ mos. county tax $_473.37_		Mortgage Payoff	$_____
_4_ mos. village tax $_127.60_		Real Estate Commission	$_____
PMI FHA Insurance $_23.56_		Water Escrow	$_____
Total: $__791.07__		....	$_____
Bank Attorney Fee	$__549.25__	....	$_____
Points	$_____	....	$_____
Title Insurance	$_____	....	$_____
Interest 9/12 – 9/30	$__268.28__	....	$_____
1985-86 school tax	$__738.24__	Legal Fee	$_____
PMI – 1 year premium	$__471.20__	Total	$_____
TAX SERVICE FEE–charged by bank	$__39.00__		
Legal Fee	$__410.00__	Cash Received:	$
Total	$__3730.79__	Less Seller's Expenses:	$_____
		Net Proceeds:	$

Cash paid to Seller: $ 2696.00
Plus Purchaser's Expenses: $ 3730.79
Total Disbursed: $ 6426.79

Monthly Payments

Principal and Interest	463.37
Taxes	146.01
Home Owners Policy	21.75
Private Mortgage Insurance	11.78
Total Monthly Payments	642.91

lender's share of the mortgage tax, the remaining real estate commission, legal costs of proving title, transfer tax, and incidental out-of-pocket expenses incurred by seller's attorney, who also deducts his or her own fee, and turns over to the seller the net proceeds.

A more complex closing statement is found in Figure 11.5. The purchaser has placed a new mortgage and carries private mortgage insurance. The down payment is small. The buyer's costs include funds to establish an escrow account with the lender.

Summary

The purpose of the recording acts is to give legal, public, and *constructive notice* to the world of parties' interests in real estate. The recording provisions have been adopted to create system and order in the transfer of real estate. The interests and rights of the various parties in a particular parcel of land must be recorded so that such rights will be legally effective against third parties who do not have knowledge, or notice, of the rights.

Possession of real estate is generally interpreted as notice of the rights of the person in possession. *Actual notice* is knowledge acquired directly and personally.

Four forms of *title evidence* are commonly in use throughout the United States: (1) abstract of title and lawyer's opinion, (2) owner's title insurance policy, (3) Torrens certificate, and (4) certificate of title.

A deed of conveyance is evidence that a grantor has conveyed his or her interest in land but it is not evidence of the kind or condition of the title. It does not *prove* that the grantor had any interest at all.

Each of the forms of title evidence bears a date and is evidence up to and including that date. All forms of title evidence show the previous actions that affect the title. Each must be *re-dated* or continued or reissued to cover a more recent date.

Title evidence shows whether or not a seller is conveying *marketable title*. Marketable title is generally one that is so free from significant defects that the purchaser can be assured against having to defend the title.

Closing a sale involves both title procedures and financial matters. The broker, as agent of the seller, is often present at the closing to see that the sale is actually concluded and to account for the earnest money deposit.

At closing a buyer may be required to prove hazard insurance coverage to a lender. A standard *homeowner's insurance policy* covers fire, theft, and liability and can be extended to cover many types of less common risks. Another type of insurance, which covers personal property only, is available to people who live in apartments and condominiums. In addition to homeowner's insurance, the federal government makes flood insurance mandatory for people living in flood-prone areas who wish to obtain federally regulated or federally insured mortgage loans. Many homeowners' policies contain a *coinsurance clause* that requires the policyholder to maintain fire insurance in an amount equal to 80 percent of the replacement cost of the home. If this percentage is not met the policyholder may not be reimbursed for the full repair costs if a loss occurs.

The federal *Real Estate Settlement Procedures Act (RESPA)* requires disclosure of all settlement costs when a real estate purchase is financed by a federally related mortgage loan. RESPA requires lenders to use a *Uniform Settlement Statement* to detail the financial particulars of a transaction.

Usually the buyer's attorney examines the title evidence to ensure that the seller's title is acceptable. The gap in time between the date of the abstract or title commitment and the closing date is covered by the seller's *affidavit of title*.

The sale may be closed in *escrow* so that the buyer can be assured of receiving good title as described in the sales contract and the seller can be assured that all funds due him or her are held in cash by the escrow agent.

The actual amount to be paid by the buyer at the closing is computed by preparation of a *closing,* or *settlement, statement*. This lists the sales price, earnest money deposit, and all adjustments and prorations due between buyer and seller. The purpose of this statement is to determine the net amount due the seller at closing. The form is signed by both parties to evidence their approval.

The buyer reimburses the seller for *prepaid* items like unused taxes or fuel oil. The seller credits the buyer for bills the seller owes that will be paid by the buyer (*accrued* items) like unpaid water bills.

Questions

1. Which of the following statements best explains why instruments affecting real estate are recorded with the recorder of deeds of the county where the property is located?
   a. Recording gives constructive notice to the world of the rights and interests in a particular parcel of real estate.
   b. The law requires that such instruments be recorded.
   c. The instruments must be recorded to comply with the terms of the statute of frauds.
   d. Recording proves the execution of the instrument.

2. The date and time a document was recorded establish which of the following?
   a. Priority
   b. Chain of title
   c. Subrogation
   d. Marketable title

3. An instrument affecting title to a parcel of real estate gives constructive notice to the world when it is filed with the:
   a. city clerk.
   b. county clerk.
   c. secretary of state.
   d. title insurance company.

4. In New York no deed may be recorded unless:
   a. it has been acknowledged.
   b. the transfer tax has been paid.
   c. there is a Real Property Transfer Report.
   d. All of the above

5. The principle of *caveat emptor* states that if the buyer buys into a title problem the fault lies with the:
   a. buyer.
   b. seller.
   c. broker.
   d. lender.

6. Chain of title refers to which of the following?
   a. A summary or history of all instruments and legal proceedings affecting a specific parcel of land
   b. A series of links measuring 7.92 inches each
   c. An instrument or document that protects the insured parties (subject to specific exceptions) against defects in the examination of the record and hidden risks such as forgeries, undisclosed heirs, errors in the public records, and so forth
   d. The succession of conveyances from some starting point whereby the present owner derives his or her title

7. In locations where the abstract system is used, an abstract is usually examined by the:
   a. broker.
   b. abstract company.
   c. purchaser.
   d. attorney for the purchaser.

8. Proof of the kind of estate and all liens against an interest in a parcel of real estate can usually be found through:
   a. a recorded deed.
   b. a court suit for specific performance.
   c. one of the four evidences of title.
   d. a foreclosure suit.

9. A fee title insurance policy generally will defend the property owner against problems arising from:
   a. unrecorded documents.
   b. facts discoverable by survey.
   c. forged documents.
   d. All of the above

10. If a property has encumbrances it:
    a. cannot be sold.
    b. can be sold only if title insurance is provided.
    c. cannot have a deed recorded without a survey.
    d. can be sold if a buyer agrees to take it subject to the encumbrances.

11. A mortgage title policy protects which parties against loss?

    a. Buyers
    b. Sellers
    c. Lenders
    d. Buyers and lenders

12. Sally Seller is frantic because she cannot find her deed and now wants to sell the property. Sally:

    a. may need a suit to quiet title.
    b. will have to buy title insurance.
    c. does not need the deed to sell if it had been recorded.
    d. should execute a replacement deed to herself.

13. At closing the seller of a single home must give the buyer an affidavit that the house has:

    a. flood insurance.
    b. title insurance.
    c. a working smoke alarm.
    d. insulation.

14. R. Crusoe is selling a two-family dwelling. The buyer's lending institution is likely to request:

    a. proof of hazard insurance.
    b. a certificate of occupancy.
    c. title insurance.
    d. All of the above

15. The terms *basic, broad,* and *comprehensive* describe types of:

    a. title insurance.
    b. attorney's services.
    c. mortgage documents.
    d. homeowner's insurance.

16. A coinsurance clause can penalize the homeowner who does not carry insurance coverage for at least what percent of replacement cost?

    a. 50 percent   c. 100 percent
    b. 80 percent   d. 125 percent

17. Flood insurance is required for mortgaging property if it is:

    a. a multiple dwelling.
    b. on a flood-prone area on a special map.
    c. owned by HUD.
    d. going to have title insurance.

18. The RESPA Uniform Settlement Statement must be used to illustrate all settlement charges:

    a. for every real estate transaction.
    b. for transactions financed by VA and FHA loans only.
    c. for transactions financed by federally related mortgage loans.
    d. for all transactions in which mortgage financing is involved.

19. A mortgage reduction certificate is executed by a(n):

    a. abstract company.
    b. attorney.
    c. lending institution.
    d. grantor.

20. The earnest money left on deposit with the broker is a:

    a. credit to the seller.
    b. credit to the buyer.
    c. debit to the seller.
    d. debit to the buyer.

21. The buyers are assuming a mortgage loan that had a principal balance of $27,496 as of June 1. Interest is at 12 percent per annum. Interest is payable in arrears. The June payment has not been made and closing is on June 15. Which of the following is true?

    a. Credit buyer $274.95; debit seller $274.95.
    b. Credit buyer $412.40; debit seller $412.40.
    c. Credit seller $137.48; debit buyer $137.48.
    d. No adjustment is necessary.

22. The year's town, county, and state taxes amount to $1,800 and have been paid ahead for the calendar year. If closing is set for June 15, which of the following is true?

    a. Credit seller $825; debit buyer $975.
    b. Credit seller $1,800; debit buyer $825.
    c. Credit buyer $975; debit seller $975.
    d. Credit seller $975; debit buyer $975.

23. Which one of the following items is *not* usually prorated between buyer and seller at the closing?

    a. Recording charges
    b. General taxes
    c. Rents
    d. Mortgage interest

24. The seller collected rent of $400 from the attic tenant on June 1. At the closing on June 15:

    a. Seller owes buyer $400.
    b. Buyer owes seller $600.
    c. Seller owes buyer $200.
    d. Buyer owes seller $200.

25. Security deposits should be listed on a closing statement as a credit to the:

    a. buyer.   c. lender.
    b. seller.   d. broker.

Appendix: Excerpts from New York State's Study Booklet for Brokers

RECORDING CONVEYANCES, ETC.

To be recordable, the document must be a conveyance of real property within the State of New York, duly acknowledged, or otherwise proved as authorized by law. The courts have held that not only deeds and mortgages, but leases for more than three years, trust agreements, releases, extensions, assignments and discharges of mortgages, are conveyances of real property eligible for recording, and this list is not exhaustive. A particular statutory provision authorizes the recording of executory contracts for the sale or purchase of real property (and powers of attorney for its conveyance).

Recording conveyances serves two purposes: Preservation of a record of the instrument in a public office for convenient reference, and to give general notice of the rights created or conveyed under it.

The latter result is, of course, exceedingly important, and is completely governed by the provisions of Article 9 of the Real Property Law, frequently referred to as the Recording Act. If the instrument is of the kind which the law permits to be recorded, and it is recorded in a county clerk's office (or register's office, in New York, Kings, Bronx and Queens counties) as provided by the statute, subsequent purchasers, from the same common source of title, acquire no greater right than as though they, in fact, knew of the instrument so recorded at the time of their purchase. If the instrument is of the kind which may be recorded, and is not recorded, it is void as against any subsequent purchaser whose conveyance is first duly recorded.

The statute creates the presumption that the subsequent good faith purchaser did not know that a previous unrecorded conveyance had been made. If it is shown that he did—as by the fact that the prior purchaser was in possession of the property—then the presumption may be lost.

Real Estate Mathematics

Overview

This review is designed to familiarize the student with some basic mathematical formulas that are most frequently used in the computations required on state licensing examinations. These same computations are also important in day-to-day real estate transactions. Some of this material has been covered in detail in the text. In these cases, reference is made to the appropriate chapter. If you feel you need additional help in working these problems, you may want to consult *Mastering Real Estate Mathematics,* Fourth Edition, by Ventolo, Allaway, and Irby. The order form at the back of this book includes this self-instructional text.

Percentages

Many real estate computations are based on the calculation of percentages. A percentage expresses a portion of a whole. For example, 50 percent means 50 parts of the possible 100 parts that comprise the whole. Percentages greater than 100 percent contain more than one whole unit. Thus, 163 percent is one whole and 63 parts of another whole. Remember that a whole is always expressed as 100 percent.

Unless a calculator with a percent key is being used, *the percentage must be converted either to a decimal or to a fraction.* To convert a percentage to a decimal, move the decimal two places to the left and drop the percent sign. Thus:

$$60\% = .6 \qquad 7\% = .07 \qquad 175\% = 1.75$$

To change a percentage to a fraction, place the percentage over 100. For example:

$$50\% = \frac{50}{100} \qquad 115\% = \frac{115}{100}$$

These fractions may then be *reduced* to make it easier to work the problem. To reduce a fraction, determine the largest number by which both numerator and denominator can be evenly divided and divide each of them by that number. For example:

$$25/100 = 1/4 \text{ (both numbers divided by 25)}$$

$$49/63 = 7/9 \text{ (both numbers divided by 7)}$$

Percentage problems contain three elements: *percentage, total,* and *part.* To determine a specific percentage of a whole, multiply the percentage by the whole. This is illustrated by the following formula:

$$\textbf{percent} \times \textbf{whole} = \textbf{part}$$
$$5\% \times 200 = 10$$

For example: A broker is to receive a seven percent commission on the sale of a $100,000 house. What will the broker's commission be?

$$.07 \times \$100,000 = \$7,000 \text{ broker's commission}$$

This formula is used in calculating mortgage loan interests, brokers' commissions, loan origination fees, discount points, amount of earnest money deposits, and income on capital investments.

A variation, or inversion, of the percentage formula is used to find the total amount when the part and percentage are known:

$$\textbf{total} = \frac{\textbf{part}}{\textbf{percent}}$$

For example: The Masterson Realty Company received a $4,500 commission for the sale of a house. The broker's commission was six percent of the total sales price. What was the total sales price of this house?

$$\frac{\$4,500}{.06} = \$75,000 \text{ total sales price}$$

This formula is used in computing the total mortgage loan principal still due if the monthly payment and interest rate are known. It is also used to calculate the total sales price when the amount and percentage of commission are known and the market value of property if the assessed value and the ratio (percentage) of assessed value to market value are known.

The formula may be used by a real estate salesperson thus: Bertha Buyer has $19,500 available for a down payment and she must make a 25 percent down payment. How expensive a home can she purchase? The question is: $19,500 is 25 percent of what figure?

$$\frac{\$19,500}{.25} = \$78,000$$

Such a problem also may be solved by the use of ratios. Thus: $19,500 is to what number as 25 percent is to 100 percent?

$$\frac{\$19,500}{?} = \frac{25}{100}$$

One type of percentage problem, which may take several forms, is often found on the New York State licensing examinations. For example: Joe Brown sold his property for $90,000. This represents a 20 percent loss from his original cost. What was his cost?

In this problem the student must resist the impulse to multiply everything in sight. Taking 20 percent of $90,000 yields nothing significant. The $90,000 figure represents 80 percent of the original cost and the question resolves itself into: $90,000 is 80 percent of what figure?

$$\frac{\$90,000}{.80} = \$112,500$$

Again: Hester Prynne clears $88,200 from the sale of her property after paying a ten percent commission. How much did the property sell for? Taking ten percent of $88,200 is an incorrect approach to the problem because the commission was based not upon the seller's net but upon the full, unknown sale figure; $88,200 represents 90 percent of the sale price.

$$\frac{\$88,200}{.90} = \$98,000$$

To determine the percentage when the amounts of the part and the total are known:

$$percent = \frac{part}{total}$$

This formula may be used to determine the tax rate when the taxes and assessed value are known or the commission rate if the sales price and commission amount are known.

Rates

Property taxes, transfer taxes, and insurance premiums are usually expressed as rates. A rate is the cost expressed as the amount of cost per unit. For example, tax might be computed at the rate of $5 per $100 assessed value in a certain county. The formula for computing rates is:

$$\frac{value}{unit} \times rate\ per\ unit = total$$

For example: A house has been assessed at $90,000 and is taxed at an annual rate of $2.50 per $100 assessed valuation. What is the yearly tax?

$$\frac{\$90,000}{\$100} \times \$2.50 = total\ annual\ tax$$

$$\$90,000 \div \$100 = 900\ (increments\ of\ \$100)$$

$$900 \times \$2.50 = \$2,250\ total\ annual\ tax$$

See Chapter 25 for a further discussion of tax computations.

Basic to investment problems is the IRV formula.

Income = Rate × Value

This formula should be memorized.

Areas and Volumes

Those in the real estate business must know how to compute the area of a parcel of land or figure the amount of living area in a house. To compute the area of a square or rectangular parcel, use the formula:

width × depth = area

The area of a rectangular lot that measures 100 feet wide by 200 feet deep would be:

$$100' \times 200' = 20,000 \text{ square feet}$$

The first figure given always represents *front feet;* a lot described as "80' × 150'" is 80 feet across and 150 feet deep.

Area is always expressed in square units.

To compute the amount of surface in a triangular-shaped area, use the formula:

area = ½ (base × height)

The base of a triangle is the bottom, upon which the triangle rests. The height is an imaginary straight line extending from the point of the uppermost angle straight down to the base:

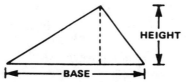

Example: A triangle has a base of 50 feet and a height of 30 feet. What is its area?

$$½ (50' \times 30') = \text{area in square feet}$$
$$½ (1500) = 750 \text{ square feet}$$

To compute the area of an irregular room or parcel of land, divide the shape into regular rectangles, squares, or triangles. Next, compute the area of each regular figure and add the areas together to obtain the total area.

Example: Compute the area of the hallway shown below:

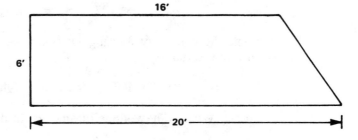

First make a rectangle and a triangle by drawing a single line through the figure as shown here:

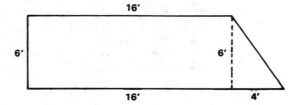

Compute the area of the rectangle:

$$\text{area} = \text{length} \times \text{width} \qquad 16' \times 6' = 96 \text{ square feet}$$

Compute the area of the triangle:

$$\text{area} = \tfrac{1}{2}(\text{base} \times \text{height}) \qquad \tfrac{1}{2}(4' \times 6') = \tfrac{1}{2}(24) = 12 \text{ square feet}$$

Total the two areas:

$$96 + 12 = 108 \text{ square feet in total area}$$

The cubic capacity of an enclosed space is expressed as volume. Volume is used to describe the amount of space in any three-dimensional area; it would be used, for example, in measuring the interior airspace of a room to determine what capacity heating unit is required. The formula for computing cubic or rectangular volume is:

$$\textbf{volume} = \textbf{length} \times \textbf{width} \times \textbf{height}$$

Volume is always expressed in cubic units.

For example: The bedroom of a house is 12 feet long, 8 feet wide, and has a ceiling height of 8 feet. How many cubic feet does the room enclose?

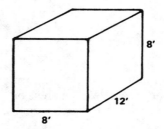

$$8' \times 12' \times 8' = 768 \text{ cubic feet}$$

To compute the volume of a triangular space, such as the airspace in an A-frame house, use the formula:

$$\text{volume} = \tfrac{1}{2}(\text{base} \times \text{height} \times \text{width})$$

For example: What is the volume of airspace in the house shown below?

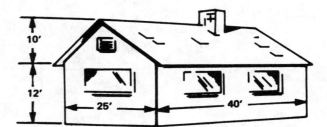

First, divide the house into two shapes, rectangular and triangular, as shown:

Find the volume of T:

$$\text{volume} = \tfrac{1}{2} (\text{base} \times \text{height} \times \text{width})$$
$$\tfrac{1}{2} (25' \times 10' \times 40') = \tfrac{1}{2} (10,000) = 5,000 \text{ cubic feet}$$

Find the volume of R:

$$25' \times 40' \times 12' = 12,000 \text{ cubic feet}$$

Total volumes T and R:

$$5,000 + 12,000 = 17,000 \text{ cubic feet of airspace in the house}$$

Cubic measurements of volume are used to compute the construction costs per cubic foot of a building, the amount of airspace being sold in a condominium unit, or the heating and cooling requirements for a building.

When either area or volume is computed, *all dimensions used must be given in the same unit of measure*. For example, one may not multiply two feet by six inches to get the area; two feet must be multiplied by ½ foot.

It is important to remember that while:

$$1 \text{ yard} = 3 \text{ feet,}$$
$$1 \text{ square yard} = 3 \times 3 = 9 \text{ square feet,}$$
$$\text{and } 1 \text{ cubic yard} = 3 \times 3 \times 3 = 27 \text{ cubic feet.}$$

Prorations. The prorating of taxes, interest, and other items is customary when a real estate transaction is closed. Instructions for calculating prorations may be found in Chapter 11 of the text.

Land Units and Measurements

It is important to know and understand land units and measurements—they are an integral part of legal descriptions. Some commonly used measurements:

1. A *rod* is 16½ feet.
2. A *chain* is 66 feet, or 100 links.
3. A *mile* is 5,280 feet.
4. An *acre* contains 43,560 square feet. **Memorize this one.**
5. A *section* of land is one square mile and contains 640 acres; a *quarter section* contains 160 acres; a *quarter of a quarter section* contains 40 acres.
6. A *circle* contains 360 degrees; a *quarter segment* of a circle contains 90 degrees; a *half segment* of a circle contains 180 degrees. One *degree* (1°) can be subdivided into 60 minutes (60′), each of which contains 60 seconds (60″). One-and-a-half degrees would be written 1°30′0″.

Table 12.1 Units of Land Measurement	Unit	Measurement	Metric Equivalent
	mile	5,280 feet; 320 rods; 1,760 yards	1.609 kilometers
	rod	5.50 yards; 16.5 feet	5.029 meters
	sq. mile	640 acres	2.590 sq. kilometers
	acre	4,840 sq. yards; 160 sq. rods; 43,560 sq. feet	4,047 sq. meters
	sq. yard	9 sq. feet	0.836 sq. meters
	sq. foot	144 sq. inches	0.093 sq. meters
	chain	66 feet or 100 links	20.117 meters
	kilometer	0.62 mile	1,000 meters
	hectare	2.47 acres	10,000 sq. meters

Questions

1. A rectangular lot measures 60 feet wide and has an area of 1,200 square yards. What is the depth of the lot?
   a. 20 feet   c. 20 yards
   b. 180 feet   d. 90 yards

2. A buyer is applying for an FHA mortgage on a house priced at $68,000. The minimum down payment required is three percent of the first $25,000 of the purchase price and five percent of the remaining purchase price. What is the minimum down payment?
   a. $2,040   c. $1,790
   b. $3,400   d. $2,900

3. Ebenezer Scrooge intends to put up a fence between his lot and his neighbor's. The fencing comes in six-foot sections. For a fence 120 feet long, how many fence posts will be required?
   a. 19   c. 21
   b. 20   d. 22

4. A house is valued at $98,000. It is to be insured for 80 percent of its cost. Insurance will cost $0.60 per $100. What is the annual insurance premium?
   a. $470.40   c. $588.00
   b. $47.04   d. $58.80

5. John Walton received a net amount of $74,000 from the sale of his house after paying $1,200 in legal and other fees and six percent sales commission. What was the selling price of the house?
   a. $80,000   c. $79,640
   b. $78,440   d. $79,000

6. A lending institution will allow its borrowers to spend 25 percent of their income for housing expense. What will be the maximum monthly payment allowed for a family with annual income of $37,000 and no other debts?
   a. $9,250   c. $925
   b. $770.83   d. None of the above

7. Sally Sellright works on a 50/50 commission split with her broker. If she lists a house at $56,000 for six percent commission and sells it for $54,000, how much will Sally receive?
   a. $3,360   c. $3,240
   b. $1,680   d. $1,620

8. Dudley Doright's monthly mortgage payment for principal and interest is $628.12. His property taxes are $1,800 a year and his annual insurance premium is $365. What is his total monthly payment for PITI (principal, interest, taxes, and insurance)?
   a. $808.54   c. $778.12
   b. $1,921.24   d. None of the above

9. A lot measuring 120' × 200' is selling for $300 a front foot. What is its price?
   a. $720,000   c. $36,000
   b. $60,000   d. $800,000

10. A five-acre lot has front footage of 300 feet. How deep is it?
    a. 145.2 feet   c. 88 feet
    b. 726 feet   d. 160 feet

11. Broker Sally Smith of Happy Valley Realty recently sold Jack and Jill Hawkins's home for $79,500. Smith charged the Hawkinses a 6½ percent commission and will pay 30 percent of that amount to the listing salesperson and 25 percent to the selling salesperson. What amount of commission will the listing salesperson receive from the Hawkins sale?
    a. $5,167.50   c. $3,617.25
    b. $1,550.25   d. $1,291.87

12. Susan Silber signed an agreement to purchase a condominium apartment from Perry and Marie Morris. The contract stipulated that the Morrises replace the damaged bedroom carpet. The carpet Silber has chosen costs $11.95 per square yard plus $2.50 per square yard for installation. If the bedroom dimensions are as illustrated, how much will the Morrises have to pay for the job?

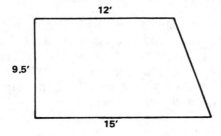

a. $170.28   c. $205.91
b. $189.20   d. $1,853.19

13. Hal Peters, Olive Gamble, Ron Clooney, and Marvin Considine decided to pool their savings and purchase a small apartment building for $125,000. If Peters invested $30,000 and Gamble and Clooney each contributed $35,000, what percentage of ownership was left for Considine?

a. 20 percent   c. 28 percent
b. 24 percent   d. 30 percent

14. Harold Barlow is curious to know how much money his son and daughter-in-law still owe on their mortgage loan. Barlow knows that the interest portion of their last monthly payment was $391.42. If the Barlows are paying interest at the rate of 11½ percent, what was the outstanding balance of their loan before that last payment was made?

a. $43,713.00   c. $36,427.50
b. $40,843.83   d. $34,284.70

15. Nick and Olga Stravinski bought their home on Sabre Lane a year ago for $68,500. Property in their neighborhood is said to be increasing in value at a rate of 12 percent annually. If this is true, what is the current market value of the Stravinskis' real estate?

a. $76,720
b. $77,063
c. $77,405
d. None of the above is within $50.

16. The DeHavilands' home on Dove Street is valued at $95,000. Property in their area is assessed at 60 percent of its value and the local tax rate is $2.85 per hundred. What is the amount of the Dehavilands' monthly taxes?

a. $1,111.50   c. $111.15
b. $926.30   d. $135.38

17. The Fitzpatricks are planning to construct a patio in their backyard. An illustration of the surface area to be paved appears here. If the cement is to be poured as a 6″ slab, how many cubic feet of cement will be poured into this patio?

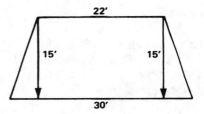

a. 660 cubic feet   c. 330 cubic feet
b. 450 cubic feet   d. 195 cubic feet

18. Happy Morgan receives a monthly salary of $500 plus three percent commission on all of his listings that sell and 2.5 percent on all his sales. None of the listings that Morgan took sold last month but he received $3,675 in salary and commission. What was the value of the property Morgan sold?

a. $147,000   c. $122,500
b. $127,000   d. $105,833

19. The Salvatinis' residence has proven difficult to sell. Salesperson Martha Kelley suggests it might sell faster if they enclose a portion of the backyard with a privacy fence. If the area to be enclosed is as illustrated, how much would the fence cost at $6.95 per linear foot?

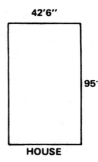

42'6"

95'

HOUSE

a. $1,911.25   c. $1,615.88
b. $1,654.10   d. $955.63

20. Andrew McTavish leases the 12 apartments in the Overton Arms for a total monthly rental of $4,500. If this figure represents an eight percent annual return on McTavish's investment, what was the original cost of the property?

a. $675,000   c. $54,000
b. $450,000   d. $56,250

21. A 100-acre farm is divided into house lots. The streets require one-eighth of the whole farm and there are 140 lots. How many square feet are there in each lot?

a. 35,004   c. 27,225
b. 31,114   d. 43,560

Part Two

Real Estate Broker

13

Opening a Broker's Office

Key Terms

Bullpen
Call diverter
Closing room
Corporation
DBA
Errors & omissions insurance
Franchise
Fringe benefits
General partnership
Limited partnership
Market share

Monolithic office
Multi-office firm
NYSAR
Phone patch
Sales manager
S corporation
Sole proprietorship
Startup expenses
Umbrella policy
Workmen's compensation insurance

Overview

An ambition to open one's own office is common among successful real estate salespersons. Any licensee contemplating such a move needs to plan well in advance, reach some basic decisions about the form the new firm will take, and carefully estimate projected expenses. This chapter will discuss matters a broker has to consider before going into business and will offer advice on planning the office itself.

Real Estate in New York

In 1985 New York State held licenses for 40,000 real estate brokers and 100,000 salespeople. Approximately one-half were licensed Downstate around New York City and the other half Upstate.

Many of the 140,000 licenses represent inactive agents. The New York State Association of Realtors (**NYSAR**) estimated that its members handle between 80 and 90 percent of all brokered sales although they constituted only 27,000 of those licensed that year.

Making the Break

The ambition to open one's own office comes readily to a successful salesperson. Sometimes the plan is to operate as a single practitioner, earning the same money more easily because one can keep the entire commission. Others have more elaborate plans, hoping to take on associates and move into sales management.

How successful these plans turn out may depend on how well the broker understands the various abilities needed for operating one's own business. The qualities that mark a star salesperson may or may not be the same as those contributing to successful management. After breaking away from an established office the new broker lacks the accustomed support system. Even with the relatively few transactions generated by one person, paperwork accumulates. Many successful salespeople are by nature uninterested in detail work, but someone must maintain accurate records, handle mail, make copies, write checks, and keep careful books. The lone broker soon discovers that even a bare-bones operation requires an extra telephone, a typewriter, new furniture, a filing cabinet, signs, stationery, promotional material, advertising, and possibly a computer terminal or copier. These expenses must be paid from that 100 percent commission that looks so inviting.

The broker who plans to move into sales management must understand that experience as a successful salesperson is not sufficient preparation for the different skills needed in hiring, training, motivating, and supervising others. When a real estate brokerage becomes large, managerial skills may not differ significantly from those needed for any other business. In many cases the new manager starts the enterprise at a disadvantage, by losing the income of one top salesperson—himself or herself. It may take the sales efforts of several associates to make up for this loss. Sometimes managing brokers find their net incomes lower than those of their top associates.

Advance Preparations

The broker's first step should be a review of the law of agency and New York's license law (Chapters 2 and 8). In addition the new broker can learn a great deal quickly by attending a national convention of the National Association of REALTORS®. These week-long gatherings are held every November. The conventioneer can choose among hundreds of educational sessions, many of them geared to office management. In addition the exhibits offer an opportunity to meet manufacturers of necessary equipment like computer hardware and software, signs and lockboxes, and service companies like franchisors, referral networks, and insurance firms. If a national convention is out of the question, a smaller version can be found in the New York State convention held every September. Management seminars are also available at different times and locations across the state.

Basic Decisions

Before opening an office the new broker must decide on specialty, groups to affiliate with, size, location, form of organization, office layout, and budgeting, among other items. The choice of specialty will come from the broker's own experience. Seven out of ten firms in this country list single-family sales as their major source of income but the broker who has acquired expertise in commercial and industrial property, multiple dwellings, or farm and land sales will be drawn to those fields.

Organizations and Franchises

The broker's first decision is whether to become a REALTOR® and whether to join any available multiple-listing arrangement. In 1985 the National Association of REALTORS® found 80 percent of surveyed firms associated with multiple-listing systems and 19 percent with franchises. Small firms were least likely to join franchises; of companies with staffs of more than 50 persons, more than one-half belonged to a franchise. The number affiliating with franchises is shown in Figure 13.1. Those offices belonging to franchises generally felt their profits had improved although impartial studies showed nonfranchised firms did at least as well as franchised ones. Asked to list the aspects of franchising that most appealed to them, member firms mentioned the national identity that made their names readily recognized and expressed satisfaction with the training programs offered by franchises. Items singled out for criticism were high franchise fees, not enough assistance with local advertising, and too few intercity referrals. Sixteen percent of the surveyed firms subscribed to a less expensive *referral network*. Many brokers, however, handle their own intercity contacts by telephone, using a national roster of REALTORS® to locate cooperating brokers. Four percent of the firms belonged to electronic mortgage market networks.

**Figure 13.1
Franchise Affiliation of
Firms: 1981–1985
(Percent of Firms)**

FRANCHISE AFFILIATION OF FIRMS: 1981-1985
(Percent of Firms)

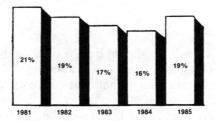

SOURCE: NATIONAL ASSOCIATION OF REALTORS®: Economics and Research Division.

Size of Office   Despite a trend toward larger offices and multi-office firms, nine out of ten real estate companies in the NAR survey had only one office and fewer than ten salespersons. Five or fewer salespersons were found in more than one-half the offices, as shown in Figure 13.2. Three percent of the firms had 50 or more associates.

Figure 13.2

Trends in the percent of firms in various size categories: 1981–1985 (Percentage Distributions)

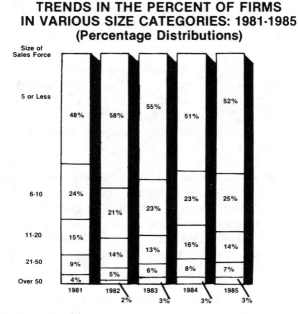

TRENDS IN THE PERCENT OF FIRMS IN VARIOUS SIZE CATEGORIES: 1981-1985 (Percentage Distributions)

SOURCE: NATIONAL ASSOCIATION OF REALTORS®: Economics and Research Division.

The survey showed the majority of small firms as having no management except that provided by the owner. Large companies usually employed part- or full-time managers most often called **sales managers** or administrative managers. Of interest to the aspiring broker is the finding that some firms achieve a sales force of 50 or more within two or three years. After five years in business no relationship was found between length of time in business and size of firm. By then the majority of brokers evidently reached the form of business they preferred and stayed there.

The *one-person office* involves less responsibility to and for others, more flexibility of hours, and lower initial investment. Its disadvantages include uneven flows of income, no backup in emergencies, and for many brokers, less prestige and ego satisfaction than a larger firm would provide. Profits are limited to one person's efforts.

Also classified as small companies are one-manager offices with a sales force of between two and ten persons. Such a firm usually employs one secretary, possibly only part-time. As the number of associates approaches ten the managing broker usually stops selling. Salespersons resent the broker who remains in competition with them, appropriates leads, and is unavailable for the management support they require. On the other hand the manager who sells remains in close contact with the market and with current financing and is in a position to spot weak points in any of the sales staff. Many managers compromise by handling only personal requests from their own past customers and clients. The advantages of this size office include a more even flow of income, more freedom to take vacations or attend conventions and seminars, availability of backup in emergency, and complete control of business decisions. Income is less limited but sometimes may not exceed that possible in the one-person office. Drawbacks include considerably more overhead, more responsibility to others, and the need for management skills. A hired manager is still not cost-effective with this size of operation.

The single **monolithic office** has ten or more associates under one roof. It furnishes central control, economy of facilities, and easy communication and it allows for specialized branches in the one firm. Space may limit the growth of this operation. Recruiting may be difficult if associates prefer working in their own neighborhoods. The monolithic office requires considerable executive ability and investment of time.

The **multi-office firm** meets many of these objections, following the residential market as it develops in different areas. The owner has more freedom in this situation, prestige accrues to the broker, and greater gain is possible. The major drawback is financial vulnerability. Overhead is high and considerable investment is necessary. Making the right decisions is crucial, the risk of losing money is ever-present, and the firm is vulnerable to bankruptcy in a falling market.

Site Selection

Site selection should follow careful analysis of the new firm's goals. The broker should study *demographics;* the population characteristics in the area should be studied and a target clientele should be identified. Research into sales activity in the area can aid the new firm in setting a goal for **market share** in terms of gross sales or number of transactions.

A *downtown* location is close to accountants, lawyers, courthouse records, and the business community. Parking costs and expensive office rentals, particularly for ground-floor locations, often make it inappropriate for residential firms. Offices specializing in commercial property are more likely to choose this type of location.

Suburban locations follow customers and clients of those brokers specializing in residential property sales. Before selecting an area the broker will consider growth patterns and present competition. A location on a well-traveled road offers high visibility and may produce some stop-ins. In addition it is easy to direct callers to a main-road address. From such a location salespersons find it possible to cover more territory. The specific site should provide easy access and ample free parking.

Shopping centers attract walk-in traffic, in some cases a mixed blessing if it ties up personnel with casual lookers. Mall locations can be expensive and a strip location offers better sign visibility. Parking density and sign regulations should be investigated before choosing shopping center space, as well as the questions: Will the mall be open after store hours and may the sign be lighted at night?

Remodeling of *existing buildings* is often successful. Historic houses or older homes can make attractive and appropriate real estate offices. Abandoned gasoline stations, found in increasing numbers across the country, can be excellent. Often located on main highways and intersections, they have high visibility for a sign, are easy to locate, and have extensive parking areas.

Status of Associates

The *independent contractor* status of salespersons, which is widely used in the real estate brokerage industry, is discussed in Chapter 2 largely from the viewpoint of the associate. The NAR survey found 92 percent of the real estate firms listing their sales associates as independent contractors. Brokers traditionally have maintained this relationship to avoid the bookkeeping problems of withholding taxes, social security payments, unemployment insurance, and other such items that become complex when based not upon a regular salary but upon unpredictable commissions. The broker who chooses independent contractor status for his or her associates should keep on file agreements signed by the associates with the wording provided by the broker's attorney. Recent "safe harbor" guidelines provide that the Internal Revenue Service will not challenge independent contractor status where the associate (1) is licensed as a real estate broker or salesperson, (2) has income based on sales output and subject to fluctuation, and (3) performs services pursuant to a written contract specifying independent contractor status.

These safe harbor rules are not, however, accepted by the State of New York. Challenges may arise on such subjects as state unemployment insurance or workmen's compensation and the traditional distinctions between employee and independent contractor relationships should be observed.

Where the broker maintains workmen's compensation insurance, which is not specifically required for independent contractors, the agreement with associates might note that it is not intended to signify an employer-employee relationship.

Employee status for salespersons has some advantages for the broker: closer control over salesperson activities and the ability to mandate sales meetings, floor duty, dress codes, and sales quotas. It also may retain skilled salespersons.

Fringe benefits like health insurance, pension plans, sick leave, and paid vacations are variously estimated to add 25 to 50 percent to base salary. The broker who chooses to regard salespersons as employees must take such costs into consideration when working out commission schedules.

Part-timers. Almost 60 percent of the firms surveyed, many of them the smaller firms, had part-time sales associates; 40 percent, more likely the larger firms, did not. In those firms that did use part-timers, one salesperson in three fit that category.

Name of Firm

The choice of a business name has an important connection with the public image planned for the firm. If a broker's name is well-known in the community it is the logical choice. Sometimes the name chosen suggests a logo for the firm or a motto. The proposed business name must be cleared in advance by the Department of State, which will veto any name too closely resembling another in the community or any deemed misleading to the public. The word "REALTOR®" is a trademark and may not be used as part of the firm name. Any **DBA** (doing business as) name must be registered with the county clerk, who will issue a certificate. Without it, the broker will have trouble opening a business bank account.

The new business will need a checking account and an escrow account. Department of State regulations stipulate that escrow deposits shall be held in a separate, special *bank* account, which may or may not be an interest-bearing one. The DOS states clearly that any interest earned does not belong to the broker. The account should be clearly identified as an escrow account to avoid any confusion with the broker's own funds in the event of a lawsuit, bankruptcy, or death.

Form of Organization

A real estate business may be run as a **sole proprietorship** with the broker as single owner. The broker may draw a regular salary or take profits as income. This type of business has the virtue of simplicity and probably offers the best tax advantage for a small office. One major drawback is the owner's unlimited financial liability if problems of damages, judgments, or bankruptcy arise.

A **corporation** offers limited personal liability in case of financial problems. Corporate profits are taxed twice, however: once to the corporation and again to stockholders as individual income. Capital gains and losses, which may not concern many brokerages, lose their special tax treatment within a corporation. Because salaries are not taxed twice, however, and generous arrangements can be made for pension funds, some flexibility is possible. The corporate form of ownership is appropriate for larger companies. The **S corporation** is often ideal for a brokerage or rental business. It avoids the tax disadvantages of a regular corporation but still offers some limited liability, continuity of life, and retirement fund advantages. It may not have more than 35 stockholders and is appropriate for proprietorships and partnerships.

General partnership in New York State requires that all partners be licensed brokers. Tax treatment of a partnership is simple: Losses, gains, and income are shared directly by each partner. A well-drafted partnership agreement is necessary; otherwise problems can arise when one partner dies, files bankruptcy, or wishes to sell his or her share. **Limited partnerships** are usually employed for acquiring investments, not for usual brokerage operations. Overall, partnership organization is used for eight percent of real estate firms (*see* Figure 13.3).

Outside Help

An ideal *attorney* for a real estate firm should be available by telephone in the evenings and on weekends to provide counsel if unusual situations arise in the course of business. Sometimes a yearly retainer is appropriate compensation. Among the attorney's contributions to the organization before operations begin will be advising which form of ownership to choose, drawing up partnership or corporation documents, reviewing a lease or a franchise contract, and assisting with independent contractor agreements and other forms to be used in the business.

While the firm's bookkeeping can be handled by the broker, *secretary,* or *bookkeeper* (often part-time), the books should be set up by an *accountant,* who should also look over the initial budget to spot any flaws. The accountant will offer advice, provide periodic reports of the firm's financial condition, and prepare income tax returns. Because tax considerations often arise in real estate brokerage, it is helpful if the accountant is also available by telephone after normal business hours.

An *insurance broker* should be consulted before the office opens. Workmen's compensation insurance is relatively inexpensive and so is an **umbrella** liability **policy,** which protects the broker over and above any automobile insurance associates

Figure 13.3
Legal Organization of
Real Estate Firms
(Percentage Distributions)

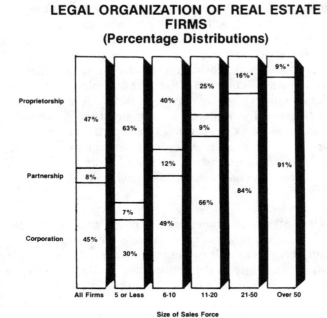

carry and also can be written to cover accidents incurred in the showing of property. More costly is **errors and omissions insurance,** increasingly necessary as society becomes more litigious. Analogous to legal or medical malpractice insurance, it is carried by about one-half of today's real estate firms.

An *artist* or *advertising agency* should be employed before a broker orders any stationery or signs. A carefully selected color scheme and logo help establish the new company's desired public image. Such matters are too important to be left to a sign painter's discretion.

If the broker prefers an *answering service* over a machine, arrangements must be made for it before the office opens. Because the telephone company charges for the wires to the answering service, the company located closest to the broker is a logical choice. *Janitorial* or cleaning service must also be secured in advance.

A *notary public* offers a useful service in a real estate office. Qualifying as a notary is a simple matter. If the broker writes appraisals that must be acknowledged, some other member of the office should become the notary. A small sign on the office wall can alert the public that a notary is on the premises; this is often a convenience for customers involved in intercity moves.

Office Layout

The bare necessities, even for the one-person office in a corner of the family room, are a *desk, restroom* for the public, *file,* and *storage space* for signs and supplies. Whether in one room or an entire building, the real estate office must provide areas for different activities. Among them: a *reception area,* with *coat storage* and a place for customers to wait in comfort, and *desk space,* preferably for each salesperson. A popular arrangement provides a number of desks in one large room known as a **bullpen.** Such an arrangement saves space and facilitates easy communication. (Recently some offices show a trend toward movable partitions for work space and telephone facilities in the bullpen.) Also needed is a private *conference area* or **closing room** for confidential interviews and the serious business of signing contracts. If residential sales are to be the company's specialty, a separate children's *play corner* is useful. A *coffee machine* is almost essential; in a larger office a kitchen area or small refrigerator is welcome. Space is needed for the *manager's desk,* often in a separate office, and for the secretary, receptionist, or bookkeeper. A computer terminal can be coupled with files, bookcases, or copier to provide a *research area.* The large office will also provide for a *training center* or *meeting room.*

Equipment

Modern office equipment and telephone gadgets can be seductive to the broker who wants to convey a good impression to the public. With rising expenses cutting brokers' profit percentages every year, every piece of equipment must be analyzed carefully to determine its cost-effectiveness. Will it contribute to the company's image, pay for itself in time saved, or produce higher sales volume?

Telephone service is the lifeblood of a real estate office. Nine out of ten firms use a telephone system and four percent have cellular telephones. The telephone company should be asked if a choice of numbers is available and several adjacent numbers can be reserved in case of later expansion. A telephone instrument at each desk is essential; some bells can be silenced and others set for pleasant low tones. An unlisted line is useful for outgoing calls so that the main line is free for incoming ones.

Telephone coverage must be provided around the clock either with an answering service or an *answering machine.* Some of the drawbacks to using a machine can be minimized if the recorded message is kept short and if the message is changed daily with the day of the week mentioned. Some offices make use of a **call diverter** that is programmed to shunt calls to the home of the broker or associate responsible for overnight coverage. Also useful is a **phone patch** device that allows two lines to be linked for conferences.

A *copier* may be rented initially rather than purchased. Copiers were found in 84 percent of the surveyed offices. The machine must take legal-size paper but high speed is not essential and a basic model is usually sufficient. An electric *typewriter* used with carbon ribbon provides a crisp, professional image.

When a *filing cabinet* is purchased a standard one can be matched later as another is required. If the startup budget is limited, however, files can be purchased secondhand or at office supply sales. *Desks, chairs,* and *tables* should be chosen for utility as well as decor. An overhang on the front of a desk allows a customer to pull up a chair to sign a contract. Usually, however, round conference tables with comfortable armchairs create a more reassuring and friendly atmosphere than an authoritative desk and straight-chair arrangement.

In the 1985 survey almost 60 percent of real estate firms had *computer* capability (*see* Figure 13.4). This figure had almost doubled since 1981. While the most common use was for access to a multiple-listing system, firms specializing in nonbrokerage activities were more likely to use in-house systems and word processors (Figure 13.5). Such offices found their software through many different sources (Figure 13.6).

The firm just starting out may find it more practical to lease a computer system than to buy one.

Figure 13.4
Computer Capability by Size of Firms (Percent of Firms)

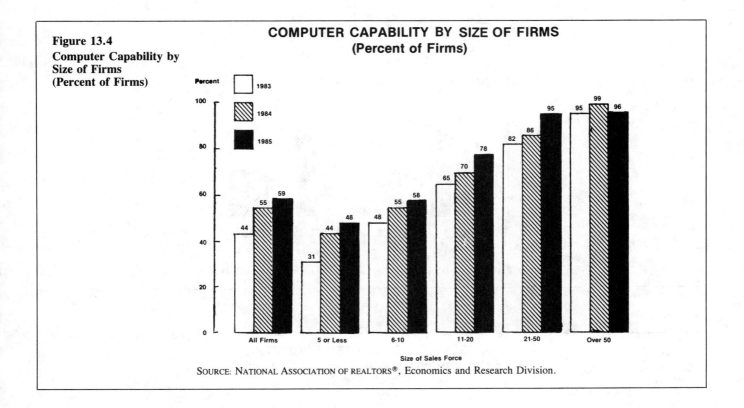

COMPUTER CAPABILITY BY SIZE OF FIRMS
(Percent of Firms)

SOURCE: NATIONAL ASSOCIATION OF REALTORS®, Economics and Research Division.

Smaller items to be purchased include lamps, bookcases, coffee or side tables, and a fireproof safe for records. The office's *outside sign* should be lighted at night. New York license law also requires that each broker be listed on a sign visible from the sidewalk or in the lobby of an office building with the words "licensed real estate broker."

Budgeting

Before the office is opened a careful budget is made to estimate **startup expenses** and costs for the first six months of operation. A sample budget for one-time and annual expenses, shown as Figure 13.7, is reprinted from *Real Estate Brokerage: A Success Guide,* by John E. Cyr and Joan m. Sobeck (Chicago: Real Estate Education Company, 1982), which also provided much of the information in this and the next chapter. The chart should be filled in carefully to reflect the decisions made regarding either the purchase or rental of equipment. Ideally the broker should have the necessary cash as indicated on the bottom line in hand before starting. A broker confident of success can sometimes borrow the money to open, however. In that case periodic repayments of the loan must be added to operating expenses.

Figure 13.5

Trends in the Use of Data Processing Equipment (Percent of Firms)

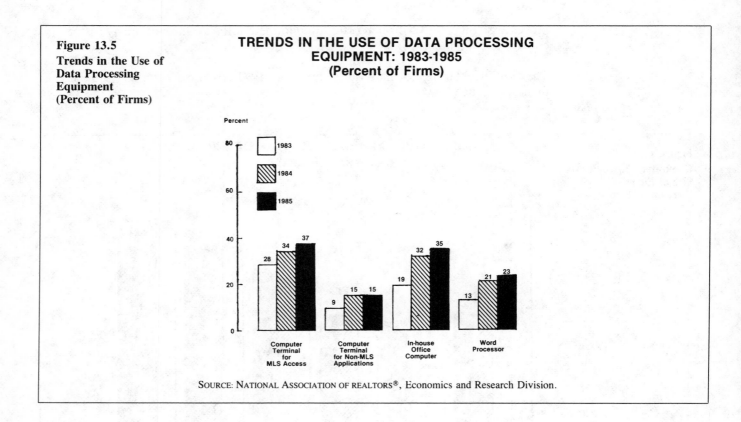

TRENDS IN THE USE OF DATA PROCESSING EQUIPMENT: 1983-1985
(Percent of Firms)

SOURCE: NATIONAL ASSOCIATION OF REALTORS®, Economics and Research Division.

Figure 13.6

Sources of Computer Software (Percent of Firms With In-House Computer Capabilities)

SOURCES OF COMPUTER SOFTWARE
(Percent of Firms With In-House Computer (Capabilities)

Obtained From Computer/Manufacturer Without/Modifications — 25%

Obtained From Computer/Manufacturer With/Modifications — 12%

Obtained From Outside Supplier Without/Modifications — 19%

Obtained From Outside Supplier With/Modifications — 12%

Obtained From MLS Or Service Bureau — 4%

Totally Custom Written — 11%

Written In-house — 16%

Obtained a Turnkey System — 9%

SOURCE: NATIONAL ASSOCIATION OF REALTORS®, Economics and Research Division.

Figure 13.7
Sample Budget

One-Time Expenses

Legal fees (to establish corporation or partnership)	$ _____
Accounting fees (advice, start-up, books)	_____
Telephone installation	_____
Initiation fees, board of REALTORS®, MLS	_____
License fees—state, city	_____
Office space costs—deposit, remodeling	_____
Office equipment—typewriters, files, desks	_____
Office supplies—stationery, cards, forms	_____
Automobile purchase or lease	_____
Artist work for logo, signs, stationery	_____
Advertising agency cost (if applicable)	_____
Stock of lawn signs	_____
Office sign—purchase or lease	_____
TOTAL ONE-TIME EXPENSES	$ _____ $ _____

Monthly Expenses

Office rent	$ _____
Office salaries	_____
Legal and accounting fees	_____
Insurance premiums	_____
Automobile cost	_____
Utilities (if applicable)	_____
Office supplies	_____
Janitorial wages (if applicable)	_____
Telephone expense	_____
Newspaper advertising	_____
Your salary	_____
Miscellaneous dues and subscriptions	_____
Sign repair and replacement	_____
Entertainment	_____
Reserve for contingencies	_____
TOTAL MONTHLY EXPENSES	$ _____ x 6 mo. $ _____
GROSS AMOUNT NEEDED	$ _____
LESS PROJECTED INCOME FOR SIX MONTHS	$ _____
MINIMUM CASH NEEDED TO START	$ _____

Opening the Office

High visibility in the community may be accomplished in several ways. Newspapers should be sent a brief, businesslike news release announcing the new firm. While the interior is being readied, a large window sign outside can announce that the brokerage is "Coming Soon. . . ." Announcements can be mailed to old customers and clients. With the first listings the office acquires, extra money should be budgeted for newspaper classified advertising, so that the firm logo is prominently displayed for a few months.

One good way to introduce the new brokerage is to hold an opening celebration complete with refreshments. Invitations can be sent to former customers, neighboring business establishments, lawyers and bankers with whom the broker has ties, and nearby real estate offices that are curious to see the new competition. Cocktail hours between the normal business day and dinnertime are probably best. The firm's brand-new Open House signs can be positioned near the door and in the office.

Summary

Operating a broker's office requires different skills beyond those needed for successful listing and selling of property. Expenses are incurred in even the most minimal operation. The new broker may prepare by reviewing law of agency and license law and by attending management seminars and REALTORS® conventions.

Among early decisions a broker needs to make are specialty, groups to affiliate with, size, location, form of ownership, office layout, and budgeting. Franchise affiliation should be considered. Even with a trend toward larger offices most real estate firms in this country are still small businesses with no sales management beyond the owner's services. Site selection must take into account ease of access, parking facilities, and the firm's desired public image.

The majority of brokers elect *independent contractor status* for associates. The name of the new firm must be cleared with the Department of State and should be registered with the county clerk. A separate bank account is required for escrow deposits.

The firm may be organized as a *sole proprietorship, corporation, S corporation,* or *general partnership.* A salesperson may not be a partner with a broker. Corporate ownership may lead to double taxation but has the advantage of limited personal liability for financial problems.

Outside assistance may include the services of an *attorney, accountant, bookkeeper, insurance broker, artist* or *advertising agency, answering service,* and *notary public.*

Office layout must provide a *reception area, desk space, research area,* and a *private conference* or *closing room.* Equipment should be carefully chosen for cost-effectiveness; expensive items like a computer terminal or copier may be rented at first.

The opening of the office can be celebrated with an open house to which clients, customers, neighbors, and business associates are invited. Newspaper releases and extra advertising of the new office's logo will increase community awareness of the firm.

Questions

1. The number of real estate licensees in New York State is approximately:
   a. 140,000. c. 650,000.
   b. 15,500. d. 31,000.

2. Approximately what portion of real estate licensees in New York State belong to the State Association of REALTORS®?
   a. Ten percent c. One-half
   b. 20 percent d. All

3. Among the requirements for successful sales management are:
   a. motivational skills.
   b. attention to detail.
   c. careful budgeting.
   d. All of the above

4. The majority of the real estate firms in this country specialize in:
   a. full-service brokerage.
   b. farm and land sales.
   c. commercial property.
   d. residential sales.

5. Approximately what proportion of REALTORS® offices are affiliated with a franchise organization?
   a. Ten percent c. One-half
   b. 20 percent d. 90 percent

6. Most REALTORS® offices in this country have how many salespersons?
   a. 1–10 c. 21–50
   b. 11–20 d. More than 50

7. The IRS allows independent contractor tax status for an associate who:
   a. holds a real estate license.
   b. is paid irregularly, by commission.
   c. works under a written contract that specifies independent contractor status.
   d. All of the above

8. The initials "DBA" are used for:
   a. Department of State.
   b. Department of Business Administration.
   c. Doing business as.
   d. Downtown Broker's Association.

9. The business name of a prospective real estate company must be cleared with the:
   a. NAR. c. DOS.
   b. NYSAR. d. IRS.

10. The broker's escrow account:
    a. may be a brokerage money-market account.
    b. must be non-interest-bearing.
    c. may also contain earned commissions.
    d. should be clearly identified as a trust account.

11. Which of the following forms of organization does *not* involve personal liability for the firm's financial debts?
    a. Sole proprietorship
    b. Corporation
    c. Monolithic office
    d. Partnership

12. Just as a physician carries malpractice insurance many real estate brokers carry:
    a. health and accident insurance.
    b. incompetence insurance.
    c. errors & omissions insurance.
    d. partnership insurance.

13. Computers are most often used by real estate firms for:
    a. word processing.
    b. playing games.
    c. in-house management systems.
    d. accessing multiple-listing information.

14. New York license law requires:
    a. an accountant's yearly report to the Department of State.
    b. a sign visible from the sidewalk with the words "licensed real estate broker."
    c. membership in the New York State Association of REALTORS®.
    d. All of the above

15. The advertising budget for a newly opened real estate office should:
    a. be held to a cautious minimum.
    b. be more lavish than usual.
    c. be discussed with the firm's attorney.
    d. include provisions for skywriting.

14

Operation of a Broker's Office

Key Terms

Caravan tours
Company dollar
Conflict of interest
Desk cost
Draw
Dual agency
Errors and omissions insurance
Floor duty

Indirect interest
Innocent misrepresentation
Intentional misrepresentation
Loss-of-bargain
Negligent misrepresentation
Nut
Policy and procedures guide
Standard of care

Overview

Careful planning, close regular supervision, and constant monitoring are essential if a real estate brokerage is to prosper in a competitive market. This chapter examines standard techniques for achieving these ends, from budgeting through selecting and training sales associates and evaluating the firm's performance. It also considers the broker's liability for breaches of fiduciary duty, conflict of interest, misrepresentation, and required standard of care.

Budgeting

When the real estate market becomes difficult, as it did in the early 1980s, the difference between firms that fail and those that stay in business is often careful financial planning, budgeting, and control of expenses. Unique to real estate brokerage is the concept of the **company dollar.** The term refers to those funds left from gross income after commissions have been shared with salespersons, other brokers, and franchise networks. The company dollar represents the money available for the firm's expenses and for profit.

Budgets for real estate companies vary widely depending on the size of the firm, methods of doing business, and type of sales management. Average figures may be of interest. A recent national survey found that the average firm paid 43 percent of commissions received to its associates, forwarded another six percent in cobrokerage commissions to other offices, credited six percent as the owner's own commissions on transactions personally negotiated, and spent approximately one percent for franchise fees, board, or MLS costs. Of gross income, therefore, 44 percent remained as company dollar for the average firm.

Breakdown of Company Dollar

Advertising accounted for an average 16 percent of the company dollar spent. Most of this went for newspaper advertising but the category also included radio and television, signs, and yellow pages advertising (often wrongly included with communications expense).

Sales promotion expense, which included entertainment, education, travel, sales awards, business gifts, and charitable contributions, totalled an average five percent of the company dollar.

Sales management expense varied widely with small firms reporting no outlay in this category and large ones about nine percent. The average was three percent.

Salary figures included managers other than sales managers, secretarial and clerical help, payroll taxes, and employee benefits. This category totalled 13 percent.

Owner's nonselling services were computed by estimating the number of hours the owner spent and their value if the same services were being performed on an hourly basis by someone else. This cost averaged eleven percent of company dollars.

Communications expense, including telephone, telegrams, long-distance networks, and answering service, averaged seven percent.

Occupancy included rent, janitorial services, and utilities. If the premises were owned the cost of occupancy was calculated from fair market rental for the space. The category accounted for about 12 percent of company dollar.

Operating expenses, which took 20 percent of the budget, covered licenses, dues, legal and accounting fees, office supplies, equipment rental, repairs and depreciation, insurance, postage, interest on business loans, auto expenses, and computer costs.

Profit was reported by a few firms to be as high as 40 percent of company dollar while others operated at a net loss. Average net income, pre-tax, was reported at around 11 percent of the company dollar, or less than 5 percent of gross income. This analysis had, of course, already compensated the owner for time spent in management and for commissions on his or her own sales.

Other Methods of Financial Analysis

Expenses in a real estate office may be analyzed in a variety of ways. If total expenses are divided by the number of associates, the resulting figure is called **desk cost** per salesperson. In a 1984–85 survey, desk cost per associate averaged $12,618. Small firms reported somewhat higher desk costs but also showed higher production per employee.

The associate who does not bring in enough company dollars to pay his or her desk cost is a drain on the firm. Besides representing a net loss, such a person costs the firm something in lost opportunities; valuable leads that might have been followed up successfully by someone else may be wasted. The inept salesperson also saps office morale and tarnishes the company's public image.

The company's revenue also may be measured by calculating the company dollar per average transaction (dividing total company dollars by number of transactions in a given period). Company figures can be calculated for items like advertising expense per salesperson or per listing, amount of money spent to produce each telephone inquiry, ratio of listings to sales, cost to service the average listing, and monthly **nut** (amount in company dollars that must be generated to cover expenses). Careful analysis of the figures is valuable in budgeting, goal-setting, and long-term planning.

Policy and Procedures Guide

In even a small office, a written **policy and procedures guide** contributes to the smooth running of the company, heads off misunderstandings, serves as a reference for settling disputes, and can be an excellent tool in recruiting and training associates. A loose-leaf format makes revisions simple. Care must be taken not to violate the salesperson's independent contractor status through inappropriate wording. "Suggested Procedures Guide" is a suitable title. Except where legal and ethical considerations are under discussion, the word "must" is inappropriate. "Sales meetings are held each Monday morning at 9:30" is better than "Associates are required to attend each Monday . . ."; "Associates may sign up for floor duty" is preferable to "Each associate must spend four hours a week on floor duty."

The guide should be as concise as possible. It should say nothing, for example, about how to secure a listing. Instead it can detail procedures to follow after the listing is obtained: how to label a key and where to store it; how to enter the listing in the computer system; arranging advertising; and whether or not leads obtained from phone calls on the property will belong to the listing agent.

Company Policy

A typical guide starts with a sketch of the company's *history* and *goals*. *Background information* on the owner and manager is appropriate, with *names* and *responsibilities* of *personnel*. A *job description* for the associates follows. *Independent contractor* status is briefly reviewed with a list of items provided by the company and another list of those to be paid by the associate. A concise treatment of *ethical* and *legal* considerations is appropriate: *civil rights* guidelines to be followed both within the office and in listing and selling (*see* Chapter 10), a review of the *fiduciary duty* to clients, the theory of *hidden defects, nonsolicitation* orders that may be in effect in the area, and local *sign restrictions* or regulations. Company policy regarding the *termination* of a salesperson is also discussed.

The associate needs knowledge of the procedures followed in relationships with *attorneys*, a *franchise* or *multiple-listing system* to which the office belongs, and *cooperating offices*. The guide may suggest (but not dictate) appropriate *goals* for an associate in terms of number of listings and sales, hours of floor duty, and attendance at sales meetings and it may discuss the desk cost per associate.

Paperwork and Housekeeping

Paperwork should be described in detail: What *forms* are available; what *reports* are to be turned in with listings, contracts, or escrow deposits, and to whom. A *sample* of each form and sales aid used in the office should be included. *Supplies, signs, lockboxes, business cards,* and use of equipment like the *copier* or computer terminal are discussed. Housekeeping information includes rules on *desk use,* lights, heat, ashtrays, coffee or kitchen equipment, *parking,* and *office hours.*

Office Procedures

Sales meetings, caravan tours, open houses, and *floor duty* (opportunity time, office time) should all be covered in the guide. The responsibilities and opportunities of the associate on floor duty are spelled out in detail to prevent misunderstandings. *Advertising* policy includes a discussion of frequency and size of ads, paperwork procedures, deadlines, individual budgets, and follow-up reports to be turned in. A section on *telephones* describes the answering service used, specifies policy on long-distance calls and entries in a long-distance log, briefly discusses standard telephone-answering techniques, and sets standards for customer rotation and the channeling of calls.

Compensation

Office morale benefits from the inclusion of a set *commission schedule.* Future disputes can be anticipated and avoided if the guide spells out commission divisions in unusual situations: when the associate buys or sells his or her own house, when the office furnishes interim financing to a buyer or seller, when unusual expenses or legal fees are incurred in the course of a transaction, or when one associate makes a sale while holding an open house at another's listing.

Antitrust

In recent years individual real estate brokers, boards of REALTORS®, and multiple-listing systems have come under close scrutiny by federal and state departments intent on ensuring free and active competition. The Sherman Antitrust Act sets penalties as high as $1 million for corporations and $100,000 and three years in prison for individuals who operate in restraint of trade. Even seemingly casual and well-meant conversations have had devastating results for some companies. Brokers are advised to refrain from any discussion, anywhere, about *commission rates* except as necessary for a specific cooperative transaction between two firms. Also suspect is any conversation with competitors about *geographical* or sociological *division* of business and *refusal to deal* with a competitor. The procedures guide should advise associates to avoid any conversation with members of another firm by leaving the premises if the talk turns to commission rates or geographical division of the market.

Recruiting

Before taking on associates the owner must consider the company's overall goals, public image, and available space. A decision should be made beforehand on whether the firm wants part-time salespersons or only full-timers. Recruiting must be coordinated with training. The small office that offers informal one-on-one training may recruit on a continuing basis. The large firm may prefer a single recruitment campaign followed by a number of classroom training sessions.

Methods of Recruiting

Advertising, career nights, and *trial training sessions* are often used for recruitment. Classified or small display ads in newspapers are common. A single sentence of invitation to discuss a real estate career may be appended to the company's other advertising. Care must be taken that advertising is not discriminatory. The phrase "experienced only," for example, has been held discriminatory in an area where experienced salespersons are almost all white, or male. "Experience desirable or we will train you" is more acceptable.

Selection

The broker who takes on anyone who walks in the door risks a loss in office morale, the financial drain of an unproductive associate, and legal problems arising from unethical associates. Common methods of selection include *application forms, aptitude tests,* and *personal interviews.*

An application form reveals, if nothing else, whether the would-be salesperson can write legibly and fill in forms, useful attributes for a real estate agent. Any application form should be reviewed by the firm's attorney before it is first used, however. Charges of discrimination in this matter can be serious. Questions about address, education, and former employment are considered relevant. Among those forbidden are queries about race, religion, age (except as necessary to meet licensure requirements), and spouse's employment. There is also a growing belief that many aptitude tests may be discriminatory; in any event the value of tests in predicting success in real estate is questionable.

Among topics explored during an interview may be the applicant's attitude toward number of hours worked, weekend and evening work, and the amount of income anticipated from commissions. Other jobs presently held should be discussed. The prospective associate's attitudes toward ethics and civil rights should be explored. The manager often cautions the applicant that no income may be forthcoming for three to six months, and explains that a regular **draw** against future commissions is inconsistent with independent contractor status. In explaining the nature of real estate brokerage the manager can stress the necessity for a salesperson to handle stress, face disappointments, and accept occasional rejection. The decision to take on a particular salesperson should consider not only the profit potential but also whether the individual fits the company image and will contribute to office harmony.

Training

A good company training program aids in recruitment and builds reputation. It allows the trainer to spot potential problems early and either cure them or suggest the neophyte leave the company. The well-trained associate requires less time-consuming attention during early transactions and is eager to try out the techniques taught. The educated salesperson is more likely to succeed and to remain with the company.

Basic Methods

An old jingle sums up the attitude in a few old-fashioned offices: "Here's the desk, there's the phone. Lots of luck, you're on your own." The small office, however, can offer excellent one-on-one *on-the-job* training with the newcomer led step-by-step through the first few transactions.

The *sales meeting* technique is often utilized in medium-sized offices. Periodic training sessions are integrated into sales meetings. Full coverage of the material requires a number of months with this method.

Organized classrooms are most often run by multiple-office companies or franchise operations. They offer efficient instruction and are one of the main inducements for franchise affiliation. Occasionally several small independent firms combine to operate an organized classroom.

Planning the Program

The instructor should set down beforehand the objectives for each session. Visual aids (blackboard, videotapes, overhead projector) greatly enhance learning. Instruction may be varied with guest speakers, perhaps a mortgage counselor or the firm's attorney. Student involvement is encouraged through discussions, questions, role-playing, and small-group work on case studies. Students may be taken on field trips to an abstract company, settlement session, or the office of the multiple-listing system or real estate board. The instructor need not be the broker; good teaching skills might be found in some other member of the staff.

Course Content

The following outline of topics is taken from Cyr and Sobeck's *Real Estate Brokerage: A Success Guide,* cited in the preceding chapter. The list can be adapted to suit the needs of the individual office.

1. The philosophy of the firm regarding ethics, Board of REALTORS® membership, MLS participation, cooperation with other firms, and the real estate sales process.
2. The jobs and duties of the broker and sales manager and what the new associate should expect of them; the jobs, duties, and responsibilities of other employees of the firm; what the trainee may ask of fellow employees and tasks they cannot expect the other employees to perform for them; and the office layout and organizational chart.
3. The job description of a professional salesperson; what is expected of the trainee in the way of objectives, goals, working habits, demeanor, dress, and attitude toward fellow associates.
4. The contract between the broker and the sales associate, what it contains and why. Independent contractor versus employer-employee relationship, with an explanation of the different responsibilities of each party. Why the company has chosen this specific form of contract and what it entails.
5. Reviewing the policy and procedures manual (if employer-employee relationship) or the suggested procedures guide (if independent contractor status).
6. How the associate can plan and manage time wisely.
7. Explanation of the company referral system; how referrals from other firms, former customers, and clients are handled.
8. The importance of communicating properly: handling letters, telephone calls, brochures, and other communication devices.
9. The law of agency and the exclusive listing. Various kinds of listings and the company's attitude toward each type.

10. The multiple-listing system to which the firm belongs, its rules and regulations, how it works, and how best to use it correctly.
11. Prospecting for listings, sources, and methods.
12. The farm method of obtaining listings—setting up a market and research program.
13. Handling objections from For-Sale-by-Owners (FSBOs), using role-playing.
14. Planning the listing presentation—use of the listing kit.
15. The first listing interview—role-playing between trainees.
16. Pricing the listing; the dangers of overpricing; and how to use the competitive market analysis form.
17. The appraisal process for residential properties.
18. The listing agreement: gathering the data, measuring the house, computing the square footage, and filling out the form properly.
19. Processing the listing by compiling the in-house records needed to service it adequately; installing the sign; lockboxes; counseling the seller about showings.
20. Servicing the listing: advertising, touring the property, holding open house for inspection—callback reports, obtaining new loan commitments.
21. How to write compelling and attention-getting classified and display ads about the listing.
22. When and how to advertise the listing by using brochures.
23. Renewing expiring exclusives.
24. Touring the listings and competing properties (improving product knowledge).
25. Prospecting for Buyers, Part One: advertising policy and techniques.
26. Prospecting for Buyers, Part Two: how to answer ad calls, getting the name and pertinent information, making the appointment, the use of "switch" sheets.
27. Prospecting for Buyers, Part Three: the use of open houses, how to conduct an open house properly, separating the buyers from the lookers.
28. Arranging for and conducting the showings correctly: cooperating with other firms, making the appointments, picking up and returning the keys, office policy regarding lockboxes.
29. Learning how to qualify buyers by using role-playing for the trainees.
30. Techniques for obtaining the offer: countering prospects' objections, when and how to close.
31. Handling offers and counteroffers, closing techniques, contingency clauses, the art of negotiating.
32. The memorandum or purchase agreement: how to fill it out correctly and pitfalls to avoid.
33. Follow-through on the transaction: obtaining required inspections, permits, and appraisals.
34. Estimating buyer and seller closing costs: how to prepare for the settlement, prorating customary charges in the locality.
35. The importance of after-sale servicing. (This is a good subject to "brainstorm.")
36. Financing, Part One: investigating and verifying the existing loan(s), obtaining the correct principal balance and interest rate; finding out if it is assumable and at what rate of interest; explaining the due-on-sale clause and use of the amortization book. Blended mortgages.
37. Financing, Part Two: finding out if the owner will carry back part of the purchase price, the use of the land contract, first and second mortgages, and wraparound or all-inclusive mortgages.
38. Financing, Part Three: explaining government-supported financing; FHA, VA, Farmers Home Administration loans, SONYMA loans.

39. Financing, Part Four: creative financing; the various sources coupled with the right tools.
40. Clauses to watch for on loans, such as subordination clause, "lock-in" loans, due-on-sale (alienation), notice of default, request for notice of default, acceleration clauses of various types, and release clause. Caution against unauthorized practice of law.
41. Income tax implications in the sale of single-family residence, the avoidance or postponement of capital gains tax, the one-time after-55 credit, and new laws affecting same.
42. The use of the installment sale method in order to spread out the capital gains tax on the sale of a home or farm.
43. Explanation of terms regarding the sale and exchange of real property; meaning of terms such as *basis, depreciation, 'like-kind' property, tax shelter, leverage,* and *accelerated cost recovery.*
44. IRS rules and regulations affecting the exchange of property and the mechanics of effecting a tax-deferred exchange.
45. Exchanges: two-party, three-party, and multiparty.
46. Listing and selling small-income properties.
47. Analyzing a Real Estate Investment, Part One: arriving at the NOI (net operating income).
48. Analyzing a Real Estate Investment, Part Two: basic knowledge.
49. Analyzing a Real Estate Investment, Part Three: advanced knowledge.
50. Discussion about and commitment to a personal success plan for each trainee.

Sales Management

Where the sales force numbers more than 12, the owner usually adds a sales manager to the staff and moves on to administrative and public relations activities. The manager handles recruiting, training, setting goals, motivating, and evaluating associates' performance. In addition the manager is readily available as a resource, providing expertise in difficult transactions, backup support when the associate must be in two places at once, and counsel for personal and professional problems. A good manager can also spot particular talents (working with transferees, obtaining listings, handling income property) and guides associates toward suitable specialties.

Compensation

The majority of nonowner sales managers are employees. As an incentive to increased production an override is sometimes offered in addition to salary. If the override is based on a percentage of net profits, the manager has an interest in controlling expenses while building volume. The manager whose primary income comes from commissions personally earned is in the difficult position of competing with the associates he or she is supposed to be helping.

Motivation

While sales associates often state they are in real estate to make money, many other important factors are also at work. Among them are the desire to belong, to be liked, to create, to achieve, and to receive recognition for achievement. These needs may be particularly strong in those individuals drawn to sales work.

Significant findings emerged from a study conducted at the University of Alberta that investigated the efficacy of various forms of motivation for real estate salespersons. Those associates who worked on a fixed 50/50 *commission split* made more money than those with sliding-rate arrangements. Firms that ran *sales contests* showed slightly lower production than those that did not. Higher earnings were found in firms that set sales *quotas* and *goals*. Associates also earned substantially more in companies that held frequent, regular *sales meetings*. Associates also earned more in offices where the sales manager did not compete for listings or sales.

Financial incentives (higher commission splits, prizes, bonuses) were found to be less effective in raising production than close supervision, goal-setting, sales meetings, and individual attention. Other studies have shown that almost any new system, if accompanied by careful individual supervision, results in increased production. The improvement shown may be simply the result of associates receiving increased attention.

Sales Meetings

Properly planned sales meetings contribute to production and to office morale. Selling can be lonely work and associates look forward to good meetings as enjoyable social occasions. Meetings impart technical knowledge, provide data on current market conditions, and disseminate information on the associates' listings, transactions, and issues of general interest.

Planning Meetings

The following guidelines can aid the broker in preparing successful meetings. *Time* should be carefully chosen so that it does not conflict with other activities. Monday morning meetings get the week off to a good start and usually associates are full of news about their weekend achievements. The *agenda* should be prepared in advance and an outline distributed to attendees. Meetings should *start promptly* so that proper attendance is rewarded and latecomers realize they have missed out on something. A sales meeting should proceed at a *brisk pace* and *finish early*. The old show business adage "Always leave them wanting more" applies here.

Typical Agenda

The sales manager might start by calling upon each associate for a brief report on new sales and listings, allowing time for questions from other salespersons. Activity at weekend open houses is then canvassed. Financial information is updated with associates sharing any news or rumors they have encountered about interest rate changes, points, and SONYMA money. Upcoming seminars and board meetings are publicized and goals and sales contests updated. A short presentation on a single training topic serves as a refresher and may stimulate discussion. An outside speaker may appear; bankers, appraisers, home inspection engineers, and Department of State examiners are often willing to address groups, even small ones. The sales meeting also can serve as a forum for ventilating office problems.

Evaluating Performance

A broker cannot require independent contractors to file regular reports but such records are valuable for analyzing each salesperson's working habits and production. Figure 14.1 is an activity report that might be used as the basis for an individual counseling session with the manager. Figure 14.2 aids in monitoring the goals set by the associate in consultation with the manager.

Figure 14.1
Monthly Activity Sheet

Name _____ Month _____

Sales . . . .
    1.
    2.
    3.
    4.
    5.

                                           _____

Listings Sold . . . .
    1.
    2.
    3.
    4.
    5.

                                           _____

New Listings . . . .
    1.
    2.
    3.
    4.
    5.

                                         _____

Total Activities . . . .   _____

Current Listing Inventory
1.
2.
3.
4.
5.
6.
7.
Total Current Listing Inventory . . . .   _____

Broker's Liability

Increasing use of litigation in our society, growing awareness of consumer rights, resentment of troubled conditions in the housing industry, all may mean trouble for real estate brokers and salespersons. It is possible to incur liability even though acting in all honesty and with goodwill. Situations that may lead to professional liability fall under four main headings:

- breach of fiduciary duties;
- failure to observe standard of care;
- conflict of interest; and
- misrepresentation.

Figure 14.2
Self-Imposed Goals and Actual Evaluation

198____	INVENTORY LISTINGS		GOALS				ACTUAL			
	Goal	Actual	Sales	Listings	Total Activities	Earnings	Sales	Actual Listings	Total Activities	Earnings
JANUARY										
FEBRUARY										
MARCH										
1st QUARTER TOTALS										
APRIL										
MAY										
JUNE										
2nd QUARTER TOTALS										
JULY										
AUGUST										
SEPTEMBER										
3rd QUARTER TOTALS										
OCTOBER										
NOVEMBER										
DECEMBER										
4th QUARTER TOTALS										
YEAR-END TOTAL										

SIGNED ______________________

Possible results include loss of client and listing, loss of customer and sale, loss of commission, civil lawsuit for damages, criminal prosecution, and suspension or loss of license. In many of the following situations full disclosure in advance will prevent liability. If on the other hand the problem is not immediately obvious, disclosure as soon as it is discovered may limit liability.

Breach of Fiduciary Duty

In essence fiduciary duty requires the agent to put the principal's interest above everyone else's, including the agent's own. Besides setting forth specific rules and regulations in this matter, New York's license law mandates "trustworthy" service.

As noted in Chapter 2, the agent owes the principal:

- care (acting in a competent manner);
- obedience (not to deviate from instructions);
- accounting (of all monies involved in a transaction);
- loyalty (acting in client's best interest, above others'); and
- notice (calling to attention any material facts).

Care

This duty requires the broker to further the client's goals by all reasonable and lawful means. If property has been listed the agent owes a sincere attempt to market it, as evinced by advertising the property, showing it to buyers, and advising the seller on ways to effect the sale.

Obedience

The agent must obey all the client's lawful instructions. Any order to conceal a hidden defect or to practice discrimination in the sale or rental of property should not be obeyed and the agent has a duty to explain to property owners their own legal liability in such cases. An agent may not advertise property below the price stipulated by the seller; thus "try the $50s" or "make an offer" may be in violation of the duty of obedience. It is also a violation to suggest that the buyer offer anything below the asking price unless the seller has authorized the broker to do whatever negotiating is necessary to effect a sale. Instructions like "24 hours' notice for showing" or "all offers through listing broker" must be scrupulously obeyed by any subagents in a multiple-listing system.

Accounting

The handling of earnest money deposits is set forth in some detail in New York's license law, rules, and regulations. A common source of trouble arises when the buyer who does not keep large sums in a checking account gives an agent a check to be held for a few days. If the seller accepts the purchase offer based on the representation that the earnest money is in the broker's possession, trouble may ensue. The broker clearly owes the seller an accounting of the exact status of the deposit.

Loyalty

Because the agent may not advance his or her interest at the expense of the principal's, any attempt to profit from a transaction except through the agreed-upon commission signals a situation in which loyalty might be breached. Profiting from a client's misfortune is forbidden. The agent who subtly discourages efforts by cobrokers in a multiple-listing system in hopes of securing a sale within the listing office is clearly not acting in the seller's best interest.

Notice

The law considers that any notice given the agent has been given to the principal. The agent therefore has a duty to pass on any material information; all offers must be presented immediately. The broker must volunteer any facts that might be of value to the seller.

Details of the buyer's financial condition should be disclosed as well as information that the buyers have indicated they might pay a higher price. The duty of notice also places on the broker an obligation to explain to the seller matters that might otherwise escape notice or be misunderstood, details of proposed financing, or drawbacks in a purchase offer.

Failure to Observe Standard of Care

Standard of care requires the agent to deliver the quality of service expected of a reasonable prudent broker. New York license law expects the broker to be "competent." Actions breaching this obligation might be failing to present an offer before it expires, neglecting to mention in the purchase contract any fixtures or personal property desired by one of the parties, neglecting the property being managed for another, improperly handling escrow deposits, or failing to obtain all necessary signatures on a contract. The cost of drapes might be sought by the buyer who was assured they would be mentioned in the contract. The seller who did not receive an offer in time to consider it might subsequently look to the broker for a sum known as **loss-of-bargain.** If the lost offer was for $80,000 and the property later sold for $75,000, the seller may look to the broker for the lost $5,000.

The courts and the New York Department of State set differing standards of care for brokers and salespersons. The broker is held to higher expectations than the salesperson. Special training, designations, education, and experience may all increase the standard required of an agent. Brokers are unwise to represent themselves as qualified appraisers or experienced syndicators if they are unable to deliver service of acceptable quality. The neophyte residential agent confronted with an opportunity to list a shopping plaza should probably approach an experienced commercial broker with a request that they work together to list and sell the property. Otherwise the duty of observing an appropriate standard of care may be breached by the inexperienced agent.

Conflict of Interest

In the mid-1980s a federal survey disclosed that approximately 75 percent of the buying public thought they were being represented by the selling broker. Even worse, some brokers had the same impression. Long discussions took place on the question of **dual agency,** sometimes designated as the *subagency* question, because of the position of a cooperating broker in a multiple-listing system. In one state after another, legislatures wrestled with the problem of informing the public and controlling the agent's fiduciary position.

New York's license law forbids the agent from representing both parties unless each knows of the arrangement and consents to it. Where the agent is being paid by both, the situation is clear. More difficult, however, is the common situation in which the agent, being paid by the seller, comes to identify with the buyer and furnishes encouragement, advice, and assistance to the buyer. Under a multiple-listing system, the selling agent may never even have met the seller. Many agents—and some lawyers—have difficulty in remembering that the seller is the principal and owed first loyalty.

Advising the buyer on how to negotiate with the seller may even put the broker in the position of serving two masters. Without such advice, of course, most transactions would not take place at all. The broker has been retained to produce a ready, willing, and able buyer; to accomplish this, negotiation and compromise are usually necessary. Nevertheless an unintended result may follow, with the agent now representing both parties. If the transaction falls through, either buyer or seller might claim damages based on the broker's conflict of interest. That the actions are performed with good intentions does not change the situation. The problem is a difficult one, faced daily by brokers and with no simple solution. One remedy might be to obtain the seller's authorization to perform whatever negotiation and service to the buyer might be necessary to secure an offer.

Conflict of interest also occurs when agents buy property on their own account. License law requires that agents disclose the facts in such situations and also forbids purchase through relatives or straw men without disclosure. The agent must also disclose personal ownership of or other interest in the property being sold.

Conflict of interest may occur when the agent is called to a listing interview and finds a seller ready to let the property go at a ridiculously low price. The courts have held that even though the property is not yet listed the seller is relying upon the broker's expertise. The broker who wants to buy the property immediately without notifying the seller of its true value is operating under a conflict between his or her own interest and that of the seller.

Indirect interest is a more subtle situation occurring where no financial advantage accrues to the agent. The agent should disclose, for example, if he is a member of a Boy Scout committee looking for a camp site or if he is trying to locate a home for his mother to purchase.

Misrepresentation

Misrepresentation covers more than simply a deliberate lie intended to mislead someone. Where that situation does exist, it is known as **intentional (fraudulent) misrepresentation.** There are two other classifications. **Negligent (unintentional) misrepresentation** covers false statements made by someone who *should* have known better. **Innocent (honest) misrepresentation** is a false statement by someone who believes the information to be true but is not expected to have expertise in the subject.

In order for the agent to be liable there must be:

- a false or misleading statement (or concealment of a material fact), by
- a person who knows (or should have known) that the information is false, with
- intent to deceive or defraud (or, where there is no such intent, the effect is still to deceive or defraud), and
- damages suffered by the party who relied on the information.

It is relatively easy for an agent to avoid intentional misrepresentation simply by sticking to the truth. But omissions and half-truths may misrepresent as readily as actual misstatements do and the offense may be committed inadvertently.

The buyer looking at rural property may be told "the septic system works well" when in fact it does not. If the agent knew the true state of affairs, *intentional misrepresentation* has occurred. If the agent did not know the condition of the system, the potential buyer is still being misled by *negligent misrepresentation*. The half-truth that might mislead would be a statement like "most people out here have septic systems." True in itself, this skirts the issue in a manner that may be misleading to an ignorant buyer. No mention at all of the septic system might also be misleading, particularly to an urban buyer who assumed sewers were present everywhere.

It will be little defense that the broker knew nothing of the condition of that system if brokers in that community *should* know about such matters. Even if the intention is not to defraud, the buyer who purchases the property and discovers the septic system inoperative has suffered damages and may seek to recover them from the broker.

In recent years buyers and sellers have become increasingly aware of the possible danger posed by urea-formaldehyde foam insulation (UFFI). Some brokers insist upon written statements from each party about the presence or absence of the insulation so that they can prove the subject was discussed. Other brokers feel that, given the difficulty in many cases of determining whether UFFI has been installed, they should not assume any responsibility for a matter they prefer to keep outside their field of expertise.

Among areas where problems frequently arise are statements about the value of property ("Sure to go up ten percent a year in this area"); title ("The judgments have all been cleared up"); utilities ("No problem hooking in to the sewers"); boundaries; zoning; and size. In a recent case in another state the buyer of a house that turned out to contain 100 square feet fewer than promised in the listing data was awarded the current construction cost of 100 square feet in that area. The buyer, who can recover from only one party, may prefer to sue the broker, who still has an office in town and who has a vulnerable reputation, rather than the seller who may have already moved out of town.

To Avoid Misrepresentation

Never present opinions as facts. Not "We can certainly get you $100,000 for this house" but "I don't see why we might not . . ." or "It should probably bring as much as these recent sales did."

Absolute statements should be avoided. Not "all copper plumbing" but "It looks from here as if. . . ." The phrases "I believe" or "I was told by the seller" are more accurate than "The roof is five years old," where the agent has no direct knowledge of its age.

Many requests for information should be met by referring the questioner directly to an expert source: city zoning bureau, mortgage counselor, building inspection engineer, or lawyer. The agent thus shifts responsibility and cuts down the chances of giving faulty information in specialized areas.

Information must be gathered with great care because the public will make important financial decisions based on the data presented. Statements of income and expense on rental property, for example, should be prepared by the seller, preferably with the aid of a certified public accountant.

Defense Against Claims of Liability

Staying alert to situations that might pose problems is a first defense. Disclaimers that "the information furnished is believed correct but not warranted" are of little value. They cannot cover spoken repetition of the material and they cannot acquit the broker of liability. The fact that the misleading material may have been furnished by the seller is also of little value in defense.

The best protection against possible damage to others and possible claims for those damages is disclosure. "This is my mother; I'm helping her look for a house" treats the seller fairly by putting him or her on notice of a possible conflict of interest. "The listing sheet says 1,600 square feet but I think it's closer to 1,500." "The contract says the buyer is putting down $2,000 earnest money; we haven't deposited the check yet." If made in time such disclosure prevents the client from making decisions based upon faulty data. Actions taken after disclosure are the client's own responsibility. The broker will not have caused damages.

Even if the problem has been discovered after the buyer or seller has acted, timely disclosure may limit the damages incurred. Consider the buyer who asks the broker to hold a deposit check for a few days "until I can get the money into my account." Subsequently the buyer tells the broker "don't cash the check at all; I'll make it good on the day of closing." Feeling that the damage already has been done, the broker hesitates to notify the seller of a potential problem. The seller meanwhile moves out of the house in anticipation of closing. If the buyer then refuses to perform, the seller may claim loss-of-the-bargain, loss of the escrow deposit that was to serve as damages, moving expenses, and rent or the cost of holding a vacant house. Damages could have been limited if the problem had been disclosed when it became apparent the transaction might be shaky. The seller's actions after that disclosure—the moving expenses and rent, for example—would not be the broker's fault and liability could have been somewhat mitigated.

Any disclosure should be made in writing, without admission of wrongdoing, in a businesslike manner. Although the letter should come from the broker, an attorney's advice and assistance with wording should be sought.

Errors and omissions insurance is the equivalent for real estate practitioners of malpractice insurance for physicians. It covers legal fees to defend against claims for liability and payment of any damages, less a deductible amount. Such insurance, however, does not cover dishonest or deliberately fraudulent acts.

Summary

Budgeting is essential to survival in today's real estate business. Unique to real estate is the concept of the *company dollar,* defined as those funds remaining after commissions have been shared with salespersons and other brokers. Nationwide, real estate firms spend the greatest share of the company dollar for advertising and operating expenses. Dividing total expenses by the number of salespersons yields a figure known as *desk cost.*

A written *policy and procedures guide* contributes to the smooth running of a real estate office. Procedures are suggested for independent contractors, who cannot be bound by specific requirements. To avoid any suspicion that they are acting in restraint of trade, brokers should avoid any discussion with competitors of *commission rates* or *geographical division* of business.

Recruiting is often done through advertising, career nights, and trial training sessions. Advertisements must be carefully worded to avoid discrimination. Application forms and aptitude tests also should be cleared with an attorney before use. The most common method of *selecting* associates is through interviews. *Training* may be informal in the small company, take place within a series of sales meetings, or follow standard classroom procedures.

A nonowner sales manager is usually found in firms with more than 12 sales associates. Most sales managers are employees, often receiving an override based on profits. Studies have shown that *sales meetings, goal-setting,* and *close supervision* motivate higher production from associates than financial incentives.

The successful *sales meeting* is prompt, brisk, and short. An agenda planned in advance may include reports on associates' activities, news of the financial market, a training topic, and outside speakers.

Liability claims against brokers for damages caused to buyers or sellers may arise from *breach of fiduciary duty, failure to observe standard of care, conflict of interest,* or *misrepresentation.* Misrepresentation need not be *intentional*; unintentional or *negligent misrepresentation* and *innocent misrepresentation* are also possible. The best defense against claims arising from such situations is *disclosure,* either before the client has acted or as soon as the problem is discovered.

Questions

1. The term "company dollar" refers to:
   a. gross commissions received.
   b. firm's share of commissions.
   c. percentage forwarded to a franchise.
   d. net profit.

2. Yellow pages costs are budgeted under:
   a. communications.
   b. advertising.
   c. operating expense.
   d. telephone.

3. The largest single expense for most real estate firms is:
   a. advertising.
   b. rent and occupancy.
   c. telephone and telegraph.
   d. sales promotion.

4. The term "desk cost" refers to:
   a. expenses for sales management.
   b. equipment rental.
   c. share of expenses for each associate.
   d. cost of training one salesperson.

5. A policy and procedures guide is best described as:
   a. a multiple-listing system's contract with brokers.
   b. board of REALTORS® rules and regulations.
   c. independent contractor agreements with associates.
   d. a statement of a company's basic philosophy and guidelines.

6. Brokers can be held guilty of restraint of trade if they are suspected of:
   a. regulating commission rates.
   b. dividing up the market geographically.
   c. refusing to deal with competitors.
   d. Any of the above

7. Violation of the Sherman Antitrust Act is punishable by:
   a. a fine of up to $1 million for a corporation.
   b. up to three years in prison.
   c. a fine of up to $100,000 for an individual.
   d. All of the above

8. Discrimination in employment has been charged where an advertisement used the phrase:
   a. "experienced only."   c. "leads furnished."
   b. "will train."   d. "high earnings."

9. Advertisements for associates, application forms, and aptitude tests must be carefully monitored for:
   a. cost effectiveness.
   b. conformity to community practice.
   c. evidence that discrimination is not practiced.
   d. goal-setting.

10. Which of the following is a legitimate question for an application form?
    a. Age
    b. Spouse's employment
    c. Religion
    d. Former employment

11. One of the main reasons cited for affiliation with a franchise is:
    a. aptitude-testing.
    b. training program.
    c. assistance with budgeting.
    d. sales contests.

12. The Alberta study found that associates earned more in firms that offered:
    a. a sliding scale of commissions.
    b. sales contests.
    c. no sales quotas.
    d. frequent sales meetings.

13. Sales meetings should be:
    a. scheduled frequently and regularly.
    b. started promptly even if not all associates have arrived.
    c. planned to allow group discussion.
    d. All of the above

14. The setting of sales quotas by a broker:
    a. results in lower production.
    b. violates the independent contractor relationship.
    c. brings up the dual agency question.
    d. involves indirect interest.

15. Misrepresentation may occur when:
    a. the speaker knows the statement is false.
    b. the speaker should know the statement is false.
    c. the speaker is not expected to have knowledge in the matter under discussion.
    d. All of the above

16. The broker charged with professional liability may suffer:
    a. civil damages.
    b. loss of commission.
    c. loss of license.
    d. All of the above

17. The duty of obedience forbids the broker from:
    a. mentioning the condition of the house in ads.
    b. placing a sign on the property.
    c. suggesting an offer under the listed price.
    d. giving information over the telephone.

18. When the buyer gives a broker information about possible financial problems in completing the purchase, the broker should:
    a. respect the confidence and let it go no further.
    b. immediately inform the seller.
    c. offer to lend the buyer extra funds needed.
    d. ask for a written confirmation of the situation.

19. Negligent misrepresentation occurs when:
    a. the speaker knows the statement is false.
    b. the speaker should know the statement is false.
    c. the speaker is not expected to have knowledge in the matter under discussion.
    d. no harm is done by the falsehood.

20. The best defense against a breach of fiduciary duty is:
    a. concealment of defects.
    b. indirect interest.
    c. timely disclosure.
    d. loss-of-bargain.

15

Advertising

Key Terms

AIDA
Annual percentage rate
Blind ads
Display advertising

Institutional advertising
Regulation Z
Triggering terms
Truth-in-Lending Act

Overview

Advertising, the largest single item in most brokerage budgets, is designed to "make the phone ring." Motivating prospective buyers and sellers to call requires skill that can be acquired. State and federal regulations call for honesty and fairness. This chapter will discuss advertising media open to the broker, techniques for creating effective advertising, and regulations to be observed.

Function of Advertising

Generally, advertising can (1) *influence or inform* the public about a particular product, service, or idea; or (2) *promote the public's confidence in a product or firm and their general goodwill toward it.* This second function is known as institutional advertising and is frequently used in the real estate field to establish and improve a broker's business image in his or her particular area.

Advertising real estate must accomplish a dual function. It attracts prospective purchasers to the real estate broker's office to inspect specific properties and it attracts prospective sellers to the office. Only by obtaining listings of property does the broker have anything to sell. Advertising therefore is both an integral part of the process of securing listings and a useful selling tool.

The dual function of advertising points out the need for the real estate broker to negotiate two sales, not just one. He or she must first sell the seller on listing the property with the office and then sell the prospective purchaser on buying. What might be called a third sale is the task the broker faces of persuading the seller to accept the purchaser's offer.

A broker pays the expenses of advertising a home. On occasion, however, a broker may persuade a homeowner to pay for some or all of the advertising, especially if special circumstances surround the sale such as the seller's need for an unusually fast transaction. Sometimes a broker has an agreement with associates whereby each salesperson may choose to place or pay for advertising on houses listed. In any case when a broker or his or her salespersons pay the cost of advertising, the profit made on a sale is reduced. The need to make advertising effective and productive is obvious.

Advertising Media

When selecting an advertising medium, aside from costs, a broker must take two important factors into consideration; (1) the *geographic area* covered by the medium and (2) the *demographic makeup* of the people that the advertising will reach. It is wise for a broker to direct advertising to a particular group of people in a select area who are most likely to be interested in the products and services offered. For example, a broker would probably be foolish to advertise a plush mansion in the local newspaper of a lower-middle income suburb. The broker, then, must *aim advertising at those people who are most likely to respond favorably and take action because of it and place this advertising where such people are likely to see it.*

Care must be taken, however, that such targeted advertising does not lay the broker open to charges of steering when the assumption that a certain group of people will be interested in a specific property is based on ethnic, religious, or other prohibited considerations.

Among the advertising tools available to the real estate broker are stationery and business cards, signs, display boards, open houses, classified ads, display ads, direct mail, press releases, billboard, and radio and television.

Stationery and business cards. A letter on business stationery and a business card are often the first items a potential prospect receives from a broker and, as such, both must create a good impression. A distinctive, easy-to-recognize company logo should be designed and incorporated into both letterheads and business cards. A printer or commercial artist usually can design company stationery and cards relatively inexpensively. Whenever possible every salesperson on a broker's staff should have personalized business cards. Such cards tend to present the salesperson as a competent, expert representative of the firm. Business cards are also an excellent way for real estate people to introduce themselves to potential clients and give contacts something to remember them by. Any item of information or memorandum should be jotted down and handed out on the back of the agent's card. Business cards are probably the least expensive form of advertising.

The New York Department of State requires that the broker's or company's name be featured more prominently on business cards than that of the salesperson. Regulations that prohibited the use of residence telephone numbers on business cards are no longer in effect.

Signs. Both For Sale and Sold signs can draw people to the real estate office that has posted them. People may interpret such signs as indications of an active and effective business and therefore one that may be able to satisfy their needs. In addition many people drive through neighborhoods in which they are thinking of living. When they notice a house they like with a lawn sign they will contact the real estate company involved.

In some areas it is against the law to post For Sale signs. One always should check local ordinances regarding this point. In New York, real estate license laws prohibit a salesperson or broker from posting a For Sale sign on listed property without the owner's express permission. The lawn sign (the "free billboard") is regarded by many as the most effective form of advertising.

Display boards. Display boards are used to attract walk-by traffic. They are usually large boards or space in the brokerage firm's front widow that display photographs of property for sale and pertinent data about the homes. The descriptions could be the same ones used in other kinds of ads. The display board may also attract the interest of walk-in buyers while they wait for someone in the office to help them.

Open houses. An open house is based on a public announcement that a particular piece of real estate is for sale and that anyone interested may visit the property at a specific time. The announcement is usually made by placing signs on major roads near the property and advertising in the newspaper. An open house may attract potential *sellers* as well as potential buyers, for people often examine the market before offering their own homes for sale.

Classified ads. Classified ads attract many potential buyers. Such advertising, generally concerning one or only a few parcels of real estate, is designed to be read line by line. It is assumed that in reading the ad, prospects will look for those words, phrases, and features that interest them or capture and stimulate their imaginations. A buyer seldom purchases the house whose ad originally attracted him or her to the real estate office. Thus ads bring in potential buyers to be qualified and then shown houses to fit their needs.

New York's license laws prohibit a broker from running **blind ads**—ads that do not identify the advertiser as a real estate broker. In addition the state license laws prohibit a salesperson from running real estate ads in his or her own name. If an ad mentions a salesperson it must also clearly show the relationship between the salesperson and his or her broker. Advertisements claiming that property is in a ''vicinity'' or geographic area must name the territorial subdivision or geographic area where the property is actually located. It should also be noted that any advertisement of a price lower than the listed price violates the broker's fiduciary duty to the seller.

Display ads. Real estate firms most often use newspaper display advertising for public relations purposes to build prestige and remind people that the firm is in business. When such an ad is intended to attract buyers, several For Sale offerings usually are combined in one attractive display. Its purpose is to describe a variety of the firm's best homes that are currently most in demand in order to create the impression that the broker can satisfy the needs of a variety of buyers. This type of ad often includes photographs of the houses along with their descriptions. An advantage of display ads is that they can be used as reprints for direct mail and other forms of promotion.

Direct mail. The usual direct-mail ad is a ''choose your neighbor'' letter sent to families in an area where the broker has one or more listings. Basically the letter notifies families in the area that a particular property is for sale and asks them to consider the possibility of having a friend or relative look at and possibly buy the available home. Those interested are invited to contact the broker. Expensive property is often marketed through direct-mail distribution of lavish color brochures.

Press releases. Press releases are considered an institutional form of publicity or advertising. Their purpose is to call attention to a real estate firm because of its involvement in a newsworthy event. For example, news releases should be sent to the real estate editors of local newspapers when a large and/or prestigious property has been either listed or sold by a firm. While a press release does not specifically advertise the proprety for sale, it does notify people in the area that a well-known property is available and calls their attention to the firm that is selling it.

Billboards. Billboard advertising is an expensive yet highly successful method of advertising. It cannot be used to sell a specific property but it is a good way to convey a short message such as a company name and service, to passersby. Some large brokerage firms use this form of advertising successfully to establish their names and reputations in a given area.

Radio and television. Some brokerages use short radio and television ads in their institutional advertising programs. Such advertising is sometimes too expensive for the average broker. Franchised brokerage firms may run a standard commercial for the chain in which the local broker's name and address will be mentioned if he or she agrees to pay a small percentage of the ad's cost.

Developing Good Advertising

The best advertisements are unusual and creative. Their wording stimulates the imagination and attracts interest. The most successful real estate firms are those that use their ads to impress the public. Every broker can build a strong public image through continuous and imaginative advertising. Consistent use of a symbol or trademark on all letterheads, advertising copy, and signs, combined with a distinctive advertising style, will contribute to this end.

It is a good idea to write ad copy several days before the newspaper's deadline, let the ad rest for a few days, and read it over critically later. Another good test is to read ads aloud.

After an advertisement appears, it can be monitored in several useful ways. A simple check to see that the ad actually ran should be routine. Publications make mistakes, particularly where last-minute classified ads are concerned. If the same classified ad is to run the next week, the broker may want to check it for *widows,* lines with only one word or part of a word on them. A slight change in wording may result in more cost-effectiveness.

Written reports on the response to individual advertisements can pinpoint surefire phrases and information of special appeal to the public. A broker can also monitor responses to estimate the amount of advertising money that has been spent to produce each phone inquiry; associates often treat phone calls with more care when they realize how expensive each one is.

The broker may distribute copies of each ad to all salespeople so they will be able to discuss the specific parcel of property when inquiries are received. It is a good practice to ask each salesperson to review the ads before they are published. This gives them the opportunity to participate in the preparation of the ad and to relate it directly to the property.

Time factors should be considered in preparing classified ads. For example, if immediate possession of the property is possible, such information could be included in the ad. During the month of August it is appropriate to relate the ad to the beginning of the school year and refer to the opening dates of both public and parochial schools. It is also possible to advertise that the seller has been transferred and that therefore the property has been priced to sell quickly. Relate the ad to the natural assets of the specific property such as proximity to lakes, availability of swim club membership, and the like.

Good advertising must: (1) attract *attention,* (2) create *interest*, (3) arouse *desire,* and, most important, (4) lead to *action.* (If you remember that the initial letters of these four goals spell the name of the opera *AIDA*, it may help your memory.)

Ad writing. Rules for effective ads: Be careful in choosing the words you use to describe a house or property offered for sale. *Words communicate images.* Some synonyms that may technically share the same meaning may communicate *widely varying images.* For example, the words "big," "substantial," "massive," "huge," "immense," "enormous," "mammoth," "colossal," "jumbo," "whoppingly big," and "king-sized" all mean the same but each conveys a strikingly different thought. Another example of this phenomenon is found in the words "charming," "polished," "refreshing," "mellow," "refined," "gracious," "cordial," "cheerful," "delightful," "lived-in," "dignified," and "inviting."

Studies have shown that ad readers look first for information about location, number of rooms, number of bedrooms, and energy-related improvements. Many of those surveyed claimed they would not read ads that gave no indication of price level.

Here are some sample ads and phrases that use price as a selling point: "$120,000 and your garden and landscaping are complete!" (excellent where the property described is in a new subdivision and competing with new homes that are not landscaped for the initial owner); "Ready to move into for $55,000"; "More than you'd expect—for only $95,000"; "No need to buy appliances—all included at $82,000."

A wise investment for anyone who writes ads is a copy of Roget's *Thesaurus*. Keep a "choose a better word chart" handy. Such a chart lists the words frequently used to describe homes and property.

There are many ways to make display and classified advertising more effective. It pays to *use a provocative lead*. Such phrases as "owner transferred," "take it away," and "don't be left out," are attention-getters. *Be sure the style and wording of ads are up-to-date*. Read professionally written classified ads and clip examples of good advertising from newspapers and magazines. Become aware of the words and phrases professional ad writers use. *Whet the reader's curiosity—don't tell everything*. Surprise the reader and make him or her want to know more so that he or she will call you. *Play upon the reader's imagination*. Use words that stimulate the imagination and encourage the reader to complete the picture. *Use emotion*. Purchasers frequently buy homes solely for emotional reasons. The pride of ownership is often cited as the primary reason. Many people also buy homes because of a strong sense of parental responsibility. They may feel a strong need to provide their children with a better way of life than they themselves had as children. *Don't waste words*. Be descriptive but pertinent. *Be sincere*. Advertising is telling the truth attractively.

Good advertising and public relations must be a continuing program based on creating new ideas, giving service, and being sincere.

The New York Department of State has prepared a pamphlet to help brokers avoid some of the more common violations of law or department policy in advertising. This pamphlet is reproduced at the end of the chapter.

Regulation Z

The federal **Truth-in-Lending Act,** known as **Regulation Z,** provides for the strict regulation of real estate advertisements that include mortgage financing terms. General phrases such as "liberal terms available" may be used but if details are given, they must comply with this act. By the provisions of the act the **annual percentage rate,** *which includes all charges, rather than the interest rate alone, must be stated.*

As revised on October 1, 1982, Regulation Z applies to all credit advertising. If any of the following *triggering terms* is used, three further items of information also must be included. The triggering terms are:

1. Amount or percentage of down payment (unless no down payment is required),
2. Number of payments or period of repayment,
3. Amount of any payment, and
4. Amount of any finance charge.

If any of the items listed above is mentioned, the advertisement also must include

1. Amount or percentage of down payment,
2. Number of payments or term of loan, and

3. ''Annual percentage rate,'' so identified, and whether that rate is to be increased after consummation.

The full disclosure would be necessary if any of the following terms were used:

- 30-year loan available,
- payment $586.23 including principal and interest,
- only five percent down, or
- assume mortgage with five years left to go.

Terms that would *not* trigger the required disclosures include:

- financing available,
- terms negotiable,
- owner may finance,
- no down payment,
- assume 13 percent annual percentage rate loan,
- attractive financing, and
- $40,000 mortgage available.

In the summer of 1983 the New York Bureau of Consumer Frauds surveyed real estate advertisements in six major newspapers from Buffalo to Long Island and found more than one-half the real estate advertisements contained triggering terms. Of those ads requiring full disclosure, only four percent were in compliance with the Truth-in-Lending Act. The most common violations were failure to disclose that an interest rate was variable and failure to mention annual percentage rate.

Summary

Advertising must perform a dual function in the real estate business—attract prospective sellers as well as prospective buyers. Forms of brokerage advertising include stationery, business cards, signs, display boards, open houses, classified ads, display ads, direct mail, press releases, billboards, radio, and television. A broker usually pays the cost of advertising a home. All real estate advertising should be aimed at those people most likely to respond favorably and take action because of it.

Effective advertising must attract attention, create interest, arouse desire, and lead to action.

New York Department of State regulations forbid blind ads, misleading geographic terms, and advertising by a salesperson that does not also identify the supervising broker.

Regulation Z sets standards to prevent misleading statements about financing.

If certain *triggering terms* are mentioned, the advertisement must disclose full loan information.

Questions

1. Institutional advertising:
   a. gives information about unique property like a school or library.
   b. keeps the firm's name before the public.
   c. meets the requirements of antidiscrimination laws.
   d. must be approved by the Department of State.

2. The least expensive form of advertising is probably a:
   a. business card.
   b. "For Sale" lawn sign.
   c. billboard.
   d. classified ad.

3. The most effective form of advertising is probably a:
   a. business card.
   b. "Sold" lawn sign.
   c. display ad.
   d. blind ad.

4. The classified ad usually:
   a. triggers a response from someone who will buy that exact house.
   b. brings in potential buyers for other property.
   c. is intended for institutional advertising.
   d. sounds as if it is run by the owner.

5. The Department of State looks with disfavor on:
   a. blind ads.
   b. vague and misleading geographic terms.
   c. ads in the salesperson's own name.
   d. All of the above

6. Buyers report they are most interested in an ad that tells about:
   a. location, number of rooms, insulation.
   b. landscaping, trees, pools, or patio.
   c. appliances, drapes, carpeting.
   d. the makeup of the neighborhood.

7. Many buyers say they will not answer ads that have no information about:
   a. school system.
   b. number of baths.
   c. price level.
   d. garages.

8. Regulation Z provides that:
   a. buyers must be provided with information on heating costs.
   b. brokers must clear all ads with the Department of State.
   c. if certain financing terms are mentioned, others also must be included.
   d. vague misleading geographic terms must not be used.

9. Which of the following is a triggering term that mandates inclusion of full details in an advertisement?
   a. Assume 12 percent FHA loan
   b. Less than ten percent down
   c. Owner may finance
   d. No down payment

10. If a triggering term is included, an ad must go on to explain:
   a. amount or percentage of down payment.
   b. number of payments.
   c. annual percentage rate.
   d. All of the above

Appendix: Department of State Guidelines on Advertising for Brokers

The fair and proper conduct of the business of a real estate broker includes advertising. There are several laws, rules and regulations, both state and federal, which affect advertising. A listing of more significant ones is provided below.

This pamphlet has been prepared in order to help brokers to avoid some of the more common violations which, although possibly unintentional, would be contrary to both the law and Department of State policy with respect to advertising in newspapers and other media. The use of business cards and stationery, while usually intended as a means of introduction, may also be construed to be advertising.

As a summary, the information contained herein is not intended to be used as a substitute for the requirements of each or any applicable law or rule; and in matters where there are questions of interpretation, licensees are directed to the actual text of such. . . .

INFORMATION FOR REAL ESTATE BROKERS. There are several aspects of advertising where a broker must maintain awareness of the specific provisions of the License law that states that "dishonest or misleading advertising" may form the basis for disciplinary action by the Department of State.

DISCRIMINATORY PRACTICES. The Executive Law, Federal Fair Housing Laws and rules governing discriminatory practices prohibit a broker from using advertisements where there is any expression of limitation because of race, creed, color, national origin, sex or disability or marital status in any of the activities defined as those of a real estate broker.

PROPERTY DESCRIPTION AND BROKER IDENTIFICATION. The General Business Law and License Law rules and regulations contain provisions which regulate both blind ads and advertising according to geographic location. A "blind ad" is one where there is no indication given in the ad that the advertiser is a broker. Property ads which give only a telephone number or a street address would be considered as blind ads. The owner of a parcel of real property might use a blind ad but brokers may not; even if they own the property advertised. Brokers may indicate their status by giving their licensed name or use the word "broker" and list an office telephone number.

Brokers are required to post a sign or directory notice at their principal and branch offices which must give their full licensed name and indicate their business to be "Licensed Real Estate Broker".

It is an important consideration for the potential home buyer to know the location of property listed in an advertisement. At the same time, when a broker is employed by a seller, there is an agency duty to present the property to be sold in the most favorable light. Whenever a broker places an ad describing the location of a property as being in the vicinity of an area or location, the actual name of the area or location of the property must also be included.

SALESPERSONS. While a real estate advertisement may include a salesperson's name as a part of the ad, such use may occur only when the name is subordinate to that of the name of the broker with whom the salesperson is associated. Additionally, ads must clearly indicate that the status is that of a* "Salesman". Substitute words such as "Salesperson", "Saleswoman", "Sales Agent" or "Sales representative" may be used but the term "Sales Associate" is unacceptable. While this does not prevent the use of additional descriptive terms such as "Relocation Manager", such should always be subordinate to the required term.

Additionally, the use of a salesperson's principal residence telephone number in advertisements is permitted as is the use of the home phone number of a broker, provided that the ad includes a notation that such is a residence number and, further, that such use is not extended to any activity that would constitute branch office operation. A separate branch office license is required for use beyond the listing of a home telephone number.

*The word "salesman" is taken from the text of Section 440 of the Real Property Law as a legal definition of one engaged in the specific activities listed and may denote either male or female gender.

Business cards and stationery should be prepared using the same guidelines that exist for advertising. The broker's name must be predominate in size of print and location, and the "salesman" identifying term should follow the salesperson's name.

BROKER ASSOCIATE. For specific application filings, a person, licensed as a real estate broker, may retain that status but perform salesperson activity in association with another broker (primary broker) and using that broker's business name and office facilities. Those so acting would follow the same guidelines applicable to salespersons except that, as an identifying term, the words "Broker Associate" would be used.

GENERAL. Any advertisement, irrespective of the medium used, should give an honest and accurate description of the property to be sold or leased; and the broker using such advertisement should include an honest and accurate representation of agency, status and associate standings. The ability and status of even unnamed competitors should not be derogated nor should there be unfair or incomplete representations of the real property involved or of others' real property by comparison.

If a broker chooses to make reference to any financing terms in an advertisement, he is required by the "Truth in Lending Law" to disclose *all* financing terms.

Excerpt from New York State's Study Booklet for Brokers

SECTION 396-b OF THE GENERAL BUSINESS LAW

Advertisements of Brokers and Dealers

Advertisements. Any person, firm, corporation or association, or agent or employee thereof, hereinafter called person, who, being engaged in the business of dealing in any property, makes, publishes, disseminates, circulates or places before the public or causes, directly or indirectly, to be made, published, disseminated, circulated or placed before the public, in this state, any advertisement respecting any such property, in any newspaper, magazine, or other publication, or over any radio station or television station, unless it is stated in any such advertisement that the advertiser is a dealer in such property or from the context of any such advertisement, it plainly appears

that such person is a dealer in such property so offered for sale in any such advertisement; or when placing or causing any such advertisement to appear in any newspaper, magazine or other publication or radio or television station as described in this section, if requested by the publisher of any such newspaper, magazine or other publication or owner or operator of such radio or television station or any agent or representative thereof to file with such owner or operator, publisher, agent or representative thereof his true name, or where he is transacting business under a name other than the true name pursuant to law, then the name under which such business is transacted, and each business address wherein any business is transacted by him, in the class of property advertised or to be advertised for sale in such advertisement, shall make any false statement in relation to any of such items; or if requested by the publisher of any such newspaper, magazine or other publication or owner or operator of such radio or television station or any agent or representative thereof to file with such owner, operator, publisher, agent or representative thereof a statement showing whether he is causing such advertisement to appear or is offering to make such sale or disposition or transaction, as herein set forth, as principal or agent, and if as agent, to set forth such information as is specified in this section, in relation to his principal as well as in relation to himself, shall make any false statement in relation to any of such items; is guilty of a misdemeanor.

Disclosure. A broker or salesperson who sells property without informing the buyers that he/she is a broker can be required to return any profit made on the sale.

Dealers. This section requiring an advertiser who is a dealer in the property advertised to indicate in some manner in the advertisement that it is a dealer's advertisement, applies to real estate brokers.

Blind ads. Section 396-b of the General Business Law makes it a misdemeanor for one engaged in the business of dealing in any property to advertise such property in any publication unless the advertisement states that the advertiser is a dealer in such property, or it is plainly apparent from the context that such person is a dealer. It also makes it a misdemeanor for any dealer to answer falsely as to his true name or business name, and his business address or addresses when requested by the publisher or publisher's agent of any medium in which he proposes to advertise, or to answer falsely, if asked, as to whether he is advertising as a principal or agent, or, if he is advertising as an agent, to make any false statement, if asked, in relation to his principal or himself, as to the true name, or business name, and business address or addresses of such party or parties.

"This evidently applies to property of any and every nature, and must include real estate brokers in its scope. The requirement is that an advertiser who is a dealer or the agent of a dealer in the property advertised must indicate in the advertisement in some manner that it is a dealer's advertisement. A mere telephone number or street address would clearly be an insufficient identification. However, a telephone number or street address accompanied by the word 'dealer' or 'broker' would suffice, in my opinion, and if the name of the broker is used I would not consider it necessary that the advertisement state expressly that he is a broker, since the public may ascertain the fact upon inquiry to the Secretary of State.'' In its discretion, the Department of State may consider a violation of section 421-a of the Penal Law as ground for the suspension or revocation of a real estate agent's license.

This statutory provision does not apply to advertisements to lease, or to obtain mortgage loans upon real property.

16

Appraisal

Key Terms

AIREA
Amenities
Appraisal
Capitalization rate
Cash equivalent
CBS
Comparables
Cost approach
CPA
Cubic-foot method
Depreciation
Designation
Economic obsolescence
Fee appraiser
Functional obsolescence
Gross rent multiplier
Highest and best use

Income approach
Locational obsolescence
Market comparison approach
Physical deterioration
Plottage
Quantity-survey method
Reconciliation
Regression
Replacement cost
Reproduction cost
Square-foot method
SRA
Staff appraiser
Subject property
Substitution
Unit-in-place method
Value

Overview

Real estate is the business of value. Members of the general public informally estimate this value when they buy, sell, or invest in real estate. A formal estimate of value generally is conducted by a real estate appraiser and serves as a basis for the pricing, financing, insuring, or leasing of real property. This chapter will examine value—what determines it, adds to it, and detracts from it. It also will discuss in detail the various methods professional appraisers use to estimate the value of residential as well as commercial and industrial real estate.

Appraising

An **appraisal** is an estimate or opinion of value. In the real estate business the highest level of appraisal activity is conducted by professional real estate appraisers who are recognized for their knowledge, training, skill, and integrity in this field. Formal appraisal reports are relied upon in important decisions made by mortgage lenders, investors, public utilities, governmental agencies, businesses, and individuals.

Not all estimates of real estate value are made by professional appraisers; often the real estate licensee must help a seller arrive at a market value for his or her property without the aid of a formal appraisal report. It is necessary for everyone engaged in the real estate business, even those who are not experts in appraisal, to possess at least a fundamental knowledge of real estate valuation.

Appraisals may be required in a number of situations. Among them:

- *Estate purposes,* to establish taxable value or facilitate fair division among heirs;
- *Divorce proceedings,* where real estate forms part of property to be shared;
- *Financing,* when the amount to be lent depends on the value of the property;
- *Taxation,* to furnish documentation for a taxpayer's protest of assessment figures;
- *Relocation,* establishing the amount to be guaranteed to a transferred employee;
- *Condemnation,* arriving at fair compensation for property taken by government;
- *Insurance,* estimating possible replacement expense in cases of loss;
- *Damage loss,* used to support income tax deductions; and
- *Feasibility,* to study possible consequences of a particular use for property.

In New York, as in most states, no license is required for real estate appraisal Brokers are cautioned, however, against the use of the phrase "free appraisal" and against undertaking appraisal work beyond their field of expertise. Both practices are unethical.

A **fee appraiser** works as an independent contractor offering services to a number of different clients. A **staff appraiser** is an in-house employee of an organization like the FHA, a lending institution, or a large corporation.

Value

Value is an abstract word with many acceptable definitions. In a broad sense **value** may be defined as the relationship between an object desired and a potential purchaser. It is the power of a good or service to command other goods or services in exchange. In terms of real estate appraisal, value may be described as the *present worth of future benefits arising from the ownership of real property.*

For a property to have a value in the real estate market it must have four characteristics:

1. *Utility:* the capacity to satisfy human needs and desires;
2. *Scarcity:* a demand that is greater than the supply;
3. *Effective demand:* the need or desire for possession or ownership backed up by the financial means to satisfy that need (when the word *demand* is used in economics, *effective demand* is usually assumed); and

4. *Transferability:* the ability to transfer ownership rights from one person to another with relative ease.

Market Value

While a given parcel of real estate may have many different kinds of value at the same time (as illustrated in Figure 16.1), generally the goal of an appraiser is an estimate of *market value*. The market value of real estate is the highest price in terms of money that a property will bring in a competitive and open market, allowing a reasonable time to find a purchaser who buys the property with knowledge of all the uses to which it is adapted and for which it is capable of being used, neither buyer nor seller under duress. Included in this definition are the following key points:

1. Market value is the *most probable* price a property will bring.
2. Payment must be made in *cash* or its equivalent.
3. Both buyer and seller must act without *undue pressure*.
4. A *reasonable length of time* must be allowed for the property to be exposed in the *open market*.
5. Both buyer and seller must be *well-informed* or *well-advised*.
6. The *present use* of the property as well as its *potential use* must be recognized.

Market value presupposes an *arms-length* transaction, one between relative strangers, each of whom is trying to do the best for himself or herself.

In the mid-1980s appraisal societies and lending institutions started taking into account the distorting effect of special financing concessions: low-interest seller financing or the payment of large numbers of points, for example. For the first time, appraisers were instructed to adjust for the **cash equivalent** of concessionary financing. Evidence of this trend can be seen in the change in the definition of the term *market value* used by Fannie Mae and Freddie Mac. Instead of defining market value as the highest price, as of July 1, 1986, they define market value as the *most probable* price a property should bring.

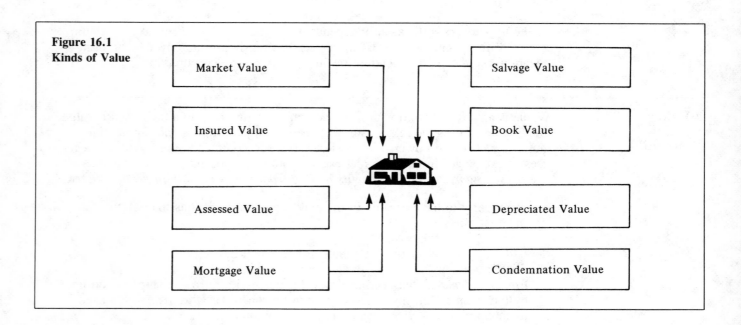

**Figure 16.1
Kinds of Value**

Market Value · Salvage Value · Insured Value · Book Value · Assessed Value · Depreciated Value · Mortgage Value · Condemnation Value

Market value versus market price. Market value is an estimated price based on an analysis of comparable sales and other pertinent market data. *Market price* on the other hand is what a property *actually* sells for—its selling price. Theoretically the ideal market price would be the same as the market value. There are circumstances under which a property may be sold below market value, however, as when a seller is forced to sell quickly or when a sale is arranged between relatives. Thus the market price can be taken as accurate evidence of current market value only after considering the relationship of the buyer and the seller, the terms and conditions of the market, and the effect of the passage of time since the sale was made.

Market value versus cost. It is also important to distinguish between market value and *cost*. One of the most common errors made in valuing property is the assumption that cost represents market value. Cost and market value *may* be equal and often are when the improvements on a property are new and represent the highest and best use of the land.

More often, cost does not equal market value. Two homes may be similar in every respect except that one is located on a street with heavy traffic and the other on a quiet, residential street. The value of the former may be less than that of the latter although the cost of each may be exactly the same.

Basic Principles of Value

Whether an appraiser observes them or not, a number of economic principles affect the value of real estate. The most important of these principles are defined in the following paragraphs.

Highest and best use. The most profitable use to which the property is adapted and needed or the use that is likely to be in demand in the reasonably near future is the **highest and best use.** For example, a highest-and-best-use study may show that a parking lot in a busy downtown area should, in fact, be replaced by an office building. To place a value on the property based on its present use would be erroneous because a parking lot is not the highest and best use of the land. In appraising a residential location the determination of highest and best use will not involve the potential rental income available. **Amenities** or owner satisfaction—an unusual view of the mountains, for instance—may be a key factor.

Substitution. The principle of **substitution** states that the maximum value of a property tends to be set by the cost of purchasing an equally desirable and valuable substitute property, assuming that no costly delay is encountered in making the substitution. For example, if two similar houses are for sale in an area, the one with the lower asking price normally would be purchased first.

Supply and demand. This principle states that the value of a property will increase if the supply decreases and the demand either increases or remains constant—and vice versa. For example, the last lot to be sold in a residential area would probably be worth more than the first lot sold in that area.

Conformity. Maximum value is realized if the use of land conforms to existing neighborhood standards. There should also be a reasonable degree of conformity along social and economic lines. In residential areas of single-family houses, for example, buildings should be similar in design, construction, size, and age to other buildings in the neighborhood and they usually will house families of similar social and economic status.

Anticipation. This principle holds that value can increase or decrease in anticipation of some future benefit or detriment affecting the property. For example, the value of a house may be affected if there are rumors that the block on which the house is located may be converted to commercial use in the near future.

Increasing and diminishing returns. Improvements to land and structures will eventually reach a point at which they will no longer have an effect on property values. As long as money spent on improvements produces an increase in income or value, the *law of increasing returns* is applicable. But at the point where additional improvements will not produce a proportionate increase in income or value, the *law of diminishing returns* applies.

Regression. The principle that, between dissimilar properties, the worth of the better property is adversely affected by the presence of the lesser-quality property is known as **regression.** Thus in a neighborhood where the homes average in the $75,000 range, a structure that would be worth at least $90,000 in another neighborhood would tend to be valued closer to $75,000. Conversely, the principle of *progression* states that the worth of a lesser property tends to increase if it is located among better properties.

Plottage. The principle of **plottage** holds that the merging or consolidation of adjacent lots held by separate landowners into one larger lot under a single land use tends to produce a higher total land value than the sum of the two sites valued separately. For example, if two adjacent lots are valued at $35,000 each, their total value if consolidated into one larger lot under a single use might be $90,000. The process of merging the two lots under one owner is known as *assemblage*.

Contribution. The value of any component of a property consists of what its addition contributes to the value of the whole or what its absence detracts from that value. For example, the cost of installing an air conditioning system and remodeling an older office building may be greater than is justified by the rental increase that may result from the improvement to the property.

Competition. This principle states that excess profits tend to attract competition. For example, the success of a retail store may attract investors to open similar stores in the area. This tends to mean less profit for all stores concerned unless the purchasing power in the area increases substantially.

Change. No physical or economic condition remains constant. Real estate is subject to natural phenomena such as tornadoes, fires, and routine wear and tear by the elements. The real estate business is also subject to the demands of its market as is any business. It is an appraiser's job to be knowledgeable about the past and, perhaps, predictable effects of natural phenomena and the behavior of the marketplace. Table 16.1 tracks changing resale prices in the first half of the 1980s. From 1982 to 1985, prices in the Northeast rose by 39 percent; in the West prices declined by three percent.

The Three Approaches to Value

In order to arrive at an accurate estimate of value, three basic approaches or techniques are traditionally used by appraisers: the market comparison approach, the cost approach, and the income approach. Each method serves as a check against the others and narrows the range within which the final estimate of value will fall. Each method is considered particularly appropriate for specific types of property.

Table 16.1

SALES PRICE OF EXISTING SINGLE-FAMILY HOMES

	United States	North-east	Midwest	South	West
	Median				
1970	$23,000	$25,200	$20,100	$22,200	$24,300
1978	48,700	47,900	42,200	45,100	66,700
1979	55,700	53,600	47,800	51,300	77,400
1980	62,200	60,800	51,900	58,300	89,300
1981	66,400	63,700	54,300	64,400	96,200
1982	67,800	63,500	55,100	67,100	98,900
1983	70,300	72,200	56,600	69,200	94,900
1984	72,400	78,700	57,100	71,300	95,800
1985	75,200	88,000	58,900	74,300	95,500

SOURCE: National Association of REALTORS®

The Market Comparison Approach

In the **market comparison approach** an estimate of value is obtained by comparing the **subject property** (the property under appraisal) with recently sold **comparables** (properties similar to the subject). This approach is most often used by brokers and salespersons when helping a seller set a price for residential real estate. Because no two parcels of real estate are exactly alike, each comparable property must be compared to the subject property and the sales prices must be adjusted for any dissimilar features. The principal factors for which adjustments must be made fall into four basic categories:

1. *Date of sale:* An adjustment must be made if economic changes occur between the date of sale of the comparable property and the date of the appraisal.
2. *Location:* An adjustment may be necessary to compensate for locational differences. For example, similar properties might differ in price from neighborhood to neighborhood or even in the more desirable locations within the same neighborhood.
3. *Physical features:* Physical features that may cause adjustments include age of building, size of lot, landscaping, construction, number of rooms, square feet of living space, interior and exterior condition, presence or absence of a garage, fireplace, or air conditioner, and so forth.
4. *Terms and conditions of sale:* This consideration becomes important if a sale is not financed by a standard mortgage procedure.

After a careful analysis of the differences between comparable properties and the subject property, the appraiser assigns either a dollar or a percentage value to each of these differences. The value of a feature present in the subject property but not in the comparable property is *added* to the total sales price. This presumes that, all other comparables being equal, a property having a feature not present in the comparable property (such as a fireplace or wet bar) would tend to have a higher market value solely because of this feature. The feature need not be a physical amenity; it may be a locational or aesthetic feature. Likewise, the value of a feature present in the comparable but not the subject property is *subtracted*. The terms **CPA** and **CBS** are useful guides: "Comparable Poorer: Add" and "Comparable Better: Subtract." The adjusted sales price represents the probable value range of the subject property. From this range a single market value estimate can be calculated using a weighted average to emphasize those properties most closely comparable.

The market comparison approach is essential in almost every appraisal of real estate. It is considered the most reliable of the three approaches in appraising residential property, where the amenities (intangible benefits) are so difficult to measure. An example of the market comparison approach is shown in Table 16.2.

The Cost Approach

The **cost approach** to value is based on the principle of substitution, which states that the maximum value of a property tends to be set by the cost of acquiring an equally desirable and valuable substitute property, assuming that no costly

Table 16.2
Market Comparison Approach to Value

	Subject Property	Comparables				
		A	B	C	D	E
Sale Price		$68,000	$67,500	$69,500	$68,000	$65,000
Location	good	same	poorer +1500	same	same	same
Age	6 years	same	same	same	same	same
Size of Lot	60' × 135'	same	same	larger -1500	same	larger -1500
Landscaping	good	same	same	same	same	same
Construction	brick	same	same	same	same	same
Style	ranch	same	same	same	same	same
No. of Rooms	6	same	same	same	same	same
No. of Bedrooms	3	same	same	same	same	same
No. of Baths	1½	same	same	same	same	same
Sq. Ft. of Living Space	1500	same	same	same	same	same
Other Space (basement)	full basement	same	same	same	same	same
Condition— Exterior	average	better -500	poorer +1000	better -500	same	poorer +500
Condition— Interior	good	same	same	better -500	same	same
Garage	2-car attached	same	same	same	same	none +2500
Other Improvements						
Financing Date of Sale	current	current	1 yr. ago +2500	current	current	current
Net Adjustments		-500	+5000	-2500	-0-	+1500
Adjusted Value		$67,500	$72,500	$67,000	$68,000	$66,500

Note: Because the value range of the properties in the comparison chart (excluding comparable B) is close, and comparable D required no adjustment, an appraiser would conclude that the indicated market value of the subject is $68,000.

delay is encountered in making the substitution. The cost approach is considered appropriate for non-income-producing property unique to the market: a church, for example, or a hospital. It can also be relevant for new residential construction and it is used for hazard insurance purposes.

The cost approach consists of five steps:

1. Estimate the value of the land if it were vacant and available to be put to its highest and best use.
2. Estimate the current cost of constructing the building(s) and site improvements.
3. Estimate the amount of accrued depreciation resulting from physical deterioration, functional obsolescence, and/or locational obsolescence.
4. Deduct accrued depreciation from the estimated construction cost of new building(s) and site improvements.
5. Add the estimated land value to the depreciated cost of the building(s) and site improvements to arrive at the total property value.

Land value (step 1) is estimated by using the market comparison approach; that is, the location and improvements of the subject site are compared to those of similar nearby sites and adjustments are made for significant differences.

There are two ways to look at the construction cost of a building for appraisal purposes (step 2): reproduction cost and replacement cost. **Reproduction cost** is the dollar amount required to construct an *exact duplicate* of the subject building at the current prices. **Replacement cost** of the subject property would be the construction cost at current prices of a property that is not necessarily an exact duplicate but serves the same purpose or function as the original. Replacement cost is most often used in appraising because it eliminates obsolete features and takes advantage of current construction materials and techniques.

An example of the cost approach to value is shown in Table 16.3.

**Table 16.3
Cost Approach to Value**

Land Valuation: Size 60 × 135 @ $450 per front foot = $27,000
    Plus site improvements: driveway, walks, landscaping, etc. = 4,000
        Total Land Valuation $31,000

Building Valuation: Replacement Cost
    1,500 sq. ft. @ $65 per sq. ft = $97,500

Less Depreciation:
Physical depreciation,
    curable
        (items of deferred maintenance)
          exterior painting $4,000
        incurable (structural deterioration)   5,200
Functional obsolescence   2,000
Locational obsolescence   -0-
        Total Depreciation   −11,200

Depreciated Value of Building $86,300
Indicated Value by Cost Approach $117,300

Determining reproduction or replacement cost. An appraiser using the cost approach computes the reproduction or replacement cost of a building by using one of the following methods:

1. **Square-foot method:** The cost per square foot of a recently built comparable structure is multiplied by the number of square feet in the subject property. Using cubic rather than linear measurement, this procedure would be known as the *cubic-foot method*. Table 16.3 is an example of the square-foot method.
2. **Unit-in-place method:** The replacement cost of a structure is estimated based on the cost of individual building components, as installed, per individual unit of use such as square or cubic footage. Computations include the costs of labor, overhead, and profit. For example, insulation might be computed at $0.13 per square foot, drywall at $2.25 per square yard, and so on. The total in-place cost per unit is multiplied by the number of such units in each building component.
3. **Quantity-survey method:** An estimate is made of the quantities of raw materials needed to replace the subject structure (lumber, plaster, brick), as well as of the current price of materials and installation costs. For example, reproduction might be stated as: 10,000 concrete slabs at $3.50 per slab, 1,500 doorknobs at $7.00 each, and so forth. These factors are added together for the total replacement cost of the structure.

Depreciation. In a real estate appraisal, **depreciation** refers to any condition that adversely affects the value of an *improvement* to real property. Land, however, does not depreciate—it retains its value indefinitely, except in such rare cases as misused farmland. For appraisal purposes (as opposed to depreciation for tax purposes, which will be discussed in Chapter 17), depreciation is divided into three classes according to its cause:

1. **Physical deterioration**—*curable:* Repairs that are economically feasible, considering the building's remaining years of life. A new roof would be a warranted expense on a 40-year-old brick building otherwise in good condition.

   Physical deterioration—incurable: Repairs that would not contribute a comparable value to the building. Near the end of a building's useful life, major repair work such as replacement of weatherworn siding may not warrant the financial investment.

2. **Functional obsolescence**—*curable:* Physical or design features that are no longer considered desirable by property buyers but could be replaced or redesigned at low cost. Outmoded fixtures such as plumbing are usually easily replaced. Room function might be redefined at no cost if the basic room layout allows for it. A bedroom adjacent to a kitchen, for instance, may be converted to a family room.

   Functional obsolescence—incurable: Currently undesirable physical or design features that could not be easily remedied. Many older multistory industrial buildings are considered less suitable than one-story buildings. An office building that cannot be air-conditioned suffers from functional obsolescence.

3. **Locational (economic) obsolescence**—*incurable only:* Caused by factors not on the subject property, this type of obsolescence cannot be considered curable. Proximity to a nuisance such as a polluting factory or a deteriorating neighborhood would be an unchangeable factor that could not be cured by the owner of the subject property.

In determining a property's depreciation, most appraisers use the *breakdown method* in which depreciation is broken down into all three classes with curable and incurable factors in each class estimated separately. Depreciation, however, is difficult to measure and the older the building, the more difficult it is to estimate. Much of functional obsolescence and all of locational obsolescence can be evaluated only by considering the actions of buyers in the marketplace.

The Income Approach

The **income approach** to value is based on the present worth of the future rights to income. It assumes that the income derived from a property will to a large extent control the value of that property. The income approach is used for valuation of income-producing properties—apartment buildings, central business district, buildings, shopping centers, and the like. In estimating value using the income approach, an appraiser must go through the following steps:

1. Estimate annual potential *gross income*.
2. Based on market experience, deduct an appropriate allowance for vacancy and rent loss in order to arrive at the *effective gross income*.
3. Based on appropriate operating standards, deduct the annual *operating expenses* of the real estate from the effective gross income in order to arrive at the annual *net operating income* (NOI). Management costs are always included as operating expenses even if the owner manages the property. Mortgage payments, however (including principal and interest), are *not* considered operating expenses.
4. Estimate the price a typical investor would pay for the income produced by this particular type and class of property. This is done by estimating the rate of return (or yield) that an investor will demand for the investment of his or her capital in this type of building. This rate of return is called the **capitalization rate** and is determined by comparing the relationship of net income to the sales prices of similar properties that have sold in the current market. For example, a comparable property that is producing an annual net income of $15,000 is sold for $100,000. The capitalization rate is $15,000 ÷ $100,000, or 15 percent. If other comparable properties sold at prices that yield substantially the same rate, it may be assumed that 15 percent is the rate that the appraiser should apply to the subject property.
5. Finally, the capitalization rate is applied to the property's annual net income, resulting in the appraiser's estimate of the property's value.

With the appropriate capitalization rate and the projected annual net income, the appraiser can obtain an indication of value by the income approach in the following manner:

$$\text{Net Income} \div \text{Capitalization Rate} = \text{Value}$$
$$\text{Example: } \$15,000 \text{ income} \div 10\% \text{ cap rate} = \$150,000 \text{ value}$$

This formula and its variations are important in dealing with income property.

$$\frac{\text{Income}}{\text{Rate}} = \text{Value} \qquad \frac{\text{Income}}{\text{Value}} = \text{Rate} \qquad \text{Value} \times \text{Rate} = \text{Income}$$

A simplified version of the computations used in applying the income approach is illustrated in Table 16.4.

Table 16.4
Income Approach
to Value

Gross Annual Income Estimate (potential rent income) = $60,000	
Less vacancy and loss of rent (estimated) 5% = −3,000	
Effective Gross Income **$57,000**	

Expense:

Real estate taxes	$9,000
Insurance	1,000
Heat	2,800
Janitor	5,200
Utilities, electricity, water, gas	800
Repairs	1,200
Decorating	1,400
Replacement of equipment	800
Maintenance	1,200
Legal and accounting	600
Management	$3,000

Total Expenses	$27,000
Annual Net Income	$30,000

Capitalization Rate = 10%

Capitalization of annual net income: $\dfrac{\$30,000}{.10}$

Indicated Value by Income Approach = $300,000

Table 16.5
Gross Rent Multiplier

Comparable No.	Sale Price	Monthly Rent	GRM
1	$70,000	$500	140.0
2	68,500	490	139.8
3	70,500	505	139.6
4	67,900	485	140.0
Subject	?	495	?

Note: Based on an analysis of these comparisons, a GRM of 140 seems reasonable for homes in this area. In the opinion of an appraiser, the estimated value of the subject property would be $495 × 140, or $69,300.

Gross rent or income multipliers. Certain properties such as single-family homes or two-flat buildings are not purchased primarily for income. As a substitute for the income approach, the **gross rent multiplier (GRM)** method is often used in appraising such properties. The GRM relates the sales price of a property to its rental income. (Gross *monthly* income is used for residential property; gross *annual* income is used for commercial and industrial property.) The formula is as follows:

$$\frac{\text{Sale Price}}{\text{Rental Income}} = \text{Gross Rent Multiplier}$$

For example, if a home recently sold for $82,000 and its monthly rental income was $650, the GRM for the property would be computed thus:

$$\frac{\$82,000}{\$650} = 126.2 \text{ GRM}$$

To establish an accurate GRM an appraiser must have recent sales and rental data from at least four properties that are similar to the subject property. The resulting

GRM then can be applied to the estimated fair market rental of the subject property in order to arrive at its market value. The formula would be:

$$\text{Rental Income} \times \text{GRM} = \text{Estimated Market Value}$$

Table 16.5 shows some examples of GRM comparisons.

As noted above, gross *annual* income is used in appraising industrial and commercial properties. The ratio used to convert annual income into market value is called a gross income multiplier (GIM).

Much skill is required to use multipliers accurately because there is no fixed multiplier for all areas or all types of properties. Many appraisers view the technique simply as a quick way to check the validity of a property value obtained by the three accepted appraisal methods: market data, cost, and income.

Reconciliation

If the three approaches to value are applied to the same property, they will normally produce three separate indications of value: **Reconciliation** is the art of analyzing and effectively weighing the findings from the three approaches.

Although each approach may serve as an independent guide to value, whenever possible all three approaches should be used as a check on the final estimate of value. The process of reconciliation is more complicated than simply taking the average of the three value estimates. An average implies that the data and logic applied in each of the approaches are equally valid and reliable and should therefore be given equal weight. In fact, however, certain approaches are more valid and reliable with some kinds of properties than with others.

For example, in appraising a home the income approach is rarely used and the cost approach is of limited value unless the home is relatively new; therefore, the market comparison approach is given greatest weight in valuing single-family residences. In the appraisal of income or investment property, the income approach would be given the greatest weight. In the appraisal of churches, libraries, museums, schools, and other special-use properties where no income is involved and there are few sales, if any, the cost approach would be assigned the greatest weight. From this analysis, or reconciliation, a single estimate of market value is produced.

The Appraisal Process

The key to an accurate appraisal lies in the methodical collection of data. The appraisal process is an orderly set of procedures used to collect and analyze all data in order to arrive at an ultimate value conclusion. Such data are divided into two basic classes:

1. *Specific data,* covering details of the subject property as well as comparative data relating to costs, sales, and income and expenses of properties similar to and competitive with the subject property; and
2. *General data,* covering the nation, region, city, and neighborhood. Of particular importance is the neighborhood, where an appraiser finds the physical, economic, social, and political influences that directly affect the value and potential of the subject property.

Figure 16.2 outlines the steps an appraiser takes in carrying out an appraisal assignment. The numbers in the following list correspond to the numbers on the flowchart.

Figure 16.2
The Appraisal Process

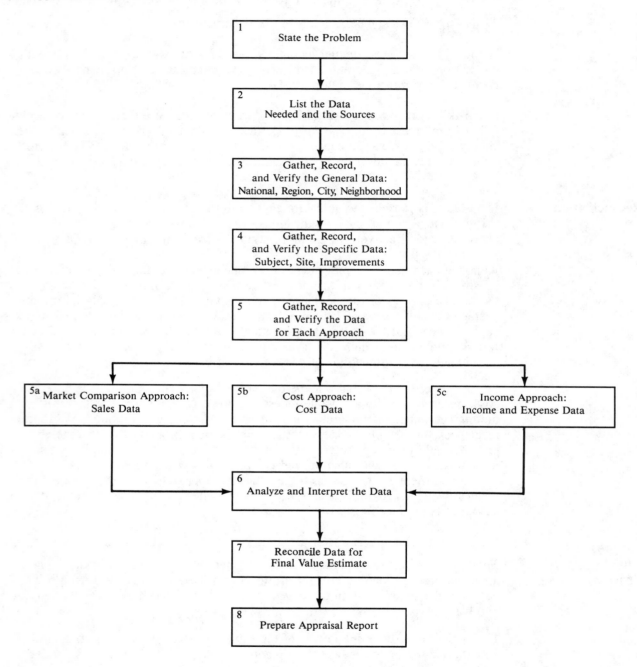

1. *State the problem:* The kind of value to be estimated must be specified and the valuation approach(es) most valid and reliable for the kind of property under appraisal must be selected.

2. *List the data needed and their sources:* Based on the approach(es) the appraiser will be using, the types of data needed and the sources to be consulted are listed.
3. *Gather, record, and verify the general data:* Detailed information concerning the economic, political, and social conditions of the region and/or city and comments on the effects of these data on the subject property must be obtained.
4. *Gather, record, and verify the specific data on the subject property:* Specific data include information about the subject site and improvements.
5. *Gather, record, and verify the data for the valuation approach used:* Depending upon the approach(es) used, comparative information relating to sales, income and expenses, and construction costs of comparable properties must be collected. As with steps 3 and 4, all data should be verified, usually by checking the same information against two different sources. In the case of sales data one source should be a person directly involved in the transaction.
6. *Analyze and interpret the data:* All information collected must be reviewed to ensure that all relevant facts have been considered and handled properly and that no errors have been made in calculations.
7. *Reconcile data for final value estimate:* The appraiser finally makes a definite statement of conclusions reached. This is usually in the form of a value estimate of the property.
8. *Appraisal report:* After the three approaches have been reconciled and an opinion of value reached, the appraiser prepares a formal written report for his or her client. The statement may be a lengthy written report, a completed form, or a simple letter and it should contain the following information:
   a. the estimate of value and the date to which it applies;
   b. the purpose for which the appraisal was made;
   c. a description of the neighborhood and the subject property;
   d. factual data covering costs, sales, and income and expenses of similar, recently sold properties;
   e. an analysis and interpretation of the data collected;
   f. a presentation of one or more of the three approaches to value in enough detail to support the appraiser's final value conclusion;
   g. any qualifying conditions;
   h. supportive material such as charts, maps, photographs, floor plans, leases, and contracts; and
   i. the certification and signature of the appraiser.

Some institutions in the secondary mortgage market require floor plans of the subject property and photographs of both subject property and comparables.

Figure 16.3 shows the FHLMC standardized form report widely used for mortgage financing.

An appraisal may take several forms. An informal *oral* report is occasionally requested by an attorney to help in the decision on whether to proceed with a more expensive investigation. Appraisers' ethics require that even for a brief telephoned report, the documentation on which the estimate is based be retained in the appraiser's files. A *letter* report may run to one or two pages. If it is to be used in court, it will be acknowledged. A full-fledged *narrative* report may run from several pages to several volumes, including floor plans, photographs of the neighborhood, and elaborate detail.

Figure 16.3
FHLMC Residential
Appraisal Report

RESIDENTIAL APPRAISAL REPORT

Property Description & Analysis   File No.

SUBJECT

Property Address	Census Tract
City County State Zip Code	
Legal Description	
Owner/Occupant	Map Reference
Sale Price $ Date of Sale Loan Term	Property Rights Appraised
Loan charges to be paid by seller $ Price/Value Considerations	☐ Fee
R.E. Taxes $ Tax Year ☐ See Comments (Y/N)	☐ Leasehold
Lender/Client	☐ Condominium (HUD/VA)
Address	☐ De Minimus PUD

VALUATION SUMMARY

Cost Approach	$
Cost New	$
Depreciation	$
Site Value	$
Comparison Approach	$
Income Approach	$
Final Value Estimate	$
Date of Value	

NEIGHBORHOOD

	Urban	Suburban	Rural
LOCATION	☐ Urban	☐ Suburban	☐ Rural
BUILT UP	☐ Over 75%	☐ 25-75%	☐ Under 25%
GROWTH RATE	☐ Rapid	☐ Stable	☐ Slow
PROPERTY VALUES	☐ Increasing	☐ Stable	☐ Declining
DEMAND/SUPPLY	☐ Shortage	☐ In Balance	☐ Over Supply
MARKETING TIME	☐ Under 3 Mos.	☐ 4-6 Mos.	☐ Over 6 Mos.

PRESENT LAND USE	%	LAND USE CHANGE	PREDOMINANT OCCUPANCY	SINGLE FAMILY
Single Family		Likely		PRICE $ (000) AGE (Yrs.)
2-4 Family		Not Likely	☐ Owner	Low
Multi-family		In process	☐ Tenant	High
Commercial		To:	☐ Vacant (0-5%)	Predominant
Industrial			☐ Vacant (over 5%)	
Vacant/Other				

NEIGHBORHOOD ANALYSIS   G A F P

- Employment Stability
- Convenience to Employment
- Convenience to Shopping
- Convenience to Schools
- Adequacy of Public Transportation
- Recreation Facilities
- Adequacy of Utilities
- Property Compatibility
- Protection from Detrimental Cond.
- Police & Fire Protection
- General Appearance of Properties
- Appeal to Market

Note: FannieMae, Freddie Mac, HUD and VA do not consider race or the racial composition of the neighborhood to be reliable appraisal factors.
COMMENTS:

SITE

Dimensions	Topography
Site Area	Size
Zoning Classification Corner Lot Zoning Compliance	Shape
HIGHEST & BEST USE: Present Use Other Use	Drainage

UTILITIES	Public	Other	SITE IMPROVEMENTS	Type	Public	Private	
Electricity	☐		Street		☐	☐	View
Gas	☐		Curb/Gutter		☐	☐	Landscaping
Water	☐		Sidewalk		☐	☐	Driveway
Sanitary Sewer	☐		Street Lights		☐	☐	Easements
Storm Sewer	☐		Alley		☐	☐	Cable TV

FEMA Flood Hazard   Yes ____ No ____

COMMENTS (Adverse encroachments, slide areas, etc.):

IMPROVEMENTS

GENERAL DESCRIPTION	EXTERIOR DESCRIPTION	FOUNDATION	BASEMENT	INSULATION
Units	Foundation	Slab grade	Area Sq. Ft.	Roof ☐
Stories	Exterior Walls	Crawl Area	% Finished	Ceiling ☐
Type Structure	Roof Surface	Basement %	Ceiling	Walls ☐
Design Name	Gutters & Dwnspts.	Outside Entry	Walls	Floor ☐
Existing	Windows Type	Cement Floor	Floor	None ☐
Proposed	Storm Sash	Sump Pump	Comments:	Adequate ☐
Under Construction	Screens	Dampness		Energy Efficient Items:
Age (Yrs.)	Manufactured House	Settlement		
Effective Age (Yrs.)		Termite Damage		

ROOM LIST

ROOMS	Foyer	Living	Dining	Kitchen	Den	Family Rm.	Rec. Rm.	Bedroom	# Baths	Laundry	Other
Basement											
1 Level											
2 Level											

Finished area above grade contains*: # Rooms ____ ; # Bedroom(s) ____ ; # Bath(s) ____   Gross Living Area*: ____ Sq. Ft.

INTERIOR

SURFACES	Materials	HEATING	KITCHEN EQUIP.	ATTIC	
Floors		Type	Refrigerator ☐	None ☐	
Walls		Fuel	Range/Oven ☐	Stairs ☐	
Trim/Finish		Condition	Disposal ☐	Drop Stair ☐	
Bath Floor		Adequacy	Dishwasher ☐	Scuttle ☐	
Bath Wainscot		COOLING	Fan/Hood ☐	Floor ☐	
Doors		Central	Compactor ☐	Heated ☐	
		Other	Washer/Dryer ☐	Finish ☐	
		Condition	Microwave ☐		
		Adequacy	Intercom ☐		

IMPROVEMENT ANALYSIS   G A F P

- Quality of Construction
- Condition of Improvements
- Room Sizes/Layout
- Closets and Storage
- Energy Efficient
- Plumbing—Adequacy & Condition
- Electrical—Adequacy & Condition
- Kitchen Cabinets—Adequacy & Cond.
- Compatibility to Neighborhood
- Overall Livability
- Appeal & Marketability
- Remaining Economic Life (Yrs.)

AUTOS

CAR STORAGE:				House Entry ☐
	Garage ☐	Attached ☐	Adequate ☐	House Entry ☐
No. Cars	Carport ☐	Detached ☐	Inadequate ☐	Outside Entry ☐
Condition	None ☐	Built-in ☐	Electric Door ☐	Basement Entry ☐

Additional features:

COMMENTS

Depreciation comments (Physical, functional and external inadequacies, repairs needed, modernization, etc.):

Price/Value Considerations—Subject/Market area (Loan discounts, interest buydowns and concessions):

Freddie Mac Form 70 (UA-Alt.) 7/85   FannieMae Form Test (UA-Alt.) 7/85

**Figure 16.3
(continued)**

Valuation Section

Purpose of Appraisal is to estimate Market Value as defined in Certification & Statement of Limiting Conditions (Freddie Mac Form 439/FannieMae Form 1004B). If submitted for FannieMae, the appraiser must attach (1) sketch or map showing location of subject, street names, distance from nearest intersection, and any detrimental conditions and (2) exterior building sketch of improvements showing dimensions.

COST APPROACH

PHOTO ATTACHMENT

Measurements	No. Stories	Sq. Ft.
___ × ___	___ × ___ = ___
___ × ___	___ × ___ = ___
___ × ___	___ × ___ = ___
___ × ___	___ × ___ = ___
___ × ___	___ × ___ = ___
___ × ___	___ × ___ = ___

Total Gross Living Area (List in Sales Comparison Analysis below.) ___
Does property conform to applicable HUD/VA minimum property standards? ☐ Yes? ☐ No?
If No, explain: _____

BUILDING SKETCH

ESTIMATED REPRODUCTION COST—NEW—OF IMPROVEMENTS:

Dwelling ___ Sq. Ft. @ $ ___	= $ ___
___ Sq. Ft. @ $ ___	= ___
Extras ___	= ___
Special Energy Efficient Items ___	= ___
Porches, Patios, etc. ___	= ___
Garage/Car Port ___ Sq. Ft. @ $ ___	= ___
Site Improvements (driveway, landscaping, etc.) ___	= ___
Total Estimated Cost New ___	= $ ___

	Physical	Functional	External	
Less Depreciation $	$	$	= $ ___
Depreciated Value of Improvements			= $ ___
ESTIMATED LAND VALUE			= $ ___
(If leasehold, show only leasehold value.)			
INDICATED VALUE BY COST APPROACH			$ ___

Construction Warranty ☐ Yes ☐ No
Name of Warranty Program ___
Warranty Coverage Expires ___

The undersigned has recited three recent sales of properties most similar and proximate to subject and has considered these in the market analysis. The description includes a dollar adjustment, reflecting market reaction to those items of significant variation between the subject and comparable properties. If a significant item in the comparable property is superior to, or more favorable than, the subject property, a minus (−) adjustment is made, thus reducing the indicated value of subject; if a significant item in the comparable is inferior to, or less favorable than, the subject property, a plus (+) adjustment is made, thus increasing the indicated value of the subject.

SALES COMPARISON ANALYSIS

ITEM	Subject Property	COMPARABLE NO. 1		COMPARABLE NO. 2		COMPARABLE NO.3	
Address							
Proximity to Subj.							
Sales Price	$	$		$		$	
Price/Gross Liv. Area	$/☑	$/☑		$/☑		$/☑	
Data Source							
Date of Sale and Time Adjustment	DESCRIPTION	DESCRIPTION	+ (−)$ Adjustment	DESCRIPTION	+ (−)$ Adjustment	DESCRIPTION	+ (−)$ Adjustment
Location							
Site/View							
Design and Appeal							
Quality of Const.							
Age							
Condition							
Living Area Room Count and Total	Total / Bdrms / Baths	Total / Bdrms / Baths		Total / Bdrms / Baths		Total / Bdrms / Baths	
Gross Living Area	Sq. Ft.	Sq. Ft.		Sq. Ft.		Sq. Ft.	
Basement & Bsmt. Finished Rooms							
Functional Utility							
Air Conditioning							
Garage/Car Port							
Porches, Patio Pools, etc.							
Special Energy Efficient Items							
Other (e.g. fireplaces, kitchen equip., remodeling)							
Sales or Financing Concessions							
Net Adj. (total)		☐ + ☐ −	$	☐ + ☐ −	$	☐ + ☐ −	$
Indicated Value of Subject			$		$		$
Comments on Sales Comparison							

INDICATED VALUE BY SALES COMPARISON APPROACH ___ $ ___
INDICATED VALUE BY INCOME APPROACH (If applicable) Economic Market Rent $ ___ /Mo. × Gross Rent Multiplier ___ = $ ___
This appraisal is made ☐ "as is" ☐ subject to the repairs, alterations, or conditions listed below ☐ completion per plans and specifications.
Comments and Conditions of Appraisal: ___

RECONCILIATION

Final Reconciliation: ___

This appraisal is based upon the above requirements, the certification, contingent and limiting conditions, and Market Value definition that are stated in
☐ Freddie Mac Form 439 (Rev. 10/78)/FannieMae Form 1004B (Rev. 10/78) filed with client ___ 19 ___ ☐ attached.
I (WE) ESTIMATE THE MARKET VALUE, AS DEFINED, OF THE SUBJECT PROPERTY AS OF ___ 19 ___ to be $ ___

I (We) certify: that to the best of my (our) knowledge and belief the facts and data used herein are true and correct; that I (we) personally inspected the subject property, both inside and out, and have made an exterior inspection of all comparable sales cited in this report; and that I (we) have no undisclosed interest, present or prospective therein.

Appraiser(s) _____   Review Appraiser (If applicable) _____
☐ Did ☐ Did Not Physically Inspect Property

Freddie Mac Form 70 (UA-Alt.) 7/85   FannieMae Form Test (UA-Alt.) 7/85

The Profession of Appraising

While appraising has existed since the origin of the concept of property, the huge number of foreclosures during the depression of the 1930s resulted in the beginning of appraising as an organized profession. Courses have been established in universities and colleges, and books, journals, and other publications devoted to various aspects of appraising have come into existence. Appraising has now become the most specialized branch of real estate.

Professional designation of qualified appraisers is made not by any licensing agency but through membership in appraisal societies. Different designations require varying levels of education, specific courses in appraisal, examinations, demonstration appraisals, experience, and continuing education. The two largest societies are the American Institute of Real Estate Appraisers (associated with the National Association of REALTORS®) and the Society of Real Estate Appraisers. **AIREA** offers the designation RM (Residential Member) and MAI (Member, Appraisal Institute). The difficulty of the coveted and relatively rare MAI level is indicated by the fact that among other qualifications, the passing of 16 hours of examinations is required. **SRA** offers the designations SRA (Senior Residential Appraiser), SRPA (Senior Real Property Appraiser), and SREA (Senior Real Estate Analyst).

The National Association of Review Appraisers awards the CRA (Certified Review Appraiser); the National Association of Independent Fee Appraisers offers the designations FA (Member) and FAS (Senior Member). Some professional appraisers belong to more than one society. Those along the Niagara Frontier, for example, may join an international society.

Where expert testimony is provided for court proceedings or before a public body such as a zoning board, specific credentials (MAI, SRA, or the like) may be required.

Summary

To *appraise* real estate to *estimate its value.* Although there are many types of value, the most common objective of an appraisal is to estimate *market value*—the most probable sale price of a property.

While appraisals are concerned with values, prices, and costs, it is vital to understand the distinctions among the terms. *Value* is an estimate of future benefits, *cost* represents a measure of past expenditures, and *price* reflects the actual amount of money paid for a property.

Basic to appraising are certain underlying economic principles such as highest and best use, substitution, supply and demand, conformity, anticipation, increasing and diminishing returns, regression, plottage, contribution, competition, and change.

A professional appraiser analyzes a property through three approaches to value. In the *market comparison approach,* the value of the subject property is compared with the values of others like it that have sold recently. Because no two properties are exactly alike, adjustments must be made to account for any differences. With the *cost approach,* an appraiser calculates the cost of building a similar structure on a similar site. Then he or she subtracts depreciation (losses in value), which reflects the differences between new properties of this type and the present condition of the subject property. The *income approach* is an analysis based on the relationship between the rate of return that an investor requires and the net income that a property produces.

A special version of the income approach called the *gross rent multiplier* (GRM) is often used to estimate the value of single-family residential properties that are not usually rented but could be. The GRM is computed by dividing the sales price of a property by its gross monthly rent.

The application of the three approaches normally will result in three different estimates of value. In the process of *reconciliation* the validity and reliability of each approach are weighed objectively to arrive at the single best and most supportable conclusion of value.

Questions

1. Jim Jordan is a fully qualified appraiser. As such he:
   a. discovers value.
   b. insures value.
   c. estimates value.
   d. sets value.

2. In order to do his work, Jim is legally required:
   a. to have a real estate license.
   b. to have a separate appraiser's license.
   c. to register with the state attorney general.
   d. to do nothing specific.

3. The appraiser who works for a number of different clients is known as an:
   a. fee appraiser.
   b. free-lance appraiser.
   c. staff appraiser.
   d. in-house appraiser.

4. Value is the:
   a. relationship between desired object and potential buyer.
   b. power of a good to command other goods in exchange.
   c. present value of future benefits.
   d. All of the above

5. A house should bring $80,000 but is sold for $75,000 by a hard-pressed seller in a hurry, is then mortgaged for $60,000, and insured for $85,000. Its market value is:
   a. $60,000.
   b. $75,000.
   c. $80,000.
   d. $85,000.

6. An example of an arm's-length transaction is one between:
   a. father and daughter.
   b. employer and employee.
   c. broker and salesperson.
   d. two strangers.

7. The seller's concessionary financing is taken into account when a comparable is adjusted for:
   a. plottage.
   b. cash equivalent.
   c. obsolescence.
   d. regression.

8. Market value and cost are often equal when property:
   a. remains in the family a long time.
   b. was recently constructed.
   c. is sold in an arm's-length transaction.
   d. receives a weighted appraisal.

9. Highest and best use of real estate is defined as the use that produces the most:
   a. benefit to the community.
   b. conformity.
   c. progression.
   d. money.

10. "Why should I pay more when I can buy almost the same house new for less?" is an example of the principle of:
    a. substitution.
    b. conformity.
    c. anticipation.
    d. competition.

11. Houses are likely to reach their maximum value when:
    a. a wide range of price levels is represented.
    b. neighbors hold a mix of executive, blue-collar, and white-collar jobs.
    c. each house is unique.
    d. jobs, houses, and price levels are similar.

12. The principle of value that states that two adjacent parcels of land combined into one larger parcel may have a greater value than the two parcels valued separately is called:
    a. substitution.
    b. plottage.
    c. highest and best use.
    d. contribution.

13. You are appraising the house at 23 Oak. The recently sold one at 54 Oak is similar but has a fireplace. What use do you make of the value of the fireplace?
    a. Subtract it.
    b. Add it.
    c. Ignore it.
    d. Reconcile it.

14. The cost approach is most useful for:
    a. a library.
    b. insurance purposes.
    c. new construction.
    d. All of the above

15. From the reproduction or replacement cost of the building an appraiser deducts depreciation, which represents:
    a. the remaining useful economic life of the building.
    b. remodeling costs to increase rentals.
    c. loss of value due to any cause.
    d. costs to modernize the building.

16. The difference between reproduction cost and replacement cost involves:
    a. functional obsolescence.
    b. estimated land value.
    c. modern vs. obsolete methods and materials.
    d. effective gross income.

17. The appraised value of a residence with five bedrooms and one bathroom would probably be reduced because of:
    a. locational obsolescence.
    b. functional obsolescence.
    c. physical deterioration—curable.
    d. physical deterioration—incurable.

18. The term *locational obsolesence* refers to:
    a. poor landscaping.
    b. faulty floor plan.
    c. wear and tear.
    d. problems beyond the property line.

19. If a property's annual net income is $37,500 and it is valued at $300,000, what is its capitalization rate?
    a. 12.5 percent   c. 15 percent
    b. 10.5 percent   d. 18 percent

20. Certain data must be determined by an appraiser before value can be computed by the income approach. Which of the following is *not* required for this process?
    a. Annual net income
    b. Proper capitalization rate
    c. Accrued depreciation
    d. Annual gross income

21. Capitalization is the process by which the estimated future annual net income is used as the basis to:
    a. determine cost.
    b. estimate value.
    c. establish depreciation.
    d. determine potential tax value.

22. Which of the following factors would *not* be important in comparing properties under the market comparison approach to value?
    a. Difference in dates of sale
    b. Difference in real estate taxes
    c. Difference in appearance and condition
    d. Difference in original cost

23. *Reconciliation* refers to which of the following?
    a. Loss of value due to any cause
    b. Separating the value of the land from the total value of the property in order to compute depreciation
    c. Analyzing the results obtained by the three approaches to value to determine a final estimate of value
    d. The process by which an appraiser determines the highest and best use for a parcel of land

24. A fully qualified appraiser will probably hold a:
    a. certification.   c. designation.
    b. license.   d. degree.

25. Some of the country's foremost appraisers have earned the designation:
    a. MAI.   c. SRE.
    b. REA.   d. ARE.

17

Real Estate Investment

Key Terms

ACRS
Adjusted basis
Appreciation
Basis
Boot
Capital gain
Cash flow
Cost recovery
Debt service
Depreciation
Exchange
General partnership
Installment sale

Leverage
Limited partnership
Marginal tax rate
Pyramiding
Real estate investment syndicate
Real estate investment trust (REIT)
Recapture
Recovery class
Recovery period
Recovery property
Return
Tax shelter

Overview

The market for real estate investment is one of the most active in the country. Besides generating income and equity buildup, real estate investment can aid in sheltering an owner's income against increasing taxes and the effects of inflation and deflation. This chapter will present a basic introduction to real estate investment; major emphasis is placed on investment opportunities open to small or beginning investors as well as the various tax shelters available to all real estate investors. The examples and computations given in this chapter are symbolic and used for *illustrative purposes only*. Such examples are included in the discussion in order to explain a particular feature or concept of investment, *not to teach the reader how, when, or what amount of money to invest*.

Investing in Real Estate

Often, customers ask a real estate broker or salesperson to act as investment counselor; too often, the licensee is placed in that role by eager, inexperienced investors with high hopes for quick profits. While it may be the real estate licensee's responsibility to analyze and discuss with the potential investor his or her financial status, future goals, and investment motivations, the broker or salesperson always should *refer a potential real estate investor to a competent tax accountant or attorney* who can give expert advice regarding the investor's specific interest.

Real estate practitioners should possess an essential knowledge of real estate investment so they can counsel customers on a basic level. Any such discussion should begin with an examination of the traditional advantages and disadvantages of investing in real estate as opposed to other commodities.

Advantages of Real Estate Investment

Traditionally, real estate investments have shown a *high rate of return,* higher than the prevailing interest rate charged by mortgage lenders. This means that an investor can use borrowed money to finance a real estate purchase and feel relatively sure that the asset will yield more money than it costs to finance the purchase.

Real estate entrepreneurs enjoy many **tax shelters** that are unavailable to investors in other money making activities. These shelters may allow an investor to reduce or defer payment of large portions of his or her federal and state income taxes. The various tax advantages—capital gains, exchanges, depreciation, cost recovery, and installment sales—will be discussed later in this chapter.

Real estate values usually rise in keeping with the ever-increasing rate of inflation. This concept, known as *inflation hedge,* provides the real estate investor with relative assurance that as the purchasing power of the dollar decreases, the value of his or her assets will increase to offset the inflationary effects. Inflation will be discussed in detail later in this chapter.

A distinct advantage of real estate investment is that an investor can use borrowed money to finance his or her assets, which significantly increases the investor's buying power. This concept of *leverage* will be discussed later. In addition to the advantage of using borrowed money, the portion of an investor's mortgage payments applied to the principal represents *equity buildup* and increases the value of the investor's ownership interest in the asset with each remittance. Sometimes the investor can refinance the property, receiving a certain amount of cash, should the need arise.

Disadvantages of Real Estate Investment

Unlike stocks and bonds, *real estate is not highly liquid* over a short period of time. An investor usually cannot sell real estate quickly without taking some sort of loss. An investor in listed stocks need only call a stockbroker in order to liquidate a portion of his or her assets quickly when funds are needed. A real estate investor, on the other hand, lists property with a real estate broker and may have to sell the property below market value in order to facilitate a quick sale.

It is difficult to invest in real estate without some expert advice. Investment decisions must be made based on a careful study of all the facts in a given situation, reinforced by a broad and thorough knowledge of real estate and the manner in which it affects and is affected by the human element. As mentioned earlier, *all investors should seek legal and tax counsel before making any real estate investments.*

A certain amount of *physical and mental effort is required* to maintain a real estate investment. Rarely can a real estate investor sit idly by and watch money grow; management decisions must be made. For example, can the investor effectively manage the property personally or would it be preferable to hire a professional property manager? How much rent should be charged? How should repairs and tenant grievances be handled? "Sweat equity" (physical and mental energy) usually must be invested to make the asset potentially profitable.

Finally, and most important, *a high degree of risk* is often involved in real estate investment. There is always the possibility that an investor's property will decrease in value during the period it is held or that it will not generate an income sufficient to make it profitable.

The Investment

The most important form of real estate investment is *direct ownership*. Both individuals and corporations may own real estate directly and manage it for appreciation, cash flow (income), and tax shelter purposes. Property held for **appreciation** is expected to increase in value and show a profit when sold at some future date. Income property is just that—property held for current income and, it is hoped, a profit upon its sale.

Appreciation

Among the avenues of investment open to those interested in holding property primarily for appreciation are purchases of agricultural and undeveloped land.

Agricultural and undeveloped land. Quite often an investor speculates in purchases of either agricultural (farm) land or undeveloped (raw) land located in what he or she expects will be a major path of growth. This type of investment carries with it many inherent risks. The investor must consider such questions as: How fast will the area develop? Will it grow sufficiently for the investor to make a good profit? Will the expected growth even occur? More importantly, will the profits eventually realized from the property be great enough to offset the costs of holding the land?

Because land cannot technically wear out, the Internal Revenue Service does not allow the tax shelter of cost recovery (depreciation). Land cannot be considered a liquid investment because few people are willing to purchase raw or agricultural land on short notice.

For this type of investment, land value must appreciate at a rate great enough to compensate the owner for the cost of holding it. For example, if an investor purchases raw land for $2,000 per acre with annual real estate taxes of $80 per acre and miscellaneous expenses of approximately ten percent per year, the land must appreciate by an average of $280 per acre each year the investor holds the property—an appreciation rate of *14 percent per year*—just to break even (ten percent of $2,000 = $200 + $80 = $280 ÷ $2,000 = 14 percent). (This is a simplistic problem used for illustrative purposes only).

Lending institutions are traditionally reluctant to lend on land; seller financing is common.

Two main factors affect appreciation: inflation and intrinsic value.

Inflation. Historically, *inflation* has been the dominant factor in the growth of our economy. Inflation is defined as the *increase in the amount of money in circulation that results in a sharp decline in its value coupled with an equally sharp rise in wholesale and retail prices.* Inflation in real estate values, high during the 1970s, leveled off in the early '80s.

In general the Northeast has recovered well from a population drain in the late 1970s and has good economic prospects. If New York were a separate country, it would rank seventh on the list of leading nations in economic terms.

Intrinsic value. Known as *situs,* intrinsic value is the result of a person's individual choices and preferences for a given geographical area based on the features and amenities that the area has to offer. For example, property located in a well-kept suburb near a shopping center would have a greater intrinsic value to most people than similar property located near a sewage treatment plant. As a rule the greater the intrinsic value, the more money a property can command upon its sale. Most land speculation is based on this principle of present versus future intrinsic value. What was farmland a few years ago very well could be a booming community today. The wise investor knows how to identify, buy, and sell such speculative properties.

Income Property

Generally, a wise initial investment is the purchase of rental income property.

Cash flow. The object of an investor's directing funds into income property is to generate spendable income, usually called cash flow. The **cash flow** is the total amount of money remaining after all expenditures have been paid, including taxes, operating costs, and mortgage payments (known as **debt service**). The cash flow produced by any given parcel of real estate is determined by at least three factors: amount of rent received, operating expenses, and method of debt repayment.

The amount of *rent* (income) that a property may command depends on a number of factors including location, physical appearance, and amenities. If the cash flow from rents is not enough to cover all expenses, a *negative cash flow* will result.

To keep cash flow high an investor must *keep operating expenses low*. Such expenses include general maintenance of the building, repairs, utilities, taxes, and tenant services (switchboard facilities, security systems, and so forth). Like inadequate rental income, poor or overly expensive management can result in negative cash flow.

Cash flow management. Cash flow may be managed either as a means of enhancing the attractiveness of a particular investment in order to command a higher selling price or as a means of producing higher or lower income levels in order to take advantage of high- and low-income years for tax purposes. Cash flow may be controlled through the use of various management techniques such as obtaining high temporary rents through short-term leases or postponing minor repairs to generate a higher cash flow for any given period of time.

Return is the sum of appreciation and amortization, plus or minus cash flow and tax benefits.

Investment opportunities. Traditional income property investments include apartment buildings, hotels, motels, small commercial properties, shopping centers, office buildings, and industrial properties. Investors in recent years have found single-family dwellings and condominium units favorable sources of income in certain situations.

Leverage

Real estate is expensive—even the most rundown property can cost tens of thousands of dollars. Regardless of cost, however, people with modest incomes are able to invest in real estate by using leverage. **Leverage** is the use of *borrowed money to finance the bulk of an investment.* As a rule an investor can receive a maximum return from his or her initial investment (the down payment) by:

1. Making a small down payment.
2. Paying low interest rates.
3. Spreading mortgage payments over as long a period as possible.

For example, assume an investor purchases a property with a selling price of $200,000 for $20,000 down and a long-term mortgage at 12 percent interest with no prepayment penalty. One year later the investor is able to sell the property for $240,000. Disregarding ownership expenses, the return based on the purchase price (if the investor had paid cash) is 20 percent. *But by using leverage,* the investor actually received a *92 percent* return on the initial $20,000 investment (before depreciation and income tax). The computations for this example are as follows:

Gross profit:
$ 240,000 selling price
 −200,000 purchase price
$ 40,000 gross profit

Less mortgage interest:
$200,000 purchase price
 −20,000 down payment
$180,000 mortgage

$180,000 mortgage
×   .12 interest
$ 21,600 mortgage interest (first and only year)

Return on investment:
$ 40,000 gross profit
 −21,600 mortgage interest
$ 18,400 net profit

$$\frac{.92}{\$20,000)\$18,400.00} = \textit{92 percent return on investment}$$
down payment   net profit

Risks are generally proportionate to leverage. A high degree of leverage gives the lending institution the highest degree of risk; low leverage results in a lower risk.

Equity. In the example using leverage, all computations were based on interest payments rather than full mortgage loan installments. This is because the equity buildup in the property is like money in the bank to the real estate investor. Equity buildup is that portion of the payment directed toward the principal rather than the interest, *plus* any gain in property value due to appreciation. Although this accumulated equity is not as liquid as money in the bank, it may be sold, exchanged, or even refinanced as leverage for other investments. This equity is not physically available to the investor until the property is sold; if the property decreases in value, it may never be realized. In addition, that portion of the buildup that is due to appreciation may be subject to capital gains taxes.

Pyramiding through refinancing. By holding and refinancing using equity and appreciation buildup, rather than selling or exchanging already-owned properties, an investor can increase his or her holdings substantially without investing any additional capital. This practice is known as **pyramiding.** By reinvesting and doubling holdings every few years, it is conceivable that an investor who started out with a small initial cash down payment could own (heavily mortgaged) properties worth approximately $1 million in a relatively short time. At the end of this period the income derived from such assets could conceivably pay off the various mortgage debts and show a handsome profit. On the other hand heavily mortgaged properties render the investor vulnerable if real estate values or rentals fall or if the local vacancy level increases.

In 1985 FNMA severely limited investors' opportunities to refinance by refusing to buy refinance mortgages placed by investors who owned more than five living units.

Tax Benefits

One of the main reasons real estate investments are so popular—and profitable—is that federal law allows investors to shelter certain portions of their incomes from taxation. Four of the more common methods of sheltering real estate profits are capital gains, exchanges, depreciation or accelerated cost recovery, and installment sales.

The discussions and examples used in this section are designed to introduce the reader to general tax concepts—a tax attorney or CPA should be consulted for further details on specific regulations. Internal Revenue Service regulations are subject to frequent change.

Any computation of projected tax savings must take into account the investor's **marginal tax rate,** that rate (state and federal combined) at which the top dollar of income is taxed.

Capital Gains

Income earned from the sale of assets (such as real estate) that are held for a specific period of time—currently more than six months—is called a *long-term capital gain* and is subject to less tax than is ordinary income. Investors may exclude *60 percent* of their long-term capital gains from their income, meaning that *only 40 percent of a capital gain is taxed as income.*

Capital gain on real estate is determined by two factors, the adjusted basis and the net selling price. **Basis** usually refers to the initial cost an investor pays for a parcel of real estate. Generally, the **adjusted basis** represents the basis plus the cost of any physical improvements to the property minus depreciation. The gain is the *difference between the adjusted basis and the net selling price.* (A property's net selling price is the sale price less the broker's commission and other selling costs.)

For example, assume an investor purchased a one-family dwelling for rental purposes ten years ago for $45,000. The value of the land was set at $10,000; the value of the improvements totaled $35,000. The investor is now selling the home for $100,000; of this sum, $20,000 represents the new value of the land. Shortly before selling the property, the investor made $3,000 worth of capital improvements to the structure. Depreciation has been taken on a straight-line 35-year basis. (Depreciation, now called "'cost recovery,'' will be discussed later in this section.) The investor paid the selling broker a seven percent commission and also paid $600 in closing costs. So the investor's capital gain would be computed as follows:

Selling price:		$ 100,000
Less:		
7% commission	$7,000	
closing costs	+ 600	
	$7,600	− 7,600
Net sales price:		$ 92,400
Less value of land:		− 20,000
		$72,400
Basis:		
building	$ 35,000	
improvements	+ 3,000	
	$ 38,000	
Less depreciation:		
($35,000 ÷ 35 years =		
$1,000; $1,000 × 10		
years' ownership)	−10,000	
Adjusted basis:	$ 28,000	−28,000
Capital gain on improvements:		$ 44,400
Plus capital gain on land:		
value at sale	$ 20,000	
less original value	−10,000	
	$ 10,000	+ 10,000
Total capital gain:		$ 54,400
		× .40
Capital gain taxable as income:		$ 21,760

Exchanges

By **exchanging** one property for another, a real estate investor can further reduce, defer, or even eliminate capital gains tax. Tax laws generally provide that an investor's capital gains are not taxed when he or she exchanges income-producing properties of like kind. Note, however, that *the tax is deferred, not eliminated.* If the investor ever sells the property, he or she will be required to pay tax on the total capital gain. Investors can keep exchanging upward in value, adding to their assets as long as they live without ever personally having to pay any capital gains tax.

To qualify as a tax-deferred exchange, the properties involved must be of *like kind*—for example, real estate for real estate. Any additional capital or personal property included with the transaction to even out the exchange is considered **boot,** and the party receiving it is taxed at the time of the exchange. The value of the boot is added to the basis of the property with which it is given.

For example, investor Smith owns an apartment building with a market value of $200,000 and an adjusted basis of $90,000. He wants to exchange it for a different apartment building owned by Jones that has a market value of $250,000 and an adjusted basis of $150,000. For Jones's building, investor Smith exchanges his building plus a cash boot of $50,000. After the exchange, investor Smith's new basis in his new building is $140,000 (the $90,000 basis of the building he exchanged plus the $50,000 cash boot he paid).

Investor Jones, on the other hand, exchanged a building worth $250,000 with an adjusted basis of $150,000 for a building worth only $200,000 plus $50,000 cash. She must pay capital gains tax on the $50,000 boot but her basis in the new building remains the same as for the building she exchanged—$150,000. If investor Jones had received all cash for her first building, her capital gains tax liability would increase to $100,000 ($250,000 minus the $150,000 basis).

Similar deferred tax benefits for homeowners are discussed in Chapter 9.

Cost Recovery (Depreciation)

Cost recovery, formerly known as **depreciation,** is an accounting concept that allows an investor to recover in tax deductions the basis of an asset over the period of its useful life. Cost recovery is an accounting concept and may have little relationship to the actual physical deterioration of the real estate. In fact *when the cost recovery deductions exceed the amount of other income received from a property, an investor may offset the loss against other sources of income.* Cost recovery deductions may be taken only on improvements to land or personal property and only if they are used in a trade or business or for the production of income. *Land cannot be depreciated*—technically it never wears out or becomes obsolete. An individual cannot claim a cost recovery deduction on his or her own personal residence.

Normally in the initial years of real estate investment the taxable loss exceeds cash outlays. This happens because the recovery deductions exceed the principal payments. It is thus possible for an investor to have a positive cash flow from an investment and still report a loss on his or her tax return. The loss is sometimes referred to as a **tax shelter.** (Too many tax preference items, of which cost recovery is one, may, however, subject the taxpayer to an alternative minimum tax.)

Recovery deductions are calculated on the basis of four factors: (1) the recoverable basis of the property (the value of the improvements to the land), (2) the recovery class of the property, and (3) the method of recovery and recovery period used.

Basis. The value of the improvements represents a property's basis only—it is not the total value of the real estate. Real estate tax statements usually separate land from improvements for tax purposes; this is helpful to an investor in determining the basis for calculating recovery deductions.

Recovery class. The Economic Recovery Tax Act of 1981 (ERTA) established two **recovery classes** for real estate investment property as follows:

1. **Five-year property** includes all items of personal property (as defined by the tax law) involved in a real estate investment, such as carpeting, appliances, and drapes.
2. **Real estate,** originally 15-year property, includes all depreciable real property except low-income housing (which may be recovered at a faster rate).

For property acquired after March 15, 1984 the recovery period was changed to 18 years. After May 8, 1985, the period became *19 years.*

Recovery period. For both recovery classes there are several possible recovery periods that an investor may elect to use. Five-year property may be recovered over 5, 12, or 25 years.

Recovery method. Five-year property placed in service before 1985 may be recovered over a five-year period according to the yearly percentages illustrated in Table 17.1.

Table 17.1
Five-Year Property Recovery

Year of Ownership	1	2	3	4	5
Recovery Percentage	15	22	21	21	21

Recapture. The main disadvantage in using an accelerated cost recovery method (**ACRS**) is that while an investor can take greater tax reductions, he or she cannot take full advantage of capital gains tax benefits. When an investor sells residential property that was depreciated using an accelerated recovery method, that portion of the gain in excess of what would have been earned using straight-line recovery will be taxed as ordinary income rather than as capital gains. This is called **recapture.** (If commercial property is recovered using an accelerated method, *all* such gain is treated as ordinary income.)

Installment Sales

An investor may defer federal income tax on a capital gain provided he or she does not receive all cash for the asset at the time of sale but instead receives payments in two or more periods. This transaction is an **installment sale.** As the name implies, the seller receives payment in installments and pays income tax each year based only on the amount received during the year. (This can be accomplished by selling through a land contract, purchase-money mortgage, or similar instrument.) Besides avoiding tax payments on money not yet collected, the installment method often saves an investor money by spreading out the gain over a number of years. The gain may be subject to a lower tax rate than if it were received in one lump sum. Depreciation, however, must be recaptured in the year of sale.

Real Estate Investment Syndicates

A **real estate investment syndicate** is a typical form of joint venture in which a group of people pool their resources to own and/or develop a particular piece of property. In this manner, people with only modest capital can invest in large-scale, high-profit operations such as high-rise apartment buildings and shopping centers. A certain amount of profit is realized from rents collected on the investment but the main return usually comes when the syndicate decides to sell the property after sufficient appreciation.

A syndicate investor enjoys the same federal and state income-tax advantages as a direct-ownership real estate investor because no matter how small his or her interest in the syndicate properties, the investor owns a certain percentage of a particular parcel of real estate. As a real estate owner, the syndicate investor is as much entitled to preferred tax treatment as is a sole owner in a similar property. However, syndicate interests may be more difficult to sell on the open market than real estate. In addition, approval by the syndicate's management may be required before an investor can sell his or her interest in the project. Some partnership agreements may even require that such interest be sold only to another member of the syndicate.

Syndicate participation can take many different legal forms, from tenancy in common and joint tenancy to various kinds of partnerships, corporations, and trusts. Private syndication, which generally involves a small group of closely associated and/or widely experienced investors, is distinguished from public syndication, which generally involves a much larger group of investors who may or may not be knowledgeable about real estate as an investment. The distinction between the two, however, is based on the nature of the arrangement between syndicator and investors, not on the type of syndicate. For this reason any pooling of individuals' funds raises questions of definition and registration of securities under state security laws, commonly referred to as *blue-sky laws*.

State security laws include provisions to control and regulate the offering and sale of securities. This is to protect members of the public who are not sophisticated investors but may be solicited to participate. Real estate securities must be registered with state officials and/or with the federal Securities and Exchange Commission when they meet the defined conditions of a public offering. The number of prospects solicited, the total number of investors or participants, the financial background and sophistication of the investors, and the value or price per unit of investment are pertinent facts.

Salespeople of real estate securities are required to obtain special licenses and registration.

Forms of Syndicates   Real estate investment syndicates are usually organized as either general or limited partnerships.

A **general partnership** is organized so that *all members of the group share equally in the managerial decisions, profits, and losses involved with the investment*. A certain member (or members) of the syndicate is designated to act as trustee for the group and holds title to the property and maintains it in the syndicate's name.

Under a **limited partnership** agreement, *one party* (or parties), usually a property developer or real estate broker, *organizes, operates, and is responsible for the entire syndicate*. This person is called the *general partner*. The other members of the partnership are merely investors; they have no voice in the organization and direction of the operation. These *passive investors are called limited partners*. The limited partners share in the profits and compensate the general partner for his or her efforts out of such profits. Unlike a general partnership, in which each member is responsible for the total losses (if any) of the syndicate, the limited partners stand to lose only as much as they invest—nothing more. The general partner(s) is totally responsible for any excess losses incurred by the investment. Limited partnerships are generally considered *investment securities* and as such are heavily regulated at the federal (Securities and Exchange Commission) and state levels.

Real Estate Trusts

By directing their funds into a real estate trust, real estate investors can take advantage of the same tax benefits as mutual fund investors. A real estate trust does not have to pay corporate income tax as long as 90 percent of its income is distributed to its shareholders. There are three types of real estate trusts: real estate investment trusts (REITs), real estate mortgage trusts (REMTs), and combination trusts.

Real estate investment trusts. Much like mutual fund operations, **real estate investment trusts** pool an assortment of large-scale income properties and sell shares to investors. This is in contrast to a real estate syndicate, through which several investors pool their funds in order to purchase *one* particular property. A REIT also differs from a syndicate in that the trust realizes its main profits through the *income* derived from the various properties it owns rather than from the sale of those properties. In order to form an REIT, a group of 100 or more members must hold shares in the trust.

Real estate mortgage trusts. REMTs operate similarly to REITs, except that the mortgage trusts buy and sell real estate mortgages (usually short-term, junior instruments) rather than real property. An REMT's major sources of income are mortgage interest and origination fees, as well as profits earned from buying and selling mortgages.

Combination trusts. Combination trusts invest shareholders' funds toward both real estate and mortgage loans. It is predicted that these types of trusts will best be able to withstand economic slumps because they can balance their investments and liabilities more efficiently than the other types of trusts.

An REIT offers a liquid way to invest in a traditionally illiquid asset. One-third of real estate trusts are traded on the New York and American stock exchanges. In 1985 $11 billion was invested in real estate securities (REITs and public limited partnerships). Table 17.2 tracks the growth of such investment, measured by filings with the National Association of Securities Dealers.

Summary

Real estate investments traditionally command a *high rate of return* while at the same time allowing an investor to take advantage of many *tax shelters* unavailable to other types of investors. In addition real estate is an effective *inflation hedge*, and an investor can make use of other people's money to make investments through *leverage*. On the other hand real estate is *not a highly liquid investment* and often carries with it a *high degree of risk*. Invest in real estate without *expert advice* and a certain amount of *mental and physical effort* is required to establish and maintain the investment.

Investment property held for *appreciation* purposes is generally expected to increase in value to a point where its selling price is enough to cover holding costs and show a profit as well. The two main factors affecting appreciation are *inflation* and the property's present and future *intrinsic value*. Real estate held for *income* purposes is expected to generate a steady flow of income, called *cash flow*, and to show a profit upon its sale.

Table 17.2
NASD Real Estate
Program Filings

Year	Real Estate Partnerships		REITs		Total Real Estate		Total Real Estate % Change	Total Real Estate Partnership % Change
	$ in thousands	Number	$ in thousands	Number	$ in thousands	Number		
1970	$ 256,485	54	$ N/A	N/A	$ 256,485	54	—%	—%
1971	523,534	139	2,540,359	71	3,063,893	210	N/A	104.1
1972	787,735	207	1,417,808	62	2,205,543	269	(28.0)	50.5
1973	849,436	172	1,320,458	51	2,169,894	223	(1.6)	7.8
1974	521,458	94	122,984	13	644,442	107	(70.3)	(36.8)
1975	341,425	76	138,911	10	480,336	86	(25.5)	(34.5)
1976	272,706	44	118,134	8	390,840	52	(18.6)	(20.1)
1977	292,973	47	81,247	9	374,220	58	(4.3)	(7.4)
1978	782,671	70	226,806	10	1,009,477	80	169.8	167.1
1979	910,176	74	246,248	18	1,156,424	92	14.6	16.3
1980	1,988,299	131	141,926	10	2,130,255	141	84.2	118.5
1981	3,587,570	159	348,442	9	3,936,012	168	84.8	80.4
1982	4,644,674	203	402,121	12	5,046,795	215	28.2	29.5
1983	7,116,198	222	925,886	12	8,042,098	234	59.4	53.2
1984	10,230,786	247	1,763,198	18	11,993,984	265	49.1	43.8
1983 3rd Q	2,404,100	57	288,975	5	2,693,075	62	—	—
1984 3rd Q	2,714,764	58	159,075	4	2,873,839	62	6.7	12.9
1985 3rd Q	3,306,404	70	1,656,073	14	4,962,477	84	72.7	21.8

SOURCES: Stephen Roulac & Company, National Association of Securities Dealers (NASD).

In order for an investor to take advantage of maximum *leverage* in financing an investment, he or she should attempt to make a small down payment, pay low interest rates, and spread mortgage payments over as long a period as possible. By holding and refinancing properties, known as *pyramiding,* an investor can substantially increase his or her holdings without investing additional capital.

An investor can take advantage of special *capital gains* tax rates, based on 40 percent of the total gain of a real estate sale, by holding investment property for longer than six months.

By *exchanging* one property for another with an equal or greater selling value an investor can *defer* paying tax on the gain realized until a sale is made. A total tax deferment is possible only if the investor receives no cash or other incentive to even out the exchange. Such cash or property is called *boot* and is taxed at the normal capital gains tax rate.

Cost recovery, or *depreciation,* is a statutory concept that allows an investor to recover in tax deductions the basis of an asset over a period of years. Only improvements to land may depreciate, not the land itself.

An investor may defer federal income taxes on gain realized from the sale of an investment property through an *installment sale.* In this situation the investor pays income tax only on the portion of the total gain he or she receives in any year.

Individuals may also invest in real estate through an *investment syndicate.* These include *general and limited partnerships, real estate investment trusts* (REITs), *real estate mortgage trusts* (REMTs), and *combination trusts.*

Questions

1. Among the advantages of real estate investment is:
   a. illiquidity.
   b. need for expert advice.
   c. hedge against inflation.
   d. degree of risk.

2. Among the disadvantages of real estate investment is:
   a. tax shelter.
   b. need for physical and mental effort.
   c. tax shelter.
   d. equity buildup.

3. Vacant land can be a good investment because:
   a. it must appreciate enough to cover expenses.
   b. it can have intrinsic value.
   c. bank financing is easily arranged.
   d. it may not be depreciated.

4. The increase of money in circulation coupled with a sharp rise in prices, resulting in an equally sharp decline in the value of money, is called:
   a. appreciation.   c. negative cash flow.
   b. inflation.   d. recapture.

5. A small multifamily property generates $50,000 in rental income with expenses of $45,000 annually, including $35,000 in debt service. The property appreciates about $25,000 a year. The owner realizes another $5,000 through income tax savings. On this property, the cash flow is:
   a. $5,000.   c. $25,000.
   b. $15,000.   d. $35,000.

6. In the example above, the owner's return is:
   a. $5,000.   c. $25,000.
   b. $15,000.   d. $35,000.

7. Leverage involves the extensive use of:
   a. cost recovery.
   b. borrowed money.
   c. government subsidies.
   d. alternative taxes.

8. A property's equity represents its current value less which of the following?
   a. Depreciation
   b. Mortgage indebtedness
   c. Physical improvements
   d. Selling costs and depreciation

9. An investor's marginal tax rate is the:
   a. total tax bill divided by net taxable income.
   b. extra tax if he has too many tax shelters.
   c. top applicable income tax bracket.
   d. percentage taxable on an installment sale.

10. The primary source of tax shelter in real estate investments comes from the accounting concept known as:
    a. recapture.
    b. boot.
    c. cost recovery.
    d. net operating income.

11. For tax purposes the initial cost of an investment property plus the cost of any subsequent improvements to the property, less depreciation, represents the investment's:
    a. adjusted basis.
    b. capital gains.
    c. basis.
    d. salvage value.

12. The money left in an investor's pocket after expenses, including debt service, have been paid is known as:
    a. net operating income.
    b. gross income.
    c. cash flow.
    d. internal rate of return.

13. The investor who secures what the IRS regards as excessive tax shelter may be subject to:
    a. recovery.
    b. recapture.
    c. alternative minimum tax.
    d. pyramiding.

14. Julia Kinder is exchanging her apartment building for an apartment building of greater market value and must include a $10,000 boot to even out the exchange. Which of the following may she use as a boot?
    a. $10,000 cash
    b. Common stock with a current market value of $10,000
    c. A parcel of raw land with a current market value of $10,000
    d. Any of the above if acceptable to the exchangers

15. In the question above:
    a. Julia will owe income tax on $10,000.
    b. each will owe tax on $10,000.
    c. the other investor will owe tax on $10,000.
    d. no one owes any tax at this time.

16. An investment syndicate in which all members share equally in the managerial decisions, profits, and losses involved in the venture would be an example of which of the following?
    a. Real estate investment trust
    b. Limited partnership
    c. Real estate mortgage trust
    d. General partnership

17. Shareholders in a real estate trust generally:
    a. receive most of the trust's income each year.
    b. take an active part in management.
    c. find it difficult to sell their shares.
    d. realize their main profit through sales of property.

18. In an installment sale, taxable gain is received and must be reported as income by the seller:
    a. in the year the sale is initiated.
    b. in the year the final installment payment is made.
    c. in each year that installment payments are received.
    d. at any one time during the period installment payments are received.

19. Cost recovery allows the investor to charge as an expense on each year's tax return part of the:
    a. purchase price.
    b. down payment.
    c. mortgage indebtedness.
    d. equity.

20. A separate license and/or registration is required for the sale of:
    a. all investment property.
    b. real estate securities.
    c. installment property.
    d. boots.

18

Subdivision and Development

Overview

As our country's population grows and shifts to new locations, the demand for housing grows and shifts. To meet this demand, subdividers and property developers convert raw land, or property that is no longer serving its highest and best use, into subdivisions for residential and other uses. These subdividers and developers, working with local officials, are largely responsible for the orderly growth of such communities. This chapter will deal with the process of developing and subdividing property and also will discuss some of the legal aspects of selling subdivided land.

Developing and Subdividing Land

Subdividing and developing land for community use are important activities that can assist the orderly growth of cities and towns. Poorly designed and located subdivisions may result in developments that are detrimental to the growth of a town or community. "Wildcat" subdividing and development practices were common during the 1920s and early 1930s. In those years, city, town, village, and county officials were not knowledgeable about good city planning methods. This resulted in the approval of scattered subdivisions without proper safeguards for water, septic fields, sewage disposal, and other health and safety factors. Today's subdividers with the help of real estate specialists are applying the economic rules of land value by determining the highest and best use of acreage before the land is actually subdivided.

Subdividers and Developers

Land in large tracts must receive special attention before it can be converted into sites for homes, stores, or other uses. As our cities and towns grow, additional land will be required for their expansion. In order for such new areas to develop soundly, the services of competent subdividers and land developers working closely with city planners are required. A **subdivider** is someone who buys undeveloped acreage, divides it into smaller, usable lots, and sells the lots to potential users. A land **developer,** on the other hand, builds homes or other buildings on the lots and sells them. A developer may use his or her own sales organization or may act through local real estate brokerage firms. City planners, working with land developers, plan whole communities that are later incorporated into cities, towns, or villages.

Regulation of Land Development

As discussed in Chapter 6, *no uniform city planning and land development legislation affects the entire country.* Laws governing subdividing and land planning are controlled by the state and local governmental bodies. New York State sets standards for villages, cities, and towns. Local governments may adopt more restrictive policies.

Land Planning

Although the recording of a plat of subdivision of land prior to public sale for residential or commercial use is usually required, land planning precedes the actual subdividing process. The land development plan must comply with the overall local plan if a *master land plan* has been adopted by the county, city, village, or town. In complying with this local plan the developer must take into consideration the zoning laws and land-use restrictions that have been adopted for health and safety purposes. Basic city plan and zoning requirements are not inflexible, but long, expensive, and frequently complicated hearings are usually required before alterations can be authorized.

As discussed in Chapter 6, most villages, cities, and other areas that are incorporated under state laws have **planning boards** or *planning commissioners.* Such boards or commissions may have only an advisory status to the councilmen or board members of the community. In other instances the commission can have authority to approve or disapprove plans. Communities establish strict criteria before approving new subdivisions. The following are frequently included: (1) *dedication* of land for streets, schools, parks; (2) assurance by *bonding* that sewer and street costs will be paid; and (3) *compliance with zoning ordinances* governing use and lot size along with fire and safety ordinances.

Because of the fear that they may pollute streams, rivers, lakes, and underground water sources, septic systems are no longer authorized in some areas and an approved sewage-disposal arrangement must be included in a land development plan. Local authorities usually require land planners to submit information on how they intend to satisfy sewage-disposal and water-supply requirements. A planner also may have to submit some sort of environmental impact statement.

Subdividing

The process of **subdivision** involves three distinct stages of development: (1) the initial planning stage, (2) the final planning stage, and (3) the disposition, or start-up.

During the *initial planning stage* the subdivider seeks out raw land in a suitable area that he or she can profitably subdivide. After the land is located the property is analyzed for its highest and best use, and preliminary subdivision plans are drawn up accordingly. As previously discussed, close contact is initiated between the subdivider and local planning and zoning officials: If the project requires zoning variances, negotiations begin along these lines. The subdivider also locates financial backers and initiates marketing strategies at this point in the process.

The *final planning stage* is a follow-up of the initial stage—final plans are prepared, approval is sought from local officials, permanent financing is obtained, the land is purchased, final budgets are prepared, and marketing programs are designed.

The *disposition, or start-up,* carries the subdividing process to a conclusion. Subdivision plans are recorded with local officials, and streets, sewers, and utilities are installed. Buildings, open parks, and recreational areas are constructed and landscaped if they are part of the subdivision plan. Marketing programs are then initiated and title to the individual parcels of subdivided land is transferred as the lots are sold.

Subdivision Plans

In plotting out a subdivision according to local planning and zoning controls, a subdivider determines the size as well as the location of the individual lots. The size of the lots, front footage, depth, and square footage are generally regulated by local ordinances. Frequently ordinances regulate both the minimum and the maximum size of a lot.

The land itself must be studied, usually in cooperation with a surveyor, so that the subdivision can be laid out with consideration of natural drainage and land contours. A site planner and an engineer are also employed.

In laying out a subdivision a subdivider should provide for *utility easements* as well as easements for water and sewer mains. Usually the water and sewer mains will be laid in the street with connecting junction boxes available for each building site. When the city, town, or village installs the water or sewer mains connecting a new building with the junction box in the street, a tie-in or connection fee is frequently charged to help the authority defray the cost of such installation.

Most subdivisions are laid out by use of *lots and blocks*. An area of land is designated as a block, and the area making up this block is divided into lots. Both lots and blocks are numbered consecutively. If a developer does not intend to subdivide an entire tract of land at one time, however, some variation from consecutive numbering may be granted.

Although subdividers customarily designate areas reserved for schools, parks, and future church sites, this practice can have some drawbacks. After a subdivision has been recorded, the purchasers of the lots have a vested interest in those areas reserved for schools, parks, and churches. If in the future any such purpose is not appropriate, it will become difficult for the developer to abandon the original plan and use that property for residential purposes. To get around this situation, many developers designate such areas as *out-lot A, out-lot B,* and so forth. This designation does not vest any rights in these out-lots in the purchasers of the homesites. Then, for example, if one of these areas is to be used for church purposes, it can be so conveyed and so used. If on the other hand the out-lot is not to be used for such a purpose, it can be resubdivided into residential properties without the burden of securing the consent of the lot owners in the area.

Plat of subdivision. The subdivider's completed **plat of subdivision,** a map of the development indicating the location and boundaries of individual properties, must contain all necessary approvals of public officials and must be recorded in the county where the land is located.

After the plat has been filed for record, all areas that have been set aside for street purposes are considered to be **dedicated.** This means that the land shown as streets now belongs to the city or town. If this is not the subdivider's intention, the plat should specify that the streets are private.

Filing the map protects the developer in the event the local government should declare a **moratorium,** a halt to further development in the area.

Because the plat will be the basis for future conveyances, the subdivided land should be carefully measured with all lot sizes and streets noted by the surveyor and accurately entered on the document. Survey monuments should be established, and measurements should be made from these monuments, with the location of all lots carefully marked.

Covenants and restrictions. Deed restrictions, discussed in Chapters 3 and 6, are originated and recorded by the subdivider as a means of *controlling and maintaining the desirable quality and character of the subdivision.* The subdivider should provide for some form of restrictions. If the subdivision plan is to be submitted for FHA approval, such restrictive covenants must comply with FHA standards. These restrictions can be included in the subdivision plat or they may be set forth in a separate recorded instrument, commonly referred to as a *declaration of restrictions.*

Subdividers place restrictions upon the use of all lots in a subdivision as a general plan for the benefit of all lot owners. Such restrictions give each lot owner the right to apply to the court for an *injunction* to prevent violation of the recorded restrictions by a neighboring lot owner.

FHA standards. FHA minimum standards have been established for subdivisions in residential areas that are to be submitted for approval for FHA loan insurance. Primary minimum standards established by the FHA are the following:

1. Streets must comply with approved widths and must be paved.
2. The area must be free from hazards such as airplane landing fields, heavy through traffic, and excessive noise or air pollution.
3. Each lot must have access to all utilities.
4. Provisions for shopping, schools, churches, recreation, and transportation must be available.
5. Lots must comply with minimum, and in some cases maximum, size requirements.
6. Plans for construction must meet local standards.
7. Uniform building setbacks and lot lines are usually required.
8. Minimum landscaping is usually required.

Personnel are available in each FHA regional office to meet with subdividers, developers, and builders to assist them in meeting the minimum FHA standards.

Development costs. The costs of developing land are not understood by most homeowners. The subdivider, developer, and builder frequently invest many hundreds of thousands of dollars (and in larger developments, several million dollars) before the subdivision is even announced to the public.

The difference between the raw land cost, usually on a per acre basis, and the asking price per front foot of subdivided lot surprises the average homeowner. An analysis of these development costs will substantiate the sales price for a typical building lot of four to six times the cost of the raw land, if the development is a financial success. These costs, of course, vary from area to area and according to the nature of the development itself.

In most areas an acre of land (43,560 square feet) will yield between two and three subdivided lots, assuming that each lot does not contain more than 10,000 square feet. (A lot 100 × 100 feet would contain 10,000 square feet.) The apparent shrinkage is due to roads, streets, parkways, and public sidewalks.

In the subdivision of a typical parcel of raw land, a lot's sales price will reflect such expenses as cost of land; installation of sewers, water mains, storm drains, landscaping, and street lights; earthworks (mass dirt removal, site grading, and similar operations); paving; engineering and surveying fees; brokers' commissions; inspections; bonding costs; filing and legal fees; sales costs; and overhead. In certain areas a subdivider also may be required to give financial assistance to school districts, park districts, and the like, either in the form of donated school or park sites or in the form of a fixed subsidy per subdivision lot. Should such further costs be incurred they must, of course, be added proportionately to the sales price of each building site.

Subdivision Density   Zoning ordinances often include covenants that control mimimum lot sizes and population density for subdivisions and land developments. For example, a typical zoning restriction may set the minimum lot area on which a subdivider can build a single-family housing unit at 15,000 square feet. This means that the subdivider will be able to build approximately 2½ houses per acre. However, many zoning authorities now establish special density zoning standards for certain subdivisions. **Density zoning** ordinances restrict the *average maximum number of houses per acre* that may be built within a particular subdivision. For example, in the previous explanation a 15,000-square-foot-lot minimum meant that the developer could build only 2.5 houses per acre. On the other hand if the area is density zoned at an average maximum of 2.5 houses per acre, the developer is free to achieve an open, clustered effect. Regardless of lot size or the number of clustered units, the subdivider will be consistent with the ordinance as long as the average number of units in the development remains at or below the maximum density. This average is called *gross density*.

By varying street patterns and clustering housing units, a subdivider can dramatically increase the amount of open and/or recreational space in a development.

Street patterns. Most subdivisions are structured around one, a combination, or a modification of the following basic street patterns: gridiron, curvilinear, loop streets, and Radburn Plan streets. These patterns are illustrated in Figure 18.1.

The **gridiron pattern** evolved out of the government rectangular survey system. Featuring large lots, wide streets, and limited-use service alleys, the system works reasonably well up to a point. However, an overabundance of grid-patterned streets often results in monotonous neighborhoods, with all lots facing busy streets. In addition, sidewalks are usually located adjacent to the streets and the system provides for little or no open, park, or recreational space.

The **curvilinear system** integrates major arteries of travel with smaller secondary and cul-de-sac streets carrying minor traffic. In addition, small open parks are often provided for at intersections.

By utilizing **loop streets** rather than a traditional grid pattern, a developer can provide residents with convenient pedestrian and auto access and attractive open space. Although the main streets are loosely patterned after the grid system, residential streets have limited access with few lots facing the busier thoroughfares.

The **Radburn Plan** originated in the New Jersey town of the same name and features clusters of housing units grouped into large cul-de-sac blocks, often called "superblocks." Pedestrian access and open space are provided for between each cluster, and pedestrian travel is well separated from auto traffic.

Clustering for open space. By slightly reducing lot sizes and **clustering** them around varying street patterns a developer can house as many people in the same area as could be done using traditional subdividing plans, but with substantially increased tracts of open space, or "conservation zoning."

For example, compare the two illustrations in Figure 18.2. The first is a plan for a conventionally designed subdivision containing 368 housing units. It uses 23,200 linear feet of street and leaves only 1.6 acres open for park areas. Contrast this with the second subdivision pictured. Both subdivisions are equal in size and terrain. But when lots are minimally reduced in size and clustered around limited-access, cul-de-sac streets, the number of housing units remains nearly the same (366), with less street area (17,000 linear feet) and drastically increased open space (23.5 acres). In addition, with modern building designs this clustered plan could be modified to accommodate 550 patio homes or 1,100 townhouses.

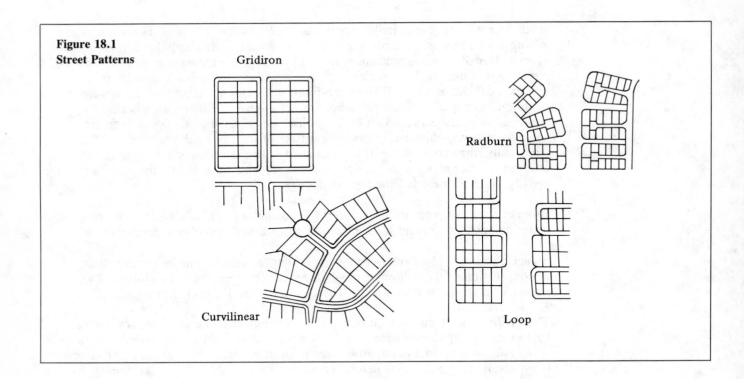

Figure 18.1
Street Patterns

Gridiron

Radburn

Curvilinear

Loop

Each of the plans in Figure 18.2 includes cul-de-sacs. As contrasted with a dead-end street, a **cul-de-sac** ends in a turning circle.

Small patio homes are sometimes developed with **zero lot line** layout, with the structure built against one side of a narrow lot.

Parking lots for a shopping plaza or apartment development are usually striped for spaces 9 or 10 feet by 20 feet. Where local authorities allow, however, more spaces may be gained by setting aside up to 40 percent of the stalls for compact cars, striped at 7.4 feet by 15 feet.

Subdivided Land Sales	Mass housing development, limited to the construction of single-family dwellings during the post–World War II years, greatly expanded in the 1950s. This expansion occurred as a result of population growth, new production techniques, and an increasing public interest in land use for future development, retirement, and recreation. As the industry grew so did the number of fraudulent acts and practices perpetrated by unscrupulous dealers and developers against the unsuspecting public.
Interstate Land Sales Full Disclosure Act	To protect the masses from such ''overenthusiastic sales promotions'' in interstate land sales, Congress passed a federal law, the **Interstate Land Sales Full Disclosure Act.** Basically a consumer protection act, the law requires those engaged in the interstate sale or leasing of 100 or more lots to register the details of the land with the U.S. Department of Housing and Urban Development (HUD).

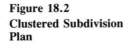

**Figure 18.2
Clustered Subdivision
Plan**

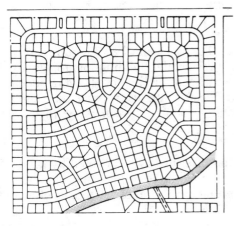
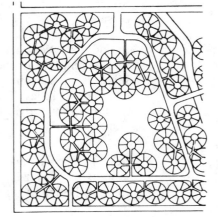

Conventional Plan
12,500-square-foot lots
368 housing units
1.6 acres of parkland
23,200 linear feet of street

Cluster Plan
7,500-square-foot lots
366 housing units
23.5 acres of parkland
17,700 linear feet of street

The seller is also required to furnish prospective buyers a **property report** containing all essential information about the property such as distance over paved roads to nearby communities, number of homes currently occupied, soil conditions affecting foundations and septic systems, type of title a buyer will receive, and existence of liens. The property report must be given to a prospective purchaser at least three business days before any sales contract is signed.

If a buyer does not receive a property report, the purchaser can cancel such a contract without further liability within two years. Any buyer of land covered by this act has the right to rescind a contract within seven days after signing.

If the seller misrepresents the property in any sales promotion, a buyer induced by such a promotion is entitled to sue the seller for civil damages under federal law. Failure to comply with the law also may subject a seller to criminal penalties of up to five years' imprisonment and a $5,000 fine.

**New York State
Subdivided Land
Sales Laws**

Land sold within New York State on the installment plan by a subdivider, and out-of-state land offered for sale in New York in any manner, may not be offered for sale until at least two documents have been filed with the Department of State. The first covers the identity and address of the offerer, the names of owners of the land, a statement on the subdivider's previous experience with vacant land, any criminal activity, a description of the land complete with maps, a title statement including any encumbrances or liens, and the terms on which the land will be sold, with a copy of the contract to be used.

The second document is a copy of the offering statement to be furnished to each buyer with a full financial statement of the assets and liabilities of the subdivider, a description of the subdivision and each lot, information on existing liens and encumbrances, existing or proposed utilities, area, community and recreational facilities and even the weather conditions of the area as well as the terms of sale.

In addition, New York's Public Health Laws require any subdivider offering for sale or rent five or more residential building lots to file a map of the proposed subdivision with the Department of Health, showing adequate water supply and sewerage facilities. The Department must approve the plan before it can be filed. A copy of any advertising to be used also must be filed with the Department of State.

New York considers land offerings to be covered by subdivision regulations as soon as a fifth lot is carved from the original parcel. The state allows any purchaser who is not represented by an attorney to cancel a contract within ten days.

In some instances, construction requires a permit from the New York **Department of Environmental Conservation (DEC).** Permits are necessary for work in a protected wetland or the 100-foot buffer zone around a wetland. Depending on the circumstances, permits may be needed for work that disturbs the banks of streams, for some water supplies, sewage discharges, and sewer extensions. The sale of more than 1,000 tons of fill dirt or gravel per year requires a DEC mining permit. **Environmental impact studies** of varying complexity may be required when the parcel is ruled environmentally sensitive: large projects or those located in flood plains, wetlands, steep slopes, or other environmentally fragile areas.

Rehabilitation

Upgrading older buildings for modern use can take different forms. Among them:

Adaptive re-use: finding a new use that varies from the building's original function—loft apartment developments in old warehouses, for example.
Preservation: careful maintenance of a building in its present state.
Reconstruction: recreation of the original building that may have been damaged or destroyed.
Recycling: any process that makes possible further use of an old building.
Rehabilitation (reconditioning): making a building sound and usable, with some consideration for original architectural features.
Renovation (restoration): reconditioning with a greater use of new materials, keeping intact or recreating original architectural elements.
Remodeling: changing the appearance of a building with the use of modern materials.
Restoration: returning a structure to the appearance it had at some point in the past, removing later additions and adding some that might have been removed.

Summary

A *subdivider* buys undeveloped acreage, divides it into smaller parcels, and sells it. A *land developer* builds homes on the lots and sells them, either through an in-house sales organization or through local real estate brokerage firms. City planners and land developers, working together, plan whole communities that are later incorporated into cities, towns, or villages.

Land development must generally comply with master land plans adopted by counties, cities, villages, or towns. This may entail approval of land-use plans by local *planning boards* or *commissioners.*

The process of subdivision includes dividing the tract of land into *lots and blocks* and providing for *utility easements,* as well as laying out street patterns and widths. A subdivider must generally record a completed *plat of subdivision* with all necessary approvals of public officials in the county where the land is located. Subdividers usually place *restrictions* upon the use of all lots in a subdivision as a general plan for the benefit of all lot owners.

By *varying street patterns and housing density* and *clustering housing units,* a subdivider can dramatically increase the amount of open and recreational space within a development.

Subdivided land sales are regulated on the federal level by the *Interstate Land Sales Full Disclosure Act.* This law requires developers engaged in interstate land sales or the leasing of 100 or more units to register the details of the land with HUD. Such developers also must provide prospective purchasers with a property report containing all essential information about the property at least three business days before any sales contract is signed.

Subdivided land sales are also regulated by New York laws. For the sale of subdivided land on an installment basis, and of any out-of-state land offered in New York, documents must be filed in advance with the Department of State, and an offering statement furnished to buyers. The sale of any subdivision of five or more lots requires approval of a water and sewage plan by the Department of Health.

Questions

1. Lila Hurwitz buys farmland near the city and turns it into usable building lots. She is a:
   a. site planner.   c. surveyor.
   b. developer.   d. subdivider.

2. Overall subdivision guidelines are set by:
   a. the federal government.
   b. New York State.
   c. the Department of Health.
   d. the Department of Environmental Conservation.

3. Local governments often regulate subdivision through their:
   a. planning boards.
   b. conservationists.
   c. site planners.
   d. building inspectors.

4. A particular subdivision plan may require the services of a(n):
   a. surveyor.   c. engineer.
   b. site planner.   d. All of the above

5. A map illustrating the sizes and locations of streets and lots in a subdivision is called a:
   a. gridiron pattern.
   b. survey.
   c. plat of subdivision.
   d. property report.

6. Which of the following items are *not* usually designated on the plat for a new subdivision?
   a. Easements for sewer and water mains
   b. Land to be used for streets, schools, and civic facilities
   c. Numbered lots and blocks
   d. Prices of residential and commercial lots

7. A subdivider turns over streets to public ownership through:
   a. development.   c. dedication.
   b. eminent domain.   d. condemnation.

8. Deed restrictions are usually placed on an entire subdivision by the:
   a. building inspector.   c. planning board.
   b. state government.   d. subdivider.

9. Which of the following would *not* be a part of the development cost of land?
   a. Curbs and gutters
   b. Installation of telephone lines
   c. Raw land cost
   d. Developer's overhead.

10. *Gross density* refers to which of the following?
    a. The maximum number of residents that may, by law, occupy a subdivision
    b. The average maximum number of houses per acre that may, by law, be built in a subdivision
    c. The maximum size lot that may, by law, be built in a subdivision
    d. The minimum number of houses that may, by law, be built in a subdivision

11. A street pattern based on the rectangular survey system is called a:
    a. Radburn plan.
    b. gridiron system.
    c. loop streets plan.
    d. cul-de-sac system.

12. A street pattern featuring clusters of housing units grouped into large, cul-de-sac blocks is generally called a:
    a. Radburn Plan.
    b. curvilinear system.
    c. loop street system.
    d. gridiron system.

13. Which of the following kinds of information need *not* be included in a property report given to a land buyer in compliance with the Interstate Land Sales Full Disclosure Act?
    a. Soil conditions affecting foundations
    b. Financial condition of the seller
    c. Number of homes currently occupied
    d. Existence of liens

14. The Marshes received a property report and consulted a lawyer a week before they signed a contract to buy a lot in a retirement community in Florida covered by the Interstate Land Sales Full Disclosure Act. They may change their minds and cancel the contract within:

   a. seven days.   c. two years.
   b. ten days.   d. They may not cancel.

15. Subdivision regulations apply in New York State as soon as one offers:

   a. the first lot.   c. the fifth lot.
   b. the third lot.   d. the seventh lot.

Appendix: Excerpt from New York State's Study Booklet for Brokers

SUMMARY OF
ARTICLE 9-A
OF THE REAL PROPERTY LAW

Subdivided Lands

No real estate broker or real estate salesperson should be involved in any way, in the State of New York, with the sale or lease of subdivided lands located within or without the State, unless the subdivider offering the property for sale or lease has complied with the provisions of Article 9-A of the Real Property Law.

Article 9-A of the Real Property Law is designed to protect the residents of New York State in the purchase or lease of subdivided lands located within the State of New York where sold on an installment plan, and located without the State of New York whether offered on the installment or any other plan, terms and conditions of sale or lease.

Safeguards are inserted into the law to prevent fraud or fraudulent practices which might be employed to induce the purchase or lease of vacant subdivided lands. Among such safeguards is the requirement that the subdividers file with the Department of State a statement, with substantiating documentation, including a certified copy of a map of the subdivided lands, a search of the title to the land reciting in detail all the liens, encumbrances and clouds upon the title which may or may not render the title unmarketable.

A subdivider, in addition to the statement required under the law, must file with the Department of State an Offering Statement. The Offering Statement must contain among other facts, detailed information about the subdivision including a description of the land, existence of utilities, area, community and recreational facilities, restriction, weather conditions and a financial statement of the subdivider. The Offering Statement must be revised yearly. It must clearly indicate that the Department of State has not passed on the merits of the offering.

The law further provides that the Department of State may in its discretion require such other and further data and information necessary to carry out the provisions of the law.

No sale or lease of subdivided lands shall be made without prior delivery of an Offering Statement to the prospective customer. Any offer to sell or lease subdivided lands prior to filing of both the Offering Statement and the statement constitutes a felony.

The Department of State is empowered to make a physical inspection of the lands offered for sale or lease.

Where the land is affected by mortgages or other encumbrances, it is unlawful for the subdivider to sell such vacant lands in the subdivision unless appropriate provisions in the mortgage or lien enable the subdivider to convey valid title to each parcel free of such mortgage or encumbrance. A mortgage on an entire subdivision will usually provide for a release of individual lots from that mortgage on payment of a specified amount of money. If the land is being sold on an installment plan, the law provides that where the amount paid to the subdivider by the purchaser reaches the point where the balance owing is the amount required to release that lot from the mortgage, all moneys thereafter received by the seller from the purchaser must be deemed trust funds, be kept in a separate account, and applied only toward clearance of title from the lien of the mortgage.

If, after investigation, the Secretary of State believes that the subdivider is guilty of fraud or that certain sales methods may constitute a fraud on the public, court proceedings to stop these practices may be instituted. The Secretary of State may also withdraw the acceptance previously granted and may order that all sales and advertising in New York State stop.

The law, as amended, also makes it mandatory that all advertising prior to publication be submitted to the Department for acceptance for filing. Misrepresentations in the sale or lease of subdivided lands constitute a misdemeanor.

The law now also provides that in every contract of sale or lease of subdivided lands, if the purchaser or lessee is not represented by an attorney, he or she has a 10-day cancellation privilege.

Sales may not be made based on the representation that the purchase of the property is a good investment, that the purchaser will or may make money on the transaction, or that the property can be readily resold. Nothing may be promised which is not contained in the written contract and Offering Statement.

For a more detailed consideration, a copy of the complete statute and the regulations promulgated thereunder will be made available upon request.

19

Construction

Key Terms

Asphalt
BTU
Blueprints
Cap insulation
Casement window
Ceiling joists
Circuit breaker
Concrete slab foundation
Crawl space
Dormer window
Double-hung window
Drywall
Eaves
Floating slab
Floor joists
Footing
Foundation walls
Framing
Gambrel roof

Heat pump
Hip roof
Insulation
Jalousie window
Mansard roof
110-volt wiring
Pier and beam foundation
Rafters
Sash windows
Sheathing
Siding
Slider windows
Solar collector
Solar heating
Studs
220-volt wiring
Urea-formaldehyde foam insulation
Veneer

Overview

A real estate licensee who has a general familiarity with basic construction details is better able to recognize and evaluate the quality of a finished house. Because most houses today are constructed with wood frames, this chapter will concentrate on the elements involved in the construction and design of wood-frame residences.

Knowledge of the following fundamentals is necessary in the planning and building of a new home:

1. municipal regulations such as building codes;
2. architectural styles and designs;
3. plans and specifications;
4. terms and trade vernacular in residential construction; and
5. practical approaches to recognizing, judging, and comparing the quality of the various house components.

| **Wood-Frame Construction** | Most houses are built with a basic underlying wood-frame construction covered with an exterior of brick, stone, wood, or vinyl siding. Wood-frame houses are preferred in New York State for several reasons: |

1. they are less expensive than other types;
2. they can be built rapidly;
3. they are easy to insulate against heat, cold, and moisture; and
4. they allow greater flexibility of design thereby enabling architects and builders to produce a variety of architectural styles.

Throughout this chapter, certain terms will be followed by a bold number in brackets. The number in the brackets refers to the numbered terms in the house diagram in Figure 19.1, which provides an overall picture of how housing components fit into the end product. For example, footing [1] means that the component is labeled one in the diagram in Figure 19.1 on the following page.

| **Regulation of Residential Construction** | Building codes for the construction industry were established when the Building Officials Conference of America (BOCA) combined with the National Board of Fire Insurance Underwriters to set forth rules to ensure both comfort and safety for homeowners. |

These standards became the forerunners of present municipal building codes. Municipal building codes place primary importance on materials, structural strength, and safe, sanitary conditions. Such building codes set the *minimum construction standards* that must be met by builders. (*See* Chapter 6 for a discussion of building codes.)

| **Architectural Styles** | Although the details of construction are rigidly specified by building codes, the architectural styles of houses may vary greatly. There are no absolute standards, and real estate values rest on what potential buyers, users, and investors think is desirable, as well as on what may be considered attractive by experts. The outward appearance of a home may rigidly adhere to one particular style or it may be a combination of several different styles. Some popular styles include colonial, Georgian, ranch, Cape Cod, contemporary, split level, Dutch colonial, French provincial, and Spanish. Examples of several typical architectural styles are shown in Figure 19.2 and 19.3. |

The architectural style of a building is one of the factors that provide long-range appeal to users and investors. The factors that affect appeal are difficult to identify and differ according to style trends and individual tastes.

| **Plans and Specifications** | In order to comply with building codes and achieve a particular architectural style, plans and specifications are required. These must be in sufficient detail to direct the builder in assembling the construction materials. Working drawings called plans or **blueprints** show the construction details of the building, while specifi- |

Figure 19.1
House Diagram

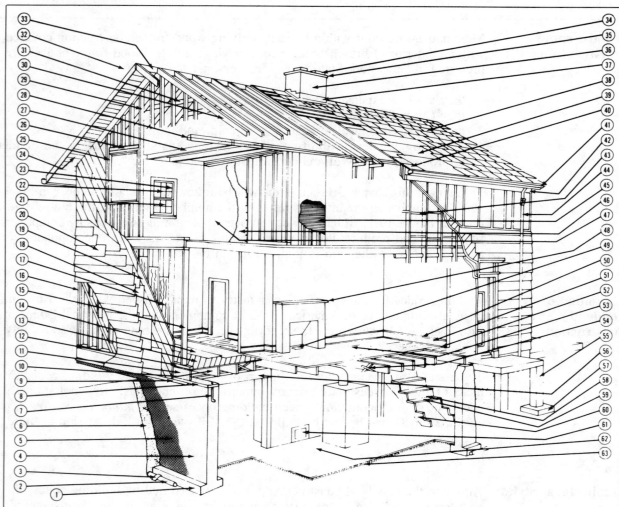

1. FOOTING
2. FOUNDATION DRAIN TILE
3. FELT JOINT COVER
4. FOUNDATION WALL
5. DAMPPROOFING OR WEATHERPROOFING
6. BACKFILL
7. ANCHOR BOLT
8. SILL
9. TERMITE SHIELD
10. FLOOR JOIST
11. BAND OR BOX SILL
12. PLATE
13. SUBFLOORING
14. BUILDING PAPER
15. WALL STUD
16. DOUBLE CORNER STUD
17. INSULATION
18. BUILDING PAPER
19. WALL SHEATHING
20. SIDING
21. MULLION

22. MUNTIN
23. WINDOW SASH
24. EAVE (ROOF PROJECTION)
25. WINDOW JAMB TRIM
26. DOUBLE WINDOW HEADER
27. CEILING JOIST
28. DOUBLE PLATE
29. STUD
30. RAFTERS
31. COLLAR BEAM
32. GABLE END OF ROOF
33. RIDGE BOARD
34. CHIMNEY POTS
35. CHIMNEY CAP
36. CHIMNEY
37. CHIMNEY FLASHING
38. ROOFING SHINGLES
39. ROOFING FELTS
40. ROOF SHEATHING
41. EVE TROUGH OR GUTTER
42. FRIEZE BOARD

43. FIRESTOP
44. DOWNSPOUT
45. LATHS
46. PLASTER BOARD
47. PLASTER FINISH
48. MANTEL
49. ASH DUMP
50. BASE TOP MOULDING
51. BASEBOARD
52. SHOE MOULDING
53. FINISH MOULDING
54. BRIDGING
55. PIER
56. GIRDER
57. FOOTING
58. RISER
59. TREAD
60. STRINGER
61. CLEANOUT DOOR
62. CONCRETE BASEMENT FLOOR
63. GRAVEL FILL

Figure 19.2
Architectural Styles

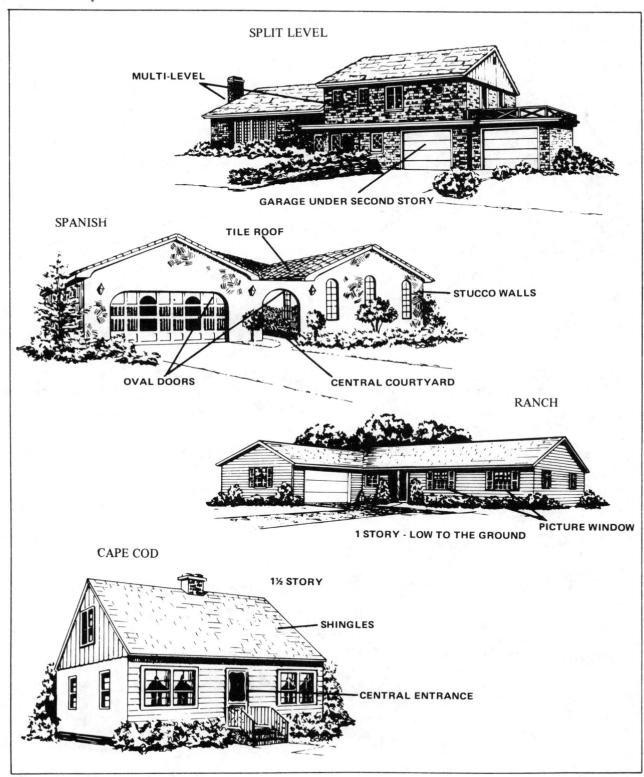

Figure 19.3
Architectural Styles

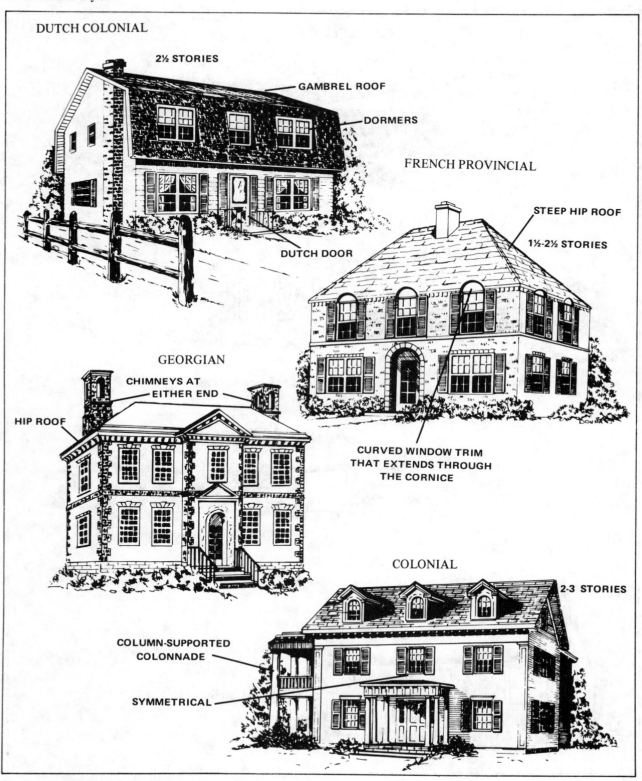

cations are written statements that establish the quality of the materials and workmanship required.

The following specialists may be involved in residential construction:

1. a mechanical engineer, who provides the heating, air conditioning, and plumbing plans and specifications;
2. a structural engineer, who ensures that the foundation will support the structure and is responsible for specifying the amount of steel required to reinforce the foundation and the type and mix of concrete to be used; and
3. a soil engineer, who may assist in determining the stability of the land on which the foundation will be built and whose investigation, coupled with the structural engineer's knowledge, will determine details of the foundation.

An owner may engage an architect to design a house and prepare plans and specifications for its construction. Professional architects are recognized as members of the American Institute of Architects (AIA). The architect's services may include negotiating with the builder and inspecting the progress of the construction as well as preparing plans and specifications. Architects' fees are usually based on the hours spent on a given project. In New York, plans must be signed by a licensed architect or engineer.

Foundations

The **foundation** of a building is the substructure on which the superstructure rests. The term *foundation* includes the footings, foundation walls, columns, pilasters, slab, and all other parts that provide support for the house and transmit the load of the superstructure to the underlying earth. Foundations are constructed of cut stone, stone and brick, concrete block, poured concrete and recently, specially treated wood. Poured concrete and concrete block are the most common foundation material because of their strength and resistance to moisture. The two major types of foundations are **concrete slab** and **pier and beam.**

Concrete slab. *A concrete slab foundation is composed of a concrete slab supported around the perimeter and in the center by concrete beams sunk into the earth.* It is made of poured concrete reinforced with steel rods. The foundation slab rests directly on the earth, with only a waterproofing membrane between the concrete and the ground. Foundations formed by a single pouring of concrete are called *monolithic*, while those in which the footings and the slab are poured separately are referred to as **floating.**

Pier and beam. In a pier and beam foundation, shown in Figure 19.4, the foundation slab rests on a series of isolated columns, called piers, that extend above ground level. The space between the ground and the foundations is called the **crawl space.** Each support of a pier and beam foundation consists of a *pier* [55], or column, resting on a **footing [1]**, or base. The pier, in turn, supports the *sill* [8], which is attached to the pier by an *anchor bolt* [7]. The **floor joists [10]** that provide the major support for the flooring are placed perpendicular to and on top of the sills.

Termite protection. In some areas of New York State the earth is infested with termites, extremely active antlike insects that are very destructive to wood. Prior to pouring the slab for the foundation, the ground should be chemically treated to poison termites and thus prevent them from coming up through or around the foundation and into the wooden structure. Chemical or pressure treatment of

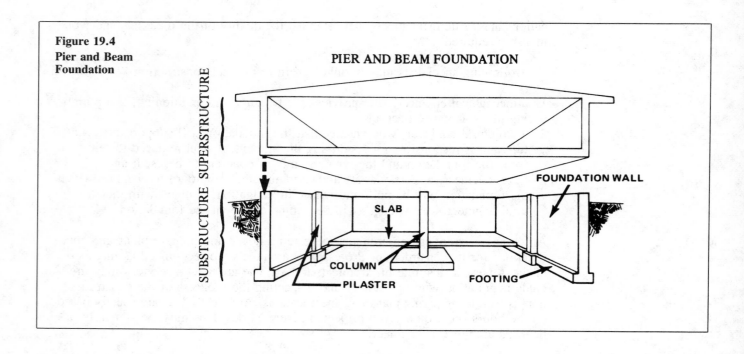

Figure 19.4
Pier and Beam
Foundation

PIER AND BEAM FOUNDATION

lumber used for sills and beams and the installation of *metal termite shields* **[9]** will also provide protection.

Exterior Construction

Walls and Framing

When the foundation is in place the exterior walls are erected. The first step in erecting exterior walls is the **framing.** The skeleton members of a building to which the interior and exterior walls are attached are called its *frame.* The walls of a frame are formed by vertical members called **studs [15].** Studs are spaced at even intervals and are attached to the sill. Normally, building codes require that for a one-story house the stud spacing not exceed 24 inches on centers. For a two-story house the spacing may not exceed 16 inches. Studs rest on *plates* **[12],** which are secured to and rest on *foundation wall* **[4].** In constructing walls and floors the builder will install *firestops* **[43]** as needed or required. These are boards or blocks nailed horizontally between studs or joists to stop drafts and retard the spread of fire.

There are three basic types of wood-frame construction: *platform, balloon,* and *post and beam,* shown in Figure 19.5.

Platform-frame construction. Today the most common type of wall-framing construction for both one- and two-story residential structures is *platform framing construction,* also known as *western frame construction.* In platform construction only one floor is built at a time, and each floor serves as a platform for the next story. The wall studs are first attached to the upper and lower plates and the entire assemblage is then raised into place and anchored to the sill.

Balloon-frame construction. The second type of wall framing is *balloon* construction, which differs from the platform method in that the studs extend continuously to the ceiling of the second floor. The second-floor joists rest on *ledger*

Figure 19.5
Frame Construction

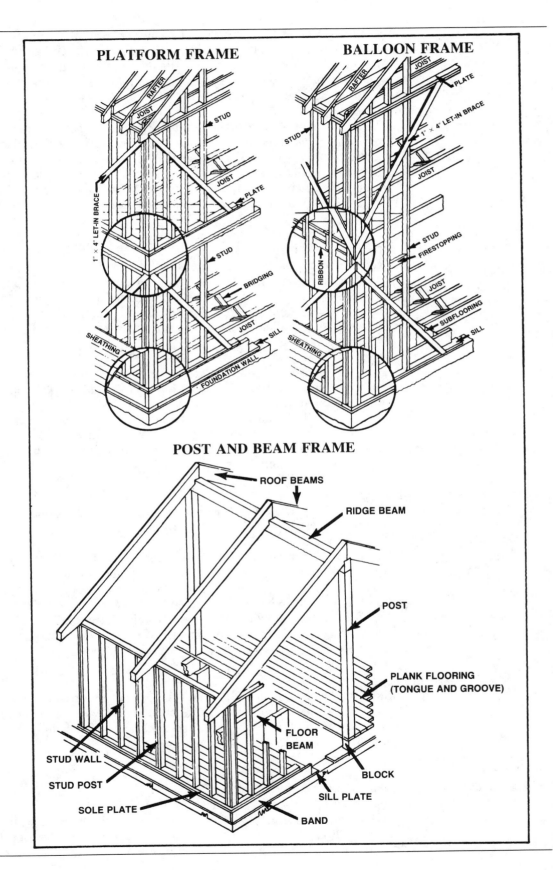

PLATFORM FRAME

BALLOON FRAME

POST AND BEAM FRAME

boards or *ribbon boards* set into the interior edge of the studs. The balloon method gives a smooth, unbroken wall surface on each floor level, thus alleviating the unevenness that sometimes results from settling when the platform method is used. The balloon method is usually employed when the exterior finish will be brick, stone veneer, or stucco.

Post and beam frame construction. The third type of frame construction is *post and beam frame construction.* With this method the ceiling planks are supported on beams that rest on posts placed at intervals inside the house. Because the posts provide some of the ceiling support, rooms can be built with larger spans of space between the supporting side walls. In some houses the beams are left exposed and the posts and beams are stained to serve as part of the decor.

Lumber. The lumber used in residential construction is graded according to moisture content and structural quality as established by the 1970 National Grade Rule. Grading rules require dimension lumber (2″ × 4″, 2″ × 6″) that is classified as *dry* to have a moisture content of 19 percent or less. Lumber that has a higher moisture content is classified as *green.* All species and grades are assigned stress ratings to indicate their strength when used in spanning distances between two supports. Actual dimensions of lumber differ from nominal measurements. A 2″ × 4″ actually measures 1½″ × 3½″.

Exterior walls. After the skeleton of the house is constructed, the exterior wall surface must be built and the **sheathing [19]** and **siding [20]** applied. The sheathing is nailed directly to the wall studs **[15]** to form the base for the siding. Sheathing is generally hardboard, insulated board, or chipboard. If the house is to have a masonry veneer, the sheathing may be gypsum board. Fabricated sheathings are available both in strip and sheet material. Sheathing is wrapped in tar paper or more recently in a plastic material.

After the sheathing is added, the final exterior layer, called *siding*, is applied. This may be vinyl, asphalt, asbestos shingles, wood, aluminum, stone, brick, or other material.

Masonry veneer versus solid brick. Brick **veneer** is a thin layer of brick often used as a covering on a frame house to give the appearance of a solid brick house. If the masonry is merely decorative and the walls are of wood, then the house is masonry veneer. If on the other hand the brick walls provide the support for the roof structure, then the house is all masonry, or solid brick. A masonry veneer house may be distinguished from a solid masonry house by the thickness of the walls. The walls of a veneered house are seldom over eight inches thick.

Small outlets evenly spaced around the base of the masonry perimeter of a brick house are called *weep holes.* These openings provide an outlet for any moisture or condensation trapped between the brick and the sheathing of the exterior walls and are essential for proper ventilation.

Insulation

Maintaining comfortable temperatures inside the home is an important factor in construction, particularly in these days of high-cost energy. To ensure adequate protection, **insulation [17]** should be placed in the exterior walls and upper floor ceilings. *Band insulation* of fiberglass is placed with a sill sealer above the foundation walls. New York's Public Service Commission requires R-19 (the equivalent of 6 inches of fiberglass) as **cap insulation,** under the attic floor and R-11 (3½ inches) in sidewalls, as well as storm windows and doors, for the installation of gas heat. For conversion of existing units to gas or electric heat, the cap insulation is required, and storm windows or insulated glass where single glazing has been used.

Commonly used insulation materials are rock wool, fiberglass, and cellulose. Combinations of material such as fiberglass wrapped in aluminum foil or rock wool formed into batt sections that can be placed between the studs are available. Proper insulation will contribute to the efficiency of both heating and air-conditioning systems.

Urea-formaldehyde foam insulation (UFFI) has been blamed for respiratory problems, nausea, and flulike illnesses. It was used in some new homes and pumped into the walls of older homes during the 1970s. Determining if it is in place can sometimes be difficult.

Window and Door Units

After the foundation has been completed and the exterior walls constructed, the next step is the construction of exterior window and door units. Windows and doors come in many styles and materials. Windows may either be side-hinged on vertical hinges **(casement)** or slide up and down **(sash).** A sash window slides up and down in a cased frame and is generally balanced by sash cords, aluminum guides, or chains passing over pulleys and attached to weights. Basic window styles include the following:

1. **Single-hung window:** A sash window of which only one sash, usually the bottom one, is movable.
2. **Double-hung window:** A sash window with two vertically sliding sashes; both single- and double-hung window sashes are held in place after movement by friction of the sash (frame) as controlled by springs or weights.
3. **Slider window:** A sash window that opens by moving horizontally.
4. **Casement window:** A window that has a sash hinged like a door and opens or closes by the action of a gear complex.
5. **Jalousie window:** A window formed by horizontal slats of glass that open or close horizontally by the action of a gear complex.

The materials most commonly found in window frames are wood, steel, and aluminum. The quality of a window depends on its construction, additional security, and insulating factors.

Door styles must of necessity be compatible with the design of the house. For example, the door style selected for an Early American house would be a six-panel door. There are six basic types of doors, each distinguished by its method of construction, as shown in Figure 19.6.

The thickness of an interior door is usually 1⅜ inches and an exterior door is usually 1¾ inches. The majority of doors are made of mahogany, birch, walnut, or oak. Glass doors, screen doors with aluminum or steel frames, and insulated metal doors are primarily exterior doors used for patios, porches, or garden areas. Energy considerations dictate triple glazing for many picture windows in recent years.

Roof Framing and Coverings

The construction of the skeleton framing for the roofing material is the next step in building a house. Residential roofs are made in several styles including gabled, shed, salt box, and flat. Roof construction includes the *rafters* [30], *sheathing* [39], and *exterior trimming* [42]. Skeleton framings are classified as either conventional or truss (*see* Figures 19.7 and 19.8).

Figure 19.6
Types of Doors

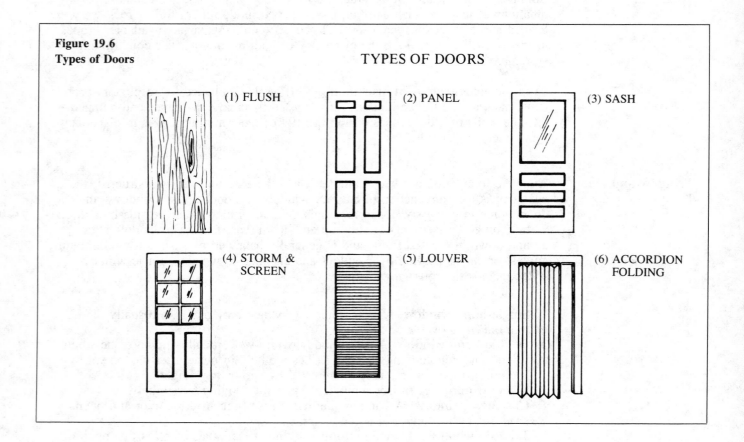

TYPES OF DOORS

(1) FLUSH

(2) PANEL

(3) SASH

(4) STORM & SCREEN

(5) LOUVER

(6) ACCORDION FOLDING

Joist and rafter roof framing. A joist and rafter roof consists of *rafters* [30], *collar beams* [31], *ceiling joists* [27], and *ridge board* [33]. **Rafters** are the sloping timbers that support the weight of the roof and establish the roof's pitch, or slant. The collar beams give rigidity to the rafters, and the ridge board aligns and receives the rafters.

Truss roof framing. A *truss* roof has four parts. It has *lower chords, upper chords,* "W" *diagonals,* and *gusset plates.* The lower chords are similar to ceiling joists, whereas the upper chords are the equivalent of the rafters in a joist and rafter roof. The "W" diagonals are the equivalent of the collar beams and are called "W" because they support the rafter chords in the form of the letter "W". The gusset plates are solid pieces of metal or wood that add rigidity to the roof. All integral parts are assembled and held in place by gusset plates, bolt connections, or nails. A truss roof is generally prefabricated at a mill and set in place in sections by a crane, whereas a joist and rafter roof is assembled piece by piece on the site.

Exposed rafter roof framing. *Exposed,* or *sloping, rafter* roofs are often used with post and beam frame construction. The rafters are supported by central support posts and by the exterior walls. However, there are no ceiling joists or lower chords to provide additional support. The rafters in this type of roof are often left exposed for decorative purposes.

Exterior trimming. The overhang of a pitched roof that extends beyond the exterior walls of the house is called the **eaves [41],** or *cornice.* The cornice is composed of the soffit, the frieze board, the facia board, and the extended rafters. The *frieze board* [42] is the exterior wood trim board used to finish the exterior wall between the top of the siding or masonry and eave, or overhang, of the roof framing. The *facia board* is an exterior wood trim used along the line of the butt end of the rafters where the roof overhangs the structural walls. The overhang of the cornice provides a decorative touch to the exterior of a house as well as some protection from sun and rain (Figure 19.9).

Roof sheathing and roofing. With the skeleton roof in place, the rafters are covered with sheathing. The type of sheathing to be used is dependent upon the choice of outside roofing material. Most shingles are composed of **asphalt** and are laid over plywood covered with tar paper. If wood shingles are used, spaced sheathing of 1″ × 4″ boards may be used to provide airspace to allow the shingles to dry after rain. Other materials, including fiberglass, may also be used for roofing.

Interior Construction

Walls and Finishing

Interior walls are the partitioning dividers for individual rooms and are usually covered with *plasterboard* [46], although *lath* [45] and *plaster* [47] may be used. The terms **drywall** and *wallboard* are synonymous with plasterboard. Plasterboard is finished by a process known as *taping and floating.* Taping covers the joints between the sheets of plasterboard. Floating is the smoothing out of the walls by the application of a plaster texture over the joints and rough edges where nails attach the plasterboard to the wall studs. Texturing may be used in some areas as a final coating applied with a roller onto the plasterboard prior to painting, wood paneling, or wallpapering.

The final features added to a home include: (1) *floor covering,* (2) *trim,* (3) *cabinet work,* and (4) *wall finishings* of paint, wallpaper, or paneling. Floor coverings of vinyl, asphalt tile, wood (either in strips or blocks), carpet, brick, stone, or terrazzo tile are applied over the wood or concrete subflooring. Trim masks the joints between the walls and ceiling and gives a finished decorator touch to the room. Cabinet work in the home may be either built in on the job or prefabricated in the mill.

Plumbing

Plumbing must be installed subject to strict inspections and in accordance with local building codes that dictate the materials to be used and the method of installation. Sewer pipes are of cast iron, concrete, or plastic, while water pipes are of copper, plastic, or galvanized iron. Recently, plastic has been used more frequently because it eliminates piping joints in the foundation slab. Domestic hot water may be supplied directly from a coil in the heating system or by a separate hot water heater. If a separate unit is used, the water is heated by electricity, gas or oil. Well water supplies may require water softeners.

Figure 19.7
Roof Construction

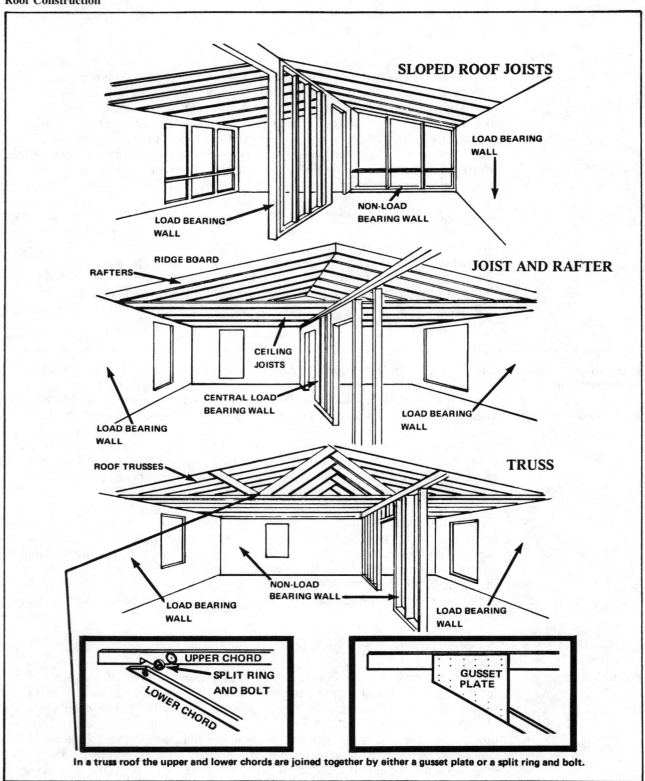

In a truss roof the upper and lower chords are joined together by either a gusset plate or a split ring and bolt.

**Figure 19.8
Roof Styles**

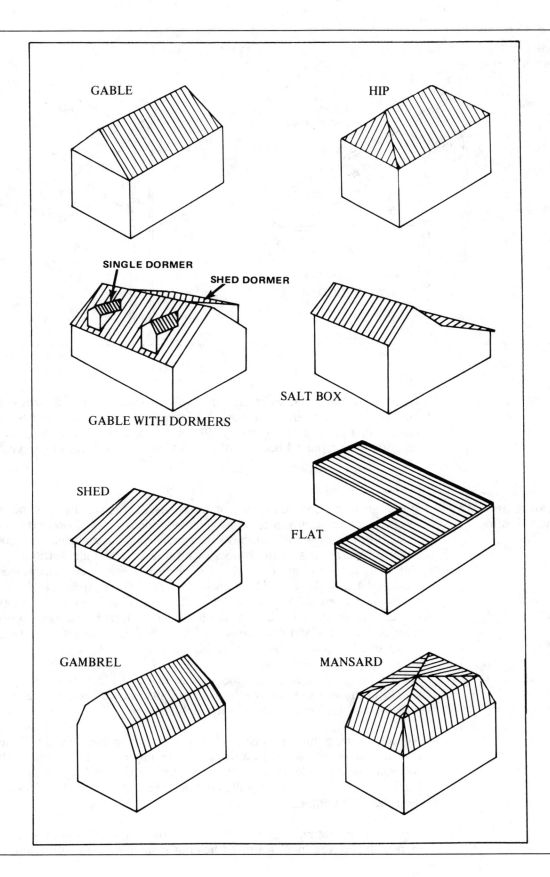

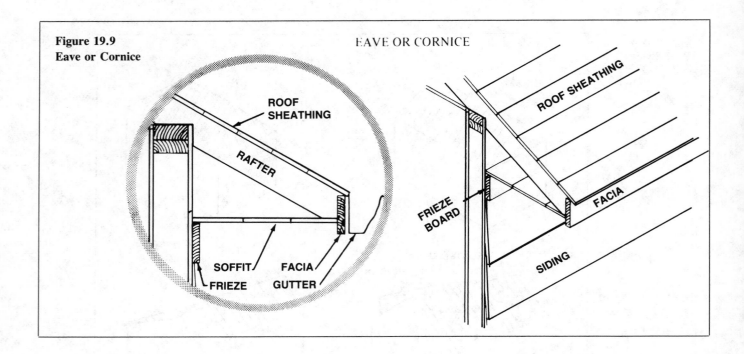

Figure 19.9
Eave or Cornice

EAVE OR CORNICE

Bathtubs, toilets, and sinks are made of cast iron or pressed steel casted with enamel, plastic, or artificial marble. Fiberglass is a new material for these fixtures and is gaining in popularity. Plumbing fixtures have relatively long lives and often are replaced because of obsolete style long before they have worn out.

Heating and Air Conditioning

Warm-air heating systems and hot water baseboards are the most common types in use today. Steam heat is found in some older homes. In recent years some areas of northern New York have seen increasing dependence on wood as a fuel. A forced warm-air system consists of a furnace, warm-air distributing ducts, and ducts for the return of cool air. Each furnace has a capacity rated in **British Thermal Units (BTUs).** The number of BTUs given represents the furnace's heat output from either gas, oil, or electric firing. A heating and cooling engineer can determine the cubic area of the building, as well as its construction, insulation, and window and door sizes, and from this data compute the furnace capacity required to provide heat for the building in the coldest possible weather.

All gas pipes for heating and cooking are made of black iron. Gas pipes are installed in the walls or run overhead in the attic where adequate ventilation is possible and are never placed in the slab.

Air-conditioning units are rated either in BTUs or in tons. Twelve thousand BTUs are the equivalent of a one-ton capacity. An engineer can determine the measurements and problems inherent in the construction and layout of the space, and from this information specify the cooling capacity required to adequately service the space or building.

Combination heating-cooling systems are common in new homes. The most common is the conventional warm-air heating system with a cooling unit attached.

The same ducts and blower that force warm air are used to force cool air. The cooling unit is similar to a large-sized air conditioner.

The technical aspects of the heating and air conditioning should be handled by an experienced and qualified authority although the homeowner should give due consideration to the operation and maintenance of the unit. The filters should be cleaned regularly and the return air grills and registers should be clear and clean for the passage of the circulating air. The thermostat controls should be well understood and properly set. The compressor and fan motors should be cared for on a regular maintenance schedule.

Solar heating. The increased demand for fossil fuels in recent years has forced builders to look for new sources of energy. One of the most promising sources of heat for residential buildings is *solar energy*. Most **solar heating** units suitable for residential use operate by gathering the heat from the sun's rays with one or more **solar collectors.** Water or air is forced through a series of pipes in the solar collector to be heated by the sun's rays. The hot air or water is then stored in a heavily insulated storage tank until it is needed to heat the house.

More immediately practical in the New York State area is *passive solar* heating. Without any additional special equipment, a house may be built or remodeled to take advantage of the sun's rays. Large areas of glass on a southern exposure and few windows on the north side of a building are typical of passive solar arrangements. Substantial savings in fuel may be obtained.

Some solar heating systems are in use but at present they are too expensive to be widely used in residential buildings. It is expected that there will be more solar energy installations in the future, however, as technology increases to reduce the initial cost of such systems.

Heat pumps, which utilize heat from outside air in a form of reverse air conditioning, are often used in conjunction with backup heating units of more conventional design. Where electricity is expensive, use of a heat pump may bring down costs. The heat pump also serves in summer for air conditioning.

Electrical Services

Electrical service from the power company is brought into the home through the transformer and the meter into a **circuit-breaker box** or fuse box. The circuit-breaker box is the distribution panel for the many electrical circuits in the house. In case of a power overload the heat generated by the additional flow of electrical power will cause the circuit breaker to open at the breaker box, thus reducing the possibility of electrical fires. It is the responsibility of the architect or the builder to adhere to local building codes that regulate electrical wiring. All electrical installations are inspected by the New York Board of Fire Underwriters.

Residential wiring circuits are rated by the voltage they are designed to carry. In the past, most residences were only wired for **110-volt** capacity. Today because of the many built-in appliances in use, **220-volt** service is generally necessary. New York State standards require at least 100-ampere service and for new home construction, a 110-volt smoke detector and a *ground fault interrupter* on each water hazard circuit (kitchen, baths, exterior outlets). The ground fault interrupter is a super-sensitive form of circuit breaker.

A typical schedule for new home construction is shown in Table 19.1.

Table 19.1
New Home Construction Schedule

Preliminary Work: Site engineering, evaluation, preliminary plan, environmental review, etc., county and local agency reviews, signatures, and filing of plan. Obtain letter of credit. Site development.

Construction Schedule:

Building permit
Surveyor stakes out lot and house.
Excavator digs basement.
Plumber installs sanitary sewer and water service.
Building inspector inspects sewer.
Excavator backfills sewer/water trench.
Mason forms the footings and pours shallow footing concrete.
Mason lays up concrete block walls.
Concrete block wall dampproofing
Backfill basement walls
Excavator digs trench footings.
Mason pours trench footing concrete.
Box out driveway and spread gravel.
Framer sets steel beams and columns.
Framer frames house.
Mason builds fireplace.
Mason lays up exterior brick or stone.
Roofing
Siding
Exterior painting/staining
Gutters
Garage door
Rough plumbing
Rough heating
Building inspector reviews framing, plumbing, and heating.

Rough electrical
Electrical inspection—rough wiring
Prewire telephone and cable TV and security system
Insulation
Drywall: hanging and finishing
Mason pours concrete floors.
Interior trim
Interior painting
Ceramic tile walls/floors
Kitchen cabinets/vanities
Finish flooring—hardwood/vinyl
Finish plumbing
Finish heating
Finish electrical
Electrical inspection—final
Mirrors/shower doors
Storms and screens
Blacktop
Landscaping
Appliances
Clean up
Certificate of occupancy inspection
Surveyor prepares instrument survey "as built."
Building department issues Certificate of Occupancy.
Final inspection and closing

Prebuilt Housing

Factory-built houses may take several forms:

Mobile home. A mobile home is complete when it leaves the factory on its own wheels. It is classed as personal property; it may be permanently installed on a foundation later or it may not.

Manufactured home. A manufactured home is factory-built to standards set by the U.S. Department of Housing and Urban Development (HUD).

Modular home. Modular homes are completely factory-built, then transported by truck to the building site, where sections are joined together.

Panelized home. Separate panels for floor, walls, and roof are factory-built and assembled on the building site, where electrical and plumbing work are added.

Prefabricated home. Factory-built panels assembled on the building site already include plumbing and electrical systems.

Looking Over an Older Home

In general, houses built after World War II are more or less modern with copper plumbing, adequate electric service, and compact furnaces. Houses built before the '40s require more stringent inspection. The buyer of such a house, where no inspection by lender, FHA, or VA will be involved, may want to retain a building inspection or construction engineer for advice before a purchase contract becomes firm.

Exterior condition. A New York State house that lacks storm windows or screens has probably seen minimal maintenance. Well-fitting older wood storms and screens, however, can be even more efficient than modern self-storing ones. Asphalt roofs can be expected to last 15 or 20 years. Binoculars can sometimes be useful in examining a roof for missing shingles, patched spots, or a dried-up, crinkled condition. Moss growing on a roof, particularly on the north side, may indicate a moisture problem within. In mid-winter a roof clear of snow often means that heat is being lost because of inadequate insulation. Downspouts should be firmly attached; gutters with holes will have to be replaced.

Electric service. State requirements call for at least 100-amp service, which is inadequate for today's needs. Modern standards call for 220 as well as 110 volts. Ideally each room should have an outlet on each wall and one every 12 feet. A tangle of extension cords signals potential problems. A circuit-breaker box in the basement indicates that the system has been modernized. An old fuse system, however, can be satisfactory if enough circuits were carefully installed.

Plumbing. Old galvanized pipes suffer from corrosion and deposits can eventually clog them enough to impede the flow of water. The classic test for water pressure is to open all taps in an upstairs bathroom and then flush the toilet to see if the flow from the faucets diminishes. Hot water lines corrode most quickly; a quick check of the water heater should show whether copper pipes have been installed. Particularly vulnerable are patch jobs, where copper has been joined to galvanized pipe to solve a particular emergency. Where kitchen and bath have been modernized, it is likely that copper plumbing was used. In rural areas a *drilled well* is preferable to a *dug well*. Water should be tested by local health officials for purity; flow also can be measured. A *percolation test,* for undeveloped land, shows whether the site is suitable for a septic system.

Basement. In much of New York State a completely dry basement is an unattainable goal. A *sump pump,* installed in a corner of the basement to pump accumulated water up into a sewer, does not necessarily signal trouble; sump pumps are routinely required by many local building codes. Inspecting an older home, one may gain some clue from the amount of material (newspapers, storage boxes) kept directly on the basement floor. Rust on the bottom of the furnace or the hot water heater or a newly-painted stripe across the bottom may indicate a former flood, which might have been a one-time occurrence.

Insulation. Many older homes show plugged holes in the attic stair risers, where insulation has been blown in. Often the owner of an older home does not know how much insulation has been installed. Inspection under the attic floor may involve prying up a floorboard; sidewalls can sometimes be accessed by removing a switchplate. Sellers are required by New York State law to make past heating bills available to prospective purchasers.

Summary

Building codes regulate residential construction by placing primary importance on materials, safe and sanitary installations, and structural strengths. FHA and VA minimum property standards tend to mold local municipal building codes.

Recent trends in architectural styling have moved away from strictly traditional styles. Greater emphasis is being put on functional design as seen in ranch, split level, and other contemporary styles. However, colonial, Georgian, Spanish, Dutch colonial, and French provincial styles are still widely used.

Working drawings and supplemental written specifications are prepared to establish the quality of materials and workmanship needed to produce the desired residence and conform to local building codes. An architect may be employed to design the building, prepare plans and specifications, and supervise construction as it progresses.

The foundation of a house forms the substructure on which the superstructure rests. Foundations include footings, foundation walls, and slabs. The two major types of foundations are *concrete slab* and *pier and beam.*

Wood-frame construction is the type most frequently used in building single-family houses. The three basic types of exterior wall framing are *platform, balloon,* and *post and beam.* Multilevel balloon construction differs from the platform method in that the studs extend continuously to the ceiling of the second floor, while with the platform method only one floor is built at a time. Post and beam construction utilizes interior posts to support the roof.

Windows may be *sash windows,* which are single-hung, double-hung, or of the slider type; *casement windows,* which are side-hinged on vertical hinges; or *jalousie windows,* which are formed of horizontal slats of glass. Door styles include *panel, slab,* and *hollow* or *solid core.*

Skeleton roof framing may be either *joist and rafter, exposed rafter,* or *truss.* The parts of the joist and rafter roof are the joists, rafters, collar beams, and ridge. The parts of the truss roof are the lower and upper chords, the ''W'' diagonals, and the gusset plates. The skeleton roof rafters or upper chords are covered with sheathing, generally plywood.

Interior walls are generally covered with plasterboard and finished with paint or wallpaper. Final interior features include wall finishings, trim, floor covering, and cabinet work. Plumbing, heating, air conditioning, and electrical wiring require careful installation to adhere to building codes.

Brokers must be alert to the possible presence of urea-formaldehyde foam insulation in residential property.

An older home in good condition should have a tight roof with no missing or patched shingles, a complete set of storm windows and screens, and firmly attached gutters and downspouts, without holes. Proper electric systems involve more than 100-amp service, an adequate number of circuits, 220 as well as 110-volt service, and outlets on each wall or every 12 feet. Plumbing should be all copper. In rural areas, well water should be tested for purity and flow. The land has to pass a percolation test for a proposed septic system. Basements should be relatively dry; adequate insulation should have been installed at least under the attic floor.

Questions

1. Most building codes place emphasis on:
   a. safety.
   b. sanitation.
   c. structural strength.
   d. All of the above

2. Which is described as a 1½-story house?
   a. Split-level   c. Colonial
   b. Ranch   d. Cape Cod

3. A gambrel roof is found on what type of house?
   a. Dutch Colonial   c. Georgian
   b. French Provincial   d. Spanish

4. In New York State, building plans must be signed by:
   a. fire underwriter.
   b. licensed architect or engineer.
   c. site planner.
   d. primary contractor.

5. Which is a type of foundation?
   a. Balloon   c. Floating slab
   b. Post and beam   d. Chord

6. The components of a pier and beam foundation include:
   a. the footings.   c. the anchor bolts.
   b. the sill or beam. d. All of the above

7. Which of the following are installed in a house in horizontal position?
   a. Joists   c. Rafters
   b. Studs   d. Posts

8. Blocks nailed between studs and joists are called:
   a. trusses.   c. bolts.
   b. firestops.   d. sills.

9. In building a frame or wooden skeleton, studs rest on:
   a. plates.   c. joists.
   b. balloons.   d. ridges.

10. Which of the following characteristics is considered when grading lumber?
    a. Age   c. Fragrance
    b. Color   d. Moisture content

11. Sheathing is found on the outside:
    a. walls.   c. foundation.
    b. windows.   d. doors.

12. Cap insulation, which has the greatest payback in lowered fuel bills, is found:
    a. under the attic floor.
    b. on the basement ceiling.
    c. in sidewalls.
    d. just under the roof.

13. Band insulation is placed:
    a. under the attic floor.
    b. above the foundation.
    c. on the basement ceiling.
    d. inside exterior walls.

14. Roof framing constructed on the site, with sloping rafters supported by ceiling joists, is called:
    a. truss.   c. exposed rafter.
    b. joist and rafter. d. platform.

15. A cornice provides some protection against:
    a. fire.   c. rain.
    b. lightning. d. cold.

16. Plasterboard is also known as:
    a. drywall.   c. sheathing.
    b. siding.   d. paneling.

17. Heat from outside air is utilized through a:
    a. reverse conditioner.
    b. passive solar system.
    c. heat pump.
    d. cold air return.

18. Buyers of an older home may want to consult a:
    a. building inspection engineer.
    b. soil engineer.
    c. framer.
    d. firestop specialist.

19. A percolation test reveals possible problems with:

    a. drilling a well.
    b. insulating sidewalls.
    c. operating a septic system.
    d. using a wood furnace.

20. Which of the following signals trouble when found on a roof?

    a. Snow   c. Birds
    b. Moss   d. Asphalt

20

Condominiums and Cooperatives

Key Terms

Black book
Board of directors
Board of managers
Bylaws
Common elements
Covenants, conditions, and restrictions (CC&Rs)
Conversion
Declaration
Disclosure statement
Eviction plan
Homeowners association

Letter of intent
Noneviction plan
Planned unit development (PUD)
Proprietary lease
Prospectus
Public offering
Red herring
Reserves
Sponsor
Timesharing
Townhouse

Overview

The advantages of home ownership and the amenities of apartment living may be combined through relatively new forms of ownership: cooperatives and condominiums. This chapter will examine these forms as well as planned unit developments, townhouses, and timesharing.

Growth of Condominiums and Cooperatives

Condominium and *cooperative* ownership of housing has been on the rise in the second half of the twentieth century, particularly in the Downstate area. Together with townhouses and *planned unit developments (PUDs),* condos and co-ops offer the emotional, financial, and tax advantages of home owning, combined with various forms of apartment living.

As inflation and interest rates escalate, the *economies* of such housing become more attractive. As opposed to traditional single-family homes, condos and co-ops offer more efficient use of ever-scarcer building land, *lower costs* for lot development, less outlay for construction per living unit, and some *savings* in maintenance and heating bills. Just as the American public learned eventually to accept smaller cars as the norm, so are homeowners learning to be content with less living space or land area per person than in the past.

Contributing to the growth of condos and co-ops are changes in population patterns with increasing numbers of single homeowners, one-parent families, and senior citizens. To such groups, community living offers *security* and *sociability,* ease of *maintenance,* and sometimes the opportunity for a share in expensive *recreational facilities* like swimming pools.

In addition, landlords plagued by rent control or by rising costs have turned to conversion of existing apartment buildings as a profitable method of disposing of property.

Looking at a shared housing complex will give no clue as to whether it is a condominium, cooperative, or (in some cases) PUD. The buildings themselves may be high-rises, townhouses, patio homes, garden apartments, or even single detached houses. The differences arise from the legal forms of ownership.

Condominium Ownership

Condominium ownership is a relatively new form of organization; in New York State it began as recently as 1963.

The buyer of a condominium receives a *deed* conveying *fee simple ownership* of two things: the apartment and an undivided interest in the **common elements** (*see* Figure 20.1). Chief among the common elements are the land and the exteriors of the buildings. Also common property are hallways, basements, elevators, stairwells, driveways, private roads, sidewalks, lawns, landscaping, and recreational facilities.

In many respects condominium owners may be regarded in the same light as owners of a single detached house. Title may be held in severalty, by the entirety, as joint tenants, or tenants in common. The unit receives an individual tax account number and tax bill and may be mortgaged as a house would be. The owners place a separate insurance policy on the living space. Income tax advantages are identical to those on single homes. The owners are free to sell the property, lease it, give it away, or leave it to heirs. Each unit is a financial entity and if an adjoining unit is foreclosed, no obligation is incurred by the other owners.

Figure 20.1
Condominium Ownership

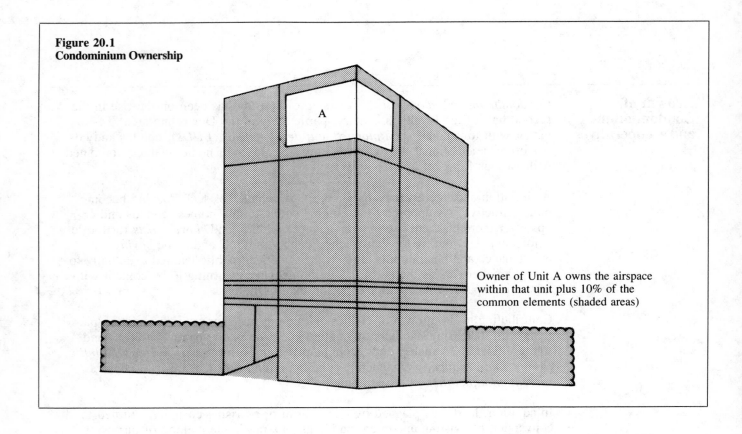

Owner of Unit A owns the airspace within that unit plus 10% of the common elements (shaded areas)

Owners are, however, bound by the bylaws of a **homeowners association** to which all belong. Monthly fees are levied for the maintenance, insurance, and management of common elements. If unpaid, these *common charges* become a lien against the individual unit and may even be enforced by foreclosure. The bylaws also set up **covenants, conditions, and restrictions (CC&Rs),** which, for example, may prohibit the display of For Sale signs or the painting of a front door bright red.

A condominium is usually managed by an elected **board of managers.** With more than 25 units, a board often hires professional management.

**Selling
Condominiums**

While the selling of new condominiums requires the broker to register with the Attorney General's office, resale is among the activities covered by a broker's or salesperson's license. The broker who deals in such properties must be concerned with some items that do not apply to the marketing of single homes. The buyer of a condominium must receive detailed statements about the property, should read the CC&Rs, and must be alerted to any unpaid common charges against the unit. Analysis of the health of a project also should include an examination of the **reserves,** those funds set aside to accumulate for large expenses like new roofs or heating units. The sale of a condominium is arranged on a special form of contract.

Although it is most widely used for residential property, condominium ownership is growing for professional buildings, office buildings, and even shopping malls.

Cooperative Ownership

Cooperative ownership, an older form of organization, is common in the New York City metropolitan area. In the city, condominium organization is generally used only for the more expensive developments. Under the usual *cooperative* arrangement, title to land and building is held by a *corporation*. Each purchaser of an apartment in the building receives stock in the corporation. The purchaser then becomes a stockholder of the corporation and, *by virtue of that stock ownership, receives a* **proprietary lease** to his or her apartment.

The cooperative building's real estate taxes are assessed against the corporation as owner. The mortgage is signed by the corporation, creating one lien on the entire parcel of real estate. Taxes, mortgage interest and principal, and operating and maintenance expenses on the property are shared by the tenant-shareholders in the form of monthly *maintenance charges*.

Thus while the cooperative tenant-owners do not actually own an interest in real estate (they own stock, which is *personal property*), for all practical purposes they control the property through their stock ownership and their voice in the management of the corporation. For example, the bylaws of the corporation generally provide that each prospective purchaser of an apartment lease must be approved by a **board of directors.**

One disadvantage of cooperative ownership became particularly evident during the Depression years and must still be considered. This is the possibility that if enough owner-occupants became financially unable to make prompt payment of their monthly assessments, the corporation might be forced to allow mortgage and tax payments to go unpaid. Through such defaults the entire property could be ordered sold by court order in a foreclosure suit. Such a sale might destroy the interests of all occupant-shareholders, even those who paid their assessments.

The tenant-owner, who does not have fee simple ownership, may not place a regular mortgage against the unit. Financing is usually arranged at a slightly higher interest rate and with perhaps a shorter term than with regular mortgages. In the mid-1980s, Fannie Mae announced that it would purchase co-op loans, thus expanding financing opportunities. Boards of directors, sensitive to the financial dependence of one tenant upon the others, sometimes set down payment requirements more stringent than those asked by lending institutions. They may even in some cases refuse prospective tenants unless the purchase is to be made for all cash. Some boards also have the right of first refusal, allowing the corporation a chance to buy back an apartment by meeting any bona fide offer from a prospective buyer.

As with a condominium, the owner of a cooperative has all the income tax advantages that accrue to the owner of a single home. That portion of maintenance charges attributable to property taxes and mortgage interest may be taken as deductions.

Outside the New York metropolitan area, cooperatives are most often found in parts of Chicago, San Francisco, Miami, and Buffalo. They are being used for conversion of resort property (motels, for example) in parts of Long Island.

Cooperative living tends to develop somewhat differently than condominium occupancy. Long-term stability of tenants is common. The corporation retains the right to accept or reject any new owner. This provision is aimed at safeguarding present owners who would share financial responsibility for a defaulting neighbor but it is often used to maintain a particular level of occupancy. Thus, not long after Watergate, residents of a New York City cooperative rejected a proposed sale to Richard Nixon on the grounds that they simply did not want him as a neighbor.

Townhouses

The term **townhouse,** as it refers to shared housing, describes a type of ownership rather than an architectural style. Although the organization, similar to a **planned unit development,** often does take the form of townhouses (attached row houses), it also may refer to attached ranch homes or even to small single dwellings in close proximity. A townhouse owner has title to the land below the individual unit; other areas are owned in common.

Construction and Conversion

Until about 1977 the majority of cooperatives and condominiums were new construction. Since then, particularly in the New York City area, most are **conversions** from rental properties. The sale of any form of shared housing is considered a **public offering** and is under the jurisdiction of the New York Attorney General's office. The **sponsor,** the organizer of the proposed project, files a **declaration** with the county clerk that contains a complete description of the proposed land, buildings, and individual units. If the proposal is for a condominium, floor plans for each unit are included. Common elements are described and the percentage of ownership for each unit is stated.

Bylaws

Also included in the enabling declaration are the plans for the governing homeowners association and its **bylaws.** By statute, the bylaws must contain numerous provisions concerning the election, term of office, compensation and powers of the **board of managers** and officers. Provisions for meetings, quorums, budget, collection of charges and assessments, use of common property, and architectural control are included, along with procedures for the collection of unpaid charges. The developer also submits a list of the covenants, conditions, and regulations.

Whether for new construction or a conversion, the developer or sponsor must file a **disclosure statement** with the Attorney General's office. The statement includes an architect's or engineer's report, statement of past or projected expenses, prices for each unit and expected amount of tax deductions, management arrangements, description of the corporation (if a cooperative), and master deed and sample unit deed (for a condominium). The declaration is also forwarded with the disclosure statement.

After it has been reviewed by the Attorney General's office, the preliminary **prospectus** (red herring) is available for inspection by present tenants. At this point it is subject to modification. When the plan is accepted for filing by the Attorney General's office, it is issued as a **black book** to potential buyers.

Conversion Restrictions

If the property is occupied, special regulations safeguarding the rights of tenants are in effect in New York City, Westchester, Nassau, and Rockland counties. Under a **noneviction plan,** unless at least 15 percent of present tenants furnish the sponsor with **letters of intent** to purchase their units, the property may not be converted to condominium or cooperative ownership. If the sponsor intends to evict present tenants (**eviction plan**) at the expiration of their leases, the requirement is that at least 51 percent of the tenants must evince their intention to purchase. Depending upon which regulations have been adopted by various communities, areas in Westchester, Rockland, and Nassau counties may require either 51 percent or 35 percent tenant participation for an eviction plan. Other communities across the state are eligible to adopt the regulations if they choose. Exempt from eviction are disabled persons and those over 62 who have occupied the apartments for at least two years and have income under $50,000 a year. To encourage tenant participation, the sponsor may offer discounts averaging one-third off the list price.

Nonpurchasers may have three-year protection from eviction, and tenants in occupancy have a 90-day exclusive-right-to-purchase and other benefits. In 1983 the state empowered town, city, and village governments elsewhere in the state to pass noneviction prohibitions for the elderly and disabled.

If the sponsor elects the noneviction (15 percent) route, all those tenants who do not wish to purchase remain as tenants under whatever rent regulations may be in effect.

The sponsor's inside sales staff, working as employees, do not require any license. In contrast, the broker who sells new condominiums, townhouses, or cooperatives, as an agent and not as an employee of the sponsor, must file with the Department of Law for a modified form of securities license. Application includes the submission of a work history and a photograph; the license is good for a four-year period and costs $100 for a broker and $25 for associates.

Timesharing

A relatively new form of ownership known as **timesharing** has become popular in resort and vacation areas in recent years, with annual sales topping $1 billion. The buyer of a timeshare receives a fraction of a year's ownership of property that might be a condominium, townhouse, single-family detached home, campground, or even a motel. In some cases only right-to-use is purchased rather than fee simple.

While the concept is most popular in resort areas such as the Caribbean, Colorado, Vermont, and Florida, it has been used in Long Island, the Catskills, and a few other areas of New York State. The property owner is entitled to some income tax deductions and can exchange, sell, or rent the time-slot subject only to any restrictions in the prospectus of the organization administering the property. As many as 13, 26, or 52 different owners might share a unit at designated times of the year. Each owner receives a deed entitling use of the property for a specified period each year.

In New York, timesharing is regulated under Article 23-A of the General Business Law (*blue-sky securities statute*) administered by the Department of Law and the Department of State. Sellers must file a public offering statement and buyers have a 10-day rescission period in which to withdraw from a contract. Real estate licenses are required of those handling such sales.

Summary

Condominium and *cooperative* arrangements for homeowning are becoming more frequent due to scarcity of land, the need for economy of construction and operation, and changing lifestyles. Both terms refer to forms of ownership and not to the type of buildings involved.

Condominiums provide *fee simple* ownership of the living unit and an undivided interest of common elements. The owner may mortgage the unit, receives individual tax bills, and arranges homeowners insurance. Owners bear no direct financial liability for adjoining units. Management of common elements is administered by a homeowners association, which levies monthly fees. Bylaws provide regulations binding upon all owners in the form of *convenants, conditions, and restrictions.*

The owner of a *cooperative* apartment receives *shares in a corporation* that owns the entire building, and a *proprietary lease* to his or her apartment. Financing is arranged through a single mortgage on the entire property; individual financing comes through personal loans. Each owner shares responsibility for the debts of the corporation. The corporation has the right to reject prospective buyers.

A *townhouse development* involves fee simple ownership of the living unit and the land below it. All other land and common elements are owned by a homeowners association in which owners are members.

Plans for construction or conversion of a condominium or cooperative must be filed with the *county recorder* and reviewed by the *Attorney General*'s office. In the New York City area at least 15 percent of present tenants must agree to buy their apartments before conversion may take place. If *eviction* is planned, at least 51 percent must agree to buy. Differing regulations in parts of Westchester, Rockland, and Nassau counties (and some Upstate communities) may require 51 percent or 35 percent tenant participation. Certain *disabled persons* and *senior citizens* are exempt from eviction in any case.

Timesharing involves the fee simple purchase of a resort or vacation property for a portion of the year.

Questions

1. Condominium living provides:
   a. economy of construction and operation.
   b. increased square footage per occupant.
   c. accelerated cost recovery.
   d. inexpensive vacations.

2. A high-rise building is most likely to be organized as:
   a. a condominium project.
   b. a cooperative development.
   c. rented apartments.
   d. Any of the above

3. A separate tax account number, insurance policy, and mortgage are available to the owner of a:
   a. cooperative apartment.
   b. condominium.
   c. Both of the above
   d. Neither of the above

4. Common elements include:
   a. stairwells.   c. foyers.
   b. swimming pool.   d. All of the above

5. The term *CC&R* refers to:
   a. clubhouse, courts, and recreation.
   b. covenants, conditions, and restrictions.
   c. Chesapeake, Charleston, and Richmond.
   d. contracts, citations, and releases.

6. The owner of a cooperative apartment receives:
   a. a deed.
   b. a property tax bill.
   c. fee simple title.
   d. shares in a corporation.

7. Condominium units in New York may be held:
   a. by one person.
   b. by joint tenants.
   c. by tenants in common.
   d. by any of the above.

8. The right to reject prospective new owners is held by the board of directors of a:
   a. townhouse.   c. cooperative.
   b. timeshare.   d. condominium.

9. The land immediately under the unit is owned individually in a:
   a. condominium.   c. townhouse.
   b. cooperative.   d. timeshare.

10. A declaration must be accepted by the:
    a. sponsor.
    b. Attorney General.
    c. homeowners association.
    d. Department of State.

11. The changing of a rental building into shared ownership is called:
    a. conversion.   c. disclosure.
    b. declaration.   d. offering.

12. Restrictions may be set on exterior architectural changes by the association of a:
    a. condominium.
    b. cooperative.
    c. planned unit development.
    d. All of the above

13. What percentage of New York City tenants must plan to buy before an existing development is changed to a condominium or cooperative under a noneviction plan?
    a. Ten percent   c. 35 percent
    b. 15 percent   d. 51 percent

14. In New York City what percentage of tenants must plan to buy before other tenants may be evicted at the expiration of leases?
    a. Ten percent   c. 35 percent
    b. 15 percent   d. 51 percent

15. Timesharing is a technique most often used for the shared ownership of:
    a. high-rise buildings.
    b. resort property.
    c. townhouses.
    d. office buildings.

21

Property Management—Rent Regulations

Key Terms

Business interruption insurance
Casualty insurance
Certified Property Manager (CPM)
Contents and personal property insurance
Decontrol
Department of Housing and Community
 Renewal (DHCR)
Fire and hazard insurance
Liability insurance

Management agreement
Multiperil policies
Property manager
Rent control
Rent stabilization
Replacement cost
Surety bond
Workers' compensation acts

Overview

A real estate owner who rents the upstairs apartment in the building where he or she resides generally has no problem with property management—setting and collecting rents, maintenance, and repairs are easy enough with only one tenant. But the owners of large, multiunit developments often lack the time and/or expertise to manage their properties successfully. Enter the *property manager*, hired to maintain the property and ensure the profitability of the owner's investment. This chapter will examine the growing property management field and will include discussions of the types of property insurance available to further protect an owner's real estate investment. It also will discuss rent control and rent stabilization in effect in some parts of New York State.

Property Management

The need for specialized property managers began to emerge during the 1930s as lending institutions found themselves owning numerous foreclosed income properties. Lenders often lacked the expertise to administer these properties and they looked to the real estate industry for expert management assistance. In recent years the increased size of buildings, the technical complexities of construction, maintenance, and repair, and the trend toward absentee ownership by individual investors and investment groups have led to the expanded use of specialized property managers for both residential and commercial properties.

Property managers are classified as either *staff managers* who work for one owner only, or independently contracted outside *fee managers*.

Some brokerage firms maintain separate management departments. Many corporate and institutional owners of real estate also have established property management departments. Many real estate investors, however, still manage their own property and must acquire the knowledge and skills of property managers. In some instances property managers must be licensed real estate brokers.

Functions of the Property Manager

In the simplest terms a **property manager** is someone who *preserves the value of an investment property while generating income as an agent for the owners.* More specifically a property manager is expected to merchandise the property and control operating expenses so as to maximize income. In addition a manager should maintain and modernize the property to preserve and enhance the owner's capital investment. The manager carries out these objectives by: (1) securing suitable tenants, (2) collecting the rents, (3) caring for the premises, (4) budgeting and controlling expenses, (5) hiring and supervising employees, and (6) keeping proper accounts and making periodic reports to the owner.

Securing Management Business

In today's market, property managers may look to corporate owners, apartments and condominiums, investment syndicates, trusts, and absentee owners as possible sources of management business. In securing business from any of these sources, word of mouth is often the best advertising. A manager who consistently demonstrates that he or she can increase property income over previous levels should have no difficulty finding new business.

Before contracting to manage any property, the property manager should be certain that the building owner has realistic income expectations and is willing to spend money on necessary maintenance. Attempting to meet impossible owner demands by dubious methods can endanger the manager's reputation and prove detrimental to obtaining future business.

The Management Agreement

The first step in taking over the management of any property is to enter into a **management agreement** with the owner. This agreement creates an agency relationship between the owner and the property manager, just as a listing agreement creates an agency relationship between selling owner and listing broker.

The property manager, usually a general agent, is charged with the same fiduciary responsibilities as a listing broker—care, obedience, accounting, loyalty, and notice (COAL-N). (Agency responsibilities were discussed at length in Chapters 2 and 14.)

The management agreement should be in writing and should cover the following points:

1. *Description* of the property.
2. *Time period* the agreement will cover.
3. *Definition of management's responsibilities:* All of the manager's duties should be stated in the contract; exceptions should be noted.
4. *Statement of owner's purpose:* This statement should indicate what the owner desires the manager to accomplish with the property. One owner may wish to maximize net income and therefore instructs the manager to cut expenses and minimize reinvestment. Another owner may want to increase the capital value of the investment, in which case the manager should initiate a program for improving the property's physical condition.
5. *Extent of manager's authority:* This provision should state what authority the manager is to have in such matters as hiring, firing, and supervising employees, fixing rental rates for space, making expenditures, and authorizing repairs within the limits established previously with the owner.
6. *Reporting:* Agreement should be reached on the frequency and detail of the manager's periodic reports on operations and financial position. These reports serve as a means for the owner to monitor the manager's work and as a basis for both the owner and the manager to assess trends that can be used in shaping future management policy.
7. *Management fee:* The fee can be based on a percentage of gross or net income, a commission on new rentals, a fixed fee, or a combination of these.
8. *Allocation of costs:* The agreement should state which of the property manager's expenses such as office rent, office help, telephone, advertising, association fees, and social security will be paid by the manager and which will be charged to the property's expenses and paid by the owner.

After entering into an agreement with a property owner, a manager must handle the property as if it were his or her own. In all activities the manager must be aware that his or her first responsibility is to *realize the highest return on the property that is consistent with the owner's instructions.*

Management Considerations

A property manager must protect the interest of the property owner by: (1) constantly *improving the reputation* as well as the *physical condition* of the property, (2) protecting the owner from *insurable losses,* (3) protecting the owner by helping the neighborhood and the community to offer the best possible *residential and business environments,* (4) keeping constant *check on all expenditures* to be sure that costs are kept as low as possible for the results that must be accomplished, and (5) *adjusting the rental rate* as necessary to produce the highest total income.

A property manager must live up to his or her side of the management agreement in both the letter and the spirit of the contract. The owner must be kept well informed on all matters of policy as well as on the financial condition of the property and its operation. Finally, a manager must keep in contact with others in the field, improving his or her knowledge of the subject and keeping informed on current policies pertaining to the field.

Budgeting Expenses

Before attempting to rent any property, a property manager should develop an operating budget based on anticipated revenues and expenses and reflecting the long-term goals of the owner. In preparing a budget a manager should begin by allocating money for such continuous fixed expenses as employees' salaries, property taxes, and insurance premiums.

Next the manager should establish a cash reserve fund for such variable expenses as repairs, decorating, and supplies. The amount allocated for the reserve funds can be computed from the previous yearly costs of the variable expenses.

Capital expenditures. If an owner and a property manager decide that modernization or renovation of the property would enhance its value, the manager should budget money to cover the costs of remodeling. In the case of large-scale construction the expenses charged against the property's income should be spread over several years. Budgets are usually prepared on an annual basis. Although they should be as accurate an estimate of cost as possible, adjustments may sometimes be necessary, especially in the case of new properties.

Renting the Property

Effective rental of the property is essential to the success of a property manager. However, the role of the manager in managing a property should not be confused with that of a broker or rental agency solely concerned with renting space. The property manager may use the services of a rental agency to solicit prospective tenants or collect rents but the rental agency does not undertake the full responsibility of maintenance and management of the properties.

Setting rental rates. In establishing rental rates for a property, a basic concern must be that, in the long term, the income from the rentable space covers the fixed charges and operating expenses and also provides a fair return on the investment. Consideration must also be given to the prevailing rates in comparable buildings and the current level of vacancy in the property to be rented. In the short term, rental rates are primarily a result of supply and demand. Decisions about rental rates should start with a detailed survey of the competitive space available in the neighborhood. Prices should be noted and judgment should be applied to adjust for differences between neighboring properties and the properties the manager will manage.

While apartment rental rates are stated in monthly amounts, office and commercial space rentals are typically stated according to either the annual or the monthly rate per square foot of space.

If a high level of vacancy exists, an immediate effort should be made to determine what is wrong with the property or what is out of line in the rental rates. *A high level of vacancy does not necessarily indicate that rents are too high.* The trouble may be inept management or defects in the property. The manager should attempt to identify and correct the problems rather than lower the rent. Conversely, *while a high percentage of occupancy may appear to indicate an effective rental program, it also could mean that rental rates are too low.* With an apartment house or office building, any time the occupancy level exceeds 95 percent serious consideration should be given to raising the costs.

Tenant selection. The highest rents can be secured from satisfied tenants. While a broker may sell a property and then have no further dealings with the purchaser, a building manager must continue to deal with each tenant, and success is dependent on sound, long-term relationships. In selecting prospective commercial or industrial tenants, a manager should be sure that each person will "fit the space." The manager should be certain that: (1) the *size of the space* meets the tenant's requirements, (2) the tenant will have the *ability to pay* for the space for which he or she contracts, (3) the *tenant's business will be compatible* with the building and the other tenants, and (4) if the tenant is likely to expand in the future, there will be *expansion space available.* After a prospect becomes a tenant *the manager must be sure that the tenant remains satisfied in all respects commensurate with fair business dealing.*

In selecting tenants the property manager must comply with all federal and local fair housing laws (*see* Chapter 10). The requirement of a bonus or *key money* for showing or renting an apartment is illegal in New York and could result in loss of license.

Collecting rents. A building will not be a profitable operation unless the property manager can collect all rents when they are due. Any substantial loss resulting from nonpayment of rent quickly will eliminate the margin of profitability in an operation.

The best way to minimize problems with rent collection is to make a *careful selection* of tenants in the first place. A property manager's desire to have a high level of occupancy should not override good judgment in accepting only those tenants who can be expected to meet their financial obligations to the property owner. A property manager should investigate financial references given by the prospect, local credit bureaus, and, when possible, the prospective tenant's former landlord.

The terms of rental payment should be spelled out in detail in the lease agreement. These details include the time and place of payment, provisions and penalties for late payment, and provisions for cancellation and damages in case of nonpayment. A *firm and consistent collection plan* with a sufficient system of notices and records should be established by the property manager. In cases of delinquency every attempt must be made to make collections without resorting to legal action. However, for those cases in which it is required, a property manager must be prepared to initiate and follow through with the necessary steps in conjunction with the property owner's or management firm's legal counsel.

Maintaining the Property

One of the most important functions of a property manager is the supervision of property maintenance. A manager must learn to balance services provided with the costs they entail so as to satisfy the tenants' needs while minimizing operating expenses.

The broad term *maintenance* actually covers several types of activities. First, the manager must *protect the physical integrity of the property* to ensure that the condition of the building and its grounds are kept at present levels. Over the long term, preserving the property by repainting the exterior or replacing the heating plant will help to keep the building functional and decrease routine maintenance costs.

A property manager must also *supervise the routine cleaning and repairs* of the building. Day-to-day duties like cleaning common areas, minor carpentry and plumbing, and regularly scheduled upkeep of heating, air conditioning, and landscaping are generally handled by regular building employees or by outside firms that have contracted with the manager to provide certain services.

In addition, especially when dealing with commercial or industrial space, a property manager will be called on to *alter the interior of the building to meet the functional demands of the tenant.* These alterations range from repainting to completely gutting the interior and redesigning the space. The property manager enlists outside help from architects, space planners, engineers, and energy specialists as necessary.

Designing interior space is especially important when renting new buildings because the interior is usually left incomplete so that it can be adapted to the needs of the individual tenants. Another portion of a manager's responsibility is the supervision of modernization or renovation of buildings that have become functionally obsolete and thus unsuited to today's building needs. (*See* Chapter 16 for a definition of *functional obsolescence*.) The renovation of a building often increases the building's marketability and its possible income.

Employees versus contracted services. One of the major decisions a property manager faces is whether to contract for maintenance services from an outside firm or hire on-site employees to perform such tasks. This decision should be based on a number of factors including size of the building, complexity of tenants' requirements, and availability of suitable labor. In a large building or one where the tenants have sophisticated needs, a property manager may find that it is necessary to keep a large on-site crew to deal with the day-to-day operations of the property; in a small apartment building, one full-time janitor can handle most everyday problems.

Tenants' Rights

New York's Multiple Dwelling Law, in effect in New York City and Buffalo, sets the following requirements for buildings with three or more living units: automatic self-closing and self-locking doors, two-way voice buzzers (for buildings with eight or more units), mirrors in each self-service elevator, and peepholes and chain door-guards on the entrance door of each apartment. Tenants may install their own additional locks but must provide the landlord with a duplicate key upon request. Heat must be provided from October 1 to May 31. Additional regulations apply in various communities.

Postal regulations require landlords of buildings with three or more units to provide secure mailboxes. The majority of municipalities have smoke detector regulations. In New York City, tenants with children under 11 years of age must receive window-guards upon request. Protective guards also must be installed on all public hall windows.

Throughout the state the landlord of a building with three or more apartments must keep the apartments and public areas in good repair, maintaining electrical, plumbing, sanitary, heating, and ventilating systems in good working order. Landlords also must maintain appliances that are furnished to tenants. Landlords have a legal duty to keep buildings free of vermin, dirt, or garbage.

A landlord may enter the tenant's apartment only with reasonable prior notice, to provide repairs or service, in accordance with the lease, or to show the apartment to prospective tenants or purchasers. The landlord may enter without prior permission only in an emergency.

Mobile home park tenants. Mobile home park tenants must be offered at least a one-year written lease. If they do not have leases, they are entitled to 90 days' written notice before rent increases. Rules must not be changed without 30 days' written notice. Late rent payment charges are limited to five percent, after a ten-day grace period.

Owners may not discriminate against mobile home tenants with children. Owners have the right to sell their homes within the park with the consent of the park owner, which consent may not be unreasonably withheld. Park owners cannot require any fee or commission in connection with the sale of a mobile home unless they act as sales agent pursuant to a written contract. Owners may not foster park monopolies.

Loft tenants. Loft tenants in New York City are protected by the rent stabilization law. The owner's costs incurred in complying with the city's building code may be passed on to tenants over a ten-year or 15-year period. Improvements made by the tenant remain the tenant's property. When tenants leave, they must first offer the improvements to the landlord at fair market value. If the landlord refuses the offer, the tenant may sell improvements to the incoming tenant.

Insurance

One of the most important responsibilities of a property manager is to protect the property owner against all major insurable risks. In some cases a property manager or a member of the firm may be a licensed insurance broker. In any case a competent, reliable insurance agent who is well-versed in all areas of insurance pertaining to property should be selected to survey the property and make recommendations. If the manager is not completely satisfied with these recommendations, additional insurance surveys should be obtained. Final decisions, however, must be made by the property owner. *An insurance broker must have passed a state examination to secure a special license to sell insurance.*

Types of Coverage

Many kinds of insurance coverage are available to the income-property owners and managers. Some of the more common types are:

1. **Fire and hazard:** Fire insurance policies provide coverage against direct loss or damage to property from a fire on the premises. Standard fire coverage can be extended to cover hazards such as windstorm, hail, smoke damage, or civil insurrection. Most popular today is the *all-risks* or *special form.*
2. **Business interruption:** Most hazard policies insure against the actual loss of property but do not cover loss of revenues from income property. Interruption insurance covers the loss of income that occurs if the property cannot be used to produce income.
3. **Contents and personal property:** *Inland marine insurance* covers building contents and personal property during periods when they are not actually located on the business premises.
4. **Liability:** Public liability insurance covers the risks an owner assumes when the public enters the building. Medical expenses are paid for a person injured in the building as a result of the landlord's negligence. Another liability risk is that of medical or hospital payments for injuries sustained by building employees hurt in the course of their employment. These claims are cov-

ered by state laws known as **Workers' Compensation Acts.** These laws require a building owner who is an employer to obtain a workers' compensation policy from a private insurance company.

5. **Casualty:** Casualty insurance policies include coverage against theft, burglary, vandalism, machinery damage, and health and accident insurance. Casualty policies usually are written on specific risks such as theft, rather than being all-inclusive.

6. **Surety bonds:** Surety bonds cover an owner against financial losses resulting from an employee's criminal acts or negligence while carrying out his or her duties. A *blanket crime policy* is most often chosen.

7. **Boiler and machinery coverage:** This covers repair and replacement of heating plants, central air-conditioning units, and major equipment.

Lower premiums may be offered property that qualifies as a *highly protected risk (HPR)* based on the quality of water supply, sprinklers, alarms, security personnel, and loss-control programs.

Many insurance companies offer **multiperil policies** for apartment and business buildings. These include standard types of commercial coverage: fire, hazard, public liability, and casualty.

Claims

When a claim is made under a policy insuring a building or other physical object, either of two methods can determine the amount of the claim. One is the *depreciated*, or actual, cash value of the damaged property and the other is replacement cost. If a 30-year-old building is damaged, the timbers and materials are 30 years old and therefore do not have the same value as new material. Thus, in determining the amount of the loss under what is called *actual cash value*, the cost of new material would be reduced by the estimated depreciation, based on the time the item had been in the building.

The alternate method is to cover **replacement cost.** This would represent the actual amount a builder would charge to replace the damaged property at the time of the loss, including materials.

When purchasing insurance, a manager must assess whether the property should be insured at full replacement cost or at a depreciated cost. As with the homeowner's policies discussed in Chapter 11, commercial policies usually carry *coinsurance clauses* that require coverage up to 80 percent of the building's replacement value.

The Management Field

For those interested in pursuing a career in property management, most large cities have local associations of building and property owners and managers that are affiliates of regional and national associations. The Institute of Real Estate Management was founded in 1933 and is part of the National Association of REALTORS®. Members may earn the designation **Certified Property Manager (CPM).** The Building Owners and Managers Association International (BOMA International) is a federation of local associations of owners and managers, primarily of office buildings. Participation in groups like these allows property managers to gain valuable professional knowledge and to discuss their problems with other managers facing similar issues. Management designation also is offered by the National Association of Home Builders, the New York Association of Building Owners, and the International Council of Shopping Centers.

A growing field is the management of cooperatives and condominiums. The manager hired by a homeowners' organization must develop different techniques because owners and tenants are one and the same. The Community Associations Institute (CAI) is a nonprofit organization founded in 1974 to research and distribute information on association living and offers training and designation for specialized management.

Rent Regulations

Rent regulation in New York State is administered by the **New York State Division of Housing and Community Renewal (DHCR)**. It includes two programs: **rent control** and **rent stabilization.**

Rent Control

Rent control dates back to the housing shortage that followed World War II and generally covers property containing three or more units constructed before February 1947 and located in one of the 64 municipalities where the system is in effect. These include New York City, Albany, Buffalo, and parts of the following counties: Albany, Erie, Nassau, Rensselaer, Schenectady, and Westchester. Table 21.1 lists participating municipalities.

**Table 21.1
Municipalities outside New York City That Are Covered by Rent Control as of 1986**

ALBANY COUNTY

Cities
Albany
Watervliet

Towns
Bethlehem
Green Island
New Scotland

Villages
Green Island
Voorheesville

ERIE COUNTY

Cities
Buffalo

Towns
Cheektowaga

Villages
Depew
Sloan

NASSAU COUNTY

Cities
Glen Cove
Long Beach

Towns
Hempstead

North Hempstead
Oyster Bay

Villages
Baxter Estates
Bayville
Bellerose
Cedarhurst
Floral Park
Freeport
Hempstead
Lawrence
Malverne
Manorhaven
Mineola
New Hyde Park
Old Westbury
Port Washington No.
Roslyn
Sea Cliff
Valley Stream
Westbury
Williston Park

RENSSELAER COUNTY

Cities
Rensselaer

Towns
Hoosick
North Greenbush

Villages
Hoosick Falls

SCHENECTADY COUNTY

Towns
Niskayuna
Princeton

WESTCHESTER COUNTY

Cities
New Rochelle
White Plains
Yonkers

Towns
Cortlandt
Eastchester
Greenburgh
Harrison
Mamaroneck
Pelham
Rye
Yorktown

Villages
Ardsley
Dobbs Ferry
Hastings-on-Hudson
Larchmont
Mamaroneck
North Tarrytown
Pelham Manor
Tarrytown
Tuckahoe

The regulations apply to an apartment continuously occupied by the present tenant since July 1, 1971 (with some exceptions in Nassau County). When such an apartment is vacated, it moves to rent stabilization status or is removed from regulation, depending on the municipality.

Rents in controlled apartments initially were based on rentals in effect when rent control was first imposed in 1943. Outside New York City the DHCR determines maximum allowable rates of rent increases, which are available to landlords every two years. Within New York City a *Maximum Base Rent (MBR)* is established for each apartment and is adjusted every two years. Landlords may raise rents by 7.5 percent each year until they reach the maximum base rental figure. Tenants may challenge proposed increases if the building has been cited for violations or the owner's expenses do not warrant an increase.

Under rent control, rent may be increased if the landlord increases services, or installs a major capital improvement, in cases of hardship, and to cover high labor and fuel costs. Rents will be reduced if the landlord fails to correct violations or reduces essential services. The law prohibits harassment of rent-controlled tenants or retaliatory eviction of tenants who exercise their right to complain to a government agency about violations of health or safety laws.

In 1985, 218,000 units in New York City remained under rent control, with another 943,000 under the later arrangement known as rent stabilization.

Rent Stabilization

In New York City, **rent stabilization** applies to apartments in buildings of six or more units constructed between February 1, 1947, and January 1, 1974. For buildings older than that, tenants are covered if they moved in after June 30, 1971. Buildings with three or more units that were constructed or extensively renovated since 1974 with special tax benefits are also subject to rent stabilization while the tax benefits continue.

Outside New York City, rent stabilization applies in those communities that have adopted the Emergency Tenant Protection Act (EPTA). Table 21.2 is a partial

---

Table 21.2
Municipalities That Have Adopted the Emergency Tenant Protection Act (Rent Stabilization) as of 1986

NASSAU COUNTY

Cities
Glen Cove
Long Beach

Towns
North Hempstead

Villages
Baxter Estates
Cedarhurst
Floral Park
Flower Hill
Freeport
Great Neck
Great Neck Estates
Great Neck Plaza
Hempstead
Lynbrook
Mineola

Rockville Center
Roslyn
Russell Gardens
Thomaston

ROCKLAND COUNTY

Towns
Haverstraw

Villages
Spring Valley

WESTCHESTER COUNTY

Cities
Mount Vernon
New Rochelle
White Plains
Yonkers

Towns
Eastchester
Greenburgh
Harrison
Mamaroneck

Villages
Dobbs Ferry
Hastings-on-Hudson
Irvington-on-Hudson
Larchmont
Mamaroneck
Mt. Kisco
North Tarrytown
Pleasantville
Port Chester
Tarrytown

list of such communities. Each community sets a limit on the size of buildings to be covered; in no case is the program applied to property with fewer than six living units.

Where rent stabilization applies, maximum allowable rent increases are set annually by local Rent Stabilization Boards. Tenants may choose one- or two-year renewal leases.

To be eligible for rent increases, owners must file an annual statement with DHCR, listing the rental for each unit under rent stabilization. Copies must be furnished to the tenants. Tenants may challenge the figures and receive a refund of any overcharges during the preceding four years. Administrative penalties for a landlord found guilty of harassment of tenants are set at $1,000 for a first offense and $2,500 thereafter.

Where units should have been registered with the DHCR and were not, any future purchaser could be liable to tenants for the refund of unauthorized rent increases. This provision is important to the real estate broker who may be handling the sale of a building that is not in compliance.

A *Senior Citizen Rent Increase Exemption (SCRIE)* is in effect for some rent-controlled and rent-stabilized apartments in New York City and in some other areas. Tenants 62 or older may qualify for full or partial exemption from rent increases if their income falls below levels set by the municipality, if they pay at least one-third of their income for rent, and if they are not on welfare. Among municipalities that have adopted the SCRIE are North Hempstead, Great Neck, Great Neck Plaza, Thomaston, Mount Vernon, New Rochelle, White Plains, Yonkers, Greenburgh, and Spring Valley.

The DHCR has set up a special unit to assist the owners of small buildings, those with fewer than 50 rental units, in filling out registration forms and with recordkeeping and bookkeeping. The Department's main office is located in the World Trade Center. District offices administering rent regulations are listed in Table 21.3.

Summary

Property management is a specialized service to owners of income-producing properties in which the managerial function may be delegated to an individual or a firm with particular expertise in the field. The manager, as agent of the owner, becomes the administrator of the property.

A *management agreement* must be carefully prepared to define and authorize the manager's duties and responsibilities.

The first step a property manager should take when managing a building is to draw up a budget of estimated variable and fixed expenses. The budget also should allow for any proposed expenditures for major renovations or modernizations. These projected expenses, combined with the manager's analysis of the condition of the building and the rent patterns in the neighborhood, will form the basis on which rental rates for the property are determined.

After a rent schedule is established, the property manager is responsible for soliciting tenants whose needs are suited to the available space and who are finan-

Table 21.3
Department of Housing and Community Renewal Offices

RENT ADMINISTRATION OFFICES

EXECUTIVE OFFICE

NEW YORK CITY
10 Columbus Circle
New York, NY 10019
(212) 307-5760

DISTRICT RENT OFFICES

LOWER MANHATTAN
(South side of 110th Street and below)
Two Lafayette Street, 12th Floor
New York, NY 10007
(212) 566-7970

UPPER MANHATTAN
(North side of 110th Street and above)
215 West 125 Street, 5th Floor
New York, NY 10027
(212) 678-2201

BRONX
260 East 161 Street, 8th Floor
Bronx, NY 10451
(212) 585-2600

BROOKLYN
91 Lawrence Street, 2nd Floor
Brooklyn, NY 11201
(718) 643-7570

QUEENS
164-19 Hillside Avenue, Ground Floor
Jamaica, NY 11432
(718) 526-2040

STATEN ISLAND
350 St. Marks Place, Room 108
Staten Island, NY 10301
(718) 816-0277

NASSAU COUNTY
50 Clinton Street, 2nd Floor
Hempstead, NY 11550
(516) 481-9494

WESTCHESTER COUNTY
99 Church Street, 4th Floor
White Plains, NY 10601
(914) 948-4434

ROCKLAND COUNTY
94-96 North Main Street
Spring Valley, NY 10977
(914) 425-6575

ALBANY, RENSSELAER AND SCHENEC-
TADY COUNTIES
Corning Tower, 22nd Floor
Empire State Plaza
Albany, NY 12220
(518) 474-8580

ERIE COUNTY
295 Main Street
Buffalo, NY 14203
(716) 847-3536

RENT HOTLINE: (212) 903-9550

cially capable of meeting the proposed rents. The manager usually is obligated to collect rents, maintain the building, hire necessary employees, pay taxes for the building, and deal with tenant problems.

One of the manager's primary responsibilities is supervising maintenance. Maintenance includes safeguarding the physical integrity of the property and performing routine cleaning and repairs as well as adapting the interior space and overall design of the property to suit the tenants' needs and meet the demands of the market.

In addition the manager is expected to secure adequate insurance coverage for the premises. The basic types of coverage applicable to commercial structures include *fire and hazard insurance* on the property and fixtures, *business interruption insurance* to protect the owner against income losses, and *casualty insurance* to provide coverage against such losses as theft, vandalism, and destruction of machinery. The manager also should secure *public liability insurance* to insure the owner against claims made by people injured on the premises and *workers' compensation policies* to cover the claims of employees injured on the job.

The Multiple Dwelling Law in New York City and Buffalo sets health and safety standards for apartment buildings. Local communities have additional regulations. The state also regulates mobile home parks.

The Institute of Real Estate Management, a branch of the National Association of REALTORS®, awards the most widely recognized designation in the field, the *CPM, Certified Property Manager.*

Rent regulations in New York are administered by the *Department of Housing and Community Renewal (DHCR). Rent control* is in effect in some localities around New York City, Albany, and Buffalo. A less rigid *rent stabilization* program applies in New York City, and as the *Emergency Tenant Protection Act* in parts of Nassau, Rockland, and Westchester counties. The tenant who successfully challenges rent overcharges may collect a rebate for *four years* past and may not be harassed or evicted.

Questions

1. An owner-manager agreement should include:

   a. a statement of the owner's purpose for the building.

   b. a clear definition of the manager's authority.

   c. agreement on what portion of the property manager's personal operating expenses will be paid by the owner.

   d. All of the above

2. An operating budget for income property usually is prepared on what basis?

   a. Daily   c. Monthly

   b. Weekly   d. Annual

3. In the absence of rent regulations the amount of rent charged is determined by:

   a. the management agreement.

   b. supply and demand.

   c. the operating budget.

   d. the toss of a coin.

4. Office rentals usually are figured by the:

   a. front foot.

   b. amount of desk space.

   c. number of rooms.

   d. square foot.

5. From a management point of view, apartment building occupancy that reaches as high as 98 percent would tend to indicate that:

   a. the building is poorly managed.

   b. the building is well-managed.

   c. the building is a desirable place to live.

   d. rents should be raised.

6. Which of the following should *not* be a consideration in selecting a tenant?

   a. The size of the space versus the tenant's requirements

   b. The tenant's ability to pay

   c. The racial and ethnic backgrounds of the tenants

   d. The compatibility of the tenant's business to other tenants' businesses

7. A property manager may be reimbursed with:

   a. a percentage of rentals.

   b. rebates from suppliers.

   c. key money.

   d. Any of the above

8. In some situations, municipal or state law may require a landlord to install:

   a. elevator mirrors.

   b. window guards.

   c. intercoms and buzzers.

   d. All of the above

9. While her tenants are at work, Laura Landlady may enter their apartment:

   a. to leave them a note.

   b. to check on their housekeeping.

   c. in case of fire.

   d. All of the above

10. Which insurance insures the property owner against the claims of employees injured on the job?

    a. Business interruption

    b. Workers' compensation

    c. Casualty

    d. Surety bond

11. A deliveryman slips on a defective stair in an apartment building and is hospitalized. A claim against the building owner for medical expenses will be made under which of the following policies held by the owner?

    a. Workers' compensation

    b. Casualty

    c. Liability

    d. Fire and hazard

12. Property manager Frieda Jacobs hires Albert
    Weston as the full-time janitor for one of
    the buildings she manages. While repairing a
    faucet in one of the apartments, Weston
    steals a television set. Jacobs could protect the
    owner against liability for this type of loss
    by purchasing:
    a. liability insurance.
    b. workers' compensation insurance.
    c. a surety bond.
    d. casualty insurance.

13. The initials CPM stand for:
    a. chargeback percentage mortgage.
    b. contract priority maintenance.
    c. Certified Property Manager.
    d. cardiopulmonary manipulation.

14. Rent regulations in this state are administered
    by:
    a. the New York City Housing Bureau.
    b. the Department of State.
    c. HUD.
    d. the New York Department of Housing and
       Community Renewal.

15. Rent control regulations are found mainly
    around:
    a. the Adirondacks.
    b. the Southern tier.
    c. the Finger Lakes.
    d. the New York City area.

16. When the original tenant dies or moves out, a
    rent-controlled apartment may become eli-
    gible for:
    a. rent control.
    b. rent stabilization.
    c. comparative hardship.
    d. freeze.

17. The rent stabilization program is known out-
    side New York City as:
    a. ETPA.   c. CPR.
    b. DHCR.   d. HPR.

18. A rent stabilization tenant may collect unau-
    thorized overcharges going back how far?
    a. Six months   c. Four years
    b. Two years   d. Indefinitely

19. Jim Ordway should have registered his Man-
    hattan apartment building for rent stabiliza-
    tion but he failed to do so. He sells it to Sam
    Simple. Tenants may file to collect their past
    rent increases from:
    a. the City of New York.
    b. the Department of Housing and Commu-
       nity Renewal.
    c. Jim.
    d. Sam.

20. The DHCR considers small apartment build-
    ings to be those with fewer than:
    a. three units.   c. 50 units.
    b. eight units.   d. 100 units.

Leases and Agreements

Key Terms

Actual eviction
Constructive eviction
Demising clause
Estate for years
Gross lease
Ground lease
Holdover tenancy
Lease
Leasehold estate
Lessee

Lessor
Month-to-month tenancy
Net lease
Percentage lease
Periodic estate
Sublease
Suit for possession
Tenancy at sufferance
Tenancy at will
Warrant of habitability

Overview

When an owner of real property does not wish to use the property personally or wants to derive some measure of income from it, he or she can allow it to be used by another person in exchange for consideration. Any type of real property may be leased. This chapter will examine the various leasehold estates a landlord and a tenant may enter into and the types and specific provisions of lease agreements commonly used in the real estate business.

Leasing Real Estate

A **lease** is a contract between an owner of real estate (known as the **lessor**) and a tenant (the **lessee**) that transfers the right to exclusive possession and use of the owner's property to the tenant for a specified period of time. This agreement sets forth the length of time the contract is to run, the amount to be paid by the lessee for the right to use the property, and other rights and obligations of the parties.

In effect the lease agreement is a combination of a conveyance (of an interest in the real estate) and a contract (to pay rent and assume other obligations). The landlord grants the tenant the right to occupy the premises and use them for purposes stated in the lease. In return the landlord retains the right to receive payment for the use of the premises as well as a *reversionary right* to retake possession after the lease term has expired.

The statute of frauds requires that a *lease for a term of more than one year must be written* to be enforceable. It also should be signed by both lessor and lessee. A lease for one year or less is enforceable if it is entered into orally.

Leasehold Estates

A tenant's right to occupy land is called a **leasehold estate.** A leasehold estate is considered personal property in New York.

Just as there are several types of freehold (ownership) estates, there are various leasehold estates. The four most important are: (1) estate for years; (2) periodic estate, or estate from period to period; (3) tenancy at will; and (4) tenancy at sufferance (*see* Table 22.1). All are recognized in New York State.

Table 22.1 Leasehold Estates

Type of Estate	Distinguishing Characteristics
Estate for Years	For Definite Period of Time
Periodic Estate	Automatically Renews
Tenancy at Will	For Indefinite Period of Time
Tenancy at Sufferance	Without Landlord's Consent

Estate for Years

A leasehold estate that continues for a *definite period of time* is an **estate for years.** When a definite term is specified in a written or oral lease and that period of time expires, the lessee is required to vacate the premises and surrender possession to the lessor. *No notice is required* to terminate such a lease at the end of the term. A lease for years may be terminated prior to the expiration date by the mutual consent of both parties but otherwise neither party may terminate without showing that the lease agreement has been breached.

An estate for years need not necessarily last for years or even for one year. Its distinguishing characteristic is that it begins and ends at a specific time.

Periodic Estates

Periodic estates, sometimes called *estates from period to period*, are created when the landlord and tenant enter into an agreement that continues for an *indefinite length of time without a specific expiration date;* rent, however, is payable at definite intervals. These tenancies generally run for a certain amount of time; for instance, month to month, week to week, or year to year. The agreement is automatically renewed for similar succeeding periods until one of the parties gives notice to terminate.

A **month-to-month tenancy** is created when a tenant takes possession with no definite termination date and pays rent on a monthly basis.

A tenancy from year to year is created when a tenant for a term of years remains in possession, or holds over, after the expiration of the lease term. When no new lease agreement has been made, the landlord may evict the tenant if he or she chooses, or may acquiesce in the **holdover tenancy.**

A New York tenant who remains in possession of leased premises after giving notice of his or her intention to quit the premises (holding over) may be held liable for double rent if he or she holds possession beyond the date stated in the notice. When the lease term is longer than one month, the landlord may commence proceedings to remove a tenant who has held over. The subsequent acceptance of rent by the landlord will create a tenancy from month to month. Some leases stipulate that in the absence of a renewal agreement, a tenant who holds over does so as a month-to-month tenant.

In order to *terminate* a periodic estate, either the landlord or the tenant must give *proper notice*. To end a month-to-month tenancy New York State requires one month's written notice; New York City requires 30 days' notice, from the day the rent is due (usually the first of the month).

Tenancy at Will

An estate that gives the tenant the right to possess with the *consent of the landlord* is a **tenancy at will.** It may be created by express agreement or by operation of law, and during its existence the tenant has all the rights and obligations of a lessor-lessee relationship including the payment of rent at regular intervals.

For example, at the end of a lease period a landlord informs a tenant that in a few months the city is going to demolish the apartment building to make way for an expressway. The landlord gives the tenant the option to occupy the premises until demolition begins. If the tenant agrees to stay, a tenancy at will is created. The term of an estate at will is indefinite but the estate may be terminated by giving proper notice. An estate at will is automatically terminated by the death of either the landlord or the tenant.

Tenancy at Sufferance

A **tenancy at sufferance** arises when a tenant who lawfully came into possession of real property continues, after his or her rights have expired, to hold possession of the premises *without the consent of the landlord.* Two examples of estates at sufferance are: (1) when a tenant for years *fails to surrender* possession at the expiration of the lease and (2) when a mortgagor, without consent of the purchaser, continues in possession after the foreclosure sale. The latter example is a tenancy at sufferance *by operation of law*. In New York a tenant may be charged up to double rent for the period while he or she was in possession as a tenant at sufferance after notice to quit the premises had been given.

Standard Lease Provisions

In determining the validity of a lease the courts apply the rules governing contracts. If the intention to convey temporary possession of a certain parcel of real estate from one person to another is expressed, the courts generally hold that a lease has been created. The lease may be written, oral, or implied, depending on the circumstances. However, the provisions of the statutes of the state where the real estate is located must be followed to assure the validity of the lease. The apartment lease shown in Figure 22.1 includes a rider required for New York City (Rent Stabilization Rider, Figure 22.2) New York State requires a *plain English* format.

The requirements for a valid lease are essentially the same as those for any other real estate contract. In New York the essentials of a valid lease are:

1. *Capacity to contract:* The parties must be sane adults.
2. A *demising clause:* The lessor to let and the lessee to take the premises.
3. *Description of the premises:* A description of the leased premises should be clearly stated. If the lease covers land, the legal description of the real estate should be used. If on the other hand the lease is for a part of the building, such as office space or an apartment, the space itself should be clearly and carefully described. If supplemental space is to be included, the lease should clearly identify it.
4. A clear statement of the *term* (duration) of the lease.
5. *Specification of the rent and how it is to be paid.* In New York, unless the lease states otherwise, rent is considered due in arrears, rather than in advance.
6. The *lease must be in writing* if it is to be for more than one year.
7. *Signatures:* To be valid a lease must be signed by both parties.

Use of Premises

A lessor may restrict a lessee's use of the premises through provisions included in the lease. This is most important in leases for stores or commercial space. For example, a lease may provide that the leased premises are to be used *only* for the purpose of a real estate office *and for no other*. In the absence of such limitations a lessee may use the premises for any lawful purpose.

Term of Lease

The term of a lease is the period for which the lease will run and it should be set out precisely. The date of the beginning of the term and the date of its ending should be stated together with a statement of the total period of the lease: for example, "for a term of thirty years beginning June 1, 1988 and ending May 31, 2018." Courts do not favor leases with an indefinite term and will hold that such perpetual leases are not valid unless the language of the lease and the surrounding circumstances clearly indicate that such is the intention of the parties.

Security Deposits

Most leases require the tenant to provide some form of security. This security, which guarantees payment of rent and safeguards against a tenant's destruction of the premises, may be established by: (1) contracting for a lien on the tenant's property, (2) requiring the tenant to pay a portion of the rent in advance, (3) requiring the tenant to post security, and/or (4) requiring the tenant to have a third person guarantee the payment of the rent. Where trade fixtures are to be installed, the landlord may want an extra deposit to ensure that the property will be restored to its original state when they are removed.

Figure 22.1
Apartment Lease

T 327—Apartment lease, stabilization clauses, plain English format, 8½ pt. type, 4-84.
PREPARED BY ARNOLD MANDELL, LL.B.

© 1978 BY JULIUS BLUMBERG, INC., PUBLISHER, NYC 10013
Use with Blumberg T326 Rent Stabilization Rider

APARTMENT LEASE

Attached to this lease are the pertinent rules and regulations governing tenants and landlords' rights under the rent stabilization law.

The Landlord and Tenant agree as of.................................... **19**......... **to lease the Apartment as follows:**

LANDLORD: ....

Address for Notices....................................

TENANT: ....

Apartment (and terrace, if any)..................... at....................................

Bank....................................

Term....................	**beginning**.................... **19**........	**ending**.................... **19**........	
Yearly Rent $....................	**Monthly Rent** $....................	**Security** $....................	

1. Use The Apartment must be used only as a private Apartment to live in as the primary residence of the Tenant and for no other reason. Only a party signing this Lease may use the Apartment. This is subject to Tenant's rights under the Apartment Sharing Law and to limits on the number of people who may legally occupy an Apartment of this size.

2. Failure to give possession Landlord shall not be liable for failure to give Tenant possession of the Apartment on the beginning date of the Term. Rent shall be payable as of the beginning of the Term unless Landlord is unable to give possession. Rent shall then be payable as of the date possession is available. Landlord must give possession within a reasonable time, if not, Tenant may cancel and obtain a refund of money deposited. Landlord will notify Tenant as to the date possession is available. The ending date of the Term will not change.

3. Rent, added rent The rent payment for each month must be paid on the first day of that month at Landlord's address. Landlord need not give notice to pay the rent. Rent must be paid in full without deduction. The first month's rent is to be paid when Tenant signs this Lease. Tenant may be required to pay other charges to Landlord under the terms of this Lease. They are called "added rent." This added rent will be billed and is payable as rent, together with the next monthly rent due. If Tenant fails to pay the added rent on time, Landlord shall have the same rights against Tenant as if Tenant failed to pay rent.

4. Notices Any bill, statement or notice must be in writing. If to Tenant, it must be delivered or mailed to the Tenant at the Apartment. If to Landlord it must be mailed to Landlord's address. It will be considered delivered on the day mailed or if not mailed, when left at the proper address. A notice must be sent by certified mail. Each party must accept and claim the notice given by the other. Landlord must notify Tenant if Landlord's address is changed.

5. Security Tenant has given security to Landlord in the amount stated above. The security has been deposited in the Bank named above and delivery of this Lease is notice of the deposit. If the Bank is not named, Landlord will notify Tenant of the Bank's name and address in which the security is deposited.

If Tenant does not pay rent or added rent on time, Landlord may use the security to pay for rent and added rent then due. If Tenant fails to timely perform any other term in this Lease, Landlord may use the security for payment of money Landlord may spend, or damages Landlord suffers because of Tenant's failure. If the Landlord uses the security Tenant, shall, upon notice from Landlord, send to Landlord an amount equal to the sum used by Landlord. That amount is due, when billed, as rent. At all times Landlord is to have the amount of security stated above.

If Tenant fully performs all terms of this Lease, pays rent on time and leaves the Apartment in good condition on the last day of the Term, then Landlord will return the security being held.

If Landlord sells or leases the Building, Landlord may give the security to the buyer or lessee. In that event Tenant will look only to the buyer or lessee for the return of the security and Landlord will be deemed released. The Landlord may use the security as stated in this section. Landlord may put the security in any place permitted by law. Tenant's security will bear interest only if required by law. Landlord will give Tenant the interest when Landlord is required to return the security to Tenant. Any interest returned to Tenant will be less the sum Landlord is allowed to keep for expenses. Landlord need not give Tenant interest on the security if Tenant is in default.

6. Services Landlord will supply: (a) heat as required by law, (b) hot and cold water for bathroom and kitchen sink, (c) use of elevator, if any, and (d) cooling if central air conditioning is installed. Landlord is not required to install air-conditioning. Stopping or reducing of service(s) will not be reason for Tenant to stop paying rent, to make a money claim or to claim eviction. Tenant may enforce its rights under the warranty of habitability. Damage to the equipment or appliances supplied by Landlord, caused by Tenant's act or neglect, may be repaired by Landlord at Tenant's expense. The repair cost will be added rent.

Tenant must pay for all electric, gas, telephone and other utility services used in the Apartment and arrange for them with the public utility company. Tenant must not use a dishwasher, washing machine, dryer, freezer, heater, ventilator, air cooling equipment or other appliance unless installed by Landlord or with Landlord's written consent. Tenant must not use more electric than the wiring or feeders to the Building can safely carry.

Landlord may stop service of the plumbing, heating, elevator, air cooling or electrical systems, because of accident, emergency, repairs, or changes until the work is complete.

If Landlord wants to change a person operated elevator to an automatic elevator, Landlord may stop service on 10 days' notice. Landlord will then have a reasonable time to begin installation of an automatic type elevator.

7. Alteration Tenant must obtain Landlord's prior written consent to install any panelling, flooring, "built in" decorations, partitions, railings, or make alterations or to paint or wallpaper the Apartment. Tenant must not change the plumbing, ventilating, air conditioning, electric or heating systems. If consent is given, the alterations and installations shall become the property of Landlord when completed and paid for. They shall remain with and as part of the Apartment at the end of the Term. Landlord has the right to demand that Tenant remove the alterations and installations before the end of the Term. The demand shall be by notice, given at least 15 days before the end of the Term. Tenant shall comply with the demand at Tenant's own cost. Landlord is not required to do or pay for any work unless stated in this Lease.

If a lien is filed on the Apartment or Building for any reason relating to Tenant's fault, Tenant must immediately pay or bond the amount stated in the Lien. Landlord may pay or bond the lien if Tenant fails to do so within 20 days after Tenant has notice about the Lien. Landlord's costs shall be added rent.

8. Repairs Tenant must take good care of the Apartment and all equipment and fixtures in it. Landlord will repair the plumbing, heating and electrical systems. Tenant must, at Tenant's cost, make all repairs and replacements whenever the need results from Tenant's act or neglect. If Tenant fails to make a needed repair or replacement, Landlord may do it. Landlord's reasonable expense will be added rent.

9. Fire, accident, defects, damage Tenant must give Landlord prompt notice of fire, accident, damage or dangerous or defective condition. If the Apartment can not be used because of fire or other casualty, Tenant is not required to pay rent for the time the Apartment is unusable. If part of the Apartment can not be used, Tenant must pay rent for the usable part. Landlord shall have the right to decide which part of the Apartment is usable. Landlord need only repair the damaged part of the Apartment. Landlord is not required to repair or replace any fixtures, furnishings or decorations but only equipment that is originally installed by Landlord. Landlord is not responsible for delays due to settling insurance claims, obtaining estimates, labor and supply problems or any other cause not fully under Landlord's control.

If the apartment can not be used, Landlord has 30 days to decide whether to repair it. Landlord's decision to repair must be given by notice to Tenant within 30 days of the fire or casualty. Landlord shall have a reasonable time to repair. In determining what is a reasonable time, consideration shall be given to any delays in receipt of insurance settlements, labor trouble and causes not within Landlord's control. If Landlord fails to give Tenant notice of its decision within 30 days, Tenant may cancel the lease as of the date of the fire or casualty. The cancellation shall be effective only if it is given before Landlord begins to repair or before Landlord notifies Tenant of its decision to repair. If the fire or other casualty is caused by an act or neglect of Tenant or guest of Tenant all repairs will be made at Tenant's expense and Tenant must pay the full rent with no adjustment. The cost of the repairs will be added rent.

Landlord has the right to demolish or rebuild the Building if there is substantial damage by fire or other casualty. Even if the Apartment is not damaged, Landlord may cancel this Lease within 30 days after the substantial fire or casualty by giving Tenant notice of Landlord's intention to demolish or rebuild. The Lease will end 30 days after Landlord's cancellation notice to Tenant. Tenant must deliver the Apartment to Landlord on or before the cancellation date in the notice and pay all rent due to the date of the fire or casualty. If the Lease is cancelled Landlord is not required to repair the Apartment or Building. The cancellation does not release Tenant of liability in connection with the fire or casualty. This Section is intended to replace the terms of New York Real Property Law Section 227.

10. Liability Landlord is not liable for loss, expense, or damage to any person or property, unless due to Landlord's negligence. Landlord is not liable to Tenant for permitting or refusing entry of anyone into the Building.

Tenant must pay for damages suffered and reasonable expenses of Landlord relating to any claim arising from any act or neglect of Tenant. If an action is brought against Landlord arising from Tenant's act or neglect Tenant shall defend Landlord at Tenant's expense with an attorney of Landlord's choice.

Tenant is responsible for all acts or neglect of Tenant's family, employees, guests or invitees.

11. Entry by Landlord Landlord may enter the Apartment at reasonable hours to: repair, inspect, exterminate, install or work on master antennas or other systems or equipment and perform other work that Landlord decides is necessary or desirable. At reasonable hours Landlord may show the Apartment to possible buyers, lenders, or tenants of the entire Building or land. At reasonable hours Landlord may show the Apartment to possible or new tenants during the last 4 months of the Term. Entry by Landlord must be on reasonable notice except in emergency.

12. Assignment and sublease Tenant must not assign all or part of this Lease or sublet all or part of the Apartment or permit any other person to use the Apartment. If Tenant does, Landlord has the right to cancel the Lease as stated in the Tenant's Default section. State law may permit Tenant to sublet under certain conditions. Tenant must get Landlord's written permission each time Tenant wants to assign or sublet. Permission to assign or sublet is good only for that assignment or sublease. Tenant remains bound to the terms of this lease after a assignment or sublet is permitted, even if Landlord accepts money from the assignee or subtenant. The amount accepted will be credited toward money due from Tenant, as Landlord shall determine. The assignee or subtenant does not become Landlord's tenant. Tenant is responsible for acts and neglect of any person in the Apartment.

13. Subordination This Lease and Tenant's rights, are subject and subordinate to all present and future: (a) leases for the Building or the land on which it stands, (b) mortgages on the leases or the Building or land, (c) agreements securing money paid or to be paid by a lender, and (d) terms, conditions, renewals, changes of any kind and extensions of the mortgages, leases or lender agreements. Tenant must promptly execute any certificate(s) that Landlord requests to show that this Lease is so subject and subordinate. Tenant authorizes Landlord to sign these certificate(s) for Tenant.

Figure 22.1 (continued)

14. Condemnation If all of the Apartment or Building is taken or condemned by a legal authority, the Term, and Tenant's rights shall end as of the date the authority takes title to the Apartment or Building. If any part of the Apartment or Building is taken, Landlord may cancel this Lease on notice to Tenant. The notice shall set a cancellation date not less than 30 days from the date of the notice. If the Lease is cancelled, Tenant must deliver the Apartment to Landlord on the cancellation date together with all rent due to that date. The entire award for any taking belongs to Landlord. Tenant assigns to Landlord any interest Tenant may have to any part of the award. Tenant shall make no claim for the value of the remaining part of the Term.

15. Tenant's duty to obey laws and regulations Tenant must, at Tenant's expense, promptly comply with all laws, orders, rules, requests, and directions, of all governmental authorities, Landlord's insurers, Board of Fire Underwriters, or similar groups. Notices received by Tenant from any authority or group must be promptly delivered to Landlord. Tenant may not do anything which may increase Landlord's insurance premiums. If Tenant does, Tenant must pay the increase in premium as added rent.

16. Tenant's default A. Landlord must give Tenant written notice of default stating the type of default. The following are defaults and must be cured by Tenant within the time stated:
(1) Failure to pay rent or added rent on time, 3 days.
(2) Failure to move into the Apartment within 15 days after the beginning date of the Term, 10 days.
(3) Issuance of a court order under which the Apartment may be taken by another party, 10 days.
(4) Improper conduct by Tenant annoying other tenants, 10 days.
(5) Failure to comply with any other term or Rule in the Lease, 10 days.
If Tenant fails to cure the default in the time stated, Landlord may cancel the Lease by giving Tenant a cancellation notice. The cancellation notice will state the date the Term will end which may be no less than 10 days after the date of the notice. On the cancellation date in the notice the Term of this Lease shall end. Tenant must leave the Apartment and give Landlord the keys on or before the cancellation date. Tenant continues to be responsible as stated in this Lease. If the default can not be cured in the time stated, Tenant must begin to cure within that time and continue diligently until cured.
B. If Tenant's application for the Apartment contains any material misstatement of fact, Landlord may cancel this Lease. Cancellation shall be by cancellation notice as stated in Section 16A.
C. If (1) the Lease is cancelled; or (2) rent or added rent is not paid on time; or (3) Tenant vacates the Apartment, Landlord may, in addition to other remedies, take any of the following steps: (a) peacefully enter the Apartment and remove Tenant and any person or property, and (b) use eviction or other lawsuit method to take back the Apartment.
D. If this Lease is cancelled, or Landlord takes back the Apartment, the following takes place:
(1) Rent and added rent for the unexpired Term becomes due and payable.
(2) Landlord may relet the Apartment and anything in it. The reletting may be for any term. Landlord may charge any rent or no rent and give allowances to the new tenant. Landlord may, at Tenant's expense, do any work Landlord reasonably feels needed to put the Apartment in good repair and prepare it for renting. Tenant stays liable and is not released except as provided by law.
(3) Any rent received by Landlord for the re-renting shall be used first to pay Landlord's expenses and second to pay any amounts Tenant owes under this Lease. Landlord's expenses include the costs of getting possession and re-renting the Apartment, including, but not only reasonable legal fees, brokers fees, cleaning and repairing costs, decorating costs and advertising costs.
(4) From time to time Landlord may bring actions for damages. Delay or failure to bring an action shall not be a waiver of Landlord's rights. Tenant is not entitled to any excess of rents collected over the rent paid by Tenant to Landlord under this Lease.
(5) If Landlord relets the Apartment combined with other space an adjustment will be made based on square footage. Money received by Landlord from the next tenant other than the monthly rent, shall not be considered as part of the rent paid to Landlord. Landlord is entitled to all of it.
If Landlord relets the Apartment the fact that all or part of the next tenant's rent is not collected does not affect Tenant's liability. Landlord has no duty to collect the next tenant's rent. Tenant must continue to pay rent, damages, losses and expenses without offset.
E. If Landlord takes possession of the Apartment by Court order, or under the Lease, Tenant has no right to return to the Apartment.

17. Jury trial and counterclaims Landlord and Tenant agree not to use their right to a Trial by Jury in any action or proceeding brought by either, against the other, for any matter concerning this Lease or the Apartment. This does not include actions for personal injury or property damage. Tenant gives up any right to bring a counterclaim or set-off in any action or proceeding by Landlord against Tenant on any matter directly or indirectly related to this Lease or Apartment.

18. No waiver, illegality Landlord's acceptance of rent or failure to enforce any term in this Lease is not a waiver of any of Landlord's rights. If a term in this Lease is illegal, the rest of this lease remains in full force.

19. Insolvency If (1) Tenant assigns property for the benefit of creditors, or (2) a non-bankruptcy trustee or receiver of Tenant or Tenant's property is appointed, Landlord may give Tenant 30 days notice of cancellation of the Term of this Lease. If any of the above is not fully dismissed within the 30 days, the Term shall end as of the date stated in the notice. Tenant must continue to pay rent, damages, losses and expenses without offset. If Tenant files a voluntary petition in bankruptcy or an involuntary petition in bankruptcy is filed against Tenant, Landlord may not terminate this Lease.

20. Rules Tenant must comply with these Rules. Notice of new Rules will be given to Tenant. Landlord need not enforce Rules against other Tenants. Landlord is not liable to Tenant if another tenant violates these Rules. Tenant receives no rights under these Rules:
(1) The comfort or rights of other Tenants must not be interfered with. This means that annoying sounds, smells and lights are not allowed.
(2) No one is allowed on the roof. Nothing may be placed on or attached to fire escapes, sills, windows or exterior walls of the Apartment or in the hallways or public areas.
(3) Tenant may not operate manual elevators. Smoking is not permitted in elevators. Messengers and trade people must only use service elevators and service entrances. Bicycles are not allowed on passenger elevators.
(4) Tenant must give to Landlord keys to all locks. Doors must be locked at all times. Windows must be locked when Tenant is out.
(5) Apartment floors must be covered by carpets or rugs. No waterbeds allowed in Apartments.
(6) Dogs, cats or other animals or pets are not allowed in the Apartment or Building.
(7) Garbage disposal rules must be followed. Wash lines, vents and plumbing fixtures must be used for their intended purpose.
(8) Laundry machines, if any, are used at Tenant's risk and cost. Instructions must be followed.
(9) Moving furniture, fixtures or equipment must be scheduled with Landlord. Tenant must not send Landlord's employees on personal errands.
(10) Improperly parked cars may be removed without notice at Tenant's cost.
(11) Tenant must not allow the cleaning of the windows or other part of the Apartment or Building from the outside.
(12) Tenant shall conserve energy.

21. Representations, changes in Lease Tenant has read this Lease. All promises made by the Landlord are in this Lease. There are no others. This Lease may be changed only by an agreement in writing signed by and delivered to each party.

22. Landlord unable to perform If due to labor trouble, government order, lack of supply, Tenant's act or neglect, or any other cause not fully within Landlord's reasonable control, Landlord is delayed or unable to (a) carry out any of Landlord's promises or agreements, (b) supply any service required to be supplied, (c) make any required repair or change in the Apartment or Building, or (d) supply any equipment or appliances Landlord is required to supply, this Lease shall not be ended or Tenant's obligations affected.

23. End of term At the end of the Term, Tenant must: leave the Apartment clean and in good condition, subject to ordinary wear and tear; remove all of Tenant's property and all Tenant's installations and decorations; repair all damages to the Apartment and Building caused by moving; and restore the Apartment to its condition at the beginning of the Term. If the last day of the Term is on a Saturday, Sunday or State or Federal holiday the Term shall end on the prior business day.

24. Space "as is" Tenant has inspected the Apartment and Building. Tenant states they are in good order and repair and takes the Apartment as is except for latent defects.

25. Landlord's warranty of habitability Landlord states that the Apartment and Building are fit for human living and there is no condition dangerous to health, life or safety.

26. Landlord's consent If Tenant requires Landlord's consent to any act and such consent is not given, Tenant's only right is to ask the Court for a declaritory judgment to force Landlord to give consent. Tenant agrees not to make any claim against Landlord for money or subtract any sum from the rent because such consent was not given.

27. Limit of recovery against Landlord Tenant is limited to Landlord's interest in the Building for payment of a judgment or other court remedy against Landlord.

28. Lease binding on This Lease is binding on Landlord and Tenant and their heirs, distributees, executors, administrators, successors and lawful assigns.

29. Landlord Landlord means the owner (Building or Apartment), or the lessee of the Building, or a lender in possession. Landlord's obligations end when Landlord's interest in the (Building or Apartment) is transferred. Any acts Landlord may do may be performed by Landlord's agents or employees.

30. Paragraph headings The paragraph headings are for convenience only.

31. Rent regulations This section applies if the Apartment is subject to the New York City Rent Stabilization Law or the Emergency Tenant Protection Act.
(1) Landlord may have proper cause to apply to the Division of Housing and Community Renewal (DHCR) for assistance. If Landlord does apply and is found to be entitled to an increase in rent or other aid, the Landlord and Tenant agree:
- (a) To be bound by the determination of the DHCR,
- (b) Tenant will pay any rent increase in the manner set by the DHCR,
- (c) Despite anything contained in Paragraphs 1a and b, it is agreed in the event that an order is issued increasing the stabilization rent because of Landlord hardship, the Tenant may, within 30 days of receipt of a copy of the DHCR order, cancel this Lease on 60 days written notice to the Landlord. During the period prior to vacating, the cancelling Tenant may continue in occupancy at no increase in rent.

(2) The rent provided for in this Lease may be increased or decreased retroactively to the commencement of the Lease to conform to the lawful Rent Guidelines or any changes in the Guidelines which apply to this Lease as issued by the New York City Rent Guidelines Board or appropriate county rent guidelines board.
(3) This Lease and all riders shall continue in full force and effect, and except as modified above, shall in no way be affected by this section.

Rider Additional terms on .... page(s) initialed at the end by the parties is attached and made a part of this Lease.

Signatures, effective date Landlord and Tenant have signed this Lease as of the above date. It is effective when Landlord delivers to Tenant a copy signed by all parties.

....

WITNESS ....

....

Figure 22.2
Rent Stabilization Rider

 A 326—Rent stabilization rider, 4-85
Use with new or renewal leases (T 327 & A 53)

JULIUS BLUMBERG, INC., PUBLISHER
62 WHITE STREET, NEW YORK, N.Y. 10013

Rent Stabilization Rider For Apartment House Tenants In New York City
Failure To Attach a Copy of This Rider To a Tenant's Lease
Without Cause May Result in a Fine or Other Sanctions

Introduction

This Rider generally informs tenants and owners about their basic rights and responsibilities under the Rent Stabilization Law. The Rent Stabilization Law protects tenants by regulating rents, services, and evictions. It also provides property owners with rent increases and remedies so that owners may meet increased maintenance costs, obtain increases for new services and equipment and otherwise properly maintain the property.

This Rider does not contain every rule applicable to rent stabilized apartments. The Appendix lists organizations which can provide assistance to tenants and owners who have inquiries, complaints or requests relating to subjects covered in this Rider.

The Rider is only informational. Its provisions are not part of the lease. However, it must be attached to the lease. The Rider does not modify the lease. It does not replace or modify the Rent Stabilization Law, the Rent Stabilization Code, any order of the New York State Division of Housing and Community Renewal (DHCR), or any order of the New York City Rent Guidelines Board.

A tenant should keep a copy of this Rider and of any lease the tenant signs.

Increases for Renewal and Vacancy Leases

Provided that the tenant's apartment is registered with the DHCR, the owner is entitled to increase the rent when a tenant renews a lease (a "renewal lease") or when a new tenant enters into a lease upon moving into an apartment (a "vacancy lease"). Each year, effective October 1, the New York City Rent Guidelines Board sets the percentage of maximum permissible increase over the September 30 rent for leases which will begin during the year that the guidelines order is in effect. The date a lease starts determines which guidelines order applies.

Guidelines orders provide increases for:

(a) **Renewal Leases:** Different percentages are set for rent increases for leases of 1 or 2 years. The renewing tenant has the choice of the length of the lease.

(b) **Vacancy Leases:** In addition to the percentage increase permitted the owner for a renewal lease, the owner may charge to a new tenant a vacancy allowance if set by the Rent Guidelines Board. The tenant has the choice of whether a vacancy lease will be for 1 or 2 years.

Security Deposits

The general rule is that an owner may collect a security deposit no greater than one month's rent. However, if the present tenant moved into an apartment prior to the date the apartment first became rent stabilized and the owner collected more than one month's rent, the owner may continue to retain a security deposit of up to two month's rent for that tenant only. When the rent is increased, the owner may charge an additional amount to bring the security deposit up to the full amount to which the owner is entitled.

Security deposits must be deposited in an interest bearing trust account. Owners may deduct a 1% service fee and must credit the balance of the interest annually, or on request of the tenant, pay the tenant the balance of the interest earned.

Other Rent Increases

In addition to guidelines increases, the rent may be permanently increased where:

(a) **Improvements, New Services or Equipment to Apartment:** While a tenant may demand serviceable used equipment at no increase in rent, an owner is generally permitted to add 1/40 of the cost of improvements, new services or equipment and its installation, such as a new stove or refrigerator, to the monthly rent. However, if a tenant is in occupancy of the apartment, the increase may be charged immediately for new equipment only with the written consent of the tenant and the subsequent approval of the DHCR. Increases for new services or improvements are only permitted after approval by the DHCR. An increase for improvements, new services or equipment installed when an apartment is vacant does not require the consent of the next tenant or an order of the DHCR. However, the tenant may challenge all or part of the increase after occupancy.

(b) **Building Wide Major Capital Improvements or Substantial Rehabilitation:** An owner is permitted a rental increase for certain types of building-wide substantial rehabilitation or major capital improvements such as the replacement of a boiler, or new plumbing. The owner must receive approval from the DHCR which will permit the owner to amortize the cost over 5 years. The owner is not required to obtain tenant consent. Tenants are served with a copy of any owner's application and have a right to respond to the application.

(c) **Hardship:** An owner may apply for a rental increase for hardship when:

1) the rent is not sufficient to enable the owner to maintain approximately the same average annual net income for a current three-year period as compared with the annual net income which prevailed on the average over the period 1968 through 1970, or for the first three years of operation if the building was completed since 1968, or for the first three years the owner owned the building if he cannot obtain records for the years 1968-1970; or

2) where the annual gross rental income does not exceed the annual operating expenses by a sum equal to at least 5% of such gross income.

If an application for a rent increase based on a building-wide major capital improvement, substantial rehabilitation, or hardship is granted, the owner may charge the increase during the term of an existing lease only if the lease contains a clause specifically authorizing the owner to do so.

An increase based on a building-wide major capital improvement or substantial rehabilitation may not exceed 15% in any 12 month period. In appropriate circumstances, the DHCR may waive the 15% limitation and authorize an increase in excess of 15%. An increase based on hardship may not exceed 6% in any 12 month period. Any increase authorized by the DHCR which exceeds these annual limitations may be collected in future years.

NOTICE

 This Rider, with this Notice, must be attached to all leases for rent stabilized apartments which commenced on or after April 1, 1984, or served on all tenants whose leases commenced since that date. The text of this Rider was approved pursuant to Section YY51-6.0 d. of the New York City Rent Stabilization Law as amended by Chapter 403 of the Laws of 1983. The text may not be modified or altered without the approval of this agency. This Rider must be in a print size larger than the print size of the lease to which the Rider is attached.

YVONNE SCRUGGS-LEFTWICH, *Commissioner*

MARIO M. CUOMO, GOVERNOR   Dated: April 1, 1985   Division of Housing and Community Renewal

**Figure 22.2
(continued)**

Status of Apartment and Last Tenant (Owner to check Box 1, 2 or 3).

1. ☐ The last tenant after April 1, 1980 was a rent stabilized tenant and had a final rent of $................per month.

OR

2. ☐ This apartment was subject to rent control until the last tenant moved out. The tenant to whose lease this Rider is attached is the first rent stabilized tenant.

OR

3. ☐ Other (please specify) ....

....

If the owner checked Box 2, the owner was entitled to bring the rent up to the "market rent" before renting it to the first stabilized tenant. That first rent charged to the first stabilized tenant becomes the initial base rent for the apartment under the rent stabilization system. If the tenant believes this rent exceeds a "fair market rent", the tenant may file a "fair market rent appeal" with the DHCR. The owner is required to give the tenant a notice of the right to file such an appeal on an official form. The notice must be served personally or by certified mail. A tenant only has 90 days after receiving the notice or 90 days from the date he or she is served with a copy of the apartment registration form, to file such an appeal. Otherwise, the rent set forth on the notice or registration form becomes final.

The "fair market rent" is computed based upon a "special guideline" established annually by the Rent Guidelines Board, or by averaging this "special guideline" with decontrolled rents charged for similar apartments (called "comparables") on June 30, 1974, updated by annual guidelines increases.

No matter which Box is checked, the owner is not entitled to a rent which is more than the legal regulated rent. That amount is the rent registered with the DHCR as set forth below, or a rent established after a "fair market rent appeal", plus increases in rent permitted to be added to the first stabilization rent.

Rent Registration

Owners are required to register the rents and services of apartments with the DHCR. To complete the rent registration process, the owner must also serve a copy of the apartment registration form upon the tenant. The tenant may challenge the correctness of the apartment's rental as stated in the registration statement within 90 days of the date that the tenant is served by the owner. Challenge forms may be obtained at any District Rent Office listed on the Appendix to this Rider.

Failure to file a timely tenant's challenge results in the rent, which is specified in the registration statement, being conclusively deemed to be the lawful rent for the apartment. However, the tenant's failure to challenge any data other than rent shall not be conclusive as to the correctness of such other data, and shall not prevent the tenant from challenging such other data at a future time. An annual update of this registration must be served on the tenant and filed with DHCR no later than September 3rd of each year.

Renewal Leases

Between 120 and 150 days before the end of a lease, the owner is required to notify the tenant in writing that the lease will soon expire. That notice must also offer the tenant the choice of a 1 or 2 year lease at the permissible guidelines increase. After receiving the notice, the tenant always has 60 days to accept the owner's offer, whether or not the offer is made within the above time period.

Any renewal lease, except for the increased rent and its length, is required to be on the same terms and conditions as the expired lease, and unless a fully executed copy of same is provided to the tenant within 30 days from the owner's receipt of the lease signed by the tenant, the owner may not collect a rent increase under the lease until such lease is provided. However, an owner may add to a renewal lease the following clauses even if such clauses were not included in the tenant's prior lease:

(a) the rent may be adjusted by the owner on the basis of Rent Guidelines Board or DHCR orders;

(b) the owner may charge a vacancy allowance for a subtenant or assignee if the owner or the lease grants permission to sublet or assign provided the prime lease is a renewal lease. (Subletting will be discussed later in this Rider);

(c) (1) if the building in which the apartment is located is receiving tax abatement benefits pursuant to Section 421-a of the Real Property Tax Law, a clause may be added providing that the owner will be permitted to charge a free market rent upon the expiration of the tax abatement period. (Such clause must state the date on which the tax abatement period is scheduled to expire, and must be in at least 12 point type);

(2) if the building in which the apartment is located is subject to Rent Stabilization solely because the owner is receiving benefits pursuant to Section J51-2.5 of the Administrative Code of the City of New York, a clause may be added providing that the owner will be permitted to charge a free market rent upon the termination of such benefits;

(d) If the Attorney General, pursuant to Section 352-eeee of the General Business Law, has accepted for filing an eviction plan to convert the building to cooperative or condominium ownership, a clause may be added providing that the lease may be cancelled upon expiration of a 3 year period after the plan is declared effective. (The owner must give the tenant at least 90 days notice that the 3 year period has expired or will be expiring).

If a tenant wishes to remain in occupancy beyond the expiration of the lease, the tenant may not refuse to sign a proper renewal lease.

An owner may refuse to offer a tenant a renewal lease only under certain conditions explained later in this Rider under the heading "When An Owner May Refuse To Renew A Lease".

Services

The owner may not decrease services which were provided or required on the date the apartment first became subject to the Rent Stabilization Law or which were added or required after that date.

Required services include building-wide services such as heat, hot water, janitorial service, maintenance of locks and security devices, and repair, and maintenance, and may include elevators, air conditioning and other amenities. Upon a finding by the DHCR that services are not being maintained on complaint of a tenant, a rent reduction shall be imposed and future rent increases shall be barred until the rent is restored.

Ancillary services provided by the owner, such as garage space or recreational facilities, whether provided with or without additional charge, may also not be decreased. Required services may also include services within the apartment, such as maintenance and repair of appliances and painting every 3 years.

Laws other than the Rent Stabilization Law also govern physical maintenance, health, safety, habitability, and sanitation standards. These laws include the Multiple Dwelling Law of the State of New York, and the New York City Housing Maintenance Code. Housing code violation complaints may be made to the New York City Central Complaint Bureau.

Subletting and Assignment

A tenant may have the right to sublet his or her apartment, even if subletting is prohibited in the lease, provided that he or she complies strictly with the provisions of Real Property Law §226-b. To comply with Real Property Law §226-b, the tenant must do all of the following to assert his or her right to sublet:

(a) Notify the owner by certified mail, return receipt requested, that he or she intends to sublet. The request to sublet must contain all of the following information:

1. The term of the sublease;

Figure 22.2
(continued)

2. The name of the proposed subtenant;
3. The business and permanent home address of the proposed subtenant;
4. The tenant's reason for subletting;
5. The tenant's address for the term of the sublease;
6. The written consent of any co-tenant or guarantor of the lease; and
7. A copy of the proposed sublease, to which a copy of the tenant's lease should be attached if available, acknowledged by both the tenant and proposed subtenant as a true copy of the sublease.

(b) If within 10 days after the mailing of the tenant's request to sublet, the owner asks for additional information about the proposed subletting, the tenant must provide the additional information if the owner's request is not unduly burdensome.

(c) The owner must respond in writing to the tenant's request to sublet within 30 days after the mailing of the tenant's request or after the mailing of the additional information asked for by the owner. If the owner does not send a written response within the 30 day period, the owner is deemed to have consented to the proposed subletting, and the tenant may proceed to sublet.

(d) If the owner has reasonable objections to the subletting and notifies the tenant in writing of his objections within the required 30 day period, the tenant cannot sublet, and the owner is not required to release the tenant from his or her lease.

(e) If the tenant believes that the owner's objections to subletting are unreasonable, the tenant may proceed to sublet in accordance with his or her request. A lawsuit may result from such action. If the court finds that the owner acted in bad faith by withholding consent, the tenant may recover court costs and attorney's fees.

If a tenant in occupancy under a renewal lease sublets his or her apartment, the owner may charge the tenant the rent the owner could have charged had the renewal lease been a vacancy lease. Thus, the rent increase is tied to the vacancy allowance available when the tenant's renewal lease commenced, but takes effect when the subletting takes place. If a tenant in occupancy under a vacancy lease sublets, the owner is not entitled to any rent increase during the subletting.

Additional Rules Which Apply When A Subletting Has Occurred:

1) A tenant who sublets his or her apartment is entitled to the rent permitted under the Rent Stabilization Law, plus a 10% surcharge payable to the tenant if the apartment sublet is fully furnished with the tenant's furniture. Any additional rent, above such surcharge which the tenant charges the subtenant, shall be considered an overcharge which may subject the tenant to civil liability to the subtenant for three times the rent overcharge plus interest and attorney's fees.

2) A tenant who sublets must maintain the apartment as his or her primary residence and must intend to reoccupy it as a primary residence when the sublease expires.

3) A tenant who sublets his or her apartment retains the right to renew the lease. The subtenant does not have a right to renew the lease. A tenant may sublet his or her apartment for a term which extends beyond the end of the lease. It is unreasonable for an owner to refuse to consent to a sublease solely because it extends beyond the end of the tenant's lease.

4) A tenant who sublets his or her apartment retains the right to purchase the shares of the apartment if the building is converted to cooperative or condominium ownership.

5) The subletting may not be for more than a total of two years out of the four year period preceding the expiration of the sublease, (for sublets occurring on or after July 1, 1983).

6) Any provision in a tenant's lease which prohibits subletting or waives the tenant's right to sublet is illegal and unenforceable.

7) A tenant who sublets his or her apartment remains the one primarily responsible to the owner for the payment of rent, and all obligations of the lease.

A tenant who does not comply with the rules regarding subletting may forfeit the right to a renewal lease or even be subject to eviction by the owner.

Assignment of Leases

In an assignment, a tenant transfers the entire remainder of his or her lease to another person (the assignee), and gives up all of his or her rights to reoccupy the apartment.

Pursuant to the provisions of Real Property Law §226-b, a tenant may not assign his or her lease without the written consent of the owner, unless the lease expressly provides otherwise. An owner is not required to have reasonable grounds to refuse to consent to the assignment. However, if the owner unreasonably refuses consent, the owner must release the tenant from the remainder of the lease, if the tenant, upon 30 days notice to the owner, requests to be released.

If the owner refuses to consent to an assignment and does have reasonable grounds for withholding consent, the tenant cannot assign and the owner is not required to release the tenant from the lease.

When An Owner May Refuse To Renew a Lease

So long as a tenant pays the lawful rent to which the owner is entitled, the tenant, except for the specific instances set forth herein, is entitled to remain in the apartment. An owner may not harass a tenant by engaging in an intentional course of conduct intended to make the tenant move from his or her apartment.

However, the owner may refuse to renew a lease and bring an action in Civil Court at the expiration of the lease on the following grounds:

(a) the tenant refuses to sign a proper renewal lease offered by the owner;

(b) the owner seeks the apartment in good faith for personal use or for the personal use of members of the owner's immediate family.

However if the tenant or the tenant's spouse is 62 years of age or older, or the tenant or the tenant's spouse is handicapped, the owner must offer to provide and if requested, provide, an equivalent or superior dwelling unit at the same or lower stabilized rent in a closely proximate area;

(c) the apartment is owned by a hospital, convent, monastery, asylum, public institution, college, school dormitory or any institution operated exclusively for charitable or educational purposes on a non-profit basis and the institution requires the apartment for its charitable or educational purposes. The institution must first send a 120-day notice of intention not to renew the tenant's lease.

1) If the institution seeks the apartment for related residential purposes the following limitations apply:

A) the institution may not refuse to renew the lease if the tenant took occupancy before the institution acquired the property;

B) even if the tenant took occupancy after the institution acquired the property, the institution may not refuse to renew the lease of a tenant who took occupancy before July 1, 1978, unless the tenant received notice at the time he or she signed his or her original lease that the tenancy was subject to non-renewal.

2) If the institutional owner requires the apartment for related non-residential use, then the limitations set forth in (c) 1) A) & B) above do not apply.

(d) the tenant does not occupy the apartment as his or her primary residence. However, an owner may not require, unless the tenant wishes to do so voluntarily, that as a condition of renewal, the tenant execute an affidavit of primary residence.

Grounds for Refusing to Renew a Lease Which Require Prior Approval From the DHCR:

There are additional grounds for refusing to renew a lease which require approval from the DHCR. A tenant will be served with a copy of the owner's application and have a right

Figure 22.2
(continued)

to object. These grounds include:

a) where the owner seeks in good faith to recover possession of the apartments for the purpose of demolishing them and constructing a new building, or

b) where the owner requires the apartment or the land for his or her own use in connection with a business which he or she owns and operates.

If the owner's application is granted, the owner may bring an action in Civil Court after sending a 30 day notice to the tenant, provided the tenant's lease has already expired.

Eviction While the Lease is in Effect

If an action is brought in Civil Court to evict a tenant during the term of the lease, the tenant will receive notice of the action and of the tenant's right to answer and appear in court.

The owner may only bring such an action in court to evict a tenant because a tenant:

(a) does not pay rent.

(b) is violating a substantial obligation of the tenancy.

(c) is committing or permitting a nuisance.

(d) is illegally using or occupying the apartment.

(e) has unlawfully refused the owner access.

(f) is occupying an apartment in a cooperative or condominium under an eviction plan. A non-purchasing tenant in a non-eviction plan may not be evicted except on the grounds set forth in (a)-(e) above. (See subdivision (d) of the paragraph titled "Renewal Leases").

Tenants are cautioned that causing violations of health, safety or sanitation standards of housing maintenance laws, or permitting such violations by a member of the family or household or by a guest may be the basis for such a court action by the owner.

Cooperative and Condominium Conversion

Any cooperative or condominium plan accepted for filing by the New York State Attorney General's Office will include specific information about tenant rights and protections. An information booklet about the general subject of conversion is available from the New York State Attorney General's Office.

Senior Citizens and Disabled Persons' Benefits

Tenants or their spouses who are 62 years of age, or older and whose "net" household income is not over $10,000 per year may qualify for an exemption from guidelines rent increases or hardship increases. The exemption will be only from that portion of the increase which causes the tenant's rent to exceed one-third of the "net" household income.

The exemption is not available for increases based on new services or equipment within the apartment or for any rent increase based upon a major capital improvement. When renewing a lease, a senior citizen eligible for an exemption or eligible to renew an existing exemption has to request a 2 year lease. When a senior citizen is granted a rent increase exemption, the owner may obtain a real estate tax credit from New York City equal to the tenant's exemption.

Notwithstanding any of the above, a senior citizen who receives a rent increase exemption is still required to pay a full month's rent as a security deposit.

Senior citizens and disabled persons in buildings which are being converted to cooperative or condominium ownership may also be eligible for exemption, in an eviction plan, from any requirement that tenants must purchase their apartment to remain in occupancy. This exemption is available to senior citizens or to disabled persons with impairments expected to be permanent, which prevent the tenant from engaging in any substantial gainful employment. A conversion plan accepted for filing by the New York State Attorney General's Office will contain specific information on this right.

Special Cases and Exceptions

Some special rules relating to stabilization rents and required services may apply to newly constructed buildings which receive tax abatement or exemption and to buildings rehabilitated under certain New York City, New York State or federal financing or mortgage insurance programs. The rules

mentioned in this Rider specifically do not apply to hotel units or units subject to the hotel stabilization system.

Appendix
Some agencies which can provide assistance
New York State Division of Housing and Community Renewal (DHCR)

The DHCR is a state agency empowered to administer and enforce the Rent Stabilization Law and the Rent Control Law. Tenants should contact the District Rent Offices for assistance. All telephone Numbers are area code 212 unless otherwise designated.

Office of Rent Administration
10 Columbus Circle, 11th Fl., N. Y., N. Y. 10019   903-9550
Registration Hot Line   488-3746
Small Business Owner Assistance Unit   903-9555

District Rent Offices:
Lower Manhattan (South side of 110 St. and below)
2 Lafayette Street, 12th Floor
New York, NY 10007   566-7970
Upper Manhattan (North Side of 110 St. and above)
215 West 125th Street, 5th Floor
New York, NY 10027   678-2201
Bronx: 260 East 161 Street, 8th Floor
Bronx, NY 10451   585-2600
Brooklyn: 91 Lawrence Street, 2nd Floor
Brooklyn, NY 11201   (718) 643-7570
Queens: 164-19 Hillside Avenue, Ground Floor
Jamaica, NY 11432   (718) 526-2040
Staten Island: 350 St. Mark's Place, Ground Floor
Staten Island, NY 10301   (718) 816-0277

Attorney General of the State of New York
Two World Trade Center
New York, NY 10047
Consumer Frauds and Protection Bureau   488-7530
—investigates and enjoins illegal or fraudulent business practices, including the overcharging of rent and mishandling of rent security deposits by owners.
Real Estate Financing Bureau   488-3310
—administers and enforces the laws governing cooperative and condominium conversions. Investigates complaints from tenants in buildings undergoing cooperative or condominium conversion, concerning allegations of improper disclosure, harassment and misleading information.

New York City Department of Housing Preservation and Development (HPD):
Office of Rent and Housing Maintenance
100 Gold St., Room 8170, New York, NY 10038   566-3918
—provides owners with assistance on housing matters.
—provides tenants considering court action to enforce housing maintenance standards with assistance at 125 Church Street, 3rd Fl., New York, NY 10007   566-6222

Senior Citizen Rent Increase Exemption Program (SCRIE)
17 John Street, 4th Floor,
New York, NY 10038   566-5414 or 5413
—administers SCRIE Program

New York City Central Complaint Bureau:
215 West 125th St., New York, NY   960-4800
—receives telephone complaints relating to physical maintenance, health, safety and sanitation standards, including emergency heat and hot water service.

New York City Rent Guidelines Board (RGB):
51 Chambers St., Rm. 201, New York, NY 10007   349-2262
—promulgates annual percentage of rent increases for rent stabilized apartments and provides information on guidelines orders.

Copies of New York State and New York City rent laws are available in the business section of some public libraries. Telephone or write to a public library to determine the exact library which has such legal material.

Under the New York General Obligations Law a landlord must hold all security deposits in trust and must not commingle them with his or her own funds because *such deposits continue to belong to the tenants who have advanced them* throughout the term of the lease. If the landlord owns six or more units, the landlord must notify tenants in writing where the security funds are being held in a New York interest-bearing bank account, and must turn over to them all but one percent of any interest earned. Any provisions in a lease requiring a tenant to waive any provisions of this law are void. The rules also apply to mobile home parks.

When a landlord conveys rental property he or she must turn over any security deposits to the new owner within five days of the deed's delivery. He or she must also notify tenants by registered or certified mail that their deposits have been turned over; such notification must include the new owner's name and address.

With a rent-stabilized apartment only one month's rent may be charged for security deposit.

Legal Principles of Leases

New York provides that leases can be recorded in the county in which the property is located when a lease runs for a period of *three years* or longer. The recording of a *long-term lease* places the world on notice of the long-term rights of the lessee. The recordation of such a lease is usually required if the lessee intends to mortgage his or her leasehold interest.

Possession of Leased Premises

Leases carry the implied covenant that the landlord will give the tenant possession of the premises. Thus, if the premises are occupied by a holdover tenant or adverse claimant at the beginning of the new lease period, it is the landlord's duty to bring whatever action is necessary to recover possession and to bear the expense of this action.

Improvements

Neither the landlord nor the tenant is required to make any improvements to the leased property. The tenant may make improvements with the landlord's permission but any such alterations generally become the property of the landlord; that is, they become fixtures. However, as discussed in Chapter 9, a tenant may be given the right to install trade fixtures or chattel fixtures by the terms of the lease. It is customary to provide that such trade fixtures may be removed by the tenant before the lease expires, provided the tenant restores the premises to the same condition as when he or she took possession.

Maintenance of Premises

Every residential New York lease, oral or written, is considered to contain an **implied warranty of habitability.** By entering into a rental agreement the landlord guarantees that the leased property is fit for human habitation and that the tenant will not be subjected to any conditions that could endanger life, health, or safety. The landlord is required to maintain dwelling units in a habitable condition and to make any necessary repairs to common elements such as hallways, stairs, or elevators. The tenant does not have to make any repairs (unless otherwise provided in the lease) but he or she must return the premises in the same condition they were received with allowances for wear and tear occasioned by ordinary use.

Assignment and Subleasing

The lessee may assign the lease or may sublease if the lease terms do not prohibit it, or if the building contains four or more units (in New York State). A tenant who transfers the entire remaining term of his or her lease *assigns* the lease. One who transfers most of the term but retains a small part of it **subleases** (*see* Figure 22.3). In most cases the sublease or assignment of a lease does not relieve the original lessee of the obligation to make rental payments unless the landlord agrees to waive such liability. Most leases prohibit the lessee from assigning or subletting without the lessor's consent; this allows the lessor to retain control over the occupancy of the leased premises. The sublessor's (original lessee's) interest in the real estate is known as a *sandwich lease*. In New York, where the lessor's consent is required for sublease or assignment, it may not be unreasonably withheld. If it is, the tenant is released from the lease with 30 days' notice.

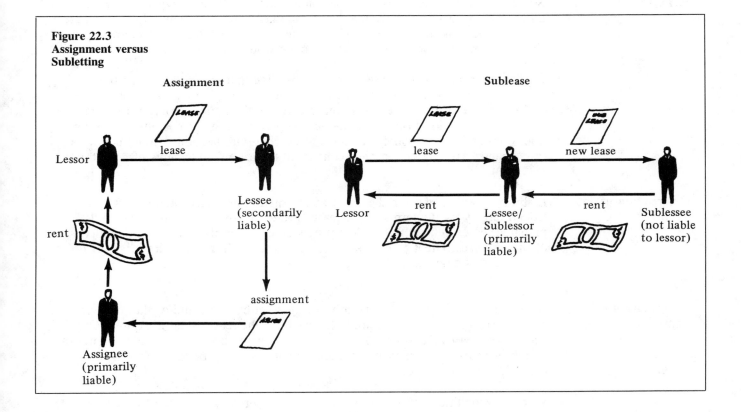

Figure 22.3
Assignment versus Subletting

New York's Real Property Law sets guidelines for a detailed written request from the tenant, the landlord's right to ask for additional information within ten days, and the landlord's written response, including the reasons for any denial, within 30 days. The landlord's failure to respond is considered consent for the sublet.

Special regulations apply to the subletting of rent-stabilized apartments: For a furnished sublet, rent may exceed the original tenant's figure by ten percent. The original tenant must establish that the apartment is his or her primary residence and will be reoccupied at the end of the sublet. A rent-subsidized apartment may not be sublet for more than one-half of any four-year period. The original tenant, not the subtenant, is entitled to the rights of a renewal lease and any right resulting from a co-op conversion.

Apartment-Sharing   In New York State a lease may not restrict occupancy of an apartment to the named tenant and that tenant's immediate family. The apartment may be shared with one additional occupant and that occupant's dependent children. If the lease names more than one tenant and one of them moves out, that tenant may be replaced with another occupant and that person's dependent children. At least one of the original tenants named in the lease, or that person's spouse, must continue to occupy the shared apartment as a primary residence.

Tenants must inform their landlords of the name of any occupant within 30 days after the occupant moves into an apartment. Landlords may, however, limit the total number of occupants to comply with health laws on overcrowding.

Renewals   Sometimes a lease contains a clause stating that it will be *automatically renewed unless* the tenant gives *notice* that he or she intends not to renew. No such clause is valid unless the landlord reminds the tenant about the automatic renewal provision 15 to 30 days before the tenant's notice would be due.

On the other hand many leases contain an *option* that grants the lessee the privilege of *renewing* the lease but requires that the lessee give *notice* on or before a specific date of his or her intention to exercise the option. Some leases grant to the lessee the option to purchase the leased premises; the provisions for the option to purchase vary widely. Options to purchase are becoming more common (*see* Chapter 5). Any option must contain all the essential elements of a contract.

Destruction of Premises   Liability of either party in the event of destruction of leased premises is controlled largely by the terms of the lease. Printed lease forms and all carefully prepared leases generally include a provision covering the subject of destruction of the premises. Great care must be exercised in reading the entire lease document before signing it.

Termination of Lease   A written lease for a definite period of time expires at the end of that time period; no separate notice is required to terminate the lease when it expires. Oral and written leases that do not specify a definite expiration date (such as month-to-month or year-to-year tenancy or a tenancy at will) may be terminated by giving proper written notice.

When the conditions of a lease are breached, or broken, a landlord may terminate the lease and evict the tenant. This kind of action must be handled through a court proceeding according to state law. The landlord who wishes to be rid of a tenant is not allowed to use threats of violence, change locks, discontinue essential services like water or heat, or seize the tenant's possessions.

It is possible for the parties to a lease to mutually agree to cancel the lease. The tenant may offer to surrender the lease and acceptance by the landlord will result in termination. A tenant who abandons leased property, however, remains liable for the terms of the lease—including the rent. The terms of the specific lease will usually dictate whether or not the landlord is obligated to try to rerent the space.

When the owner of leased property dies or the property is sold, *the lease does not terminate.* The heirs of a deceased landlord are bound by the terms of existing valid leases. In addition, if a landlord conveys leased real estate, the new landlord takes the property subject to the rights of the tenant. The lease *survives* the sale. If a tenant dies, the lease will remain in effect; the deceased lessee's heirs will be bound by the terms of the lease.

Breach of Lease

When a tenant breaches any lease provision, the landlord may sue the tenant to obtain a judgment to cover past due rent, damages to the premises, or other defaults. Likewise, when a landlord breaches any lease provision the tenant is entitled to remedies. The landlord's nonperformance of some obligation under the lease, short of eviction, does not, however, affect the tenant's obligation to pay rent.

In this state, grounds for which the landlord can institute proceedings include nonpayment of rent, illegal use of the premises, tenant remaining in possession after expiration of the lease without permission, and bankruptcy or insolvency of the tenant.

Suit for possession—actual eviction. When a tenant breaches a lease or improperly retains possession of leased premises the landlord may regain possession through a **suit for possession** or *summary proceeding to recover possession of real estate.* This process is known as **actual eviction.** Law requires the landlord to serve *notice* on the tenant before commencing the suit. In New York only a three-day notice must be given before filing a suit for possession based on a default in payment of rent. When a court issues a judgment for possession to a landlord, the tenant must peaceably remove or the landlord can have the judgment enforced by a sheriff, constable, or marshal, who will *forcibly remove* the tenant and his or her possessions.

Tenants' remedies—constructive eviction. If a landlord breaches any clause of a lease agreement, the tenant has the right to sue, claiming a judgment for damages against the landlord. If an action or omission on the landlord's part results in the leased premises becoming uninhabitable for the purpose intended in the lease, the tenant may have the right to abandon the premises. This action, called **constructive eviction,** terminates the lease agreement if the tenant can prove that the premises have become uninhabitable because of the landlord's neglect. In order to claim constructive eviction the tenant must actually move from the premises while the uninhabitable condition exists.

For example, a lease requires the landlord to furnish steam heat; because of the landlord's failure to repair a defective heating plant, the heat is not provided. If this results in the leased premises becoming uninhabitable, the tenant may abandon them. Some leases provide that if the failure to furnish heat is accidental and not the landlord's fault, it is not grounds for constructive eviction.

Pro-Tenant Legislation

In New York State a landlord may not legally retaliate because a tenant joins a tenants' organization. The landlord or his or her agent may not willfully violate any provision of a lease requiring the furnishing of heat, lights, water, and like utilities. If the landlord fails to furnish heat as stipulated in the lease, tenants in New York may pay a utility company directly and deduct the sum from rent due. In New York City at least one-third of the tenants of a multiple-unit dwelling, having agreed to participate together, may start a special court proceeding to use their rent money to remedy conditions dangerous to life, health, or safety.

The federal government also took steps to increase tenants' protection with the implementation of the Tenants' Eviction Procedures Act in 1976. This act establishes standardized eviction procedures for people living in *government-subsidized housing*. It requires that the landlord have a valid reason for evicting the tenant and that the landlord give the tenant proper notice of eviction. This act does not supersede state laws in this area; however, it does provide recourse for tenants in states that have no such laws. The act applies only to multiunit residential buildings that are owned or subsidized by the Department of Housing and Urban Development and to buildings that have government-insured mortgages.

Types of Leases

The three primary types of leases are; (1) the gross lease, (2) the net lease, and (3) the percentage lease (*see* Table 22.2)

Table 22.2
Types of Leases

Type of Lease	Lessee Pays	Lessor Pays

Gross Lease
    Residential (also small
        commercial)
	Basic Rent	Property Charges (taxes,
		    repairs, insurance, etc.)

Net Lease
    Commercial/Industrial
	Basic Rent Plus Most or
	    All Property Charges
		Few or No Property Charges

Percentage Lease
    Commercial/Industrial
	Basic Rent Plus Percent of
	    Gross Sales (may pay some or
	    all property costs)
		Any Agreed Property Charges

Gross Lease

In a **gross lease** the tenant's obligation is to pay a *fixed rental* and the landlord pays all taxes, insurance, mortgage payments, repairs, and the like connected with the property (usually called *property charges*). This type of lease most often is used for residential rentals.

Net Lease

The **net lease** provides that in addition to the rent, the *tenant pays some or all of the property charges*. The monthly rental paid to the landlord is in addition to these charges and so is net income for the landlord. Leases for entire commercial or industrial buildings and the land on which they are located, ground leases, and long-term leases are usually net leases. With a *triple-net* lease, the tenant pays taxes, insurance and all other expenses except debt service.

Percentage Lease

Either a gross lease or a net lease may be a **percentage lease.** A percentage lease provides that the rental is based on a *percentage of the gross or net income* received by the tenant doing business on the leased property. This type of lease is normally used in the rental of retail business locations.

The percentage lease provides for a minimum fixed rental fee plus a percentage of that portion of the tenant's business income that exceeds a stated minimum. For example, a lease might provide for a minimum monthly rental of $1,200 with the further agreement that the tenant pay an additional amount each month equivalent to five percent of all gross sales in excess of $30,000. The percentage charged in such leases varies widely with the nature of the business and it is negotiable between landlord and tenant. A tenant's bargaining power is determined by the volume of business.

Other Lease Types

Variable leases. Several types of leases allow for increases in the fixed rental charge during the lease period. Two of the more common ones are the *graduated lease,* which provides for increases in rent at set future dates, and the *index lease,* which allows rent to be increased or decreased periodically based on changes in the government cost-of-living index.

Ground leases. When a landowner leases his or her land to a tenant who agrees to *erect a building* on it, the lease is referred to as a **ground lease.** Such a lease must be for a long enough term to make the transaction desirable to the tenant making the investment in the building. These leases are generally *net leases* that require the lessee to pay rent as well as real estate taxes, insurance, upkeep, and repairs. Net ground leases often run for terms of 50 years or longer and a lease for 999 years is not impossible. Although these leases are considered to be personal property, law may give leaseholders some of the rights and obligations of real property owners.

Oil and gas leases. When oil companies lease land to explore for oil and gas, a special lease agreement must be negotiated. Usually the landowner receives a cash payment for executing the lease. If no well is drilled within the period stated in the lease, the lease expires; however, most oil and gas leases provide that the oil company may continue its rights by paying another flat rental fee. Such rentals may be paid annually until a well is produced. If oil and/or gas is found, the landowner usually receives a fraction of its value as a royalty. In this case the lease will continue for as long as oil or gas is obtained in significant quantities. Oil and gas leases are common across the Southern Tier and in the western part of New York State.

An oil or gas lease constitutes a cloud on title, and a buyer may refuse to consummate a purchase unless he or she has specifically agreed to take title subject to such a lease.

Summary

A *lease* grants one person the right to use the property of another for a certain period in return for consideration. The lease agreement is a combination of a conveyance creating a leasehold interest in the property and a contract outlining the rights and obligations of landlord and tenant.

A leasehold estate that runs for a specific length of time creates an *estate for years,* while one that runs for an indefinite period creates a *periodic tenancy* (year to year, month to month) or a *tenancy at will.* A leasehold estate is generally classified as personal property.

The requirements of a valid lease include the capacity to contract, a demising clause, description of premises, statement of terms, rent, and signatures. The state statute of frauds requires that any lease that will not be executed within one year be in writing. Most leases also include clauses relating to such rights and obligations of the landlord and tenant as the use of the premises, subletting, judgments, maintenance of the premises, and termination of the lease period.

In New York an oral lease is valid if it is for a period of less than one year. A lease for three years or more, if properly acknowledged, may be entered in the public records. State regulations require the owner of six or more units to hold security deposits in an interest-bearing New York bank account with all interest less a one-percent fee due the tenant. State law gives the tenant in any building with four or more units the right to sublet, subject to the landlord's consent, which may not be unreasonably withheld.

Leases may be terminated by the expiration of the lease period, the mutual agreement of the parties, or a breach of the lease by either landlord or tenant. Neither the death of the tenant nor the landlord's sale of the rental property terminates a lease.

Upon a tenant's default on any of the lease provisions, a landlord may sue for a money judgment or for *actual eviction* in a case where a tenant has improperly retained possession of the premises. If the premises have become uninhabitable due to the landlord's negligence, the tenant may have the right of *constructive eviction*, the right to abandon the premises and refuse to pay rent until the premises are repaired.

Basic types of leases include *net leases, gross leases,* and *percentage leases.* These leases are classified according to the method used in determining the rental rate of the property.

Questions

1. In order to be considered valid in New York a two-year lease must:
   a. be in writing.
   b. be signed by the parties involved.
   c. state the terms of the agreement.
   d. All of the above

2. A lease for more than one year must be in writing because:
   a. the landlord or tenant may forget the terms.
   b. the tenant must sign the agreement to pay rent.
   c. the statute of frauds requires it.
   d. it is the customary procedure to protect the tenant.

3. A lease is considered to be:
   a. a freehold estate.
   b. personal property.
   c. a rerversionary interest.
   d. real property.

4. Willie James agrees to rent Dana Gibson her upstairs apartment for the next six months. Dana has a(n):
   a. estate for years.
   b. periodic estate.
   c. tenancy at will.
   d. tenancy at sufferance.

5. Willie James agrees to rent Dana Gibson her upstairs apartment from month to month. To end the arrangement Willie must:
   a. file a court suit to recover possession.
   b. give at least 60 days' notice from the day the rent is due.
   c. give at least 30 days' notice from the day the rent is due.
   d. simply refuse to accept the next month's rent, on the day it is due.

6. A tenant's lease has expired, the tenant has neither vacated nor negotiated a renewal lease, and the landlord has declared that she does not want the tenant to remain in the building. The tenancy is called:
   a. estate for years.
   b. periodic estate.
   c. tenancy at will.
   d. tenancy at sufferance.

7. Mary Withers sells her six-unit apartment building in Queens to George Brown. Now:
   a. George may give all the tenants 30 days' notice.
   b. tenants should collect their security deposits from Mary.
   c. George must renegotiate all leases with the tenants.
   d. Mary must turn over security deposits to George.

8. A lease, properly acknowledged, may be recorded if it is for a period of at least:
   a. one year.   c. three years.
   b. two years.   d. four years.

9. Steve Jackson rents a single-family house under a one-year lease. Two months into the rental period Jackson installs awnings over the front windows to keep the sun from some delicate hanging plants. The awnings:
   a. may be removed by Jackson any time before the year is over.
   b. are classified as trade fixtures.
   c. are now the property of the landlords.
   d. are known as chattels.

10. If a tenant is unable to receive hot water because of a faulty hot-water heater, which of the following remedies may the tenant take if the landlord refuses to fix the equipment?
    a. The tenant may sue the landlord for damages.
    b. The tenant may abandon the premises.
    c. The tenant may terminate the lease agreement.
    d. All of the above

11. A tenant who transfers the entire remaining term of his or her lease to a third party is:

   a. a sublettor.
   b. assigning the lease.
   c. automatically relieved of any further obligation under it.
   d. giving the third party a sandwich lease.

12. Unless otherwise stated in the lease, in New York State:

   a. rent is payable in arrears.
   b. the tenant is not entitled to interest on the security deposit.
   c. the tenant may not sublet.
   d. the lease is automatically terminated when the property is sold.

13. An automatic renewal clause in a lease:

   a. is not allowed on rent-stabilized apartments.
   b. is granted every tenant in a building with four or more units.
   c. is illegal in New York State.
   d. requires notice from the landlord calling the tenant's attention to the clause.

14. Jane Miller's apartment lease agreement states that it will expire on April 30, 1989. When must her landlord give notice that her tenancy is to terminate?

   a. January 31, 1989
   b. March 31, 1989
   c. April 1, 1989
   d. No notice is required.

15. If a tenant falls three months behind in rent payments, a landlord may:

   a. turn down the heat.
   b. move out the tenant's possessions, storing them carefully.
   c. start a court suit for possession.
   d. All of the above

16. In the example above, the landlord who turns down the heat has terminated the lease through:

   a. the demising clause.
   b. constructive eviction.
   c. payment in arrears.
   d. assigning the lease.

17. A gross lease is most likely to be used for rental of:

   a. an apartment.
   b. a factory building.
   c. land under a post office.
   d. a farm.

18. With a triple-net lease, the tenant pays:

   a. rent only.
   b. rent plus a share of business profits.
   c. rent plus any increase in property taxes.
   d. everything but the mortgate.

19. A percentage lease provides for:

   a. a rental of a percentage of the value of a building.
   b. a definite periodic rent not exceeding a stated percentage.
   c. a definite monthly rent plus a percentage of the tenant's gross receipts in excess of a certain amount.
   d. a graduated amount due monthly and not exceeding a stated percentage.

20. A ground lease is usually:

   a. terminable with 30 days' notice.
   b. based on percentages.
   c. long-term.
   d. a gross lease.

Appendix: Excerpts from New York State's Study Booklet for Brokers

LEASES

A lease is a contract whereby, for a consideration, usually termed rent, one who is entitled to the possession of real property grants such right to another for life, for a term of years, or at will.

Essentials of a valid lease. These are:

1. Competent parties (sane adults):
2. A definite demising clause, whereby the lessor (landlord) leases and the lessee (tenant) takes the property leased;
3. A reasonably definite description of the property leased;
4. A clear statement of the term (duration) of the letting;
5. Specification of the rent payable and how it is to be paid;
6. If the term of the lease is for more than one year it must be in writing, signed by all parties thereto and duly delivered.

Generally. There is no limitation upon the length of the term for which property may be leased. It is not necessary that the wife of the lessor join him in executing a lease even if its term is for 99 years, or longer.

A net lease is one that provides that the tenant, in addition to paying the agreed rent, shall defray the expense of all repairs, taxes, water rents, insurance, premiums, and such other items of the carrying charges upon the leased property, as may be specified.

Leases usually include numerous covenants, conditions of limitations, collateral to the letting and containing such provisions as the parties may agree upon as necessary to define their respective rights and responsibilities. Many of such collateral agreements are incorporated in all leases. Others are used only in connection with the letting of a particular class of property, such as apartments, lofts or offices.

All clauses or conditions contained in a lease are binding on the parties thereto because they are part of the contract entered into between the landlord and tenant. However, one of the exceptions to this rule of law exists with relation to the clause which is known as the "automatic renewal clause."

Section 5—905 of the General Obligations Law reads as follows: "No provision of a lease of any real property or premises which states that the term thereof shall be deemed renewed for a specified additional period of time unless the tenant gives notice to the lessor of his intention to quit the premises at the expiration of such term shall be operative unless the lessor, at least fifteen days and not more than thirty days previous to the time specified for the furnishing of such notice to him, shall give to the tenant written notice, served personally or by registered or certified mail, calling the attention of the tenant to the existence of such provision in the lease."

The results that may flow from the omission of a necessary or desirable covenant or condition are often annoying and, sometimes, may prove serious to the landlord or the tenant, as the case may be. *For instance, rent is not payable in advance unless the lease so provides.* So, too, a landlord has no right to send mechanics into leased premises, to make alterations or to install new equipment, unless the lease authorizes the landlord to do so. On the other hand, the tenant should carefully consider the negative covenants the lease contains. A negative covenant binds the tenant not to do specified acts, such as assigning the lease, subletting, or using the premises for other than a specified purpose, etc. The tenant should also bear in mind that, unless the lease provides that the landlord shall make all repairs, or such of them as the landlord has agreed to make, the tenant must bear the cost of even the most necessary repairs to the leased premises. Under section 226-b of the Real Property Law, a tenant of a residence of four or more units is given the right to sublet the premises or to assign his or her lease, such subletting or assignment being subject to the landlord's prior approval. If, however, the landlord unreasonably withholds consent, the landlord upon request must release the tenant from the lease. These provisions are applicable to all leases or renewals of leases now entered into. Every residential lease is also deemed to contain a covenant by the landlord that the premises are fit for human habitation and for the uses for which they were reasonably intended by the parties.

The tenant's rights under this covenant cannot be waived.

Form. There is no statutory form of lease. The law does require, however, that a residential lease be written in a clear and coherent manner, using words with every day meaning—that is, in plain language.

Recording leases. A lease is not recordable unless it is for a term of three years, or more, and has been duly signed and acknowledged by the parties thereto.

23

Voluntary and Involuntary Alienation

Key Terms

Descent
Escheat
Executor
Heir
Intestate
Involuntary alienation

Last will and testament
Probate
Testate
Testator
Title
Voluntary alienation

Overview

A parcel of real estate may be transferred from one owner to another in a number of different ways. It may be given *voluntarily* by sale or gift, or it may be taken *involuntarily* by operation of law. In addition it may be transferred by the living or it may be transferred by will or descent after a person has died. In every instance, however, a transfer of title to a parcel of real estate is a complex legal procedure involving a number of laws and documents. This chapter will discuss the four methods of title transfer.

| **Title** | **Title** to real estate means the right to or ownership of the land; in addition it represents the *evidence* of ownership. The term *title* has two functions: It represents the "bundle of rights" the owner possesses in the real estate and it also denotes the facts that, if proven, would enable a person to recover or retain ownership or possession of a parcel of real estate. |

Titles are either *original* or *derivative*. Original title to real property can be vested only in the state and is usually obtained through discovery, occupancy, conquest, or cession to the state. All other titles are derivative and are vested in individuals (or corporations, partnerships, and the like).

The laws of each state govern real estate transactions for land located within its boundaries. Each state has the authority to pass legislative acts that affect the methods of transferring title or other interests in real estate. Title to real estate may be transferred in most states by the following methods: (1) voluntary alienation, (2) involuntary alienation, (3) will, and (4) descent.

| **Voluntary Alienation** | **Voluntary alienation** (transfer) of title may be made by either gift or sale. To transfer title by voluntary alienation during his or her lifetime, an owner must use some form of deed of conveyance, as discussed in detail in Chapter 4. |

In New York the following deeds are used to convey title to property: (1) deeds with full covenants (warranty deeds); (2) bargain and sale deeds, without covenant against grantor's acts; (3) bargain and sale deeds, with covenant against grantor's acts; (4) quitclaim deeds; (5) executor's deeds; and (6) referees' deeds.

The full covenants and warranty deed contains the following five covenants:

1. that the grantor is *seized* of (owns) the premises and has good right to convey the same (covenant of seizin);
2. that the grantee will have the right to a property free of interference from the acts or claims of third parties (covenant of quiet enjoyment);
3. that the premises are free from *encumbrances* (covenant against encumbrances);
4. that the grantor will execute or procure any *further* necessary *assurance* of the title to the premises (covenant of further assurances); and
5. that the grantor will *forever warrant* the title to the premises (covenant of warranty forever).

Title to land may be transferred voluntarily between an individual and the government through dedication or public grant. A developer passes ownership of subdivision lands earmarked for streets and roads to a city, town, or village through the process of *dedication*. Lands owned by the government may be transferred to individuals through *public grant,* as when available public land is earned through the process of homesteading.

Involuntary Alienation

Title to property can be transferred by **involuntary alienation,** that is, without the owner's consent (*see* Figure 23.1). Such transfers are usually carried out by operations of law ranging from government condemnation of land for public use to the sale of property to satisfy delinquent tax or mortgage liens. When a person dies intestate and leaves no heirs, the title to his or her real estate passes to the state by operation of law based on the principle of **escheat.**

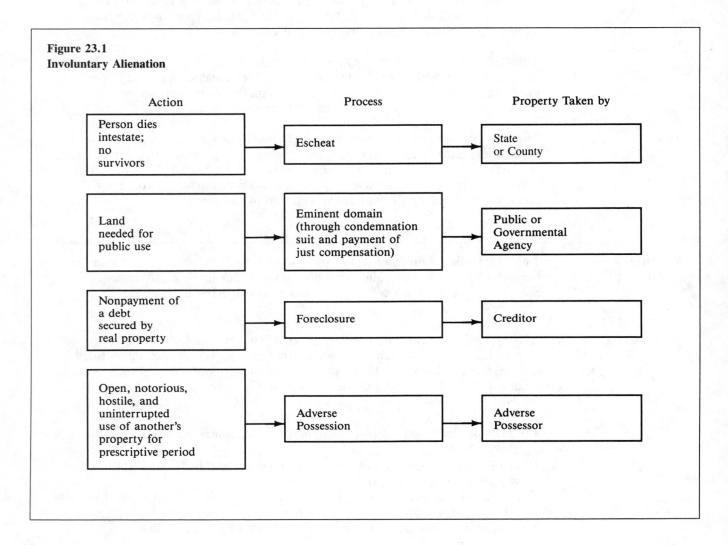

Figure 23.1
Involuntary Alienation

Action	Process	Property Taken by
Person dies intestate; no survivors	Escheat	State or County
Land needed for public use	Eminent domain (through condemnation suit and payment of just compensation)	Public or Governmental Agency
Nonpayment of a debt secured by real property	Foreclosure	Creditor
Open, notorious, hostile, and uninterrupted use of another's property for prescriptive period	Adverse Possession	Adverse Possessor

Federal, state, and local governments, school boards, some government agencies, and certain public and quasi-public corporations and utilities (railroads and gas and electric companies) have the power of *eminent domain.* Under this power, private property may be taken for public use through a *suit for condemnation.* The exercise of eminent domain is subject to a court's determination of two necessary conditions: (1) that the use is for the benefit of the public and (2) that an equitable amount of compensation, as set by the court, will be paid to the owner. Whenever private property is taken in New York, the owner is given the opportunity to challenge in court the amount of money offered for the interest taken.

Land also may be transferred without an owner's consent in order to satisfy debts contracted by the owner. In such cases the debt is foreclosed, the property is sold, and the proceeds of the sale are applied to pay off the debt. Debts that could be foreclosed include mortgage loans, real estate taxes, mechanics' liens, or general judgments against the property owner (*see* Chapter 24).

In addition to the involuntary transfer of land by legal processes, land may be transferred by natural forces. Owners of land bordering on rivers, lakes, and other bodies of water may acquire additional land through the process of *accretion*, the slow accumulation of soil, rock, or other matter deposited by the movement of water on an owner's property. The opposite of accretion is *erosion*, the gradual wearing away of land by the action of water and wind. In addition property may be lost through *avulsion*, the sudden tearing away of land by natural means like earthquakes or tidal waves.

Involuntary alienation also may occur as a result of court action. In a *partition proceeding* one co-owner seeks to force another to divide or sell property. An *action to quiet title* requests that the court rule on a clouded or disputed title, quashing one claim in favor of another.

Adverse Possession

Adverse possession is another means of involuntary transfer. An owner who does not use his or her land or does not inspect it for a number of years may lose title to another person who has some claim to the land, takes possession, and, most importantly, uses the land. In New York a person may acquire title by adverse possession to land owned by another by the continuous, open, notorious, hostile, and exclusive occupation of the property for *ten years*. After that time the user may perfect the claim of title to land by adverse possession by bringing a court suit to quiet title.

Through a process known as *tacking*, continuous periods of adverse possession may be combined by successive users, thus enabling a person who had not been in possession for the entire ten years to establish a claim of adverse possession. The process is not automatic; legal action is necessary to *perfect* the claim. Adverse possession is not possible against publicly owned property.

Through adverse possession the law recognizes that the use of land is an important function of its ownership. In many cases an adverse user's rights may supersede those of a fee owner. The subject of adverse possession is extremely technical because the right is statutory, and state requirements must be carefully followed in order to establish ownership. When a transaction involves the possibility of title by adverse possession, the parties should seek legal counsel. A claimant who does not receive title may acquire an easement by prescription (*see* Chapter 24).

Transfer of a Deceased Person's Property

Every state has a law known as the *statute of descent and distribution*. When a person dies **intestate** (without having left a will), the decedent's real estate and personal property pass to his or her heirs according to this statute. In effect the state makes a will for such decedents. In contrast a person who dies **testate** has prepared a will indicating the way his or her property will be disposed of after his or her death.

Legally, when a person dies, title to his or her real estate immediately passes either to the heirs by descent or to the persons named in the will. However, the will must be probated and all claims against the estate must be satisfied.

Probate Proceedings   **Probate** or administration is a legal process by which a court determines who will inherit the property of a deceased person and what the assets of the estate are. Surrogate's court proceedings must take place in the county where the deceased person lived. In the case of a person who has died testate, the court also rules on the validity of the will. If the will is upheld, the property is distributed according to its provisions. If a person has died without a will, the court determines who inherits by reviewing a *proof of heirship*. This statement, usually prepared by an attorney, gives personal information regarding the decedent's spouse, children, and relatives. From this document the court decides which parties will receive what portion of the estate.

To initiate probate or administration proceedings, the custodian of the will, an heir, or another interested party must petition the court. The court then holds a hearing to determine the validity of the will and/or the order of descent, should no valid will exist. If for any reason a will is declared invalid by the court, any property owned by the decedent will pass by the laws of descent. The court will appoint an **executor**, usually named in the will, or an *administrator* to oversee the administration and distribution of the estate. Probate proceedings vary and local procedures must be followed.

The court gives the administrator or executor the authority to appraise the assets of the estate and satisfy all debts that were owed by the decedent. He or she is also responsible for paying federal estate taxes and state inheritance taxes. After all these liens against the property have been satisfied, the executor distributes the remaining assets of the estate according to the provisions of the will or the state law of descent.

Transfer of Title by Will   A **last will and testament** is an instrument made by an owner to voluntarily convey title to the owner's property after his or her death. A will takes effect only after the death of the decedent; until that time, any property covered by the will can be conveyed by the owner.

A party who makes a will is known as a **testator,** or (female) *testatrix;* the gift of real property by will is known as a *devise,* and a person who receives real property by will is known as a *devisee.* In addition a gift of personal property is a *legacy* or *bequest;* the person receiving the personal property is a *legatee.*

In New York, children may be disinherited but a surviving spouse is entitled to at least one-third of the estate. In a case where a will does not provide the minimum statutory inheritance, the surviving spouse has the option of informing the court that he or she will take the minimum statutory share rather than the lesser share provided in the will. This practice, called a right of election, is a right reserved only to a surviving spouse.

A will differs from a deed in that a deed conveys a present interest in real estate during the lifetime of the grantor, while a will conveys no interest in the property until after the death of the testator. To be valid a deed *must* be delivered during the lifetime of the grantor. The parties named in a will have no rights or interests as long as the party who has made the will is still alive; they acquire interest or title only after the owner's death. State laws require that upon the death of a testator, his or her will must be filed with the court and *probated* in order for title to pass to the devisees.

Legal requirements for making a will (*see* Figure 23.2). A person must be of *legal age* and of *sound mind* when he or she executes the will. There are no rigid tests to determine the capacity to make a will. Usually the courts hold that to make a valid will the testator must have sufficient mental capacity to understand the nature and effect of his or her acts and to dispose of the property according to some plan. The courts also hold that the drawing of a will must be a voluntary act, free of any undue influence by other people.

**Figure 23.2
Requirements for a
Valid Will**

WILL

1. Legal Age
2. Sound Mind
3. Proper Wording
4. No Undue Influence
5. Witnesses

New York law provides that any person of sound mind who is 18 years of age or older can make a will devising his or her real property. All wills must be in writing and signed by the testator in the presence of at least two witnesses. A holographic will is one that is written entirely in the testator's own handwriting and is not properly attested in the manner just described. Such a document will be enforced by New York courts only under limited circumstances.

Transfer of Title by Descent

By law the title to real estate and personal property of a person who dies intestate passes to his or her heirs. Under the **descent** statutes the primary **heirs** of the deceased are his or her spouse and close blood relatives such as children, parents, brothers, and sisters. The closeness of the relationship to the decedent determines the specific rights of the heirs. As previously discussed, the relative's right to inherit must be established by proof of heirship during the probate process.

When children have been legally adopted, most states consider them to be heirs of the adopting parents but not heirs of ancestors of the adopting parents. In most states illegitimate children inherit from the mother but do not inherit from the father unless he has admitted parentage in writing or parentage has been established legally. If he legally adopts such a child, that child will inherit as an adopted child.

Intestate property will be distributed according to the laws of the state in which the property is located. The New York law of descent and distribution provides that real property belonging to an individual who has died intestate is distributed in the order listed below. This law and the estate discussed apply only to what remains of the estate after payment of all debts.

If a decedent is survived by:

1. a spouse and children or grandchildren, the spouse receives money or personal property not to exceed $4,000 in value and one-third of what remains of the estate. The balance of the estate passes to the children or to grandchildren.
2. a spouse and only one child, or a spouse and the children of only one child, the spouse receives money or personal property not to exceed $4,000 in value and one-half of what remains of the estate. The balance passes to the child or his or her children.
3. a spouse and both parents only, $25,000 and one-half the estate passes to the spouse. The parents or parent receive the balance, or the whole estate if there is no surviving spouse.
4. a spouse only, the spouse receives the entire estate.
5. children only, the children receive the entire estate.
6. siblings only, or their children, they receive the entire estate.

If there are no heirs, the decedent's property escheats to the state of New York.

Summary

Title to real estate is the right to and evidence of ownership of the land. It may be transferred in four ways: (1) voluntary alienation, (2) involuntary alienation, (3) will, and (4) descent.

An owner's title may be transferred without his or her permission by a court action such as a *foreclosure* or judgment sale, a tax sale, *condemnation* under the right of eminent domain, *adverse possession,* or *escheat.* Land also may be transferred by the natural forces of water and wind, which either increase property by *accretion* or decrease it through *erosion* or *avulsion.*

The real estate of an owner who makes a valid *will* (who dies testate) passes to the devisees through the probating of the will. Generally, an heir or a devisee does not receive a deed, because title passes by the law or the will. The title of an owner who dies without a will (intestate) passes according to the provisions of the *law of descent* of the state in which the real estate is located.

Questions

1. Title to real estate may be transferred during a person's lifetime by:
   a. devise.
   b. descent.
   c. involuntary alienation.
   d. escheat.

2. Title to an owner's real estate can be transferred at the death of the owner by which of the following documents?
   a. Warranty deed
   b. Quitclaim deed
   c. Referee's deed
   d. Last will and testament

3. Matilda Fairbanks bought acreage in a distant county, never went to see the acreage, and did not use the ground. Harold Sampson moved his mobile home onto the land, had a water well drilled, and lived there for 12 years. Sampson may become the owner of the land if he has complied with the state law regarding:
   a. requirements for a valid conveyance.
   b. adverse possession.
   c. avulsion.
   d. voluntary alienation.

4. Which of the following is *not* one of the manners in which title to real estate may be transferred by involuntary alienation?
   a. Eminent domain
   b. Escheat
   c. Erosion
   d. Seizin

5. A person who has died leaving a valid will is called a(n):
   a. devisee.
   b. testator.
   c. legatee.
   d. intestate.

6. Claude Johnson, a bachelor, died owning real estate that he devised by his will to his niece, Annette. In essence, at what point does title pass to his niece?
   a. Immediately upon Johnson's death
   b. After his will has been probated
   c. After Annette has paid all inheritance taxes
   d. When Annette executes a new deed to the property

7. An owner of real estate who was adjudged legally incompetent made a will during his stay at a nursing home. He later died and was survived by a wife and three children. His real estate will pass:
   a. to his wife.
   b. to the heirs mentioned in his will.
   c. according to the state law of descent.
   d. to the state.

8. In New York, land may be acquired by adverse possession after a period of:
   a. three years.
   b. seven years.
   c. ten years.
   d. 20 years.

9. The acquisition of land through deposit of soil or sand washed up by water is called:
   a. accretion.
   b. avulsion.
   c. erosion.
   d. condemnation.

10. The person whose land is taken for public use in New York State:
    a. may or may not receive compensation.
    b. may refuse to give up the property.
    c. may still devise it by will.
    d. may challenge a money award in court.

24

Liens and Easements

Key Terms

Corporation franchise tax
Easement appurtenant
Easement by prescription
Easement in gross
Equitable lien
Estate taxes
General contractor
General lien
Inheritance taxes
Involuntary lien
Internal Revenue Service tax lien
Judgment
Lien

Mechanics' liens
Mortgage lien
Notice of pendency
Priority
Specific lien
Statutory lien
Subcontractor
Subordination agreement
Surety bail bond
Tacking
Vendee's lien
Vendor's lien
Voluntary lien

Overview

The ownership interest a person has in real estate can be diminished by the interests of others. Taxing bodies, creditors, and courts can lessen an ownership interest by making a claim—called a *lien*—against a person's property to secure payment of taxes, debts, and other obligations. In addition, rights to use another's real estate can be acquired; these rights are called *easements*. This chapter will discuss the nature of liens and easements that affect both real and personal property.

Liens

A **lien** is defined as a charge against property that provides security for a debt or obligation of the property owner. A lien allows a creditor (lienor) to force the sale of the property given as security by the debtor (lienee) to satisfy the lienee's debt in case of default. A lien does not constitute ownership; it is a type of *encumbrance*—a charge or burden on a property that may diminish its value. While all liens are encumbrances, encumbrances are not necessarily liens. As discussed in Chapter 3, encumbrances that are not liens (easements and deed restrictions) are *incorporeal rights* in real estate and give the parties in question certain rights, or interests, in the real estate.

Generally liens are enforced by court order. A creditor must institute a legal action for the court to sell the real estate in question for full or partial satisfaction of the debt.

A lien may be voluntary or involuntary. A **voluntary lien** is created by the owner's action such as taking out a mortgage loan. An **involuntary lien** is created by law. Involuntary liens are either statutory or equitable. A **statutory lien** is created by statute. An **equitable lien** arises out of common law. A real estate tax lien, for example, is an involuntary, statutory lien; that is, it is created by statute without any action by the property owner. A court-ordered judgment requiring payment of the balance on a delienquent charge account would be an involuntary, equitable lien on the debtor's property.

Liens may be classified into two categories: general and specific. As illustrated in Figure 24.1, **general liens** usually affect all the property of a debtor, both real and personal, and include judgments, estate and inheritance taxes, debts of a deceased person, corporation franchise taxes, and Internal Revenue Service taxes. **Specific liens** on the other hand are secured by a specific parcel of real estate and affect only that particular property. As illustrated in Figure 24.2, these include mechanics' liens, mortgages, taxes, special assessments, liens for certain public utilities, vendors' liens, vendees' liens, and surety bail bond liens.

Effects of Liens on Title

Although the fee simple estate held by a typical real estate owner can be reduced in value by the lien and encumbrance rights of others, the owner is still free to convey his or her title to a willing purchaser. This purchaser, however, will buy the property subject to any liens and encumbrances of the seller because, after properly established, liens *run with the land;* that is, they will bind successive owners if steps are not taken to clear the liens.

Liens attach to property, not to the property owner. Although a purchaser who buys real estate under a delinquent lien is not responsible for payment of the debt secured by the lien, he or she faces a possible loss of the property if the creditors take court action to enforce payment of their liens.

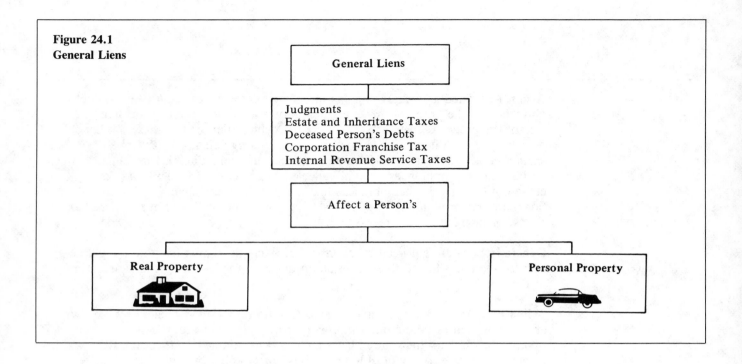

**Figure 24.1
General Liens**

General Liens

Judgments
Estate and Inheritance Taxes
Deceased Person's Debts
Corporation Franchise Tax
Internal Revenue Service Taxes

Affect a Person's

Real Property

Personal Property

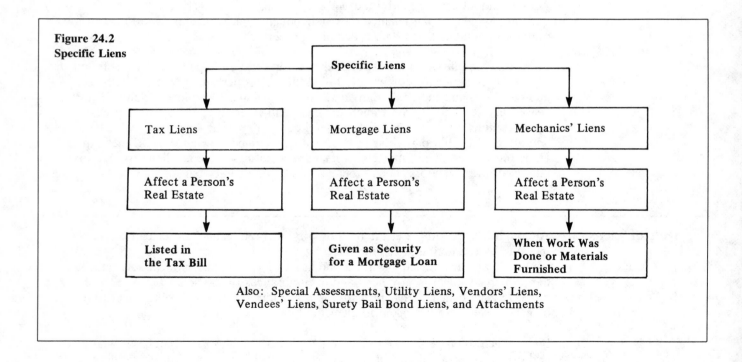

**Figure 24.2
Specific Liens**

Specific Liens

Tax Liens	Mortgage Liens	Mechanics' Liens
Affect a Person's Real Estate	Affect a Person's Real Estate	Affect a Person's Real Estate
Listed in the Tax Bill	Given as Security for a Mortgage Loan	When Work Was Done or Materials Furnished

Also: Special Assessments, Utility Liens, Vendors' Liens,
Vendees' Liens, Surety Bail Bond Liens, and Attachments

Priority of Liens   **Tax liens.** Real estate taxes and special assessments generally take **priority** over
all other liens. If the property goes through a court sale to satisfy unpaid debts
or obligations, outstanding real estate taxes and special assessments will be paid

from the proceeds *first*. The remainder of the proceeds will be used to pay other outstanding liens in the order of their priority.

For example, if the courts ordered a parcel of land sold to satisfy a judgment lien entered in the public record on February 7, 1986, subject to a first mortgage lien recorded January 22, 1984, and to this year's as-yet unpaid real estate taxes, the proceeds of the sale would be distributed in the following order:

1. to the taxing bodies for this year's real estate taxes.
2. to the mortgage lender for the entire amount of the mortgage loan outstanding as of the date of the sale (if proceeds remain after payments of taxes).
3. to the creditor named in the judgment lien (if any proceeds remain after paying the first two items).
4. to the foreclosed-upon landowner (if any proceeds remain after paying the first three items).

Liens other than general taxes and special assessments take priority from the date of recording in the public records of the county where the property is located (*see* Figure 24.3.).

Figure 24.3 Priority of Liens

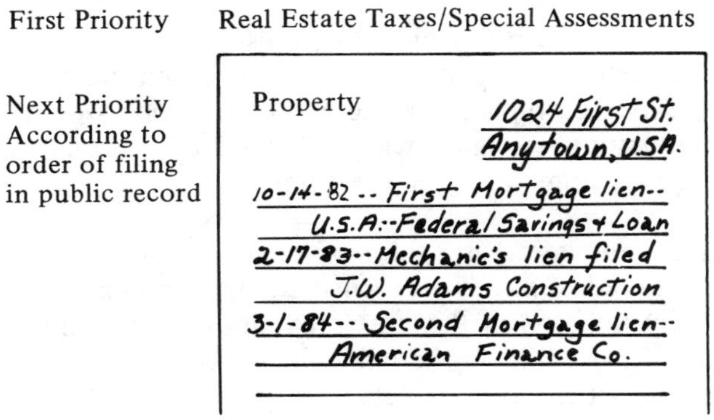

First Priority   Real Estate Taxes/Special Assessments

Next Priority According to order of filing in public record

Property   *1024 First St. Anytown, USA.*

10-14-82 -- First Mortgage lien-- U.S.A.--Federal Savings + Loan
2-17-83--Mechanic's lien filed J.W. Adams Construction
3-1-84 -- Second Mortgage lien-- American Finance Co.

Subordination agreements are written agreements between lienholders to change the priority of mortgage, judgment, and other liens under certain circumstances. Priority and recording of liens are discussed in detail in Chapter 11.

Liens Other than Taxes

Aside from real estate tax and special assessment liens, the following types of liens may be charged against real property either voluntarily or involuntarily: mortgage liens, mechanics' liens, judgments, estate and inheritance tax liens, vendors' liens, vendees' liens, liens for municipal utilities, surety bail bond liens, corporation franchise tax liens, and Internal Revenue Service tax liens.

Mortgage Liens

In general a **mortgage lien** is a voluntary lien on real estate given to a lender by a borrower as security for a mortgage loan. It becomes a lien on real property when the mortgage funds are disbursed and when the lender files or records the mortgage in the office of the county clerk or registrar of the county where the property is located. Mortgage lenders generally require a preferred lien, referred to as a *first mortgage lien;* this means that (aside from taxes) no other major liens against the property would take priority over the mortgage lien. This requirement does not apply to second mortgages.

Mortgages and mortgage liens are discussed in detail in Chapter 7.

Mechanics' Liens
The purpose of the **mechanic's lien** is to *give security to those who perform labor or furnish material in the improvement of real property.* In general the mechanic's lien right is based on the *enhancement of value theory.* Because of the labor performed and material furnished, the real estate has been enhanced in value. Therefore the parties who performed the work or supplied materials are given a right of lien on the real estate on which they worked as security for the payment of their proper charges. A mechanic's lien is a specific, involuntary lien.

In order for a person to be entitled to a mechanic's lien, the work that was done must have been by contract (express or implied consent) with the owner or owner's authorized representative. Such a lien is relied on to cover situations in which the owner has not fully paid for the work or when the general contractor has been paid but has not paid the subcontractors or suppliers of materials.

A notice of a mechanic's lien must be filed in the office of the clerk of the county in which the property is located. The lien must be filed within four months for work on a single residence and eight months on all other property, from the date the last item of labor was performed or material furnished. The mechanic's lien attaches immediately upon filing.

If a landowner has paid a **general contractor** in full and the general contractor has failed to pay the **subcontractor** or materialmen, the general contractor may be in violation of the trust provisions of the New York State lien law. Proof of payment in full by the landowner will be a defense to the claim under the mechanic's lien law; the subcontractor must look to the contractor.

A mechanic's lien does not have priority over any prior recorded lien provided the prior liens are proper in all respects. A mechanic's lien for private improvements is valid for one year from the date of filing and can be renewed by a court order.

New York's lien law was amended at the end of 1982 to allow certain brokers' claims for commissions to be filed as mechanics' liens. On the theory that the negotiation of a long-term lease constitutes an improvement of commercial property, a broker may enter a mechanic's lien in the public records for unpaid commissions. Such a lien may be filed only if the property is to be used for other than residential purposes and if the lease is for three years or longer. The broker must file the claim only after execution of the lease by the lessor and lessee and must append a copy of the written contract of employment or agreement for compensation.

A similar amendment of the real property law, made at the same time, allows a broker to file an affidavit of entitlement to commission for negotiation of a contract for the purchase or lease of any real property. Such an affidavit, although entered in the public records, does not become a lien against the property and does not invalidate any transfer or lease.

Judgments

A **judgment** is a *decree issued by a court*. When the decree provides for the awarding of money and sets forth the amount of money owed by the debtor to the creditor, the judgment is referred to as a *money judgment*.

A judgment becomes a *general, involuntary lien on both real and personal property* owned by the debtor. A lien covers only property located within the county in which the judgment is issued. Therefore transcripts of the lien must be filed in other counties when a creditor wishes to extend the lien coverage. A judgment differs from the mortgage in that a *specific* parcel of real estate was not given as security at the time that the debtor-creditor relationship was created.

A judgment becomes a lien against the debtor's real property in each county where the judgment is docketed—a judgment acquired in one county can be docketed in any county of New York. A judgment is a lien against the property for ten years and can be renewed for ten more. (A judgment remains a valid lien against *personal* property for 20 years.)

A judgment takes its priority as a lien on the debtor's property from the date the judgment was filed for record in the county clerk's office. Judgments are enforced through the sale of the debtor's real or personal property by a sheriff. When the property is sold to satisfy the debt, the debtor may demand a legal document known as a *satisfaction of judgment,* or *satisfaction piece,* which should be filed with the clerk of the court and the county clerk where the judgment was filed or docketed so that the record will be cleared of the judgment. Normally the sheriff files a writ of execution showing that it has been returned satisfied; this is generally sufficient.

Lis pendens. A judgment or other decree affecting real estate is rendered at the conclusion of a lawsuit. Generally, considerable time elapses between the filing of a lawsuit and the rendering of a judgment. When any suit is filed that affects title to a specific parcel of real estate (such as a foreclosure suit), a notice known as a *lis pendens* is recorded. A lis pendens is not a lien but rather a *notice of a possible future lien*. Recording of the lis pendens gives notice to all interested parties such as prospective purchasers and lenders and establishes a priority for the later lien, which is dated back to the date the lis pendens was filed for record. The lis pendens creates a cloud on the title until the lawsuit is determined. In New York a lis pendens is also known as a **notice of pendency.**

Estate and Inheritance Tax Liens

Federal **estate taxes** and state **inheritance taxes** (as well as the debts of deceased persons) are *general, statutory, involuntary liens* that encumber a deceased person's real and personal property. These are normally paid or cleared in probate court proceedings. Probate and issues of inheritance are discussed in Chapter 23.

Vendors' Liens

A **vendor's lien** is a *seller's claim* against the title of property he or she conveyed to a buyer; it occurs in cases where the seller did not receive the full, agreed-upon purchase price. This is a *specific, equitable, involuntary lien* for the amount of the unpaid balance due the seller but is not enforceable without the decree of a court of competent jurisdiction.

Vendees' Liens

A **vendee's lien** is a *buyer's claim* against a seller's property in cases where the seller failed to deliver title. This usually occurs when property is purchased under an installment contract (contract for deed, land contract) and the seller fails to deliver title after all other terms of the contract have been satisfied. A vendee's lien is a *specific, equitable, involuntary lien* for any money paid plus the value of any improvements made to the property by the buyer.

The buyer has a lien against the property covered by the contract of sale to the extent of his or her down payment. The contract terms often define the lien and extend it to include the costs of a survey and title examination as well. This lien does not have to be filed in the clerk's office. If it is not filed, however, it will be subordinate to those liens that have been filed. The vendee may notify third parties of the claim by filing a lis pendens or the contract itself.

Liens for Municipal Utilities

Municipalities that furnish water or services like refuse collection to property owners are given the right to a *specific, involuntary lien* on the property of an owner who refuses to pay bills for water or any other such municipal utility services.

Surety Bail Bond Liens

A real estate owner charged with a crime for which he or she must face trial may choose to put up real estate instead of cash as surety for bail. The execution and recording of such a **surety bail bond** creates a *specific, voluntary lien* against the owner's real estate. This lien is enforceable by the state through a sheriff or other court officer if the accused person does not appear in court as required.

Corporation Franchise Tax Liens

State governments levy a **corporation franchise tax** on corporations as a condition of allowing them to do business in the state. Such a tax is a *general, involuntary, statutory* lien on all property, real and personal, owned by the corporation and need not be specifically filed.

IRS Tax Lien

An **Internal Revenue Service (IRS) tax lien** results from a person's failure to pay any portion of his or her federal IRS taxes such as income and withholding taxes. A federal tax lien is a *general, statutory, involuntary lien* on all real and personal property held by the delinquent taxpayer.

Miscellaneous Liens

Other possibilities include liens for New York State Tax Commission Warrants, special liens in the City of New York such as parking violations and emergency repairs, and certain UCC filings where real estate is specifically included in the lien.

Easements

A right acquired by one party to use the land of another party for a special purpose is an **easement.** Although this is the common definition of an easement, a party may also have an easement right in the air above a parcel of real estate or land.

Since 1979 the New York Real Property Law provides for the recording of solar energy easements.

Because *an easement is a right to use land* it is classified as an interest in real estate, but it is not an estate in land. The holder of an easement has only a right. He or she does not have an estate or ownership interest in the land over which the easement exists. An easement is sometimes referred to as an *incorporeal right* in land (a nonpossessory interest). An easement may be either appurtenant or in gross.

Easement Appurtenant

An easement that is *annexed to the ownership and used for the benefit of another's parcel of land* is an **easement appurtenant.** For example, if A and B both own adjacent properties in a resort community and only A's property borders the lake, A may grant B a right-of-way across A's property to the beach.

For an easement appurtenant to exist there must be two adjacent tracts of land owned by different parties. The tract over which the easement runs is known as the *servient tenement;* the tract that is to benefit from the easement is known as the *dominant tenement.*

An easement appurtenant is considered part of the dominant tenement, and if the dominant tenement is conveyed to another party, the easement passes with the title. In legal terms it is said that *the easement runs with the land.* However, title to the land over which an easement actually runs is still retained by the servient tenement.

Easement in Gross

A *mere personal interest* in or right to use the land of another is an **easement in gross.** Such an easement is not appurtenant to any ownership estate in land. Examples of easements in gross are the easement rights a railroad has in its right-of-way or the right-of-way for a pipeline or high-tension power line. Commercial easements in gross may be assigned or conveyed and may be inherited. However, personal easements in gross usually are not assignable and terminate upon the death of the easement owner. Easements in gross are often confused with the similar personal right of license. A license may be withdrawn; it is not an estate.

Easement by Necessity

An appurtenant easement that arises when an owner sells part of his or her land that has no access to a street or public way except over the seller's remaining land is an **easement by necessity.**

Easement by Prescription

When the claimant has made use of another's land for a certain period of time as defined by state law, an **easement by prescription** may be acquired. This *prescriptive period* is ten years in New York. The claimant's use must have been continuous, adverse to owner's title, exclusive, and without the owner's approval. Additionally the use must be visible, open, and notorious so that the owner could readily learn of it.

Through the concept of **tacking,** a party not in possession of real property for the entire required statutory period may successfully establish a claim of an easement by prescription. Successive periods of continuous, uninterrupted occupation by different parties may be tacked on, or combined, to reach the prescriptive period. In order to tack on one person's possession to that of another, the parties must have been *successors in interest* such as an ancestor and his or her heir, landlord and tenant, or seller and buyer. Legal action must be taken to perfect the easement.

Party Walls
A party wall is an exterior wall of a building that straddles the boundary line between two owners' lots. Each lot owner owns half of the wall (on his or her own side) and each has an easement right in the other half of the wall for support of the building. A written party-wall agreement should be used to create these easement rights. Each owner must pay half of expenses to build and maintain the wall.

Creating an Easement
Easements are commonly created by written agreement between the parties establishing the easement right. They also may be created in a number of other ways: (1) by express grant from the owner of the property over which the easement will run; (2) by the grantor in a deed of conveyance either *reserving* an easement over the sold land or *granting* the new owner an easement over the grantor's remaining land; (3) by longtime usage, as in an easement by prescription; (4) by necessity; and (5) by *implication;* that is, the situation or the parties' actions may imply that they intend to create an easement. Again, court action would be necessary to perfect the easement.

To create an easement there must be *two separate parties*, one of whom is the owner of the land over which the easement runs. It is impossible for the owner of a parcel of property to have an easement over his or her own land. Thus where a valid easement exists and the dominant tenement is acquired by the owner of the servient tenement, the easement becomes dormant. The easement will not be considered terminated unless it is either the express or the implied intention of the user to terminate it.

Terminating an Easement
Easements may be terminated:

1. when the purpose for which the easement was created no longer exists;
2. when the owner of either the dominant or the servient tenement becomes the owner of the other, providing there is an express intention of the parties to extinguish the easement (this is called a *merger*);
3. by release of the right of easement to the owner of the servient tenement; and
4. by abandonment of the easement (again, the intention of the parties is the determining factor).

Summary
Liens are claims, or charges, of creditors or tax officials against the real and personal property of a debtor. A lien is a type of encumbrance. All liens are encumbrances but not all encumbrances are liens. Liens are either *general,* covering all real and personal property of a debtor-owner, or *specific,* covering only the specific parcel of real estate described in the mortgage, tax bill, or building or repair contract or other document.

With the exception of real estate tax liens and mechanics' liens, the priority of liens is generally determined by the order in which they are placed in the public record of the county in which the debtor's property is located.

Mortgage liens are voluntary, specific liens given to lenders to secure payment for mortgage loans. *Mechanics' liens* protect general contractors, subcontractors, and material suppliers whose work enhances the value of real estate.

A *judgment* is a court decree obtained by a creditor, usually for a monetary award from a debtor. The lien of a judgment can be enforced by issuance of a *writ of execution* and sale by the sheriff to pay the judgment amount and costs.

Lis pendens, or *notice of pendency,* is a recorded notice of a lawsuit that is awaiting trial in court and may result in a judgment that will affect title to a parcel of real estate.

Federal estate taxes and *state inheritance taxes* are general liens against a deceased owner's property.

Vendors' liens and *vendees' liens* are liens against a specific parcel of real estate. A vendor's lien is a seller's claim against a purchaser who has not paid the entire purchase price, and a vendee's lien is a purchaser's claim against a seller under an installment contract who has not conveyed title.

Liens for *water charges or other municipal utilities* and *surety bail bond liens* are specific liens, while *corporation franchise tax liens* are general liens against a corporation's assets.

Internal Revenue Service tax liens are general liens against the property of a person who is delinquent in payment of income tax.

An *easement* is the right acquired by one person to use another's real estate. Easements are classified as interests in real estate but are not estates in land. *Easements appurtenant* involve two separately owned tracts. The tract benefited is known as the *dominant tenement;* the tract that is subject to the easement is called the *servient tenement.* An *easement in gross* is a personal right such as that granted to utility companies to maintain poles, wires, and pipelines.

Easements may be created by agreement, express grant, grant or reservation in a deed, implication, necessity, prescription, or party-wall agreement. They can be terminated when the purpose of the easement no longer exists, by merger of both interests with an express intention to extinguish the easement, by release, or by an intention to abandon the easement.

Questions

1. Which of the following is (are) considered liens on real estate?

    a. Easements running with the land
    b. Unpaid mortgage loans
    c. Public footpaths
    d. A license to erect a billboard

2. General contractor Ralph Hammond was hired to build a room addition to Thom and Harriet Elkin's home. Hammond completed the work several weeks ago but still has not been paid. In this situation Hammond is entitled to a mechanic's lien; it will be a:

    a. general lien.   c. statutory lien.
    b. specific lien.   d. voluntary lien.

3. When the Micawbers failed to pay for their bedroom furniture the store secured a judgment against them. The judgment becomes what kind of lien?

    a. Specific   c. Voluntary
    b. General   d. Statutory

4. Which of the following best refers to the type of lien that affects all real and personal property of a debtor?

    a. Specific lien   c. Involuntary lien
    b. Voluntary lien   d. General lien

5. Which of the following is a voluntary, specific lien?

    a. IRS tax lien   c. Mortgage lien
    b. Mechanic's lien   d. Vendor's lien

6. Which of the following liens usually would be given higher priority?

    a. A mortgage dated last year
    b. The current real estate tax
    c. A mechanic's lien for work started before the mortgage was made
    d. A judgment rendered yesterday

7. Jim Chard was not paid for roofing the Hills' ranch home. How long does he have to file a mechanic's lien?

    a. Four months   c. One year
    b. Eight months   d. Ten years

8. Jim's mechanic's lien will remain against the property for at least:

    a. four months.   c. one year.
    b. eight months.   d. ten years.

9. In New York a lis pendens:

    a. is known as a notice of pendency.
    b. gives notice of a lawsuit involving a particular property.
    c. is filed in the county clerk's office.
    d. All of the above

10. General contractor Kim Kelly is suing homeowner Bob Baker for nonpayment of services; suit will be filed in the next few weeks. Recently Kelly learned that the homeowner has listed his property with a local real estate broker for sale. In this instance which of the following will probably be used by Kelly and her attorneys to protect her interest?

    a. Lis pendens
    b. Prescription
    c. Affidavit of entitlement
    d. Satisfaction piece

11. Suzy Soldsine secured an excellent buyer for the Tightes' split-level home but she suspects they will not pay her commission. Suzy may file a(n):

    a. mechanic's lien.
    b. lis pendens.
    c. affidavit of entitlement.
    d. statutory lien.

12. When the Cratchetts failed to pay for Tim's orthopedic surgery Dr. Kildare obtained a money judgment, which he can now file against the Cratchetts':

    a. car.   c. apartment house.
    b. home.   d. All of the above

13. Donny Prelate sold Ernest Tully a parcel of real estate; title has passed but to date Tully has not paid the purchase price in full as originally agreed upon. If Prelate does not receive payment, which of the following could he sue to enforce?

    a. Mortgage lien   c. Lis pendens
    b. Vendee's lien   d. Vendor's lien

14. Which of the following is classified as a general lien?

    a. Vendor's lien
    b. Surety bail bond lien
    c. Debts of a deceased person
    d. General real estate taxes

15. When the Cratchetts pay off their doctor's judgment they should:

    a. record a satisfaction certificate.
    b. put a lis pendens on the apartment house.
    c. notify their mortgagee.
    d. grant an easement appurtenant.

16. In New York City, property may receive a lien for the owner's:

    a. jaywalking.   c. shoplifting.
    b. traffic tickets.   d. public disturbance.

17. A telephone company runs its poles and wires with the rights granted by an:

    a. easement by necessity.
    b. easement appurtenant.
    c. easement by prescription.
    d. easement in gross.

18. A license differs from an easement in that it:

    a. runs with the land.
    b. requires a court order.
    c. may be withdrawn.
    d. allows use of someone else's land.

19. The farmer who allowed promoters to run the Woodstock rock festival on his land granted them a(n):

    a. easement by necessity.
    b. dominant tenement.
    c. equitable lien.
    d. license.

20. To establish an easement by prescription in New York a person must use another's property for an uninterrupted period of:

    a. five years.   c. 15 years.
    b. ten years.   d. 20 years.

25

Taxes and Assessments

Key Terms

Ad valorem tax
Assessment roll
Equalization factor
Full-value assessment
In rem
Mill
Redemption

Special assessment
Statutory redemption period
Tax foreclosure
Tax lien
Tax sale
True tax

Overview   Among the powers of government over ownership of real estate in the right to levy taxes. This chapter will discuss real estate tax liens, which affect every owner of real estate.

Tax Liens

As discussed in Chapter 6, the ownership of real estate is subject to certain government powers. One of these powers is the right of state and local governments to impose **tax liens** for the support of their governmental functions. Because the location of real estate is permanently fixed, the government can levy taxes with a rather high degree of certainty that the taxes will be collected. Because the annual taxes levied on real estate usually have priority over other previously recorded liens, they may be enforced by the court-ordered sale of the real estate.

Real estate taxes can be divided into two types: (1) *general real estate tax,* or **ad valorem tax,** and (2) **special assessment,** or *improvement tax.* Both of these taxes are levied against specific parcels of property and automatically become liens on those properties.

General Tax (Ad Valorem Tax)

The general real estate tax is made up of the taxes levied on real estate by various governmental agencies and municipalities. These include cities, towns, villages, and counties. Other taxing bodies are school districts, park districts, lighting districts, drainage districts, water districts, and sanitary districts. Municipal authorities operating recreational preserves such as forest preserves and parks also may be authorized by the legislature to levy real estate taxes.

General real estate taxes are levied for the *general support or operation* of the governmental agency authorized to impose the levy. These taxes are known as *ad valorem* taxes because the amount of the tax varies in accordance with the *value of the property being taxed.*

Exemptions from general taxes. Certain real estate is exempt from real estate taxation. Certain property owned by cities, various municipal organizations (schools, parks, and playgrounds), the state and federal governments, and religious corporations, hospitals, or educational institutions is tax exempt. The property must be used for tax-exempt purposes by the exempted group or organization. If it is not so used, it will be subject to tax.

New York also allows special exemptions to reduce real estate tax bills for certain property owners or land uses. Veterans and senior citizens may be eligible for set reductions in some property taxes. Real estate tax reductions are sometimes granted to attract industries. In specific agricultural districts New York may offer reductions for agricultural land to encourage the continuation of agricultural uses.

The real estate broker taking the listing of a parcel of real estate should be alert to the possibility of exemptions and exercise diligence in ascertaining the **true tax** figure.

Special Assessments (Improvement Taxes)

Special assessments are *special taxes levied on real estate that require property owners to pay for improvements that benefit the real estate they own.* These taxes are often levied to pay for such improvements as streets, alleys, street lighting, curbs, and similar items and are enforced in the same manner as general real estate taxes.

The authority to recommend or initiate the *specific improvement* is vested in either the property owners, who may petition for an improvement, or in a proper legislative authority such as the city council or board of trustees, who may initiate the proposal for an improvement. Hearings are held and notices are given to the owners of the property affected.

After the preliminary legal steps have been taken, the legislative authority authorized by statute to act in such cases adopts an *ordinance* that sets out the nature of the improvement, its cost, and a description of the area to be assessed.

The proper authority spreads the assessment (called the **assessment roll**) over the various parcels of real estate that will benefit. The amount of the assessment for each parcel is determined by the estimated benefit each tract will receive by reason of the assessment. The assessment usually will vary from parcel to parcel, as all will not benefit equally from the improvement.

After hearing the benefits and nature of improvements to be made and after hearing any objections from members of the local community affected by the improvements, the local authority will either approve or reject the proposal. This is usually referred to as *confirming the assessment roll*.

After all of these steps have been taken, the assessment becomes a lien on the land assessed. When the improvement has been completed, a *warrant* is issued by the proper authority. This warrant gives the local collector the authority to issue special assessment bills and begin collection. An assessment becomes a *lien* following the confirmation of the roll.

If a benefit charge is unpaid the town can add that charge to its general tax levy by requesting an appropriate resolution from the county board of supervisors or the county legislature. In that way the town can collect in full any delinquent charges, often for water.

The Taxation Process

Assessment. Assessments in New York are made by municipal officials known as assessors. Assessments are made by towns, villages, and cities and, in a few cases, by counties. The assessment roll contains an assessment for land and a total value for land and improvements, if any.

In 1788 New York law mandated **full-value assessment.** The requirement was largely ignored, with most municipalities assessing at less than full value. In 1975 the court of appeals ordered the state either to enforce the law or to change it. More than 400 communities then went to full-value assessment voluntarily or under court order. In 1982 the legislature repealed the 200-year-old requirement. Under the regulations that went into force at that time, Upstate communities were simply required to assess all property at a "*uniform* percentage of value" while New York City and Long Island were allowed to divide real property into four different classes for tax purposes. The question of full-value assessment remains controversial and hotly debated, with court challlenges frequent.

Property owners who claim that errors were made in determining the assessed value of their property may present their objections, usually to a local board of review. Protests or appeals regarding tax assessments ultimately may be taken to court.

Such cases generally involve a proceeding whereby the court reviews the certified assessment records of the tax assessment official. Since 1982, a simple, inexpensive "small claims" procedure is available in New York.

Equalization. When it is necessary to correct general inequalities in statewide tax assessments, uniformity is achieved by use of an **equalization factor.** The New York State Board of Equalization and Assessment issues an equalization rate for each municipality. This factor is intended to equalize the assessments in every taxing jurisdiction across the state. No equalization factor applies where full-value assessment is used. Westchester County also establishes its own equalization rate. The assessed value of each property is multiplied by the equalization factor and the tax rate is then applied to the equalized assessment. For example, the assessments in one district are determined to be 20 percent lower than the average assessments throughout the rest of the state. This underassessment can be corrected by decreeing the application of an equalization factor of 125 percent to each assessment in that district. Thus a parcel of land assessed for tax purposes at $63,000 would be taxed based upon an equalized assessment of $78,750 in this district ($63,000 × 1.25 = $78,750).

Tax rates. The process of arriving at a real estate tax rate begins with the *adoption of a budget* by each county, city, school board, or other taxing district (*see* Figure 25.1). Each budget covers the financial requirements of the taxing body for the coming fiscal year, which may be the January to December calendar year or some other 12-month period designated by statute. The budget must include an estimate of all expenditures for the year and indicate the amount of income expected from all fees, revenue-sharing, and other sources. The net amount remaining to be raised from real estate taxes is then determined from these figures.

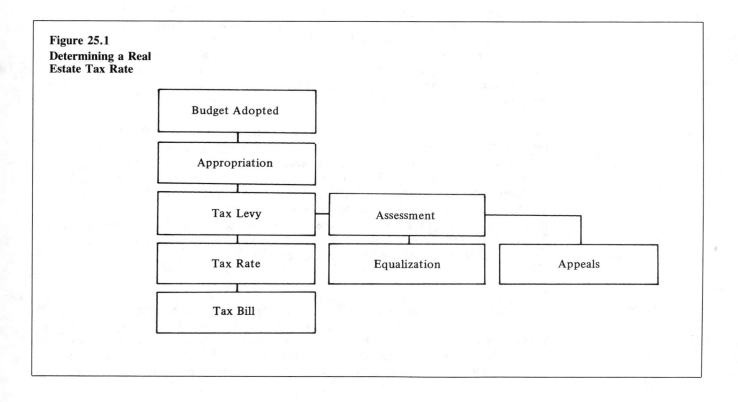

**Figure 25.1
Determining a Real
Estate Tax Rate**

The next step is *appropriation,* the action taken by each taxing body that authorizes the expenditure of funds and provides for the sources of such monies. Appropriation involves the adoption of an ordinance or the passage of a law setting forth the specifics of the proposed taxation.

The amount to be raised from the general real estate tax is then imposed on property owners through a *tax levy,* the formal action taken to impose the tax, by a vote of the taxing district's governing body.

The *tax rate* for each individual taxing body is computed separately. To arrive at a tax rate, the total monies needed for the coming fiscal year are divided by the total assessments of all real estate located within the jurisdiction of the taxing body. For example, a taxing district's budget indicates that $300,000 must be raised from real estate tax revenues, and the assessment roll (assessor's record) of all taxable real estate within this district equals $10,000,000. The tax rate is computed thus:

$$\$300,000 \div \$10,000,000 = .03, \text{ or } 3\%$$

The tax rate may be expressed in a number of different ways. In some areas it is expressed in mills. A **mill** is *1/1,000 of a dollar, or $.001.* The tax rate computed in the above example could be expressed as follows:

$3.00 per $100.000 assessed value

or

30 mills ($30 per $1,000 of assessed value)

Tax bills. A property owner's tax bill is computed by applying the tax rate to the assessed valuation of the property. For example, on a property assessed for tax purposes at $60,000 at a tax rate of 30 mills, or $30 per thousand, the tax will be $1,800 (60 × $30 = $1,800). Taxing bodies operate on different taxing years, so the homeowner may receive separate bills for various taxes at different times during the year. (Where a lending institution maintains an escrow account to meet a mortgagor's taxes, tax billls may be sent directly to the lender. After the taxes are paid the receipted bills are forwarded to the property owner.) Penalties in the form of monthly interest charges are added to all taxes that are not paid when due. The due date is also called the *penalty date.*

New York cities, towns, villages, and school districts generally send out their own tax bills that in many municipalities often include the county tax levy. Improvement district charges are usually included in the town tax bill; benefit charges are often billed separately. State, town, and county taxes run from January to December and are payable in advance. Villages may begin their tax year either in March or, more commonly, in June. School taxes are levied from July 1 through June 30 but the tax may not be payable until September or October in some areas. School taxes, therefore, are paid in arrears for several months. City taxes frequently are payable in two or four installments during the year.

Enforcement of Tax Liens

To be enforceable, real estate taxes must be valid, which means they must be: (1) properly levied; (2) used for a legal purpose; and (3) applied equitably to all affected property. Real estate taxes that have remained delinquent for the period of time specified by state law can be collected by the tax-collecting officer through either **tax foreclosure** (similar to mortgage foreclosure) or **tax sale.** Many cities and villages enforce their own tax liens through tax sales; in most cases towns do not.

Tax sales are held pursuant to a published notice and often are conducted by the tax collector as an annual public sale. The purchaser must pay at least the amount of delinquent tax and penalty owing.

Some foreclosures are **in rem,** against the property on which taxes are delinquent, without proceeding against the individual owner.

The delinquent taxpayer can redeem the property at any time before the tax sale by paying the delinquent taxes plus interest and charges (any court costs or attorney's fees); this is known as an *equitable right of redemption.* State laws also grant a period of redemption *after the tax sale* during which the defaulted owner or lienholders (creditors of the defaulted owner) may redeem the property by paying the amount paid at the tax sale plus interest and charges. This is known as the *statutory right of redemption.*

During the **statutory redemption period** the property owner and other parties who have an interest in the property, including a mortgagee, can redeem the property by payment of the back taxes together with penalties and interest. Counties, cities, and villages have different statutory redemption periods.

County tax sales. The owner of the property encumbered by the delinquent tax lien is entitled to redeem the property from the tax lien (as sold) within one year following the date of the tax sale.

If the property is actually occupied (not vacant land) or if the property is mortgaged, the period for redemption is extended for an additional two years (three years total, following the date of the tax sale). This period may be shortened by a procedure involving service of a notice to redeem upon the owner.

Village tax sales. The owner of the property encumbered by the delinquent tax lien is entitled to redeem the property from the tax lien (as sold) within two years following the date of the tax sale and further until either:

(1) an action is commenced by the tax lien purchaser *by filing of a lis pendens* for foreclosure of the tax lien similar in procedure to a mortgage foreclosure; such lis pendens cannot be filed within the two years following the date of the tax sale; or (2) a deed is given by the Village Treasurer pursuant to the sale of the tax lien; the deed is given after application to the Treasurer for such deed and the application cannot be made within the two years following the date of the tax sale; service on the owner of the property of a notice to redeem within six months of service of the notice is a prerequisite to the making of an application for a deed.

In most cases the purchasers of tax titles in New York secure title insurance or bring actions to quiet any outstanding claims against the property and do not rely only on the tax deed issued by the municipality when the property is purchased at a tax sale.

Summary

Real estate taxes are levied by local taxing authorities. Tax liens are generally given priority over other liens. Payments are required before stated dates, after which penalties accrue. An owner may lose title to his or her property for nonpayment of taxes because such tax-delinquent property can be sold at a tax sale. New York allows a time period during which a defaulted owner can redeem his or her real estate from a tax sale.

Special assessments are levied to spread the cost of such improvements as new sidewalks, curbs, or paving to the real estate that benefits from them.

The appraisal process begins with assessment of the taxable value of each parcel. New York mandates either *equitable* or *full-value assessment* with variations from one jurisdiction to another adjusted through the use of equalization rates. The money budgeted to be raised through taxation is then divided by the total assessment roll to arrive at the *tax rate*. The tax bill for each parcel is determined by multiplying the tax rate by assessed valuation.

Various taxing authorities send tax bills at different times of the year. Unpaid taxes become a lien against property, usually taking precedence over other liens, and may be enforced through tax foreclosure or sale.

Questions

1. Some exemptions from real estate taxes may be granted to certain:
   a. veterans.
   b. senior citizens.
   c. religious organizations.
   d. Any of the above

2. Which of the following taxes is used to distribute the cost of civic services among real estate owners?
   a. Personal property tax
   b. Inheritance tax
   c. Ad valorem tax
   d. Sales tax

3. A lien on real estate made to secure payment for specific improvements made to a local community is a(n):
   a. mechanic's lien.
   b. special assessment.
   c. ad valorem tax.
   d. utility lien.

4. Which of the following steps is usually required before a special assessment becomes a lien against a specific parcel of real estate?
   a. The state of New York must verify the need.
   b. An ordinance is passed.
   c. The improvement is completed.
   d. A majority of affected property owners must approve.

5. New York statutes require that property be assessed for taxes at which percentages of its value?
   a. 33⅓
   b. 50
   c. Any uniform percentage
   d. 100

6. When real estate is assessed for tax purposes:
   a. the homeowner may appeal to a local board of review.
   b. a protest must take the form of a personal suit against the assessor.
   c. the appeal process must start in state court.
   d. no appeal is possible.

7. A specific parcel of real estate has a market value of $80,000 and is assessed for tax purposes at 25 percent of market value. The tax rate for the county in which the property is located is 30 mills. The tax bill will be:
   a. $500.   c. $600.
   b. $550.   d. $700.

8. What is the annual real estate tax on a property that is valued at $135,000 and asessed for tax purposes at $47,250 with an equalization factor of 125 percent, when the tax rate is 25 mills?
   a. $1,417.50   c. $4,050.00
   b. $1,476.56   d. None of the above

9. An *in rem* foreclosure proceeds against:
   a. the property.
   b. the owner of the property.
   c. the mortgagee on the property, if any.
   d. All of the above

10. During the statutory period of redemption, New York property sold for delinquent taxes:
    a. may be redeemed by payment of back taxes, penalties, and interest.
    b. may be redeemed by payment of four times the delinquent taxes.
    c. may be redeemed only through a court proceeding.
    d. may not be redeemed.

General Business Law

Key Terms

Administrator
Appellate divisions
Bankruptcy
Blind pool
Board of directors
Bulk transfers
Certificate of incorporation
Chapter 7
Chapter 11
Chapter 13
Civil law
Commercial paper
Common law
Complaint
Court of appeals
Criminal law
Defendant
Depositions
Endorsement
Executor

Financing statement
Holder in due course
Injunction
Involuntary bankruptcy
Marital deduction
Negotiable instrument
Personal representative
Plaintiff
Precedent
Procedural law
Real estate investment trust (REIT)
Secured debt
Security agreement
Small claims court
Substantive law
Torts
Unified credit
Uniform Commercial Code (UCC)
Voluntary bankruptcy

Overview

Real estate brokers and salespersons must have a broad understanding of law and how various laws affect real estate. The broker is already familiar with several aspects of this topic, including Law of Agency, Law of Contracts, and Real Property Law. This chapter will discuss the sources of law, commercial paper, business organizations, the court system, torts, process of a lawsuit, bankruptcy, and the settlement of estates.

Sources of Law

There are *seven sources of law* in the United States, all of which affect the ownership and transfer of real estate (*see* Figure 26.1). These are: *the Constitution of the United States; laws passed by Congress; federal regulations adopted by the various agencies and commissions created by Congress; state constitutions; laws passed by state legislatures; ordinances passed by cities, towns, and other local governments; and court decisions.*

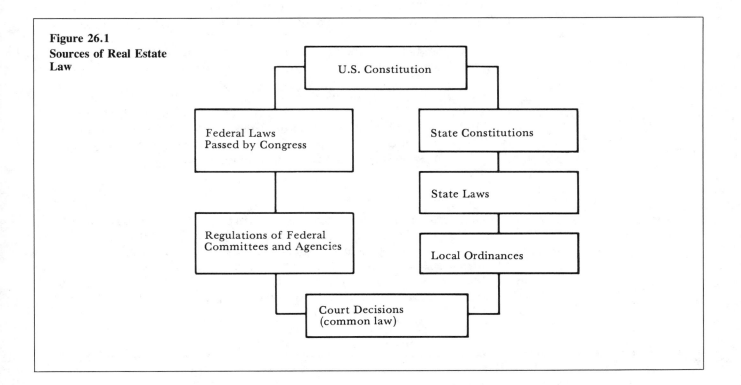

Figure 26.1
Sources of Real Estate Law

The primary purpose of the *U.S. Constitution and the individual state constitutions* is to establish the rights of citizens and delineate the limits of governmental authority.

Laws passed by Congress and by state and local legislative bodies may establish specific provisions on any issue or they may simply set broad standards of conduct and establish administrative and enforcement agencies.

Governmental agencies that enact rules and regulations range from the Federal Housing Administration through state real estate commissions to local zoning boards. These regulations are a means of implementing and enforcing legislative acts; they provide detailed information on legal and illegal actions and practices and they designate penalties and violations. These regulations have the effect of law.

Court decisions of federal, state, and municipal courts serve to clarify and interpret laws, regulations, and constitutional provisions. By applying and interpreting the laws in relation to a specific event, a court decision expands the meaning of the law. For example, an attorney draws up what he considers to be a valid contract under the provisions of state law. If the court disallows the contract, it will render an opinion as to why the contract does not fulfill the legal requirements for such a document. Future contracts in that state then will be based on the **precedent** of the requirements established by prior court decisions as well as on the statutes governing contracts.

The courts are not always bound by the established precedent. Courts in one jurisdiction (area of authority) may not be bound by the decisions of courts in other jurisdictions. In addition, a court with superior authority in its jurisdiction may at its discretion reverse the ruling of a lower court.

Common law. In addition to the aforementioned sources of law, real estate ownership and transfer are indirectly affected by what is known as the common law.

The **common law** is the body of rules and principles founded on custom, usage, and the decisions and opinions of the courts. It is derived mainly from practices developed in England and, as it applies to the United States, dates back to the practices that were in effect at the time of the American Revolution. Today the common law includes not only custom but the previous decisions of courts.

Commercial Paper	A written promise to pay money is known as **commercial paper.** *Promissory notes, checks, drafts,* and *certificates of deposit,* all forms of commercial paper, are also known as **negotiable instruments.** Negotiability means that they can be freely transferred from one person to another. Commercial paper serves as a convenient substitute for actual money and also can be used to extend credit. The *Uniform Commercial Code (UCC)* divides commercial paper into four types: notes, drafts, checks, and certificates of deposit.
Promissory Notes	The simplest form of commercial paper, the note, is a promise by one person (the *maker*) to pay money to another (the *payee*). A promissory note may be made payable to a specific payee or simply to anyone who presents it for payment (the *bearer*). If it can be collected at any time, it is a *demand* note. Often, however, notes are used as a device for extending credit and are not due until a specified time in the future. The bond or note accompanying a mortgage, for example, is a form of promissory note.
Drafts	A *draft* is a form of commercial paper involving three parties. Sometimes known as a *bill of exchange,* a draft is issued by the *drawer,* who orders another party (the *drawee*) to pay money to the payee. Like a note, a draft may be payable either to a specific payee or to a bearer and may be payable on demand or on a certain date. Drafts are often used in connection with goods being shipped from seller to buyer. A *trade acceptance* is a form of time draft.
Checks	A check is a special type of draft, ordering a bank to pay money to the payee upon demand. A check may name a specific payee or be payable to the bearer (often, in that case, made out to ''cash''). A *cashier's check,* issued by the bank,

is a type of draft in which two of the three parties (drawer and drawee) are the same party: the bank.

Certificates of Deposit

A *certificate of deposit* is a bank's receipt for a sum of money with a promise to repay it. Certificates of deposit (CDs) are devices for investing large amounts of cash, often at relatively high rates of interest. They run for a specific length of time.

Negotiability

The Uniform Commercial Code (UCC) sets standards for a negotiable instrument. It must be in writing, signed by the maker or drawer, containing an unconditional promise or order to pay a specific sum of money either on demand or at a definite time, and payable either to order or to bearer. If a third-party instrument, it must identify the drawee.

Writing. The instrument must be written on material relatively permanent and portable. It may be written in ink or pencil, typed, or printed. Standard printed forms are used most often.

Signed. A simple X made by a person unable to write can constitute a legal signature. Initials or a thumbprint are also acceptable. A trade name or a rubber stamp, when used by someone authorized to do so, is also permitted.

Promise. The promise or order to pay must be unconditional. Because it may pass from one person to another and be used in place of money, the instrument cannot be dependent on other happenings. The promise or order to pay must be clear. A simple IOU acknowledging that ''I owe you $1,000'' is not a promise to pay and not a negotiable instrument. A promise to pay ''to Mary Doe'' implies no promise to pay to anyone else. In order for Mary to sell the instrument or otherwise turn it over to someone else, it should contain a promise to pay ''*to the order of* Mary Doe.'' Mary could then order the sum paid to another party.

Specific sum. Negotiable paper must be payable only in money. It cannot promise payment in goods or services. If interest is involved, it must be stated so clearly that a computation of the sum promised is possible. Any recognized foreign currency may be stipulated in place of U.S. currency.

Demand or time. A negotiable instrument must be payable ''on *demand*'' or at a definite time. Most checks are payable immediately (*on sight,* or upon presentation). A note also may be payable *after sight,* for example, one month after it is presented for payment. It may state that it will be paid ''on or before'' a specific date. If it is payable in installments, it may contain an acceleration clause, allowing the full amount to fall due immediately if some event occurs, like default on payment.

Endorsement. Instruments payable to bearer may be transferred by *delivery*. Instruments payable to order must be transferred by **endorsement.** A note may be transferred from one party to another by one of four types of endorsements (illustrated in Figure 26.2):

1. *Blank endorsement,* in which the payee signs the back of the note without further explanation. It is the riskiest form of endorsement because the note remains negotiable for any purpose, even if the holder acquired it illegally. It is almost equivalent to cash.

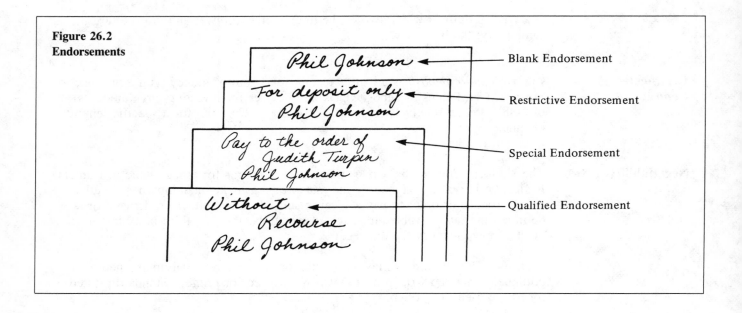

Figure 26.2
Endorsements

Phil Johnson — Blank Endorsement

For deposit only Phil Johnson — Restrictive Endorsement

Pay to the order of Judith Turpin Phil Johnson — Special Endorsement

Without Recourse Phil Johnson — Qualified Endorsement

2. *Restrictive endorsement,* in which the negotiability of the instrument is restricted to a specific purpose, stated in the endorsement.
3. *Special endorsement,* in which the payee specifically names the next holder in due course.
4. *Qualified endorsement,* in which the phrase ''without recourse'' is written as part of the endorsement in order to relieve the person making the endorsement from any liability if the check or note is not honored. A qualified endorsement specifies that the person who originated the check remains liable for the note.

If an instrument is payable to John or Mary Doe, one endorsement is sufficient to transfer it. If it is payable to John and Mary Doe, both must endorse it.

Holder in due course. The holder of an instrument is the person in possession of it, but only if the instrument is payable to bearer or properly endorsed to the person holding it. That person is entitled to receive payment. Special rights accrue to a **holder in due course,** who has more claim than an ordinary holder against potential conflicting claims to the payment. A holder in due course must meet specific requirements, taking the instrument for *value exchanged,* in *good faith,* and *without having notice* that it was *overdue, dishonored* (payment previously refused), or *having a claim against it.* A holder in due course has a stronger legal case for enforcing payment than an ordinary holder.

Defenses. Legal defense against paying on an instrument might include claims that the maker was under duress, that the instrument was intended for some illegal purpose (payment of a gambling debt or for the purchase of illegal drugs), that the instrument was obtained by fraud, or that the instrument had been altered after it was signed.

Discharge   The most common method of discharging commercial paper is by *payment.* It also may be *cancelled* by the holder either by marking it paid or by destroying it. The destruction must be deliberate, not accidental, for the instrument to be discharged. The instrument also may be *renounced* by the holder or, in the case of a check, the maker may issue a *stop-payment* order.

Uniform Commercial Code

The **Uniform Commercial Code (UCC)** is a codification of commercial law that has been adopted, wholly or in part, in all states. While this code generally does not apply directly to real estate, it has replaced state laws relating to chattel mortgages, conditional sales agreements, and liens on chattels, crops, or items that are to become fixtures. In many areas UCC filings have replaced chattel mortgages as financing instruments for personal property.

To create a security interest in a chattel, including chattels that will become fixtures, the code requires the use of a **security agreement,** which must contain a complete description of the items against which the lien applies. A short notice of this agreement, called a **financing statement** or UCC-1, which includes the identification of any real estate involved, must be filed with the clerk of the county where the debtor resides and in Albany in some instances. The recording of the financing statement constitutes notice to subsequent purchasers and mortgagees of the security interest in chattels, and fixtures on the real estate. Many mortgagees require the signing and recording of a financing statement when the mortgaged premises include chattels or readily removable fixtures (washers, dryers, and the like) as part of the security for the mortgage debt. If the financing statement has been properly recorded, upon the borrower's default the creditor could repossess the chattels and cause them to be sold and apply the proceeds to the debt payment.

Article 6 of the code covers **bulk transfers,** which are defined as the sale of the major part of the materials, supplies, merchandise, or other inventory of an enterprise *not* made in the ordinary course of the transferor's business. The purpose of this article is to outlaw the fraud perpetrated when a business person who is in debt sells all stock in trade (personal property) and disappears without having paid his or her creditors. Under Article 6, a bulk sale does not give the purchaser of such goods a clear title unless the purchaser complies with the article's requirements, which include giving notice of the sale to the seller's creditors. Some sales of business property involve the sale of the business and all of the owner's stock in trade, which may constitute a bulk sale.

Business Organizations

Partnerships

Partnership is defined by the Partnership Law as an association of two or more persons to carry on a business for profit as co-owners. Each partner is considered an agent of the other as concerns the partnership and each shares the profits or losses. While the stockholders of a *corporation* are liable only to the extent of their investment in the firm, the members of a *partnership* are personally liable for debts and losses and liable for each other's acts within the scope of the business.

A specific *partnership agreement* sets up the powers and duties of the partners. Unless the agreement specifies otherwise, some common arrangements are that new members must be approved by all the existing partners and every member is entitled to equal participation in the management and to a specific share of profits.

When the question arises as to whether two persons are in fact partners, the chief test is whether each receives a share of profits. Partners have a fiduciary duty to each other. Notice given to one is considered as given to all.

Partnership property. Property contributed to the partnership when it is formed is considered to be partnership property. Property acquired with the firm's assets is also partnership property. No one partner can assign partnership property unless all consent. Creditors of the individual partners may not attach the assets of the partnership for a partner's personal debts but may attach the partner's interest in the partnership.

If one partner assigns his or her share of profits to a third person, that person may be entitled to profits but does not become a partner and has no right to share in management or examine the firm's books.

Dissolution. The partnership is dissolved at a specific time originally agreed upon or if any one partner requests *dissolution*. It is also dissolved on the death or bankruptcy of a partner. A court order can dissolve the partnership if it is shown that one partner is insane or incapacitated, that the business cannot be operated at a profit, or that one partner is involved in impropriety affecting the partnership.

Upon dissolution the partnership may no longer transact new business but the partnership continues through the process of *winding-up*. Assets are distributed first to creditors who are not partners, next to partners who have lent money to the partnership, then in a refund of capital contributed by each partner. Anything remaining is distributed among the partners according to their respective interests.

Limited partnerships. Limited partnerships, to be discussed more fully later in this chapter, are generally formed for commercial investment. The general partner takes management responsibility and unlimited personal liability for the partnership's debts; the limited partners contribute cash but do not share in management and are liable only to the amount of their contributions.

Corporations

A corporation is an organization that is recognized by the law as a legal person. It may buy, sell, lease, mortgage, make contracts, and perform most other acts allowed to persons. It is entitled to most of the same protection guaranteed other persons by the Bill of Rights.

Its authority to act is separate from the persons who own shares in it and, in most cases, they bear no individual liability for the corporation's actions or debts. Likewise, the corporation cannot be held liable for the shareholders' debts.

Creation of a corporation. A corporation is created by the filing of a **certificate of incorporation** with the secretary of state. The incorporator(s) must sign the certificate, giving their names and addresses, the name of the intended corporation and its purposes, intended duration (usually perpetual), address, and number of shares of stock authorized to be issued. Upon payment of a fee and approval of the secretary of state, the corporation becomes a legal entity. Bylaws, the rules and regulations under which the corporation will operate, are usually adopted at the first organizational meeting after the certificate of incorporation has been secured.

Management. A corporation is managed by a **board of directors** elected by shareholders. Shareholders who cannot attend meetings, which are usually held annually, may vote by *proxy*. Once elected, the board of directors selects officers who administer the business of the corporation. Directors and officers have a fiduciary duty to the corporation and may not profit personally at its expense. Each shareholder has the right to examine the company's books.

A *closely held corporation* is one owned by a single individual or a small number of shareholders, perhaps members of the same family. The shareholders usually manage the business themselves.

Corporations, considered as persons, are subject to income tax on profits. One of the major disadvantages to corporate organization is double taxation, with profits taxed once to the firm and again when received (in the form of dividends) by shareholders. Corporations are also subject to the New York State franchise tax (another term for corporate income tax).

One of the major advantages of corporate organizations, however, is the ability to shelter some income through pension and profit-sharing plans and to consider as business expense fringe benefits like health or life insurance. In recent years, however, liberalized tax-deferment possibilities for individuals through various retirement plans, have lessened the appeal of this aspect of incorporation.

S corporations. The S corporation, intended for a small group of shareholders, allows the firm to be taxed as a partnership would be—passing profit and loss directly to shareholders, so that profits are taxed only once. Losses also may be passed to shareholders, although only to the limit of their investments, and used to offset ordinary income. An S corporation may have no more than 35 shareholders.

Termination. *Dissolution* is the legal death of the corporation. *Liquidation* is the winding-up process. A corporation may be dissolved by an act of the legislature, expiration of the time originally planned for the business, approval of the shareholders and board of directors, unanimous action of all the shareholders, or court order. A *certificate of dissolution* is filed with the secretary of state and assets are distributed first to creditors, next to holders of preferred stock, and last to holders of common stock.

Real Estate Investment Trusts and Limited Partnerships	Both **real estate investment trusts (REITS)** and limited partnerships are methods for pooling cash so that small investors may participate in real estate investments. REITs have developed since the early 1960s; limited partnerships, originally small groups, are now being sold as public offerings. Some differences and similarities between the two are summarized in Table 26.1.
Public vs. Private Offerings	*Public offerings* (more often REITs) must be approved by the Securities and Exchange Commission and blue-sky laws in the states where they are offered. *Private offerings* are exempt from that requirement but must make comparable disclosures except to investors with $1 million net worth or $200,000 annual income ("rich but dumb" rule). Public offerings are more often large, averaging about $200 million in size; private offerings are considered small, at $1–$2 million. The larger offerings are often **blind pools** with property to be purchased after the money is raised as an ongoing process. Private offerings usually are formed for one specific project.

**Table 26.1
REITs vs. Limited
Partnerships**

	Real Estate Investment Trust	Real Estate Limited Partnership
Tax strategy	Shelter dividends. Not much use for losses.	Pass cash and tax losses to partners.
Liquidity	Often traded on stock exchanges.	Generally illiquid. Partners stay until end.
Investment required	Often $1,000 initial, $100 for reorders	Generally $3,000 to $5,000 minimum
Financial suitability of investors	No specific requirements beyond a stockbroker's usual guidelines	Investor must have financial suitability (for example, $75,000 net worth or specific income).
Management	Board of directors (majority must not be sponsors of the project)	General partner runs project as fiduciary.
Dividends	Reinvestment plan	No reinvestment plan
Payout	Generally pays out 95% of income to avoid corporate tax.	Usually pays out cash flow.
Main goal	Stresses income because traded on exchanges.	Stresses growth and appreciation.
Duration	Can stay in business indefinitely by investing in further projects.	Usually liquidates one project in 5–7 years.
How sold	Publicly sold (need 100 shareholders for tax purposes)	Sold privately or, in recent years, publicly.
Meetings	Annual stockholders meeting (proxy solicitation) to renew advisory contract and compensation for management	Informational meetings only

Public offerings, with many more partners, are more liquid and easier to resell. They are more diversified and carry less risk than private offerings and are usually structured for profit. Private offerings are more often structured for tax shelter (*soft dollars*).

The Federal Court System

The federal court system includes specialized courts, district courts, courts of review (appellate courts), and the Supreme Court, as shown in Figure 26.3. All federal judges receive lifetime appointments, subject to confirmation by the Senate.

District courts cover specific geographical areas, with at least one in each state. New York as four *districts,* known as the northern, eastern, southern, and western districts. District courts are the point of origin for civil cases arising from

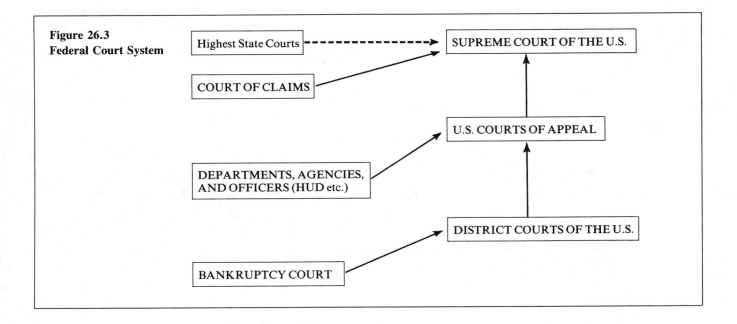

**Figure 26.3
Federal Court System**

federal law and for federal crimes. They also serve as appellate courts for the U.S. bankruptcy court.

Specialized courts are established by Congress. Among them are tax court, court of claims, and bankruptcy court. The *U.S. court of appeals* provides review for district courts and for decisions made by federal agencies such as HUD. The United States is divided into 11 judicial circuits. Appeals from district courts located in this state are heard by the 2nd court of appeals, which also covers part of Connecticut. Decisions of this court are generally final, with further appeal to the Supreme Court the only possibility.

The *Supreme Court of the United States* consists of nine justices. While it serves mainly as a court of appeals for cases involving federal law or constitutionality, it also has original, or trial, jurisdiction in a few situations.

New York Court System

In New York State the supreme court is paradoxically one of the lowest courts in the system, so named because of its wide jurisdiction and because it originates most lawsuits. New York's court system is complicated by differing arrangements in the New York City area (first and second departments) and Upstate (third and fourth departments) as diagrammed in Figure 26.4. The highest court in the state is the **court of appeals.** *Supreme court* is the lowest court of unlimited jurisdiction and unlimited dollar amount of claims. It has branches in every county. Supreme court justices are also assigned to criminal cases when the caseload requires it.

County court is a court of criminal jurisdiction, also handling some civil cases and appeals from lower courts. *Surrogate court* handles decedents' estates, will contests, probates, adoptions (with family court), and incompetency proceedings.

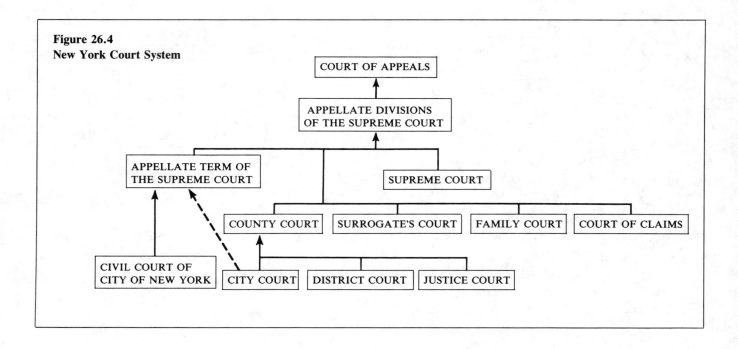

Figure 26.4
New York Court System

Family court combines the old domestic relations and children's courts for family complaints, delinquencies, child abuse, and adoptions. Divorces, however, are heard in supreme court.

The *court of claims* has jurisdiction over claims against the state. **Small claims courts** are set up for prompt and informal treatment of disputes and complaints involving less than $1,500. Fees and paperwork are nominal and the parties generally appear for themselves, with no lawyers involved except in the case of corporations. Small claims court may issue monetary awards and judgments but may not compel specific performance. They are part of *city, town,* and *village justice courts.*

The **appellate divisions** of the supreme court handle appeals by parties dissatisfied with lower court findings. The state is divided into four departments: First appellate department covers Manhattan and the Bronx; second covers Brooklyn and part of Long Island. The third is based in Albany and the fourth in Rochester. Five judges serve, taking no testimony but basing their decisions on the record and arguments by the parties' attorneys. Appeals are usually based on questions of law and procedure and not on disputes about the facts in the case. Occasionally the appellate division will rule, however, that the original verdict was against the weight of evidence. The appellate divisions serve as an intermediate level of review in some cases and as final arbiter in others. Those unsatisfied can, in some instances, take the case further, to the court of appeals.

The *court of appeals* is the highest court in the state. Seven judges sit. There is generally no further appeal from this court although constitutional questions can be taken to the Supreme Court of the United States.

Substantive and Procedural Law

The whole body of law falls into two categories, **substantive law,** which defines the rights of individuals, and **procedural law,** which establishes the methods of enforcing those rights. *Substantive law* includes some subjects with which the real estate broker is already familiar, among them Law of Agency and Real Property Law. Other major areas of substantive law include Administrative Law, Commercial Law, Constitutional Law, Law of Contracts, Corporation Law, Criminal Law, Personal Property Law (Uniform Commercial Code), Partnership, Trusts and Wills, Torts, and Taxes.

Procedural law includes Law of Evidence, Civil Procedure, Criminal Procedure, Administrative Procedure, and Appellate Procedure.

Torts

The state prosecutes criminals who commit acts that injure the state or society as a whole under the provisions of **criminal law. Civil law,** on the other hand, is concerned with **torts,** the injuries one person does another. While criminal law concentrates on punishing the culprit, the law of torts is intended to compensate the injured party. A single act may result in both civil and criminal court action as well as administrative procedure. The commission of a fraud, for example, may result in criminal prosecution, a civil suit by the defrauded person, and administrative action such as the revocation of a real estate license.

For a tort to be committed, three factors must exist: The plaintiff must have suffered a loss or injury; the damage must have been caused by the defendant; and the defendant must have failed to exercise reasonable care. Torts are generally classified into three groups: intentional torts, negligence, and strict liability. Wrongs against the person include *assault* (threatening behavior), *battery* (physical contact, even without actual injury), *false imprisonment* (sometimes charged, for example, in the detention of a suspected shoplifter), and the *infliction of mental distress* through harassment. *Defamation* covers *slander* (oral) and *libel* (written) actions that tend to hold a person up to contempt, ridicule, or hatred. Slander or libel arise when third parties can read or overheard the material. Among the grounds for libel that may concern real estate brokers are statements that another person has committed improprieties while engaging in a profession or trade. In a lawsuit the truth of the statement is almost always a complete defense. False statements about products, businesses, or title to property also can result in torts if actual damages occur. Torts against the person also include *misrepresentation, fraud,* and *invasion of the right to privacy.*

Wrongs against property include *trespass,* unauthorized intrusion upon another's land. No actual damage need be shown; the landowner's right to exclusive possession has been violated by the trespass. Damage to landscaping by workers who could have avoided it through reasonable care becomes a tort against the property. *Trespass to personalty* occurs when personal property is injured or the owner's right to enjoyment of it is interfered with. When property is stolen, the tort of *conversion* (to someone else's use) had occurred. Conversion also can occur if another's property is mistakenly taken or accidentally damaged.

Nuisances are acts that interfere with another's enjoyment or health. Barking dogs, searchlights that shine onto another's property, and business activities that cause unpleasant odors are typical nuisances. In addition to seeking money damages, the plaintiff will usually ask the court for an **injunction,** an order forbidding the offending activity.

Negligence covers actions that tend to wrong another through carelessness without any intent to cause damage. Such torts are often committed in accidents and the court may apportion negligence between the parties. *Business torts* include infringement of copyrights, patents and trademarks, and unfair competition. A business venture that is entered into for the single purpose of harming another established business becomes the tort known as *malicious injury to business*. *Strict liability* (usually in product liability cases) covers damages caused by unusual and abnormally dangerous activities in the course of business such as improper manufacturing procedures that create dangerous products. Failure to warn the user of the dangers in using such an item is also covered by strict liability.

Process of a Civil Lawsuit

In New York State a lawsuit begins when the aggrieved party *(plaintiff)*, usually through an attorney, arranges for the service of a *summons* upon the person accused of wrongdoing. The summons must be accompanied or shortly followed by a **complaint.** The complaint is a recital of the facts and a request for a remedy. The defendent is given a period of time, usually 20 days, in which to serve an *answer* with the plaintiff's attorney. If the defendant has a claim against the plaintiff, he or she may include a *counterclaim* in the answer, alleging wrongdoing by the plaintiff. If there is a counterclaim, the plaintiff responds with a *reply*. The complaint and answer, together with any counterclaim and reply, are known as the *pleadings*. They inform each party of the position taken by the opposing side and aid in preparations for the forthcoming trial.

Pretrial motions may follow in which either side requests dismissal of the suit, perhaps on the grounds that insufficient legal grounds exist for trial. If no dispute exists about the facts in the case, either side may ask for a summary judgment, requesting the judge to apply the law without a trial. Other pretrial motions are possible as well.

Discovery (often known in New York as *disclosure*) is a process before trial begins for obtaining relevant information from witnesses and from the opposing party. Disclosure includes the procedure known as *examination before trial (EBT)* under which the parties are brought into the lawyers' offices and examined under oath. The information is recorded in stenographic record as *oral depositions*. Written *interrogatories (written depositions)* are written questions submitted by one party to which the other party must respond in writing and under oath. Medical examinations also may form part of the discovery process. Documents and physical evidence relevant to the case also can be obtained.

Either party or the court itself may request a *pretrial conference*. An informal proceeding among the opposing attorneys and the judge, a pretrial conference clarifies which matters are in dispute and may lead to an out-of-court settlement.

A trial may be held without a jury *(bench trial)* with the judge rendering a verdict, or may be tried before a jury, which determines the facts. Jurors are selected from a panel after questioning by both attorneys, and occasionally by the judge to determine impartiality.

Each attorney, at the start of the trial, makes an *opening statement*. The plaintiff's attorney then calls the first witness for *direct examination* or questioning. The defendant's attorney questions the plaintiff's witness through *cross-examination*. Each attorney may then return for *redirect* or *recross-examination*. The process is repeated for each of the plaintiff's witnesses.

The defendant's witnesses are called and examined in the same fashion. At the close of the defendent's evidence, the plaintiff's attorney may offer a *rebuttal* and the defendant's attorney a *rejoinder*. The trial ends with *closing statements* from each side and the judge's instructions or *charges* to a jury, if one is being used, on the law involved in the suit. *Judgment* follows, either from a jury or from the judge. The case is closed unless one party, unsatisfied, *appeals* the suit to a higher court.

Bankruptcy

Bankruptcy is a legal proceeding through which a debtor may seek relief from overwhelming financial problems and a chance at a fresh start. Creditors are assured a fair share of any assets that may be available. Bankruptcy is a federal proceeding brought in bankruptcy court, a special federal court. Three general types of bankruptcy are usually known by the chapter numbers in the Bankruptcy Reform Act of 1978. **Chapter 7** provides for the total liquidation of the debtor's assets (less certain exempt items available to individuals). **Chapter 11** and **Chapter 13** provide for the debtor's retention of assets and a corresponding adjustment in the payment of the outstanding debts. The purposes of bankruptcy law are to allow a debtor whose debts have become unmanageable to be protected from the creditors, to give the debtor a chance to start over, and to distribute the debtor's available assets fairly to the creditors.

Chapter 7, often known as straight bankruptcy, requires the debtor (either an individual or a corporation) to disclose all debts and to disclose and surrender all assets to a trustee. The process starts with the filing of a petition in the bankruptcy court, either **voluntarily** (by the debtor) or **involuntarily** (by creditors). Filing of the petition automatically freezes actions against the debtor, providing temporary relief. *The filing of any bankruptcy case automatically halts any pending foreclosure suit.* Lawsuits in progress and other actions against the debtor are halted, and no new actions may be commenced. However, if a creditor is *secured* (where his debt is backed by a lien on debtor's real property or personal property), the secured creditor may request the court to permit the creditor to pursue foreclosure or repossession remedies. The bankruptcy judge may or may not grant this request or may require the debtor to make some payments to the secured creditor to forestall foreclosure.

At the time of the filing of the petition for bankruptcy, an interim trustee is appointed. A meeting of the creditors provides an opportunity for questioning of the debtor and confirmation of the amounts owed. The creditors also may vote for the election of a permanent trustee. The trustee takes over the debtor's assets and distributes the net proceeds proportionately to creditors. The balance of the debts are canceled or *discharged.* The law provides guidelines for the priority of payment of the claims. The debtor is allowed by law to retain up to $5,000 worth of household furnishings, equity in an automobile up to $2,400, and up to $10,000 equity in a homestead. If husband and wife file bankruptcy together, they may protect up to $20,000 in homestead equity. To exercise the homestead equity, it is required that the debtor reside in the real property.

The property of the debtor at the time the bankruptcy petition is filed is known as the *property of the estate.* Any property the debtor acquires after the bankruptcy petition is filed is not included in the property of the estate and belongs to the debtor (with the exception of an inheritance within six months after the petition was filed).

A *corporation* filing for *Chapter 11* relief receives the same automatic stay or freeze on creditors' actions as provided by Chapter 7 proceedings. The goal of Chapter 11, however, is not immediate liquidation of the debtor's business or total distribution of assets. Instead, the debtor and a creditors' committee formulate a plan for paying a portion of the debts while the debtor continues in business under the scrutiny of the bankruptcy court and the creditors' committee. Chapter 11 plans may provide for a gradual, orderly winding-up of the business or may aim at total recovery.

Persons holding mortgages on real property may be delayed in foreclosing those mortgages by order of the bankruptcy judge until a plan is proposed by the bankrupt party and either accepted or rejected by the creditors and the court. Thus although a creditor holds a mortgage on real property of the debtor, the mortgagee may have to wait a considerable time, sometimes years, before the mortgage can be foreclosed.

After the Chapter 11 petition is filed, the debtor continue to operate the business, free of the claims and judgments that beset the debtor prior to such filing. *Debtor-in-possession* (DIP) is the term used to designate this situation. The court may allow the debtor to continue in the operation of the business or upon a showing of fraudulent practices or waste may appoint a trustee to do so. In either event a creditors' committee is appointed to oversee the management. After a plan is proposed (by the debtor or by the creditors' committee) a vote of the creditors is taken. If the creditors' vote favors the plan and the court approves it, it is put into effect. If no plan is presented or the creditors and/or the court turn down the plan, the proceeding is generally converted into a straight Chapter 7 bankruptcy.

Chapter 13 is available only to *individuals* with regular income (including those on welfare, social security, and retirement income) or those who operate a small business. It offers a chance to work out financial problems over a period of up to five years. Creditors may be paid in part or in full as in Chapter 11 but under Chapter 13 the proposed plan is not voted on by creditors. The court, in its sole discretion, makes the decisions on the viability of the plan and the best interests of the creditors. Chapter 13 can be initiated only by a voluntary petition and tends to avoid the stigma of bankruptcy. The automatic stay halting all pending actions and prohibiting new actions exists just as under Chapters 7 and 11.

The trustee appointed in a bankruptcy replaces the debtor in exercising control over the debtor's property. His or her function is to take control of the debtor's (bankrupt's) assets, manage them until they are disposed of, and then distribute the net proceeds pro rata among the creditors in the order of the statutory priorities.

If the secured creditor is permitted by the bankruptcy court to foreclose the lien on the secured property (real or personal property or both) and the value of the foreclosed property is less than the amount of mortgagee's debt, the secured creditor becomes unsecured for the excess amount and to that extent shares pro rata with the other unsecured creditors in the property of the estate.

Certain claims cannot be discharged in bankruptcy:

• income taxes accruing within three years of the bankruptcy filing;
• sales taxes and withholding taxes collected from customers and employees but not paid over to the taxing authorities;
• claims not listed on the bankruptcy schedule;

- claims based on fraud (misrepresentation or false pretenses);
- alimony and child support;
- claims based on willful injury (except under Chapter 13);
- some fines or penalties due to the government; and
- some student loans (except where the court determines there is undue hardship or under Chapter 13).

Occasionally debtors do not receive their discharge. Discharges may be withheld where proof is offered that the debtor has concealed assets, obtained credit under false financial statements, or failed to cooperate with the trustee.

Estates

A decedent's estate is administered and settled by a **personal representative** appointed by surrogate's court. A will may name an **executor** to serve as personal representative. If no will can be found or no executor is named, the court will appoint an **administrator,** who serves as a personal representative and performs the same duties as an executor. The executor first inventories the estate to determine its extent and value. The will, insurance policies, deeds, car registrations, birth and marriage certificates are located. Safe deposit boxes are inventoried and the executor takes possession of property such as bank accounts, real estate, and personal property. Names, addresses, and social security numbers of all heirs are obtained. The executor files claims for social security, pension, and veterans benefits.

The personal representative then administers the estate as the decedent would have done, collecting debts, mananging real estate, collecting insurance proceeds, continuing a family business, and arranging for the support of a family pending final distribution of the estate. The executor also pays rightful claims against the estate, negotiates the most favorable treatment for taxes, and sells selected assets to pay taxes in time to avoid any penalties.

Final winding-up of the estate involves arranging proper division of the assets, selling some to pay cash bequests, and transferring title to real and personal property. Final estate costs are paid and an accounting is prepared.

Estate and Gift Taxes

Both the federal government and New York State government may levy taxes on the assets of the decedent's estate. The executor or other personal representative of the estate generally pays estate taxes from the assets of the estate. Under the Economic Recovery Tax Act of 1981, any amount may be transferred between spouses during a lifetime or by will with no federal gift or estate tax due. This transfer to a spouse by will is known as the **marital deduction.** The remainder of an estate, beyond property passing through the marital deduction and certain other deductions, is subject to federal estate tax if it exceeds limits that rose to $600,000 in 1987.

Gifts made during a lifetime in excess of the *annual exclusion* ($10,000 to any individual each year, or $20,000 if the donor's spouse joins in the gift) are subject to federal gift tax. They may, however, be subtracted from the **unified credit.** A gift of $100,000 during the decedent's lifetime, for example, would be free of gift tax but if death occurred in 1987, only $500,000 would be covered by the remaining unified exclusion.

New York also allows annual gifts of $10,000 each to any number of individuals, free of any gift tax. Gifts of up to $100,000 may go to a spouse during one's lifetime, untaxed. A limited amount of unified credit is also available at the state level.

For those dying after October 1, 1983, an unlimited amount may pass to the spouse free of New York estate tax. After this marital deduction and certain other deductions, approximately $108,000 of the estate's assets are free from estate tax.

If estate or gift tax is due and not paid, the federal government and New York State may impose a lien on property. With certain exceptions, after a tax lien attaches to property, it continues even though the property is transferred to another. Thus until taxes are paid, a cloud on the title may render the property subject to the lien unmarketable.

Summary

The *seven sources of law* in the United States are the U.S. Constitution, laws passed by Congress, federal regulations, state constitutions, laws passed by state legislatures, local ordinances, and court decisions.

Common law in the United States evolved predominantly from custom and usage in early England. Gradually the basis of common law expanded to include the precedent of prior court decisions as well as custom. Much of real property law is founded in common law.

Commercial paper, or *negotiable instruments*, are written promises or orders to pay money that may be transferred from one person to another. The Uniform Commercial Code divides commercial paper into *notes, drafts, checks*, and *certificates of deposit*. Commercial paper must be in writing, signed by the maker or drawer, payable either to bearer or a specific payee, for a specific sum of money at a definite time or on demand. It may be transferred by four types of *endorsement: blank, restrictive, special*, or *qualified*. A *holder in due course* has a stronger claim to payment in case of dispute than an ordinary holder.

Under the Uniform Commercial Code, security interests in chattels must be recorded using a *security agreement* and *financing statement*. The recording of a financing statement gives notice to purchasers and mortgagees of the security interests in chattels and fixtures on the specific parcel of real estate.

A *partnership* is an association of two or more persons to carry on a business for profit as co-owners. Profit and loss are passed directly through to individual partners for taxation. Partners have unlimited individual liability for the partnership's debts. *Limited partnerships* have one general partner who takes on management and unlimited debt liability, and limited partners who are liable only to the extent of their investment.

A *corporation* is a legal person, owned by any number of shareholders, who have limited individual liability for the corporation's debts. It is formed through the approval of a *certificate of incorporation* by the secretary of state. A *board of directors*, elected by the shareholders, selects officers to manage the business. Profits are taxed twice, once to the corporation and once to the shareholder who receives dividends.

Real estate investment trusts and limited partnerships are formed to pool small investors' funds for real estate ventures. They differ in size, tax strategy, management, duration, and liquidity, as well as in other ways.

The federal court system includes *district court, specialized courts, courts of review,* and the *Supreme Court.* New York State has four federal judicial district courts, which originate federal cases. Appeals from this state are heard by the *second circuit court of appeals.*

In New York State different court systems originate cases in the New York City area and Upstate. *Small claims court* is part of a court of local jurisdiction for the prompt and informal treatment of disputes. *Appeals* from lower courts are handled by the *appellate divisions of the supreme court.* The highest court in the state is the *court of appeals.*

The whole body of law falls into two categories, *substantive* law, which defines the rights of individuals, and *procedural* law, which establishes methods for enforcing those rights. *Criminal law* covers acts that injure society or the state; *civil law* is concerned with *torts,* the injuries one person does another. Torts may be against the person or against property. Civil lawsuits are intended to recompense the injured party.

A lawsuit starts with a *summons* and *complaint* served by the *plaintiff* on the *defendant,* who files an *answer.* These initial documents are known as the *pleadings. Pretrial motions* may follow and before trial begins, information is obtained from witnesses and the opposing party, in the process known as *discovery* or *disclosure.* A *pretrial conference* may be held to clarify the matter at dispute.

A trial may be held before a judge or jury. After *opening statements* by both parties, the plaintiff's case is presented, followed by the defendant's. *Rebuttal, rejoinder,* and *closing statements* may be followed by the judge's *charge* to the jury. The trial concludes wth a *judgment,* which may in some cases be *appealed* to a higher court by an unsatisfied party.

Bankruptcy is a federal proceeding through which a debtor seeks relief from overwhelming financing problems. *Chapter 7* provides for immediate liquidation of debts, *Chapter 11* for reorganization or the orderly winding-down of *businesses,* and *Chapter 13* for gradual payment over a period of time, either in part or in full, by *individual* debtors.

A decedent's estate is settled by a *personal representative,* either an *executor* named in a will or an *administrator* appointed by the court. The executor inventories the estate, administers it, collects debts and pays claims, divides the assets, and distributes them to heirs. The federal and state governments levy *estate taxes.*

Questions

1. Among the seven sources of law are:
   a. court decisions.
   b. governmental agencies' regulations.
   c. state laws.
   d. All of the above

2. A written promise to pay money made by one individual directly to another is most often a:
   a. promissory note.
   b. draft.
   c. check.
   d. certificate of deposit.

3. To be negotiable, an instrument:
   a. must mention a consideration.
   b. must conform with Chapter 11 rules.
   c. must mention a specific sum of money.
   d. must qualify for dissolution.

4. In case of a dispute, the person with the best claim to payment is a(n):
   a. ordinary holder.
   b. holder in due course.
   c. drawer.
   d. maker.

5. The Uniform Commercial Code covers:
   a. bequests.   c. chattels.
   b. realty.   d. services.

6. Writing "for deposit only" on a check constitutes a:
   a. blank endorsement.
   b. special endorsement.
   c. qualified endorsement.
   d. restrictive endorsement.

7. Co-owners have no individual liability for the debts of a:
   a. corporation.   c. tort.
   b. partnership.   d. private offering.

8. The general partner has unlimited liability in a:
   a. corporation.
   b. real estate investment trust.
   c. limited partnership.
   d. closely held corporation.

9. Most federal lawsuits and prosecution for federal crimes originate in:
   a. supreme court.   c. district court.
   b. court of claims.   d. court of appeals.

10. New York State's highest court is:
    a. supreme court.   c. district court.
    b. court of claims.   d. court of appeals.

11. Disputes of limited dollar value may be settled at nominal cost and without the use of lawyers in:
    a. small claims court.
    b. court of claims.
    c. civil court.
    d. justice court.

12. Law of Agency and Real Property Law fall under the category known as:
    a. substantive law.   c. criminal law.
    b. procedural law.   d. law of contracts.

13. Slander, libel, assault, and battery are types of torts known as:
    a. negligence.
    b. wrongs against property.
    c. wrongs against the person.
    d. strict liability.

14. A court order forbidding a certain activity is known as:
    a. specific performance.
    b. an injunction.
    c. coversion.
    d. a rejoinder.

15. Legal relief through the immediate cancelling of most debts can be sought through which form of bankruptcy?
    a. Chapter 1   c. Chapter 11
    b. Chapter 7   d. Chapter 13

16. The debtor who files bankruptcy is allowed to keep:
    a. household furnishings.
    b. income-producing real estate.
    c. a vacation home worth up to $20,000.
    d. All of the above

17. Bankruptcy proceedings are heard in:
    a. federal court.
    b. small claims court.
    c. surrogate's court.
    d. family court.

18. The personal representative who handles a decedent's estate may be a(n):
    a. referee.   c. plaintiff.
    b. administrator.   d. proxy.

19. Federal tax law provides that one spouse may give another:
    a. any amount without gift or estate taxes due.
    b. up to $100,000 without estate taxes due.
    c. no more than $250,000 tax-free during a lifetime.
    d. up to $20,000 tax-free in any year.

20. New York's estate tax allows a spouse to inherit without any estate tax due:
    a. any amount.
    b. up to $250,000 or one-half the estate.
    c. $100,000.
    d. up to $20,000.

Glossary of Real Estate Terms

Abandonment The voluntary surrender or relinquishment of possession of real property without the vesting of this interest in any other person.

Abstract of title The condensed history of a title to a particular parcel of real estate.

Abstract of title with lawyer's opinion An abstract of title that a lawyer has examined and has certified to be, in his or her opinion, an accurate statement of fact.

Accelerated cost recovery Accounting concept for recovering capital invested over a short period of years.

Acceleration clause The clause in a mortgage or trust deed that can be enforced to make the entire debt due immediately if the mortgage defaults.

Accession Acquiring title to additions or improvements to real property as a result of the annexation of fixtures or the accretion of alluvial deposits.

Accretion The increase or addition of land by the deposit of sand or soil washed up naturally from a river, lake, or sea.

Accrued items On a closing statment, items of expense that have been incurred but are not yet payable, such as interest on a mortgage loan.

Acknowledgment A formal declaration made before a duly authorized officer, usually a notary public, by a person who has signed a document.

ACR Accelerated cost recovery.

Acre A measure of land equal to 43,560 square feet; 4,840 square yards; 4,047 square meters; 160 square rods; or 0.4047 hectare.

Actual eviction. Action whereby a defaulted tenant is physically ousted from rented property pursuant to a court order. (*See also* Eviction.)

Actual notice Express information or fact; that which is known; actual knowledge.

Adjacent Lying near to but not necessarily in actual contact with.

Adjoining Contiguous; attaching, in actual contact with.

Adjustable rate mortgage A mortgage loan in which the interest rate may increase or decrease at specific intervals, following an economic indicator.

Administrator A person appointed by court to administer the estate of a deceased person who left no will, i.e., who died intestate.

Ad valorem tax A tax levied according to value; generally used to refer to real estate tax. Also called the *general tax*.

Adverse possession The actual, visible, hostile, notorious, exclusive, and continuous possession of another's land under a claim of title. Possession for ten years may be a means of acquiring title.

Affidavit A written statement sworn to before an officer who is authorized to administer an oath or affirmation.

Affirm To confirm, to ratify, to verify.

Agency That relationship wherein an agent is employed by a principal to do certain acts on the principal's behalf.

Agency coupled with an interest An agency relationship in which the agent is given an estate or interest in the subject of the agency (the property).

Agent One who undertakes to transact some business or to manage some affair for another by authority of the latter.

Air rights The right to use the open space above a property, generally allowing the surface to be used for another purpose.

Alienation The act of transferring property to another.

Alienation clause The clause in a mortgage stating that the balance of the secured debt becomes immediately due and payable at the mortgagee's option if the property is sold.

Allodial system A system of land ownership in which land is held free and clear of any rent or service due to the government; commonly contrasted to the feudal system. Land is held under the allodial system in the United States.

Amortized loan A loan in which the principal as well as the interest is payable in monthly or other periodic installments over the term of the loan.

Annual percentage rate Rate of interest charged on a loan, calculated to take into account up-front loan fees and points. Usually higher than the *contract interest rate*.

Antitrust laws Laws designed to preserve the free enterprise of the open marketplace by making illegal certain private conspiracies and combinations formed to minimize competition.

Appeals Complaints made to a higher court requesting the correction of errors in law made by lower courts.

Appellate division Courts of appeals.

Apportionments Adjustment of the income, expenses, or carrying charges of real estate usually computed to the date of closing of title so that the seller pays all expenses to that date.

Appraisal An estimate of a property's valuation by an appraiser who is usually presumed to be expert in this work.

Appraisal by capitalization An estimate of value by capitalization of productivity and income.

Appraisal by comparison An estimate of value based on the sale prices of other similar properties.

Appreciation An increase in the worth or value of a property due to economic or related causes.

Appurtenances Those rights, privileges, and improvements that belong to and pass with the transfer of real property but are not necessarily a part of the property such as rights-of-way, easements, and property improvements.

APR *See* Annual percentage rate.

ARM *See* Adjustable rate mortgage.

Arm's length transaction A transaction between relative strangers, each trying to do the best for himself or herself.

Article 12A The section of New York State's Real Property Law relating to real estate licenses.

Assessed valuation A valuation placed upon property by a public officer or a board as a basis for taxation.

Assessment The imposition of a tax, charge, or levy, usually according to established rates.

Assignment The transfer in writing of interest in a bond, mortgage, lease, or other instrument.

Assumption of mortgage Acquiring title to property on which there is an existing mortgage and agreeing to be personally liable for the terms and conditions of the mortgage, including payments.

Attest To witness to; to witness by observation and signature.

Avulsion The removal of land from one owner to another when a stream suddenly changes its channel.

Balloon payment The final payment of a mortgage loan that is considerably larger than the required periodic payments because the loan amount was not fully amortized.

Bargain and sale deed A deed that carries with it no warranties against liens or other encumbrances but that does imply that the grantor has the right to convey title.

Bargain and sale deed with covenant A deed in which the grantor warrants or guarantees the title against defects arising during the period of his or her tenure and ownership of the property and not against defects existing before that time.

Basis The cost that the Internal Revenue Service attributes to an owner of an investment property for the purpose of determining annual cost recovery and gain or loss on the sale of the asset. The cost of property plus the value of any capital expenditures for improvements to the property, minus any cost recovery allowable or actually taken. This new basis is called the *adjusted basis*.

Benchmark A permanent reference mark or point established for use by surveyors in measuring differences in evaluation.

Beneficiary The person who receives or is to receive the benefits resulting from certain acts.

Bequeath To give or hand down by will; to leave by will.

Bequest That which is given by the terms of a will.

Bilateral contract *See* Contract.

Bill of sale A written instrument given to pass title of personal property from vendor to vendee.

Binder An agreement that may accompany an earnest money deposit for the purchase of real property as evidence of the purchaser's good faith and intent to complete the transaction.

Black book Offering plan for a cooperative or condominium as accepted for filing by the attorney general and used for marketing.

Blanket mortgage A mortgage covering more than one parcel of real estate.

Blockbusting. The illegal practice of inducing homeowners to sell their properties by making representations regarding the entry or prospective entry of minority persons into the neighborhood.

Blue-sky laws Common name for those state and federal laws that regulate the registration and sale of investment securities.

Board of directors Elected managing body of a corporation, specifically of a cooperative apartment building.

Board of managers Elected managing body of a condominium.

Bona fide In good faith, without fraud.

Bond The evidence of a personal debt that is secured by a mortgage or other lien on real estate.

Boot Money or property given to make up any difference in value or equity between two properties in an *exchange*.

Branch office A secondary place of business apart from the principal or main office from which real estate business is conducted.

Breach of contract Violation of any terms or conditions in a contract without legal excuse, for example, failure to make a payment when it is due.

Broker One who buys and sells for another for a commission. *See also* Real estate broker.

Brokerage. The business of buying and selling for another for a commission.

Building codes Regulations established by local governments stating fully the structural requirements for building.

Building line A line fixed at a certain distance from the front and/or sides of a lot, beyond which no building can project.

Building loan agreement An agreement whereby the lender advances money to an owner with provisional payments at certain stages of construction.

Bulk transfer *See* Uniform Commercial Code.

Buyer's broker A real estate broker retained by a prospective purchaser, who becomes the broker's principal or client and to whom fiduciary duties are owed.

Bylaws Rules and regulations adopted by an association.

Cap With an adjustable rate mortgage, a limit, usually in percentage points, on how much the interest rate or payment might be raised in each adjustment period. For *lifetime cap, see* Ceiling.

Capital gains *Long-term* capital gains are profits realized from the sale of assets like real estate that have been held for a statutory period (variously six months or one year) and are partially exempted from income tax according to percentages (40 percent, 50 percent) that are also liable to changes in tax law. Short-term gains are taxed as ordinary income.

Capital investment The initial capital and the long-term expenditures made to establish and maintain a business or investment property.

Capitalization A mathematical process for estimating the value of a property using a proper rate of return on the investment and the annual net income expected to be produced by the property. The formula is expressed:

$$\frac{Income}{Rate} = Value$$

Capitalization rate The rate of return a property will produce on the owner's investment.

Cash equivalent An appraisal technique that takes into account the influence of concessionary financing.

Cash flow The net spendable income from an investment.

Casualty insurance A type of insurance policy that protects a property owner or other person from loss of injury sustained as a result of theft, vandalism, or similar occurrences.

Caveat emptor A Latin phrase meaning "Let the buyer beware."

CC&R Covenants, conditions, and restrictions of a condominium or cooperative development.

Cease and desist petition A statement filed by a homeowner showing address of premises, that notifies the Department of State that such premises are not for sale and the owner does not wish to be solicited.

Ceiling With adjustable rate mortgages, a limit, usually in percentage points, beyond which the interest rates or monthly payment on a loan may never rise. Sometimes known as a *lifetime cap*.

Certificate of occupancy Document issued by a municipal authority stating that a building complies with building, health, and safety codes and may be occupied.

Certificate of title A statement of opinion of the status of the title to a parcel of real property based on an examination of specified public records.

Chain of title The conveyance of real property to one owner from another, reaching back to the original grantor.

Chapter 7, Chapter 11, Chapter 13 Different forms of bankruptcy.

Chattel Personal property such as household goods or fixtures.

Chattel mortgage A mortgage on personal property.

Checkers. *See* Testers.

Client The one by whom a broker is employed and by whom the broker will be compensated on completion of the purpose of the agency.

Closing date The date upon which the buyer takes title to the property.

Closing statement A detailed cash accounting of a real estate transaction showing all cash received, all charges and credits made, and all cash paid out in the transaction.

Cloud on the title An outstanding claim or encumbrance that, if valid, would affect or impair the owner's title.

Clustering The grouping of homesites within a subdivision on smaller lots than normal with the remaining land used as common areas.

CMA *See* Comparative market analysis.

C of O *See* Certificate of occupancy.

Coinsurance clause A clause in insurance policies covering real property that requires the policyholder to maintain fire insurance coverage generally equal to at least 80 percent of the property's actual replacement cost.

Collateral Additional security pledged for the payment of an obligation.

Color of title That which appears to be good title but which is not title in fact.

Commingling The illegal act of a real estate broker who mixes the money of other people with his or her own money.

Commission Payment to a broker for services rendered, such as in the sale or purchase of real property; usually a percentage of the selling price.

Commitment A pledge or a promise or affirmation agreement.

Common elements Parts of a property that are necessary or convenient to the existence, maintenance and safety of a condominium or are normally in common use by all of the condominium residents.

Common law The body of law based on custom, usage, and court decisions.

Community property A system of property ownership not in effect in New York.

Company dollar A broker's net commission income after cooperating brokers and the firm's own salespersons have been paid.

Comparables Properties listed in an appraisal report that are substantially equivalent to the subject property.

Comparative market analysis. A study, intended to assist an owner in establishing listing price, of recent comparable sales, properties that failed to sell, and parcels presently on the market.

Competent parties People who are recognized by law as being able to contract with others; usually those of legal age and sound mind.

Complaint The first pleading brought in a civil lawsuit.

Condemnation A judicial or administrative proceeding to exercise the power of eminent domain through which a government agency takes private property for public use and compensates the owner.

Condition A contingency, qualification, or occurrence upon which an estate or property right is gained or lost.

Condominium The absolute ownership of an apartment or a unit (generally in a multi-unit building) plus an undivided interest in the ownership of the common elements, which are owned jointly with the other condominium unit owners.

Consideration 1. That which is received by the grantor in exchange for his or her deed. 2. Something of value that induces a person to enter into a contract. Consideration may be *valuable* (money) or *good* (love and affection).

Constructive eviction Actions of the landlord that so materially disturb or impair the tenant's enjoyment of the leased premises that the tenant is effectively forced to move out and terminate the lease without liability for any further rent.

Constructive notice Notice given to the world by recorded documents. Posessesion of property is also considered constructive notice.

Contract An agreement entered into by two or more legally competent parties by the terms of which one or more of the parties, for a consideration, undertakes to do or refrain from doing some legal act or acts. A contract may be either *unilateral*, where only one party is bound to act, or *bilateral*, where all parties to the instrument are legally bound to act as prescribed.

Contract for deed A contract for the sale of real estate wherein the purchase price is paid in periodic installments by the purchaser, who is in possession of the property even though title is retained by the seller until final payment. Also called an *installment contract* or *land contract*.

Conventional loan A loan that is not insured or guaranteed by a government.

Conveyance The transfer of the title of land from one to another. The means or medium by which title of real estate is transferred.

Cooperative A residential multi-unit building whose title is held by a corporation owned by and operated for the benefit of persons living within the building, who are the stockholders of the corporation, each possessing a proprietary lease.

Corporation An entity of organization created by operation of law whose rights of doing business are essentially the same as those of an individual.

Cost approach. The process of estimating the value of property by adding to the estimated land value the appraiser's estimate of the reproduction or replacement cost of the building, less depreciation.

Cost basis. *See* Basis.

Cost recovery Accounting system for recovering capital invested in property over a period of time. Formerly *depreciation*.

Counteroffer A new offer made as a reply to an offer received.

County clerk's certificate When an acknowledgment is taken by an officer not authorized in the state or county where the document is to be recorded, the instrument that must be attached to the acknowledgment is called a county clerk's certificate. It is given by the clerk of the county where the officer obtained his or her authority and certifies to the officer's signature and powers.

Covenants Agreements written into deeds and other instruments promising performance or nonperformance of certain acts or stipulating certain uses or nonuses of the property.

CPM Certified Property Manager, a designation awarded by the Institute of Real Estate Management.

Credit On a closing statement, an amount entered in a person's favor.

Criminal law That branch of law defining crimes and providing punishment.

Cubic-foot method A technique for estimating building costs per cubic foot.

Curtesy A life estate given to the surviving husband in real estate owned by his deceased wife. New York has abolished curtesy.

Damages The indemnity recoverable by a person who has sustained an injury, either to person, property, or rights, through the act or default of another.

DBA ''Doing business as''; an assumed business name.

Dealer An IRS classification for a person whose business is buying and selling real estate on his or her own account.

DEC The New York Department of Environmental Conservation.

Decedent A person who has died.

Declaration A formal statement of intention to establish a condominium.

Dedication The voluntary transfer of private property by its owner to the public for some public use such as for streets or schools.

Deed A written instrument that, when executed and delivered, conveys title to or an interest in real estate.

Deed restriction An imposed restriction in a deed for the purpose of limiting the use of the land by future owners.

Default The nonperformance of a duty whether arising under a contract or otherwise; failure to meet an obligation when due.

Defendant The person accused in a lawsuit or criminal trial.

Deficiency judgment A personal judgment levied against the mortgagor when a foreclosure sale does not produce sufficient funds to pay the mortgage debt in full.

Delinquent taxes Unpaid taxes that are past due.

Delivery The transfer of the possession of a thing from one person to another.

Demising clause A clause in a lease whereby the landlord (lessor) leases and the tenant (lessee) takes the property.

Department of Housing and Community Renewal The New York State department charged with administering rent regulations.

Deposition Sworn testimony that may be used as evidence in a suit or trial.

Depreciation In appraisal, a loss of value in property due to any cause including physical deterioration, functional depreciation, and locational obsolescence.

Descent Process by which when an owner of real estate dies intestate, property descends by operation of law to the owner's natural heirs.

Determinable fee estate A fee simple estate in which the property automatically reverts to the grantor upon the occurrence of a specified event or condition.

Developer One who improves land with buildings, usually on a large scale, and sells to homeowners and/or investors.

Devise A gift of real property by will.

Devisee One who receives a bequest of real estate made by will.

Devisor One who bequeaths real estate by will.

Discount points An added loan fee charged by a lender to make the yield on a lower-than-market-value loan competitive with higher-interest loans.

Discovery A procedure for uncovering pertinent facts before a trial.

Distributee Person receiving or entitled to receive land as representative of the former owner.

Documentary evidence Evidence in the form of written or printed papers.

Dominant tenement A property that includes in its ownership the right to use an easement over another person's property for a specific purpose.

DOS New York Department of State; administers license law.

Dower The legal right or interest, no longer recognized in New York, that a wife acquires in the property her husband held or acquired during their marriage.

Dual agency Representing both parties to a transaction.

Due-on-sale *See* Alienation clause.

Duress Unlawful constraint or action exercised upon a person who is forced to perform an act against his or her will.

Earnest money deposit An amount of money deposited by a buyer under the terms of a contract, that is to be forfeited if the buyer defaults but applied on the purchase price if the sale is closed.

Easement A right to use the land of another for a specific purpose as for a right-of-way or utilities; an incorporeal interest in land. An *easement appurtenant* passes with the land when conveyed.

Easement by necessity An easement allowed by law as necessary for the full enjoyment of a parcel of real estate; for example, a right of ingress and egress over a grantor's land.

Easement by prescription An easement acquired by continuous, open, uninterrupted, exclusive, and adverse use of the property for the period of time prescribed by state law.

Easment in gross An easement that is not created for the benefit of any *land* owned by the owner of the easement but that attaches *personally to the easement owner.*

EBT Examination before trial; *See* Discovery.

Economic obsolescence *See* Locational obsolescence.

Emblements Growing crops, such as grapes and corn, that are produced annually through labor and industry; also called *fructus industriales.*

Eminent domain The right of a government or quasipublic body to acquire property for public use through a court action called *condemnation.*

Employment contract A document evidencing formal employment between employer and employee or between principal and agent. In the real estate business this generally takes the form of a listing agreement or management agreement.

Encroachment A building or some portion of it—a wall or fence for instance—that extends beyond the land of the owner and illegally intrudes upon some land of an adjoining owner or a street or alley.

Encumbrance Any claim by another—such as a mortgage, tax, or judgment lien, an easement, encroachment, or a deed restriction on the use of the land—that may diminish the value of a property.

Endorsement An act of signing one's name on the back of a check or note with or without further qualifications.

Equalization The raising or lowering of assessed values for tax purposes in a particular county or taxing district to make them equal to assesments in other counties or districts.

Equitable title The interest held by a vendee under a land contract or an installment contract; the equitable right to obtain absolute ownership to property when legal title is held in another's name.

Equity The interest or value that an owner has in his or her property over and above any mortgage indebtedness.

Equity of redemption A right of the owner to reclaim property before it is sold through foreclosure by the payment of the debt, interest, and costs.

Erosion The gradual wearing away of land by water, wind, and general weather conditions; the diminishing of property caused by the elements.

Errors and omissions insurance A form of malpractice insurance for real estate brokers.

Escheat The reversion of property to the state or county, as provided by state law, in cases where a decedent dies intestate without heirs capable of inheriting or when the property is abandoned.

Escrow The closing of a transaction through a third party called an *escrow agent*. Also can refer to earnest money deposits or to mortgagee's trust account for insurance and tax payments.

Estate The degree, quantity, nature, and extent of interest that a person has in real property.

Estate at will The occupation of lands and tenements by a tenant for an indefinite period, terminable by one or both parties at will.

Estate for years An interest for a certain, exact period of time in property leased for a specified consideration.

Estate in land The degree, quantity, nature, and extent of interest that a person has in real property.

Estate in reversion The residue of an estate left for the grantor, to commence in possession after the termination of some particular estate granted by the grantor.

Estate tax Federal tax levied on property transferred upon death.

Estoppel certificate A document in which a borrower certifies the amount he or she owes on a mortgage loan and the rate of interest.

Eviction A legal process to oust a person from possession of real estate.

Evidence of title Proof of ownership of property; commonly a certificate of title, a title insurance policy, an abstract of title with lawyer's opinion, or a Torrens registration certificate.

Exchange A transaction in which all or part of the consideration for the purchase of real property is the transfer of *like kind* property (that is, real estate for real estate).

Exclusive-agency listing A listing contract under which the owner appoints a real estate broker as his or her exclusive agent for a designated period of time to sell the property, on the owner's stated terms, for a commission. The owner reserves the right to sell without paying anyone a commission.

Exclusive right to sell A listing contract under which the owner appoints a real estate broker as his or her exclusive agent for a designated period of time, to sell the property on the owner's stated terms, and agrees to pay the broker a commission when the property is sold, whether by the broker, the owner, or another broker.

Executed contract A contract in which all parties have fulfilled their promises and thus performed the contract.

Execution The signing and delivery of an instrument. Also, a legal order directing an official to enforce a judgment against the property of a debtor.

Executor A male person or a corporate entity or any other type of organization designated in a will to carry out its provisions.

Executory contract A contract under which something remains to be done by one or more of the parties.

Executrix A woman appointed to perform the duties of an executor.

Expressed contract An oral or written contract in which the parties state the contract's terms and express their intentions in words.

Extension agreement An agreement that extends the life of a mortgage to a later date.

Fee simple estate The maximum possible estate or right of ownership of real property, continuing forever. Sometimes called a *fee* or *fee simple absolute*.

Feudal system A system of ownership usually associated with precolonial England in which the king or other sovereign is the source of all rights.

FHA loan A loan insured by the Federal Housing Administration and made by an approved lender in accordance with the FHA's regulations.

Fiduciary relationship A relationship of trust and confidence as between trustee and beneficiary, attorney and client, or principal and agent.

Financing statement. *See* Uniform Commercial Code.

Fixture An item of personal property that has been converted to real property by being permanently affixed to the realty.

Foreclosure A procedure whereby property pledged as security for a debt is sold to pay the debt in the event of default in payments or terms.

Franchise An organization that leases a standardized trade name, operating procedures, supplies, and referral service to member real estate brokerages.

Fraud Deception that causes a person to give up property or a lawful right.

Freehold estate An estate in land in which ownership is for an indeterminate length of time, in contrast to a leasehold estate.

Front foot A standard measurement, one foot wide, of the width of land, applied at the frontage on its street line. Each front foot extends the depth of the lot.

Functional obsolescence A loss of value to an improvement to real estate due to functional problems, often caused by age or poor design.

Future interest A person's present right to an interest in real property that will not result in possession or enjoyment until some time in the future.

Gap A defect in the chain of title of a particular parcel of real estate; a missing document or conveyance that raises doubt as to the present ownership of the land.

GEM *See* Growing equity mortgage.

General agent One who is authorized to act for his or her principal in a specific range of matters.

General contractor A construction specialist who enters into a formal contract with a landowner or lessee to construct a building or project. The general contractor often contracts with several *subcontractors* specializing in various aspects of the building process.

General lien The right of a creditor to have all of a debtor's property—both real and personal—sold to satisfy a debt.

General partnership *See* Partnership.

General tax *See* Ad volarem tax.

Grace period Additional time allowed to perform an act or make a payment before a default occurs.

Graduated lease A lease that provides for a graduated change at stated intervals in the amount of the rent to be paid; used largely in long-term leases.

Grantee A person who receives a conveyance of real property from the grantor.

Granting clause Words in a deed of conveyance that state the grantor's intention to convey the property. This clause is generally worded as "convey and warrant," "grant," "grant, bargain, and sell," or the like.

Grantor The person transferring title to or an interest in real property to a grantee.

Gross income Total income from property before any expenses are deducted.

Gross lease A lease of property under which a landlord pays all property charges regularly incurred through ownership, such as repairs, taxes, and insurance.

Gross rent multiplier A figure used as a multiplier of the gross rental income of a property to produce an estimate of the property's value.

Ground lease A lease of land only, on which the tenant usually owns a building or constructs a building as specified in the lease.

Growing equity mortgage An arrangement with mortgage payments increasing regularly, usually by a given percentage each year, with the extra amount credited to principal, thus shortening the term of the loan.

Habendum clause That part of a deed beginning with the words "to have and to hold" following the granting clause and defining the extent of ownership the grantor is conveying.

Heir One who might inherit or succeed to an interest in land under the state law of descent when the owner dies without leaving a valid will.

Highest and best use That possible use of land that would produce the greatest net income and thereby develop the highest land value.

Holdover tenancy A tenancy whereby a lessee retains possession of leased property after his or her lease has expired and the landlord, by continuing to accept rent, agrees to the tenant's continued occupancy.

Holographic will A will that is written, dated, and signed in the testator's handwriting but is not witnessed.

Homeowners' association A nonprofit group of homeowners in a condominium, cooperative, or PUD that administers common elements and enforces covenants, conditions, and restrictions.

Homeowner's insurance policy A standardized package insurance policy that covers a residential real estate owner against financial loss from fire, theft, public liability, and other commercial risks.

Homestead Land that is owned and occupied as the family home. The right to protect a portion of the value of this land from unsecured judgments for debts.

Hypothecate To give a thing a security without the necessity of giving up possession of it.

Implied contract A contract under which the agreement of the parties is demonstrated by their acts and conduct.

Improvement Any structure erected on a site to enhance the value of the property—buildings, fences, driveways, curbs, sidewalks, or sewers.

Imputed interest An IRS concept that treats some concessionary low-interest loans as if they had been paid and collected at a statutory rate.

Income approach The process of estimating the value of an income-producing property by capitalization of the annual net income expected to be produced by the property during its remaining useful life.

Incompetent A person who is unable to manage his or her own affairs by reason of insanity, imbecility, or feeble-mindedness.

Incumbrance Any right to or interest in land that diminishes its value. *See also* Encumbrance.

Independent contractor Someone who is retained to perform a certain act but who is subject to the control and direction of another only as to the end result and not as to the way in which he or she performs the act; contrasted with employee.

Index With an adjustable rate mortgage, a measure of current interest rates, used as a basis for calculating the new rate at time of adjustment.

Infant A person who has not reached 18; a minor.

Informed consent exception A provision in state real estate license law that permits a broker to represent both buyer and seller to a transaction if he or she has their prior mutual consent to do so.

Inheritance tax New York State tax levied upon those who inherit property located in the state.

Injunction An order issued by a court to restrain one party from doing an act that is deemed to be unjust to the rights of some other party.

In rem A proceeding against the realty directly; as dinstinguished from a proceeding against a person. (Used in taking land for nonpayment of taxes, etc.)

Installment contract *See* Contract for deed.

Installment sale A method of reporting income received from the sale of real estate when the sales price is paid in two or more installments over two or more years.

Instrument A written legal document, created to effect the rights of the parties.

Interest A charge made by a lender for the use of money.

Interest rate The percentage of a sum of money charged for its use.

Intestate The condition of a property owner who dies without leaving a valid will.

Involuntary alienation *See* Alienation.

Involuntary bankruptcy A bankruptcy proceeding initiated by one or more of the debtor's creditors.

Involuntary lien A lien imposed against property without consent of the owner, i.e., taxes, special assessments.

Irrevocable consent An agreement filed by an out-of-state broker in the state in which he or she wishes to be licensed, stating that suits and actions may be brought against the broker in that state.

Joint tenancy Ownership of real estate between two or more parties who have been named in one conveyance as joint tenants. Upon the death of a joint tenant, his or her interest passes to the surviving joint tenant or tenants by the right of survivorship.

Joint venture The joining of two or more people to conduct a specific business enterprise.

Judgment The formal decision of a court upon the respective claims of the parties to an action. After a judgment has been recorded, it usually becomes a general lien on the property of the defendant.

Junior lien An obligation such as a second mortgage that is subordinate in priority to an existing lien on the same realty.

Laches Loss of a legal right through undue delay in asserting it.

Land The earth's surface, extending downward to the center of the earth and upward infinitely into space.

Land contract *See* Contract for deed.

Landlord One who rents property to another.

Law of agency *See* Agent.

Lease A written or oral contract between a landlord (the lessor) and a tenant (the lessee) that transfers the right to exclusive possession and use of the landlord's real property to the lessee for a specified period of time and for a stated consideration (rent).

Leasehold estate A tenant's right to occupy real estate during the term of a lease; generally considered to be personal property.

Legacy A disposition of money or personal property by will.

Legal description A description of a specific parcel of real estate complete enough for an independent surveyor to locate and identify it.

Lessee Tenant.

Lessor Landlord.

Leverage The use of borrowed money to finance the bulk of an investment.

License 1. A privilege or right granted to a person by a state to operate as a real estate broker or salesperson. 2. The revocable permission for a temporary use of land—a personal right that cannot be sold.

Lien A right given by law to certain creditors to have their debt paid out of the property of a defaulting debtor, usually by means of a court sale.

Life estate An interest in real or personal property that is limited in duration to the lifetime of its owner or some other designated person.

Life tenant A person in possession of a life estate.

Like kind property. *See* Exchange.

Limited parnership. *See* Partnership.

Liquidity The ability to sell an asset and convert it into cash at a price close to its true value in a short period of time.

Lis pendens A recorded legal document giving constructive notice that an action affecting a particular property has been filed in court.

Listing agreement A contract between a landowner (as principal) and a licensed real estate broker (as agent) by which the broker is employed as agent to sell real estate on the owner's terms within a given time, for which service the landowner agrees to pay a commission or fee.

Listing broker The broker in a multiple-listing situation from whose office a listing agreement is initiated, as opposed to the *selling broker* from whose office negotiations leading up to a sale are initiated.

Litigation. The act of carrying on a lawsuit.

Littoral rights. 1. A landowner's claim to use water in large navigable lakes and oceans adjacent to his or her property. 2. The ownership rights to land bordering these bodies of water up to the high-water mark.

Locational obsolesence Reduction in a property's value caused by factors outside the subject property such as social or environmental forces or objectionable neighboring property.

Lot-and-block description A description of real property that identifies a parcel of land by reference to lot and block numbers within a subdivision as specified on a plat of subdivision duly recorded in the county recorder's office.

Margin With an adjustable rate mortgage, the number of points over an *index* at which the interest rate is set.

Marginal tax rate Percentage at which the last dollar of income is taxed; top tax bracket.

Marketable title Good or clear title reasonably free from the risk of litigation over possible defects.

Market comparison approach The process of estimating the value of a property by examining and comparing actual sales of comparable properties.

Market price The actual selling price of a property.

Market value The probable price a ready, willing, able, and informed buyer would pay and a ready, willing, able, and informed seller would accept, neither being under any pressure to act.

Master plan A comprehensive plan to guide the long-term physical development of a particular area.

Mechanic's lien A statutory lien created in favor of contractors, laborers, and materialmen who have performed work or furnished materials in the erection or repair of a building.

Meeting of the minds *See* Offer and acceptance.

Metes-and-bounds description A legal description of a parcel of land that begins at a well-marked point and follows the boundaries, using direction and distances around the tract back to the place of beginning.

Mill One-tenth of one cent. A tax rate of 52 mills would be $.052 tax for each dollar of assessed valuation of a property.

Minor A person under 18 years of age.

MIP Mortgage insurance premium.

Month-to-month tenancy A periodic tenancy; that is, the tenant rents for one period at a time. In the absence of a rental agreement (oral or written), a tenancy is generally considered to be month to month.

Monument A fixed natural or artificial object used to establish real estate boundaries for a metes-and-bounds description.

Moratorium An emergency act by a legislative body to suspend the legal enforcement of contractual obligations.

Mortgage A conditional transfer or pledge of real estate as security for the payment of a debt. Also, the document creating a mortgage lien.

Mortgagee A lender in a mortgage loan transaction.

Mortgage lien A lien or charge on the property of a mortgagor that secures the underlying debt obligations.

Mortgage reduction certificate An instrument executed by the mortgagee, setting forth the present status and the balance due on the mortgage as of the date of the execution of the instrument.

Mortgagor A borrower who conveys his or her property as security for a loan.

Multiple listing An exclusive listing with the additional authority and obligation on the part of the listing broker to distribute the listing to other brokers in the multiple-listing organization.

Negative amortization Gradual building up of a larger mortgage debt when payments are not sufficient to cover interest due and reduce the principal.

Negligence An unintentional tort caused by failure to exercise reasonable care.

Negotiable instrument A signed promise to pay a sum of money.

Net lease A lease requiring the tenant to pay not only rent but also some or all costs of maintaining the property, including taxes, insurance, utilities, and repairs.

Net listing A listing based on the net price the seller will receive if the property is sold. Under a net listing the broker is free to offer the property for sale at the highest price he or she can get in order to increase the commission. This type of listing is outlawed in New York.

Nonconforming use A use of property that is permitted to continue after a zoning ordinance prohibiting it has been established for the area.

Nonhomogeneity A lack of uniformity; disimilarity. Because no two parcels of land are exactly alike, real estate is said to be nonhomogeneous.

Notary public A public officer who is authorized to take acknowledgments to certain classes of documents such as deeds, contracts, and mortgages, and before whom affidavits may be sworn.

Note An instrument of credit given to attest a debt.

Nuisance An act that disturbs another's peaceful enjoyment of property.

NYSAR New York State Association of REALTORS®.

Obligee The person in whose favor an obligation is entered into.

Obligor The person who binds himself/herself to another; one who has engaged to perform some obligation; one who makes a bond.

Obsolescence *See* Locational and Functional obsolescence.

Offer and acceptance Two essential components of a valid contract; a "meeting of the minds," when all parties agree to the exact terms.

Open-end mortgage A mortgage loan that is expandable by increments up to a maximum dollar amount, the full loan being secured by the same original mortgage.

Open listing A listing contract under which the broker's commission is contingent upon the broker's producing a ready, willing, and able buyer before the property is sold by the seller or another broker.

Open market An economic model that allows the price of a commodity to respond freely to the forces of supply and demand.

Open mortgage A mortgage that has matured or is overdue and, therefore, is "open" to foreclosure at any time.

Option An agreement to keep open for a set period an offer to sell or purchase property.

Ostensible agency A form of implied agency relationship created by the actions of the parties involved rather than by written agreement or document.

Package mortgage A method of financing in which the loan that finances the purchase of a home also finances the purchase of certain items of personal property such as a washer, dryer, refrigerator, stove, and other specified appliances.

Parcel A specific piece of real estate.

Participation financing A mortgage in which the lender participates in the income of the mortgaged venture.

Partition The division that is made of real property between those who own it in undivided shares.

Partnership An association of two or more individuals who carry on a continuing business for profit as co-owners. A *general partnership* is a typical form of joint venture, in which each general partner shares in the administration, profits, and losses of the operation. A *limited partnership* is administered by one or more general partners and funded by limited or silent partners who are by law responsible for losses only to the extent of their investments.

Party wall A wall that is located on or at a boundary line between two adjoining parcels of land and is used by the owners of both properties.

Percentage lease A lease commonly used for commercial property whose rental is based on the tenant's gross sales at the premises.

Periodic estate An interest in leased property that continues from period to period— week to week, month to month, or year to year.

Personal property Items, called *chattels,* that do not fit into the definition of real property; movable objects.

Personal representative The administrator or executor appointed to handle the estate of a decedent.

Physical deterioration Loss of value due to wear and tear or action of the elements.

PITI Principal, interest, taxes, and insurance components of a regular mortgage payment.

Plaintiff The person who brings a lawsuit against another.

Planned unit development A planned combination of diverse land uses such as housing, recreation, and shopping, in one contained development or subdivision.

Planning board Municipal body overseeing orderly development of real estate.

Plat A map of a town, section, or subdivision indicating the location and boundaries of individual properties. ,

Pleadings Formal written documents defining the issues in dispute in advance of a trial.

PMI Private mortgage insurance.

Point A unit of measurement used for various loan charges; one point equals one percent of the amount of the loan. *See also* Discount points.

Point of beginning In a metes-and-bounds legal description, the starting point of the survey, situated in one corner of the parcel.

Police power The government's right to impose laws, statutes, and ordinances including zoning ordinances and building codes, to protect the public health, safety, and welfare.

Policy and procedures manual A broker's compilation of guidelines for the conduct of the firm's business.

Power of attorney A written instrument authorizing a person, the *attorney-in-fact,* to act as agent on behalf of another person to the extent indicated in the instrument.

Precedent A court decision that serves as authority for later cases.

Premises Lands and tenements; an estate; the subject matter of a conveyance.

Prepayment clause A clause in a mortgage that gives mortgagor the privilege of paying the mortgage indebtedness before it becomes due.

Prepayment penalty A charge imposed on a borrower who pays off the loan principal early.

Price-fixing *See* Antitrust laws.

Principal 1. A sum lent or employed as a fund or investment as distinguished from its income or profits. 2. The original amount (as in a loan) of the total due and payable at a certain date. 3. A main party of a transaction—the person for whom the agent works.

Principal broker *See* Supervising broker.

Priority The order of position or time.

Private mortgage insurance Insurance that limits a lender's potential loss in a mortgage default, issued by a private company rather than by the FHA.

Probate To establish the will of a deceased person.

Property manager Someone who manages real estate for another person for compensation.

Proprietary lease A written lease in a cooperative apartment building, held by the tenant/shareholder, giving the right to occupy a particular unit.

Prorations Expenses, either prepaid or paid in arrears, that are divided or distributed between buyer and seller at the closing.

Prospectus A printed statement disclosing all material aspects of a real estate project.

PUD Planned unit development.

Puffing Exaggerated or superlative comments or opinions not made as representations of fact and thus not grounds for misrepresentation.

Pur autre vie For the life of another. A life estate pur autre vie is a life estate that is measured by the life of a person other than the grantee.

Purchase-money mortgage A note secured by a mortgage given by a buyer, as mortgagor, to a seller, as mortgagee, as part of the purchase price of the real estate.

Quiet enjoyment The right of an owner or a person legally in possession to the use of property without interference of possession.

Quiet title suit *See* Suit to quiet title.

Quitclaim deed A conveyance by which the grantor transfers whatever interest he or she has in the real estate, without warranties or obligations.

Ready, willing, and able buyer One who is prepared to buy property on the seller's terms and is ready to take positive steps to consummate the transaction.

Real estate A portion of the earth's surface extending downward to the center of the earth and upward infinitely into space including all things permanently attached thereto, whether by nature or by a person.

Real estate board An organization whose members consist primarily of real estate brokers and salespersons.

Real estate broker Any person, partnership, association, or corporation who sells (or offers to sell), buys (or offers to buy), or negotiates the purchase, sale, or exchange of real estate, or who leases (or offers to lease) or rents (or offers to rent) any real estate or the improvements thereon for others and for a compensation or valuable consideration.

Real estate investment trust (REIT) Trust ownership of real estate by a group of at least 100 individuals who purchase certificates of ownership in the trust.

Real property Real estate plus all the interests, benefits, and rights inherent in ownership. Often referred to as *real estate*.

REALTOR® A registered trademark term reserved for the sole use of active members of local REALTOR® boards affiliated with the National Association of REALTORS®.

Reconciliation The final step in the appraisal process in which the appraiser reconciles the estimates of value received from the market data, cost, and income approaches to arrive at a final estimate of value for the subject property.

Recording The act of entering or recording documents affecting or conveying interests in real estate in the recorder's office established in each county.

Rectangular survey system A system established in 1785 by the federal government providing for surveying and describing land by reference to principal meridians and base lines, outside the 13 original colonies.

Redemption period A period of time established by state law during which a property owner has the right to redeem his or her real estate from a tax sale by paying the sales price, interest, and costs.

Red herring Preliminary offering plan for a cooperative or condominium project submitted to the attorney general and to tenants and subject to modification.

Redlining The illegal practice of a lending institution denying loans or restricting their number for certain areas of a community.

Regulation Z Law requiring credit institutions and advertisers to inform borrowers of the true cost of obtaining credit; commonly called the *Truth-in-Lending Act*.

Release The act or writing by which some claim or interest is surrendered to another.

Remainder The remnant of an estate that has been conveyed to take effect and be enjoyed after the termination of a prior estate, as when an owner conveys a life estate to one party and the remainder to another.

Remainderman The person who is to receive the property after the death of a life tenant.

Rent A fixed, periodic payment made by a tenant of a property to the owner for possession and use, usually by prior agreement of the parties.

Replacement cost The construction cost at current prices of a property that is not necessarily an exact duplicate of the subject property but serves the same purpose or function as the original.

Reproduction cost The construction cost at current prices of an exact duplicate of the subject property.

Reserves Money set aside to accumulate for future expenses.

Restriction A limitation on the use of real property, generally originated by the owner or subdivider in a deed.

Return The income from a real estate investment, calculated as a percentage of cash invested.

Reverse discrimination *(Benign discrimination)* Housing discrimination, usually based on quotas, designed by a municipality to achieve a racial balance perceived as desirable.

Reversion The remnant of an estate that the grantor holds after he or she has granted a life estate to another person—the estate will return, or revert, to the grantor; also called a *reverter*.

Reversionary right An owner's right to regain possession of leased property upon termination of the lease agreement.

Revocation An act of recalling a power of authority conferred, as the revocation of a power of attorney, a license, or an agency.

Right of survivorship *See* Joint tenancy.

Right-of-way The right to pass over another's land more or less frequently according to the nature of the easement.

Riparian rights An owner's rights in land that borders on or includes a stream, river, lake, or sea. These rights include access to and use of the water.

Sale and leaseback A transaction in which an owner sells his or her improved property and, as part of the same transaction, signs a long-term lease to remain in possession of the premises.

Sales contract A contract containing the complete terms of the agreement between buyer and seller for the sale of a particular parcel of real estate.

Salesperson A person who performs real estate activities while employed by or associated with a licensed real estate broker.

Satisfaction price. A document acknowledging the payment of a debt.

S Corporation A simple form of corporation, taxed as a partnership.

Secondary mortgage market A market for the purchase and sale of existing mortgages, designed to provide greater liquidity of mortgages.

Section A portion of a township under the rectangular survey (government survey) system. A section is a square with mile-long sides and an area of one square mile, or 640 acres.

Seizin The possession of land by one who claims to own at least an estate for life therein.

Selling broker *See* Listing broker.

Servient tenement Land on which an easement exists in favor of an adjacent property (called a dominant estate); also called *servient estate*.

Setback The amount of space local zoning regulations require between a lot line and a building line.

Severalty Ownership of real property by one person only; also called *sole ownership*.

Shared appreciation mortgage A mortgage loan in which the lender, in exchange for a loan with a favorable interest rate, participates in the profits (if any) the mortgagor receives when the property is eventually sold.

Situs The personal preference of people for one area over another, not necessarily based on objective facts and knowledge.

Small claims court A special local court for settling disputes without the need for attorneys or extensive court costs.

Special agent One who is authorized by a principal to perform a single act or transaction. A real estate broker is usually a special agent authorized to find a ready, willing, and able buyer for a particular property.

Special assessment A tax or levy customarily imposed against only those specific parcels of real estate that will benefit from a proposed public improvement like a street or sewer.

Specific lien A lien affecting or attaching only to a certain, specific parcel of land or piece of property.

Specific performance suit A legal action brought in a court of equity in special cases to compel a party to carry out the terms of a contract.

Sponsor The developer or owner organizing and offering for sale a condominium or cooperative development.

Statute of frauds The part of state law requiring certain instruments such as deeds, real estate sales contracts, and certain leases to be in writing in order for them to be legally enforceable.

Statute of limitations That law pertaining to the period of time within which certain actions must be brought to court—in New York, six years for contracts.

Statutory lien A lien imposed on property by statute—a tax lien, for example—in contrast to a voluntary lien such as a mortgage lien that an owner places on his or her own real estate.

Steering The illegal practice of channeling home seekers to particular areas for discriminatory ends.

Straight-line method A method of calculating cost recovery for tax purposes, computed by dividing the adjusted basis of a property by the number of years chosen.

Subagent A broker's sales associate, or cooperating broker in a multiple-listing system, in relationship to the principal who has designated the broker as an agent.

Subchapter S Corporation *See* S Corporation.

Subcontractor *See* General contractor.

Subdivision A tract of land divided by the owner, known as the *subdivider,* into blocks, building lots, and streets according to a recorded subdivision plat that must comply with local ordinances and regulations.

Subject property The property being appraised.

Subletting The leasing of premises by a lessee to a third party for part of the lessee's remaining term. *See also* Assignment.

Subordination Relegation to a lesser position, usually in respect to a right or security.

Subrogation The substitution of one creditor for another with the substituted person succeeding to the legal rights and claims of the original claimant.

Subscribing witness One who writes his or her name as witness to the execution of an instrument.

Substitution An appraisal principle stating that the maximum value of a property tends to be set by the cost of purchasing an equally desirable and valuable substitute property.

Subsurface rights Ownership rights in a parcel of real estate to the water, minerals, gas, oil, and so forth that lie beneath the surface of the property.

Suit for possession A court suit initiated by a landlord to evict a tenant from leased premises after the tenant has breached one of the terms of the lease or has held possession of the property after the lease's expiration.

Suit to quiet title A court action intended to establish or settle the title to a particular property, especially when there is a cloud on the title.

Summons A formal document notifying a person that a lawsuit has been started against him or her, and directing a court appearance.

Supervising broker The one broker registered with the Department of State as in charge of a real estate office, responsible for the actions of salespersons and associate brokers.

Surface rights Ownership rights in a parcel of real estate that are limited to the surface of the property and do not include the air above it (air rights) or the minerals below the surface (subsurface rights).

Surrender The cancellation of a lease by mutual consent of the lessor and the lessee.

Surrogate's court (probate court) A court having jursidiction over the proof of wills and the settling of estates.

Survey The process by which a parcel of land is measured and its area ascertained; also, the blueprint showing the measurements, boundaries, and area.

Syndicate A combination of people or firms formed to accomplish a joint venture of mutual interest.

Tacking Adding or combining successive periods of continuous occupation of real property by several different adverse possessors.

Taxation The process by which a government or municipal quasipublic body raises monies to fund its operation.

Tax deed An instrument, similar to a certificate of sale, given to a purchaser at a tax sale.

Tax lien A charge against property created by operation of law. Tax liens and asssessments take priority over all other liens.

Tax rate The rate at which real property is taxed in a tax district or county. For example real property may be taxed at a rate of .056 cents per dollar of assessed valuation (56 mills).

Tax sale A court-ordered sale of real property to raise money to cover delinquent taxes.

Tax shelter An investment yielding paper losses that may be used to shield other income from taxation. In real estate, often the result of *depreciation* or *cost recovery*.

Tenancy at will An estate that gives the lessee the right to possession until the estate is terminated by either party; the term of this estate is indefinite.

Tenancy by the entirety The joint ownership property acquired by husband and wife during marriage. Upon the death of one spouse, the survivor becomes the owner of the property.

Tenancy in common A form of co-ownership by which each owner holds an undivided interest in real property as if he or she were sole owner. Each individual owner has the right to partition. Tenants in common have no right of survivorship.

Tenant One who holds or possesses lands or tenements by any kind of right or title.

Tenant at sufferance One who comes into possession of lands by lawful title and keeps it afterwards without any title at all.

Testate Having made and left a valid will.

Testers Members of civil rights and neighborhood organizations, often volunteers, who observe real estate offices to assess compliance with fair housing laws.

Time is of the essence A phrase in a contract that requires the performance of a certain act within a stated period of time.

Timesharing Undivided ownership of real estate for only a portion of the year.

Title Evidence that the owner of land is in lawful possession thereof; evidence of ownership.

Title insurance A policy insuring the owner or mortgagee against loss by reason of defects in the title to a parcel of real estate, other than the encumbrances, defects, and matters specifically excluded by the policy.

Title search An examination of the public records to determine the ownership and encumbrances affecting real property.

Torrens system A method of evidencing title by registration with the proper public authority, generally called the registrar.

Tort A civil wrong done by one person against another.

Townhouse A hybrid form of real estate ownership in which the owner has fee simple title to the living unit and land below it, plus a fractional interest, either cooperative or condominium, in common elements.

Township The principal unit of the rectangular survey (government survey) system. A township is a square with six-mile sides and an area of 36 square miles.

Trade fixtures Articles installed by a tenant under the terms of a lease and removable by the tenant before the lease expires. These remain personal property and are not true fixtures.

Transfer tax Tax stamps required to be affixed to a deed by state and/or local law.

Trespass An unlawful intrusion upon another's party.

Trust A fiduciary arrangment whereby property is conveyed to a person or institution, called a *trustee*, to be held and administered on behalf of another person, called a *beneficiary*.

Trust account Escrow account for money belonging to another.

Trust deed An instrument used to create a mortgage lien by which the mortgagor conveys his or her title to a trustee, who holds it as security for the benefit of the note holder (the lender); also called a *deed of trust*.

Trustee *See* Trust.

Umbrella policy An insurance policy that covers additional risk beyond several underlying policies.

Undivided interest *See* Tenancy in common.

Unenforceable contract A contract that seems on the surface to be valid, yet neither party can sue the other to force performance of it. For example, an unsigned contract is generally unenforceable.

Uniform Commercial Code A codification of commercial law, adopted in most states, that attempts to make uniform all laws relating to commercial transactions, including chattel mortgages and bulk transfers. Security interests in chattels are created by an instrument known as a *security agreement*. Article 6 of the code regulates *bulk transfers*—the sale of a business as a whole, including all fixtures, chattels, and merchandise.

Unilateral contract. *See* Contract.

Unity of ownership The four unities that are traditionally needed to create a joint tenancy—unity of title, time, interest, and possession.

Universal agent One who is empowered by a principal to represent him or her in all matters that can be delegated.

Urban property City property; closely settled property.

Urban renewal The acquisition of run-down city areas for purposes of redevelopment.

Useful life In real estate investment the number of years a property will be useful to the investors.

Usury Charging interest at a higher rate than the maximum rate established by law.

Valid contract A contract that complies with all the essentials of a contract and is binding and enforceable on all parties to it.

VA loan A mortgage loan on approved property made to a qualified veteran by an authorized lender and guaranteed by the Veterans Administration in order to limit the lender's possible loss.

Valuation Estimated worth or price. The act of valuing by appraisal.

Value The power of a good or service to command other goods in exchange for the present worth of future rights to its income or amenities.

Variance Permission obtained from zoning authorities to build a structure or conduct a use that is expressly prohibited by the current zoning laws; an exception from the zoning ordinances.

Vendee A buyer under a land contract or contract of sale.

Vendor A seller under a land contract or contract of sale.

Violations Act, deed, or conditions contrary to law or permissible use of real property.

Voidable contract A contract that seems to be valid on the surface but may be rejected or disaffirmed by one of the parties.

Void contract A contract that has no legal force or effect because it does not meet the essential elements of a contract.

Voluntary transfer *See* Alienation

Waiver The renunciation, abandonment, or surrender of some claim, right, or privilege.

Warranty deed A deed in which the grantor fully warrants good clear title to the premises.

Waste An improper use or an abuse of a property by a possessor who holds less than fee ownership, such as a tenant, life tenant, mortgagor, or vendee.

Will A written document, properly witnessed, providing for the transfer of title to property owned by the deceased, called the *testator*.

Without recourse Words used in endorsing a note or bill to denote that the future holder is not to look to the endorser in case of nonpayment.

Wraparound mortgage An additional mortgage in which another lender refinances a borrower by lending an amount over the existing first mortgage amount without disturbing the existence of the first mortgage.

Year-to-year tenancy A periodic tenancy in which rent is collected from year to year.

Zone An area set off by the proper authorities for specific use subject to certain restrictions or restraints.

Zoning ordinance An exercise of police power by a municipality to regulate and control the character and use of property.

Answer Key

Chapter 1:
What Is Real Estate?
1. b
2. d
3. b
4. d
5. c
6. b
7. b
8. c
9. a
10. c
11. c
12. c
13. c
14. d
15. d
16. b
17. d
18. b
19. a
20. d

Chapter 2:
Law of Agency
1. c
2. a
3. a
4. a
5. b
6. b
7. b
8. c
9. c
10. c
11. d
12. d
13. c
14. b
15. c
16. c

17. d
18. c
19. a
20. d

Chapter 3:
Real Estate Instruments:
Estates and Interests
1. b
2. a
3. a
4. a
5. d
6. d
7. a
8. d
9. d
10. a
11. c
12. c
13. b
14. b
15. b
16. d
17. b
18. b
19. c
20. b
21. a
22. a
23. a
24. b
25. c

Chapter 4:
Real Estate Instruments:
Deeds and Mortgages
1. c
2. d
3. d
4. b

5. a
6. c
7. b
8. b
9. c
10. b
11. b
12. a
13. d
14. a
15. c
16. b
17. b
18. b
19. a
20. d

Chapter 5:
Law of Contracts
1. c
2. b
3. d
4. d
5. b
6. a
7. b
8. d
9. a
10. d
11. c
12. d
13. d
14. b
15. b
16. b
17. a
18. b
19. d
20. d

Chapter 6:
Land-Use Regulations
1. d
2. c
3. b
4. d
5. d
6. c
7. a
8. c
9. b
10. d

Chapter 7:
Real Estate Financing
1. b
2. b
3. c
4. b
5. b
6. b
7. a
8. b
9. d
10. a
11. b
12. b
13. c
14. d
15. d
16. c
17. b
18. b
19. d
20. b
21. b
22. a
23. c
24. b
25. a

Chapter 8:
License Law and Ethics
1. d
2. c
3. b
4. c
5. b

6. d
7. c
8. b
9. d
10. a
11. d
12. b
13. d
14. d
15. d
16. a
17. b
18. a
19. c
20. c
21. c
22. b
23. c
24. a
25. c

Chapter 9:
Valuation and Listing
Procedures
1. a
2. a
3. a
4. b
5. d
6. c
7. a
8. c
9. d
10. a
11. b
12. d
13. d
14. d
15. d
16. a
17. b
18. c
19. d
20. d
21. c
22. d
23. b
24. c
25. d

Chapter 10:
Human Rights and Fair
Housing
1. d
2. c
3. d
4. b
5. c
6. b
7. c
8. c
9. a
10. a
11. b
12. a
13. c
14. d
15. d

Chapter 11:
Closing and Closing Costs
1. a
2. a
3. b
4. d
5. a
6. d
7. d
8. c
9. c
10. d
11. c
12. c
13. c
14. d
15. d
16. b
17. b
18. c
19. c
20. b
21. b
22. d
23. a
24. c
25. a

Chapter 12:
Real Estate Mathematics

1. 1,200 square yards × 9 = 10,800 square feet
   area = length × width
   10,800 = length × 60
1. b. 180 feet   10,800 ÷ 60 = 180 feet

2. $25,000 × 3% = $25,000 × .03 = $750
   $68,000 – $25,000 = $43,000 remaining purchase price
   $43,000 × 5% = $43,000 × .05 = $2,150
2. d. $2,900 $750 + $2,150 - $2,900 total down payment

3. 120 feet ÷ 6 feet per section = 20 sections
   One fence post must be added to anchor the other end
3. c. 21   20 + 1 = 21 fence posts

4. $98,000 × 80% = $98,000 × .80 = $78,400 insured value
   $78,400 ÷ 100 = 784 hundreds
4. a. $470.40   784 × $.60 per hundred = $470.40

5. $74,000 + $1,200 = $75,200 sale price less commission
   $75,200 = 94% of sale price
5. a. $80,000 $75,200 ÷ .94 = $80,000 sale price

6. $37,000 ÷ 12 = $3,083.33 monthly income
6. b. $770.83 $3,083.33 × .25 = $770.83 permissible mortgage payment

7. $54,000 × .06 = $3,240 total commission
7. d. $1,620 $3,240 × .50 = $1,620 Sally's share

8. $1,800 ÷ 12 = $150 monthly property taxes
   $365 ÷ 12 = $30.42 monthly insurance premium
8. a. $808.54 $150 + $30.42 + $628.12 = $808.54 total monthly payment

9. c. $36,000   9. 120 front feet × $300 = $36,000 sale price.

10. 43,560 feet per acre × 5 = 217,800 square feet
10. b. 726 feet   217,800 ÷ 300 = 726 feet depth

11. $79,500 sale price × 6½% commission =
    $79,500 × .065 = $5,167.50 Happy Valley's commission
    $5,167.50 × 30% or $5,167.50 × .30 = $1,550.25 listing salesper-
11. b. $1,550.25   son's commission

12. 12′ × 9.5′ = 114 square feet, area of rectangle
    ½ (3′ × 9.5′) = ½ (28.5) = 14.25 square feet, area of triangle
    114 + 14.25 = 128.25 square feet
    to convert square feet to square yards divide by 9
    128.25 ÷ 9 = 14.25 square yards
    $11.95 carpet + $2.50 installation = $14.45 cost per square yard
12. c. $205.91 $14.45 × 14.25 square yards = $205.9125

13. $30,000 Peters + $35,000 Gamble + $35,000 Clooney = $100,000
$125,000 − $100,000 = $25,000 Considine's contribution

$$\frac{\text{part}}{\text{total}} = \text{percent}$$

13. a. 20% $25,000 ÷ $125,000 = .20, or 20%

14. 391.42 × 12 = $4,697.04, annual interest

$$\frac{\text{part}}{\text{percent}} = \text{percent}$$

14. b. $40,843.83 $4,697.04 ÷ 11½% or $4,697.04 ÷ .115 = 40,843.826

15. $68,500 × 12% = $68,500 × .12 = $8,220, annual increase in value
15. a. $76,720 $68,500 + $8,220 = $76,720, current market value

16. $95,000 × 60% or $95,000 × .60 = $57,000, assessed value
divided by 100 because tax rate is stated per hundred dollars
$57,000 ÷ 100 = 570
570 × $2.85 = $1,624.50, annual taxes
divide by 12 to get monthly taxes
16. d. $135.38 $1,624.50 ÷ 12 = $135.375

17. 22′ × 15′ = 330 square feet, area of rectangle
½ (4′ × 15′) = ½ (60) = 30 square feet, area of each triangle
30 × 2 = 60 square feet, area of two triangles
330 + 60 = 390 square feet, surface area to be paved
6″ deep = ½ foot
17. d. 195 cubic feet   390 × ½ = 195 cubic feet, cement needed for patio

18. $3,675 − $500 salary = $3,175 commission on sales
18. b. $127,000 $3,175 ÷ 2.5% = $3,175 ÷ 025 = $127,000, value of property sold

19. two sides of 95′ plus one side of 42′6″
95′ × 2 = 190 feet
42′6″ = 42.5 feet
190 + 42.5 = 232.5 linear feet
19. c. $1,615.88   232.5 × $6.95 = $1,615.875

20. $4,500 × 12 = $54,000 annual rental
20. a. $675,000 $54,000 ÷ 8% or $54,000 ÷ .08 = $675,000, original cost of property

21. 100 acres × 43,560 square feet per acre = 4,356,000 total square feet.
4,356,000 × ⅞ available for lots = 3,811,500 square feet
21. c. 27,225 square feet   3,811,500 ÷ 140 lots = 27,225 square feet per lot

Chapter 13:
Opening a Broker's Office
1. a
2. b
3. d
4. a
5. b
6. a
7. d
8. c
9. c
10. d
11. b
12. c
13. d
14. b
15. b

Chapter 14:
Operation of a Broker's Office
1. b
2. b
3. a
4. c
5. d
6. d
7. d
8. a
9. c
10. d
11. b
12. d
13. d
14. b
15. d
16. d
17. c
18. b
19. b
20. c

Chapter 15:
Advertising
1. b
2. a
3. b
4. b
5. d
6. a
7. c
8. c
9. b
10. d

Chapter 16:
Appraisal
1. c
2. d
3. a
4. d
5. c
6. d
7. b
8. b
9. d
10. a
11. d
12. b
13. a
14. d
15. c
16. c
17. b
18. d
19. a
20. c
21. b
22. d
23. c
24. c
25. a

Chapter 17:
Real Estate Investment
1. c
2. b
3. b
4. b
5. a
6. d
7. b
8. b
9. c
10. c
11. a
12. c
13. c
14. d
15. c
16. d
17. a
18. c
19. a
20. b

Chapter 18:
Subdivision and Development
1. d

2. b
3. a
4. d
5. c
6. d
7. c
8. d
9. b
10. b
11. b
12. a
13. b
14. a
15. c

Chapter 19:
Construction
1. d
2. d
3. a
4. b
5. c
6. d
7. a
8. b
9. a
10. d
11. a
12. a
13. b
14. b
15. c
16. a
17. c
18. a
19. c
20. b

Chapter 20:
Condominiums and Cooperatives
1. a
2. d
3. b
4. d
5. b
6. d
7. d
8. c
9. c
10. b
11. a
12. d
13. b

14. d
15. b

Chapter 21:
Property Management—Rent Regulations

1. d
2. d
3. b
4. d
5. d
6. c
7. a
8. d
9. c
10. b
11. c
12. c
13. c
14. d
15. d
16. b
17. a
18. c
19. d
20. c

Chapter 22:
Leases and Agreements

1. d
2. c
3. b
4. a
5. c
6. d
7. d
8. c
9. c
10. d
11. b
12. a
13. d
14. d
15. c
16. b
17. a
18. d
19. c
20. c

Chapter 23:
Voluntary and Involuntary Alienation

1. c

2. d
3. b
4. d
5. b
6. a
7. c
8. c
9. a
10. d

Chapter 24:
Liens and Easements

1. b
2. b
3. b
4. d
5. c
6. b
7. a
8. c
9. d
10. a
11. c
12. d
13. d
14. c
15. a
16. b
17. d
18. c
19. d
20. b

Chapter 25:
Taxes and Assessments

1. d
2. c
3. b
4. b
5. c
6. a
7. c
8. b
9. a
10. a

Chapter 26:
General Business Law

1. d
2. a
3. c
4. b
5. c
6. d

7. a
8. c
9. c
10. d
11. a
12. a
13. c
14. b
15. b
16. a
17. a
18. b
19. a
20. a

Index

STRAIGHT $ TALK
Don't go into the real estate business without it!

It takes hard work to get your real estate license. It will take more than that to make your license pay off. You'll need facts, figures, inside information, and timely forecasts of coming industry trends.

It's all in *STRAIGHT TALK* — the real estate newsletter filled with the help you need to turn hard work into results, effort into dollars.

YES! Please send me a free issue of *STRAIGHT TALK*, without obligation.

Name _____

Address _____ Apt. _____

City/State/Zip _____

Telephone (___) _____

REAL ESTATE   324

——15-DAY FREE EXAMINATION ORDER CARD——

Longman Financial Services Publishing, Inc.

Please send me the books I have indicated. I'll receive a refund with no further obligation for any books I return within the 15-day period.

Detach, Sign, and Mail in the Postage-Paid envelope today!

NAME _____

ADDRESS _____

CITY/STATE/ZIP _____

TELEPHONE # (___) _____

═══ TEXTBOOKS ═══

		Order #		Price	Total Amount
☐	1.	1970-04	Questions & Answers to Help You Pass the Real Estate Exam, 2nd ed.	$19.95	_____
☐	2.	1970-02	Guide to Passing the Real Estate Exam (ACT), 2nd ed.	$19.95	_____
☐	3.	1970-01	The Real Estate Education Company Real Estate Exam Manual, 3rd ed. (ETS)	$19.95	_____
☐	4.	1970-06	Real Estate Exam Guide (ASI)	$19.95	_____
☐	5.	1970-03	How To Prepare for the Texas Real Estate Exam, 3rd ed.	$19.95	_____
☐	6.	1556-10	Fundamentals of Real Estate Appraisal, 3rd ed.	$31.95	_____
☐	7.	1557-10	Essentials of Real Estate Finance, 4th ed.	$31.95	_____
☐	8.	1559-01	Essentials of Real Estate Investment, 2nd ed.	$31.95	_____
☐	9.	1595-01	Essentials of Real Estate Taxation	$24.50	_____
☐	10.	1513-01	Real Estate Fundamentals	$22.50	_____
☐	11.	1551-10	Property Management, 2nd ed.	$31.95	_____
☐	12.	1560-01	Real Estate Law	$32.95	_____
☐	13.	1965-01	Real Estate Brokerage: A Success Guide	$29.95	_____
☐	14.	1510-01	Modern Real Estate Practice, 10th ed.	$31.50	_____
☐	15.	1510-	Supplements for Modern Real Estate Practice are available for many states. Indicate the state you're interested in _____	$ 9.95	_____
☐	16.	1510-02	Modern Real Estate Practice Study Guide, 10th ed.	$11.95	_____
☐	17.	1961-01	The Language of Real Estate, 2nd ed.	$23.95	_____
☐	18.	1512-10	Mastering Real Estate Mathematics, 4th ed.	$21.95	_____
☐	19.	1512-15	Practical Real Estate Financial Analysis: Using the HP-12C Calculator	$19.95	_____

═══ PROFESSIONAL BOOKS ═══

☐	20.	1926-01	Classified Secrets	$29.95	_____
☐	21.	1909-01	New Home Sales	$24.95	_____
☐	22.	1907-01	Power Real Estate Listing	$15.95	_____
☐	23.	1907-02	Power Real Estate Selling	$15.95	_____
☐	24.	1974-01	Protecting Your Sales Commission: Professional Liability in Real Estate	$24.95	_____

PAYMENT MUST ACCOMPANY ALL ORDERS: (check one)

☐ Check or money order payable to Longman Financial Services Publishing, Inc.
☐ Charge to my credit card (circle one) **Visa** or **MasterCard** or **AMEX**

Account No. _____ Exp. date _____

Signature _____

Or call toll-free 1-800-428-3846; In Illinois, 1-800-654-8596 (charge orders only).

Book Total _____
IL Res. Add 8% Sales Tax _____
Postage/Handling $2.75 + .50 postage for each additional book _____
TOTAL _____

PRICES SUBJECT TO CHANGE WITHOUT NOTICE

234

LONGMAN FINANCIAL SERVICES PUBLISHING

FUNDAMENTALS OF REAL ESTATE APPRAISAL, 3rd Edition
By William L. Ventolo, Jr., and Martha R. Williams; James Boykin, MAI, Consulting Editor

This thorough and concise explanation of real estate appraisal covers—in detail—the cost approach . . . market comparison approach . . . and income approach to appraising. NEW TO THIS EDITION . . .

- Information on the ways financing techniques affect appraised value—provides numerous examples to give a hands-on feel for this critical element in current appraisals.
- Complete, up-to-date discussion of zoning and depreciation and the way each affects a parcel's value.

Numbers and figures have been updated throughout the text to reflect current costs and values of real estate. Features end-of-chapter exams plus glossaries of appraisal and construction terms.

Check box #6 on the order card $31.95   order number 1556-10

QUESTIONS AND ANSWERS TO HELP YOU PASS THE REAL ESTATE EXAM, 2nd Edition
By John W. Reilly and Paige Bovee Vitousek

Designed to help readers become confident, this popular manual features up-to-date financing and taxation questions, as well as a new practice exam. Also included is a challenging Broker Bonus Quiz.

Special features of *Questions and Answers,* 2nd Edition . . .

- More than 1,600 practice questions with the answers fully explained and clarified . . . students learn the correct answer and why that answer is preferable.
- A special real estate math appendix to help the math-shy.
- Information on licensing law appears in the appendix.
- Five subject areas of the ETS exam are covered: ownership . . . brokerage . . . contract . . . financing . . . valuation.
- One sample salesman and broker exam, plus an additional exam for both candidates.
- Vocabulary appendix tests student's knowledge of terms.

Check box #1 on order card $19.95   order number 1970-04

ESSENTIALS OF REAL ESTATE TAXATION
By Thomas V. Novak and Jeffrey M. Wells

Regardless of its type, size, or nature, every real estate transaction has a tax consequence. *Essentials of Real Estate Taxation* provides an overall view of the tax implications resulting from a wide range of real estate dealings—from buying a home to making a "tax-free" exchange.

Essentials of Real Estate Taxation will provide you with:

- An overall look at positive and negative implications to make better use of professional advice.
- Preparation for unexpected tax penalties.
- A review of tax benefits inherent in the ownership of real property.
- An introduction to methods that reduce, defer, and avoid negative tax consequences.

Make your "tax awareness" work for you!

Check box #9 on the order card $24.50   order number 1595-01

PROPERTY MANAGEMENT, 2nd Edition
By Robert C. Kyle with Floyd M. Baird, RPA, Consulting Editor

An in-depth study of the professional management of apartment buildings, cooperatives, condominiums, office buildings, and commercial and industrial property. The text covers the major functions of property management, from creation of the management plan through control of the office. It also features sections on subsidized housing and creative management alternatives.

These special features help introduce readers to the field . . .

- A complete glossary of terms.
- Text written at basic level to increase understanding of subject matter.
- Covers full range of property manager's duties and responsibilities.

Check box #11 on the order card $31.95   order number 1551-10